SPORTS

IN

NORTH

AMERICA

Volumes in This Series

SPORTS

IN
NORTH AMERICA

A DOCUMENTARY HISTORY

EDITED BY
THOMAS L. ALTHERR

VOLUME I

PART 1—SPORTS IN THE COLONIAL ERA
1618–1783

Academic International Press
1997

DEDICATION

To my grandfather, Norbert,

Who blocked the plate with the best of them,

To my father, Henry,

Who embodied the term Sportsman,

To my brothers, Douglas, Paul, and James,

Athletes all.

SPORTS IN NORTH AMERICA. A DOCUMENTARY HISTORY
VOLUME 1. PART 1—SPORTS IN THE COLONIAL ERA, 1618–1783
Edited by Thomas L. Altherr

Copyright © 1997 by Academic International Press

ISBN: 0-87569-188-9

Composition by Ethel Chamberlain

Printed in the United States of America

By direct subscription with the publisher

A list of Academic International Press publications is found at the end of this volume

ACADEMIC INTERNATIONAL PRESS
POB 1111 • Gulf Breeze FL 32562–1111 • USA

CONTENTS

5 BLOOD SPORTS   58

Cockfighting

The Carolinas and Georgia

Maryland and Virginia

PREFACE

The purpose of this volume is to provide a comprehensive collection of extant primary source documents pertaining to sport on the North American continent during colonial and Revolutionary times. These documents consist mainly of journal and diary entries, newspaper stories and advertisements, and contemporary descriptions of sports, games, amusements, and similar diversions. There are poems as well as sermons, essays, and nonfiction pieces that promote or deliver moral judgments about a particular sport. Additionally the anthology excerpts colonial, territorial, and state laws and city ordinances that attempted to restrict or regulate sport.

The first chapter focuses on the general aspects of sports and recreation during the colonial period and includes general laws and ordinances governing them. Subsequent chapters address specific sports in alphabetical order, primary sources in each appearing in chronological order. The emphases reflect what the writers themselves chose to stress. Large sections on blood sports (bear baiting, bull baiting, cockfighting, and gander pulling), contact sports (boxing, cudgeling, gouging, and wrestling), fishing, horse racing, and hunting dominate. The sections on aquatics (swimming, bathing, rowing, and boating), fencing, and gymnastics (general running, leaping, track and field, throwing, climbing, and walking) are also large, primarily because sizeable portions of large treatises on those topics are included. Other sports have smaller sections because it proved impossible to locate more references. I have included children's games because writers in those eras saw them as sport. I am aware of the controversy among sports historians and sociologists as to the definition of a sport. Games or means of subsistence are included if the residents and travelers of that era called them a sport; competitiveness was not a requisite. Some of the distinctions may seem arbitrary. For example, the collection omits sources about chess, card playing, and billiards, although at least one later volume in the series includes billiards under "Pub Sports." Bowling, one form of which was a tavern diversion, is included. There is material about fencing but not about dueling, descriptions of marksmanship, but not in a battle setting.

The headnote preceding each document is set in a different typeface than the document for greater readability. No attempt was made to reproduce the documents in their original form. Whenever possible I have tried to present the source with its original spelling, grammar, and paragraphing. Because writers in those centuries had quite different notions of orthography, sentence structure, and paragraphization, the sources will look strange to modern readers. Typefaces within the documents were standardized. Newspaper advertisements often utilized different sizes of type and, on occasion, illustrations such as a horse or pointing hand. Sources with modern spelling, punctuation, and grammar emendations were available only in a format edited by a modern editor. Rather than reproduce the penmanship in diaries and journal, we leave the reader to envision, in the mind's eye, these sources in their original form. An attempt to excerpt only the pertinent parts was made, unless it threatened to destroy the sense of context. Included in a few documents are certain words that are objectionable today, but those words were retained in an effort to remain true to the document.

A few words about arrangement within the chapters. Following the brief introduction, documents are listed chronologically. In larger chapters general documents, treating the sport as a whole or including multiple activities, are listed immediately following the introduction. Then subheads are utilized to group the remaining documents, either by a particular sport, ethnic group, or by naturally occuring geographic regions. Whenever a writer made more than one reference to a sport, I list them chronologically under that person starting with the earliest date. Occasionally items encompassing a span of many years will follow the first notation. The reader must be alert to this, although the index at the rear of the volume will help.

Within each section there are sources that are positive, neutral, or hostile toward that sport, so the reader must search for the desired interpretation. The sources are presented without editorial content, knowing some are definitely or probably satirical. Among the fishing and hunting stories, there are some "tall tales." The reader must judge the truthfulness or intent of the writer.

Many of the sources are familiar to the handful of colonial and Revolutionary historians who chronicled sport in those areas, and I am thankful for their previous efforts which helped me locate them again for this volume. There are many other sources that I have rediscovered—that no other historian has reprinted or referenced. Only a few are from primary source manuscript collections; most come from various historical collections, periodicals, journals, printed diaries, and similar books, sadly overlooked until now. For example, many of the sources in the "Baseball and Similar Ball Games" chapter are unknown to baseball historians. Indeed, I unearthed one in Cooperstown itself under the very nose of the National Baseball Library! This volume makes these new sources easily available for general readers and scholars alike.

There were many difficulties in gathering these sources, far more than I expected when I agreed to this project. First, the very scope—two centuries, numerous indigenous tribal groups, five major Euroamerican colonist groups and a few minor ones, three major racial groups, several regions—mandated that I locate a vast number of journals, newspapers, diaries, travelers accounts, poems, essays, and similar materials. Even so I found it very frustrating to find sources about sport in the Hispanic colonies and about African-Americans whether free or slave. If there is ever a second or supplemental edition of this volume, perhaps another editor will have better luck locating such valuable sources.

Second, sources about sport appeared in the unlikeliest places, unpredictable provenances. Then, in sources that seemed to promise description of sport, there was nary a word. Sometimes a long diary yielded only a snippet, albeit a revealing one, hence its inclusion. Occasionally I was at the mercy of old indexing systems; most often I trudged through the whole volume to find sport references that the indexer considered too mundane to index. Even with all the searching and reading I was unable to locate many, or even any, primary sources. The sources, for example, about golf and ice hockey are exasperatingly thin, even though nearly every secondary sports history refers to them in colonial and Revolutionary America.

Third, because sport in those centuries was so informal or irregular, there are no constitutions of sporting associations and very few lists of rules or regulations, descriptions of technique or strategy. Often there is simply a brief mention of someone playing a game or witnessing one. For my purposes that is important enough in its own right to establish the presence of that sport. The reader may note that the advertisements for horse races in that chapter have a relentless sameness, but the more observant will detect intriguing nuances over time. I included so many of them to show how frequently racing was happening and to advance what I consider is one of the major "arguments" of this volume: sport existed and mattered in colonial and Revolutionary America.

Fourth, because some of the original sources were in Spanish, French, German, or Dutch, I tried to locate an English translation. In some cases I translated a French or German source, but I cannot vouch for the complete accuracy or grace of any of these translations.

Fifth, because book publishing of the day was a very transatlantic industry, there are many sources here with European publishers and imprints; I chose only sources that were directly about America. Conversely, if I found a book about sport with the imprint of an American publisher, even if the content were about sport in England or another part of Europe, I considered it an American source. Obviously that publisher reckoned there was a market for his book, even though the sport occurred infrequently in America.

The following collection represents the fruits of nearly five-and-a-half years of fairly steady research in archives and through interlibrary loan. I can't pretend that I have found all or nearly all the extant sources about colonial and Revolutionary sports in America. It is my fondest hope that this collection will encourage scholars, who view sport history as important, to research other journals, primary source manuscripts, and newspapers and compile a fuller, richer record.

There are several people, or groups of people, who helped immensely or in smaller ways along the way, and I wish to extend my full thanks here. First, I want to thank Berndt von Wahlde at Academic International Press for his patience waiting for this compilation and Ethel Chamberlain, also of AIP, for her critical copy editing skills. The staff of Connie Whitson's Auraria Library Interlibrary Loan office was unflaggingly persistent in locating sources. The curators and staff at the American Antiquarian Society, Dartmouth College Library, the Vermont Historical Society and especially Barney Bloom, the National Baseball Hall of Fame Library at Cooperstown, the C.C. Morris Cricket Library at Haverford College, and especially Amar Singh, Denver Public Library, and Norlin Library at the University of Colorado at Boulder all were courteous and helpful. Conversations about early American baseball with Tom Heitz and other "regulars" at the annual Cooperstown "Baseball and American Culture" symposium were always enjoyable. At a couple of North American Society for Sport History conferences, George Kirsch got me started on the right foot, and some incidental conversations with other NASSH scholars were of great aid. "Rawhide" Jim McClain, Kay Sheehan, and my sister-in-law Patricia Altherr clearly explained certain terms from early horseracing. Among my departmental colleagues at Metropolitan State College of Denver, I would like to thank Stephen Leonard, Jeremiah Ring, Shirley Fredricks, Monys Hagen, Vincent C. De Baca, and George Archuleta for source suggestions, and Steve O'Bryan, who kindly translated some Attic Greek phrases and words. I also thank my college, which allowed me some travel money and a sabbatical in the fall term of 1995 to continue and complete research at the archives. Teresa Mariska McGuinness, a former work-study student, typed up four of the larger documents at a point when the project needed a boost, and our always dependable secretary Gloria

Kennison provided numerous instances of logistical aid. Much gratitude goes to my dear friend, Peggy "the Lieutenant" Combs, who typed up one of the large documents and was always unstinting with her computer and moral support. Last but not least, my thanks go to my family, who were rooting this one on all the way.

Thomas L. Altherr

Metropolitan State College of Denver

INTRODUCTION

Whenever most Americans consider the history of sports in American culture, they tend to overlook or outrightly ignore the early periods. Bedazzled by the electronic glitter of current megasports whose seasons rapidly cannibalize each other, these same Americans barely recall these sports had previous phases, histories, and precursors. Increasingly even the sporting feats of the last decade seem misty and hoary, relegated to the sports trivia bins. The exploits of the early twentieth century seem downright ancient and those of the distant nineteenth century almost prehistoric. Historians were not much more attentive to American sports before 1820. American sports history courses hustle past the colonial and Revolutionary eras with scarcely a cursory comment, maybe a nod toward King James I's *Book of Sports*, maybe a mention of Ben Franklin as a swimmer, George Washington as a fox hunter, or the Marquis de Chastellux at a cockfight, but nothing resembling any sustained treatment of the topic. Students in these courses likewise push their professors to concentrate on the near present.

The neglect of early American sport has resulted partly from a common misconception that every man, woman, and child in those times worked unrelievedly from before dawn until after dusk, barely lived above a subsistence existence, and thus had few or no leisure moments for frolic. A sort of perverse nostalgia takes some odd comfort in embellished beliefs that the so-called pioneers labored so unstintingly and really did walk through eight feet of snow, ten miles, uphill both ways, to attend church, town meetings, school, training days, and markets. Filiopietism and similar types of ancestor worship would demand nothing less! In reality, early Americans were far less heroic. Frontier conditions could be grueling indeed, but settlers sought out sports and other entertainment to alleviate the tedium. Spontaneous frolics and barbecues supplemented the more or less regular holiday, training day, and court day festivities. Even those activities directly related to sustenance, such as hunting, fishing, and trapping, often took on the outward characteristics of sport, and occasionally other work, such as plowing and spinning, blended into play and competition. The human need for sport persisted in all these periods.

In plain fact, colonial and Revolutionary era Americans indulged in sports, games, and similar amusements as participants and spectators. Indigenous tribal peoples across the continent played and watched a variety of ball and hoop games and were inveterate foot racers. Euroamerican colonists brought along their own sporting traditions intact or modified them to meet American conditions. And although the record is very sketchy, Africans and African-Americans must have enjoyed some sport in the occasional breaks from the dreadful and relentless business of slavery. Many travelers, military officers, soldiers, missionaries, and other sojourners remarked from time to time about the presence of sports and amusements, if only to criticize the inhabitants for supposed immorality. Newspapers listed upcoming sporting events and reported the results of them, albeit irregularly, and sporadically advertised sporting equipment for sale. Colonial and state laws and city ordinances attempted to regulate sport, especially the gaming that accompanied it often, and preserve the concept of the inviolate

Sabbath. Undoubtedly matters of economics and safety from the enemy during wars predominated, but these Americans were hardly strangers to sport and leisure.

The roots of several modern sports are easily discernible in the colonial variations. Hunters and fishermen chased down and angled for their prey in American woods, fields, lakes, rivers, and seas with techniques and strategies, if not equipment, a modern shooter or angler would recognize. Shooters and archers squared off in front of different types of targets, but the principle was the same: hit the center of the target. Runners sprinted the short races or paced long distances with the age-old spirit of competition. Boys and men played a form of football that evolved into soccer and rugby, and in the game of "fives" developed the forerunner to playground handball. Cricketeers bowled and batted as later generations would do. Skaters flocked to the frozen waterways on bone and then metal skates. Sledders hurtled down hills on rudimentary toboggans and sleighers skidded across the fields and down the lanes in more elaborate carrioles. Those interested in swimming consulted Ben Franklin's swimming manual for hints on floating and strokes. Children frolicked with a variety of tag, hiding, spinning, and jumping games that remained nearly unchanged over the centuries. And many a modern would find little surprise at the gambling, drinking, and similar types of masculine carousing that surrounded the sports, particularly horseracing and cockfighting.

Colonial and Revolutionary sports did differ in several important ways from those after the turn of the century. First, the availability of time and leisure for sport was variable. Certainly, early Americans lacked the constantly regular opportunities for sport that beckon modern Americans. They lived pre-industrial lifestyles that often escape the understanding of industrial or post-industrial-age Americans. Time flowed for them in different rhythyms based on agricultural seasons, daylight and moonlight, and sidereal schedules. In some cases periods of leisure were predictable, such as on the Sabbath days and holidays, some of which varied according to the agricultural calendar but happened roughly the same time each year. At other times farmers and artisans broke off from work and set their own workday paces. Idleness was never a virtue, but episodes of relaxation and recreation accompanied the work regimen. The availability of leisure varied seasonally and regionally. Soldiers and officers out on campaigns, especially during the wars for empire and the Revolutionary War, found themselves with unpredictable stretches of time between battles and marches that lent themselves to the occasional ball game or shooting match.

Second, although early American sports displayed often resembled their later versions, many other aspects of those diversions were different, not necessarily unrecognizable but still different. Race horses were invariably smaller and slower than those that churn today's tracks. Hunters and anglers hunted and fished with less sophisticated equipment, materials, and clothing. Similarly marksmen and archers made do without the greater accuracy of modern high-tech rifles and bows. Golf courses, hockey rinks, and bowling greens and alleys were not omnipresent. Despite Ben Franklin's entreaties, relatively few Americans swam for pleasure, fearing or generally shunning the water. Lacrosse was a game which virtually only indigenous people played. Baseball was in its infant stage, amidst a welter of prototype games in several configurations. Blood sports such as cockfighting, bear baiting, bull baiting, and gander pulling were far more common than in later decades when humane societies and laws forced those activities out of existence or underground. Boxing and wrestling were quite inchoate; usually an absence of rules prevailed and combatants grappled in no-holds-barred fashion, often seriously maiming each other in a vicious activity called gouging. Fencing, long connected with self-protection, warfare, military science, and duelling, became a necessary gentlemanly activity often linked with dancing and French-speaking capabilities. Boats were available for rowing and yachts for sailing, but except for the occasional canoe race, colonial and Revolutionary Americans seem to have capitalized only rarely on the recreational potentials of both. Tennis was mostly an indoor game, played in a courtyard of sorts. Golf may have resembled field hockey more than the current "great walk spoiled," and hockey itself was in a murky status of its own, midway between the Celtic games of shinty and hurling and the continental style of ice hockey. And although the football of those times, often associated with Shrove Tuesday ceremonies, would be the basis for soccer and rugby, there was very little yet visible of the modern sport called football in the United States.

Third, most of the sporting activity of the times was on the folk game or folk sport level. Many of the matches were spontaneous or irregularly scheduled. Rules were subject to revision and adaptation, often on whim and mutual preference. Some courts for fives and tennis existed, as did specific tracks for horseracing and bowling greens and alleys, but for the most part wouldbe players and contestants selected any field or commons for the games. What public architecture did exist was mostly for religious and governmental needs. Newspapers and periodicals followed sport only haphazardly; none had anything resembling a "sports section" or sportswriter. No one kept more than the most elementary statistics or compared them seriously over time. Fame for athletic achievement was most often a local matter, although occasionally certain race horses and game cocks had widespread reputations. Professionalization was likely nonexistent; short of maintaining a long streak of large gambling wins it would have been hard for anyone to make a living at sport alone. There were no formalized leagues, standings, divisions, or regular championships. Uniforms or sports attire was nearly absent, perhaps visible only at some private academies, but even there may not have differed from regular clothing. Even training days which were necessary with a militia tradition did not always involve sport, especially if the weather was bad. Perhaps only the lacrosse and other ball plays that tribal people engaged in approximated any degree of formality. Nancy Struna, the historian who did the most and best work analyzing colonial and Revolutionary sport, detected an increasing movement toward formalization after 1720, but even then sport had much more in common with its medieval predecessors than the regularized and regimented formulations which followed .

Fourth, and perhaps quite obviously, certain sports were either nonexistent or only marginally popular. There was no basketball or volleyball yet. Cycling awaited the improvement of that contraption and automobile racing was only a distant glimmer in the eye of the most farsighted visionary. Asian sports such as judo, jujitsu, karate, and tae kwan do were far in the future. Bullfighting and walk racing, or pedestrianism, each became more popular later. Even work sports, somewhat surprisingly, were infrequent. Despite thriving cattle industries on the Spanish northern frontier, especially southern California, in the English colonies in the East, and French Louisiana, rodeo didn't appear until the mid-1840s according to some accounts, or not until after the Civil War, according to others. Similarly logging did not immediately spawn woodsmen and woodswomen contests, fire company races came along with larger cities, and in spite of the pervasiveness of the plow in the heavily agricultural regions, plowing demonstrations and matches were much more frequent after the turn of the century.

Collegians played at sports, sometimes under the baleful eye of administrators, but these activities were intramural as intercollegiate matches were also far in the future.

Fifth, sports of the colonial and Revolutionary periods were mostly available to males and less frequently to females. Occasionally women participated in fishing and hunting, rode horses in a genteel manner, ran a foot race for a smock, a pair of gloves or shoes, or a hat, dipped their presumably very covered bodies in bathing tanks or the ocean, or played relatively nonstrenuous children's games such as badminton (called battledores and shuttlecocks in those days), but sport was a masculine province. Contemporary descriptions barely mention women except as spectators at some of the horse races and fairs. Blood sport exhibitions, boxing, wrestling, shooting, and many other sports were in venues generally off limits to moral females, though the lower sort may have attended. Some women complained about the lack of exercise; other women derived some aerobic benefits from walking, housework, farm work, spinning matches, barbecues, or the occasional dance or ball. But for the most part affluent women contented themselves with sewing, reading, singing, playing musical instruments, visiting, conversation, and similar arts to fill leisure time.

Sixth, but not least, colonial and Revolutionary sports operated under greater clouds of suspicion and moral disapproval than afterwards. Although it would be erroneous to characterize the English Puritans, Presbyterians, Methodists, and Quakers as total enemies of pleasure and sport, northern colonies and states did pass strict laws and ordinances that proscribed certain types of recreation or penalized excess gaming. Some of the motivation was anti-Catholic and anti-pagan as well as part and parcel of the internecine interdenominational struggles with the Anglicans. Much of the energy of prohibition and restriction centered on preserving the Sabbath as a day of rest and reflection. Additionally the unsavory association many sports had garnered upset the moralists who reckoned that even innocent sport contributed to wrack and ruin, intemperance, idleness, and loitering. An incipient humanitarianism attacked blood sports and eye gouging, although at least one later historian suggested the reformers' real fear was not for the animal or human victims, but that the crowd derived pleasure from the torments. Some progressive sportsmen sought to clean out unsportsmanlike hunting and fishing practices to upgrade the public image in those sports. Some areas of the country, especially the South and the backcountry frontiers, ignored these moral strictures, but during Revolutionary times in many sectors of the Northeast and Midwest, the so-called Blue Laws continued.

Yet for all of this restriction, sport continued to exist and even expand during that period. Travelers and inhabitants left frequent enough detailed accounts and references so that historians can rest assured that sport was not covert, a crazy or random aberration, nor any completely atypical activity. Even though several concrete areas of difference existed, sport mattered to the Americans of the colonial and Revolutionary eras. As several anthropologists have demonstrated about a variety of cultures and peoples, sports, as "deep play," served important ritualistic needs, attempted to provide satisfactory catharses for the resolution of conflicts between humans and nature, humans and animals, the individual and the community, life and death. Early Americans may not have commented about these functions of sport, or even particularly realized them on a conscious level, but even in spite of restrictions, may Americans of that era took pleasure participating or watching others competing in the sports of the times.

Chapter 1

GENERAL ATTITUDES TOWARD EXERCISE AND SPORT

Matters of sport, games, recreations, pastimes, amusements, diversions, and leisure were controversial in colonial and Revolutionary North America. Spanish colonists and missionaries confronted the games and pastimes of indigenous tribal peoples in the Caribbean, the Gulf Coast region, Mexico, and the northern frontiers, declared them idolatrous and attempted to abolish them. The best the Spaniards could secure was a blending of indigenous and European culture. The French met with roughly similar experiences in eastern Canada, although the fewer French were in little position to coerce the indigenous peoples to give up their major sports, such as lacrosse. In the more northerly reaches of the Canadian colonies, the conflict centered on the tribal peoples' penchant for hunting. French Jesuits tried to persuade them to give up the chase for more sedentary pursuits, with limited success. Many British colonists were more curious than judgmental, finding the habits of indigenous people interesting and worthy of note as is demonstrated in the many diary entries regarding them.

In the more populous English colonies, sport was likewise problematic. Jamestown settlers who were accustomed to lives of leisure preferred to bowl in the streets rather than work, setting the pattern of more lax attitudes about sport in the South. Conversely, the Puritans, those Congregationalist Protestant reformers who sought to ready England and New England for the expected millenium, generally condemned sport as irreligious and profane. Sports reminded the Congregationalists of the many pre-Christian and Catholic feast day games and frolics. Even so, not all Puritans were hostile toward sport—some saw a place for moderate and lawful recreation, if only to keep workers productive and happy. In England the issue came to a head by 1618, when King James I, angered by Puritan prohibitions on sport in Lancashire, proclaimed the "King's Book of Sport." This proclamation authorized a variety of traditional sports and games as necessary to the health, well-being, and military readiness of the populace. The Puritans gritted their teeth about such a prospect and whenever possible tried to undercut the proclamation in England and New England.

The typical strategy to forbid sport or control the lower classes or unchurched in the colonies was the passage of Sabbath observance laws. Almost every colony and province declared sports and games on the Sabbath a profanation and levied fines or jail time on offenders. During the Revolution, the states and territories carried over this principle of Sabbath observance into law. The Quaker colony of Pennsylvania, and those colonies and states with large populations of the Society of Friends, added their protests to sports, reckoning them debauchery attended by every other vice. The legislatures in those colonies and states enacted laws protecting Friends meetings from nearby sports. The following sources contain the pertinent sections from some of these laws, although space constraints prevent reprinting each Sabbath and anti-gaming law.

Within these limits, and often in direct opposition to them, colonial Americans played a variety of games and sports. Inns and taverns became usual places of sport. Patrons practiced games such as bowling, skittles, ninepins, quoits, pitching the bar, slinging long bullets, cockfighting, wrestling, and fives indoors and outside these establishments. The surrounding fields hosted occasional sports such as cricket and other ball games, some of which were actually baseball or its forerunners. The pubs were often staging grounds for foxhunts and other hunting, fishing expeditions, shooting contests, and horse racing. Militias and military units were fertile grounds for the development of a sporting consciousness. Officers tried to control the excesses of gaming, but allowed recreation as necessary physical exercise for the troops.

Works sports along the model of plowing contests, oxen pulls, fire company races, rodeos, woodsmen competitions, and similar matches did not exist in the formalized way they would after the turn of the century. If they were more common, newspapers and travelers did not take notice, for the concept of work sports failed to materialize significantly in the record. This volume includes a mention of yarn-spinning contests, especially noteworthy in that the participants were women. Girls and women did not have as many opportunities to partake in sports and games as boys and men.

Although the Puritan opinion concerning exercise and sport continued to dominate until the Revolution, the attitude of enlightened individuals softened by the mid-1700s. Philadelphians Benjamin Franklin and Benjamin Rush began to recommend various sports and recreations as physical activity vital to the complete citizen. Some sports were given more validity by the issuance of rule books, and institutions which offered sport instruction appeared. The anti-sport legacy persisted in the various Sabbath and anti-gaming laws, but by 1783 there was a definite trend toward acceptance and support of sports as a whole.

THE OFFICIAL VIEW

King James I proclaims sports as healthful and necessary recreation, *The Book of Sports,* 24 May 1618, in James I, *The Kings Maiesties Declaration to His Subiects Concerning Lawfull Sports to bee Vsed* (London: Robert Barker, 1618), reprinted in Henry A. Parker, "The Reverend Josse Glover and the Book of Sports," *Publications of the Colonial Society of Massachusetts, Volume VIII, Transactions 1902-1904* (Boston: The Colonial Society of Massachusetts, 1906), 337-339.

"By the King.

"WHEREAS vpon Our *returne the last yere out of Scotland, We did publish our Pleasure touching the recreations of Our people in those parts under Our hand: For some causes Us thereunto moouing, Wee haue thought good to command these Our Directions then given in* Lancashire *with a few words thereunto added, and most appliable to these parts of Our Realmes, to bee published to all Our Subjects.*

"Whereas We did iustly in Our *Progresse through* Lancashire, *rebuke Some Puritanes and Precise people, and tooke order that the like vnlawful carriage should not bee vsed by any of them hereafter, in the prohibiting and vnlawful punishing of Our good people for vsing their lawfull Recreations, and honest exercises vpon Sundayes and other Holy dayes, after the afternoone Sermon or Seruice: Wee now finde that two sorts of people wherewith that Countrey is much infested, (Wee meane Papists and Puritanes) have maliciously traduced and calumniated those Our iust and honourable proceedings. And therefore lest Our reputation might upon the one side (though innocently) have some aspersion layd vpon it, and that vpon the other part Our good people in that Countrey be misled by the mistaking and misinterpretation of Our meaning: We have therefore thought good hereby to cleare and make Our pleasure to be manifested to all Our good People in those parts.*

"It is true that at Our first entry to this Crowne, and Kingdome, Wee were informed, and that too truely, that Our County of Lancashire *abounded more in Popish Recusants then any County of England, and thus hath still continued since to Our great regret, with little amendment, saue that now of late, in Our last riding through Our said County Wee find both by the report of the Iudges, and of the Bishop of that diocesse that there is some amendment now daily beginning, which is no small contentment to Vs.*

"The report of this growing amendment amongst them, made Vs the more sorry, when with Our owne Eares We heard the generall complaint of Our people, that they were barred from all lawfule Recreation, & exercise vpon the Sundayes afternoone, after the ending of all Diuine Seruice, which cannot but produce two euils: The one, the hindering of the conuersion of many, whom their Priests will take occasion hereby to vexe, perswading them that no honest mirth or recreation is lawfull or tolerable in Our Religion, which cannot but breed a great discontentment in Our peoples hearts, especially of such as are peraduenture vpon the point of turning; The other inconuenience is, that this prohibition barreth the common and meaner sort of people from vsing such exercises as may make their bodies more able for Warre, when Wee or Our Successours shall have occasion to vse them. And in place thereof sets vp filthy tiplings and drunkennesse, & breeds a number of idle and discontented speeches in their Alehouses. For when shall the common people have leaue to exercise, if not upon the Sundayes & holydaies, seeing they must apply their labour, & win their liuing in all working daies?

"Our expresse pleasure therefore is, that the Lawes of Our Kingdome, & Canons of Our Church be aswell obserued in that Countie, as in all other places of this Our Kingdome. And on the other part, that no lawfull Recreation shall bee barred to Our good People, which shall not tend to expresse more particularly, Our pleasure is, That the Bishop, and all other inferiour Churchmen, and Churchwardens, shall for their parts bee carefull and diligent, both to instruct the ignorant, and conuince and reforme them that are mis-led in Religion, presenting them that will not conforme themselues, but obstinately stand out to Our Iudges and Iustices: Whom We likewise command to put the Law in due execution against them.

"Our pleasure likewise is, That the Bishop of that Diocesse take the like straight order with all the Puritanes and Precisians within the same, either constraining them to conforme themselues, or to leaue the Countrey according to the Lawes of Our Kingdome, and Canons of Our Church, and so to strike equally on both hands, against the contemners of Our Authority, and aduersaries of Our Church. And as for Our good peoples lawfull Recreation, Our pleasure likewise is, That after the end of Diuine Seruice, Our good people not be disturbed, letted, or discouraged from any lawful

*recreation; Such as dauncing, either men or women, Archery for men, leaping, vault-
ing, or any other harmelesse Recreation, nor from hauing of May-Games, Whitson
Ales, and Morris-dances, and the setting vp of May-poles & other sports therewith
vsed, so as the same be had in due & conuenient time, shall haue leaue to carry rushes
to the Church for the decoring of it, according to their custome. But withall We doe
here account still as prohibited all vnlawfull games to bee vsed vpon Sundayes onely,
as Beare and Bullbaitings, Interludes, and at all times in the meaner sort of people by
Law prohibited, Bowling.*

*"And likewise We barre from this benefite and liberty, all such knowne recusants,
either men or women, as will abstaine from comming to Church or diuine Seruice,
being therefore unworthy of any lawfull recreations after the said Seruice, that will not
first come to the Church, and serue God: Prohibiting in like sort the said Recreations
to any that, though conforme in Religion, are not present in the Church at the Seruice
of GOD, before going to the said Recreations. Our pleasure likewise is, That they to
whom it belongeth in Office, shall present and sharpely punish all such as in abuse of
this Our liberty, will vse these exercise before the ends of all Diuine Seruices for that
day. And We likewise straightly command, that euery person shall resort to his owne
Parish Church to heare Diuine Seruice, and each Parish by it selfe to vse the said
Recreation after Diuine Seruice. Prohibiting likewise any Offensiue weapons to bee
carried or vsed in the said times of Recreations. And Our pleasure is, That this Our
Declaration shall bee published by order from the Bishop of the Diocesse, through all
the parish Churches, and that both Our Iudges of Our Circuit, and Our Iustices of Our
Peace be informed thereof.*

"Giuen at Our Mannour of Greenwich the foure and twentieth of May, in the sixteenth yeere of Our Raigne of England, France and Ireland, and of Scotland the one
and fiftieth."

OBSERVANCE OF THE SABBATH AND RELIGIOUS HOLIDAYS

William Bradford, Plymouth, Massachusetts elder, objects to several types of sport, 25
December 1621, in Bradford, *Of Plymouth Plantation,* ed. by Harvey Wish (New York:
Capricorn Books, 1962), 82-83.

"One the day called Chrismasday, the Governor caled them out to worke, (as was
used,) but the most of this new-company excused them selves and said it wente against
their consciences to work on that day. So the Governor tould them that if they made
it a mater of conscience, he would spare them till they were better informed. So he led-
away the rest and left them; but when they came home at noone from their worke, he
found them in the streete at play, openly; some pitching the barr, & some at stoole-ball,
and shuch like sports. So he went to them, and took away their implements, and tould
them that if they made the keeping a mater of devotion, let them kepe their houses, but
ther should be no gameing or revelling in the streets. Since which time nothing has
been atempted that way, at least openly."

The Dutch Director and Council in New Amsterdam, probibits many sports and games on the Sabbath, 29 April 1648, reprinted in Esther Singleton, *Dutch New York* (New York: Benjamin Blom, 1968), 200.

"On the Lord's day of rest, usually called Sunday, no person shall be allowed to do the ordinary and customary labors of his calling, such as Sowing, Mowing, Building, Sawing Wood, Smithing, Bleeching, Hunting, Fishing, or any works allowable on other days, under the penalty of One Pound Flemish, for each person so offending; much less any idle or unallowed exercises and sports, such as Drinking to excess, frequenting Inns or Taphouses, Dancing, Card-playing, Tick-tacking, Playing at ball, Playing at bowls, Playing at nine-pins, taking jaunts in Boats, Wagons, or Carriages, before, between, or during Divine Service, under the penalty of a double fine (Two Pounds, Flemish); and in order to prevent all such accidents and injuries, there shall be a fine of Twelve Guilders for the first offence; Twenty-four Guilders for the second offence; and arbitrary correction for the third offence; the One-third for the Officers; One-third for the Poor; and the remaining One-third for the Prosecutor."

* * *

Rhode Island and Providence Plantations statute, 1 September 1654, in John Russell Bartlett, ed., *Records of the County of Rhode Island and Providence Plantations in New England, Vol. I, 1636 to 1663* (Providence, R.I.: A. Crawford Greene and Brother, 1856), 279-280.

"6. Whereas, there have been severall complaints exhibited to this Assemblie against ye incivilitie of persons exercised upon ye first day of ye weeke which is offensive to divers amongst us. And whereas it is judged that ye occasion thereof ariseth because there is noe day apoynted for recreation. It is therefore referred to ye consideration and determination of each Towne to alow what dayes they shall agree uppon for theire men servants maid servants and children to recreate themselves, to prevent ye incivilities which are amongst us exercised on that day."

* * *

Peter Stuyvesant, New Amsterdam Governor, prohibits many sporting activities on the Sabbath, 27 January 1656, reprinted in Esther Singleton, *Dutch New York* (New York: Benjamin Blom, 1968), 302.

"[Sunday is] a day of fasting and prayer for God's blessing protection and prosperity in trade and agriculture but principally for a righteous and thankful use of his blessings and benefits. The which better to observe and practice with greater unanimity, We interdict and forbid, on the aforesaid day of Fasting and Prayer during Divine Service, all labour, Tennis-playing Ball-playing, Hunting, Fishing, Travelling, Ploughing, Sowing, Mowing and other unlawful games as Gambling and Drunkenness, on pain of arbitrary correction and punishment already enacted against the same."

* * *

New Netherland ordinance, 26 October 1656, reprinted in Edmund B. O'Callaghan, ed., *Laws and Ordinances of New Netherland, 1638-1674* (Albany, N.Y.: Weed, Parsons and Company, 1868), 258-259.

"First, all persons [are prohibited] from performing or doing on the Lord's day of rest, by us called Sunday, any ordinary labor, such as Ploughing, Sowing, Mowing, Building, Woodsawing, Smithing, Bleaching, Hunting, Fishing, or any other work which may be lawful on other days, on pain of forfeiting One pound Flemish for each person; much less any lower or unlawful exercise and Amusement, Drunkenness, frequenting Taverns or Tippling houses, Dancing, playing Ball, Cards, Tricktack, Tennis, Cricket or Ninepins, going on pleasure parties in a Boat, Car or Wagon, before, between or during Divine Service, on pain of a double fine;...."

* * *

Massachusetts colonial law, circa 1660, in *The Book of the General Lavves and Libertyes Concerning the Inhabitants of the Massachusets, Collected out of the Records of the General Court, for the several Years Wherin They Were Made and Established* (Cambridge, Mass.: The General Court, 1660), 33.

"Sabbath.

"....That if any perfon or perfons henceforth, either on the Saturday night, oron the Lords day night, after the Sun is fet, fhall be found fporting in the ftreets or fields of any town in this Jurisdiction, Drinking, or being in any houfe of publick entetainment...and cannot give a fatisfactory Reafon to fuch Magiftrate or Comifhioner, in the feverall Towns, as fhall have the cognizance thereof. Every fuch Perfon fo found Complained of and Prooved Transgreffing, fhall pay *Five fhillings* for evey fuch Transgreffion or Suffer Corporal Punifhment, as Authority Aforefayd fhall Determine."

* * *

New York provincial law, October 1695, in *New York Province, Acts of the Sixth Assembly, First Sessions* (New York, 1695), 112.

"*An Act againft the Prophanation of the Lords Day, called*, Sunday"

"WHEREAS the true and fincere Service and Worfhip of God, according to his Holy Will and Commandments, is often Prphaned and neglected by many of the Inhabitants and Sojourners within this Province, who do not keep holy the Lords Day, but in a Diforderly manner, accuftom themfelves to Travel, Labouring, Working, Shooting, Fifhing, Sporting, Playing, Horfe-Racing, Frequenting of Tipling-houfes, and ufing many other Unlawful Exercifes and Paftimes upon the Lords day, To the great fcandal of the holy *Chriftian Faith, Be it therefore Enacted by the Governor and Council, and Reprefentatives, Convened in General Affembly, and by the Authority of the Same*, That from and after forty days next after the Publication therof, There fhall be no Travelling, Servile Labouring and Working, Shooting, Fifhing, Sporting, Playing, Horfe-Racing, Hunting or Frequenting of Tipling-houfes, or the ufing of any other Unlawful Exercifes or Paftimes by any of the Inhabitants or Sojourners within this Province, or by any of their Slaves or Servants, on the Lords day; and that every Perfon or Perfons offending In the premiffes, fhall Forfit for every Offence the Sum of fix Shillings Current Money of this Province,...."

* * *

Connecticut law, circa 1702, in *Acts and Laws of His Majefties Colony in Connecticut in New-England* (Boston: Bartholomew Green and John Allen, 1702), 103-104.

"An Act for the better Obfervation and Keeping the Lords-Day

Be it Enacted & Ordained by the Governour, Council and Reprefentatives Convened in General Court of Affembly, and it is Enacted by the Authority of the fame, That all and every perfon and perfons whatfoever, fhall on that day carefully apply themfelves to Duties of Religion and Piety, publickly and privately; and that no Trades man, Artificer, Labourer, or other perfon whatfoever, fhall upon the Land or Water, do or exercife any Labour, Bufinefs or Work of their ordinary Callings: Nor ufe any

Game, Sport, Play or Recreation on the Lords Day, or any part thereof (works of neceffity and mercy only excepted) upon pain that every perfon fo offending, fhall forfeit *Ten Shillings.*"

* * *

Cotton Mather, Boston, Massachusetts Congregationalist minister, protests against sports on the Sabbath, 4 January 1703, in Mather, *The Day Which the Lord Hath Made. A Discourse Concerning the Institution and Observation of the Lords-Day* (Boston: Bartholomew Green and John Allen, 1703), 27.

"*Sports on the Lords day!* Never did any thing found more forrowfully or more odioufly, fince the day that the World was firft blefs'd with fuch a day."

* * *

Benjamin Colman, Massachusetts Congregationalist minister, warns against sports on the Sabbath, circa 1707, in Colman, *The Government & Improvement of Mirth* (Boston: Samuel Philips, 1707), 51, 79.

"Sports and Paftimes are deteftable on the *Lords-Day*, whoever tolerate and authorize 'em: Work and Labour is rather fufferable; for to make it a *Play-day* is worfe than to make it a *Reft.*"

"It [profane mirth] cramps Induftry, and is big with Idlenefs; it affects fuch Company as are the Grafs and Gaming; it wou'd make the Year one long *Holiday*, & dooms the *Sabbath to Sport & Paftime*, as well as the Six dayes of Labour."

* * *

New York City ordinance, 28 March 1707, in *Several Laws, Orders and Ordinances Eftablifhed by the Mayor, Recorder, Alder-men and Affiftants of the City of New-York* (New York: William Bradford, 1707), 3.

"*For the Obfervation of the Lords Day.*
"*No Children &c. to play on the Sabbath.*
"And be it further Ordained by the Authority aforefaid, That no Children, Youths, Maids, or other perfons whatfoever, do meet together on the Lords Day in any of the Streets or places within this City or Liberties thereof, and there fport, play, make noife or difturbance, under the penalty of One Shilling for each Offence, to be paid by the Parents of all under Age."

* * *

South Carolina provincial law, circa 1712, in *The Public Laws of the State of South-Carolina, from its First Establishment as a British Province Down to the Year 1790, Inclusive* (Philadelphia: R. Aitken and Son, 1790), 19.

"An Act for the better obfervation of the Lord's Day, commonly called Sunday.
"§ V. No public fports or paftimes, as bear-baiting, bull-baiting, foot-ball playing, horfe-racing, interludes or common plays,or other unlawful games, exercifes, fports or paftimes whatfoever fhall be ufed on the Lord's-Day by any perfon or perfons what-foever, and that every perfon or perfons offending in any of the premifes fhall forfeit for every offence, the fum of 5s. current money."

* * *

New Hampshire provincial law, circa 1716, in *Acts and Laws, Paffed by the General Court or Assembly of His Majefties Province of New-Hampfhire in New-England* (Boston: Bartholomew Green, 1716), 7-8.

"An Act for the better Obfervation and Keeping the Lords Day.

"Be it Enacted & Ordained by the Lieutenat Governour, Council, and Reprefent-atives, Convened in General Affembly, and ıt is Enacted by the Authority of the fame, That all and every perfon and perfons whatfoever, fhall on that Day carefully apply themfelves to Duties of Religion and Piety, Publickly and Private: And that no Trades-man, Artificer, or other perfon whatfoever, fhall upon the Land or Water, do or exercife, any labour, bufinefs, or workof their ordinary Calling, nor ufe any Game, Sport, Play, or Recreation on the Lords Day, or any part thereof (works of Neceffity and Mercy only excepted:) upon pain that every perfon fo ffending fhall forfeit *Five Shillings*."

"And all and every Juftices of the Peace, Conftables, and Select-men are required to take effectual care, ad indeavour that this Act in all the particulars thereof be duely obferved; As alfo to reftrain all perfons from Swimming in the Water, unneceffarily; and unfeafonable walking in Streets, or Fields, in any part of this Province: Keeping open their Shops, or following their Secular Occafions, or Recreations in the Evening preceeding the Lords day, or any part of the faid day, or Evening following."

* * *

Maryland provincial law, circa 1718, in *The Laws of the Province of Maryland Collected into One Volumn, By Order of the Governor and Affembly of the Province* (Philadelphia: Bradford, 1718), 6.

"An Act for fanctifying and keeping Holy the Lord's Day, commonly called *Sunday*.

"FORASMUCH as the Sanctifying and keeping Holy of the Lord's Day commonly called Sunday, hath been and is efteemed by the prefent and all Primative Chriftians and People, to be a principal Part of the Worfhip of Almighty God, and the Honour which is due to his holy Name.

"*Be it Enacted by the King's moft Excellent Majefty, by and with the Advice and Confent of this prefent General Affembly and by the Authority of the fame*, That from and after the Publication of this Law, no Perfon or perfons whatfoever, within this Province, fhall...fuffer or permit any of his, her, or their Children, Servants or Slaves, or any other under their Authority to abufe or prophane the Lord's day as aforefaid, by Drunkenefs, Swearing, Gaming, Fowling, Fifhing, Hunting, or any other Sports or paftimes or Recreations, whatfoever. And if any Perfon or Perfons within this Prov-ince,..., fhall offend in all or any the Premiffes; he, fhe or they fo offending fhall forfeit and pay, for every Offence, the Sum of one hundred Pounds of Tobacco,...."

* * *

New York City law, 18 November 1731, in *Laws, Orders & Ordinances Eftablifhed by the Mayor, Recorder, Aldermen and Affiftants of the City of New-York* (New York: William Bradford, 1731), 3-4.

"A Law for the Obfervation of the Lords Day, called *Sunday*.

"*And be it Ordained by the Authority aforefaid*, That no Children, Youths, Maids, or other Perfons whomfoever, do meet together on the Lords Day, called *Sunday*, in any of the Streets or Places within this City o Liberties thereof, and there fport, play, make noife or difturbance, under the Penalty of *One Shilling* for each Offence, to be paid by the Parent, Mafter, or thofe to whofe care fuch Children, Youth, or Maids are commit-ted, of all under Age, who fuffer their Children Servants or Apprentices fo to do; and on failure of fuch Payment, fuch Child, Children, Servants or Apprentuces to be fent to the Houfe of Correction or to the Cage, at the difcretion of the faid Mayor, Recorder and Aldermen, or any one of them."

"*And be it further Ordained by the Authority aforefaid*, That no Negro, Mullatto or Indian Slaves, above the Number of Three, do affemble or meet together on the Lords Day, call'd *Sunday*, and fport, play or make any Noife or Difturbance, or at any Time or any Place from their Mafters Service, within this City and Liberties thereof;...."

* * *

Delaware provincial law, circa 1741, in *Laws of the Government of New-Caftle, Kent and Suffex Upon Delaware* (Philadelphia: Benjamin Franklin, 1741), 121-122.

"*An* ACT to *prevent the Breach of the Lord's Day commonly called* Sunday.

"AND BE IT FURTHER ENACTED by the Authority aforefaid, That if any Perfon fhall be duly convicted of Fifhing, Fowling, Oyftering Horfe-hunting or Horfe-racing on the Lord's Day, the Perfon fo offending, fhall, for every fuch Offence, forfeit the Sum of *Ten Shillings*, or upon Refufal to pay the faid Fine, be fet in the Stocks, there to remain the Space of four Hours.

"AND BE IT FURTHER ENACTED by the Authority aforefaid, That if any Number of perfons fhall meet to game, play or dance on the Lord's-Day, every Perfon fo offending fhall forfeit the Sum of *Five Shillings*, or upon Refufal to pay the faid Fine, be fet in the Stocks, there to remain for the Space of four Hours."

* * *

North Carolina provincial law, circa 1741, in *A Collection of All the Acts of Assembly, of the Province of North-Carolina, Now in Force and Use,* 2 vols., Vol. 1 (Newbern, N.C.: James Davis, 1765), 85-86.

"*An Act, for the better Obfervation and keeping of the Lord's Day, commonly called* Sunday, *and for the more effectual Suppreffion of Vice and Immorality.*

"I. WHEREAS in well regulated Governments, effectual Care is always taken, that the Day fet apart for Publick Worfhip, be obferved and kept holy, and to fupprefs Vice and Immorality: Wherefore,

"II. WE pray that it may be Enacted, *and Be it Enacted, by his Excellency* Gabriel Johnfton, *Efq*; *Governor, by and with the Advice and Confent of his Majefty's Council and General Affembly of this Province, and it is hereby Enacted, by the Authority of the fame,* That all and every Perfon and Perfons whatfoever fhall on the Lord's Day, commonly called *Sunday*, carefully apply themfelves to the Duties of Religion and Piety; and that no Tradefman, Artificer, Planter, Labourer or other Perfon whatfoever, fhall upon the Land or Water, do or exercife any Labour, Bufinefs or Work, of their ordinary Callings (Works of Neceffity and Charity only excepted;) nor employ themfelves either in hunting, fifhing or fowling, nor ufe any Game, Sport or Play, on the Lord's Day aforefaid, or any Part thereof, upon Pain that every Perfon fo offending being of the age of Fourteen Years, and upwards, fhall forfeit and pay the Sum of Ten Shillings, Proclamation Money."

* * *

William Stephens, Georgia Trustee, comments on recreation, December 1741, March 1744, and April 1745, in E. Merton Coulter, ed., *The Journal of William Stephens, 1741-1743,* and *The Journal of William Stephens, 1743-1745* (Athens, Ga.: University of Georgia Press, 1958), 1:24; 2:86-87, 216.

26 December 1741: "How irregular so ever we may be in many things, very few were to be found who payd no regard to Xmas Holy days, and it was a slight which would ill please our Adversaries, had they seen what a number of hail young Fellows were got together this day, in, and about the Town, at Crickett, and such kinds of Exercise."

26 and 27 March 1744: "Little to be taken notice of During these Holidays when the common sort of people pass'd most of their time in Sports, Cricket Quoits and such like Exercise."

15 and 16 April 1745: "These Holy Days would not afford any thing material to observe but passed away among the Common Juvenile people in rural Sports of various kinds, according to Custom."

* * *

Devereux Jarratt, Anglican rector, Bath Parish, Dinwiddie County, Virginia, concerning the Sabbath in Albemarle County and his own indulgence in sport in New Kent, Virginia, circa 1751, in [Jarratt], *The Life of the Reverend Devereux Jarratt, Rector of Bath Parish, Dinwiddie County, Virginia* (Baltimore: Warner & Hanna, 1806 [1969 reprint]), 28, 44.

"But in Albemarle, there was no minister of any persuasion, or any public worship, within many miles. The Sabbath day was usually spent in *sporting:* and whether *this* was right or wrong, I believe, no one questioned."

"I thought it vain for me to attempt a religious life any more (at least, as yet) and therefore I might as well give a loose to my passions and, and get what little happiness I could in sports and sensual gratifications."

* * *

Rhode Island colonial law, circa 1752, in *Acts and Laws of His Majesty's Colony of Rhode-Ifland, and Providence Plantations, in New-England, in America. From* Anno *1745, to* Anno *1752* (Newport, R.I.: J. Franklin, 1752), 69.

"*BE it enacted, and and by the Authority of this Affembly, It is Enacted,* That from and after the Publication of this Act, if any Perfon or Perfons in this Colony, fhall play or game at Cards, Dice, Tables, Bowls, Billiards, Wheel of Fortune, Shuffle-board, or Cock-fighting, for Money, or any other valuable Confideration, the Perfon lofing [or winning] at any fuch Game or games, fhall pay a Fine of *Ten Pounds,...* for the firft Offence, and for the fecond Offence, *Twenty Pounds...,* and for the third Offence, *Forty Pounds....*"

* * *

Georgia provincial law, circa 1762, in A*cts Passed by the General Assembly of Georgia, At a Seffion begun and holden at* Savannah, *on* Wednefday *the 11th Day of* November, Anno Dom. *1761...; and from thence continued by feveral Adjournments to the 4th Day of* March, *1762, being the fecond Seffion of this prefent Affembly* (Savannah, Ga.: James Johnston, 1763), 11.

"AN ACT *For preventing and punifhing Vice, Profanenfs, and Immorality, and for keeping holy the Lord's Day, commonly called* Sunday.

"IV. And be it further Enacted, by the authority aforefaid, That no publick fports, or paftimes, as bear-baiting, bull-baiting, foot-ball, playing, horfe-racing, fhooting, hunting or fifhing, interludes or common plays, or other games, exercifes, fports, or paftimes whatfoever, fhall be ufed on the Lord's day, by any perfon or perfons whatfoever, and that all and every perfon and perfons in any of the premifes, fhall forfeit for every fuch offence the fum of five fhillings *Sterling.*"

Rhode Island provincial law, February 1769, in *Acts and Laws of the Englifh Colony of Rhode-Island and Providence-Plantations, in New-England, in America. Made and Paffed fince the Revifion in June, 1767* (Newport, R.I.: Solomon Southwick, 1772), 13.

"An ACT prohibiting the Sale of Liquors, and for preventing Sports, Plays and Recreations, on the Days, and near the Places where, the Friends hold their General Meetings for Worfhip, in this Colony.

"*BE it Enacted by this General Affembly, and, by the Authority of the fame, It is Enacted,* That whoever fhall, from and after the Twentieth Day of *May* enfuing,... fhall run Horfes, play at Quoits, wreftle, or be exercifed in other Games, Plays, Sports or Recreations, in the Highway, Yard or Field, on either of the Days, and within the Diftance of Four Miles from the Place or Places, where fuch Meeting or Meetings, for religious Worfhip, fhall be held (excepting in the Towns of *Newport* and *Providence,* where the Diftance fhall be One Mile) fhall, for every fuch Offence, forfeit and pay the Penalty of Twenty Shillings;...."

* * *

Pennsylvania state law, 30 March 1779, in *Laws Enacted in the Second Sitting of the Third General Assembly, of the Commonwealth of Pennsylvania* (Philadelphia? 1779), 190-192.

"*An* ACT *for the fuppreffion of vice and immorality.*

"SECTION 1. WHEREAS fufficient provifion hath not hitherto been made by law for the due obfervation of the Lord's Day, commonly called Sunday, and the preventing of profane fwearing, curfing, drunkenefs, cock-fighting, bullet-playing, horfe-racing, fhooting matches, and the playing or gaming for money or other valuable things, fighting of duels, and fuch evil practices, which tend greatly to debauch the minds and corrupt the morals of the fubjects of this commonwealth: For remedy whereof.

"SECT. 2. *Be it enacted, and it is hereby enacted, by the Reprefentatives of the Freemen of the commonwealth of Pennfylvania, in General Affembly met, and by the authority of the fame,* That if any perfon fhall do any kind of work of his or her ordinary calling, or follow or do any worldly employment or bufinefs whatfoever, on the Lord's day commonly called Sunday (works of necessity and mercy only excepted) or fhall ufe or practice any game, play, fport or diverfion whatfoever on the faid day, and be convcted thereof before any Juftice of the Peace, each and every perfon fo offending, fhall for every fuch offence, be fined the fum of Three Pounds,...or in the cafe the offender fhall have none, he or fhe fhall be committed to the common Jail or Work-houfe of the County, there to remain without bail or mainprize for the term of ten days."

* * *

Marquis de Chastellux, French officer, sailing away from Virginia in Chesapeake Bay, January 1783, laments the American restrictions on sport on the Sabbath, in de Chastellux to James Madison, 12 January 1783, in [de Chastellux], *Travels in North-America, in the Years, 1703, 1781, and 1782, by the Marquis de Chastellux,* 2nd ed., 2 vols., Vol. 2 (London: G.G.J. and J. Robinson, 1787), 383-385.

"What a gloomy filence reigns in all your towns on Sunday! a ftranger would imagine that fome epidemic or plague had obliged every one to confine himfelf at home. —Tranfport yourfelf to Europe, and efpecially to a Catholic country; behold [frequent displays of merriment, music, and sport]. In America, it is the reverfe; as there is nothing but idlenefs without the refource of either fport or dance,...."

Charleston, South Carolina city ordinance, 22 November 1783, in *Ordinances of the City Council of Charleston in the State of South Carolina, Passed in the First Year of the Incorporation of the City* (Charleston, S.C.: J. Miller, 1784), 19.

"AN ORDINANCE
For the better OBSERVANCE of the LORD'S-DAY, commonly called SUNDAY, and to prevent DISTURB-
ANCES at any Place of PUBLIC WORSHIP
within the City of CHARLSTON.

"And be it further ordained by the authority aforefaid, That no fports or paftimes, as bear-baiting, bull-baiting foot-balls, horfe-racing,... fhall be allowed on the Lord's-Day, and every perfon fo offending fhall forfeit for every fuch offence the fum of Five Pounds."

SPORTS IN EDUCATION

Harvard College records, April 1712 and April 1737, in "Meeting of the President and Fellows of Harvard College, April 28, 1712" and "A Meeting of the Corporation of Harv^d College, April 19, 1737," in *Harvard College Records, Part II. Corporation Records, 1636-1750, Publications of the Colonial Society of Massachusetts,* Vol. 16 (Boston, 1925), 401, 656.

"9. Voted, That the Orchard purchased of Michael Spencer & lately fenced, be assign'd for a place of recreation & exercise for the Scholars."

"3 The northerly part of the Land improved by the Late President and that adjoynes the playing pasture for the Schollars be Layd open to the said playing pasture for the Enlargement of the same and If this should be any damage to Dr Wigglesworths or Mr Appletons fences or Lands adjacent the Corporation wil give it a just Consideration"

* * *

Benjamin Franklin, Pennsylvania editor, concerning physical education, recommends sports as healthful recreation, circa 1749, in [Franklin], *Proposals Relating to the Education of Youth in Pensilvania* (Philadelphia: pvt. ptg?, 1749), 10-11.

"That to keep them [pupils] in Health, and to ftrengthen and render active their Bodies, they be frequently* exercis'd in Running, Leaping, Wreftling, and Swimming, &c."

*Milton propofes, that an Hour and half before Dinner fhould be allow'd for Exercife, and recommends among other Exercifes, the handling of Arms, but perhaps this may not be thoughtneceffary here. *Turnbull*, p. 318. fays, 'Corporal Exercife invigorates the Soul as well as the Body; let one be kept clofely to Reading, without allowing him any Refpite from Thinking, or any Exercife to his Body, and were it poffible to preferve long, by fuch a Method, his Liking to Study and Knowledge, yet we fhould foon find fuch an one become no lefs

foft in his Mind than in his outward Man. Both Mind and Body would thus become gradually too relaxed, too much unbraced for the Fatigues and Duties of
active Life. Such is the Union between Soul and Body, that the fame Exercifes
which are conducive, when rightly managed, to confolidate or ftrengthen the
former, are likewife equally neceffary and fit to produce Courage, Firmnefs, and
manly Vigour, in the latter. For this, and other Reafons, certain hardy Exercifes
were reckoned by the Antients an Effential Part in the Formation of a liberal
Character; and ought to have their Place in Schools where Youth are taught the
Languages and Sciences.' See p. 318 to 323."

* * *

Ordinance at William and Mary College, Virginia, 29 August 1754, in "Journal of the
Meetings of the President and Masters of William and Mary College," William and Mary
College Quarterly, 1st Series, Vol. 2, No. 2 (October 1893), 123-124.

"August 29, 1754
At a Meeting of the President and Masters of William and Mary College:
Present,

The Rev. W. Stith, President,

Mr Dawson, Mr Robinson, Mr Preston, Mr Graham and Mr Camm.
....

Ordered I^{st} , That no Boy shall be permitted to saunter away his Time upon any of
the College Steps or to be seen playing during School Hours under a severe animadversion f^m ye President, or any of the Masters."

* * *

John Adams, Braintree, Massachusetts politician and later United States President, con-
cerning recreation and study, circa January 1759, in Lyman H. Butterfield, ed., Diary and
Autobiography of John Adams, Volume 1. Diary, 1755-1770 (Cambridge, Mass.: Harvard
University Press, 1962), 72.

"Let Virtue address me—'Which, dear Youth, will you prefer? a Life of Effeminacy,
Indolence and obscurity, or a Life of Industry, Temperance, and Honour? Take my
Advice, rise and mount your Horse, by the Mornings dawn, and shake away amidst the
great and beautiful scenes of Nature, that appear at that Time of thr day, all the Cru-
dities that are left in your stomach, and all the obstructions that are left in your Brains.
Then return to your Study, and bend your whole soul to the Institutes of the Law, and
the Reports of cases, that have been adjudged by the Rules, in the Institutes. Let no
trifling Diversion or amuzement or Company decoy you from your Books, i.e. let no
Girl, no Gun, no Cards, no flutes, no Violins, no Dress, no Tobacco, no Laziness, decoy you from your Books.'"

* * *

Eleazer Wheelock, Dartmouth College president, proposes work instead of recreation for
his indigenous students, circa 1771, in Wheelock, A Continuation of the Narrative of the
Indian Charity School, in Lebanon, in Connecticut; From the Year 1768, to the Incorporation of It with Dartmouth College, and Removal and Settlement of It in Hanover, in the
Province of New Hampshire, 1771 (Hanover, N.H.?: pvt. ptg.?, 1771), 33.

"2. That they turn the courfe of their diverfions, and exercifes for their health, to
the practice of fome manual arts, or cultivation of gardens, and other lands, at the

proper hours of leisure, and intermiffiom from ftudy, and vacancies in the college and school."

SPORTS AS HEALTHFUL RECREATION

John Hammond, British traveler, mentions recreation for men and women, concerning Virginia, circa 1656, in Hammond, *Leah and Rachel, or, the Two Fruitful Sisters Virginia, and Mary-land. Their Present Condition, Impartially Stated and Related* (London: T. Mabb, 1656), 12.

"...and both men and women have times of recreations, as much or more than in any part of the world besides,...."

* * *

Thomas Shepard, Jr., Puritan minister, advises his son at Harvard College on recreation, circa 1670, in [Shepard], "A Letter from the Revd Mr Thos Shephard to His Son att His Admission into the College," reprinted in *Publications of the Colonial Society of Massachusetts, Volume XIV, Transactions 1911-1913* (Boston: The Colonial Society of Massachusetts, 1913), 104.

"6, Come to your Studies with an Appetite, and weary not your body, mind, or Eyes with long poreing on your book, but break off & meditate on what you have read, and then to it again; or (if it be in fitt season) recreate your Self a little, and so to yur work afresh; let your recreation be such as may stir the Body chiefly, yet not violent, and whether such or sedentry, let it be never more than may Serve to make your Spirit the more free and lively in your Studies."

* * *

Increase Mather, Harvard College president, refers to the skating deaths of two Harvard students, December 1696, in *A Discourse Concerning the Uncertainty of the Times of Men, and the Neceffity of being Prepared for Sudden Changes and Death. Delivered in a Sermon Preached at Cambridge in New England Decemb. 6, 1696. On Occafion of the Sudden Death of Two Scholars belonging to Harvard College* (Boston: Bartholomew Green and John Allen, 1697), 39-40.

"3*ly*, and Finally, be always able to give a good Anfwer to this Queftion, *What am I doing?* Is the thing that I am about a Lawful thing? Am I ufing Recreations for my Health fake? And is it Lawful Recreation, which no Law neither of God nor man has forbidden? The two young men that were Drowned the other day, Death found them in Recreation: It's well, it was a Lawful one *Skating* on the ice is fo, if ufed feafonably & with due difcretion and moderation. But how difmal is it when Death fhall furprife Perfons when they are diverting themfelves with *Scandalous Paftimes*."

* * *

Reasons for repeal of "An Act Against Riotous Sports, Plays and Games," Pennsylvania, circa 1709 and 1713, reprinted in Samuel Hazard, ed., *Pennsylvania Archives* (Philadelphia: Joseph Severns and Company, 1852), Vol. 1, 155, 159.

Circa 1709:   "An Act against Riotous Sports, Plays and Games

"Her Majesty was pleased by her order in Council of the 7th of February, 1705, for the Reasons then laid before Her, to repeal several Laws of Pennsylvania, among which was one with the same Title and Contents with this before mentioned, which is lyable to the same Objection as the former, viz., That it restrains her Ma^{tys} Subjects from Innocent Sports and Diversions; However, if the Assembly of Pennsylvania shall pass an Act for preventing of Riotous Sports, and for restraining such as are contrary to the Laws of this Kingdom, there will be no Objection thereunto, so it contain nothing else."

Circa 1713:   "As to the Act ag^t Riotous Sports, Plays & Games"

It restrains persons from several innocent Sports & healthy diversions and the penalties in it are to great, & therefore I humbly c+onceive it ought to be repealed."

* * *

Cotton Mather, Boston Congregationalist minister, comments on recreation, circa 1726, in [Mather], *A Serious Address to those who unnecessarily frequent the Tavern* (Boston, 1726), 10.

"Men and Brethren, We would not be misunderstood, as if we meant to insinuate, that a due Pursuit of Recreation is inconsistent with all manner of Diversion: No, we suppose there are Diversions undoubtedly innocent, yea profitable and of use, to fit us for Service, by enlivening & fortifying our frail Nature, Invigorating the Animal Spirits, and brightning the Mind, when tired with a close Application to Business."

* * *

George Milligen-Johnston, South Carolina doctor, comments on recreation in South Carolina, circa 1763, in [Milligen-Johnston], *A Short Description of the Province of South-Carolina, with An Account of the Air, Weather, and Diseases, at Charles-Town, Written in the Year 1763* (London: John Hinton, 1770), in Chapman J. Milling, ed., *Colonial South Carolina. Two Contemporary Descriptions* (Columbia, S.C.: University of South Carolina Press, 1951), 135.

"The Weather is much too hot in Summer, for any Kind of Diverfion or Exercife, except Riding on Horfeback, or in Chaifes, (which few are without) in the Evenings and Mornings;...."

* * *

Benjamin Rush, Philadelphia physician, recommends horseback riding as healthful recreation, circa 1772, in Rush, *Sermons to Gentlemen upon Temperance and Exercise* (Philadelphia: John Dunlap, 1772), 36-37.

"RIDING ON HORSEBACK is the moft manly and ufeful fpecies of exercife for gentlemen. Bifhop Burnet expreffes his surprize at the lawyers of his own time, being fo much more long-lived (*caeteris paribus*) than other people, confidering how much thofe of them who become eminent in their profeffion, are obliged to devote themfelves to conftant and intenfe study. he attributes it entirely to their RIDING the circuits fo frequently, to attend the different courts in every art of the kingdom. This no doubt has a chief fhare in it: But we fhall hereafter mention another caufe which concurs with this, to protract their lives. It may be varied according to our ftrength, or natiure of our diforder, by walking—pacing—trotting—or cantering our horfe. All thofe difeafes which are attended with a weaknefs of the nerves, fuch as the hyfteric and hypochondriac diforders, which fhow themfelves in a weaknefs of the ftomach and bowels— indigeftion—low fpirits, &c. require this exercife. It fhould be ufed with caution in the confumption, as it is generally too violent, except in the early ftage of that diforder. In riding, to preferve haelth, eight or ten miles a day are fufficient to anfwer all the purpofes we would wifh for. But in riding, to reftore health, thefe little excurfions will avail nothing. The mind as well as the body muft be roufed from its languor. In *taking an airing*, as it is called, we ride over the fame ground for the moft part every day. We fee no new objects to divert us, and the very confideration of our riding for health finks our fpirits fo much, that we receive more harm than good from it. Upon this accunt I would recommend long journies to fuch people, in rder, by the variety or novelty of the journey to awaken and divert the mind. Many people have by thefe means been furprifed into health. Perfons who labour under hyfteric or epileptic diforders, fhould be fent to cold; thofe who labour under hypochondriac or confumptive complaints fhould vifit warm climates."

* * *

George Washington, Virginia planter, Revolutionary War general, and later United States President, Norristown, Pennsylvania, encourages sports, 26 May 1777, in "Orderly Book of Gen. John Peter Gabriel Muhlenberg, March 26–December 20, 1777," Pennsylvania Magazine of History and Biography, Vol. 33, No. 3 (1909), 263.

"Games of Exercise for amusem[t] may not only be permitted but encouraged."

SPORTS AS IMMORAL ACTIVITIES

Massachusetts colonial laws, circa 1660, in *The Book of the General Lavves and Libertyes Concerning the Inhabitants of the Massachusets, Collected out of the Records of the General Court, for the several Years Wherin They Were Made and Established* (Cambridge, Mass.: The General Court, 1660), 33.

"Gaming and Dauncing.

"UPON Complaint of the diforders, by the play of the Games, of fhuffle-board and Bowling, in and about houfes of common entertainment, whereby much precious time is fpent unprofitably, & much waft of wine and beer occafioned; It is Ordered by this Court and the Authority thereof, That no Perfon fhall henceforth, ufe the faid Games of fhuffle-board, or bowling, or any other play or game, in, or about fuch houfe, nor in any other houfe ufed as Common for fuch purpofe, upon paine for every keeper of fuch houfe to forfeit for every fuch Offence *Twenty Shillings*, &c every perfon Playing at the fayd Games &c: in or about any fuch houfe fhall forfeit for every fuch Offence *Five Shillings*."

* * *

Resolutions of the Yearly Meetings of the Society of Friends, circa 1719 and circa 1739, in Society of Friends, *The Book of Discipline Agreed on by the Yearly-Meeting of Friends for New-England* (Providence, R.I.: John Carter, 1785), 135.

Circa 1719: "ADVISED that such [persons] be dealt with as run races, either or horfeback or on foot; or otherwife lay wagers or ufe any kind of gaming, or needless and vain fports and paftimes: For our time fwiftly paffeth away, and our pleafure and delight ought to be in the law of the Lord."

Circa 1739: "WE earneftly befeech our friends, and efpecially the youth among us, to avoid all fuch converfation as may tend to draw out their minds into the foolifh and wicked paftimes with which this age aboundeth (particularly balls, gaming-places, horfe-races, and play-houfes) thofe nurferies of debauchery and wickednefs, the burthen and grief of the fober part of other focieties, as well as of our own; practices wholly unbecoming a people under the Chriftian profeffion, contrary to the tenor of the doctrine of the gofpel, and the examples of the beft men in the earlieft ages of the church."

* * *

Alexander Harvey, Vermont colonel, comments on recreation in Sunbury, Pennsylvania, 2 October 1774, in [Harvey], "The Journal of Alexander Harvey," in *The Upper Connecticut. Narratives of its Settlement and its Part in the American Revolution,* 2 vols., Vol. 1 (Montpelier: Vermont Historical Society, 1943), 231.

"[I]n this toun and for manie miles in the / Nighbourhood of it there is no minister / nor any publick worship and I Belive / very little privet the Method they take / to supy this Defect is they meet in / the taverns and spend the former part / of the Day (viz the Sabath) in Drinking / wrestling and swearing and in the / afternoon they betake themselves to / the more sober Excercise of Vomiting / and Sleeping...."

* * *

Colonel William Henshaw, Leicester, Massachusetts officer, notes Army order regarding sports, exercise and recreation 3 October 1775, in "The Orderly Books of Colonel William Henshaw, October, 1775, through October 3, 1776," *Proceedings of the American Antiquarian Society,* Vol. 47, Part 1 (1948), 29-30.

"Any Officer, Non Commission'd Officer or Soldier, who shall hereout be detected playing at Toss up, Pitch & Hurtle or any other Games of Chance in or near the Camps or Villages bordering our Encampments, shall without delay be confin'd & punish'd for disobedience of Orders. The General does not mean by the above Order to discourage Sports of Exercise & Recreation he only means to discountenance & punish Gaming."

* * *

Robert Proud, historian of Pennsylvania, circa 1776-1780, concerning the Pennsylvania Quakers' antipathy toward sports, in Proud, *The Hiftory of Pennfylvania, in North America, from the Original Inftitution and Settlement of that Province, under the firft Proprietor and Governor William Penn, in 1681, till after the Year 1742,* 2 vols., Vol. 1 (Philadelphia: Zachariah Poulson, Junior, 1797), 55-56.

"*First,* Their *difufe of all gaming,* and *vain fports*; as the frequenting of *plays, horfe-races,* &c. was a cuftom ftrictly and conftantly adhered to by them; as being moft confiftent with a truly chriftian life; the ufe of thefe, and fimilar things, having, in their eftimation, a manifeft and infallible tendency to draw away, and alienate the human mind from the moft important object of true happinefs, as thus expreffed by *R. Barclay,* viz.

"'.... And again, that thefe games, fports, plays, dancings, comedies, &c. do naturally tend to draw men from *God's fear;* to make them forget *heaven, death* and *judgment;* to fofter *lust, vanity* and *wantonnefs;....*'"

Pennsylvania state law, 30 March 1779, in *Laws Enacted in the Second Sitting of the Third General Assembly, of the Commonwealth of Pennsylvania* (Philadelphia? 1779), 190-192.

"An ACT *for the fuppreffion of vice and immorality.*

"SECT. 8. *And be it further enacted by the authority aforefaid,* That if any perfon or perfons fhall promote or encourage any match or matches of cock-fighting or bullet-playing, or appear in any public or private place with a cock or cock prepared to fight for any bet or prize; or, in like manner, affembled to play at bullets for any bet or prize; or fhall enter, ftart, or run any horfe, mare or gelding, for any bet or prize; or fhall promote or be concerned in any fhooting match,for any plate, prize, fum of money, or other thing of value whatfoever; or fhall make, print, publifh, or proclaim any advvertifement or notice, of any plate, prize, fum of money, or other thing of value, for the ufe of cock-fighting, bullet-playing, horfe racing, or to be fhot for, by any perfon or perfons whofoever; he, fhe, or they upon conviction thereof by indictment in any Court of Quarter Seffions of the Peace and Jail Delivery, to be held for the city or county where the offence is or fhall be committed, fhall forfeit and pay the fum of Five hundred Pounds."

"SECT. 10. *Be it therefore enacted by the authority aforefaid,* That if any public houfekeeper, or other retailer of ftrong liquors, fhall promote or encourage any horfe race, cock fight, bullet match, fhooting match, or other fuch idle fport; or fhall fell any wine, rum, whifkey, beer, cyder, or other ftrong liquors whatfoever, to any perfon or perfons affembled or met for the purpofe of attending any horse race, cock fight, bullet match, fhooting match, or other idle fport; or fhall permit or fuffer any kind of playing or gaming for money or other valuable thing, either at cards, dice, billiards, bowls, fhuffle-board, or in any other manner whatfoever to be ufed, practifed, or carried on within his or her houfe, or in any place in his or her occupancy; every fuch offence, whereof he or fhe fhall be legally convicted upon indictment in any court of Quarter Seffions of the Peace and Jail Delivery, forfeit and pay the fum of Twenty Pounds...."

* * *

Virginia state law, circa 1779, in *Acts Passed at a General Assembly, Begun and Held at the capitol, in the City of Williamsburg, on Monday the Fourth Day of October, in the Year of Our Lord, One Thousand Seven Hundred and Seventy Nine* (Williamsburg, Va.: John Dixon & Thomas Nicolson, 1779), 41.

"An ACT *to* SUPPRESS *exceffive* GAMING.

"*BE it enacted by the General Affembly,* that every promife, agreement, note, bill, bond, or other contract to pay, deliver, or fecure money or other thing won, or obtained by playing at cards, dice, tables, tennis, bowles, or other games; or by betting or laying on the hands or fides of any perfon who fhall play at fuch games; or won or obtained by betting or laying on any horferace, or cockfighting, or at any other fport or paftime,...fhall be void."

WORK SPORTS

Ezra Stiles, Yale College president, chronicles local yarn spinning matches, April 1769, May 1770, May and June 1771, May 1772, May 1773, and May 1774, in Franklin Bowditch Dexter, ed., *The Literary Diary of Ezra Stiles, D.D., LL.D. President of Yale College,* 3 vols., Vol. 1 (New York: Charles Scribner's Sons, 1901), 8-9, 53, 106-107, 237, 376, 440.

26 April 1769: "Spinning Match at my House, *thirty-seven Wheels*; the Women bro't their flax—& spun *ninety-four* fifteen-knotted skeins: about five skeins & half to the pound of 16 ounces. They made us a present of the whole. The Spinners were two Quakers, six Baptists, twenty-nine of my own Society. There were beside fourteen Reelers, &c. In the evening & next day, Eighteen 14-knotted skeins more were sent in to us by several that spun at home the same day. Upon sorting & reducing of it, the whole amounts to One hundred & eleven fifteen-knotted skeins. We dined sixty persons."

30 May 1770: "This day a voluntary Bee or Spinning Match at my house. Begun by Break o'day, & in fornoon early were sixty-four Spinning Wheels going. Afternoon seventy wheels going at the same Time for part of the time. Ninety-two daughters of Liberty spun and reeled, respiting and assisting one another. Many brought their flax, especially of my Society—the Spinners were of all Denominations, Chh., Quakers, Bapt. & Cong. &c. They spun One hundred & seventy Skeins (fourteen-knotted) and seven Knots. They found two-thirds of the flax. The 170 Skeins weighed thirty-two Averd. Of the 70 stationed to the 70 Wheels, 41 or more were of my Meet^g, and of the 92 about 53 were mine. The yarn very good."

24 May 1771: This day a Spinning Match at Mr Hopkins' about eighty Wheels."

5 June 1771: "Spinning Match at my house, 70 Wheels; spun & brot in 187 fourteen-knotted Skeins of fine Linnen yarn."

21 May 1772: "My kind People had a spinning Match at my House. We had *seventy seven* Wheels going all day, which delivered in at Night 224 fourteen knotted skeins of Linnen; which they gave us."

28 May 1773: "This Day we had a Spinning Match at my House, about 60 Wheels—they spun and made us a present of 183 fourteen knotted Skeins."

18 May 1774: "This day a Spinning Match at my House—68 Wheels—delivered in to us 172 fourteen-knotted skeins of Linnen Yarn."

Chapter 2

AQUATICS

Americans in the colonial and revolutionary periods lived close to many bodies of water, oceans, bays, rivers, creeks, ponds, and lakes. Many traversed these waters or fished in them. Surprisingly, few Americans in those times could swim or enjoyed the water for recreation. Perhaps that is why they were impressed with the seemingly natural abilities of indigenous peoples in the water, and why they took note of their swimming methods.

When the peripatetic Benjamin Franklin became an expert swimmer himself and starting in the 1760s advocated swimming as a safety measure and healthful amusement, he was a rare voice. Most Americans feared swimming. Many of the swimming, or bathing, accounts in these earlier times contained stories of drownings or near-drownings. Likely these narratives were lamentable reminders of the danger that attended any careless pastime, and probably there were Americans who did swim or bathe safely, thus never making the newspaper.

By the 1760s and 1770s the leisure industry in several cities, particularly New York City, consisted of public baths and swimming tanks or "machines" for swimming and bathing. These were either private clubs or open by subscription, but probably were accessible to the privileged and not the average citizen. It is unclear from the advertisement how much actual swimming occurred as opposed to more sedentary bathing, but the times labelled even the latter as sport. Much of what went under the term "bathing" during this period was likely to be submergings in cold or hot water baths.

Other water-based recreation was similarly scarce. Unless boating, rowing, yachting, and canoeing were so incredibly commonplace experiences that no one thought to write about them, the overall record barely indicates these pastimes. Occasionally a group of friends sailed a boat for fun and a challenge match spurred some competitive rowing, but infrequency seemed to be the rule. Oddly enough, given the Dutch origin of the word "yacht," New Netherlanders left no writings about regattas. Probably some canoeists in the fur trade engaged each other in contests, "work sport" of sorts, but again the chronicles are bare of references. It was not until after 1820 that water-based sports gained popularity. The following sources provide an extended glimpse at these activities in colonial and revolutionary America.

[Consult the general writings about sports, recreation, and the various colonial, provincial, territorial, and state Sabbath and gaming laws in Chapter One for other sources about the specific sports or games in this chapter.]

Yale College law, circa 1774, in *The Laws of Yale-College, in New-Haven, in Connecti-cut, Enacted by the President and Fellows* (New Haven, Conn.: Thomas and Samuel Green, 1774), 14.

"19. If any Scholar fhall go a Fifhing or Sailing, or undrefs himfelf for Swimming, in any Place expofed to public View...he may be fined not exceeding two Shillings;...."

* * *

Philip Vickers Fithian, tutor at Nomini Hall, Virginia, chronicles boat races, pleasure boating, and swimming in Virginia, July, August, and September 1774, and in east central Pennsylvania near the Susquehanna River, June and July 1775, in Hunter Dickinson Farish, ed., *Journal and Letters of Philip Vickers Fithian, 1773-1774. A Plantation Tutor of the Old Dominion* (Charlottesville, Va.: University Press of Virginia, 1957 [1943]), 145, 146-147, 151, 154, 189, 192; and Robert Greenhalgh Albion and Leonidas Dodson, eds., *Philip Vickers Fithian. Journal, 1775-1776 Written on the Virginia-Pennsylvania Frontier and in the Army around New York* (Princeton, N.J.: Princeton University Press, 1934), 40, 51.

16 July 1774: "I have forgot to remark before that from the time of our setting out as we were going down Machodock, & along the Potowmack-Shore, & especially as we were rowing up Nominy we saw Fishermen in great numbers in Canoes,...."

20 July 1774: "At *Coffee* The Colonel & myself entered somehow into Dispute upon the advantage in working an Oar—He asserted & tried to prove that the advantage lies in having the Oar longer from the *Thole-pin* or where it lies on the Boat to the water than from the *Thole-pin* to the Rowers hand in a mathematical sense; He allow'd the Water to the Fulcrum or Prop, & the Boat to be the weight, & the Rower to be a secondary Power—But the resistance of the Water to the Oar hecall'd the chief & primary Power—"

30 July 1774: "He [Captain Dobby] acquainted us that at Hobb's-Hole this Day is a Boat-Race on the River Rappahannock Each Boat is to have 7 Oars: to row 2 Mile out & 2 Miles in round a Boat lying at Anchor—The Bett 50£—And that in the Evening there is a great Ball to be given—I believe both the *Rowers* & *dancers*, as well *Ladies* as *Gentlemen* will perspire freely—Or in plain English they will soak in Sweat! The Captain invited us on Board his Ship next Tuesday to Dine with him & wish them a pleasant Passage as the Ship is to Sail the day following—If the Weather is not too burning hot I shall go provided the Others go likewise."

2 August 1774: "The Boats were to Start, to use the Language of Jockeys, immediately after Dinner; A Boat was anchored down the River at a Mile Distance—Captain *Dobby* and Captain *Benson* steer'd the Boats in the Race—Captain *Benson* had 5 Oarsmen; Captain *Dobby* had 6—It was Ebb-Tide—The Betts were small—& and chiefly given to the Negroes who rowed—Captain Benson won the first Race—Captain Purchace offered to bett ten Dollars that with the same Boat & same Hands, only having Liberty to put a small Weight in the Stern, he would beat Captain *Benson*—He was taken, & came out best only half the Boats length—About Sunset we left the Ship, & went all to Hobb's Hole, where a *Ball* was agreed on...."

11 September 1774: "Towards evening, I took a book in my hand, & strolled down to the Pasture quite to the Bank of the River—Miss *Stanhope, Priss, Nancy, Fanny* &

Betsy Carter were just passing by—They walked to the *Mill;* there they entered a Boat, & for exercise & amusement were rowed down the River quite to the granary, & then went to angling—I walked to them, & together we all marched Home to *Coffee*."

18 September 1774: "The Morning was fine, & Nomini-River alive with Boats Canoes &c some going to Church, some fishing, & some Sporting—...."

29 June 1775: "...—After Dinner, with two of Mr. *Gibson's* I went down the River for Exercise & Diversion, in a small Boat."

7 July 1775: "Towards Evening, I took a pleasant Turn on the River: I wish'd to leave the Boat & swim, but Spectators from every Part prevented me—...."

SWIMMING

William Wood, English settler, concerning swimming by indigenous people in New England, circa 1634, in Wood, *New England's Prospect, A True, Lively and Experimentall Defcription of that Part of America, Commonly Called Nevv England. Difcovering the Ftate of that Countrie, Both As It Ftands to Our New-Come* Englifh *Planters; and to the Old Native Inhabitants* (London: Thomas Cotes, 1634), reprinted as *Wood's New-England Prospect, Publications of the Prince Society, Volume 1* (Boston: The Prince Society, 1865), 96-98.

"For their fports of activitie they have commonly but three or foure; as footeball, fhooting, running and fwimming...."

"It is moft delight to fee them play, in fmaller companies, when men may view their fwift fotemanfhip, their curious Toffings of their Ball, their flouncing into the water...."

"For their fwimming it is almoft naturall, but much perfected by continuall practife; their fwimming is not after our *Englifh* fafhion of fpread armes and legges which they hold too tiresome, but like dogges their armes before them cutting through the liquids withe their right fhoulder; in this manner they fwimme very fwift and farre, either n rough or fmooth waters, fometimes for their eafe lying as ftill as a log; fometimes they will play the dive-doppers, and come up in unexpected places. Their children likewife be taught to fwimme when they are yong."

* * *

Samuel Sewall, Boston magistrate, swims in Boston Bay, 15 August 1687, and in the Thames River in London, July 1689, in M. Halsey Thomas, ed., T*he Diary of Samuel Sewall, 1674-1729, Volume I. 1674-1708* (New York: Farrar, Straus and Giroux, 1973), 146, 226-227.

15 August 1687: "Went into the Water alone at Blackstone's Point."

8 July, 1689: "Went with Mr. Brattle and swam in the Thames, went off from the Temple Stairs, and had a Wherry to wait on us: I went in in my Drawers. I think it hath been heathfull and refreshing to me."

John Barnard, Marblehead, Massachusetts clergyman, circa 1767, concerning a summer, 1697 swimming accident near Harvard College, in Barnard, "Autobiography of the Rev. John Barnard [1767]," *Collections of the Massachusetts Historical Society,* Third Series, Vol. 5 (Boston, 1836), reprinted in John Demos, ed., *Remarkable Providences. Readings on Early American History* (Boston: Northeastern University Press, 1991), 76-77.

"The other instance happened the summer following, when a great number of the scholars went to bathe and cool themselves in the river, upon a very hot day. George Curwin, a freshman, who could not swim, went up to his waist near the foot of the bridge, ducking and trying to learn to swim. It being near high water, the tide came round the foot of the bridge with a strong current and, ere he was aware, carried him past his depth, and soon hurried him into the current of the arch, which threw him a great way into the river, where he was dabbling and drowning. One of the tallest and stoutest young men immediately swam off to his relief, [and] bid him get upon his back, and he would carry him ashore. He got upon the back of the young man, but unhappily, instead of taking him round the neck, he embraced both the arms of the young man so strongly that he could not extend them to swim, who became now as much in danger of drowning as Curwin. He tried to shake him off but could not, and both were now tumbling in the water. I happened to be upon a pier of the bridge, and called to the company now on shore (who cared not to go off to their help lest they should be alike entangled) to wade, the tallest up to his chin, and make a string to the shore, and I would try to save them. Upon which I immediately swam away to the helpless couple, kept myself from their laying hold on me, and continually pushed them forward till they were got within the reach of the outmost man and were recovered, seemingly at the last gasp, and thus, through divine goodness, they were both preserved."

* * *

William Byrd, Westover, Virginia planter, goes swimming locally, July and August 1710 and June 1711, in Louis B. Wright and Marion Tinling, eds., *The Secret Diary of William Byrd of Westover, 1709-1712* (Richmond, Va.: The Dietz Press, 1941), 207, 220, 221, 360.

21 July 1710: "I drank some milk and water after I came out of the river where I had been to swim."

19 August 1710: "We went into the river."

22 August 1710: "I went into the river."

15 June 1711: "Then I took a walk about the plantation and then swam in the river to wash and refresh myself."

* * *

Joshua Hempstead, New London, Connecticut carpenter, notes a swimming accident, 3 July 1712, in [Hempstead], *Diary of Joshua Hempstead of New London, Connecticut Covering a Period of Forty-Seven Years from September, 1711, to November, 1758, Collections of the New London County Historical Society, Volume I* (New London, Conn.: New London County Historical Society, 1901), 12.

"Little Thomas Avery drownded in a Swiming."

John Fontaine, Irish Huguenot immigrant to Virginia, swims in the Rappahannock River, 10 September 1716, in [Fontaine], "Journal of John Fontaine," in Ann Maury, *Memoirs of a Huguenot Family. Translated and Compiled from the Original Autobiography of Rev. James Fontaine* (New York: George P. Putnam & Company, 1853), 290.

I went at five to swim in the Rappahannoc River, and returned to the town."

* * *

Antoine Le Page du Pratz, French traveler, concerning swimming by indigenous people in Louisiana, circa 1720-1728, in du Pratz, *The History of Louisiana, or of the Western Parts of Virginia and Carolina. Containing a Description of the Countries that lie on both Sides of the River Mississippi. With an Account of the Settlements, Inhabitants, Soil, Climate, and Products* (London: T. Becket, 1774), 341.

"…and left of all they go and bathe; an exercife of which they are very fond of when they are heated or fatigued."

* * *

Roger Wolcott, Connecticut lawyer and politician, refers to swimming in a poem, circa 1725, in Wolcott, "Some Improvement of Vacant Hours," in *Poetical Meditations, Being the Improvement of Some Vacant Hours* (New London, Conn.: L. Green, 1725), 32.

"The Waters Frefh and Sweet, & he that fwims
In it, Recruits and Cures his Surfeit Limbs."

* * *

Notice of a swimming accident in Philadelphia, South Carolina Gazette, No. 35, 9-16 September 1732.

"*Philadelphia, July* 27. On Tuefday Morning laft about one o'Clock, one John M'Donnal attempting to fwim over Skuylkil Ferry, commonly called Roach's Ferry, was drowned. The Body was taken up the fame Day."

* * *

William Byrd, Virginia Planter, near the Roanoke River in Virginia, 30 September 1733, in [Byrd], "A Journey to the Land of Eden," in Louis B. Wright, ed., *The Prose Works of William Byrd of Westover. Narratives of a Colonial Virginian* (Cambridge, Mass.: Harvard University Press, 1966), 397.

"This being Sunday, we were glad to rest from our labors; and, to help restore our vigor, several of us plunged into the river, notwithstanding it was a frosty morning. One of our Indians went in along with us and taught us their way of swimming. They strike not out both hands together but alternately one after another, whereby they are able to swim both farther and faster than we do."

* * *

Notice of a drowning near Boston, Boston News-Letter, No. 1637, 26 June 26-3 July 1735.

"On Saturday laft about Noon the only Son of Mr. *Robert Hadwin* of this Town, a promifing Lad near 13 Years of Age, going in the Water to Swim at the Bottom of the Common, venturing out too far, fank down, and was drowned: His Body was foon taken up, and very decently buried on Monday laft, a great number of his School-Mates following him to the Grave, many of them feeming to be much affected with this forrowful Providence; which 'tis hop'd will caufe others to be more careful for the future."

John Adams, Massachusetts lawyer, politician, and later United States President, concerning his boyhood swimming, circa 1740s, in [Adams], "The Autobiography of John Adams," in Lyman H. Butterfield, ed., *Diary and Autobiography of John Adams, Volume 3. Diary, 1782-1804, Autobiography, Part One To October 1776* (Cambridge, Mass.: Harvard University Press, 1962), 257; and Adams to Skelton Jones, 11 March 1809, reprinted in Adrienne Koch and William Peden, eds., *The Selected Writings of John and John Quincy Adams* (New York: Alfred A. Knopf, 1946), 153.

"[A]nd I spent my time as idle Children do in making and sailing boats and Ships upon the Ponds and Brooks, in making and flying Kites, in driving hoops, playing marbles, playing Quoits, Wrestling, Swimming, Skaiting and above all in shooting, to which Diversion I was addicted to a degree of Ardor which I know not that I ever felt for any other Business, Study or Amusement.

"My Enthusiasm for Sports and Inattention to Books, allarmed my father, and he frequently entered into conversation with me upon the Subject...."

"17. Under my first Latin master, who was a churl, I spent my time in shooting, skating, swimming, flying kites, and every boyish exercise and diversion I could invent. Never mischievous. Under my second master, who was kind, I began to love my books and neglect my sports."

* * *

Benjamin Franklin, Pennsylvania editor, proposes swimming as a part of physical education, circa 1749, in [Franklin], *Proposals Relating to the Education of Youth in Pensilvania* (Philadelphia: pvt. ptg?, 1749), 10-11.

"That to keep them [pupils] in Health, and to ftrengthen and render active their Bodies, they be frequently exercis'd in Running, Leaping, Wreftling, and Swimming,† &c."

    † 'Tis fuppos'd that every Parent would be glad to have their Children fkill'd in *Swimming*, if it might be learnt in a Place chofen for its Safety, and under the Eye of a careful Perfon. Mr. *Locke* fays, p. 9. in his *Treatife of Education*; "'Tis that faves many a Man's Life; and the *Romans* thought it fo neceffary, that they rank'd it with Letters; and it was the common Phrafe to mark one ill educated, and good for nothing, that he had neither learnt to read nor to fwim; *Nec Literas didicit nec Natare.* But befides the gaining a Skill which may ferve him at Need, the Advantages to Health by often Bathing in cold Water during the Heat of the Summer, are fo many, that I think nothing need be faid to encourage it.'

    'Tis fome Advantage befides, to be free from the flavifh Terrors many of thofe feel who cannot fwim, when they are oblig'd to be on the Water even in croffing a ferry."

* * *

Henry Alline, Nova Scotia Baptist minister, about his boyhood swimming in Rhode Island in 1758, in James Beverly and Barry Moody, eds., *The Life and Journal of The Rev. Mr. Henry Alline* (Hantsport, N.S.: Lancelot Press, 1982 [1806]), 33.

"Whenever I went a swimming with my mates, I would pray, that I might not be drowned."

* * *

Paul Coffin, Wells, Massachusetts schoolteacher, goes swimming near Palmer, Massachusetts, 20 July 1760, in [Coffin], "A Tour to Connecticut River, through the Colony of

Massachusetts from Wells," New England Historical and Genealogical Register, Vol. 9, No. 4 (October 1855), 340.

"Went into Swimming; and, after that, had a Night of Sweet Rest."

* * *

Advertisement for a bathing house in New York City, New York Gazette, No. 79, 11 August 1760.

"A COLD BATHING-HOUSE

Oppofite to Mr. *Nicholas Roofevelt*, at the *North River*,

IS kept in order for the Ufe of Gentlemen, or Ladies by ABRAHAM FINCHER,

Who takes Care to have the Water let in frefh every Tide, and has it convenient for Ufe from half Flood to half Ebb. Thofe who chufe to engage for the Ufe of it, by the Year, or otherways, may apply to faid *Fincher*."

* * *

Thomas Hutchinson, Massachusetts politician and historian, circa 1765, lists the recreations of New England indigenous peoples, in Hutchinson, *The History of the Province of Massachusetts Bay,* 2nd ed., 2 vols., Vol. 1 (London: M. Richardson, 1765) 471.

"Swimming, running, and wrestling they [Massachusetts indigenous people] were, as early [as childhood], accustomed to."

* * *

A children's book draws a moral about swimming, in *A Little Pretty Pocket-Book, Intended for the Amusement and Instruction of Little Master Tommy and Pretty Miss Polly* (London: J. Newbery, 1767), 89.

"SWIMMING.

WHEN the Sun's Beams have warm'd the Air,
Our Youth to fome cool Brook repair;
In whofe refrefhing Streams they play,
To the laft Remnant of the Day.

RULE *of* LIFE.

Think ere you fpeak; for Words, once flown,
Once utter'd, are no more your own."

* * *

Benjamin Franklin, Philadelphia printer, inventor, and politician, advises on swimming techniques, before 1769, in Franklin to Oliver Neave, in William B. Willcox, ed., *The Papers of Benjamin Franklin, Volume 15, January 1 through December 31, 1768* (New Haven: Yale University Press, 1972), 295-298.

"Dear Sir,   [Before 1769]

I Cannot be of opinion with you that 'tis too late in life for you to learn to swim. The river near the bottom of your garden affords you a most convenient place for the purpose. And as your new employment requires your being often on the water, of which you have such a dread, I think you would do well to make the trial; nothing being so likely to remove those apprehensions as the consciousness of an ability to swim to the shore, in case of an accident, or of supporting yourself in the water till a boat could come to take you up.

"I do not know how far corks or bladders may be useful in learning to swim, having never seen much trial of them. Possibly they may be of service in supporting the body while you are learning what is called the stroke, or that manner of drawing in and striking out the hands and feet that is necessary to produce progressive motion. But you will be no swimmer till you can place some confidence in the power of the water to support you; I would therefore advise acquiring that confidence in the first place; especially as I have known several who by a little of the practice necessary for that purpose, have insensibly acquired the stroke, taught as it were by nature.

"The practice I mean is this. Chusing a place where the water deepens gradually, walk coolly into it till it is up to your breast, then turn round, your face to the shore, and throw an egg into the water between you and the shore. It will sink to the bottom, and be easily seen there, as your water is clear. It must lie in water so deep as that you cannot reach it to take it up but by diving for it. To encourage yourself in undertaking to do this, reflect that your progress will be from deeper to shallower water, and that at any time you may by bringing your legs under you and standing on the bottom, raise your head far above the water. Then plunge under it with your eyes open, throwing yourself towards the egg, and endeavouring by the action of your hands and feet against the water to get forward till within reach of it. In this attempt you will find, that the water buoys you up against your inclination; that it is not so easy a thing to sink as you imagined; that you cannot, but by active force, get down to the egg. Thus you feel the power of the water to support you, and learn to confide in that power; while your endeavours to overcome it and to reach the egg, teach you the manner of acting on the water with your feet and hands, which action is afterwards used in swimming to support your head higher above water, or to go forward through it.

"I would the more earnestly press you to the trail of this method, because, though I think I satisfyed you that your body is lighter than water, and that you might float in it a long time with your mouth free for breathing, if you would put yourself in a proper posture, and would be still and forbear struggling; yet till you have obtained this experimental confidence in the water, I cannot depend on your having the necessary presence of mind to recollect that posture and the directions I gave you relating to it. The surprize may put all out of your mind. For though we value ourselves on being reasonable knowing creatures, reason and knowledge seem on such occasions to be of little use to us; and the brutes to whom we allow scarce a glimmering of either, appear to have the advantage of us.

"I will, however, take this opportunity of repeating those particulars to you, which I mentioned in our last conversation, as by perusing them at your leisure, you may possibly imprint them so in your memory as on occasion to be of some use to you.

"1. That though the legs, arms and head, of a human body, being solid parts, are specifically something heavier than fresh water, yet the trunk, particularly the upper part from its hollowness, is so much lighter than water, as that the whole of the body taken tgether is too light to sink wholly under water, but some part will remain above, untill the lungs become filled with water, which happens from drawing water into them instead of air, when a person in the fright attempts breathing while the mouth and nostrils are under water.

"2. That the legs and arms are specifically lighter than salt-water, and will be supported by it, so that a human body would not sink in salt-water, though the lungs were filled as above, but from the greater specific gravity of the head.

"3. That therefore a person throwing himself on his back in salt-water, and extending his arms, may easily lie so as to keep his mouth and nostrils free for breathing; and by a small motion of his hands may prevent turning, if he should perceive any tendency to it.

"4. That in fresh water, if a man throws himself on his back, near the surface, he cannot long continue in that situation but by proper action of his hands on the water. If he uses no such action, the legs and lower part of the body will gradually sink till he comes into an upright position, in which he will continue suspended, the hollow of the breast keeping the head uppermost.

"5. But if in this erect position, the head is kept upright above the shoulders, as when we stand on the ground, the immersion will, by the weight of that part of the head that is out of water, reach above the mouth and nostrils, perhaps a little above the eyes, so that a man cannot long remain suspended in water with his head in that position.

"6. The body continuing suspended as before, and upright, if the head be leaned quite back, so that the face looks upwards, all the back part of the head being then under water, and its weight consequently in a great measure supported by it, the face will remain above water quite free for breathing, will rise an inch higher every inspiration, and sink as much every expiration, but never so low as that the water may come over the mouth.

"7. If therefore a person unacquainted with swimming, and falling accidentally into the water, could have presence of mind sufficient to avoid struggling and plunging, and to let the body take this natural position, he might continue long safe from drowning till perhaps help would come. For as to the cloathes, their additional weight while immersed is very considerable, the water supporting it; though when he comes out of the water, he would find them very heavy indeed.

"But, as I said before, I would not advise you or any one to depend on having this presence of mind on such an occasion, but learn fairly to swim; as I wish all men were taught to do in their youth; they would, on many occurrences, be the safer for having that skill, and on many more the happier, as freer from painful apprehensions of danger, to say nothing of the enjoyment in so delightful and wholesome an exercise. Soldiers particularly should, methinks, all be taught to swim; it might be of frequent use in surprising an enemy, or saving themselves. And if I had now boys to educate, I should prefer those schools (other things being equal) where an opportunity was afforded for acquiring so advantageous an art, which once learnt is never forgotten. I am, Sir, &c. B.F."

* * *

Advertisement for swimming equipment in New York City, 1769, reprinted in Esther Singleton, *Social New York under the Georges* (New York: D. Appleton and Company, 1902), 266.

[Jarvis Roebuck, a cork-cutter informed the public that he had] "cork jackets of different prices for swimming, which has saved many from drowning."

* * *

Benjamin Franklin, Philadelphia statesman and inventor, circa 1771, remembers swimming during his childhood and 1726 trip to London, in [Franklin], *The Autobiography of Benjamin Franklin*, ed. by Leonard W. Labaree, Ralph L. Ketcham, Helen C. Boatfield, and Helene H. Fineman (New Haven, Conn.: Yale University Press, 1964), 53-54, 103-104, 105-106.

"I dislik'd the Trade [as a candlemaker] and had a strong Inclination for the Sea; but my Father declar'd against it; however, living near the Water, I was much in and about it, learnt early to swim well, and to manage Boats, and when in a Boat or Canoe with other Boys I was commonly allow'd to govern, especially in any case of Difficulty;...."

"I taught him, and a Friend of his, to swim, at twice going to the River, and they soon became good Swimmers. They introduc'd me to some Gentlemen from the Country who went to Chelsea by Water to see the College and Don Saltero's Curiosities. In our Return, at the Request of the Company, whose Curiosity Wygate had excited, I stript and leapt into the River, and swam from near Chelsea to Blackfryars, performing on the Way many Feats of Activity both upon and under Water, that surpriz'd & pleas'd those to whom they were Novelties. I had from a Child been ever delighted with this Exercise, had studied and practis'd all Thevenot's Motions and Positions, added some of my own, aiming at the graceful and easy, as well as the Useful. All these I took Occasion of exhibiting to the Company, and was much flatter'd by their Admiration."

"He [Sir William Wyndham] had heard by some means or other of my Swimming from Chelsey to Blackfryars, and of my teaching Wygate and another young Man to swim in a few Hours. He had two Sons about to set out on their Travels; he wish'd to have them first taught Swimming; and propos'd to gratify me handsomely if I would teach them. They were not yet come to Town and my Stay was uncertain, so I could not undertake it. But from this Incident I thought it likely, that if I were to remain in England and open a Swimming School, I might get a good deal of Money. And it struck me so strongly, that had the Overture been sooner made me, probably I should have not so soon have returned to America."

* * *

Benjamin Rush, Philadelphia physician, recommends swimming as a recreation, circa 1772, in Rush, *Sermons to Gentlemen upon Temperance and Exercise* (Philadelphia: John Dunlap, 1772), 32-33.

"Too much cannot be faid in praife of SWIMMING, or as the poet of Avon expreffes it—'buffeting the waves with lufty sinews.' Befides exercifing the limbs, it ferves to wafh away the duft, which is apt to mix itfelf with the fweat of our bodies in warm weather. Wafhing frequently in water, we find, was enjoined upon the Jews and Mahometans, as a part of their religious ceremonies. The Hollanders are cleanly in their houfes and ftreets, without remembering, or perhaps knowing, that cleanlinefs was absolutely neceffary at firft, to guard againft the effects of thofe inundations of mire, to which their country is always expofed—fo a Jew and a Muffulman contend for, and practife their ablutions, without remembering that they were inftituted only to guard them againft thofe cutanious difeafes, to which the conftant accumulation of fordes upon their fkins in a warm climate, naturally expofed them. For the fame reafon, I would ftrongly recommend the practife of bathing, and fwimming, frequently in the fummer feafon. But remember, you fhould not ftay too long in the water at one time, leaft you leffen inftead of increafing the vigour of the conftitution."

* * *

John Ferdinand Dalziel Smyth, British traveler, discusses swimming in Virginia, November? December? 1772? or January? February? 1773?, in Smyth, *A Tour in the United*

States of America. Containing an Account of the Present Situation of that Country, 2 vols., Vol. 1 (London: G. Robinson, 1784), 131-132.

"I accuftomed myfelf to go out along with them a hunting, fifhing, fwimming, fowling, &c. for my amufement and diverfion.

"Being once on a vifit at a Mr. Glen's, he and I went to the river to fwim, it being a very fhort diftance from his houfe; whilft we were there, his wife and her fifter, who were both young and handfome, came down to the water-fide and in a frolic hid our cloaths.

"After they had laughed at us for fome time, they informed us where they were, and I put mine on; but he ran out of the water, and purfued the women ftark naked."

* * *

John Long, American trader, concerning swimming by indigenous peoples in the Great Lakes region, circa 1777, in Milo Milton Quaife, ed., *John Long's Voyages and Travels in the Years 1768-1788* (Chicago: Lakeside Press, 1922), 48.

"They are also admirable swimmers, and are not afraid of the strongest currents."

* * *

Jabez Fitch, Connecticut lieutenant, swims on Long Island, June and August 1777, in [Fitch], *The New-York Diary of Lieutenant Jabez Fitch of the 17th (Connecticut) Regiment from August 22, 1776 to December 15, 1777,* ed. by W.H. Sabine (New York: pvt. ptg., 1954), 180, 183, 198.

17 June 1777: "…, Capt: Bissel Mr: Eells & I went in a swimming;…."

26 June 1777: "…, & then went with Mestrs: Brewster Eells & Bilderback, down to the Creeck where we stript & went in a Swimming,…."

9 August 1777: "…; Emediately after dinner we went down to Wychofs, where we found Mestrs: Brewster & Eells, with whom we went down to the Crick & went in a swimming according to a plan, form'd for that purpose in the forenoon;…."

* * *

Joseph Joslin, Jr., South Killingly, Connecticut teamster, goes swimming, July 1777 and June, July, and August 1778, in [Joslin], "Journal of Joseph Joslin Jr. of South Killingly A Teamster in the Continental Service March 1777–August 1778," in "Orderly Book and Journals Kept by Connecticut Men While Taking part in the American Revolution 1775-1778," *Collections of the Connecticut Historical Society,* Vol. 7 (Hartford: Connecticut Historical Society, 1899), 318, 361, 363, 365.

10 July 1777: "…and at Even went in a Swiming…."

27 June 1778: "was Various hot indeed I hoed Corn & pertators and at Even went in Swiming…."

11 July 1778: "we hoed in the forenoon it was Cloudy and in the afternoon we Raked hay and got one load into the barn then it Raind a littel Swiming very hot day"

6 August 1778: "got there Jut before knight and I went Swiming…."

* * *

Advertisements for a swimming tank in New York City, [Rivington's] *Royal Gazette,* 1778.

"A BATHING MACHINE,

Upon the plan of thofe ufed at Margate, and other Watering-places in England, is propofed to be eftablifhed by fubfcription at the North River, near Vauxhall, being only a pleafant walk from moft parts of the city.

"CONDITIONS.

"I. Subfcribers to pay ONE GUINEA each, for which they will receive a Ticket, entitling them to the ufe of the Machine for the feafon; which ticket may be transferred or lent to others.

"II. Non-fubfcribers, having no Ticket, to pay FIVE SHILLINGS each time of bathing; but they are not to be admitted while any of the fubfcribers are in waiting.

"III. The number of Subfcribers fhall not exceed fifty, without another machine is fet up.

"IV. The machine will be ready for bathing by the firft of June, and attend daily till the laft of September, from fix in the morning till twelve at noon.

"V. It is expected that Gentlemen Subfcribers will rife early enough to difmifs the machine for the ufe of the Ladies, and thofe that do not, will wait till the Ladies retire.

"THE benefit of bathing in Salt-Water, being univerfally acknowledged, is it not aftonifhing that the Inhabitants of New-York, who have the means at hand fhould never yet have provided a coveniency for the purpofe. The Gentlemen could fcarce find a place to bathe in with decency, and the Ladies, though it is known to be of the greatest advantage to their delicate frames, have been totally excluded. Phyficians in general recommend Salt-Bathing as the beft prefervative againft difeafes in a hot climate, and they are known to have a more than genial warmth from the Sun's beams, at leaft two months in the year. In fhort, the defign being purely to ferve the public, and defray the incidental charges, there is no doubt it will meet the encouragement it deferves.

Subfcriptions are received by Mr. Rivington."   (No. 166, 25 April 1778)

"The Bathing Machine

WILL certainly be ready at the North River, on Saturday Morning next, behind Mr. Harrifon's Brewhoufe, when Attendance will be given every Morning during the Summer Seafon.

Subfcribers are defired to fend to Mr. Rivington for their Tickets."

"BATHING MACHINE

THE proprietor finding that the prefent number of fubfcriptions inadequate to the expence, is under a neceffity of declaring that the fubfcription will clofe on Saturday next, the 27th inft. after which time, fubfcriptions for the feafon will be raifed to two Guineas, and none but fubfcribers will be permitted to bathe. The machine will be ready as foon as poffible.

Subfcriptions are received by Mr. Rivington."   (No. 185, 8 July 1778)

"The Bathing Machine

IS ready at the North River, behind Mr. Harrifon's Brewhoufe, when Attendance will be given every Morning during the Summer Seafon. Subfcribers are defired to fend to Mr. Rivington for their Tickets."   (No. 190, 25 July 1778)

* * *

Samuel Dewees, Pennsylvania captain, goes swimming near West Point, New York, circa 1779, in John Smith Hanna, ed., *A History of the Life and Services of Captain Samuel Dewees, A Native of Pennsylvania, and Soldier of the Revolutionary and Last Wars* (Baltimore: Robert Neilson, 1844), 204-205.

"Sometime after we returned to West Point, a circumstance transpired which nearly cost me my life. There was a vessel laden with apples lying near the New England shore. Myself and comrades were very anxious to become possessed of some of them. As none of the musicians but myself could swim to any great distance, I volunteered to swim across the river for that purpose. I placed a knapsack upon my back and put the money into the lining of my cap, and plunged into the river and swam across to the vessel. When I arrived on the deck of the vessel, all hands were surprised when I asked them for apples. Some of them cried out 'where the d—l have you come from.' I told them I had come from West Point encampment for the purpose of buying apples, stating at the same time that I had brought money along to pay for them, as also a knapsack to carry them over in. The master of the vessel then filled my knapsack with apples, for which I paid him his price. He and the hands aboard fastened my knapsack upon my back, and assisted me in descending the wooden steps to the water's edge. To the steps there were ropes attached on each side to hold on by. When I had descended the steps to the edge of the water, the master and crew advised me not to venture, saying that I would be drowned and offered to carry my apples and myself over the river in their boat. This offer I rejected, being perhaps a little vain of my abilities as a swimmer. But if I was a little proud of my performances, I possessed something worth being proud of, for no man I ever met with could go me in swimming. It seemed to me that I could walk (tread) in the water, as long and as far as it might please me, and could swim upon my back any distance I chose to swim to.

"Notwithstanding the generous offer made to me by the crew, I dashed off into the water in fine spirits, and swam off with my load and had succeeded in reaching better than half way across the river. I do not recollect the width of the river at West Point, but suppose I had swam fully half a mile. All at once a monster of a Sturgeon jumped up out of the water very near to me, and making a great splashing and noise about me at the same time. Being frightened at this moment, thinking it might be a Shark, '*I began to pull away for life.*' This swimming in so hurried and hard a manner caused me to let water into my throat, which strangled me very much, and I began to sink. But as a kind Providence would have it, the *tide* was out at the time, and when I began to sink, I found bottom with my feet. This so encouraged me at the moment that my strength renewed itself, and by making a powerful effort I succeeded in reaching the land and my comrades in safety with my apples. As is with the jacktar in a storm, it was with me then. This made a deep impression for the moment, but I suppose it was soon lost (as are their impressions in a calm over a flowing cann) in making our eager repast —that of feasting upon my cargo of mellow and delicious apples. The ship's crew cheered tremendously when they saw me reach the shore in safety."

BOATING AND SAILING

Notices of boating accidents in Philadelphia, Boston News-Letter, 1728.

"Philadelphia, March 14. *On the* 10th Inft. *about* 3 *a Clock in the Afternoon, the following unhappy Accident happen'd to fix Boys who went from this City in an open Boat Pleafuring; they defign'd to crofs the River over to* Gloucefter, *and in their way one of them loft his Hat over-board, the Wind being very high at* N.W. *and they not underftanding how to manage the Boat, tack'd about all of a fudden and endeavour'd to take up the Hat, with their Sails haul'd clofe abaft, which occafion'd the Boat to over-fet, and three of them were drowned, and the other three were faved from perifhing in the Waves, (thro' the Divine Providence of the moft Merciful God) by fome Perfons who went in Boats from this City to their Affiftance.*"

(No. 65, 22-28 March 1728)

"We hear from Philadelphia, That not long fince, Three Young Men and Five Young Women, went out in a Boat to take their Pleafure on the River there on the Lords-Day, when a fudden fquall of Wind came and over-fet the Boat, and one of the Men with three of the Women were Drowned."   (No. 93, 3-10 October 1728)

* * *

Notice of a boating accident in New Hampshire, Boston News-Letter, No. 1439, 19-26 August 1731.

"*New-Hampfhire, Aug.* 20. On Wednefday laft the 18th Inftant, Two Men in a Boat who were to Sail for Pleafure here, was overfet, both were drowned, and the Boat found ftove to pieces."

* * *

Notice about a boating accident in Boston, Maryland Gazette, No. 431, 9 August 1753.

"BOSTON

July 9. Thurfday Laft, about twenty Perfons of both Sexes, went in a Two-Maft Boat from this Town on a Party of Pleafure to *Deer Ifland*, and anchored the Boat at fome Diftance from the Shore, and being impatient to Land, two Men and as many Women got into a Float, not much bigger than a Kneading Trough, and put off from the Bat, but had not gone far from her, before the Float overfet, and turned Bottom upwards, by which Accident one of the Men was drowned, but the other getting upon her Bottom, faved himfelf. At this Inftant a fifhing Schooner was coming through the Gut, and the People feeing the two Women in Diftrefs, immediately threw out their Boat and took them up, as they afterwards did the Man. The Women were fo far gone that they had no Senfe or Motion, but are now in a fair Way of Recovery. It is greatly to be wifhed, that People upon a Frolick, efpecially on the Water, would be *careful* and *wife*, as well as *merry*."

* * *

John Adams, Massachusetts lawyer, politician, and later United States President, sails near Boston, 25 June 1760, in Lyman H. Butterfield, ed., *Diary and Autobiography of John Adams, Volume 1*. Diary, *1755-1770* (Cambridge, Mass.: Harvard University Press, 1962), 140-141.

"Went out with the Coll., in his Canoe, after Tom Codd. Rowed down, in a still calm, and smooth Water, to Rainsford Island, round which we fished in several Places, but had no Bites. Then we went up the Island, and round the Hill....

"and then we dined expecting with much Pleasure an easy sail Home before the Wind, which hen bread fresh at East. After Diner we boarded and hoisted sail, and sailed very pleasantly a Mile, when the Wind died away into a Clock Calm and left us to row against the Tide, and presently against the Wind too for that sprung up at south, right a Head of us, and blew afresh. This was hard work. Doubtful what Course to steer, whether to Nut Island, or to Half Moon, or to Hangmans Island or to Sunken Island, Coll. Q. grew sick which determined us to go to ashore at Hangmans for that was nearest…. When the Coll. awoke and found himself strengthened and inspirited, we rowed away, under Half Moon, and then hoisted sail and run home. So much for the Day of Pleasure, The fishing frolick, and the Water frolick. We had none of the Pleasure of Angling, very little of the Pleasure of Sailing. We had much of the fatigue of Rowing, and some of the Vexation of Disappointment. However the Exercise and the Air and smell of salt Water is wholesome."

* * *

Ann MacVicar Grant, American lady, describes pleasure boating near Albany, New York, circa 1769, in [Grant], *Memoirs of an American Lady. With Sketches of Manners and Scenery in America, As They Existed Previous to the Revolution*, 2 vols., Vol. 1 (London: Longman, Hurst, Rees, and Orme, 1808), 97.

"Their amufements were marked by a fimplicity which, to ftrangers, appeared rude and childifh, (I mean thofe of the younger clafs.) In fpring, eight or ten of the young people of one company, or related to each other, young men and maidens, would fet out together in a canoe on a kind of rural excurfion, of which amufement was the object. Yet fo fixed were their habits of induftry, that they never failed to carry their work-bafkets with them, not as a form, but as an ingredient neceffarily mixed with their pleafures."

* * *

George Washington, Virginia planter, Revolutionary War general, and later President, mentions a boat race in Virginia, 7 May 1774, in Donald Jackson, ed., *The Diaries of George Washington*, 6 vols., Vol. 3 (Charlottesville, Va.: University Press of Virginia, 1978), 248.

"Went with the above Company to a Boat Race & Barbicue at Johnson's Ferry."

Chapter 3

ARCHERY AND SHOOTING

Two of the most common stereotypes associated with the colonial and Revolutionary eras of American history are the Noble, or Ignoble, Savage, replete with arrow notched, ready to let it fly at a deer or an unlucky settler, and the sturdy citizen-soldier, musket shouldered, drawing a bead on a bear or a British soldier. Although peaceful stretches actually did occur on the various frontiers, Americans have retained the attachment to images of violence in these formative years. Victuals needed securing, varmints needed plugging, and virtue and virility defending. Bows and arrows symbolized the lives of a sometimes hostile people; rifles and muskets ranked equally with the axe and the plow as symbols of conquest.

But the use of the bows and arrows and the firearms furnished some sport for those Americans. How many Americans of this period were actually familiar and proficient with these weapons is a matter of debate among historians. Certainly many, if not most, indigenous males, and some females, trained with the bow. Some of the Europeans brought with them a knowledge of archery from Europe's wars. Muskets and rifles were commonplace, but accuracy was accidental or scarce. Most males were subject to militia training requirements several times a year, but how often that improved skills is unknown at this point. Some military historians believe in battle a gun served better as a club or bayonet extender, given the accuracy, reloading, and misfire problems of early American firearms.

These problems notwithstanding, interest in archery and shooting techniques and exploits continued through the period. European explorers commented on indigenous bow and arrows styles, their accuracy, and the occasional contests in which tribal peoples shot at targets, stationary or moving. The English, remembering back to Robin Hood, Agincourt, and other British longbow heroics, at least gave attention to the idea of archery, and at one time required archery training for defense on the Rhode Island frontier. Still, no formal or genteel tradition of archery emerged. Occasionally, William Byrd, the Westover squire, carried a bow and arrows about his Virginia grounds attempting to shoot partridge, and several times he and friends shot at targets, but he apparently lost interest quickly.

Shooting contests were another matter. Travelers reported on local matches and repeated rumors of incredible feats of accuracy and distance shooting. Tales of challenges and jokes occasionally reached print. As much of the interest was attached to military prowess, soldiers honed or demonstrated their skills. Some accounts of training days told who won the ribbon or the hat shooting at marks in the afternoon. Horse races, fairs, and court days all became excuses to fire at targets, for prizes or just the pleasure of it. In some instances contests rewarded the winner with a gold watch, tack, a piece of furniture, or even a property lot in New York; on the frontiers, shooting for the beef or for the turkey was commonplace. The following selections illustrate the colonial and Revolutionary interest in the bow and the firearm as tools of conquest, defense, and hunting, as well as implements of sport.

[Consult the general writings about sports, recreation, and the various colonial, provincial, territorial, and state Sabbath and gaming laws in Chapter One for other sources about the specific sports or games in this chapter.]

ARCHERY AMONG COLONISTS

Edward Winslow, English settler and chronicler of Plymouth, Massachusetts, refers to archery, 11 December 1621, in [Winslow], "Gov. Bradford's History of Plymouth Colony," in Alexander Young, ed., *Chronicles of the Pilgrim Fathers of the Colony of Plymouth from 1602 to 1625* (Boston: George C. Little and James Brown, 1841), 231.

"At which time, amongst other recreations, we exercised our arms,...."

* * *

A Rhode Island and Providence Plantations statute requires archery practice in that colony, circa 1647, in John Russell Bartlett, ed., R*ecords of the Colony of Rhode Island and Providence Plantations in New England, Volume I. 1636 to 1663* (Providence, R.I.: A. Crawford Greene and Brother, 1856), 186-187.

"Archerie.

"Forasmuch, as we are cast among the Archers, and know not how sonne we may be deprived of Powder and Shott, without which our guns will advantage vs nothing; to the end also that we may come to outshoot these natives in their owne bow; Be it enacted by the authoritie of this present Assembly, that that statute touching Archerie, shall be revived and propagated throwout the whole Colonie; and that every person from the age of seventeen yeares, to the age of seventy, that is not lame, debilitated in his body, or otherwise exempted by the Colonie, shall have a Bow and for arrowes, and shall vse and exercise shooting; and every Father having Children, shall provide for every man-child from the age of seven years, till he come to seventeen yeares, a Bow and two Arrowes or shafts, to induce them, and to bring them up to shooting; and every sonn, servant, or master, thus appointed and ordered to have a Bow and Arrowes, that shall be remiss and negligent in the observance hereof, and shall be found to lack a bow and so many arrowes for the space of a month together after the last of the fourth month, commonly called June, shall forfeit three shillingsand four pence; the father shall pay for the son, the master for the servant, and deduct it out of his wages.

It is also ordered, that each Towne shall have a pair of Butts [embankments on which to place targets] before the last of the fourth Month, vnder the penaltie of ten shillings."

* * *

William Byrd, Virginia planter, practices archery, December 1709, February, March, and April 1710, and December 1711, in Louis B. Wright and Marion Tinling, eds., *The Secret Diary of William Byrd of Westover, 1709-1712* (Richmond, Va.: The Dietz Press, 1941), 114, 144, 157, 161, 454, 461.

5 December 1709: "In the afternoon we shot in a bow but none of us could hit the mark."

21 February 1710: "In the afternoon we shot with bow and arrow and I hit the mark."

27 March 1710: "Then we played at shooting with arrows till about 4 o'clock when we went all toMr. Harrison's,...."

3 April 1710: "In the afternoon we shot with a bow and then played at cricket."

17 December 1711: "Robin Bolling was better and he and I went to shoot with bows and arrows."

29 December 1711: "In the afternoon I set my razor, and then went out to shoot with bow and arrow till the evening...."

An account of a wedding near Saybrook, Connecticut, circa 1726, mentions archery as a recreation, reprinted in Helen Evertson Smith, *Colonial Days and Ways as Gathered from Family Papers by Helen Evertson Smith of Sharon, Connecticut* (New York: The Century Company, 1901), 180.

"[The men at wedding participated in] rastling, quoits, running, leaping, archery and firing at a mark, but on the last day no muskets were allowed by reason of the Indians."

* * *

John Armstrong, British writer refers to archery, circa 1757, in Armstrong, *The Art of Preserving Health*, 4th ed. (London and Boston: Green & Russell, 1757), 37.

"and there are,
Whom ftill the meed of the green archer charms."

* * *

Fray Miguel Venegas, Mexican Jesuit, mentions archery among other recreations at California rancherias, circa 1758, in Venegas, *A Natural and Civil History of California*, 2 vols., Vol. 1 (London: James Rivington and James Fletcher, 1759), 84.

"To thefe feftivities the rancherias ufually invite one another; and likewife often fend challenges for wreftling, leaping, running, fhooting with their bow, and trials of ftrength; and in thefe and the like fports, days and nights, weeks and months were often fpent in times of peace."

* * *

Ann MacVicar Grant, an American lady, observes archery near Albany, New York, circa 1769, in [Grant], *Memoirs of An American Lady. With Sketches of Manners and Scenery in America, As They Existed Previous to the Revolution*, 2 vols., Vol. 1 (London: Longman, Hurst, Rees, and Orme, 1808), 124.

"Boys on the verge of manhood, and ambitious to be admitted into the hunting parties of the enfuing winter, exercifed themfelves in trying to improve their fkill in archery, fhooting birds, fquirrels, and racoons."

* * *

Jabez Fitch, Connecticut lieutenant, notices archery on Long Island, 11 April 1777, in William H. Sabine, ed., *The New-York Diary of Lieutenant Jabez Fitch of the 17th (Connecticut) Regiment from August 22, 1776 to December 15, 1777* (New York: pvt. ptg., 1954), 161.

"...; After Breakfast I went over to Sherrv: lots where I observ'd Mestrs: Statten & Fisher, much Engag'd in shooting Arrows at a Dollar;...."

* * *

Samuel Dewees, Pennsylvania captain, practices archery at Lancaster, Pennsylvania, 1781? 1782?, in John Smith Hanna, ed., *A History of the Life and Services of Captain Samuel Dewees, A Native of Pennsylvania, and Soldier of the Revolutionary and Last Wars* (Baltimore: Robert Neilson, 1844), 271.

"..., I frequently amused myself with a bow and arrows, in shooting at rats in the stoccades. They were very numerous, and of an enormous size. This kind of sport I enjoyed very well. I one day shot at one which was nearly the size of a cat. I had shot my arrow through his body and he bit off the arrow."

ARCHERY AMONG INDIGENOUS PEOPLES

James Rosier, British explorer, concerning the bows and arrows of indigenous people in New England, circa 1605, in Rosier, *A Trve Relation of the Moft Profperous Voyage* Made this Prefent Yeere *1605, by Captaine* George Waymouth, *in the Difcouery of the land of* Virginia (London: George Bishop, 1605), C-C1.

"When we went on fhore to trade with them, in one of their Canoas I saw their bowes and arrowes, which I tooke up and drew an arrow in one of them, which I found to be of strength able to carry an arrow five or sixe score stronglie: and one of them tooke it and drew as we draw our bowes, not like the Indians. Their bow is made of Wich Hazell, and some of Beech in fashion much like our bowes, but they want nocks, onely a ftring of leather put through a hole at one end, and made faft with a knot at the other. Their arrowes are made of the fame wood, fome of Afh, big and long, with three feathers tied on, and nocked very artificiallie: headed with the long shanke bone of a Deere, made very sharpe with two fangs in manner of a harping iron."

* * *

Edward Winslow, English settler and chronicler of Plymouth, Massachusetts, concerning indigenous peoples' archery, circa 1620s, in [Winslow], "Gov. Bradford's History of Plymouth Colony," in Alexander Young, ed., *Chronicles of the Pilgrim Fathers of the Colony of Plymouth, from 1602 to 1625* (Boston: Charles C. Little and James Brown, 1841), 363.

"The [indigenous] men themselves wholly in hunting, and other exercises of the bow, except at some times they take some pains in fishing."

* * *

William Wood, English settler, concerning indigenous peoples' archery skills in New England, circa 1634, in Wood, *New Englands Prospect, A True, Lively and Experimentall Defcription of that Part of* America, *Commonly Called Nevv England. Difcovering the Ftate of that Countrie, Both As It Ftands to Our New-Come* Englifh *Planters; and to the Old Native Inhabitants* (London: Thomas Cotes, 1634), reprinted as *Wood's New-England Prospect, Publications of the Prince Society, Volume 1* (Boston: The Prince Society, 1865), 97-98.

"For their fports of activitie they [the indigenous people] have commonly but three or foure; as footeball, fhooting, running and fwimming:.... For their fhooting they be moft defperate markfmen for a point blancke object, and if it may bee poffible *Cornicum oculos configere* they will doe it; fuch is their celerity and dexterity in Artillerie, that they can fmite the fwift running Hinde and nimble winked Pigeon without a ftanding paufe or left eyed blinking; they draw their Arrowes between the fore fingers and the thumbe; their bowes be quicke, but not very ftrong, not killing above fix or feven fcore. Thefe men fhoot at one another, but with fwift conveighance fhunne the Arrow; this they doe to make them expert againft time of warre. It hath beene often admired how they can finde their Arrowes, be the weede as high as themfelves, yet they take fuch perfect notice of the flight and fall that they feldome loofe any. They are trained up to their bowes even from their childhood; little boyes with Bowes made of little ftickes and Arrowes of great bents, will fmite downe a peece of Tobacco pipe every fhoot a good way off: as thefe *Indians* be good markemen, fo are they well experienced where the very life of every creature lyeth, and know where to fmite him to make hime dye prefently."

Father Andrew White, British Jesuit missionary, about Maryland indigenous peoples' bows and arrows, circa 1634, in White, "A Briefe Relation of the Voyage unto Maryland, by Father Andrew White, 1634," in Clayton Colman Hall, ed., *Narratives of Early Maryland, 1633-1684* (New York: Barnes & Noble, Inc., 1918), 43.

"Their weapons are a bow and a bundle of arrowes, an ell long, feathered with turkies feathers, and headed with points of deered hornes, peeces of glasse, or flints, which they make fast with an excellent glew which they have for that purpose. The shaft is a small cane or sticke, wherewith I have seene them kill at 20 yards distance, little birds of the bignesse of sparrows, and they use to practise themselves by casting up small stickes in the aire, and meeting it with an arrow before it come to ground. Their bow is but weake and shoots level but a little way. They daily catch partridge, deere, turkies, squirrels and the like of which there is wonderfull [plenty?],...."

* * *

Peter Lindestrom, Swedish geographer, concerning the archery of Delaware indigenous people, circa 1654-1656, in Amandus Johnson, trans. and ed., *Geographia Americae with An Account of the Delaware Indians Based on Surveys and Notes Made in 1654-1656* (Philadelphia: Swedish Colonial Society, 1925), 215.

"In this their convention they [also] practice shooting. He who is sachem has a turkey placed very high in the air, whose entrails are removed and [the body] filled again with their money. And the one who then can shoot it down, he receives the money, *et talia*, etc."

* * *

Samuel Clarke, British writer, concerning the archery of Virginia area indigenous peoples, circa 1670, in Clarke, *A True and Faithful Account of the Four Chiefest Plantations of the English in America. Of Virginia, New England, Bermudus, Barbados* (London: R. Clavel and T. Passenger, 1670), 8.

"They much ufe their Bows and Arrows in Fifhing, Hunting, and the Wars. They bring their Bows to the form of ours, by fcraping them with a Shell: Their Arrows are made of ftrait young Sprigs, which they head with a bone, two or three inches log: With thefe they fhoot at *Squirils*. Other Arrows they have made of Reeds, pieced with Wood, and headed with Chriftals or Flint, &c..... To make the notch of their Arrows, they have the Tooth of a *Bever* fet in a ftick, with which they grate it by degrees. Their Arrow heads they quickly make with a little bone, which they ever wear at their bracer, of a fplint of ftone or glafs, in the form of a Heart, which they glew to their Arrows; their Glew they make of the Sinews of Deer, and the tops of Deer Horns which will not diffolve in cold water."

* * *

Charles Wooley, British clergyman, concerning the archery skills of New York area indigenous people, circa 1678, in W[ooley], *A Two Years Journal in New-York. And Part of its Territories in America* (London: John Wyat and Eben Tracy, 1701), reprinted in Cornell Jaray, ed., *Historic Chronicles of New Amsterdam, Colonial New York and Early Long Island, First Series,* Empire State Historical Publications Series No. 35 (Port Washington, N.Y.: Ira J. Friedman, 1968), 31.

"Before the Christians especially the Dutch came amongst them they were very dexterous Artists at their Bows, insomuch I have heard it affirm'd that a Boy of seven years old would shoot a Bird flying...."

Francis Louis Michel, Swiss traveler, witnesses an archery exhibition in Virginia, 1701? 1702?, in William J. Hinke, trans. and ed., "Report of the Journey of Francis Louis Michel from Berne, Switzerland to Virginia, October 2, 1701-December 1, 1702," Virginia Magazine of History and Biography, Vol. 24, No. 2 (April 1916), 129.

"When most of the shooting was done, two Indians were brought in, who shot with rifles and bows so as to surprize us and put us to shame."

* * *

John Fontaine, Irish Huguenot immigrant, describes the archery exploits of Saponi indigenous youths in Virginia, 6 April 1716, in [Fontaine], "Journal of John Fontaine," in Ann Maury, Memoirs of a Huguenot Family. Translated and Compiled from the Original Autobiography of Rev. James Fontaine (New York: George P. Putnam & Company, 1853), 278.

"The Governor sent for all the young boys, and they brought with them their bows, and he got an axe, which he made them all shoot by turn at the eye of the axe, which was about twenty yards distant. Knives and looking glasses were the prizes for which they shot, and they were very dexterous at this exercise, and often shot through the eye of the axe. This diversion continued for about an hour."

* * *

Father Sebastien Rasles, French Jesuit missionary, concerning the archery of Quebec area indigenous peoples, 12 October 1723, in "From Father Sebastien Rasles, Missionary of the Society of Jesus in New France, to Monsieur His Brother," reprinted as "The Wanderings of Father Rasles. 1689-1723," in William Ingraham Kip, ed., The Early Jesuit Missions in North America, Part 1 (London: Wiley and Putnam, 1847), 26.

"No sooner have the children begun to walk, than they exercise them in using the bow, and in this they become so skilful that at ten or twelve years of age they scarcely ever fail to kill the bird at which they aim. I was very much surprised, and should have had difficulty in believing it, if I had not myself been a witness of their skill."

* * *

Father Joseph Lafitau, French Jesuit missionary, concerning Northeastern indigenous peoples' burial customs, circa 1724, in Lafitau, Customs of the American Indians Compared with the Customs of Primitive Times, ed. and trans. by William N. Fenton and Elizabeth L. Moore, 2 vols., Vol. 2 (Toronto: The Champlain Society, 1977), 249-250.

"People busy themselves also with different games. The young men on one side, and the young women on the other, exercise from morning to evening separately, either shooting arrows for a prize or exercising with the handspike. Each exercise has a prize for the victor...."

* * *

Jean-Bernard Bossu, French traveler, notes archery among the Choctaw, 30 September 1759, in Seymour Feiler, ed., Jean-Bernard Bossu's Travels in the Interior of North America, 1751-1762 (Norman, Okla.: University of Oklahoma Press, 1962), 170.

"The children shoot arrows for prizes. The winner of the first prize is praised by an old man and is given the title of 'apprentice warrior.'"

* * *

Joseph Doddridge, Pennsylvania Episcopal minister, comments on the archery of indigenous peoples in western Pennsylvania, circa 1763-1783, in Doddridge, Notes on the Settlement and Indian Wars of the Western Parts of Virginia and Pennsylvania from 1763 to 1783, inclusive, together with a Review of the State of Society and Manners of the

First Settlers of the Western Country (Pittsburgh: John S. Ritenour and William T. Lindsey, 1912), 122.

"Many of the sports of the early settlers of this country were imitative of the exercises and stratagems of hunting and war. Boys were taught the use of the bow and arrow at an early age, but although they acquired considerable adroitness in the use of them, so as to kill a bird or squirrel sometimes, yet it appeared to me that in the hands of the white people the bow and arrow could never be depended upon for warfare or hunting, unless made and managed in a different manner from any specimens of them which I ever saw. In ancient times the bow and arrow must have been deadly instruments in the hands of the barbarians of our country; but I much doubt whether any of the present tribes of Indians could make much use of the flint arrow heads which must have been so generally used by their forefathers."

* * *

Thomas Hutchinson, Massachusetts politician and historian, circa 1765, concerning the archery capabilities of New England indigenous youth, in Hutchinson, *The History of the Province of Massachusetts Bay,* 2nd ed., 2 vols. (London: M. Richardson, 1765), 471.

"Shooting at marks was a diverfion for their children, as foon as they were capable of drawing a bow."

* * *

Bernard Romans, French captain, mentions archery among the Choctaw, circa 1775, in Romans, *A Concise Natural History of East and West Florida* (New York: pvt. ptg., 1775), 76.

"Their exercises agree pretty much with what I have feen among other nations: from their infancy they learn the ufe of bows and arrows;...."

* * *

Robert Honyman, Scottish doctor resident of Virginia, records an archery exhibition in Philadelphia, 8 March 1775, in Philip Padelford, ed., *Colonial Panorama 1775. Dr. Robert Honyman's Journal for March and April* (San Marino, Cal.: The Huntington Library, 1939), 16.

"In the afternoon likewise amused myself, looking at some [Tuscarora, Nanticoke, and Conoy] Indians, who were shooting with Bows & Arrows before the state house; their mark was a Halfpenny put on top of a Post; & though they often mist it, yet they hit it so often & shot so true & with such force as was very surprising."

* * *

John Long, American trader, concerning the archery skills of indigenous youths in the Great Lakes region, circa 1777, in Milo Milton Quaife, ed., *John Long's Voyages and Travels in the Years 1768-1788* (Chicago: Lakeside Press, 1922), 69-70.

"The boys are very expert at trundling a hoop, particularly the Cahnuaga Indians, whom I have frequently seen excel at this amusement. The game is played by any number of boys who may accidentally assemble together, some driving the hoop, while others with bows and arrows shoot at it. At this exercise they are surprisingly expert, and will stop the progress of the hoop when going with great velocity, by driving a pointed arrow into its edge; this they will do at a considerable distance, and on horseback as well as on foot. They will also kill small birds at fifty yards' distance, and strike a half-penny off a stick at fifteen yards."

SHOOTING AMONG COLONISTS

George Morton, British settler, observes shooting at Plymouth, Massachusetts, 5 July 1621, in Henry Martyn Dexter, ed., *Mourt's Relation or Journal of the Plantation at Plymouth* (Boston: John Kimball Wiggin, 1865), 108.

"The next day being Thurfday, many of their Sachims, or petty Governours came to fee vs, and many of their men alfo. There they went to their manner of Games for skins and kniues. There we challenged them to fhoote with them for skins; but they durft not: onely they defired to fee one of vs fhoote at a marke, who fhooting with Haile-fhot, they wondred to fee the marke fo full of holes."

* * *

John Smith, British explorer, concerning New England, recommends training in marksmanship, circa 1631, in Smith, *Advertisements for the Unexperienced Planters of New-England, or Anywhere or the Path-way to Experience to Erect a Plantation* (London: Robert Milbourne, 1631), reprinted in Charles Herbert Levermore, ed., *Forerunners and Competitors of the Pilgrims and Puritans*, 2 vols., Vol. 2 (Brooklyn: The New England Society, 1912), 799-800.

"..., and be not sparing of a little extraordinary shot and powder to make them markmen, especially your Gentlemen, and those you finde most capable, for shot must be your best weapon: yet all this will not doe unlesse you have at least 100. or as many as you can, of expert, blouded, appreoved good Souldiers, who dare boldly lead them; not to shoot a ducke, a goose or a dead marke, but at men, from whom you must expect such as you send."

* * *

Court order at Fort Orange and Beverwyck, New Netherland, 9 May 1655, in A.J.F. van Laer, ed. and trans., *Minutes of the Court of Fort Orange and Beverwyck, 1652-1656* (Albany: The University of the State of New York, 1920), 220.

"Hendrick Jochemsz is granted permission to have the burghers shoot the target provided he keeps good order and takes care that no accidents occur or result therefrom."

* * *

Thomas Nairne, Swiss traveler, comments on marksmanship capabilities in South Carolina, circa 1710, in [Nairne], *A Letter from South Carolina* (London: A. Baldwin, 1710), reprinted in Jack P. Greene, ed., *Selling a New World. Two Colonial South Carolina Promotional Pamphlets* (Columbia: University of South Carolina Press, 1989), 52.

"The Inhabitants of *Carolina*, especially those born there, are dextrous and expert in the Use of Fire-Arms. If regular Troops excel in performing the Postures, this Militia is much superiour in making a true Shot. The Habit of Shooting so well is acquir'd by the frequent Pursuit of Game in the Forests."

* * *

John Fontaine, Irish Huguenot immigrant, practices shooting in Virginia, 26 August 1716, in Edward Porter Alexander, ed. *The Journal of John Fontaine. An Irish Huguenot Son in Spain and Virginia, 1710-1719* (Williamsburg, Va.: Colonial Williamburg Foundation,1972), 102.

"In the morning I diverted myself shooting at a mark with the other gentlemen."

An account of a wedding near Saybrook, Connecticut, circa 1726, mentions marksman-ship as a recreation, reprinted in Helen Evertson Smith, *Colonial Days and Ways as Gathered from Family Papers by Helen Evertson Smith of Sharon, Connecticut* (New York: The Century Company, 1901), 180.

"[The men at wedding participated in] rastling, quoits, running, leaping, archery and firing at a mark, but on the last day no muskets were allowed by reason of the Indi-ans."

* * *

Harvard College law, circa 1734, in "College Laws, 1734, Chapter 8th, Concerning Mis-cellaneous Matters," in *Harvard College Records, Part I. Corporation Records, 1636-1750, Publications of the Colonial Society of Massachusetts*, Vol. 15 (Boston, 1925), 154.

"15. No Undergraduate shall keep a Gun or pistol in the College, or any where in Cambridge; nor shall he go a guning, fishing, or Scating over deep waters, without leave from the President or one of the Tutors, under the penalty of three Shillings. And if any scholar shall fire a Gun or pistol, within the College walls Yard, or near the College; he shall be fined not exceeding ten Shillings; or be admonishe[d] degraded or expelled, according to the Aggravation of the Offence."

* * *

Peter Kalm, Swedish naturalist, evaluates the marksmanship in Quebec, 14 October 1749, in Adolph B. Benson, trans. and ed., *Peter Kalm's Travels in North America*, 2 vols., Vol. 2 (New York: Dover Publications, 1966), 563.

"The Canadians are generally good marksmen. I have seldom seen any people shoot with such dexterity as they. A bird that flew so close to them that they could reach it with their bullet or shot, had difficulty in escaping with its life. There was scarcely one of them who was not a clever marksman and who did not own a rifle."

* * *

Jeduthan Baldwin, Brookfield, Massachusetts soldier, shoots at marks in eastern New York, 17 February 1756, in Thomas Williams Baldwin, ed., *The Revolutionary Journal of Col. Jeduthan Baldwin, 1775-1778* (Bangor, Me.: The De Burians, 1906), 8.

"Wagons came in. Shot at marks. 2 frenchmen Came in from Crn poit."

* * *

Joseph Doddridge, Pennsylvania Episcopalian minister, concerning shooting in western Pennsylvania, circa 1763-1783, in Doddridge, *Notes on the Settlement and Indian Wars of the Western Parts of Virginia and Pennsylvania from 1763 to 1783, Inclusive, Together with a Review of the State of Society and Manners of the First Settlers* (Pittsburgh: John S. Ritenour and William T. Lindsey, 1912), 124.

"Shooting at marks was a common diversion among the men, when their stock of ammunition would allow it; this, however, was far from being always the case. The present mode of shooting off hand was not then in practice. This mode was not con-sidered as any trial of the value of a gun; nor, indeed, as much of a test of the skill of a marksman. Their shooting was from a rest, and at as great distance as the length and weight of the barrel of the gun would throw a ball on a horizontal level. Such was their regard to accuracy, in these sportive trials of their rifles, and of their own skill in the use of them, that they often put moss, or some other soft substance, on the log or stump from which they shot, for fear of having the bullet thrown from the mark, by the spring of the barrel. When the rifle was held to the side of a tree for a rest, it was pressed against it as lightly as possible, for the same reason."

* * *

William Mylne, Scottish traveler, describes shooting in the colonies in the Southern back country, 1 March 1775, in Mylne to Miss Ann Mylne (from New York), in Ted Ruddock, ed., *Travels in the Colonies in 1773-1775 Described in the Letters of William Mylne* (Athens, Ga.: University of Georgia Press, 1993), 75.

"In the back parts the[y] have several companies whose exercise is shooting with rifled guns at a dollar fixed to a tree at a distance of 120 paces, these are the most dangerous, being accustomed to fighting amongst trees with the Indians they are very dextorous, I have seen one of them take of[f] the head of a hawk at the distance of a hundred yards with a single bullet."

* * *

Daniel Boone, Kentucky settler, demonstrates his shooting abilities among the Shawanese near Chillicothe, Ohio, in late winter or early spring 1778, in Boone, "The Adventures of Col. Daniel Boon," in John Filson, *The Discovery, Settlement, and Present State of Kentucky,* Volume II and supplement to Gilbert Imlay, *A Topographical Description of the Western Territory of North America* (New York: Samuel Campbell, 1793), 62.

"I often went a hunting with them, and frequently gained their applaufe for my activity at our fhooting-matches. I was careful not to exceed many of them in fhooting; for no people are more envious than they in this fport. I could obferve, in their countenances and geftures, the greateft expreffions of joy when they exceeded me; and, when the reverfe happened, of envy."

* * *

George Hanger, Hessian colonel, tells of a humorous conversation about shooting, in Virginia, circa 1780, in Hanger, *The Life, Adventures, and Opinions of Col. George Hanger,* 2 vols., Vol. 1 (New York: Johnson and Stryker, 1801), 183-184.

"I cannot refrain from relating a ludicrous conversation which took place between Sir Guy Carleton and myself, one day when I had the honour of dining at head-quarters, immediately after his arival, which strongly evinced his good humour and affability. The great skill which, from years of practice, (even from a lad when educated in Germany,) I had acquired in the knowledge of a rifle-gun, and the precision and perfection to which I had brought the art of shooting with a rifle, was well known to the army, and Sir Guy Carleton had been informed of it. At dinner, he said to me, sitting opposite to him, 'Major Hanger, I have been told that you are a most skilful marksman with a rifle-gun. I have heard of astonishing feats that you have performed in shooting!' —Thanking him for the compliment, I told his Excellency, that I was vain enough to say, with truth, that many officers in the army had witnessed my adroitness. I then began to inform Sir Guy how my old deceased friend, Col. Ferguson, and myself, had practised together, who, for skill and knowledge of that weapon had been so celebrated, and that Ferguson had ever acknowledged the superiority of my skill to his, after one particular day's practice, when I had shot *three* balls running into one hole. —Sir Guy replied to this, 'I know you are very expert in this art.' Now, had I been quiet and satisfied with the compliment the Commander in Chief paid me, and not pushed this affair farther, it had been well for me; but I replied, 'Yes, Sir Guy, I really have reduced the art of shooting with a rifle to such a nicety, that, at a moderate distance, I can *kill a flea* with a single ball.' At this Sir Guy began to stare not a little, and seemed to indicate, from the smile on his countenance, that he thought I had rather outstepped my usual outdoings in the art. Observing this, I respectfully replied, 'I see, by your Excellency's countenance, that you seem doubtful of the singularity and perfection of my art; but, if I may presume so much as to dare offer a wager to my Commander in Chief, I will bet your Excellency five guineas that I kill a flea with a single ball once in eight shots, at eight yards;' —(and, reader, I will bet you fifty guineas I do; and, what is more, the person who wagers with me shall decide the bet, to shew that there is no bubble in it.) Sir Guy replied, 'My dear Major, I am not given to lay wagers; but for once I will bet you five guineas, provided you will let *the flea hop*.' —A loud laugh ensued at the table; and, after laughing heartily myself, I placed my knuckle under the table, said, 'Sir Guy, I knock under, and will never speak of my skill in shooting with a rifle-gun again before you."

SHOOTING AMONG INDIGENOUS PEOPLES

Peter Lindestrom, Swedish geographer, writes of shooting (or possibly archery) among the Delaware indigenous people, circa 1654-1656, in Lindestrom, *Geographia Americae with An Account of the Delaware Indians Based on Surveys and Notes Made in 1654-1656,* trans. and ed. by Amandus Johnson (Philadelphia: Swedish Colonial Society, 1925), 215.

"In this their convention they [also] practice shooting. He who is sachem has a turkey placed very high in the air, whose entrails are removed and [the body] filled again with their money. And the one who then can shoot it down, he receives the money, *et talia*, etc."

* * *

John Lawson, Carolina Surveyor-General and historian, describes marksmanship among the indigenous peoples in South Carolina, 14 January 1701, in Lawson, *A New Voyage to Carolina; Containing the Exact Defcription and Natural Hiftory of That Country. Together with the Present State Thereof. And a Journal of a Thoufand Miles, Travel'd thro' feveral Nations of Indians. Giving a Particular Account of their Cuftoms, Manners, &c.* (London: pvt. ptg., 1709), 27.

"Our *Indian* having this Day kill'd good Store of Provifion with his Gun, he always fhot a fingle Ball, miffing but two Shoots in above forty; they being curious Artifts in managing a Gun, to make it carry either Ball, or Shot, true. When they have bought a Piece, and find it to fhoot any Ways crooked, they take the Barrel out of the Stock, cutting a Notch in a Tree, wherein they set it ftreight, fometimes fhooting away above 100 Loads of Ammunition, before they bring the Gun to fhoot according to their Mind."

* * *

Robert Beverly, Virginia plantation owner and historian, refers to the shooting skills of indigenous peoples, circa 1705, in Louis B. Wright, ed., *The History and Present State of Virginia* (Charlottesville, Va.: University Press of Virginia, 1947), 269.

"The People there are very Skilful in the use of Fire-Arms, being all their Lives accustom'd to shoot in the Woods."

John Brickell, Irish doctor, comments on the shooting abilities of indigenous peoples in North Carolina, circa 1737, in Brickell, *The Natural History of North-Carolina* (Dublin: James Carson, 1737), 344-345.

"Thefe *Indians* are generally the beft marks Men with *Guns* that are to be met with in moft parts of the World, and commonly kill what they Shot at with a fingle Ball; this is principally owing to the fteadinefs in their Limbs and the fharp Sight with which they are endued. They take a great deal of pains when they buy a *Gun* firft, to find out if it has any fault in the Barrel, which they generally take out of the ftock and cut a Notch in a Tree where they make it ftreight, if there be occafion, and after fhoot feveral times at markes, that they may be acquainted with its faults and perfections, this they do before they go to kill *Deer*, or any other kind of Game that is to be met with as they hunt in Woods."

SHOOTING AMONG THE MILITARY

William Strachey, British settler, concerning shooting in Virginia, 22 June 1611, in [Strachey?], "Instructions of the Marshall, for the Better inabling of a Captaine, to the executing of his charge in this present Colonie. Iune the 22, 1611," in *For the Colony in Virginea Britannia. Lavves Diuine, Morall and Martiall, &c.* (London: Walter Burre, 1612), 43-44.

"And because that, during the watch, that time is appointed for the exercising of his men, and fashioning them to their armes, he shall set vp a conuenient marke by his court of guard, where hee shall teach his men the exercise of their armes, both for the comely and needful vse thereof, as the offensiue practise against their enemies, at which marke his men shall discharge their pieces twice, both morning and euening, at the discharge of the watch, hauing procured from the Gouernor some prize of incouragement due vnto him that shall shoot neerest,...."

* * *

Joshua Hempstead, New London, Connecticut carpenter, chronicles shooting contests at the militia training days, October 1716, October 1717, September 1731, October 1736, and September 1748, in [Hempstead], *Diary of Joshua Hempstead of New London, Connecticut Covering a Period of Forty-Seven Years from September, 1711, to November, 1758, Collections of the New London County Historical Society, Volume I* (New London Conn.: New London County Historical Society, 1910), 60, 70, 240, 310, 506.

29 October 1716: "a Trayning day both Companys in arms Shooting at Marks."

29 October 1717: "A Trayning day a also it was yesterday. I was at it al day. I bought a Silk hankerchief price 5s od on ye Companys acctt to Shoot for. It was won by Wm Waterhouse."

14 September 1731: "Trayning day again. wee Shot at a Mark by Samll Richards. Jos Merrills hitt the Spot & Received 10s"

26 October 1736: ""I was at Trayning. our Company Shot at markt Each man to fire his own Gun & he that Shot Nearest the Center was to winn the Prize wch was 10s & Corpll Silas Whipple got the Prize."

20 September 1748: "in the aftern I went to Trayning. both Comps were marcht up to ye Plain by Samll Richards's to Shoot at a mark...."

* * *

Robert Honyman, Scottish doctor resident of Virginia, notes the marksmanship in Boston, March 1775, in Philip Padelford, ed., *Colonial Panorama 1775. Dr. Robert Honyman's Journal for March and April* (San Marino, Cal.: The Huntington Library, 1939), 44, 50.

22 March 1775: "I saw a Regiment & the Body of marines, each by itself, firing at marks. A Target being set up before each company, the soldiers of the regiment stept out singly, took aim & fired, & the firing kept up in this manner by the whole regiment till they had all fired ten rounds. The Marines fired by Platoons, by Companies, & sometimes by files, & made some general discharges, taking aim all the while at Targets the same as the Regiment."

25 March 1775: "Lookt at five companies on the common firing at Targets. A little dog happened to be on the beach where the balls fell thickest, & continued to run backwards & forwards after the balls, being much diverted by the noise they made, & the dirt flying about; & kept doing so, till they had done firing their 10 rounds apiece without being hurt."

* * *

Charles Biddle, Philadelphia soldier and later politician, describes a shooting match and accident, May 1775, in [Biddle], *Autobiography of Charles Biddle, Vice-President of the Supreme Executive Council of Pennsylvania, 1745-1821* (Philadelphia: E. Claxton and Company, 1883), 73-74.

"Captain [Alexander] Graydon, of Shee's Regiment, and myself went out one morning about this time to fire at a mark with our pistols. After we had each fired several times at a piece of papers on a fence, a man came running up to us, his face as white as a sheet, and cried to beg we would not fire again; that we had shot his child. Inquiring where the child was, he pointed to a house a considerable distance back of the fence. We had observed the house, but did not suppose it within reach of our shot. He desired us to go with him to his house; however, as we thought that might occasion some trouble we refused. But told him we would call next day. He said it was no matter, he knew Captain Biddle very well. After consulting together, we thought, as he knew me, it would be best to go with him. We found the ball had gone through a pane of glass and struck the child, who was in its mother['s] arms, in the side, but had not entered the body. Probably it would have been killed but for the thick woollen clothes it had on. After expressing our concern, and giving the mother some money, they were perfectly satisfied. I called several times afterwards, and found the child had received no injury whatsoever. The pistol was fired by me—the ball must have passed through a hole in the fence.... He [the father] kept the ball, which he said he would preserve for the child, and probably it is still kept in the family."

Thomas Lynch, Philadelphia lawyer, notes the rifle accuracy of soldiers in Philadelphia, July 1775, in Lynch to Ralph Izard, 7 July 1775, in *Correspondence of Mr. Ralph Izard, of South Carolina, from the Year 1774 to 1804; with a Short Memoir*, 2 vols., Vol. 1 (New York: Charles S. Francis and Company, 1844), 100.

"There are now marching to the camp, a thousand riflemen. They are, at listing rejected, unless they can hit a playing-card, without a rest, at one hundred and twenty yards distance."

* * *

John Harrower, a Virginia indentured servant, discusses the shooting skills of soldiers in Virginia, 28 August 1775, in Edward Miles Riley, ed., *The Journal of John Harrower, An Indentured Servant in the Colony of Virginia, 1773-1776* (Williamsburg, Va.: Colonial Williamsburg, 1963), 111.

"The commanding officer chuse his Compty. by the following method Vizt. He took a board of a foot squar[e] and with Chalk drew the shape of a moderate nose in the center and nailed it up to a tree at 150 yds. distance and those who came nighest the mark with a single ball was to go [in the company]. But by the first 40 or 50 that fired the nose was all blown out of the board, and by the time his Compy. was up the board shared the same fate."

* * *

Simeon Lyman, Sharon, Connecticut soldier, shoots at New London, Connecticut, 25 December 1775, in [Lyman], "Journal of Simeon Lyman of Sharon Aug. 10 to Dec. 28, 1775," in "Orderly Book and Journals Kept by Connecticut Men While Taking Part in the American Revolution, 1775-1778," *Collections of the Connecticut Historical Society*, Vol. 7 (Hartford: Connecticut Historical Society, 1899), 133.

"Monday, 25th. I tried my gun, and we had a fine Christmas a shooting at a mark."

* * *

James Thacher, Massachusetts military surgeon, describes shooting near Fishkill in the Hudson River valley, 20 July 1778, in Thacher, *Military Journal of the American Revolution, from the Commencement to the Disbanding of the American Army* (Hartford, Conn.: Hurlbut, Williams and Company, 1862), 139-140.

"Having a number of sheep running at large in the woods belonging to our hospital, and being in want of mutton, I was induced to assist the slaughterers with my gun against these harmless animals. In pursuit of this game, I devoted most of the day, and a single sheep only was the reward of my labor and fatigue. On my return, I was accused of want of skill as a marksman, and Dr. Prescott challenged me to decide our superiority by firing at a mark; the challenge accepted, we placed an object at the end of our garden. After the third fire, we were checked by an unpleasant incident. Several horses were grazing in a field directly in our range, and one of them, a valuable animal, received a ball through his body. The wound on examination was found to be fatal, the skill of the surgeon could avail nothing,.... "but the event is sufficiently unfortunate to dter us from again sporting with our guns at random shot."

* * *

Henry Hamilton, British officer, chronicles shooting by his soldiers near the Wabash and Tippecanoe Rivers in Indiana, November 1778, in John D. Barnhart, ed., "The Unpublished Journal of Lieut. Gov. Henry Hamilton," in *Henry Hamilton and George Rogers Clark in the American Revolution* (Crawfordsville, Ind.: R.E. Banta, 1951), 120, 125, 133.

12 November 1778: "Exercised the Cannon and small arms at Marks —The arms are in very good order—...."

19 November 1778: "I broke off the meeting abruptly, and told them I was going to exercise my young men, and gave orders for the men to turn out and fire ball at a mark, which they did, and shewed great dexterity firing very quick and making excellent shots—...."

30 November 1778: "The Men were exercised in firing at a Mark—...."

* * *

Erkuries Beatty, Pennsylvania lieutenant, notes marksmanship in central Pennsylvania, 3 August 1779, in [Beatty], "Journal of Lt. Erkuries Beatty," in Frederick Cook, ed., *Journals of the Military Expedition of Major General John Sullivan against the Six Nations of Indians in 1779* (Freeport, N.Y.: Books for Libraries Press, reprint of 1885 ed.), 22.

"Nothing of consequence as I know of to day the Rifle men went down by the side of the lake to try their Rifles which they did by Shooting at marks."

SHOOTING EXHIBITIONS AND MATCHES

Edward Bland, Virginia merchant, describes a shooting exhibition in the Carolina area, 30 August 1651, in Edward Bland, et al., "The Discovery of New Brittaine 1650," in Alexander S. Salley, Jr., ed., *Narratives of Early Carolina, 1650-1708* (New York: Barnes & Noble, 1967 [1911]), 12.

"This day in the morning the Maharineck great men spake to heare some of our guns go off: Whereupon we shot two guns at a small marke, both hitting it, and at so great a distance of a hundred paces, or more, that the Indians admired at it: And a little before night the old King Maharineck came to us, and told us, that the people in the Towne were afraid when the guns went off, and ran all away into the Woods."

* * *

Virginia Governor Francis Nicholson proclaims a shooting match, circa 1691, in "Nicholson's Proclamation about the College and Orders for Prize Games for Bachelors, etc.," William and Mary Quarterly, 1st. Series, Vol. 11, No. 2 (October 1902), 87.

"To the Sheriffe of Surry County,

I desire that you give public notice that I will give first and second prizes to be shott for, wrastled, played at backswords, & Run for by Horse and foott, to begin on the 22^d. day of Aprill next s^{et}. [Saint] Georges day being Satterday all which prizes are to be shott for &c by the better sort of Virginians onely, who are Batchelers."

* * *

Francis Louis Michel, Swiss traveler, notes a rifle match in Virginia, 1701? 1702?, in William J. Hinke, trans. and ed., "Report of the Journey of Francis Louis Michel from Berne, Switzerland to Virginia, October 2, 1701-December 1, 1702," Virginia Magazine of History and Biography, Vol. 24, No. 2 (April 1916), 129.

"After it [dinner] was over, the Governor showed his liberality by arranging a rifle match. When the soldiers had finished no one was allowed to shoot except those born in the country and some Indians. The prizes consisted of rifles, swords, saddles, bridles, boots, money and other things. When most of the shooting was done, two Indians shot rifles and bows so as to surprize us and put us to shame."

* * *

Sarah Knight, traveler in Connecticut, describes marksmanship, circa 1704, in Knight, *The Private Journal Kept by Madame Knight on a Journey from Boston to New-York, in the Year 1704* (Boston: Small, Maynard and Company, 1920), 36-37.

"Their Diversions in this part of the Country are on Lecture days and Training days mostly: on the former there is Riding from town to town.

"And on training dayes The Youth divert themselves by Shooting at the Target, as they call it, (but it very much resembles a pillory,) where hee that hitts neerest the white has some yards of Red Ribbin presented him wch being tied to his hattband, the two ends streeming down his back, he is Led away in Triumph, wth great applause, as the winners of the Olympiack Games."

* * *

Advertisement for a shooting match, New York Journal, No. 72, 24 March 1735.

"To be Shot for.

"A Lott of Land belonging to *Robert Bennett*, in Sacket's Street, it contains in breath front and rear 37 Feet 6 Inches. It is to be shot for on *Eafter* Munday, Tuefday, Wednefday & Thurfday, the 7, 8, 9, & 10th of *April* next, with a fingle Ball, at a 100 Yards Diftance, at the Sign of *Marlborough*'s Head in the Bowery Lane Every Perfon that inclines to fhoot for the above-mentioned Lot of Land is to lay in 5 *s*. before he fires his Piece for every Shot, and whoever makes the beft Shot in the four Days mentioned fhall receive a good and warrantable Bill of Sale of the afore-mentioned Lot of Land from *Robert Bennett*.

"And to prevent all Difputes, if it fhall fo Happen that two or more of the Shooters fhall be adjudged to have fhot equally well, then and in fuch Cafe the Competitors are again to try their Skill on the next Day, among themfelves; and if at this fecond Shooting any Equallity of Shots fhall be adJudged, the Competitors are to Shoot the third Time; but if any Equallity then remains, then thofe fo adjudged equall fhall fill up for it. Provided always thas none fhall be adjudged Equals but thofe neareft to the Mark.

"And if it fhould happen that the money received for the above mentioned fhooting Match fhould not amount to the Value of the faid Lott of Land, (which is l 125) then the faid *Robert Bennett* will on the laft Day of Shooting return every Perfon his own Money again, unlefs the the beft Marks Man, or he who has fhot ofteneft at the Mark, will advance the Remainder, fo as to make up what Money has been received the fum of *l*. 125, which fhall intitle him to the Land."

* * *

Advertisement for a shooting match, South Carolina Gazette, No. 714, 14-21 December 1747.

"TO BE RUN, RAFFLED, OR SHOT FOR, on Friday the 20th of *January* next, at the Houfe of *Ifaac Peronneau* at *Goofe Creek*, a very handfome Silver-mounted *Gun*, with a water Pan, value 140 *l*. Alfo a neat Silver watch, value 55 l. and a handfome Saddle, Bridle, and Houfings, value 25 *l*. with Silver Spurs, Boots and Sundry other Things."

* * *

Advertisement for a shooting contest, New York Gazette, No. 570, 31 December 1753.

"TO be SHOT for, on the 22d of January *next, a good Mahogany Cheft of Drawers, with Eagle's Claw feet, a Shell on each Knee, and fluted Corners, with good brafs Work and Locks. Thofe that intend to try their Fortune for the fame, may apply to Mr.* George Peters, *next Door to Mr.* Peter Marfchalk'*s, in* Broad-Street, *at the Corner of* Marten-Barragh, *where they may fee the above: There will be Twenty Chances, at* 14 *Shillings each Chance."*

* * *

Account of a shooting match that resulted in lethal violence, Maryland Gazette, No. 456, 31 January 1754.

"We *hear from* Queen Anne'*s County, that on a Monday, a few Weeks ago, at a private Tippling-Houfe on* Chefter *River, a Number of People met on a Shooting Match, which they turn'd into a Drinking Match, and held it 'til the Thurfday* [during which time the crowd tortured a feeble-minded young man to death]."

* * *

James Parker, Shirley, Massachusetts farmer, chronicles local shooting matches, January, October, and December 1770, January 1771, January 1772, December 1774, February 1775, November 1800, and November 1819, in [Parker], "Extracts from the Diary of James Parker of Shirley, Mass.," *New England Historical and Genealogical Register,* Vol. 69 (January 1915), 9, 12, 13, 15, (April 1915), 122, 123; Vol. 70 (April 1916), 142, (October 1916), 302.

31 January 1770: "I strew mould at Mr Ivorys. Mose went to a shooting at Landod Sawtells"

24 October 1770: "Iwent to Groton trooping & shot a Pistell full & hurt my hand & stayed all Night at my Mothers & Wallace Little with me"

19 December 1770: "Went to Oliver Farwell's shooting."

16 January 1771: "Samll Hazen had a Shooting this Day"

1 January 1772: "I went to Lunenburg to Dodges shooting. I had very sore eyes"

14 January 1772: "Joshua Longley had a shooting"

1 December 1774: "I plowed along by ye Ledge of rocks in Order to make a road in ye afternoon I went to Silas Davises Shooting of [illegible]"

1 February 1775: "Jonathan Davis had a Shooting I was there a Little While"

15 February 1775: "Henry Haskell had a great shooting"

24 November 1800: "I at Jonas Parkers Shooting"

23 November 1819: "I at shootings at Edes"

* * *

Advertisement for a shooting match, Boston Evening Post, No. 1946, January 11, 1773.

"This is to give Notice,

That there will be a BEAR, and a Number of TURKEYS fet up as Marks, next Thurfday beforenoon, at the PUNCH-BOWL Tavern in Brookline."

* * *

Advertisement for a turkey shoot at Beverly, Massachusetts, circa 1773?, reprinted in Ruth E. Painter, "Tavern Amusements in Eighteenth Century America," Americana, Vol. 11 (1916), 107.

"SHARP SHOOTING.

Thos. D. Ponsland informs his Friends and the Friends of *Sport* that he will on Friday, 7th day of December next, set up for SHOOTING a number of

FINE FAT TURKEYS

and invites all *Gunners* and others who would wish to recreate themselves to call on the day after Thanksgiving at the Old Baker's Tavern, Upp. Parish Beverly, where every accommodation will be afforded."

* * *

John Andrews, Boston merchant, comments to his Philadelphia brother-in-law on a shooting contest in Boston, 1 October 1774, in Winthrop Sargent, ed., "Letters of John Andrews, Esq., of Boston," Proceedings of the Massachusetts Historical Society, Vol. 7 (July 1865), 371-372.

"It's common for the Soldiers to fire at a target fixed in the stream at the bottom of the *common*. A countryman stood by a few days ago, and laugh'd very heartily at the whole regiment's firing, and not one being able to hit it. The officer observ'd him, and ask'd why he laugh'd? Perhaps you'll be affronted if I tell you, reply'd the countryman. No, he would not, he said. *Why then* says he, I laugh to see how awkward they fire. *Why*, I'll be bound I hit it ten times running. Ah! will you, reply'd the officer; come try: Soldiers, go and bring five of the best guns, and load 'em for this honest man. Why, you need not bring so many: let me have any one that comes to hand reply'd the other, but I chuse to load *myself*. He accordingly loaded, and asked the officer where he should fire? He reply'd, to the right —when he pull'd tricker, and drove the ball as near the right as possible. The officer was amaz'd — said he could not do it again, as that was only by chance. He loaded again. Where shall I fire? To the *left* —when he perform'd as well as before. Come! once more, says the officer. — He prepar'd the third time. —Where shall I fire *naow*? *In the center*. He took aim, and the ball went as exact in the middle as possible. The officers as well as soldiers *star'd*, and tho't the Devil was in the man. *Why*, says the countryman, I'll tell you *naow*. I have got a *boy* at home that will toss up an apple and shoot out all the seeds as it's coming down."

* * *

Advertisement for a shooting contest, [Rivington's] Royal Gazette, No. 163, 4 April 1778.

"TO BE SHOT FOR
A GOLD WATCH,

VALUED at Thirty-two Dollars at the houfe of Mr. Deal, the Sign of the Hand and Flower, at Greenwich, on Thurfday the 9th of this month; the particulars may be known by enquiring as above."

Chapter 4

BASEBALL AND SIMILAR BALL GAMES

Although most Americans may still believe that baseball originated one June day in 1839 in Elihu Phinney's farm field in Cooperstown, New York when Abner Doubleday supposedly invented the game for boys, Americans were playing baseball and its variants before the Revolutionary War. Some of the "ball games" may have been soccer or a combination of foot-and-hand ball sports, but absent firm proof, it is reasonable to assume that "ball play" among Euroamericans involved a stick and a ball. Bat and ball games, as historians Erwin Mehl and Robert Henderson have demonstrated, are actually quite ancient. Certainly Europeans, perhaps mostly the children, but probably even adult men and women, took a swing at a variety of pre-baseball folk games: stool ball, trap ball, one o'cat, rounders, town ball, and base, or baste, ball, and possibly others called whirl and chermany. Balls were made easily from rags and leather, and bats were paddles or tree branches. Farm fields or the cozier confines of streets and alleys sufficed for playing fields. Bases were trees, chairs (hence "stool ball"), stones, and stakes. Rules were immensely flexible. These games fit into the interstices of work patterns, ceremonial days, and longer leisure stretches.

Two groups in particular, soldiers and students, seem to have contributed to spreading the game. Revolutionary war troops were apparently enthusiasts for ball, even walking for miles to find ground level enough for play, as the following documents show. One historian surmises that ball play was no more formal than frisbee or hacky-sack is today, that soldiers carried a ball or two in their packs and threw it amongst themselves during breaks. Certainly there were no organized teams nor leagues, but the embryonic pattern for such may have lain behind what soldiers saw played and played themselves at Valley Forge and in the Wyoming valley. Students probably played the games, taking advantages of study breaks and lapses in college discipline to pour onto the common for matches. Some colleges, cities, and towns attempted to ban the ball games because of potential property damage to windows and buildings, but as history shows, baseball's predecessors were entrenched. The following documents, although few in number, reveal the early presence of baseball-like games in the colonial and Revolutionary periods.

[Consult the general writings about sports, recreation, and the various colonial, provincial, territorial, and state Sabbath and gaming laws in Chapter One for other sources about the specific sports or games in this chapter.]

William Bradford, Plymouth, Massachusetts elder, scolds some Pilgrims for playing stool ball, 25 December 1621, in Bradford, *Of Plymouth Plantation,* ed. by Harvey Wish (New York: Capricorn Books, 1962), 82-83.

"One the day called Chrismasday, the Governor caled them out to worke, (as was used,) but the most of this new-company excused them selves and said it wente against their consciences to work on that day. So the Governor tould them that if they made it a mater of conscience, he would spare them till they were better informed. So he led-away the rest and left them; but when they came home at noone from their worke, he found them in the streete at play, openly; some pitching the barr, & some at stoole-ball, and shuch like sports. So he went to them, and took away their implements, and tould them that if they made the keeping a mater of devotion, let them kepe their houses, but ther should be no gameing or revelling in the streets. Since which time nothing has been atempted that way, at least openly."

* * *

Samuel Sewall, Boston magistrate, refers to trapball, 6 June 1713, in M. Halsey Thomas, ed., *The Diary of Samuel Sewall, 1674-1729, Volume II. 1709-1729* (New York: Farrar, Straus and Giroux, 1973), 718.

"The Rain-water grievously runs into my son Joseph's Chamber from the N. Window above. As went out to the Barber's I observ'd the water to run trickling down a great pace from the Coving. I went on the Roof, and found the Spout next Salter's stop'd, but could not free it with my Stick. Boston went up, and found his pole too big, which I warn'd him of before; came down a Spit, and clear'd the Leaden-throat, by thrusting out a Trap-Ball that stuck there."

* * *

John Brickell, Irish doctor, traveling in North Carolina, refers to trapball, circa 1737, in Brickell, The *Natural History of North-Carolina* (Dublin: James Carson, 1737), 336.

"They [indigenous peoples] have another Game which is managed with a *Battoon*, and very much refembles our *Trap-Ball*;...."

* * *

Yale College statute, circa 1765, quoted and translated in Clarence Deming, *Yale Yesterdays* (New Haven, Conn.: Yale University Press, 1915), 192.

"'*Siquis Pila pedali vel palmeria, aut globis, in area academica laserit ....multetur non plus sex denariis et damna rescariat.*' [Playing ball by hand or foot in the college yard was forbidden under penalty of making restitution for any damage and a maximum fine of sixpence]."

* * *

A children's book describes stool ball, baseball, and trapball, in *A Little Pretty Pocket-Book, Intended for the Amusement and Instruction of Little Master Tommy and Pretty Miss Polly* (London: J. Newbery, 1767), 88, 90, 91.

"STOOL-BALL

THE *Ball* once ftruck with Art and Care,
And drove impetuous through the Air,
Swift round his Courfe the *Gamefter* flies,
Or his Stool's taken by *Surprife.*

RULE *of* LIFE.
Beftow your Alms whene'er you fee
An Object in Neceffity."

"BASE-BALL.	"TRAP-BALL.
THE *Ball* once ftruck off,	TOUCH lightly the *Trap*,
Away flies the Boy	And ftrike low the *Ball*;
To the next deftin'd Poft,	Let none catch you out,
And then Home with Joy.	And you'll beat them all.
MORAL.	MORAL.
Thus *Britons* for Lucre	Learn hence, my dear Boy,
Fly over the Main;	To avoid ev'ry Snare,
But, with Pleafure tranfported,	Contriv'd to involve you
Return back again."	In Sorrow and Care."

* * *

New Hampshire law, 23 December 1771, in *New Hampshire (Colony) Temporary Laws, 1773* (Portsmouth, N.H. [1773-1774]), 53.

"An Act to prevent and punifh
Diforders ufually committed on the twenty-fifth Day of December, commonly called Chriftmas-Day, the Evening preceding and following faid Day, and to prevent other Irregularities committed at other Times.

WHEREAS as it often happens that many diforders are occafioned within the town of Portfmouth,...by boys and fellows playing with balls in the public ftreets:....
And any boys playing with balls in any ftreets,whereby there is danger of breaking the windows of any building, public or private, may be ordered to remove to any place where there fhall be no fuch danger."

* * *

Simeon Lyman, Sharon, Connecticut soldier, in New London, Connecticut, plays ball, 6 September 1775, in [Lyman], "Journal of Simeon Lyman of Sharon Aug. 10 to Dec. 28, 1775," in "Orderly Book and Journals Kept by Connecticut Men While Taking Part in the American Revolution, 1775-1778," *Collections of the Connecticut Historical Society,* Vol. 7 (Hartford: Connecticut Historical Society, 1899), 117.

"Wednesday the 6. We played ball all day."

* * *

Lieutenant Ebenezer Elmer, New Jersey officer, chronicles ball playing in New York state, September 1776 and in New Jersey, May 1777, in [Elmer], "Journal of Lieutenant Ebenezer Elmer, of the Third Regiment of New Jersey Troops in the Continental Service," Proceedings of the New Jersey Historical Society, Vol. 1, No. 1 (1848), 26, 27, 30, 31; Vol. 3, No. 2 (1848), 98.

18 September 1776: "...The Regiment exercised 'fore and afternoon, and in the afternoon the Colonel, Parsons, and a number of us played whirl...."

20 September 1776: "At 9 o'clock, A. M., the Regiment was paraded, and grounded their arms to clear the parade; after which we had a game or two more at whirl; at which Dr. Dunham gave me a severe blow on my mouth which cut my lip, and came near to dislocating my under jaw...."

In the afternoon again had exercise,.... Played ball again."

28 September 1776: "We had after exercise a considerable ball play—Colonel, Parsons and all. Parade again at 2 o'clock, but soon dismissed."

30 September 1776: "The day was so bad and so much labor going on, that we had no exercise, but some ball play—at which some dispute arose among the officers, but was quelled without rising high."

14 May 1777: "Played ball, &c., till some time in the afternoon, when I walked up to Mr. DeCamp's, where I tarried all night."

* * *

Lieutenant Jabez Fitch, Connecticut officer, observes ball playing as a prisoner-of-war in the New York city area, March and April 1777, in William H.W. Sabine, ed., *The New-York Diary of Lieutenant Jabez Fitch of the 17th (Connecticut) Regiment from August 22, 1776 to December 15, 1777* (New York: pvt. ptg., 1954), 126, 127, 162.

14 March 1777: "In the Morning Lt: Blackleach made us a short Visit; this forenoon I went with Capt: Bissell down to Capt: Wells's Quarters where I procured some paper &c; on our way we lit of a number of our Offrs: who were Zealously Engaged at playing Ball, with whom we staid some time; We came home to our Quarters at about one."

15 March 1777: "This Forenoon Col. Hart & Majr: Wells came to our Quarters, & we went with them down Street as far as Johanes Lotts, where there was a large number of our Offrs: collected, & spent some Time at playing Ball."

12 April 1777: "Toward Night I took a walk with Lt: Brewster down as far as Capt: Johnsons Quarters, where there was a number of our Offrs: Assembled for playing Ball; I came home alittle after Sunset."

* * *

Charles Herbert, Newburyport, Massachusetts sailor, refers to ball playing as a prisoner of war in Plymouth, England, 2 April 1777, in [Herbert], *A Relic of the Revolution, Containing a Full and Particular Account of the Sufferings and Privations of All the American Prisoners Captured on the High Seas, and Carried into Plymouth, England, During the Revolution of 1776* (Boston: Charles H. Peirce, 1847), 109.

"Warm, and something pleasant, and the yard begins to be dry again, so that we can return to our former sports; these are ball and quoits, which exercise we make use of to circulate our blood and keep us from things that are worse."

* * *

George Ewing, New Jersey ensign, plays baseball at Valley Forge, Pennsylvania, April 1778, in [Ewing], *The Military Journal of George Ewing (1754-1824) a Soldier of Valley Forge* (Yonkers, N.Y.: Thomas Ewing, 1928), 35.

"Attested to my Muster Rolls and delivered them to the Muster Master excersisd in the afternoon in the intervals playd at base...."

* * *

Joseph Joslin, Jr., South Killingly, Connecticut teamster, observes ball playing, 21 April 1778, in [Joslin], "Journal of Joseph Joslin Jr. of South Killingly A Teamster in the Continental Service March 1777–August 1778," in "Orderly Book and Journals Kept by Connecticut Men While Taking part in the American Revolution 1775-1778," *Collections of the Connecticut Historical Society,* Vol. 7 (Hartford: Connecticut Historical Society, 1899), 353-354.

"I took care of my oxen & then I went to Capt grinnels after oats and for a load of goods and then S W Some cloudy and I See them play ball...."

* * *

Benjamin Gilbert, Brookfield, Massachusetts sergeant, chronicles ball playing in the lower Hudson River valley, April 1778 and April 1779, in Rebecca D. Symmes, ed., *A Citizen-Soldier in the American Revolution. The Diary of Benjamin Gilbert in Massachusetts and New York* (Cooperstown, N.Y.: New York State Historical Association, 1980), 30, 49.

28 April 1778: "In the fore noon the Serjt went Down the hill and plaid Ball."

30 April 1778: "In the Morning I went Down the Hill to play Ball and was Called up immediately to Gather watch coats."

5 April 1779: "Our Regt Mustered at 3 oClock after noon. After Muster went to the store and plaid Ball with serjt. Wheeler."

6 April 1779: "In the after noon the serjt. of our Regt. Went to the Comsy. store to play Ball."

14 April 1779: "Fair and Clear. In the afternoon we went to the Comissary Store and Plaid Ball."

* * *

Enos Stevens, Charlestown, New Hampshire loyalist lieutenant, plays baseball 2 and 31 May 1778, in Charles Knowlton Bolton, ed., "A Fragment of the Diary of Lieutenant Enos Stevens, Tory, 1777-1778," *New England Quarterly*, Vol. 11, No. 2 (June 1938), 384-385.

2 May 1778: "2^d. At home. Play ball."

31 May 1778: "31st Lords dy. I omit puting down every dy when their is nothing meteriel happens. Good weather for ball play."

* * *

Henry Dearborn, New Hampshire officer, plays ball in north central Pennsylvania, April 1779, in Lloyd A. Brown and Howard H. Peckham, eds., *Revolutionary War Journals of Henry Dearborn 1775-1783* (Freeport, N.Y.: Books for Libraries Press, 1969 [1939]), 149-150.

3 April 1779: "all the Officers of the Brigade turn'd out & Play'd a game at ball the first we have had this yeare.—"

17 April 1779: "we are oblige'd to walk 4 miles to day to find a place leavel enough to play ball."

* * *

Samuel Shute, New Jersey lieutenant, plays ball in central Pennsylvania, 9-22 July 1779, in [Shute], "Journal of Lt. Samuel Shute," in Frederick Cook, ed., *Journals of the Military Expedition of Major General John Sullivan against the Six Nations of Indians in 1779* (Freeport, N.Y.: Books for Libraries Press, rpt. of 1885 ed.), 268.

"..., until the 22nd, the time was spent in playing Shinny and Ball."

* * *

Dartmouth College law, circa 1780, in *Dartmouth College Laws and Regulations,* Dartmouth College Library, Special Collections MS 782415.

"If any student shall play at ball or use any other diversion the College or Hall windows within 6 rods of either he shall be fined two shilling for the first offence 4 for the 2^d and so no [on] at the discretion of the President or Tutors—"

Samuel Dewees, Pennsylvania captain, describes ball playing at Lancaster, Pennsylvania, 1781?, 1782?, in John Smith Hanna, ed., *A History of the Life and Services of Captain Samuel Dewees, A Native of Pennsylvania, and Soldier of the Revolutionary and Last Wars* (Baltimore: Robert Neilson, 1844), 265, 266.

"These officers [British prisoners of war] were full of cash, and frolicked and gamed much. One amusement in which they indulged much, was playing at ball. A Ball- Alley was fitted up at the Court-House, where some of them were to be seen at almost all hours of the day. When I could beg or buy a couple of old stockings, or two or three old stocking feet, I would set to work and make a ball. After winding the yarn into a ball, I went to a skin-dressers and got a piece of white leather, with which I covered it. When finished, I carried it to the British officers, who would *'jump at it'* at a quarter of a dollar. Whilst they remained at Lancaster, I made many balls in this way, and sold them to the British officers, and always received a quarter a-piece."

"Whilst the game of ball was coming off one day at the Court House, an American officer and a British officer, who were among the spectators, became embroiled in a dispute."

* * *

Joel Shepard, Montague, Massachusetts farmer, recalls baseball near Albany, New York, circa 1782, in John A. Spear, ed., "Joel Shepard Goes to the War," New England Quarterly, Vol. 1, No. 3 (July 1928), 344.

"We passed muster and layed in Albany about six weeks and we fared tolerable well, and not much to doo, but each class had his amusement. The officers would bee a playing at Ball on the comon, their would be an other class piching quaits, an other set a wrestling,...."

Chapter 5

BLOOD SPORTS

Americans of the colonial and Revolutionary periods were in closer contact with animals and the animal world than modern Americans can grasp today. Most Europeans and Euroamericans were farmers who reared livestock for a variety of human usages. Indigenous peoples felt the brunt of cultural pressure to convert to the "white man's ways" by taking up stockraising themselves. The pastoral vision for the new republic included a panorama of small farmers with their everpresent sheep and cows. Civilization equalled domestication and vice versa.

The world of animals and men rarely resembled the 1830s "Peaceable Kingdom" portrayals of Quaker artist Edward Hicks. Few colonial Americans evinced much sympathy for beasts. The Bible's book of Genesis accorded humans dominion over animals.

For every St. Francis of Assisi there were hundreds of churchmen like St. Thomas Aquinas asserting the absence of souls in animals. Bereft of the "hope of heaven," such animals were vulnerable to human needs and whimsies. Undoubtedly a few creatures lived privileged lives as pets, but most did not.

Hence it was hardly surprising that "blood sports" flourished. "If animals were going to die or meet the butcher's blade, why not subject them to some torture or combat to provide humans with spectacle and sport?" went the logic. If one could win some money gambling all the better. Drink, perhaps some fisticuffs, and other immoralities would attend the merriment. At the very least it would be a social occasion. Thus numerous cockfights, bearbaitings, bullbaitings, dogfights, and other assorted animal "worryings" took place, not just in the Southern colonies and states, but north to south. Perhaps the most ingenious development was gander-pulling in which a rider bearing down on a tied live goose attempted to pull off its head. Turkey shoots blended marksmanship and animal-based amusement. Such was the stuff of blood sports. Some might consider hunting and even fishing as blood sports, and there are distinct similarities, but two separate chapters in this volume cover those sports.

Cultural anthropologists, such as Clifford Geertz and his classic study of Balinese cockfighting, argue that such rituals are evidence of a form of deep play within the societies. Probably such forces were at work in colonial blood sports. The "battles royal" reminded the watchers of the larger combats of human life at that time, served as allegorical matches of vice and virtue on display, accomplished some social class leveling in the taverns, and acted as catharses for other deep-seated tensions. New England Puritans and some moralists in other regions disagreed totally and sought to abolish these blood sports, although as the old historical chestnut supposed, not because the practices caused the animals pain, but because they gave pleasure to humans. Even with the various anti-blood sports laws, the activities continued. For Americans of this era, as the following documents testify, such brutality was commonplace and even condoned.

[Consult the general writings about sports, recreation, and the various colonial, provincial, territorial, and state Sabbath and gaming laws in Chapter One for other sources about the specific sports or games in this chapter.]

COCKFIGHTING

Samuel Sewall, Boston magistrate, attempts to control cockfighting, February 1686 and March 1690, in M. Halsey Thomas, ed., *The Diary of Samuel Sewall, 1674-1729, Volume I. 1674-1708* (New York: Farrar, Straus and Giroux, 1973), 96, 252.

16 February 1686: "Great disorder in the Town by Cock-skailing: I grant 2 warrants. Tho. Barnard has one, and James Barns the other, whereby several Companies broke up: but for want of a Law and Agreement shall find much ado to supress it."

2 March 1690:   "TO THE CONSTABLES OF BOSTON,
                          AND EVERY OF THEM.

You are Required in their Majesties Names to Walk through the several parts of the Town this day, and take effectual care to suppress and dissipate all unlawful Assemblies, or tumultuous gathering together of people for Skailing or throwing at Cocks, and such like Disorders, tending to the disturbance of their Majesties Liege People, and breach of the Peace, contrary to the wholsom Laws on that behalf made and provided, those entituled Cruelty, and Prescriptions."

* * *

Hugh Jones, Virginia Anglican minister, decries the local custom of cockfighting, circa 1724, in Jones, *The Present State of Virginia* (New York: Joseph Sabin, 1865, reprint of 1724 ed.), 48.

"The common Planters leading eafy Lives don't much admire Labour, or any manly Exercife, except Horfe-Racing, nor Diverfion, except Cock-Fighting, in which fome greatly delight. This eafy Way of Living, and the Heat of the Summer makes fome very lazy, who are then faid to be Climate-ftruck."

* * *

Advertisement for a cockfight, South Carolina Gazette, No. 58, 17-24 February 1733.

"ON *Eafter Monday*, at the Houfe of Mrs. ELDRIDGE on the Green, there will be a Match of COCK-FIGHTING, Five pair of COCKS to fight five Battles for 20*l.* each, and 50*l.* the odd Battle."

* * *

Advertisements for cockfights, South Carolina Gazette, 1735.

"A Certain perfon on the 29th Inft. will fhew at the Houfe of Mr. *Jo: Wilks* at Habeaw Ferry Eleven Cocks; whoever will undertake to match them fhall have one Ounce given in the weight of each Cock, and will fight 110 1. againft 100, provided they will fight Ten Battles for 50 1 each, and 100 the odd: Whoever will take up theis Challenge, let him leave his Name in writing at the Houfe of the faid *Wilks* by the 20ft Inft. that the Challenger may have time to get his Cocks."

(No. 68, 10-17 May 1735)

"To *the Gentlemen of* Port-Royal.

THere is at the Houfe of Mr. *Ch: Shepheard* a muffled Cock, named BOUGRE DE SOT, that will fight againft any Cock in the Province, give an Ounce and take an Ounce, for 100 £. Currency: Whoever has the *Punk* to take up the aforefaid *Bougre de Sot*, may come to the faid *Shepheard*, and agree about Time and Place."

(No. 97, 22 November- 6 December 1735)

* * *

John Brickell, Irish doctor, discusses cockfighting customs in North Carolina, circa 1737, in Brickell, *The Natural History of North-Carolina* (Dublin: James Carson, 1737), 40.

"*Cock-Fighting* they greatly admire, which Birds they endeavour to procure from *England* and *Ireland*, and to that intent, employ Mafters of Ships, and other Trading Perfons to fupply them."

* * *

William Byrd, Westover, Virginia planter, refers to a cockfight, 26 March 1740, in Maude H. Woodfin, ed., *Another Secret Diary of William Byrd of Westover, 1739-1741,* (Richmond, Va.: The Dietz Press, 1942), 50.

"The Secretary was gone to the cockfight."

John Randolph, Virginia planter, describes a cockfight, 25 February 1747, in "Personal Items, 1746-1749," William and Mary Quarterly, 1st Series, Vol. 20, No. 1 (July 1911), 16.

"1746-7. feb. 25. Main of Cocks between the gent of Gloster & of Ja[S]. R. 20 pr. matched & fought for 5 gs a battle & 50 gs the odd. Gloster won 13; afterw'd another match between the Cocks of the aforesaid gent for 3 pistoles the battle & 30 pistoles the odd, in which James R. won two out of 3, besides several byes which major Littlepage said would have been the case the first day if Bacon's *Thunderbolts* had fallen in the match."

* * *

Robert Rose, Virginia Anglican minister, mentions a cockfight, 26 February 1749, in Ralph Emmett Fall, ed., *The Diary of Robert Rose. A View of Virginia by a Scottish Colonial Parson, 1746-1751* (Falls Church, Va.: McClure Press, 1977), 74.

"..., and lodged at Lomax's who is gone to a Cock fight at New Castle—...."

* * *

Francis Jerdone, Virginia merchants' agent, refers to a cockfight in Virginia near New Castle, February 1750, in Jerdone to Buchanan and Hamilton, London merchants, 24 February 1750, in "Letterbook of Francis Jerdone," William and Mary College Quarterly, 1st Series, Vol. 11, No. 2 (October 1902), 155.

"..., but of this I shall write you by Cap[t] Teage who will sail in ten or twelve days, before which time I shall have an opportunity of seeing many Gentlemen at a grand Cock Fight which is to be at New Castle in a few days."

* * *

Advertisement for a cockfight, Virginia Gazette, No. 7, 14 February 1751.

"ON *Tuefday* next will be fought, at *George and Dragon*, in *Williamsburg*, a Match of Cocks, for Ten Piftoles the firft Battle, Five Piftoles the Second, and Two Piftoles and a Half the Third, &c. As likewife feveral other Matches."

* * *

John Blair, Virginia politician, mentions a cockfight, 19 February 1751, in [Blair], "Diary of John Blair," William and Mary College Quarterly Historical Magazine, Vol. 7, No. 3 (January 1899), 136.

February 19, 1751: "a fine warm sunny day for ye cock fight."

* * *

Essay against cockfighting, Virginia Gazette, No. 53, January 2, 1752.

"To the PRINTER.

SIR,

"If you'll pleafe to communicate to the Public the following Obfervations on one of the reigning Diverfions of this Country, you'll oblige

Your very humble Servant.

"THE Right Mankind has to deprive an Innocent Animal of Life, muft depend upon the Property every refpective Individual has therein. Now, I fay, that the Property Men have in every Thing they poffefs, is limited, or that no Man may ufe any of the Things they poffeth, according to his own Pleafure, unlefs fuch Ufing be agreeable to the Divine Law. There fore the depriving an innocent Animal of Life, muft be under certain Limitations.

"Whether the Dominion God gave the firft Man over the Creatures extended to the taking away their Lives for any other Ufe than Sacrifice or for Cloathing; or whether the Allowance was only given to *Noah* after the Deluge, to kill them for Food, I fhall not here enquire, fince I fhall take it for granted that Mankind has a Licence to kill them for the Neceffities and Conveniences of Life. The Opinion of fome *Calvinifts*, that none but the Elect have fuch Property, not being worth confuting. But then the Queftion is, how far this Property extends, or where it ftops. Now the Way to find this out, is to examine where the Exercife thereof is fupported by any Divine Law, or where it contradicts the fame. For Inftance... The Domeftick, or innocent Animals are not to be killed to gratify an extravagant Paffion for Money, out of Wantonnefs, or with Circumftances of Cruelty attending fuch killing. Becaufe this is a Tranfgreffion of the Laws that forbid fuch Crimes. For even the Law of Nature forbids Cruelty. It is grievous to fee, or even hear of an Animal in Torment. Our very Make and Conftitution (if it is not vitiated) reftrains us from being infenfible to the Pains of others. *Plutarch* fays, 'If we kill an Animal for our Provifion, let us do it with the Meltings of Compaffion, and without tormenting it. Let us confider that 'tis, in its own Nature, Cruelty, to put a living Creature to Death; we at leaft deftroy a Soul that has Senfe and Perception.' And again, 'It is no more than an obligation of our very Birth, to practife Humanity to our own Kind, but Humanity may be extended through the Whole Order of Creatures, even to the Meaneft.'

"The Scripture tells us, *Prov.* xii. 10 That the Righteous Man regardeth the Life of his Beaft. Then, by the Rule of Contraries, He that regardeth not the Life of his Beaft, is not a righteous Man. But how can he, who wantonly puts a poor innocent Animal to a cruel and lingering Death, be faid to regard its Life. Certainly in no Senfe. Therefore I infer, that he who does fo, is an unrighteous Man, or fo far Tranfgreffor of the Divine Law.

"To apply this to the Practice fo much in Vogue here, of late, of Cock-fighting. I would beg Leave to afk the Advocates for that Diverfion, upon what Law is it founded? It it be anfwered, by afking another Queftion, viz. Does not the Laws of the Country allow a Man to ufe his own Property, as he pleafes? I anfwer, By no Means. For either fuch Laws are agreeable to the Divine Law, or they are not. To fay they are not agreeable to the Divine Law, is faying in other Words, no Man ought to obferve them. Which is a poor Compliment to the Laws of our Country. It follows therefore that they are agreeable to the Divine Law. And if fo, I have endeavoured to fhew that the above Practice is contrary as well to the Divine Law revealed, as to that of Nature.

"But it may perhaps be objected, That the Animals, for which fo tender a Regard is pleaded, are of fuch a Nature, that they will tear and deftroy one another whenever they meet; therefore Cock-fighting is only giving further Scope to this natural Inftinct. To which I anfwer, admitting the Truth of the Fact contained in the Objection, it will by no Means follow, that becaufe fome of the brute Animals are naturally fierce, therefore Men are to cultivate and improve that Quality in them. On the contrary, it is obfervable, that the moft civilized Part of Mankind has always tam'd and render'd ufeful many of the fierce Animals, as they ought to have done.

"And if it be a juft Obfervation (as I think it is) that moft of the domeftick Animals are only apt to quarrel with fuch of their own Species as they don't ufually fee, but are commonly fond of thofe they affociate with, then I think the Objection turns againft the Objectors.

"And as the Circumftances of an Action very much affect its Nature, this Practice will be found attended with Circumftances fhockingly prophane and impious. This I can affert from my own Obfervation. For having actually been prefent at a Cock-fight, fome time ago, I could not but take Notice, with much Concern, that fome Gentlemen, who, upon other Occafions, behav'd with great Decency, and as if they had been influenced with fuitable Impreffions of the awful and tremendous Name of GOD, did then fpeak and act if the Divine Law had beenfor that Time abrogated, opening their Mouths with horrid Oaths, and dreadful Imprecations. And all this when their Paffions were not much nflam'd, being early in the Day, and their high Bets not yet begun. I, for my Part was foon tir'd with the Place and *Diverfion,* as 'tis called, and left it, with a firm Purpofe, never to be prefent at another fuch. To it fucceeded Drinking and Gaming, an uninterrupted Violation both of Divine, and Human Laws, for fome Days and Nights.

"Now admitting that the Practice of Cock-fighting were lawful in itfelf, which I abfolutely deny; yet when 'tis attended with fuch Circumftances, and follow'd by fuch terrible Confequences, is it not a Shame that it fhould be allowed in a Chriftian Country. Were one of the primitive Chriftians but to revifit this Globe, and be dropt at a modern Cock-fight, he would hardly be persuaded, that he was among Chriftains; but upon his being affured, athat he was in the pureft Part of the Chriftian Church, how great muft his Surprize and Concern be, to find fuch a dreadful Diffolution of Manners, among thofe that bear the Redeemer's Name.

"If then this Practice be fo unjuftifiable, is it not fit, the more fober and regular Part of Mankind, who have, without duly examining the Nature thereof, or viewing it in the Light in which I have placed it, given too much Countenance thereto, fhould abandon the fame; and thereby difcountenance, if they canot entirely remove the growing Evil: For I'm perfuaded, atht if thofe in eminent Stations, would fhew their Diflike, not only to that, but to every other diffolute Practice, the Vulgar, who are very apt to mimick them, would foon give it up alfo, at leaft it would become fo infamous, that none who regarded their Character, would be found publickly to practife it.

"It may perhaps be thought, that I have exaggerated the Malignity of the above Practice, and that many who love the Diverfion, abhor the Confequences thereof. But I would have fuch confider, what has been faid as to the Lawfulnefs thereof; and then, though the Circumftances attending be not effential thereto, yet if they are fo infeparable therefrom, as the World goes, that they are become almoft what Logicians call fecondary Qualities, then I will leave it to their Confciences to determine, what is fafeft to be done in fuch a Cafe.

"Upon the whole, if any one, who has aught to offer in Support of the above mentioned Diverfion, will pleafe communicate his Thoughts to the Public, I fhall duly confider and endeavour to anfwer them, if they contain any Thing like Reafon and Argument. But if no better Reafon can be given for it, than that it is an old Cuftom, in itfelf indifferent, and not to be parted with, becaufe fome People of fcrupulous Confciences diflike it; then, I hope, Men of Senfe will not think it beneath them, to follow good Advice, from whatever Quarter it comes, and abandon a Practice for which fo little can be pleaded."

* * *

Advertisement for a cockfight, Virginia Gazette, No. 61, February 27, 1752.

"A COCK-MATCH will be fought on the 7th Day of *April*, next, at the Ordinary formerly *Seayre*'s Ordinary, near *Hobb*'s-*Hole*, in *Effex* County, for Sixty Piftoles."

George Washington, Virginia plantation owner, Revolutionary War general, and later President, mentions a cockfight, circa 1752, in Donald Jackson, ed., *The Diaries of George Washington, Volume I, 1748-1765* (Charlottesville, Va.: University Press of Virginia, 1976), 115.

"A Great Main of cocks [was fought] in Yorktown between Glouster & York for 5 pistoles each battle 100 ye odd. I left it with Colo Lewis before it was decided."

* * *

George Hume, Virginia surveyor, refers to cockfights in Culpepper County, Virginia, August 1754, in Hume to his brother John Hume, 22 August 1754, in "Letters of Hume Family," William and Mary College Quarterly, 1st Series, Vol. 8, No. 1 (July 1899), 89.

"I have no oy^r news to tell you —money is so scarce it is a rare thing to see a dollar, and at the publick places where great monied men will bet on cock fights, horse races, etc., ye noise is not now as it used to be—...."

* * *

Ordinance at William and Mary College, Virginia, 14 September 1754, in "Journal of the Meetings of the President and Masters of William and Mary College," William and Mary Quarterly, 1st Series, Vol. 2, No. 1 (July, 1893), 54-55.

"At a meeting of ye President & Masters of William & Mary College, Sepr ye 14th, 1754, present,

Y^e Revd Mr Stith, President, Mr Dawson, Mr Robinson, Mr Preston & Mr Graham, ye following orders were unanimously agreed to....

2. Ordered —y^t no scholar belonging to ye College of w^t Age, Rank, or Quality, soever, or wheresoever residing, within, or without ye College, do presume to appear playing or Betting at ye Billiard or other gaming Tables, or be any way concern'd in keeping or fighting cocks under Pain of ye like severe Animadversion or Punishment."

* * *

Account of a cockfight, Virginia Gazette, No. 228, March 23, 1755.

"On *Tuesday* the 20th of this Instant, was determined at the *New-Kent* Court Houfe, the great Cock Match between *Gloucester* and *New-Kent*, for Ten Piftoles a Battle and an Hundred the Main, there fell Eighteen in the Match, of which the *New-Kent* men won Ten and *Gloucester* Seven, one a drawn Battle; Some *James* Rivers Cocks that fell on the *New-Kent* Side diftinguished themfelves in a very extraordinary Manner."

* * *

Robert Page's will refers to cockfights, Hanover County, Virginia, 15 August 1765, reprinted in "Wills of Robert and John Page," Virginia Magazine of History and Biography, Vol. 34, No. 3 (July 1926), 276.

"I desire my brother Mann and John Page with my dearest wife may be my Executors and I desire neither of my sons may ever be allowed to go to Horse Races or Cock Fights, or to any other public diversion as they are only consuming of time & that all my children may be piously brought up to that one and only thing necessary religion.
                              Robert Page, Thursday, Augt. 15, 1765."

* * *

Advertisement for a cockfight, Virginia Gazette, No. 878, 17 March 1768.

"*On* Monday *the 4th of* April *will be fought at* Suffex *court-house.*

A MATCH OF
COCKS,

between the *Brunfwick* and *Suffex* Gentlemen; to fhow 30 cocks a fide, for 5 l. a battle, and 50 l. the odd. At night there will be a ball, for the reception of the Ladies and Gentlemen."

* * *

Account of a servant transaction at a cockfight, Rind's Virginia Gazette, No. 167, July 20, 1769.

"SOME days before the cock-fight which was made by Meff. *Price* and *Underwood*, and to be at Major *John Bofwell*'s, on *Eafter Tuefday* laft paft, Mr. *John Aylett* came to the fubfcriber's houfe, and had with him a flave, a boy of a yellow complexion named *Will*, which he the faid *Aylett* told him, he had purchafed of Mr. *John McKeind*, merchant at *Shockoes*; and further told him, that he intended to fell the faid boy at the cock fight above-mentioned, in order to difcharge a debt he owed to the above named *Underwood*, and *George Clough*; after the faid cock fight, the faid *Aylett* told him, that he had actually fold the faid boy to the faid *Underwood*, for fixty three pounds, and was to deliver him according to agreement the next *Hanover* court day, and that the faid *Underwood* had affumed the payment of the debt owe[d] by him the faid *Aylett* to *George Clough*. Witnefs my hand this 29th day of *May*, 1769

N. W. DANDRIDGE.

Teft. Peter Strachan,
Robert Wilfon."

* * *

Francis Hopkinson, Philadelphia poet, chastises cockfighters, circa 1770, in Hopkinson, "The Cock-Fighter, an Elegy," unpublished poem reprinted in The Pennsylvania Magazine of History and Biography, Vol. 44, No. 1 (1920), 74-75.

"The Cock-Fighter, an Elegy

"Ah me! what means this cackling all around?
Hen cries to Hen & Chicken shrilly sound;
A Father *these, those* mourn a Husband dead,
By cruel Hands to bloody Battle led.

"See from N—— Y—— D—— comes in state,
And twenty *fighting Cocks* around him wait,
All arm'd with steel & ready for the War—
Chicks fly amaz'd & Hens the Sight abhor.

"From yonder Barn sad sounds salute mine Ear,
And thus methinks the Notes of Woe I hear:
'Curs'd be the Hour that bro't him to this place,
That savage Foe to all our harmless Race!

"'Attend my little Brood, & whilst I sing,
Oh gather close beneth my shelt'ring Wing!
A Father *you*, a Husband *I* deplore—
D—— came, & Dicky is no more.

"'At Yester-Morn, while yet the Morn was grey,
My Dicky rose and hail'd the rising Day:
Ah, what avail'd his Voice so clear & shrill,
His glossy Neck, gay Plumage, polish'd Bill.

"'Or coral Comb that grac'd his lofty Head,
Or cockly Strut when forth our Train he led?
For ere the Sun to hastening Night could yield,
Poor Dicky lay, all mangled, on the Field.

"'Thus are we left —Oh barb'rous Sport of Men!
Poor Orphans you, and I a widow'd Hen.
Is't not enough our hamrless Race must bleed
To crown your Feasts, ev'n luxury to feed?

"'That ere our pretty Cockling learn to crow,
To pamper Lust they must to Market go?
But will you thus, on fatal Mischief bent,
For our destrcution cruel Sports invent?

"'Hence! hence away, & leave this bloody Plan,
Pusure some nobler purpose, worthy Man!
Think'st thou that Heav'n was to thy Fortunes kind,
Gave Wealth & Pow'r, gave an immortal Mind,

"'With boasted Reason, & a ruling Hand
To make thee first Cock-Fighter in the Land?
With crimson Dye our blood shall spot thy Fame
And Chickens yet unhatch'd shall curse D——'s Name.'"

* * *

Advertisements for cockfights, Virginia Gazette, 1770.

"A Match of Cocks
to be fought at *Suffex* courthoufe, on Monday the 16th of *April*, between the *Charles City* and *Suffex* Gentlemen; to fhow 25 cocks for 10l. a battle, and 50l. the odd battle. At night there will be a ball for the reception of the Ladies and Gentlemen.
ROBERT OWING."
(No. 979, 22 February 1770)

"*A MATCH of COCKS will be fought at* Goochland *courthoufe on* Whitfun Tuefday; *to fhow* 30 *Cocks of a fide,* 5 *l. a battle, and* 50l. *the odd one.*
ROBERT COLEMAN."
(No. 992, 24 May 1770)

* * *

Charles Jeffery Smith, Virginia educator, on plans to outlaw cockfighting at a new academy at New Kent, Virginia, 1 March 1770, in Smith, "Plans for an Academy at Providence, in New Kent," William and Mary Quarterly, 2nd Series, Vol. 3, No. 1 (January 1923), 54.

"The *morals* of the pupils, that capital part of *education*, will be watched with pious vigilance, and formed with unremitting assiduity: But no licentious amusements, which are real vices, however polite and fashionable they may appear to some, will be tolerated or connived at, such as *card-playing, horse-racing, cock-fighting, wrestling, &c.*"

* * *

Jacob Hiltzheimer, Philadelphia area farmer and politician, mentions a cockfight, 6 March 1770, in Jacob Cox Parsons, ed., *Extracts from the Diary of Jacob Hiltzheimer* (Philadelphia: William Fell Company, 1893), 20.

"Today James DeLancey, from New York, and Timothy Matlack, had a great cock fight at Richardson's, up Germantown Road."

* * *

Advertisement for a cockfight, Rind's Virginia Gazette, No. 206, 19 April 1770.

"To *be* FOUGHT *at* King William *courthoufe, on* Tuefday *the 8th day of* May,
A Match of COCKS,
For FIVE POUNDS a battle, and FIFTY POUNDS the main; made between the *Charles* and *James City* Gentlemen, and the *King William* and *Caroline* Gentlemen. To fhow 21 cocks."

* * *

Advertisement for a cockfight, Virginia Gazette, No. 1046, 15 August 1771.

"A MATCH of COCKS to be fought at *Lunenburg* Courthoufe, on Tuefday the 17th of *September* between the *Dinwiddie* and *Lunenburg* Gentlemen; to fhow fifteen Cocks for five Pounds a Battle, and fifty Pounds the odd Battle. There will be good Entertainment for all Gentlemen that are difpofed to come.

JAMES COLL."
* * *

John Ferdinand Dalziel Smyth, British traveler, concerning Virginians, mentions cockfighting, August 1772?, in Smyth, *A Tour in the United States of America. Containing an Account of the Present Situation of that Country*, 2 vols., Vol. 1 (London: G. Robinson, 1784), 67.

"They are all exceffively attached to every fpecies of fport, gaming, and diffipation, particularly horfe-racing, and that moft barbarous of all diverfions, that peculiar fpecies of cruelty, cock-fighting."

* * *

Philip Vickers Fithian, tutor at Nomini Hall, Virginia, chronicles the local cockfighting, April, June, and September 1774, in Hunter Dickinson Farish, ed., *Journal and Letters of Philip Vickers Fithian, 1773-1774. A Plantation Tutor of the Old Dominion* (Charlottesville, Va: University Press of Virginia, 1957 [1943]), 91, 97, 121, 161-162, 190.

4 April 1774: "Easter Monday; a general holiday; Negroes now are all disbanded till Wednesday morning & are at Cock Fights through the County;...."

"I was before Dinner very strongly urged, by Mr Taylor, Mr Randolph, & some others to attend a Cock-Fight, where 25 Cocks are to fight, & large Sums are betted, but I choose rather to stay at Home. I read to day, & am much charmed with a Speech of Plato's over Alexander the *Great* lying dead before him—'O thou, who deceived by vain-Glory didst think of grasping at every thing, others are now going to gather the fruits of thy labours & thy Fatigues. Of so many conquests, there remains of thee but the terrible account, which thou art obliged to render unto the sovereign Judge'!—"

10 April 1774: "Before Breakfast I saw a Ring of Negroes at the Stable, fighting Cocks...."

18 June 1774: "At twelve *Bob* [Robert Carter, Jr.] teaz'd me for leave to go to a Cock-Fight & Horse-Race about two Miles off, I gave him Leave with his promising to be home by Sun Set."

12 August 1774, [Fithian to John Peck]: "But whenever you go from Home, where you are to act on your own footing, either to a Ball; or to a *Horse-race*, or to a *Cock-Fight*, or to a *Fish-Feast*, I advise you that you rate yourself very low...."

15 September 1774: "*Harry's* Genius seems towards Cocks, & low Betts, much in company with the waiting Boys...."

* * *

Letter from Wilmington, North Carolina, concerning amusements such as cockfighting, 26 November 1774, reprinted in Francis Barnum Culver, *Blooded Horses* of *Colonial Days. Classic Horse Matches* in *America before the Revolution* (Baltimore: pvt. ptg., 1922), ?.

"The Continental Congress lately held at Philadelphia, representing the several American colonies from Nova Scotia to Georgia, associated and agreed among other things, for themselves and their constituents, to 'discontinue and discourage every species of extravagance and dissipation, especially all horse-racing, and all kinds of gaming, cock-fighting, exhibitions of shows and plays and other expensive diversions and entertainments.'"

* * *

Ebenezer Hazard, postal inspector for the Continental Congress, describes cockfighting near Jamestown, Virginia, June 1777, in Fred Shelley, ed., "The Journal of Ebenezer Hazard in Virginia, 1777," The Virginia Magazine of History and Biography, Vol. 62 (1954), 411, 414.

10 June 1777: "At Nelson's (where I dined) a Cock Match is to be fought next Thursday: great Betts are depending. Met some Men who were going to race their Horses. Horse-Racing & Cock-fighting seem to be the principal Objects of Attention between Williamsburgh & Smithfield at present.... I find that the Cock Match is between the Counties of Isle of Wight & Surry."

13 June 1777: "The Virginians ...[are] much addicted to Gaming, drinking, swearing, horse-racing, Cock-fighting, & most Kinds of Dissipation."

* * *

Announcement for a cockfight, Royal Pennsylvania Gazette, No. 7, 24 March 1778.

"THOSE Gentlemen who are fond of COCKING, and have COCKS, may have an opportunity of matching them, either to fight in the main, or by battles, at the Cock-Pit, in Moore's Alley, in Front-Street, near Carr's ftore, on Saturday the 28th inftant.

"N.B. Cocks received by Tho. Wildman of the 17th dragoons."

* * *

Thomas Anburey, British officer, at Mystic, Connecticut, moralizes about cockfighting, 20 May 1778, in [Anburey], *Travels through the Interior Parts of America*, 2 vols., Vol. 2 (London: William Lane, 1791), 199-200.

"I need not tell you of what a reftlefs difpofition we Englifh are of, and that we muft be employed on fomething, fituated as we are, without books, newfpapers, or any other amufement: fome officers, who came from the Weft of England, have inftituted the diverfion of fighting of cocks; for my own part, you know, I ever efteemed it a barbarous cuftom, and a difgrace to our nation, and cannot but fay I was a little pleafed at a reprimand that fome officers met with from an old woman, to whom they had applied for a couple of fine birds that were in the yard; fhe enquired if they were to fight, or to kill for eating; being told the former, fhe in a moft violent rage exclaimed, 'I fwear now you fhall have neither of them; I fwear now I never faw any thing fo bloodthirfty as you Britonions be; if you can't be fighting and cutting other people's throats, you muft be fetting two harmlefs creatures to kill one another; Go along, go; I have heard of your cruel doings at Watertown (the place where the cocks fought) cutting off the feathers, and the poor creature's comb and gills, and putting on iron things upon their legs; go along, I fay.' I could not help laughing to fee them decamp in hafte, as the old woman had worked herfelf into fuch a paffion, that they expected fhe would have ftruck them with her crutch, which fhe lifted to give the greater energy to her language. This is the only inftance in my memory, that can reflect credit on American humanity."

* * *

Advertisement for cockfighting equipment, [Rivington's] Royal Gazette, No. 232, 19 December 1778.

"COCK GAFFS,
SILVER and STEEL,
Enquire of the Printer."

* * *

Andrew Jackson, future United States President, copies down a recipe on what to feed a gamecock in North Carolina, 22 March 1779, in John Spencer Bassett, ed., *Correspondence of Andrew Jackson,* 4 vols., Vol. 1 (Washington: Carnegie Institution of Washington, 1926), 2.

"A Memorandum How to Feed a Cock before You Him Fight.
"Take and give him some Pickle Beaf Cut fine 3 times a Day and give him sweet Milk Instead of water to Drink give him dry Indian Corn that hase been Dryn Up in smoke give him lighte wheat Bread Soked in sweet Milk feed him as Much as he can Eat for Eight Days   Orrange Town in Orange County
   March the 22d 79
Mr. Mabee Merchant."

* * *

Advertisement for a cockfighting manual, [Rivington's] Royal Gazette, No. 494, 23 June 1781.

"To the COCK-FIGHTERS.
DIRECTIONS FOR BREEDING
GAME COCKS,
With the Methods of treating them from the time of their being hatched, till fit to fight; including inftructions for the choice of a Cock and Hens to breed from; place to breed at; and remarks worthy obfervation previous to fighting a match.
   Articles for a Cock-Match; Key to a Match; Rules and Orders in Cocking, abided by at the Cock Pit Royal, with

CALCULATIONS for BETTING,
May be had of the PRINTER, price 6f."
* * *
Jean-Baptiste-Antoine de Verger, French officer, comments on cockfighting near Williamsburg, Virginia, 18 January 1782, in [Verger], "Journal of Jean-Baptiste-Antoine de Verger," in Howard C. Rice, Jr. and Anne S. K. Brown, trans. and eds., *The American Campaigns of Rochambeau's Army, 1780, 1781, 1782, 1783*, 2 vols., Vol 1 (Princeton, N.J.: Princeton University Press, 1972), 157-158.

"They have another sport, which is cock-fighting. Here is how it is conducted: Certain inhabitants raise cocks that look very strong and that they bring in a covered cage to the battlefield. Those disposed to bet choose one, which is then weighed, and if he is of the same weight as his adversary, the neck feathers that might hinder him are plucked out. The cocks are next fitted with very sharp, long, curved steel spurs which are attached to their natural spurs. Then they are put into a ring enclosed by a rope, around which the circle of spectators sits. Each man lauches his cock, and the fight is on. The moment one falls a man picks him up and makes him take a drink. The fight continues until one of the combatants is killed. I heard that after one of these fights Messrs. Graves and Nicholson, got into a fist-fight—the usual outcome of disputes between Americans."
* * *

Baron Ludwig von Closen, French captain, discusses cockfighting in Virginia, 16 February 1782, in Evelyn M. Acomb, trans. and ed., *The Revolutionary Journal of Baron Ludwig von Closen, 1780-1783* (Chapel Hill, N.C.: University of North Carolina Press, 1958), 176-177.

"There are endless balls; the women love dancing with as much passion as the men hunting and horse-racing, and sometimes cock-fights too.

"As for the cock-fights, they are something to see once out of curiosity, but the spectacle is a little too cruel for one to enjoy; one sees these poor things knocked about, pricked, blinded, and finally killed with their steel spurs. I have seen some very dexterous ones who played with this instrument with the greatest daring and skill; thus they often win a reputation for fifty miles or more. Some breeds of cocks are very expensive. I will bring back with me some of these spurs to satisfy the curiosity of those who would like to see a cock-fight. Those in North America are pointed like the *aal* of shoemakers; those in Spain are like pen knives with a double edge.
    [diagram] Spain   [diagram] Virginia"
* * *

Marquis de Chastellux, French officer, describes a cockfight at Willis's Ordinary, Virginia, 12 April 1782, in [Chastellux], *Travels in North-America, in the Years 1780, 1781, and 1782, by the Marquis de Chastellux*, 2nd ed., 2 vols., Vol. 2 (London: G.G.J. and J. Robinson, 1787), 28-32.

"As foon as I alighted, I enquired what might be the reafon of this numerous affembly, and was informed it was a *cock-match*. This diverfion is much in fafhion in Virginia, where the Englifh cuftoms are more prevalent than in the reft of America. When the principal promoters of this diverfion, propofe to watch [match?] their champions, they take great care to announce it to the public, and although there are neither pofts, nor regular conveyances, this important news fpreads with fuch facility, that the planters for thirty or forty miles round, attend, fome with cocks, but all with money for betting, which is fometimes very considerable. They are obliged to bring their own provifions, as fo many people with good appetites could not poffibly be fupplied with them at the inn. As for lodgings, one large room for the whole company, with a blanket for each individual, is fufficient for fuch hearty countrymen, who are not more delicate about the conveniences of life, than the choice of their amufements.

"Whilft our horfes were feeding, we had an opportunity of feeing a battle. The preparation took up a great deal of time; they arm the cocks with long fteel fpurs, very fharp, and cut off a part of their feathers, as if they meant to deprive them of their armour. At last they fought and one of them remained dead on the battlefield. The ftakes were very confiderable; the money of the parties was depofited in the hands of one of the principal perfons, and I felt a fecret pleafure in obferving that it was chiefly French [money]. I know not which is most aftonifhing, the infipidity of fuch diverfion, or the ftupid intereft with which it animates the parties. This paffion appears almoft innate among the Englifh, for the Virginians are still Englifh in many refpects. Whilft the interefted parties animated the cocks to battle, a child of fifteen, who was near me, kept leaping for joy, and crying, Oh! it is a *charming diverfion*."

* * *

An English gentleman, moralizes about cockfighting in Virginia, circa 1782-1787, quoted in Marquis de Chastellux, *Travels in North-America, in the Years 1780, 1781, and 1782,* 2nd ed., 2 vols., Vol. 2 (London: G.G.J. and J. Robinson, 1787), 192.

"The indolence and diffipation of the middling and lower claffes of white inhabitants of Virginia, are fuch as to give pain to every reflecting mind. Horfe-racing, cockfighting, and boxing-matches, are ftanding amufements, for which they neglect all bufinefs;...."

* * *

Advertisement for cockfighting equipment, [Rivington's] Royal Gazette, No. 657, 11 January 1783.

"COCK GAFFS,
FOR THE ROYAL PASTIME OF
COCK FIGHTING.
TO BE SOLD.
Enquire of the Printer."

* * *

Johann David Schoepf, German physician, comments about youths and cockfighting in Virginia, December 1783, in Schoepf, *Travels in the Confederation. Pennsylvania, Maryland, Virginia, the Carolinas, East Florida, the Bahamas,* trans. and ed. by Alfred J. Morrison, 2 vols., Vol. 2 (Cleveland: Arthur H. Clark, 1911), 95.

"A Virginia youth of 15 years is already such a man as he will be at twice that age. At 15, his father gives him a horse and a negro, with which he riots about the country, attends every fox-hunt, horse-race, and cock-fight, and does nothing else whatever;...."

* * *

Advertisement for cockfighting equipment, [Rivington's] New-York Gazette, and Universal Advertiser, No. 755, 20 December 1783.

"COCK-FIGHTING.
The Profeffors of this Sport, are informed, that the fineft and beft finifhed

Affortment of
GAFFS, or COCK-SPURS,
HITHERTO IMPORTED,
ARE now to be feen and purchafed, either in fingle Pairs, or boxes of eight or twelve Pairs, with Saws, Sciffars, &c. &c. at Mr. RIVINGTON's.
WHO HAS FOR SALE,
A book, entitled, DIRECTIONS for Breeding GAME COCKS; with the Method of treating them, from the time they are hatched, till fit to Fight. Including Inftructions for the Choice of a Cock and Hens to breed from, Place to breed at; and Remarks worthy Obfervation previous to Fighting a Match; Articles for a Cock Match; Key to a Match-Bill; Rules and Orders in Cocking, abided by at the Cock-Pit Royal, in St. James's Park; with CALCULATIONS for BETTING. Being the refult of many year's experience. —*Price Four Shillings.*"

OTHER BLOOD SPORTS

Unnamed English travelers describe a bullfight on Hispaniola, circa 1585, in "Anonymous Journal of the 1585 Virginia Voyage [by Sir Richard Greenvile]," in David B. Quinn and Alison M. Quinn, eds., *The First Colonists. Documents on the Planting of the First English Settlements in North America, 1584-1590* (Raleigh, N.C.: North Carolina Department of Cultural Resources, Division of Archives and History, 1982), 16.

July 5, 1585: "Which banquet being ended, the Spanyardes in recompense of our curtesie, caused a great herd of white buls, and kyne, to be brought together from the Mounteines, and appointed for every Gentlemen and Captaine that would ride, a horse ready sadled, and then singled out three of the best of them to be hunted by horsemen after their manner, so that the pastime grew very plesant for the space of three houres, wherein all three of the beasts were killed, whereof one tooke the sea, and there was slaine with a musket. After this sport, many rare presents and gifts were given and bestowed on both partes,...."
                                                        * * *

William Wood, English settler, depicts sport with bears in New England, circa 1634, in [Wood], *New England's Prospect. A True, Lively, and Experimental Defcription of that Part of America, Commonly Called Nevv England. Difcovering the Ftate of that Countrie, both as it ftands to our New-Come* Englifh *Planters; and to the Old Native Inhabitants* (London: Thomas Cotes, 1634), reprinted as *Wood's New-England Prospect, Publications of the Prince Society, Volume 1* (Boston: The Prince Society, 1865), 22.

"For Beares they be common, being a great blacke kind of Beare, which be moft fierce in Strawberry time, at which time they have young ones; at this time likewife they will goe upright like a man, and clime trees, and swimme to the Iflands; which if the *Indians* fee, there will be more fportfull Beare bayting than Paris Garden can affoard. For feeing the Beares take water, an *Indian* will leape after him, where they goe to water cuffes for bloody nofes, and fcratched fides; in the end the man gets the victory, riding the Beare over the watery plaine till he can beare him no longer."

* * *

John Dunton, London traveler, in Boston, 25 March 1686, quotes a sermon by minister Increase Mather, concerning sport with animals, in [Dunton], *A Summer's Ramble, Through Ten Kingdomes, Occasionally Written by John Dunton, Citizen of London*, 2 vols. (London: A. Baldwin, 1686), reprinted as W.H. Whitmore, ed., *Letters Written from New-England, A.D. 1686, by John Dunton* (Boston: The Prince Society, 1867), 130-131.

"The Scripture faith, That a good Man is merciful to his Beaft: they then that make themfelves fport with putting dumb Creatures to mifery, do very finfully: Yet that has been practiced here of later years in the open ftreets, efpecially on one day in the year: (I mean the Cock-Scalings on Shrove-Tuefday.) To do it at fuch a time is vanity and heathenifh Superftition: Befides, to make fport with exercifing Cruelty on dumb Creatures, which had never been miferable had not the Sins of Man made them fo, it is a wicked thing, and ought not to be amongst thofe that call themfelves Chriftians."

* * *

Josiah Cotton, Haverhill, Massachusetts resident, writes to Rowland Cotton about a bull-baiting, 17 October 1702, in Robert E. Moody, ed., *The Saltonstall Papers, 1607-1815, Volume 1. 1607-1789* (Boston Massachusetts Historical Society, 1972), 271.

"Last Monday here was a Training, Tuesday a Bullbaiting as they do in England. A poor Fellow had brought a Bull and pretended after he had baited him he would give him to the poor, and therefore was suffered to do it just before the Schoolhouse, where were an abundance of People, but he has turned him out and intends to bait him again at Novr. 5, and then give him to the poor."

* * *

Benjamin Colman, Massachusetts Congregationalist minister, warns against bear-baiting, circa 1707, in Colman, *The Government and Improvement of Mirth* (Boston: Samuel Philips, 1707), 73.

"Woe be to the *Church-Member*, who muft now be content to a Knave and a Fool, and like fome *Martyrs* of old, be drefs'd up to be worry'd without pity, nay with all the rude pleafures of a *Bear-baiting*."

* * *

Advertisement for a bear-baiting, Boston Gazette, 23-30 May 1726, reprinted in George Francis Dow, *Every Day Life in the Massachusetts Bay Colony* (New York: Benjamin Blom, 1935), 114.

"On Thursday next the 2d of June, at 3 o'clock P.M., in Staniford's Street, near the Bowling Green, will be Baited a Bear, by John Coleson; where all Gentlemen and others that would divert themselves may repair."

* * *

William Byrd, Westover, Virginia planter, describes a bull-baiting near the Roanoke River in Virginia, 8 October 1733, in [Byrd], "A Journey to the Land of Eden," in Louis B. Wright, ed., *The Prose Works of William Byrd of Westover. Narratives of a Colonial Virginian* (Cambridge, Mass.: Harvard University Press, 1966), 404-405.

"In coming back to the camp we discovered a solitary bull buffalo, which boldly stood his ground, contrary to the custom of that shy animal. We spared his life, from a principle of never slaughtering an innocent creature to no purpose. However, we made ourselves some diversion by trying if he would face our dogs. He was so far from retreating at their approach that he ran at them with great fierceness, cocking up his ridiculous little tail and grunting like a hog. The dogs in the meantime only played about him, not venturing within reach of his horns, and by their nimbleness came off with a whole skin."

* * *

Excerpt from an advertisement about a fair and horse racing at Williamsburg in the Virginia Gazette, No. 175, 30 November-7 December 1739.

"A Pig, with his Tail foap'd, to be run after; and to be given to the Perfon that catches him, and lifts him off the Ground fairly by the Tail."

* * *

Advertisement for a pig race, South Carolina Gazette, No. 598, September 9, 1745.

"On *Tuefday the* 24th *Infant, Afhley Ferry* Fair will be held as ufual, where will be a Shoat to be run for, the Property of the Perfon who catches him, and a Goofe to be rid for under Gallop, the Property of him who pulls off his Head, and a Watch and plate to be raffled for, likewife Horfe racing, at the Houfe of   *Thomas Stoakes.*"

* * *

Advertisement for a bear and turkey shoot, Boston Evening Post, No. 1946, 11 January 1773.

"This is to give Notice,
That there will be a BEAR, and a Number of TURKEYS fet up as marks, next Thurfday beforenoon, at the PUNCH-BOWL Tavern in Brookline."

* * *

Advertisement for a bull-baiting, Rivington's New-York Gazetteer, No. 63, 30 June 1774.

"BULL-BAITING.
JOHN CORNELL,
Near St. GEORGE's Ferry, LONG-ISLAND,
GIVES this public notice that there will be a Bull-baited on Tower-Hill, at three o'clock in the afternoon, every Thurfday during the feafon.
Said CORNELL alfo attends the Fly-Market with fweet milk every night and morning, and is to be found at ftall near Alderman Leftert's. He has good ftabling for horfes; and has waggons, chairs, and faddle horfes to hire at the fhorteft notice."

[Bull tossing dog illustration with advertisement, 28 July 1774, No. 67.]

* * *

Tench Tilghman, Maryland lieutenant-colonel, describes a bull-baiting among the Onondagas in New York, circa 1775, in [Tilghman], Memoir of Lieut. Col. Tench Tilghman, Secretary and Aid to Washington (Albany, N.Y.: Joel Munsell, 1876), 94.

"In the evening we turned out a Bull for the young Indians to hunt after their manner, with arrows, knives, and hatchetts. The Beast was not of the furious spanish bred for he suffered himself to be despatched in a very few minutes without ever turning upon his assailants."

* * *

Landon Carter, Virginia plantation owner, discussing a general muster of the militia, refers to bull-baiting, 29 March 1776, in Jack P. Greene, ed., The Diary of Colonel Landon

Carter of Sabine Hall, 1752-1778, 2 vols., Vol. 2 (Charlottesville, Va.: University Press of Virginia, 1965), 1006.

"The front rank [was] more crowded with Spectators than I ever saw [at] a boxing match or a bull bating,...."

* * *

Advertisements for bull-baitings, [Rivington's] Royal Gazette, 1781.

"A Bull Baiting,

"After the true Englifh Manner.

"TAURUS will be brought to the Ring at half paft Three o'Clock; fome good Dogs are already provided, but every affiftance of that fort will be efteemed a favour.

"A Dinner exactly Britifh will be upon LOOSLEY's Table at 11 o'Clock, after which there is not the leaft doubt but that the Song called 'O! the Roaft Beef of Old England,' will be fung with harmony and glee.

This notice gives to all who covet	*Taurus is steel to the back bone,*
Baiting the Bull, and dearly love it:	*And Canine cunning does difown.*
To-morrow's very afternoon,	*True Britifh blood runs thro' his veins,*
At Three—or rather not fo foon—	*And barking numbers he difdains.*
A Bull of magnitude and fpirit	*Sooner than knavifh dogs fhall rule,*
Will dare the dogs prefuming merit.	*He'll prove himfelf a true JOHN BULL.*
Brooklyn-Hall	*June 19, 1781"*

(No. 493, 20 June 1781)

"A BULL BATE,
AUGUST, 30.

"THE Subfcriber having procured a Stout BULL, propofes bateing him to morrow, at four o'clock in the afternoon, at his houfe, the fign of his prefent Majefty, near the frefh Water Pump. The Bull is active, and very vicious, therefore hopes the fpectators will have fatisfactory diverfion.   THOs. McMULLAN."

(No. 513, 29 August 1781)

"A BULL-BAIT.

THE fubfcriber, having been at great pains in providing a very ftout active bull, propofes baiting him to-morrow, at his houfe, the fign of his prefent Majefty, near the Tea-Water Pump. As the Bull is both ftout and active, there can be little doubt but that he will afford great fport to the fpectators.   THOs. McMULLIN."

(No. 517, 12 September 1781)

* * *

Advertisement for a bull-baiting, [Rivington's] Royal Gazette, No. 701, 14 June 1783.

"A BULL to be baited at the public Slaughter-Houfe, on Monday next, if fair, or the firft fair day after; the Ring to be ftaked off, and it is earneftly defired that no perfon will enter it, except the Owner of the Bull, and the Owner of the Dog that runs.

The Bull to be at the ftake at Three o'Clock."

* * *

Charleston, South Carolina city ordinance, 22 November 1783, in *Ordinances of the City Council of Charleston in the State of South Carolina, Passed in the First Year of the Incorporation of the City* (Charleston, S.C.: J. Miller, 1784), 19.

"AN ORDINANCE
For the better OBSERVANCE of the LORD'S-DAY, commonly called SUNDAY, and to prevent DISTURB-
ANCES at any Place of PUBLIC WORSHIP
within the City of CHARLESTON.

"And be it further ordained by the authority aforefaid, That no fports or paftimes, as bear-baiting, bull-baiting foot-balls, horfe-racing,... fhall be allowed on the Lord's-Day, and every perfon fo offending fhall forfeit for every fuch offence the fum of Five Pounds."

Chapter 6

BOWLING AND PITCHING SPORTS

Luxuriating in what leisure they had, many colonial Americans took up the pastimes of rolling balls, knocking over pins, and tossing projectiles for sport. Bowling, presumably street bowling, appeared as early as Jamestown. Later gentlemen designed and built their own bowling greens on their estates, and as the case of William Byrd shows, became avid bowlers. Entrepreneurs in cities also established and advertised their bowling greens. Taverns offered a variety of nine pins, ten pins, and skittle (or skettles) bowling for the local and traveling patrons. Betting, carousing, and general idleness and loitering of course, often accompanied these matches and irritated critics. Even though gentlemen dignified the game, the tavern versions picked up an unsavory reputation. Some governments and a couple of colleges sought to limit or abolish bowling, especially on the Sabbath. Public houses also offered shuffleboard (for which there is a sample entry below) and billiards (outside the scope of this collection) which critics grouped with the tavern types of bowling.

Other pitching sports involved pitching the bar, throwing a heavy piece of iron for distance. This activity appeared infrequently in primary sources, although several secondary sources refer to it matter-of-factly.

More frequent in the record was a pastime called "long bullets," a game unfamiliar to most readers. "Bullets" were artillery projectiles that weighed from 16 to 20 ounces up to two-and-a-half pounds. Players slung or "jerked" the bullets up a street or road cleared for this purpose. Nineteenth-century writers differ over the rules and object of the game. One authority claimed that two matched teams drew a starting line, then slung or jerked the bullet three consecutive times, each sling from the end point of the previous one. The second team, starting where the first team finished, slung the bullets back toward the starting line. The team whose bullet was ahead at the end of the sixth throw was the victor. Another nineteenth-century writer's description of long bullets resembled modern shotputting. Slingers received one, two, or three points, depending on the distance their slings rolled past predetermined markings. Players ran quickly toward the starting line to give their projectiles maximum velocity. For more information see letters by M.A. Ross and George Johnston in the "Notes & Queries" section of the Pennsylvania Magazine of History and Biography, Vol. 6 (1882), 370, and Vol. 8 (1884), 351-352, respectively. Allegedly the game was dangerous, as cities and towns outlawed it. Revolutionary war soldiers liked to sling bullets, but drew occasional disciplinary frowns. Undoubtedly these pitching sports inspired betting, drinking, and enough other loose behavior to warrant the opprobrium of the moralists.

Pitching quoits was yet another popular pastime. Quoits were iron or wooden rings which the players would attempt to toss on posts, although in some cases, references to quoits made the game seem more related to classical discus throwing for distance, with solid wooden, metal, or stone discs. Presumably there were indoor and outdoor, urban and rural versions of this game which most resembles modern horseshoe pitching. Playing quoits often was associated with taverns or barbecues and other frolics, thus making it a target for some "blue law" restrictions. Several commentators mention the game matter-of-factly, suggesting its popularity overrode the restrictions. The following documents demonstrate the diversity of these bowling and pitching sports in America's early times.

[Consult the general writings about sports, recreation, and the various colonial, provincial, territorial, and state Sabbath and gaming laws in Chapter One for other sources about the specific sports or games in this chapter.]

BOWLING

William Stith, Virginian rector and Governor of William and Mary College, writing in 1747 concerning bowling in Jamestown, Virginia, circa 1611, in Stith, *The History of the Firft Discovery and Settlement of Virginia* (Williamsburg: William Parks, 1747), 122.

"And having taken Order for his Bufinefs, and committed the Care of it to his Under-Officers, he [Lord Delaware] hafted back to *James-Town*; where he found moft of the Company, at their daily and ufual Work, bowling in the Streets. But he foon employed them about things more neceffary;...."

* * *

Samuel Sewall, Boston magistrate, in London, May and July 1689, and in Boston, August 1715, in M. Halsey Thomas, ed., The *Diary of Samuel Sewall, 1674-1729, Volume I. 1674-1708* (New York: Farrar, Straus and Giroux, 1973), 216, 227; and M. Halsey Thomas, ed., *The Diary of Samuel Sewall, 1674-1729, Volume II. 1709-1729* (New York: Farrar, Straus and Giroux), 795.

14 May 1689: "Went to a Garden at Mile End and drunk Currant and Rasbery Wine, then to the Dog and Partrige's, and plaid Nine-Pins."

9 July 1689: "Saw a Bowling Green where is 3 or 4 Sets of Bowls. The Lord help me aright to improve my Flesh, Bones and Spirits, which are so soon to become useless, and it may be expos'd in one part or other of God's Creation."

8 August 1715: "Set out at 11 at night on Horseback with Tho. Wallis to inspect the order of the Town.

"Constable Eady, Mr. Allen, Salter, Herishor Simson, Howel, Mr. John Marion. Dissipated the players at Nine Pins at Mount-Whoredom."

* * *

William Byrd, Westover, Virginia planter, plays nine pins, 13 June 1709, in Louis B. Wright and Marion Tinling, eds., *The Secret Diary of William Byrd of Westover, 1709-1712* (Richmond, Va.: The Dietz Press, 1941), 47.

"About 11 o'clock we rode to Drury Stith's where we met Mr. Anderson and his wife and Mr. Eppes. I ate pork and turnips for dinner. Then we played at nine-pins."

* * *

Advertisement for a bowling green, Boston News-Letter, No. 524, 26 April–3 May 1714.

"THis is to give Notice, that the Bowling Green, formerly belonging to *Mr. James Ivers* in Cambridge-Street, Bofton, does now belong to *Mr. Daniel Stevens* at the Britifh Coffee Houfe in Queen-Street, Bofton, which Green will open'd, on Monday next the Third Day of this Inftant May, where all Gentlemen, Merchants and others, that have a Mind to Recreate themfelves, fhall be well accommodated by the faid *Stevens.*"

* * *

Elizabeth Brooks' inventory, York County, Virginia, circa 1716, reprinted in Ulrich Troubetzkoy, "Bowls and Skittles," Virginia Cavalcade, Vol. 9, No. 4 (Spring 1960), 12.

"I Sett Nine pins, bowl & frame, valued at 5 shillings."

* * *

Satirical poem on Harvard College's commencement, refers to bowling, circa 1718, in *A Satyrical Description of Commencement. Calculated to the Meridian of Cambridge in New-England* (Boston: The Heart and Crown, 1718), reprinted in Samuel Eliot Morison, *Three Centuries of Harvard, 1636-1936* (Cambridge, Mass.: Harvard University Press, 1946), 122.

> "...To Taverns some repair;
> And who can tell what Pranks are acted there.
> Some spend the Time at Pins (that toilsome Play)...."

* * *

Judge's order, Maryland, June 1722, excerpted in George and Virginia Schaun, *Everyday Life in Colonial Maryland* (Annapolis, Md.: Greenberry Publications, 1960), 68.

"[T]he Public Houses in the County shall be hindered from Keeping their Nine Pins on the Streets during the Sitting of the Court; and that no persons whatsoever shall be suffered to play at them during the term aforesaid."

* * *

Advertisement for a bowling green, Boston Gazette, 10-17 June 1734, reprinted in George Francis Dow, *Every Day Life in the Massachusetts Bay Colony* (New York: Benjamin Blom, 1935), 115.

"Hanover Bowling Green, at the Western Part of the Town of Boston, is now open and in good order for the Reception of all Gentlemen who are disposed to Recreate themselves with that Healthful Exercise."

* * *

Advertisement for bowling equipment, South Carolina Gazette, No. 262, 8 February 1739.

"This is to give Notice, that George Bridge living in Tradd ſtreet, Turner in Brass, Iron or Ivory, makes and fells ſcrews of all ſizes, Preſſes of any ſort, Tea boards of all ſizes, Peſtils and Mortars, Billiard Balls, Nine pins and Bowls,...."

* * *

William Byrd, Westover, Virginia planter, chronicles his bowling, August and September 1739, May, June, July, and August 1740, and April, May, June, July, and August 1741, in Maude H. Woodfin, ed., *Another Secret Diary of William Byrd of Westover, 1739-1741,* (Richmond, Va.: The Dietz Press, 1942), 3-7, 9-14, 66, 72-74, 80-91, 93, 96, 148-149, 161, 164, 171-177, 180-181.

10 August 1739: "In the evening we played bowls and walked."

13 August 1739: "After dinner read more Latin till the evening, when we played bowls for an hour and then walked."

15 August 1739: "After dinner I put things in order, read more Latin and played at bowls."

18 August 1739: "After dinner I put matters in order, read more Latin till 5, then played bowls."

21 August 1739: "After dinner put several things in order, read English, and then played bowls with my son."

27 August 1739: "After dinner we talked, then came Tom Short and I wrote letters to the Governor, then played bowls,...."

29 August 1739: "After dinner I put things in order and read Latin till the evening when I played bowls and then walked."

30 August 1739: "After dinner I put things in order, read Latin till the evening, then played bowls."

31 August 1739: "After dinner we played billiards and then at bowls...."

1 September 1739: "After dinner I put things in order, read Latin, and then played bowls and walked."

3 September 1739: "I read more Latin and then played bowls."

7 September 1739: "After dinner all went away but Captain Randolph, who played bowls and then played piquet till 10."

12 May 1740: "The parson went away but the young gentlemen stayed to dinner, till which we played billiards and bowls,...."

3 June 1740: "After dinner we played bowls and walked."

4 June 1740: "In the afternoon we had tea and then played bowls...."

5 June 1740: "In the evening Mrs. Carter returned home in our chariot and we played bowls and walked."

6 June 1740: "We played bowls and walked."

7 June 1740: "After dinner we talked and played bowls and walked."

26 June 1740: "After dinner we talked and had coffee, then played bowls and walked."

28 June 1740: "After dinner played billiards and then at bowls,...."

3 July 1740: "After dinner we talked and played bowls and walked."

5 July 1740: "After dinner took a nap, played bowls and walked."

9 July 1740: "In the evening played bowls...."

10 July 1740: "We played bowls."

11 July 1740: "After dinner I put things in order, played bowls,...."

12 July 1740: "After dinner took a nap and then read more English till evening when we played bowls."

14 July 1740: "After dinner put things in order and read more Latin till the evening, when we played bowls."

15 July 1740: "...; then played bowls and walked."

17 July 1740: "After dinner I took a nap and then put things in order till the evening, when we played bowls."

18 July 1740: "We played bowls and walked."

19 July 1740: "In the evening played bowls,...."

21 July 1740: "In the evening played bowls and walked."

22 July 1740: "After dinner I took a nap and had tea, then played bowls and walked."

25 July 1740: "In the evening played bowls and walked."

28 July 1740: "In the evening played bowls."

29 July 1740: "...; then played bowls."

30 July 1740: "After dinner took a nap and read more Latin till the evening, when we played bowls and walked."

31 July 1740: "In the evening played bowls."

2 August 1740: "After dinner the company went away and we played bowls."

8 August 1740: "After dinner we played cards till the evening and then bowls."

9 August 1740: "After dinner we talked and played again till the evening when we played bowls."

20 August 1740: "After dinner I put things in order and read more Latin till the evening when we played bowls...."

23 August 1740: "...; then played bowls and walked."

6 April 1741: "After dinner we played bowls."

10 April 1741: "However Mr. Spalding stayed this day and we played bowls till dinner when I ate fish. After dinner we played bowls again."

26 May 1741: "After dinner I put things in order, played at bowls and walked about."

4 June 1741: "After dinner we had coffee and then played bowls."

5 June 1741: "After dinner we played bowls and then all the company went away."

3 July 1741: "After dinner we talked and played bowls...."

4 July 1741: "...; however we played bowls."

6 July 1741: "After dinner we talked and in the evening played bowls."

7 July 1741: "In the evening we played bowls."

8 July 1741: "After dinner we played bowls, notwithstanding it had rained."

9 July 1741: "After dinner I put several matters in order and played bowls."

10 July 1741: "I played bowls."

15 July 1741: "After dinner we talked and had tea: then we played bowls."

16 July 1741: "After dinner put things to rights in the library and in the evening we bowled and walked."

17 July 1741: "After dinner I took a nap and then played bowls."

18 July 1741: "After dinner put several things, read more Latin and then played bowls."

20 July 1741: "After dinner I took a nap and in the evening played bowls and walked."

21 July 1741: "After dinner I put things in order till the evening and then played bowls and walked."

22 July 1741: "After dinner we played [piquet] again till the evening and then played bowls."

23 July 1741: "After dinner I put things in order and played bowls."

27 July 1741: "After dinner we talked and had tea and in the evening played bowls and walked."

7 August 1741: "After dinner we played bowls."

10 August 1741: "We played bowls and I prayed."

* * *

Advertisement for a bowling green, South Carolina Gazette, No. 748, 16-25 July 1748.

"The BOWLING-GREEN at BRAMPTON-BRYAN, was open'd on Saturday the 23d Inftant; where Gentlemen that favour me with their Cuftom, may depend on the beft Ufage, and will oblige   Their humble Servant,
Anne Shepheard."

* * *

Landon Carter, Virginia plantation owner, refers to bowling in a metaphorical sense, 11 April 1752, in Jack P. Greene, ed., *The Diary of Colonel Landon Carter of Sabine Hall, 1752-1778*, 2 vols.,Vol. 1 (Charlottesville, Va.: University Press of Virginia, 1965), 99.

"'Tis a pity men should run like Bowls. The famous Mr. Richd. Bland is a Shuttle Cock and without faith."

* * *

George Fisher, British visitor, observes bowling, near Williamsburg, Virginia, 13 May 1755, in "Narrative of George Fisher," William and Mary Quarterly, 1st Series, Vol. 17, No. 3 (January 1909), 165.

"Set out a little after Nine, past Ashleys, something after Ten, where was a number of Planters at Nine Pins;...."

* * *

Notice of a bowling match, Connecticut Courant, No. 71, 5 May 1766.

"A CHALLENGE is hereby given by the Subfcribers, to ASHBEL STEEL, and JOHN BARNARD, with 18 Young Gentlemen, South of the Great Bridge, in this Town, to play a Game at BOWL for a Dinner and Trimmings, with an equal Number North of faid Bridge, on Friday Next.   WILLIAM PRATT,
                    DANIEL OLCOTT,

"N. B. If they accept the Challenge, they are defired to meet us at the Court-Houfe by 9 o'Clock in the Morning."

* * *

Benjamin Rush, Philadelphia physician, recommends bowling as a recreation, circa 1772, in Rush, *Sermons to Gentlemen upon Temperance and Exercise* (Philadelphia: John Dunlap, 1772), 33.

"To all thefe fpecies of exercife which we have mentioned, I would add, SKEATING, JUMPING, alfo, the active plays of TENNIS, BOWLES, QUOITS, GOLF, and the like. The manner in which each of thefe operate, may be underftood from what we faid under the former particulars."

Yale College law, circa 1774, in *The Laws of Yale-College, in New-Haven, in Connecticut, Enacted by the President and Fellows* (New Haven, Conn.: Thomas and Samuel Green, 1774), 11.

"9. If any Scholar fhall play at Hand-Ball, or Foot Ball, or Bowls in the College-Yard, or throw any Thing againft College, by which the Glafs may be endangered,... he fhall punifhed fix Pence, and make good the Damages."

* * *

Philip Vickers Fithian, tutor at Nomini Hall, Virginia, notes a bowling green, 18 March 1774, in Hunter Dickinson Farish, ed., *Journal and Letters of Philip Vickers Fithian, 1773–1774. A Plantation Tutor of the Old Dominion* (Charlottesville, Va.: University Press of Virginia, 1957 [1943]), 81.

"The Area of the Triangle made by the Wash-House, Stable, & School-House is perfectly levil, & designed for a bowling-Green,...."

* * *

Samuel Shute, New Jersey lieutenant, bowls (or slings bullets) in central Pennsylvania, 13, 14, 15, 16, and 17 June 1779, in [Shute], "Journal of Lt. Samuel Shute," in Frederick Cook, ed., *Journals of the Military Expedition of Major General John Sullivan against the Six Nations of Indians in 1779* (Freeport, N.Y.: Books for Libraries Press, reprint of 1885 ed.), 268.

"Spent in Bowling bullets and playing fives."

* * *

Claude Blanchard, French officer, observes bowling in Rhode Island, 19 August 1780, in William Duane, trans., and Thomas Balch, ed., *The Journal of Claude Blanchard, Commissary of the French Auxiliary Army Sent to the United States during the American Revolution, 1780-1783,* (Albany, N.Y.: Joel Munsell, 1876), 56.

"On the 19th, General Varnum took me two miles from the city to a sort of garden where different persons had met and were playing nine-pins; they made us drink punch and tea. The place was pleasant and rural, and this little jaunt gave me pleasure."

* * *

Jeremiah Greenman, Rhode Island officer, refers to bowling, May? early June? 1783, in Robert C. Bray and Paul E. Bushnell, eds., *Diary of a Common Soldier in the American Revolution, 1775-1783. An Annotated Edition of the Military Journal of Jeremiah Greenman* (DeKalb, Ill.: Northern Illinois University Press, 1978), 264.

"Nothing happing worthy remarks, implying our selves in a skettle & ball Alle[y]—...."

LONG BULLETS

Boston, Massachusetts town by-law, 19 April 1723, in *Orders and By-Laws made and Agreed Upon by the Freeholders and Inhabitants of the Town of Boston, on May 14, 1719, on March 11, 1722, April 19, 1723, and March 8, 1724* (Boston, 1725), 27.

"*For Preventing Throwing Bullets in the Common,* &c.

"*WHEREAS the Throwing, Rowling or Flinging of the Bullets, commonly called the Throwing of the Long-bullet, in the common Training Field, High-ways, Streets, Lanes or Alleys of the Town, is attended with divers Inconveniences, and may be of Pernicious Confequence, to his Majesties good Subjects, in Walking about their neceffary affairs and bufinefs.*

"For Preventing wherof.

"IT is Ordered, that whofoever fhall prefume to Ufe and Exercife themfelves, in Throwing, Rowling or Flinging the Bullet, or any fuch like Inftrument whether made of Iron, Lead, Brafs, Stone, Wood or any other matter or fubftance, that may Endanger the Lives or Limbs, of any of His Majefties Subjects in the Common Training Field, High-ways, Lanes, Street or Alleys in the Town; fhall Forfeit and Pay, the Sum of *Twenty Shillings,* upon Conviction, before any of his Majefties Juftices of the Peace for faid County, for every fuch Offence."

* * *

Philip Vickers Fithian, Virginia tutor, witnesses long bullets playing near Newark, Delaware, 7 September 1775, in Robert Greenhalgh Albion and Leonidas Dodson, eds., *Philip Vickers Fithian. Journal, 1775-1776, Written on the Virginia-Pennsylvania Frontier and in the Army around New York* (Princeton, N.J.: Princeton University Press, 1934), 128-129.

"Newark reminded me of old Days at Princeton—Full of antic School-Boys—It was Play Hours—Some gallopping out—Some coupled Walking—Some throwing long-Bullets—Some Strutting at the Doors before Girls—Others playing at Fives at the End of the Academy &c—...."

* * *

Samuel Shute, New Jersey lieutenant, in central Pennsylvania, plays at long bullets, 13, 14, 15, 16, and 17 June 1779, in [Shute], "Journal of Lt. Samuel Shute," in Frederick Cook, ed., *Journals of the Military Expedition of Major General John Sullivan against the Six Nations of Indians in 1779* (Freeport, N.Y.: Books for Libraries Press, reprint of 1885 ed.), 268.

"Spent in Bowling bullets and playing fives."

* * *

Christopher Marshall, Lancaster, Pennsylvania soldier, observes long bullets playing, May and August 1780, in William Duane, ed., *Extracts from the Diary of Christopher Marshall, Kept in Philadelphia and Lancaster, During the American Revolution, 1774-1781* (Albany, N.Y.: Joel Munsell, 1877) 242, 261.

15 May 1780: "I went nowhere from home this day although it's a very high holiday in this place, and as it was a most pleasant, agreeable, fine day, numbers were diverting themselves abroad, some riding, some walking, others playing long bullets, &c."

16 August 1780: "A great number of young men, Menonists, met at Kap's tavern, as usual, to play sling bullets, &c., early in the afternoon."

* * *

Samuel Dewees, Pennsylvania captain, comments on long bullets playing near York, Pennsylvania, circa 1780, in John Smith Hanna, ed., *A History of the Life and Services of Captain Samuel Dewees, A Native of Pennsylvania, and Soldier of the Revolutionary and Last Wars* (Baltimore: Robert Neilson, 1844), 228.

"In a few days after we arrived at York, a soldier by the name of Jack Smith, and another soldier whose name I do not now remember, were engaged in playing *long bullets*. Whilst thus engaged some of the officers were walking along the road, where they were throwing the bullets. The bullets passing near to the officers they used very harsh language to Smith and his comrade, who immediately retorted by using the same kind of indecorous language."

* * *

Pittsburgh residents petition Fort Pitt Brigadier General William Irvine to prohibit the playing of long bullets, circa 1782, reprinted in Soeren Stewart Brynn, "Some Sports in Pittsburgh during the National Period," Western Pennsylvania Historical Magazine, Vol. 51, No. 4 (October 1968), 347.

"The Humble Petition of part of the Inhabitance of the Town of Pittsburgh Most Humbly Begett; that your Honour will be pleased to take it into Consideration, That as Several of the Officers, Soldiers, of the Town has of late made a Constant Practice, in Playing at Long Bullets, in the Street that goes up by the Brewhouse, and that a Number of Children belonging to us, who are Dwellers in the Same Street, are in Danger of their Lives, by the said evil Practice, We therefore hope (since we have no Civil Magistrate to Apply too) that your Honour will Condesend to put a Stop to such Practice, in the Streets, by your Own Special Orders;...."

QUOITS

An account of a wedding near Saybrook, Connecticut, circa 1726, mentions quoits playing as a recreation, reprinted in Helen Evertson Smith, *Colonial Days and Ways as Gathered from Family Papers by Helen Evertson Smith of Sharon, Connecticut* (New York: The Century Company, 1901), 180.

"[The men at wedding participated in] rastling, quoits, running, leaping, archery and firing at a mark, but on the last day no muskets were allowed by reason of the Indians."

* * *

John Adams, Massachusetts lawyer, politician, and later United States President, concerning playing quoits in his boyhood, circa 1740s, in [Adams], "The Autobiography of John Adams," in Lyman H. Butterfield, ed., *Diary and Autobiography of John Adams, Volume 3. Diary, 1782-1804, Autobiography, Part One To October 1776* (Cambridge, Mass.: Harvard University Press, 1962), 257.

"[A]nd I spent my time as idle Children do in making and sailing boats and Ships upon the Ponds and Brooks, in making and flying Kites, in driving hoops, playing marbles, playing Quoits, Wrestling, Swimming, Skaiting and above all in shooting, to which Diversion I was addicted to a degree of Ardor which I know not that I ever felt for any other Business, Study or Amusement."

William Stephens, Georgia Trustee, lists quoits as a holiday recreation, 26 and 27 March 1744, in E. Merton Coulter, ed., *The Journal of William Stephens, 1743-1745*, 2 vols., Vol. 2 (Athens, Ga.: University of Georgia Press, 1958), 86-87.

"Little to be taken notice of During these Holidays when the common sort of people pass'd most of their time in Sports, Cricket Quoits and such like Exercise."

* * *

Benjamin Rush, Philadelphia physician, recommends quoits as recreation, circa 1772, in Rush, *Sermons to Gentlemen upon Temperance and Exercise* (Philadelphia: John Dunlap, 1772), 33.

"To all thefe fpecies of exercife which we have mentioned, I would add, SKEATING, JUMPING, alfo, the active plays of TENNIS, BOWLES, QUOITS, GOLF, and the like. The manner in which each of thefe operate, may be underftood from what we faid under the former particulars."

* * *

Philip Vickers Fithian, Virginia minister, notices quoit playing near the Juniata River in Pennsylvania, 22 August 1775, in Robert Greenhalgh Albion and Leonidas Dodson, eds., *Philip Vickers Fithian. Journal, 1775-1776, Written on the Virginia-Pennsylvania Frontier and in the Army around New York* (Princeton, N.J.: Princeton University Press, 1934), 114.

"The Men, for Exercise, play at Quoits, hunt Deer, Turkeys, Pheasants &c—...."

* * *

Charles Herbert, Newburyport, Massachusetts sailor, plays quoits as a prisoner of war in Plymouth, England, 2 April 1777, in [Herbert], *A Relic of the Revolution, Containing a Full and Particular Account of the Sufferings and Privations of All the American Prisoners Captured on the High Seas, and Carried into Plymouth, England, During the Revolution of 1776* (Boston: Charles H. Peirce, 1847), 109.

"Warm, and something pleasant, and the yard begins to be dry again, so that we can return to our former sports; these are ball and quoits, which exercise we make use of to circulate our blood and keep us from things that are worse."

* * *

Jabez Fitch, Connecticut lieutenant, observes quoit playing on Long Island, 13 September 1777, in William H. Sabine, ed., *The New-York Diary of Lieutenant Jabez Fitch of the 17th (Connecticut) Regiment from August 22, 1776 to December 15, 1777* (New York: pvt. ptg., 1954), 215.

"After Breakfast I took a walk down to the old Shop, where I met considerable Compy: who spent most of the forenoon in playing Quates Cards &c...."

* * *

Joel Shepard, Montague, Massachusetts farmer, recalls quoits-pitching near Albany, New York, circa 1782, in John A. Spear, ed., "Joel Shepard Goes to the War," New England Quarterly, Vol. 1, No. 3 (July 1928), 344.

"We passed muster and layed in Albany about six weeks and we fared tolerable well, and not much to doo, but each class had his amusement. The officers would bee a playing at Ball on the comon, their would be an other class piching quaits, an other set a wrestling,...."

OTHER PITCHING SPORTS

William Bradford, Plymouth, Massachusetts elder, scolds some Pilgrims for pitching the bar instead of working, 25 December 1621, in Bradford, *Of Plymouth Plantation,* ed. by Harvey Wish (New York: Capricorn Books, 1962), 82-83.

"One the day called Chrismasday, the Governor caled them out to worke, (as was used,) but the most of this new-company excused them selves and said it wente against their consciences to work on that day. So the Governor tould them that if they made it a mater of conscience, he would spare them till they were better informed. So he led-away the rest and left them; but when they came home at noone from their worke, he found them in the streete at play, openly; some pitching the barr, & some at stoole-ball, and shuch like sports. So he went to them, and took away their implements, and tould them that if they made the keeping a mater of devotion, let them kepe their houses, but ther should be no gameing or revelling in the streets. Since which time nothing has been atempted that way, at least openly."

* * *

Advertisement for shuffleboard, South Carolina Gazette, No. 476, 9 May 1743.

"THIS is to give Notice that a SHUFFLE BOARD, ready to play at, is fet up in the Home of Mr. *Laurans* (in the *Market Square,*) wherein Captain *Lewis Lormier* lately dwelt, where Gentlemen may enjoy their Bowl and Bottle with Satisfaction and be handfomely ferved by   JOHN MANDEVILE."

Chapter 7

CHILDREN'S GAMES

As historians of childhood and life cycle stages have noted, most colonial and Revolutionary era American children lacked carefree, play-filled childhoods. Chores and child care duties for younger siblings beckoned constantly. Apprenticeship came early for too many. Indentured servitude was bleak, as recent studies report on abuse, neglect, and privation. Slave children saw their destiny harden as chattel system laws imprisoned the offspring of a slave. But even children from the more affluent and fortunate classes lived rushed, supervised lives. The cultural pressure to produce serious-minded young adults in a rapid transition from childhood bypassed adolescence and pushed children into an adult status usually before their biological maturation.

  Much of the play that existed was structured play, task or skill-enhancing games that trained the child for adult responsibilities. Hunting and fishing are obvious, but other activities such as shooting, riding, fencing, and gymnastics prepared youths for adulthood.

Other sports imbued messages in children in less manifest ways. In team sports, the values of cooperation, competency, position status, loyalty, patience, and endurance often overrode the natural ebullience of children in spontaneous play. Add to this the heavy religious didacticism of the day which imparted a basic distrust of recreation.

Even so, children always managed to create their own play styles around the fringes of structured play. Folk games are flexible; the absence of rigid rules invited inventiveness. Many games required little time, space, or money. Some did require more than one or two participants which penalized isolated children. But often enough players appeared for a spontaneous game of marbles or leapfrog or blindman's buff. And one group of children, indigenous youth, suffered less repression. Travelers and missionaries usually described happier children in the tribal cultures. The following selections exhibit the variety of children's games available for the more fortunate Toms and Pollys of those days.

Father Paul Le Jeune, Jesuit missionary, comments on indigenous children's games in New France, circa 1634, in [Le Jeune], "Le Jeune's Relation, 1634," in Reuben Gold Thwaites, ed., *The Jesuit Relations and Allied Documents. Travels and Explorations of the Jesuit Missionaries in New France, 1610-1791,* Vol. 7 (New York: Pageant Book Company, 1959), 95, 97.

"As the bow and arrow seem to be weapons invented by Nature, since all the Nations of the earth have made use of them, so you might say there are certain little games that children find out for themselves without being taught. The little Savages play at hide-and-seek as well as the little French children. They have a number of other childish sports that I have noticed in our Europe; among others, I have seen the little Parisians throw a musket ball into the air and catch it with a little bat scooped out; the little montagnard Savages do the same, using a little bunch of Pine sticks,which they receive or throw into the air on the end of a pointed stick. The little Hiroquois have the same pastime, throwing a bone with a hole in it, which they interlace in the air with another little bone. I was told this by a young man of that nation as we were watching the montagnard children play."

* * *

Antoine Le Page du Pratz, French traveler, notes indigenous children's games in Louisiana Territory, circa 1720-1728, in Le Page du Pratz, *The History of Louisiana, or of the Western Parts of Virginia and Carolina. Containing a Description of the Countries that lie on both Sides of the River Mississippi. With an Account of the Settlements, Inhabitants, Soil, Climate, and Products* (London: T. Becket, 1774), 347.

"The young people, especially the girls, have hardly any kind of diversion but that of the ball; this consists in tossing a ball from one to the other with the palm of the hand, which they perform with a tolerable address."

James Jeffry, Salem, Massachusetts resident, mentions a children's game, 14 February 1724, in [Jeffry], "James Jeffry's Journal for the Year 1724," Essex Institute Historical Collections, Vol. 37 (October 1900), 333.

"Piercce at night was at Mad^m Brownes Playing hide & Goe Seek with Olive Parker, Wibird &c^a"

* * *

John Adams, Massachusetts lawyer, politician, and later United States President, recalls the children's games of his boyhood, circa 1740s, in [Adams], "The Autobiography of John Adams," in Lyman H. Butterfield, ed., *Diary and Autobiography of John Adams, Volume 3. Diary, 1782-1804, Autobiography, Part One To October 1776* (Cambridge, Mass.: Harvard University Press, 1962), 257.

"And I spent my time as idle Children do in making and sailing boats and Ships upon the Ponds and Brooks, in making and flying Kites, in driving hoops, playing marbles, playing Quoits, Wrestling, Swimming, Skaiting and above all in shooting, to which Diversion I was addicted to a degree of Ardor which I know not that I ever felt for any other Business, Study or Amusement."

* * *

A children's book draws moral stories from several children's games, in *A Little Pretty Pocket-Book, Intended for the Amusement and Instruction of Little Master Tommy and Pretty Miss Polly* (London: J. Newbery, 1767), 71, 72, 73, 74, 75, 76, 78, 81, 82, 86, 92, 94, 98, 100.

"CHUCK-FARTHING.
AS you value your Pence,
At the Hole take your Aim;
Chuck all fafely in,
And you'll win the Game.
MORAL.
Chuck-Farthing, like Trade,
Requires great Care;
The more you obferve,
The better you'll fare."

"*Flying the* KITE.
UPHELD in Air, the gaudy Kite
High as an Eagle takes her Flight;
But if the Winds their Breath reftrain,
She tumbles headlong down again.
RULE *of* LIFE.
Soon as thou feest the Dawn of Day,
To God thy Adoration pay."

"*Dancing round the* MAY-POLE.
WITH Garlands here the May-Pole's
crown'd,
And all the Swains a dancing round

Compofe a num'rous jovial Ring,
To welcome in the chearful Spring.
RULE *of* LIFE.
Leave God to manage, and to grant
That which his Wifdom fees thee want."

"TAW.
KNUCKLE down to your *Taw*,
Aim well, fhoot away;
Keep out of the *Ring*,
And you'll foon learn to play.
MORAL.
Time rolls like a *Marble*,
And awes ev'ry State;
Then hufband each Moment,
Before 'tis too late."

"HOOP *and* HIDE.
GO hide out, and hoop,
Whilft I go to fleep;
If you I can't find,
My Poft I muft keep.
MORAL.
With Carefulnefs watch

Each Moment that flies,
To keep Peace at Home,
And ward off Surprife."

THREAD *the* NEEDLE.
HERE Hand in Hand the Boys unite,
And form a very pleafing Sight;
Then thro' each other's Arms they fly,
As Thread does thro' the Needle's Eye.
RULE *of* LIFE.
Talk not too much; fit down content,
That your Difcourfe be pertinent."

BLINDMAN'S BUFF.
BEREFT of all Light,
 I ftumble alone;
But, if I catch you,
 My Doom is your own.
MORAL.
How blind is that Man,
 Who fcorns the Advice
Of Friends, who intend
 To make him more wife!"

PEG-FARTHING.
SOON as the Ring is once compos'd,
The Coin is in the Centre clos'd;
And then with the wifh'd-for Prize
 to win,
The Top that drives it out muft fpin.
RULE *of* LIFE.
Be filent if you doubt your Senfe,
And always fpeak with Diffidence."

KNOCK OUT *and* SPAN.
STRIKE out your *Taw* ftrong;
 For the very next man
Will bear off the Prize,
 If you come to a Span.
MORAL.
This *Span*, my dear Boy,
Shou'd your Monitor be:
'Tis the Length of a Life,
As we oftentimes fee."

PITCH *and* HUSSEL.
POISE your Hand fairly,
 And pitch plump your Slat;

Then fhake for all Heads,
And turn down the Hat.
MORAL.
How fickle this Game!
 So Fortune or Fate
Decrees our Repentance,
When oft 'tis too late."

TIP-CAT.
THE *Gamefter* here his Art difplays,
And drives the Cat a thoufand Ways;
For fhould he mifs, when once 'tis
 tofs'd,
He's out—And all his Sport is loft.
RULE *of* LIFE.
Debates and Quarrels always fhun;
No one by Peace was e'er undone."

"LEAP-FROG.
THIS ftoops down his Head,
 Whilft that fprings up high;
But then you'll find,
 He'll stoop by and by.
MORAL.
Juft fo 'tis At Court;
 To-day you're in Place;
To-morrow, perhaps,
 You're quite in Difgrace."

"HOP-HAT.
O'ER this *Hat,* and that,
Boys hop to the laft;
Which, once in their Mouths,
Behind them is caft.
MORAL.
Thus Men often ftruggle,
 Some Blifs to obtain;
Which, once in their Pow'r,
 They treat with Difdain."

"HOP-SCOTCH.
FIRST make with Chalk an oblong Square,
With wide Partitions here and there;
Then to the firft a *Tile* convey;
Hop in—then kick the *Tile* away.
RULE *of* LIFE.
Strive with good Senfe to ftock your Mind,
And to that Senfe be Virtue join'd."

Chapter 8

CONTACT SPORTS

Early Americans, according to the evidence, were fairly ferocious in their recreation. Supposedly these settlers would fight with each other at the drop of a hat, sometimes for a hat as a prize. Not all of the fighting qualified as sport, but even the most spontaneous outbreak of fisticuffs drew a crowd that bet and egged on the combatants to bloodier deeds. Modern readers may recoil at many of these descriptions, only to remember that some of the current "pro wrestling," Ultimate Fighting, and gang fighting styles are no more civilized than what was boxing or wrestling in earlier times. Peoples with disregard for fellow humans have in all centuries, often cloaking their aggression in the guise of sport.

Boxing, as later Americans knew it, barely existed in the colonial period. Few accounts of prize fights appear. In many instances one-on-one fighting was used to settle a personal grievance, but it was known that men exchanged blows just for the sport of it. These pugilistic efforts were all bare knuckle, and despite the formalization of a boxing code called Broughton's Rules in the 1740s, often violent affairs.

In the early eighteenth century, cudgeling was popular. Images of Robin Hood and Little John squaring off for supremacy of Sherwood Forest come to mind, but there are no details in the meager mentionings. Presumably the participants exchanged blows with large sticks or branches until one submitted. Whether there was any padding on the person or cudgel, or whether these contests took place on logs or other unstable places, is unclear. What is clear is that cudgeling contests occurred at some fairs and militia training days.

More frequent was the custom of a no-holds-barred form of wrestling known as "gouging" or "eye-gouging." In this brutal combat, grapplers agreed either to "fight fair" and leave each other intact, or to attack each other with intent to deprive the other of his eye or eyes, ear or ears, or nose. Colonial anti-maiming laws hint that sometimes the adversaries targeted each others' genitals for destruction. Southern states were notorious for this wrestling style, although apparently it existed in most if not all of the colonies and early states. Foreign travelers could not resist giving their readers gruesome depictions of gouging or reporting that there was a suspiciously high percentage of one-eyed men in the vicinity. Some Americans challenged this image and contended that the claims were exaggerated. Whatever the case, the colonial and territorial legislatures recognized it as a problem and began to enact specific laws to prevent and severely punish maiming and disfiguring, often with a specific clause referring to gouging.

Classical wrestling, as with formal boxing, hardly existed in colonial America. Aside from the brief allusion to wrestling in Greece or Rome, not until after the turn of the century was there any systematic description of Olympic-style grappling. Presumably this less violent type of wrestling was on the mind of Benjamin Franklin when he recommended it as recreation in 1749, and that at the various Maryland and Virginia fairs and training days was likely less bloody, given their supervision by community elders. Classical style wrestling would not emerge for many years. The following sources detail, often graphically, the presence of these varied combative contests. [Consult the general writings about sports, recreation, and the various colonial, provincial, territorial, and state Sabbath and gaming laws in Chapter One for other sources about the specific sports or games in this chapter.]

William Byrd, Westover, Virginia planter, describes cudgeling and wrestling at training days, September and October 1711, in Louis B. Wright and Marion Tinling, eds, *The Secret Diary of William Byrd of Westover, 1709-1712* (Richmond, Va.: The Dietz Press, 1941), 405, 415, 417.

14 September 1711: "When I came to Captain Stith's I found Joe Harwood and his troopers which are in good order. I told them of the prizes and set them immediately to running and wrestling. I stayed to see them about an hour and then returned home,...."

3 October 1711: "About 11 o'clock I ate some mutton for breakfast, and several of my captains came to go over the river with me, where we got about 2 o'clock but in the meantime the Major had exercised his men on the north side. Then I ordered the men to be drawn in single [file] along the path where the men were to run for the prize, and John Hatcher, one of Captain Randolph's men, won the pistol. Then I caused the men to be drawn into a square to see the men play at cudgels and Dick O-l-n won the sword, and of the wrestling Will Kennon won the gun. Just as the sun went down our games ended...."

6 October 1711: "About 2 o'clock our prizes began and Will M-r-l got the prize of running and John S-c-l-s the prize of cudgels and Robin Easely the prize [of] wrestling. All was finished about 4 o'clock...."

* * *

Excerpt from a horse racing advertisement mentions cudgeling and wrestling, Virginia Gazette, No. 61, 30 September–7 October 1737.

"2. That a Hat of the Value of 20s. be cudgell'd for, and that after the first Challenge made, the Drums are to beat once every Quarter of an hour, for Three Challenges round the Ring; on no Answer, the Person challenging to be entitled to the Prize; and none to Play with their Left hand."

"10. That a Pair of Silver Buckles be Wrestled for, by a certain Number of brisk young Men."

* * *

Excerpt from an advertisement about a fair and horse racing at Williamsburg offers cudgeling contests, Virginia Gazette, No. 175, 30 November-7 December 1739.

"A good Hat to be Cudgell'd for; and to be given to the Perfon that fairly wins it, by the common Rules of Play...."

Excerpt from advertisement for a fair at Baltimore offers wrestling and cudgeling contests, Maryland Gazette, No. 24, 20 September 1745.

"A Hat and Ribbon of Twenty-five Shillings Value to be cudgelled for on the fecond Day, and a pair of *London* Pumps to be wreftled for on the third Day."

* * *

Excerpt from a horse racing advertisement mentions wrestling and cudgeling matches, Maryland Gazette, No. 100, 24 March 1747.

"And on the third Day, Wreftling, Cudgelling, and feveral other Diverfions."

* * *

Excerpt from an advertisement for a fair at Baltimore mentions wrestling and cudgeling matches, Maryland Gazette, No. 124, 8 September 1747.

"On Saturday the third Day, a Hat and Ribbon will be cudgell'd for; a Pair of Pumps wreftled for; and a white Shift to be run for by Negro Girls."

* * *

Philip Vickers Fithian, tutor at Nomini Hall, Virginia, chronicles local wrestling and gouging, December 1773 and February and September 1774, and mentions boxing in a letter to a friend, 12 August 1774, in Hunter Dickinson Farish, ed., *Journal and Letters of Philip Vickers Fithian, 1773-1774. A Plantation Tutor of the Old Dominion* (Charlottesville, Va.: University Press of Virginia, 1957 [1943]), 29-30, 63, 161, 183.

3 December 1773: "Evening Ben Carter and myself had a long dispute on the practice of fighting—He thinks it best for two persons who have any dispute to go out in good-humour & fight manfully, & says they will be sooner and longer friends than to brood and harbour malice—...."

6 February 1774: "This day two Negro Fellows the Gardiner & cooper, wrangled; & at last fought; It happened hard however for the Cooper. who is likely to lose one of his Eyes by that Diabolical Custom of gouging which is in common practise among those who fight here—...."

12 August 1774: "...; because any young Gentleman travelling through the Colony, as I said before, is presum'd to be acquainted with Dancing, Boxing, playing the Fiddle, & Small-Sword, & Cards."

2 September 1774: "By appointment today is to be fought this Day near Mr Lanes two fist Battles between four young Fellows. The Cause of the battles I have no yet known; I suppose either that they are lovers, & one has in Jest or reality some way supplanted the other; or has in a merry hour call'd him a *Lubber*, or a *thick-Skull*, or a *Buckskin*, or a *Scotchman*, or perhaps one has mislaid the others hat, or knocked a peach out of his Hand, or offered him a dram without wiping the mouth of the Bottle; all these, & ten thousand more quite as triffling & ridiculous, are thought & accepted as just Causes of immediate Quarrels, in which every diabolical stratagem for Mastery is allowed & practised, of Bruising, Kicking, Scratching, Pinching, Biting, Butting, Tripping, Throtling, Gouging, Cursing, Dismembring, Howling, &c. This spectacle, (so loathsome & horrible!) generally is attended with a crowd of People! In my opinion, (others may think for themselves) animals which seek after & relish such odious and filthy amusements are not of the human species, they are destitute of the remotest pretension to humanity;...."

* * *

Francisco de Miranda, Spanish aristocrat, mentions a friendly fist fight at a barbecue in eastern North Carolina, 17 June 1783, in Judson P. Wood, trans., and John S. Ezell, ed., *The New Democracy in America. Travels of Francisco de Miranda in the United States, 1783-1784* (Norman, Okla.: University of Oklahoma Press, 1963), 8.

"There were some drunks, some friendly fisticuffs, and one man was injured."

BOXING

Broughton's Rules for boxing, circa 1743, reprinted in Nat Fleischer, *The Heavyweight Championship. An Informal History of Heavyweight Boxing from 1719 to the Present Day* (New York: G.P. Putnam's Sons, 1949), 279-280.

"1. That a square of a yard be chalked in the middle of the stage; and at every fresh set-to after a fall, or being parted from the rails, each second is to bring his man to the side of the square and place him opposite to the other, and till they are fairly set-to at the lines, it shall not be lawful for the one to strike the other.

"2. That, in order to prevent any disputes, the time a man lies after a fall, if the second does not bring his man to the side of the square, within the space of half a minute, he shall be deemed a beaten man.

"3. That in every main battle, no person whatever shall be upon the stage, except the principals and their seconds; the same rule to be observed in by-battles, except that in the latter, Mr. Broughton is allowed to be upon the stage to keep decorum and to assist gentlemen to get to their places; provided always he does not interfere with the battle; and whoever presumes to infringe these rules, to be turned immediately out of the house. Everybody is to quit the stage as soon as the champions are stripped, before they set to.

"4. That no champion be deemed beaten unless he fails coming up to the line in the limited time; or that his own second declares him beaten. No second is to be allowed to ask his man's adversary any questions, or advise him to give out.

"5. That, in by-battles, the winning man to have two thirds of the money given, which shall be publicly divided upon the stage, notwithstanding any private agreements to the contrary.

"6. That, to prevent disputes, in every main battle, the principals shall, on the coming on the stage, choose from among the gentlemen present, two umpires, who shall absolutely decide all disputes, that may arise about the battle; and if the two umpires cannot agree, the said umpires to choose a third, who is to determine it.

"7. That no person is to hit his adversary when he is down, or seize him by the ham, or breeches, or any part below the waist; a man on his knees is to be reckoned down."

* * *

Landon Carter, Virginia plantation owner, discussing a general muster of the militia, refers to a boxing match, 29 March 1776, in Jack P. Greene, ed., *The Diary of Colonel Landon Carter of Sabine Hall, 1752-1778,* 2 vols., Vol. 2 (Charlottesville, Va.: University Press of Virginia, 1965), 1006.

"The front rank [was] more crowded with Spectators than I ever saw [at] a boxing match or a bull bating,...."

* * *

Jabez Fitch, Connecticut lieutenant, observes a boxing match on Long Island, 6 November 1777, in William H. Sabine, ed., *The New-York Diary of Lieutenant Jabez Fitch of the 17th (Connecticut) Regiment from August 22, 1776 to December 15, 1777* (New York: pvt. ptg., 1954), 234.

"..., perceiving a large collection of people on the plain, a number of us had the curiosity to join the compy:, where the diversion of the of the day seem'd to be Introduc'd by a severe Combat in Boxing way, between the famous Polhames, & some Refugees; this scene demanded the attention of the people for a considerable time;..."

* * *

Joseph Plumb Martin, Connecticut soldier, describes a boxing match, near New Milford, Connecticut, December 1778, in [Martin], *Narrative of Some of the Adventures, Dangers and Sufferings of a Revolutionary Soldier* (1830), reprinted as James Kirby Martin, ed., *Ordinary Courage. The Revolutionary War Adventures of Joseph Plumb Martin* (St. James, N.Y.: Brandywine Press, 1993), 87.

"I had often heard of some of the low bred Europeans, especially Irishmen, boxing with each other in good fellowship, as they termed it; but I could not believe it till I was convinced by actual demonstration. While we tarried here, I was one day at a sutler's tent, or hut, where were a number of what we Yankees call 'Old Countrymen.' Soon after entering the hut, I observed one who was to appearance 'pretty well over the bay.' Directly there came in another who, it appeared, was an old acquaintance of the former's; they seemed exceeding glad to see each other, and so must take a drop of 'the cratur' together; they then entered into conversation about former times. The first-mentioned was a stout athletic fellow; the other was a much smaller man. All of a sudden the first says, 'Faith, Jammy, will you take a box?' 'Aye, and thank ye too,' replied the other. No sooner said than done, out they went, and all followed to see the sport, as they thought it, I suppose.

"It was a cold, frosty day in the month of December. The ground all around the place was ploughed and frozen as hard as a pavement. They immediately stripped to the buff, and a broad ring was directly formed for the combatants (and they needed a broad one), when they prepared for the battle. The first pass they made at each other, their arms drawing their bodies forward, they passed without even touching either; the first that picked them up was the frozen ground, which made the claret, as they called the blood, flow plentifully, They, however, with considerable difficulty put themselves into a position for the second bout, when they made the same pass-by as at the first. The little fellow, after getting upon his feet again, as well as he could, cried out, 'I am too drunk to fight,' and crawled off as fast as he was able to the sutler's hut again; the other followed, both as bloody as butchers, to drink friends again where no friendship had been lost. And there I left them and went to my tent, thankful that Yankees, with all their follies, lacked such a *refined* folly as this."

* * *

Johann David Schoepf, German physician, comments on a boxing match in eastern North Carolina, 31 December 1783, in Schoepf, *Travels in the Confederation. Pennsylvania, Maryland, Virginia, the Carolinas, East Florida, the Bahamas,* trans. and ed. by Alfred J. Morrison, 2 vols., Vol. 2 (Cleveland: Arthur H. Clark, 1911), 123-124.

"Of what dignity is a North Carolina Justice in these times the following incident will show, which happened immediately after our arrival. A young man who rode up after us, offered his hand to another whom he found here but it was not accepted, because the latter fancied the man had injured him on some former occasion. After a brief exchange of words there was a challenge, and both men, laying aside their coats and shirts, hurriedly prepared themselves for a boxing-match, which took place on the spot, in front of the house and in the presence of the Justice of the Peace. Women, children, and blacks gathered around, the women exclaiming at the contempt shown for the officer's house. The Justice himself stepped forward with folded arms and tranquil demeanor, and once, twice, three times bade the combatants to keep the peace. The boxers paid no attention, and the Justice having fulfilled his duty by thrice commanding the peace, withdrew with the same measured step, and looked on in cold blood. Outraged at the disobedience, the Justice's wife appeared and repeated the commands of her husband, but was received with derision. Finally the antagonists cooled, shook hands by the fighting code, and each rode on his way."

GOUGING

An unidentified English traveler describes gouging in South Carolina, February 1734, in *A New Voyage to Georgia. By A Young Gentleman Giving an Account of his Travels to South Carolina, and Part of North Carolina. To which is added, A Curious Account of the Indians, by an Honourable Person.* (London, 1737), reprinted as "A Gentleman's Account of His Travels," in H. Roy Merrens, ed., *The Colonial South Carolina Scene Contemporary Views, 1697-1774* (Columbia, S.C.: University of South Carolina Press, 1977, 117.

"Two men being in liquor, they quarrelled till they came to blows, when one had the fortune to throw the other down; the underm ost, finding the other to be too strong for him, bit off his nose, which made the other immediately let him go; upon which the fellow made his escape, and was not then to be heard of."

* * *

Elkanah Watson, Massachusetts traveler, describes a gouging match in Georgia, late January? February? 1778, in Winslow C. Watson, ed., *Men and Time of the Revolution, or, Memoirs of Elkanah Watson, Including Journals of Travels in Europe & America from 1777 to 1842* (New York: Dana & Company, 1856), 47.

"In the evening of this day we were much annoyed by the quarrel of two overseers in an adjoining room, who soon gave us a fair (or rather foul) specimen of a genuine Georgia gouging-match. They rushed upon each other with the fury and ferocity of bull-dogs, and made every effort to gouge out each other's eyes. We at length succeeded in separating them."

* * *

Thomas Anburey, British officer, comments on gouging in Richmond, Virginia, February 1779 and at Jones' plantation near Charlottesville, Virginia, April and May 1779, in

[Anburey], *Travels through the Interior Parts of America*, 2 vols., Vol. 2 (London: William Lane, 1791), 309-311, 333-334, 350.

12 February 1779: "As I was walking with fome officers, I was fhewn a gentleman of the town, a Mr. Fauchée, a furgeon and apothecary, who had the misfortune to have one of his eyes gouged out; it was happily replaced, and there were hopes that he would recover the ufe of it. I fhall relate the way the accident happened, to fhew the ferociousnefs of the lower clafs in this country: this gentleman was at play in the billiard-room, where there were a number of gentleman, and feveral of our officers; a low fellow, who pretends to gentility, came in, and in the courfe of play, fome words arofe, in which he firft wantonly abufed, and afterward would infift on fighting Mr. Fauchée, defiring at the afme time, to know upon what terms he would fight, as the lower fort have various modes: Mr. Fauchée declined any, faying, that he was totally ignoarnt as to boxing, but the other calling himfelf a gentleman, he would meet him in a gentleman-like manner; he had fcarcely uttered thefe words, before the other flew at him, and in an inftant turned his eye out of the focket, and while it hung upon his cheek, the fellow was barbarous enough to pluck it entirely out, but was prevented. You can eafily imagine what the officers who were prefent, muft have felt, as fpectators of fuch a fcene, who were obliged to fuffer fuch a wretch to go off with impunity, their hands being reftrained, by their parole, from any interference.

"This moft barbarous cuftom, which a favage would blufh at being accufed of, is peculiar to the lower clafs of people in this province; at one time it was fo prevalent, that the Governor and Affembly were obliged to pafs a law which made it criminal, and that law is now in force, but the rabble are fuch a lawlefs fet, efpecially thofe in the back woods, that they are little reftrained by any laws the State can pafs, and in the back fettlement, this favage cuftom prevails.—I have feen a fellow, reckoned a great adept in gouging, who conftantly kept the nails of both his thumbs and fecond fingers very long and pointed; nay, to prevent their breaking or fplitting, in the execution of his diabolical intentions, he hardened them every evening in a candle."

10 April 1779: "Their amufements are the fame with thofe of the middling fort, with the addition of boxing matches, in which they difplay fuch barbarity, as fully marks their innate ferocious difpofition. An Englifh boxing match, though a difgrace to a polifhed nation, is humanity itfelf, compared with the Virginian mode of fighting; for, previous to the combatants falling-to, they enter into an agreement, whether all advantages are allowable, which are, biting, gouging, and (if I may fo term it) Abelarding each other. If thefe three preliminaries are agreed upon, they inftantly fall to, an, after fome little ftruggling, feize upon their adverfaries with their teeth. What is very remarkable, and fhews what coolnefs there muft be in thefe difputes, and that they are not wholly the effect of anger is, that whatever terms are fpecified, if only one or two out of the three conditions, let the conflict be ever fo fevere, they never infringe on any other."

12 May 1779: "We ftaid and faw feveral [horse races], and then returned, as we were given to underftand, that after the races were finifhed, the day was to be concluded with feveral of thofe horrid boxing-matches I defcribed to you in my laft; and that two or three daring fellows had faid they would feek a quarrel with the Britifh officers; therefore we left thefe buck-fkins to fight by themfelves;...."

* * *

An unnamed English gentleman comments on Virginian amusements, circa 1782-1787, quoted in Marquis de Chastellux, *Travels in North-America, in the Years 1780, 1781, and 1782,* 2nd ed., 2 vols., Vol. 2 (London: G.G.J. and J. Robinson, 1787), 192-193.

"The indolence and diffipation of the middling and lower claffes of white inhabitants of Virginia, are fuch as to give pain to every reflecting mind. Horfe-racing, cock-fighting, and boxing-matches, are ftanding amufements, for which they neglect all bufinefs; and in the latter of which they conduct themfelves with a barbarity worthy of their favage neighbours. The ferocious practice of ftage-boxing in England, is urbanity, compare with the Virginian mode of fighting. In their combats, unlefs fpecially precluded, they are admitted (to ufe their own term) 'to bite, b-ll-ck, and goudge;' which operations, when the firft onfet with fifts is over, confifts in faftening on the nofe or ears of their adverfaries with their teeth, feizing him by the genitals, and dexteroufly fcooping out an eye; on which account it is no uncommon circumftance to meet men in the prime of youth, deprived of one of thofe organs. This is no traveller's exaggeration, I fpeak from knowledge and obfervation. In the fummer months it is very common to make a party on horfeback to a limeftone fpring, near which there is ufually fome little hut with fpirituous liquors, if the party are not themfelves provided, where their debauch frequently terminates in a boxing match, a horfe-race, or perhaps both. During a day's refidence at Leefburg, I was myfelf accidentally drawn into one of thefe parties,.... While we were feated round the fpring, at the edge of a delightful wood, four or five countrymen arrived, headed by a veteran cyclops, the terror of the neighbourhood, ready on every occafion to rifk his remaining eye. We foon found ourfelves under the neceffity of relinquifhing our pofts, and making our efcape from thefe fellows, who evidently fought to provoke a quarrel."

LAWS AGAINST MAIMING

Delaware provincial law, circa 1719, reprinted in *Laws of the State of Delaware, From the Fourteenth Day of October, One Thousand Seven Hundred, to the Eighteenth Day of August, One Thousand Seven Hundred and Ninety-Seven,* 2 vols., Vol. 1 (New Castle, Del.: Samuel and John Adams, 1797), 64.

"SECT. 8. *And be it further enacted by the authority aforefaid,* That if any perfon or perfons on purpofe, and of malice fore-thought, and by lying in wait, fhall unlawfully cut out, or difable the tongue, put out an eye, flit the nofe, cut off the nofe or lip, or cut off or difable any limbs or member s of any of the King's fubjects, with intention in fo doing to maim or disfigure in any of the manners before-mentioned, fuch his Majefty's fubjects; that then and there in every fuch cafe the perfon or perfon fo offending, their counsellors, aiders and abetters, knowing of and privy to the offence as aforefaid, fhall fuffer death, as in cafes of felony, without benefit of the clergy."

* * *

Virginia statute against maiming, February 1752, in "An Act to prevent malicious Maiming and Wounding," February 1752–25th George II, in William Waller Hening, comp., *The Statutes at Large; Being a Collection of All the Laws of Virginia from the the First Session of the Legislature in 1619*, 13 vols., Vol. 6 (Richmond, Va.: Franklin Press, 1819), 250.

An Act to prevent malicious Maiming and Wounding.

Preamble.   I. WHEREAS many mischievious and ill disposed persond have of late, in a malicious and barbarous manner, maimed, wounded, and defaced, many of his majesty's subjects, for the prevention of which in human practices:

What maiming is.   II. BE *it enacted, by the Lieutenant-Governor, Council and Burgesses of this present general Assembly, and it is hereby enacted, by the authority of the same,*That if any person or persons, from and after the first day of June, which shall bein the year of our Lord, one thousand seven hundred and fifty three, on purpose, shall unlawfully cut out, or disable, the tongue, put out an eye, slit the nose, bite orcut off a nose, or lip, or cut off or disable any limb, or member, of any subject of his majesty, in so doing, to maim, or disfigure, in any of the manners before mentioned, such his majesty's subject, that then, and in every such case, the person or persons so offending, their counsellors, aiders, and

Penalty.   abettors, knowing of and privy to the offence as aforesaid, shall be, and are hereby declared to be be felons, and shall suffer as in the case of felony.

Proviso.   III. *Provided,* That no attainder of such felony, shall extend to corrupt the blood, or forfeit the dower of the wife, or the lands, goods, or chattels, of the offender."

* * *

North Carolina provincial law, circa 1755, in *Session Laws at a General Assembly* [12 December 1754+] (Newbern, N.C., 1755), 63.

"CHAP. XV.
"An Act, to prevent Malicious Maiming and Wounding.

"I. WHEREAS many mifchievous and ill difpofed Perfons, have of late, in a malicious and barbarous Manner, maimed, wounded, and defaced many of his Majefty's Subjects: For the Prevention of which inhuman Practices:

"II. BE *it Enacted, by the Governor, Council, and Affembly, and by the Authority of the fame,* That if any Perfon or Perfons, from and after the Ratification of this Act, on Purpofe, fhall unlawfully cut out, or difable the Tongue, put out an Eye, flit the Nofe, bite off or cut off a Nofe, or Lip, bite off or cut off or difable any Limb or Member of any Subject of his Majefty, in fo doing to maim or disfigure, in any of the Manners before mentioned fuch his Majefty's Subject; that then and in every fuch Cafe, the Perfon or Perfons fo offending, their Councellors, Abbettors, and Aiders, knowing of, and privy to the Offence as aforefaid, fhall be, and are hereby declared to be Felons, and fhall fuffer as in Cafe of Felony:..."

* * *

Virginia provincial law, February 1772, in *Acts of the General Assembly, 12 Geo. II* (Williamsburg, Va.: William Rind, 1772), 8-9.

"CHAP. VIII.

"An Act to amend an Act, intitled An act to prevent malicious maiming and wounding.

"I. WHEREAS many diforderly and quarrelfome Perfons do frequently moleft, difturb, and ill treat many of his Majefty's peaceable and quiet Subjects, often wounding and doing them great Injury, yet not in fuch a Manner as to come within the Defcription and Penalties of the Act of Affembly, made in the twenty-fecond Year of his late Majefty's Reign, to prevent malicious maiming and wounding, and the Offenders, upon Suits brought againft them, and Damages recovered, do fecrete their effects, fo that no Satisfaction can be obtained for fuch Injuries: For remedy whereof, *Be it enacted, by the Governor, Council, and Burgeffes, of this prefent General Affembly, and it is hereby enacted, by the Authority of the same,* That if any Perfon or Perfons, from and after the first day of *June* next, fhall wound, by gouging, plucking or putting out an eye, biting, kicking, or ftamping upon any of his Majefty's Subjects, and a Suit fhall be brought to recover Damages for the fame, the Defendant or Defendants fhall give Bail to anfwer fuch Suit, and if the Jury, by whom fuch Suit fhall be tried, fhall find that the Wounding was wilful and malicious, the Defendant or Defendants fhall immediately pay, in Court, the Damages affeffed by the Jury, with the Cofts of Suit, or give fufficient Security to pay the fame within three Months; and every Perfon failing to do fo, fhall, by Order of fuch Court, receive on his bare back fo many Lashes, well laid on, at the Public Whipping Poft, as the Court fhall think fit to order, not to exceed thirty-nine."

WRESTLING

William Wood, English settler, concerning wrestling by New England indigenous people, circa 1634, in Wood, *New England's Prospect. A True, Lively, and Experimental Defcription of that Part of* America, *Commonly Called Nevv England: Difcovering the Ftage of the Countrie, Both as it Ftands to our New-Come* Englifh *Planters; and to the Old Native Inhabitants* (London: Thomas Cotes, 1634), reprinted as *Wood's New-England's Prospect, Publications of the Prince Society, Volume 1* (Boston: The Prince Society, 1865), 97.

"It is moft delight to fee them play, in fmaller companies, when men may view their fwift footemanfhip, their curious toffings of their Ball, their flouncing into the water, their lubberlike wreftling, having no cunning at all in that kind, one *Englifh* being able to beate ten *Indians* at footeball."

* * *

Virginia governor Francis Nicholson proclaims a wrestling match, circa 1691, reprinted in "Nicholson's Proclamation about the College and Orders for Prize Games for Bachelors, etc.," William and Mary Quarterly, 1st Series, Vol. 11, No. 2 (October 1902), 87.

"To the Sheriffe of Surry County

I desire that you give public notice that I will give first and second prizes to be shott for, wrastled, played at backswords, & Run for by Horse and foott, to begin on the 22^{d}.

day of Aprill next s^{et}. [Saint] Georges day being Satterday all which prizes are to be shott for &c by the better sort of Virginians onely, who are Batchelers."

* * *

Satirical poem about Harvard's commencement, circa 1718, in *A Satyrical Description of Commencement. Calculated to the Meridian of Cambridge in New-England* (Boston: The Heart and Crown, 1718), reprinted in Samuel Eliot Morison, *Three Centuries of Harvard, 1636-1936* (Cambridge, Mass.: Harvard University Press, 1946), 122.

> "In Rings some Wrestle till they're mad out-right,
> And then with their Antagonists they fight.
> For Fighting is the Effect of Wrestling, as
> *Men draw Conclusion from the Premises.*"

* * *

An account of a wedding near Saybrook, Connecticut, circa 1726, mentions wrestling as a recreation, reprinted in Helen Evertson Smith, *Colonial Days and Ways as Gathered from Family Papers by Helen Evertson Smith of Sharon, Connecticut* (New York: The Century Company, 1901), 180.

"[The men at wedding participated in] rastling, quoits, running, leaping, archery and firing at a mark, but on the last day no muskets were allowed by reason of the Indians."

* * *

John Brickell, Irish doctor, mentions wrestling by the colonists in North Carolina, circa 1737, in Brickell, *The Natural History of North-Carolina* (Dublin: James Carson, 1737), 40.

"*Wreftling, Leaping*, and fuch Activities are much ufed by them;...."

* * *

Excerpt from a story about a St. Andrew's Day festival in Hanover County mentions wrestling, Virginia Gazette, No. 68, 11–18 November 1737.

"With divers other confiderable Prizes, for Dancing, Singing, Foot-ball-play, Jumping, Wreftling, &c."

* * *

John Adams, Massachusetts lawyer, politician, and later United States President, concerning wrestling during his boyhood, circa 1740s, in [Adams], "The Autobiography of John Adams," in Lyman H. Butterfield, ed., *Diary and Autobiography of John Adams, Volume 3. Diary, 1782-1804, Autobiography, Part One To October 1776* (Cambridge, Mass.: Harvard University Press, 1962), 257.

"And I spent my time as idle Children do in making and sailing boats and Ships upon the Ponds and Brooks, in making and flying Kites, in driving hoops, playing marbles, playing Quoits, Wrestling, Swimming, Skaiting and above all in shooting, to which Diversion I was addicted to a degree of Ardor which I know not that I ever felt for any other Business, Study or Amusement."

* * *

Ebenezer Parkman, Congregationalist minister, mentions wrestling in Westborough, Massachusetts, 14 February 1744, in Francis G. Walett, ed., *The Diary of Ebenezer Parkman, 1703-1782* (Worcester, Mass.: American Antiquarian Society, 1974), 91.

"At the Same Meeting [to divide the town of Westborough into north and south townships] Eliezer Rice broke his legg wrestling with Silas Pratt."

Thomas Lewis, Virginia surveyor, chronicles wrestling in the Blue Ridge mountains of Virginia, October and November 1746, in John W. Wayland, ed., *The Fairfax Line. Thomas Lewis's Journal of 1746* (New Market, Va.: The Henkel Press, 1925), 51, 65.

28 October 1746: "Several of the Inhabitants Came to see us whom our men Engaged to wrestle with them."

8 November 1746: "This Evining we were very much Diverted By Terrable & hoorer (?) of Death, two of our hands, who had some Differance the former offring apiece of Eight to the other to feight him wc the Last agreed too & was So Succesfull that he Beat the other & gained the piece of Eight wc. he afterwards Recovered Before a justice in Orange"

* * *

Benjamin Franklin, Pennsylvania editor, recommends wrestling as a form of physical education, circa 1749, in [Franklin], *Proposals Relating to the Education of Youth in Pensilvania* (Philadelphia: pvt. ptg?, 1749), 10-11.

"That to keep them [pupils] in Health, and to ftrengthen and render active their Bodies, they be frequently exercis'd in Running, Leaping, Wreftling, and Swimming, &c."

* * *

Fray Miguel Venegas, Mexican Jesuit missionary, mentions wrestling among other recreations at California rancherias, circa 1758, in Venegas, *A Natural and Civil History of California,* 2 vols., Vol. 1 (London: James Rivington and James Fletcher, 1759), 84.

"To thefe feftivities the rancherias ufually invite one another; and likewife often fend challenges for wreftling, leaping, running, fhooting with their bow, and trials of ftrength; and in thefe and the like fports, days and nights, weeks and months were often fpent in times of peace."

* * *

Joseph Doddridge, Pennsylvania Episcopalian minister, mentions wrestling in the western settlements of Virginia and Pennsylvania, circa 1763-1783, in Doddridge, *Notes on the Settlement and Indian Wars of the Western Parts of Virginia and Pennsylvania from 1763 to 1783, inclusive, together with a Review of the State of Society and Manners of the First Settlers of the Western Country* (Pittsburgh: John S. Ritenour and William T. Lindsey, 1912), 123.

"The athletic sports of running, jumping and wrestling, were the pastimes of boys, in common with the men."

* * *

Thomas Hutchinson, Massachusetts politician and historian, circa 1765, refers to wrestling by New England indigenous peoples, in Hutchinson, *The History of the Province of Massachusetts Bay,* 2nd ed., 2 vols., Vol. 1 (London: M. Richardson, 1765), 471.

"Swimming, running, and wrestling they were, as early [as childhood], accustomed to."

* * *

Charles Jeffery Smith, Virginia educator, on plans to prevent wrestling at a new academy at New Kent, Virginia, 1 March 1770, in Smith, "Plans for an Academy at Providence, in New Kent," William and Mary Quarterly, 2nd Series, Vol. 3, No. 1 (January 1923), 54.

"The *morals* of the pupils, that capital part of *education*, will be watched with pious vigilance, and formed with unremitting assiduity: But no licentious amusements, which

are real vices, however polite and fashionable they may appear to some, will be tolerated or connived at, such as *card-playing, horse-racing, cock-fighting, wrestling, &c.*"

* * *

Samuel Hearne, British explorer, describes wrestling among indigenous peoples in the
Canadian Northwest, 27? May 1771, in Samuel Hearne, *Journey from Fort Prince Wales,
in Hudson's Bay, to the Northern Ocean, for the Discovery of Copper Mines and a North-
West Passage, Performed between the Years 1769 and 1772, by Mr. Samuel Hearne*
(Philadelphia: Joseph and James Crukshank, 1802), 23-25.

"Time immemorial, it has been a cuftom among thofe people [the Copper Indians]
to wreftle for the woman to whom they are attached; and of courfe, the strongeft carries off the prize. Indeed without a confsiderable fhare of bodily ftrength, or fome
natural or acquired confequence, it is feldom permitted to keep a wife, whom a ftronger
man thinks worth his notice,or whom he wants to affift in carrying his goods.

"This favage and unnatural cuftom prevails throughout all their tribes, and excites
a fpirit of emulation among youth to diftinguifh themfelves in gymnaftic exercifes, to
enable them to protect their wives and property.

"The manner in which they tear the women an[d] other property from each otheir
[sic], is not fo much by fighting as by hauling each other by the hair of the head. Seldom any hurt is done in thofe rencounters. Before the conteft begins, it is not unufual
for one or both of the combatants to cut of[f] his hair, and to greafe his ears in private.
If one only is fhorn, though he be the weakeft man, he generally obtains the victory;
fo that it is evident, addrefs will never exceed mere ftrength among all nations.

"The by-ftanders never interfere on thefe occasions: not even the neareft relations,
[illegible word] by advice to purfue or abandon the conteft. Scarcely a day paffes without fome overtures being made for contefts of this kind; and our author fays, it often
affected him much, to fee the object of the difpute, fitting in penfive filence, and await-
ing the termination of the combat, which was to decide her fate. Sometimes a woman
happens to be won by a man whom fhe mortally hates; but even in this cafe, fhe muft
be paffive, fhould fhe at the fame time be torn from a man fhe really loves."

* * *

Alexander Harvey, Vermont colonel, notes wrestling in Sunbury, Pennsylvania, 2 October 1774, in [Harvey], "The Journal of Alexander Harvey," in *The Upper Connecticut.
Narratives of its Settlement and its Part in the American Revolution*, 2 vols., Vol. 1 (Montpelier: Vermont Historical Society, 1943), 231.

"[I]n this toun and for manie miles in the / Neighbourhood of it there is no minister /
nor any publick worship and I Belive / very little privet the Method they take / to supy
this Defect is they meet in / the taverns and spend the former part / of the Day (viz the
Sabath) in Drinking / wrestling and swearing and in the / afternoon they betake themselves to / the more sober Excercise of Vomiting / and Sleeping...."

* * *

Paul Lunt, Massachusetts soldier, notes wrestling near Boston, 26 October 1775, in
Samuel A. Green, ed., *Paul Lunt's Diary. May-December, 1775* (Boston: pvt. ptg., 1872),
15.

"Pleasant for the season, and all still with the enemy. A wrestling-match between
Winter Hill brigade and Prospect before our regiment; ours carried the ring."

* * *

Henry Tufts, Massachusetts soldier, recalls his wrestling at Wallingford, Vermont, circa 1776, in Edmund Pearson, ed., *Henry Tufts. The Autobiography of a Criminal* (London: Jarrolds Publishers, 1931), 103-104.

"I was, at this time of life, both strong and athletic; valued myself much, as a wrestler, and was, to boot, quite fond of this exercise, which, however, is a pernicious one, and attended with evil consequences, as experience has proved. A few of the misfortunes, that, first and last, have befallen me, while pursuing these practices, I will here enumerate. At one time I had my wrist put out of place by wrestling; at another, one of my arms was broken; at a third my elbow joint was dislocated, after which my collar bone was broken, and again tow of my ribs; all done, at different times, by wrestling.

"About this period I went to Wallingford in Vermont, where at the raising of two buildings, was a great wrestling match. A certain mulatto man threw all out who had the *hardiesse* to engage him. At his success he exulted immoderately, and continued calling out to the company to bring in their *trash*. I had been standing, as a quiet spectator the whole time, without a wish to intermeddle in the business. But at length a number of bystanders requested me to enter the lists. I declined, to little purpose; they still absolutely insisted upon my taking a turn with the champion, who was yet in possession of the ring, and boasting of his prowess. At last, to gratify the company, I yielded to their persuasions, and approached the ring. My opponent, vaunted excessively, accosting me in terms none of the politest. We engaged with equal animosity, but I had the satisfaction to bring him upon his back, twice successively. He insisted upon a third trial; I complied, but now my antagonist was more unsuccessful than before, for finding himself likely to fall, he clapped out his hand to prevent it. At that moment I struck, his arm with my foot, and snapped it short off. This, for the present cured my hero of his athletic disposition, but I was seriously agitated at his misfortune, and the more so, as I had been the unlucky cause of it. No surgeon being near, I undertook the office of setting the bone, and performed it adroitly; three months, however, elapsed, as I afterwards learned, before the fellow was capable of ordinary labor.

"At another time I wrestled with a black fellow (belonging to Col. Smith, of Newmarket) when, unluckily, he was so much hurt by the receipt of a fall I gave him, that he died within the first fortnight. I understood that the poor fellow did not acquaint his master with the true state of the affair, but pretended to have fallen from a hay loft; yet the fact was, as here represented...."

* * *

Pliny H. White on Samuel Cobb, Revolutionary War soldier from Coventry, Vermont, circa 1777, in White, *A History of Coventry, Orleans County, Vermont* (Irasburgh, Vt.: A.A. Earle, 1859), 9.

"While in the army he acquired much distinction for his prodigious strength and his great skill in wrestling, an exercise in which our athletic ancestors very freely indulged. Tradition says that on one occasion when a wrestling match was held to determine the championship of that division of the army to which he belonged, he was victorious over all competitors."

* * *

Levi Beardsley, Otsego County, New York lawyer, concerning wrestling in the Cooperstown area, circa the 1780s, in Beardsley, *Reminiscences; Personal and Other Incidents; Early Settlement of Otsego County; Notices and Anecdotes of Public Men; Judicial, Legal and Legislative Matters; Field Sports; Dissertations and Discussions* (New York: Charles Vinten, 1852), 34-35, 53-54.

"Wrestling, running, jumping, and hopping always constituted part of the amusements...."

"After the building was raised, or the bee concluded, the party collected to take the last drink, and then the sports commenced. Almost invariably a ring was formed for wrestling, and frequently commenced with boys, the men looking on. The boy thrown, would bring in one to wrestle with the victor, and so on till all had wrestled, and the one was victor, who could keep the ring against all comers; so also with the men, who never expected to separate without a goodly number of wrestling matches. This practice was very generally continued as late as 1807. I have never seen so good wrestlers as those early settlers in Richfield. The Colwell family, take them as a whole, were the best in town. Isaac and Robert, who have been dead many years, were very powerful; Samuel, yet alive, about four years older than myself, was master among the boys.

"I became skilful in all these sports, understood them well, and in a rough and tumble scuffle, or at side hold, there were but few of my age I could not throw. Every lock, in wrestling, was familiar, and I knew how and when to take them, and how and when to lay out my strength to accomplish my object. I was quick and but few men, even much larger and stronger than myself, but could I more than match.....

"As Judge Cooper has been introduced, I may as well relate an incident witnessed by my father, not far from this time,.... I have thought it strange that James F. Cooper, the novelist, has not introduced it in some of his works, and once spoke to him about it and related the circumstances, as my father described them. A wrestling match was got up, in front of Griffins; where a ring was formed, and the parties matched for the contest. Judge Cooper said he was a wrestler himself; and believed he could throw any man in the county; and further, that he wanted to find a man on his patent, who could throw him at arms length. Timothy Morse, who I have elsewhere mentioned as a strong man, steeped up and laying his hands on the judge's shoulder, said, 'Cooper, I believe I can lay you on your back.' Cooper replied 'If you can I will give you one hundred acres.' A ring was formed, and at it they went, and Morse soon brought him to the position indicated. The judge got up and ordered Richard Smith, his clerk, to make out the necessary papers for one hundred acres.

"This Richard Smith was the first sheriff of the county. Whether a deed was executed for this one hundred acres, or the value of the land deducted from a previouis or other purchase, I am not positive; but have always supposed Morse resided on the identical hundred acres in Burlington. There is no doubt, I presume, of the wrestling match, and that one hundred acres was at stake; for the contest is till remembered by some of the old inhabitants, who point out the place where they wrestled, near the corner of the present Eagle tavern, formerly Griffin's.

"When I mentioned this to James F. Cooper, he remarked 'that it used to be fashionable to wrestle where his father was brought up, and from whence he removed to Otsego county; and that William Penn was a celebrated wrestler, and introduced and encouraged this with other athletic sports among his colonists.'"

* * *

Joel Shepard, Montague, Massachusetts farmer, recalls wrestling near Albany, New York, circa 1782, in John A. Spear, ed., "Joel Shepard Goes to the War," *New England Quarterly*, Vol. 1, No. 3 (July 1928), 344.

"We passed muster and layed in Albany about six weeks and we fared tolerable well, and not much to doo, but each class had his amusement. The officers would bee a playing at Ball on the comon, their would be an other class piching quaits, an other set a wrestling,...."

Chapter 9

COURT SPORTS

In the colonial and Revolutionary period Americans had limited interest in three sports played on courts, specifically badminton, fives, and tennis. The record is fragmentary regarding all three, so it is difficult to judge if they were more popular than sources indicate. Undoubtedly all three games had their devotees, but none were major sports in the times.

Badminton, also known as battledores and shuttlecock, was most likely a children's game. How much adults indulged in the game is unknown. It is unclear if players played with a net or merely hit the shuttlecock back and forth to each other. Similarly there is no reference to the size of a court or even if there were any formal court. But no rules are extant. Clearly the term shuttlecock became a metaphor for anyone who was weak-willed, revealing the game's overlap with non-sport areas of American life. Some stores offered badminton equipment, indicating some popularity for the game, but other information is absent.

The game of fives perhaps was more known and widespread. This recreation most resembles modern playground styles of handball. Players chose a building wall or played in specially designated courts or "alleys" to hit the ball against. Fives was probably flexible enough to allow a variety of play venues. Presumably they hit the ball off the wall with the intent to deceive or overwhelm the opponent and score points. The game was somewhat popular with college students, judging from the occasional prohibition against it, and with academy scholars. Because a precise description of the game is still wanting, fives remains an intriguing but little understood game.

Even harder to grasp is what tennis meant in colonial and Revolutionary America. As Robert Henderson demonstrated in *Ball, Bat, and Bishop*, tennis in its several variants was an aristocratic game in Europe played in an enclosed courtyard or room, off roofs and walls. But early Americans knew of tennis, often comparing indigenous peoples' lacrosse sticks and snowshoes with tennis rackets. Some colonial Sabbath observance laws prohibited tennis, but there is little other contemporary commentary. Generally the sport was probably too lofty or complex for Americans of this period.

The following documents demonstrate the limited presence these three court sports occupied in the realm of amusement.

[Consult the general writings about sports, recreation, and the various colonial, provincial, territorial, and state Sabbath and gaming laws in Chapter One for other sources about the specific sports or games in this chapter.]

BADMINTON

Landon Carter, Virginia plantation owner, refers to badminton in a metaphorical sense, 11 April 1752, in Jack P. Greene, ed., *The Diary of Colonel Landon Carter of Sabine Hall, 1752-1778*, 2 vols., Vol. 1 (Charlottesville, Va.: University Press of Virginia, 1965), 99.

"'Tis a pity men should run like Bowls. The famous Mr. Richd. Bland is a Shuttle Cock and without faith."

* * *

Advertisement for badminton equipment, Rivington's New-York Gazetteer, circa 1766, reprinted in Esther Singleton, *Social New York under the Georges* (New York: D. Appleton and Company, 1902), 265.

"James Rivington imported battledores and shuttlecocks, cricket-balls, pillets, best racquets for tennis and fives, backgammon tables with men, boxes and dice."

* * *

A children's book draws a moral from badminton, in *A Little Pretty Pocket-Book, Intended for the Amusement and Instruction of Little Master Tommy and Pretty Miss Polly* (London: J. Newbery, 1767), 79.

"SHUTTLE-COCK.

THE *Shuttle-Cock* ftruck   MORAL. Thus chequer'd in Life,
Does backward rebound;   As Fortune does flow;
But, if it be mifs'd,   Her Smiles lift us high,
It falls to the Ground.   Her Frowns fink us low."

* * *

Advertisements for shuttlecocks, New York Gazette and Weekly Mercury, 1769.

"JAMES RIVINGSTON,

Bookfeller, at the lower End of Wall-Street, amongft a large Variety of Articles, has the following to fell very cheap,
"...Shuttlecocks,...."

(No. 923, 3 July 1769)

"JAMES RIVINGTON,
BOOKSELLER,

... will fell...
Fiddle Strings, Mathematical Inftruments, Shuttle Cocks,...."

(No. 941, 6 November 1769)

* * *

Advertisement for badminton equipment, [Rivington's] The Royal Gazette, No. 566, 2 March 1782.

"Battledores and Shuttlecocks,
For the Seafon.
To be had of the Printer."

FIVES

Prohibition against playing fives at Princeton College, May 1761, reprinted in Varnum Lansing Collins, *Princeton* (New York: Oxford University Press, 1914), 207.

"The Trustees having on their own View been sensible of the Damages done to the President's House by the Students playing at Ball against it, do hereby strictly forbid all and any of the Sd Students, the Officers & all other Persons belonging to the College playing at Ball against the sd President's House under the Penalty of Five Shillings for every offence to be levied on each Person who shall offend in the Premises."

* * *

Advertisement for fives equipment in Rivington's New-York Gazetteer, circa 1766, reprinted in Esther Singleton, *Social New York under the Georges* (New York: D. Appleton and Company, 1902), 265.

"James Rivington imported battledores and shuttlecocks, cricket-balls, pillets, best racquets for tennis and fives, backgammon tables with men, boxes and dice."

* * *

A children's book draws a moral from fives, in *A Little Pretty Pocket-Book, Intended for the Amusement and Instruction of Little Master Tommy and Pretty Miss Polly* (London: J. Newbery, 1767), 93.

"FIVES.

WITH what great Force the little Ball	RULE *of* LIFE.
Rebounds, when ftruck againft the Wall!	Know this (which is enough to know)
See how intent each Gamefter ftands;	Virtue is Happinefs below."
Mark well his Eyes, his Feet, his Hands!	

* * *

Yale College law, circa 1774, in *The Laws of Yale-College, in New-Haven, in Connecticut, Enacted by the President and Fellows* (New Haven, Conn.: Thomas and Samuel Green, 1774), 11.

"9. If any Scholar fhall play at Hand-Ball, or Foot Ball, or Bowls in the College-Yard, or throw any Thing againft College, by which the Glafs may be endangered,... he fhall punifhed fix Pence, and make good the Damages."

* * *

Philip Vickers Fithian, Virginia tutor, observes fives playing near Newark, Delaware, 7 September 1775, in Robert Greenhalgh Albion and Leonidas Dodson, eds., *Philip Vickers Fithian. Journal, 1775-1776, Written on the Virginia-Pennsylvania Frontier and in the Army around New York* (Princeton, N.J.: Princeton University Press, 1934), 128-129.

"Newark reminded me of old Days at Princeton—Full of antic School-Boys—It was Play Hours—Some gallopping out—Some coupled Walking—Some throwing long-Bullets—Some Strutting at the Doors before Girls—Others playing at Fives at the End of the Academy &c—...."

* * *

Account of a fives game in Gloucester County, New Jersey, in (Purdie's) Virginia Gazette, No. 64, 19 April 1776.

"WE hear from Gloucefter county, that as the fheriff was opening the court of commiffions in that county, to try a TORY, as ufual, he was going to conclude with *God fave the King*, when, juft as he was about pronouncing the words, a *five's ball*, ftruck by a foldier of the 7th regiment, entered the window, and knocked him in the mouth, which prevented him from being guilty of fo much impiety."

* * *

Albigense Waldo, American surgeon, mentions fives playing at Valley Forge, Pennsylvania, 26 April 1778, reprinted in Alfred Hoyt Bill, *Valley Forge. The Making of an Army* (New York: Harper and Brothers, 1952), 155.

> "One choix at Fives are earnest here,
> Another furious at Cricket there."

* * *

Samuel Shute, New Jersey lieutenant, plays fives in central Pennsylvania, 13, 14, 15, 16, and 17 June 1779, in [Shute], "Journal of Lt. Samuel Shute," in Frederick Cook, ed., *Journals of the Military Expedition of Major General John Sullivan against the Six Nations of Indians in 1779* (Freeport, N.Y.: Books for Libraries Press, reprint of 1885 ed.), 268.

"Spent in Bowling bullets and playing fives."

TENNIS

Eliza Lucas Pinckney, Charleston, South Carolina planter, refers to tennis in a metaphorical sense, June 1742, in Elise Pinckney, ed. , *The Letterbook of Eliza Lucas Pinckney, 1739-1762* (Chapel Hill, N.C.: University of North Carolina Press, 1972), 53.

"But if the diver should pretend each of these perls as big as a Tennis ball...."

* * *

John Armstrong, poet, refers to tennis playing, in Armstrong, *The Art of Preserving Health*, 4th ed. (London and Boston: Green & Russell, 1757), 37.

> "WHATE'ER you ftudy, in whate'er you fweat,
> Indulge your tafte. Some love the manly foils;
> The tennis fome; and fome the graceful dance."

* * *

Jean-Bernard Bossu, French traveler, in the Southeast, compares indigenous peoples' lacrosse to tennis, 30 September 1759, in Seymour Feiler, ed., *Jean-Bernard Bossu's*

Travels in the Interior of North America, 1751-1762 (Norman, Okla.: University of Oklahoma Press, 1962), 169-170.

"The Choctaws are very fresh and alert. They play a game similar to our tennis and are very good at it."

* * *

Advertisement for tennis rackets in Rivington's New-York Gazetteer, circa 1766, reprinted in Esther Singleton, *Social New York under the Georges* (New York: D. Appleton and Company, 1902), 265.

"James Rivington imported battledores and shuttlecocks, cricket-balls, pillets, best racquets for tennis and fives, backgammon tables with men, boxes and dice."

* * *

Benjamin Rush, Philadelphia physician, recommends tennis as recreation, circa 1772, in Rush, *Sermons to Gentlemen upon Temperance and Exercise* (Philadelphia: John Dunlap, 1772), 33.

"To all thefe fpecies of exercife which we have mentioned, I would add, SKEATING, JUMPING, alfo, the active plays of TENNIS, BOWLES, QUOITS, GOLF, and the like. The manner in which each of thefe operate, may be underftood from what we faid under the former particulars."

* * *

Advertisement for a rule book about tennis, [Rivington's] Royal Gazette, No. 437, 6 December 1780.

"For the Advantage of Young Adventurers,Spooners, and all others rated in the lower clafs of Card Players, &c.

HOYLE's GAMES,

BEING Practical Treatifes on the following fafhionable Games:——

Whift,	Chefs,	Cricket,	Hazard,
Quadrille,	Backgammon,	Tennis,	Lanfquenet,
Picquet,	Draughts,	Quinze,	Billiards.

Enquire of the Printer."

Chapter 10

CRICKET

Cricket historian George Kirsch writes, "Although a few cricket clubs were organized in the British colonies and during the inaugural decades of the new republic, the sport's modern era in America did not really begin until the 1830s." Cricket, a definitely

English game datable to the 1300s, appeared almost everywhere the British colonized in North America. Military garrisons were the first major force in promoting the transatlantic migration. British officers, and perhaps enlisted soldiers, too, defended wickets at Nova Scotia and Quebec in Canada, and at New York and points southward in what became the United States. American soldiers and officers, too, played the game, as evidence from Valley Forge shows. So, too, did the commander-in-chief, George Washington, who was known to take a turn at bat.

Civilians in the colonies did their part to preserve and enliven the cricket tradition. The Virginia gentry, as represented by William Byrd of Westover, played cricket at least as early as 1709. The sport conferred an aura of genteel refinement in England, an attribute the squires wished to cultivate in themselves and convince others to believe. But civilians other than the landed developed some level of affection for the game. It is clear that the players William Stephens witnessed playing cricket on holidays in Georgia weren't all patricians; probably neither were the groups of men in Hartford and Maryland, who were challenging each other to matches by the 1750s. Newspaper announcements reveal some continuity of interest, even during the war years. The rising anti-British feelings may have led to an attitude whereby players discriminated against cricket, leading to the sport's ultimate stagnation.

Although the game was never formalized, it enjoyed a certain popularity among the folk. It may be that some of the ball games that cities and towns, colleges and villages restricted were cricket or wicket. Maybe there was a little more cricket in bandy wicket than known. The answers are presently unknown as the diaries and newspapers of the time left a spotty record. Suffice it to say some colonial Americans knew how to bowl over the batsman, when to run for the wickets, and how to keep wicket. Baseball enthusiasts are grateful that the slower paced British game lost favor to the more frenetic one that Alexander Cartwright and Henry Chadwick engineered, but sport historians should recall that Cartwright, Chadwick, and several other early diamond stars, such as the brothers Wright, Harry and George, played cricket enthusiastically as well. The following documents give some glimpse into the existence of colonial and Revolutionary cricket.

[Consult the general writings about sports, recreation, and the various colonial, provincial, territorial, and state Sabbath and gaming laws in Chapter One for other sources about the specific sports or games in this chapter.]

William Byrd, Westover, Virginia planter, plays cricket, April, May, and November 1709, February, March, and April 1710, in Louis B. Wright and Marion Tinling, eds., *The Secret Diary of William Byrd of Westover, 1709-1712* (Richmond, Va.: The Dietz Press, 1941), 25, 27, 31, 111, 137, 144-146, 149, 151, 153, 155-158, 161.

25 April 1709: "Then we played at cricket, Mr. W-l-s and John Custis against me and Mr. [Hawkins], but we were beaten."

27 April 1709: "After dinner we played at cricket...."

6 May 1709: "I rose about 6 o'clock and Colonel Ludwell, Nat Harrison, Mr. Edwards and myself played at cricket, and I won a bit."

27 November 1709: "About 8 'clock we played at cricket and lost five shillings."

1 February 1710: "The Colonel and Mr. Harrison were just going to court but I stayed with Mr. Anderson and he and Colonel Eppes played with Isham Randolph and me at cricket but we beat them."

20 February 1710: "We rode to Colonel Hill's where we were kindly received. We played at cricket and I sprained my backside. I ate bacon and fowl for dinner. In the afternoon we played at the same sport again but I could not run. When we came away I was forced to get on my horse by a chair."

22 February 1710: "In the afternoon Colonel Randolph came. We played at cricket and the Colonel Randolph and Mr. Anderson went away."

25 February 1710: In the afternoon they played at cricket, at which the Captain sprained his thigh."

4 March 1710: "In the afternoon we played at cricket and then rode home where I found all was well,...."

10 March 1710: "In the afternoon we played at cricket a little while but Mr. Anderson was sent for to Mrs. Harrison who was worse."

15 March 1710: "In the afternoon we played at cricket but Mr. Harrison was soon tired."

17 March 1710: "We played at cricket."

22 March 1710: "In the afternoon played at cricket, four of a side, and Mr. Harrison among us, who looked exceedingly red a great while after it."

23 March 1710: "Then we played several games of cricket and after a little rest played several games till it began to rain."

27 March 1710: "After I had given them a glass of sack we played at cricket and after that at billiards till dinner.... Here we went to cricket again till dark;...."

28 March 1710: "About 10 o'clock Major Harrison, Hal Harrison, James Burwell and Mr. Doyley came to play at cricket. Isham Randolph, Mr. Doyley, and I played with them three for a crown. We won one game, they won two..... We played a game at cricket again."

3 April 1710: "In the afternoon we shot with a bow and then played at cricket."

* * *

Samuel Sewall, Boston magistrate, mentions cricket playing, 15 March 1726, in M. Halsey Thomas, ed., *The Diary of Samuel Sewall, 1674-1729, Volume II. 1709-1729* (New York: Farrar, Straus and Giroux, 1973), 1043.

"Sam. Hirst got up betime in the morning, and took Ben Swett with him and went into the Common to play at Wicket. Went before any body was up, left the door open; Sam came not to prayer; at which I was much displeased."

* * *

William Stephens, Georgia Trustee, observes cricket, December 1741, April and November 1742, and March 1744, in E. Merton Coulter, ed., *The Journal of William Stephens, 1741-1743* (Athens, Ga: University of Georgia Press, 1958), 24, 67, 145; and Coulter, ed., *The Journal of William Stephens, 1743-1745* (Athens, Ga.: University of Georgia Press, 1958), 86-87.

26 December 1741: "How irregular so ever we may be in many things, very few were to be foundwho payd no regard to Xmas Holy days, and it was a slight which would ill please our Adversaries, had they seen what a number of hail young Fellows were got together this day in, and about the Town, at Crickett, and such kinds of Exercise,...."

28 December 1741: "During so great a Pother about Rights and Priviledges, among our wise men of Gotham the Common People (who would be quiet enough, if left to themselves) had no other Contest, but at Foot Ball and Crickett, and resolved to see the utmost extent this day of the Holy days."

19 April 1742: "Divers Sports, Cricket, and the like, was mostly the Employment of the Day."

30 November 1742: "When most of the North Britons in Town Assembled in the Square, diverting themselves at Cricket &c,...."

26 and 27 March 1744: "Little to be taken notice of During these Holidays when the common sort of people pass'd most of their time in Sports, Cricket Quoits and such like Exercise."

* * *

Rules of cricket, circa 1744, reprinted, with spelling apparently modernized somewhat, in Neville Cardus, *Cricket* (London: Longmans, Green and Company, 1930), 8-12.

"Ye pitching of ye first Wicket is to be determined by ye cast of a piece of Money.

"When ye first Wicket is pitched and ye popping Crease cut, which must be exactly three Foot 10 Inches from ye Wicket ye other Wicket is to be pitched, directly opposite, at 22 Yards distance, and ye other popping Crease cut 3 Foot 10 Inches before it.

"Ye bowling Creases must be cut, in a direct line, from each Stump.

"Ye Stumps must be 22 Inches, and ye Ball 6 Inches.

"Ye Ball must weigh between 5 and 6 Ounces.

"When ye Wickets are both pitched and all ye Creases cut, ye Party that wins the toss up may order which side shall go in first at his option.

"Laws for Ye Bowlers 4 Balls and Over

"Ye Bowler must deliver ye Ball with one foot behind ye Crease even with ye Wicket, and when he has bowled one ball or more shall bowl to ye number 4 before he changes Wickets, and he shall change but once in ye same Innings.

"He may order ye Player that is in his Wicket to stand on which side of it he pleases at a reasonable distance.

"If he delivers ye Ball with his hinder foot over ye bowling Crease, ye Umpire shall call No Ball, though she be struck, or ye Player is bowled out, which he shall do without being asked, and no Person shall have any right to ask him.

"Laws for ye Strikers, or those that are in

"If ye Wicket is Bowled down, its Out.

"If he strikes, or treads down, or falls himself upon ye Wicket in striking, but not in over running, its Out.

"A stroke or nip over or under his Batt, or upon his hands, but not arms, if ye Ball be held before she touches ye ground, though she be hug'd to the body, its Out.

"If in striking both his feet are over ye popping Crease and his Wicket put down, except his Batt is down within, its Out.

"If he runs out of his Ground to hinder a Catch, its Out.

"If a ball is nipp'd up and he strikes her again, wilfully, before she comes to ye Wicket, its Out.

"If ye Players have cross'd each other, he that runs for ye Wicket that is put down is Out. If they are not cross'd he that returns is Out.

"Batt Foot or Hand over ye Crease

"If in running a notch ye Wicket is struck down by a throw, before his hand or Batt is over ye popping Crease, or a stump hit by ye Ball though ye Ball was down, its Out. But if ye Ball is down before, he that catches ye Ball must strike a Stump out oif ye ground, Ball n hand, then its Out.

"If ye Striker touches or takes up ye Ball before she is lain quite still unless asked by ye Bowler or Wicket-keeper, its Out.

"When ye Ball has been in hand by one of ye Keepers or Stopers, and ye Player has been at home, He may go where he pleases till ye next ball is bowled.

"If either of ye Strikers is cross'd in his running ground designedly, which design must be determined by the Umpires, N.B. The Umpire(s) may order that Notch to be scored.

"When ye Ball is hit up, either of ye Strikers may hinder ye catch in his running ground, or if she's hit directly across ye wickets, ye other Player may place his body anywhere within ye swing of his Batt, so as to hinder ye Bowler from catching her, but he must neither strike at her nor touch her with his hands.

"If a Striker nips a ball up just before him, he may fall before his Wicket, or pop down his Batt before she comes to it, to save it.

"Ye Bail hanging on one Stump, though ye Ball hit ye Wicket, its Not Out.

"Laws for Wicket Keepers

"Ye Wicket Keepers shall stand at a reasonable distance behind ye Wicket, and shall not move till ye Ball is out of ye Bowlers hand, and shall not by any noise incommode ye Striker, and if his hands knees foot or head be over or before ye Wicket, though ye Ball hit it, it shall not be Out.

"Laws for ye Umpires

"To allow 2 Minutes for each man to come in when one is out, and 10 minutes between each Hand.

"To mark ye Ball that it may not be changed.

"They are sole judges of all Outs and Ins, of all fair and unfair play, of frivolous delays, of all hurts, whether real or pretended, and are discretionally to allow what time they think proper before ye Game goes on again.

"In case of a real hurt to a Striker, they are to allow anther tocome in and ye Person hurt to come in again, but are not to allow a fresh Man to play, on either Side, on any Account.

"They are the sole judges of all hindrances, crossing ye Players in running, and standing unfair to strike, and in case of hindrance may order a Notch to be scored.

"They are not to order any Man out unless appealed to by any one of ye Players.

"(These Laws are to ye Umpires jointly.)

"Each Umpire is sole judge of all Nips and Catches, Ins and Outs, good or bad Runs, at his own Wicket, and his determination shall be absolute, and he shall not be changed for another Umpire without ye consent of both Sides.

"When 4 Balls are bowled, he is to call Over.

"(These Laws are Separately.)
"When both Umpires shall call Play, 3 times, 'tis at ye peril of giving ye Game from them that refuse to Play."

* * *

Notice of a cricket match, Maryland Gazette, No. 481, 25 July 1754.

"We hear there is to be a great Cricket Match, for a good Sum, play'd on Satur-day next, near Mr. Aaron Rawling's Spring, between Eleven young Men of this City, and the fame Number of Prince George's County."

* * *

Accounts of cricket matches, Maryland Gazette, 1754.

"Saturday laft the Cricket Match, between Eleven from Prince George's County, and Eleven from Annapolis, was play'd near Mr. Rawling's cool Spring, and Won by the former; the Difference being very few."   (No. 482, 1 August 1754)

"Laft Week a Cricket Match was Play'd, in Mr. Murdock's old Field, in Prince George's County, between Eleven of that County, and Eleven South River Gentlemen (Anne Arundel County) *and that the Prince Georgians were Beat."*   (No. 497, 14 November 1754)

* * *

Challenge for a cricket match, Maryland Gazette, No. 483, 8 August 1754.

"To Mr. JONAS GREEN, in Annapolis.

Auguft 3, 1754.

SIR,

I AM defired by the *Prince George's* County Gentlemen (including Mr. *John Duckett*, who lately left the County), to make a Challenge of Fifteen of the County for Fifteen Piftoles, and from that Sum to Fifty, at the Game called *Cricket*, againft the fame Number in any one County of the Province. *I am, with great Efteem, Yours, &c.*

THOMAS HARWOOD, junior."

* * *

Advertisement for cricket equipment in Rivington's New-York Gazetteer, circa 1766, re-printed in Esther Singleton, *Social New York under the Georges* (New York: D. Appleton and Company, 1902), 265.

"James Rivington imported battledores and shuttlecocks, cricket-balls, pillets, best racquets for tennis and fives, backgammon tables with men, boxes and dice."

* * *

Challenge for a cricket match, Connecticut Courant, No. 71, 5 May 1766.

"A CHALLENGE is hereby given by the Subfcribers, to ASHBEL STEEL, and JOHN BARNARD, with 18 Young Gentlemen, South of the Great Bridge, in this Town, to play a Game at BOWL for a Dinner and Trimmings, with an equal Number North of faid Bridge, on Friday Next.

WILLIAM PRATT,
DANIEL OLCOTT,

N.B. If they accept the Challenge, they are defired to meet us at the Court-Houfe by 9 o'Clock in the Morning."

* * *

A children's book draws a moral from cricket, *A Little Pretty Pocket-Book, Intended for the Amusement and Instruction of Little Master Tommy and Pretty Miss Polly* (London: J. Newbery, 1767), 87.

"CRICKET.

THIS Leffon obferve,	MORAL.	This Maxim regard,
When you play at *Cricket,*		Now you're in your Prime;
Catch *All* fairly out,		Look ere 'tis too late;
Or bowl down the *Wicket.*		By the Fore-lock take Time."

* * *

Challenge for a cricket match, Connecticut Courant, No. 124, 11 May 1767.

"FIFTEEN Young Men on the South-Side the Great Bridge, hereby challenge an equal Number on the North-Side faid Bridge, to play a Game of Cricket, the Day after the Election, to meet about IX o'Clock, Forenoon, in Cooper-Lane, then and there to agree on Terms, & appoint Proper Judges to fee Fair-Play."

* * *

Account of a cricket match, Connecticut Courant, No. 127, 1 June 1767.

"WHEREAS a Challenge was given by Fifteen Men South of the Great Bridge in Hartford, to an equal Number North of faid Bridge, to play a Game at Cricket the Day after the laft Election —the Public are hereby inform'd, that the Challenged beat the Challengers by a great Majority. And faid North Side hereby acquaint the South Side, that they are not afraid to meet them with any Number they fhall chufe, and give them not only the Liberty of picking their Men among themfelves but alfo the beft Players both in the Weft-Divifion and Weathersfield. Witnefs our Hands (in the Name of the Whole Company)   William Pratt,

Niell McLean, Jun."

* * *

Advertisement for a cricket bat and ball maker, 20 March 1778, in Royal Pennsylvania Gazette, No. 6, 20 March 1778.

"ANY Perfon acquainted with the making of CRICKETT BATS or BALLS, may have good encouragement. Enquire of the Printer."

* * *

Albigense Waldo, American surgeon, mentions cricket at Valley Forge, Pennsylvania, 26 April 1778, reprinted in Alfred Hoyt Bill, *Valley Forge. The Making of an Army* (New York: Harper and Brothers, 1952), 155.

"One choix at Fives are earnest here,
Another furious at Cricket there."

* * *

George Ewing, New Jersey ensign, plays cricket, at Valley Forge, Pennsylvania, May 1778, in [Ewing], *The Military Journal of George Ewing (1754-1824) a Soldier of Valley Forge* (Yonkers, N.Y.: Thomas Ewing, 1928), 47.

"2nd Removed my quarters to the Aty [artillery] Park in the afternoon playd a game at Wicket with a number of Gent of the Arty—...."

"4 This day His Excellency dined with G[eneral] Nox [Knox?] and after dinner did us the honor to play at Wicket with us—...."

* * *

Announcements for cricket matches, [Rivington's] Royal Gazette, 1778.

"CRICKET.

"THE GAME of CRICKET, to be played on Monday next, the 14th inftant, at CANNON's TAVERN, at Corlear's Hook. Thofe Gentlemen that choofe to become Members of the Club, are defired to attend. The Wickets to be pitcht at at two o'Clock."   (No. 178, 13 June 1778)

"CRICKET.

THOSE gentlemen of the army and navy, who wifh to play a match at CRICKET, are requefted to meet every Saturday morning, at X o'clock, at the encampment of the British Legion, near Greenwich."   (No. 217, 28 October 1778)

* * *

Ebenezer Elmer, New Jersey surgeon, plays cricket, in central Pennsylvania, 26 July 1779, in [Elmer], "Journal of Dr. Ebenezer Elmer," in Frederick Cook, ed., *Journals of the Military Expedition of Major General John Sullivan against the Six Nations of Indians in 1779* (Freeport, N.Y.: Books for Libraries Press, reprint of 1885 ed.), 83.

"Drisly weather in the forenoon, the afternoon of the day more fair—All hands dined at the Colonels to day & after dinner we took a hearty game of Bandy wicket."

* * *

Announcements for cricket matches, [Rivington's] Royal Gazette, 1779.

"CRICKET.

"A CRICKET MATCH for FIFTY GUINEAS, between the Brooklyn Club and Greenwich Club, to be played on Monday next, at the Houfe of Loofley and Elms. To begin at 10 o'Clock in the Morning."   (No. 312, 25 September 1779)

"CRICKET.

A CRICKET MATCH for Twenty Two Guineas, to be played for at the houfe of WILLIAM DEAL, at Greenwich, on Wednefday next, at ten o'Clock, between the Greenwich Club and the Brooklyn Club.
New-York, October 1, 1779."   (No. 314, 2 October 1779)

"THE Weather proving unfavourable, the Match intended to be played on Wednefday laft between the Brooklyn and Greenwich Clubs will be played on Monday next at the Cricket ground at Mr. Deal's on the Greenwich Road, the wickets to be pitched, and begin playing at Ten o'Clock.
New-York, October 9."   (No. 316, 9 October 1779)

* * *

Announcements for cricket matches, [Rivington's] Royal Gazette, 1780.

"CRICKET.

"A MATCH will be played every Monday during the Summer Seafon (weather permitting) on the ground where the late Reviews were, near the Jews Burying Ground. The Company of all Gentlemen who are lovers of that noble and manly exercife will be very acceptable.
"N.B. The wickets will be pitched at Three o'Clock in the afternoon."
                                                  (No. 388, 17 June 1780)

"CRICKET.

"A MATCH will be played to-morrow and every Thurfday during the feafon, (weather permitting) at Greenwich. The compnay of all gentlemen who are fond of that noble and manly exercife, is particularly requefted at Mr. Deal's by three o'clock in the afternoon the day intended for playing." (No. 403, 9 August 1780)

"CRICKET,

"At the Jew's Burying-ground.
"WILL be played on Monday next, and continued on that Day during the Seafon.
—The Wickets to be pitched at Two o'Clock." (No. 411, 6 September 1780)

Challenges for cricket matches, [Rivington's] Royal Gazette, 1780.

"CRICKET.

"AS four Americans having fome time ago challenged four Englifhmen at the above-mentioned game, but through ill luck, (not bad play) had the misfortune to be beat. We have fince had the courage to challenge them to play ELEVEN on a fide, but receiving no fatisfactory anfwer, WE, in this public manner, challenge the beft ELEVEN Englifh-men in the city of New-York, to play the game of Cricket with them for any fum they think proper to ftake, on giving us timely notice."
(No. 406, 19 August 1780)

"CRICKET.

"AN advertifement appeared in Mr. Rivington's laft Saturday's paper, challenging the beft 11 Englifhmen in the city of New. York to play at the above mentioned game for any fum of money. In confequence of which the Englifhmen applied to the four Americans alluded to in faid advertifement to accept the challenge, but they declared they knew nothing about the matter. We then had recourfe to the Printer to difcover the author, were inform'd a Mr. Vandeufer was the publifher, who, upon enquiry, is not to be found in the city. We the 11 Englifhmen now call upon Mr. Vandeufer in this public manner, if he is TRUE GAME, to produce his 11 Americans to play the faid match for the fum of one hundred guineas, The Sons of John Bull are to be found by applying at Mr. Bain's, at the Checkers, in Cherry ftreet.

"N.B. If Mr. Vandeufer's non-appearance is occafioned by the lofs of his batts and balls, the Englifhmen welcome him to the ufe of theirs, and hope he mayy retain his boafted courage until the money is once ftaked." (No. 408, 26 August 1780)

* * *

Advertisement for a rule book on cricket, [Rivington's] Royal Gazette, No. 437, 6 December 1780.

"For the Advantage of Young Adventurers, Spooners, and all others rated in the lower clafs of Card Players, &c.

HOYLE's GAMES,

BEING Practical Treatifes on the following fafhionable Games:——

Whift,	Chefs,	Cricket,	Hazard,
Quadrille,	Backgammon,	Tennis,	Lanfquenet,
Picquet,	Draughts,	Quinze,	Billiards.

Enquire of the Printer."

* * *

Announcement for a cricket match, [Rivington's] Royal Gazette, No. 476, 21 April 1781.

"CRICKET.

"ON Monday the 23rd inftant will be played the Game of Cricket, near the Jews burying ground, and continued every Monday during the feafon. The prefence of any Gentlemen who are fond of that noble, and truly manly exercife, will be very acceptable. The ftumps will be pitched at two o'clock."

* * *

Jeremiah Greenman, Rhode Island adjutant, plays cricket, at Philadelphia, 20 April 1782 [Greenman], *Diary of a Common Soldier in the American Revolution, 1775-1783. An Annotated Edition of the Military Journal of Jeremiah Greenman*, ed. by Robert C. Bray and Paul E. Bushnell (DeKalb, Ill.: Northern Illinois University Press, 1978), 247.

"The fore noon spent in playing wicket ball...."

* * *

Announcement for a cricket match, [Rivington's] Royal Gazette, No. 604, 13 July 1782.

"CRICKET.

"A NUMBER of gentlemen intending playing a Match on Monday the 15th inftant, on the Green, near the Ship Yards. Any gentleman that would wifh to join their company will be very acceptable; the Balls and Bats, and every thing for their accommodation, at Henry Brinckman's Marquee, on the Field.

"N.B. To continue playing every Monday during the feafon."

Chapter 11

FENCING

Romance novels and enthralling images of bold swashbucklers notwithstanding, few colonial Americans were expert fencers. Fencing was an aristocratic sport that did not migrate well to the new continent. Fencing instructors complained about the disregard for their art or science. Some broadsword play undoubtedly took place at fairs and military training days, but the more precise display of skills and discipline required in fencing needed more attention and practice than most early Americans possessed. The complete fencing manual by Edward Blackwell, reprinted below, shows fencing was a very rigorous and meticulous sport, relying on tradition, technique, and a code of gentlemanliness that descended to medieval times in Europe. Different schools of fencing style apparently existed, but a core curriculum of guards, thrusts, parries, ripostes, parades, slips, bindings, and other maneuvers commanded the student's respect and attention.

Fencing indeed was intertwined with notions of gentlemanliness. As some Americans developed greater sophistication and aspired to be gentlemen, the desire for fencing instruction increased. Fencing academies sporadically appeared in cities, and some tutors took their skills to plantations or became semi-itinerant around the city's outskirts. The instructors were usually from Europe and former military personnel. Many of the schools offered teaching in other gentlemanly arts, such as dancing, French language, and occasionally boxing. If the instructor was married, his wife sometimes provided lessons in gentlewomen's skills, such as needlework, the art of conversation, etiquette, and again dancing and French. It is unclear from the advertisements in newspapers how these schools fared or how long they existed. They may have been somewhat ephemeral enterprises.

One other type of fencing, one that drew great amounts of opprobrium, occurred in these earlier centuries. Antagonists with a grievance occasionally chose swords for the duel. Dueling was such a fact throughout colonial and revolutionary times that most colonies tried to outlaw it. Some laws to prevent murder or mayhem had a specific chapter on dueling prohibiting the use of foils, epées, sabers, or other swords to settle disagreements. None of these appear below because dueling was surely not sport, but deadly combat akin to war. The sport of fencing always carried the undertone of violence and self-defense from potentially lethal assaults. The following selections display the intensity of fencing in colonial times.

[Consult the general writings about sports, recreation, and the various colonial, provincial, territorial, and state Sabbath and gaming laws in Chapter One for other sources about the specific sports or games in this chapter.]

John Dunton, British traveler in Boston, refers to a fencer, March 1686, in [Dunton], *A Summer's Ramble, Through Ten Kingdomes, Occasionally Written by John Dunton, Citizen of London,* 2 vols. (London: A. Baldwin, 1686?, reprinted as W.H. Whitmore, ed., *Letters from New-England, A.D. 1686. by John Dunton* (Boston: The Prince Society, 1867), 91.

25 March 1686: "Another was Mr. Mallinfon; He is one of thofe unfortunate Gentlemen that fled from Monmouth: One that is a great Fencer, who has yet found there was no Fence againft a Flail: And was in England, fo fenfible that the Weakeft his fkill in fencing, for his fafety."

* * *

Samuel Sewall, Boston magistrate, mentions swordplay, 28 April 1687, in M. Halsey Thomas, ed., *The Diary of Samuel Sewall, 1674-1729, Volume I. 1674-1708* (New York: Farrar, Straus and Giroux, 1973), 138.

"After the Stage-fight, in the even, the Souldier who wounded his Antagonist, went accompanyed with a Drumm and about 7. drawn Swords, Shouting through the streets in a kind of Tryumph."

* * *

Virginia Governor Francis Nicholson, proclaims a fencing contest, circa 1691, reprinted in "Nicholson's Proclamation about the College and Orders for Prize Games for Bachelors, etc.," William and Mary Quarterly, 1st Series, Vol. 11, No. 2 (October 1902), 87.

"To the Sheriffe of Surry County

"I desire that you give public notice that I will give first and second prizes to be shott for, wrastled, played at backswords, & Run for by Horse and foott, to begin on the 22^d. day of Aprill next s^{et}. [Saint] Georges day being Satterday all which prizes are to be shott for &c by the better sort of Virginians onely, who are Batchelers."

* * *

John Dunton, British traveler in Boston, refers to a fencer in London, circa 1705, in [Dunton], *The Life and Errors of John Dunton Late Citizen of London* (London: S. Malthus, 1705), 132.

Circa 1705: "The next I'll mention shall be Mr. *Malinfon*, he is a ftiff Independent, (which is rare in a FENCER,) and so great a *Critick*, that he would even find a KNOT in a Bull-rufh. *Malinfon* was one of those *unfortunate Gentlemen that engag'd with* Monmouth, and (I'm told) this Day, at the *Royal-Exchange*, he now teaches young Gentlemen to Fence in *Bofton*, &c."

* * *

William Byrd, Westover, Virginia planter, fences, 25 April 1709, in Louis B. Wright and Marion Tinling, eds., *The Secret Diary of William Byrd of Westover, 1709-1712* (Richmond, Va.: The Dietz Press, 1941), 25.

"Mr. W-l-s and I fenced and I beat him."

* * *

Edward Blackwell, Virginian? fencing instructor, publishes a fencing manual, in Blackwell, *A Compleat Syftem of Fencing. Or, The Art of Defence, in the Ufe of the* Small-Sword (Williamsburg, Va.: William Parks, 1734).

"THE DEDICATION.

"To all Gentlemen, Promoters, and Lovers of the ART *of* FENCING, *in* North America.
Gentlemen,

"THE Genteel Treatment, and Good Enouragement I had the Honour of, in the Profeffion of this NOBLE SCIENCE amongft you, induce me to a Publication of this fmall *TREATISE*; in Hopes that it will, in fome Meafure, be found Advantageous; or, at leaft, will meet with a generous and good natured Acceptance; efpecially from You, who have permitted me to give You fome Inftructions herein: And if it gains the Approbation of other Gentlemen, as well as my Scholars, it will doubly contribute to my Satisfaction, in that I have been thus far capable of obliging thefe Provinces with my mean Ability. Let me then humbly intreat my Readers to perufe thefe Papers with the fame Candor and Good Will in which they will be publifhed: Which will compleat my Pretenfions, and crown my Work with Honour.

I am, Gentlemen,
Your moft obedient Servant,
       Edward Blackwell.

"THE PREFACE.

"HAVING, in my fmall Practce in fundry Parts of America, *met with much Difficulty in Introducing this* ART *of the* SMALL-SWORD, *I almoft defpaired of its Succefs, and that due Efteem which fo ingenious an Art deferves; or that I ever fhould become inftrumental in the general Admittance it now has in thefe Parts of* America. *But notwithftanding the many groundlefs Objections furmized and advanced againft it,*

(which I was the Pains of Clearing up by fuch demonftrable Proofs, as made the very fame Reafons, at firft offer'd againft it, plainly prove the Reafonablenefs and Ufefulnefs of it,) I hope, it won't be thought improper, to give my Readers a fhort Intimation of thefe groundlefs Objections, with this fmall Digreffion.

"THE *Profeffion of this SCIENCE being my proper Employment, I often found Gentlemen flow in giving me encouragement therein; which obliged me to intreat them to learn of me: To which fome would reply,* They were of too Hot and Paffionate a Temper; and were they to learn this Art, it would make them the more quarrelfome: *To which I fay, That the Knowledge of this Art made always a very different Impreffion on very difcreet Perfon, from what they imagined; for, knowing the Danger and difmal Confequences attending the rafh Ufe of it, they will rather put up an Affront, and difpence with a little ill Treatment, than imprudently rufh themfelves, or fend others, into Eternity. Thus it mollifies Heat and Paffion, inftead of exciting Rage and Fury; So that it neceffarily follows, That fuch furious men have the greater Occafion to learn it; fince the Knowledge of this Accomplifhment, teaches them to moderate their Paffions. Others fay,* They never intend to ufe the Sword; therfor Knowledge therein would be of no Service to them: *I anfwer, That the Knowledge of the Sword is never burtherfome; but may often prove ufeful; Befides, the proper management of this Art depends on a Man's own Difcretion; and his Skill never obliges him to the difhonourable practice of it. Some again, are of the Opinion, That,* were they to learn the Small-Sword, they fhould be under a Neceffity of drawing it on every flight Occafion that offer'd; whereby they fhould be deprived of the Advantage of Apologizing for their Ignorance; which humble Submiffion perhaps might have been fufficient Satisfaction to a reafonable Man. *But fince Men do not at all Times truly exercife their Senfes, it is highly neceffary that a Gentleman fhould be qualified to defend himfelf from the Ignorance and Infults of abufive Perfons; which, in my humble Opinion, cannot be compleatly done without this noble Art. Some Gentlemen, alfo, who wear Swords, have thus surprizingly argued,* That Skill is of fo little Service at the Point, that the Bold Ignorant has as good a Chance as the Artift. *This needs no other Anfwer, I think, than that (if a double Advantage be allow'd,) Skill with Courage is better than Courage alone: Unlefs it prov'd, that a Man can be indued with only one of them at the fame Time; and that the Learning of this Art makes Cowards of its Learners; which, I dare fay, was never found to be the Confequence of it; tho' I muft own, (as I in Anfwer to my firft Objection faid,) it makes difcreet Men cautious; which, I hope, will be efteemed a great Addition to its Excellency. Some will alfo affirm,* That an Artift may be eafily beat out of his Play by a Bold Stout Fellow, intirely ignorant of the Sword. *Now, what I apprehend by fuch a Man's being beat out of his Play, is, when he's hurry'd into a confufed, irregular Manner of Performance; which muft be the Effects of Fear, or too much Paffion; but that can't be apply'd as an Imperfection in the Art: For, when a Man has acquired a little Knowledge therein, by being a Month or Two at the* Fencing School, *he is too apt to flatter himfelf, that he's Swordfman enough to defend himfelf: But, in my Opinion, the niceft Part of* Fencing *confifts in the Defenfive, and particularly againft the Bold Ignorant; and fo fmall a Matter of this Accomplifhment will prove more fatal than ferviceable; for a Man is apt to depend on that little Judgment which he has acquir'd, very often at the Expence of his Life, and fuch are the Swordfmen that are to beat out of their Play: In fine, No Perfon ought ever to make any other Ufe of his Skill in* Fencing, *than in his own Defence; and then in fuch a cool and temperate*

Manner, as neither to be exafperated by Paffion, or afraid to exert his Judgment; then a Gentleman will reap the Benefit of his Inftructions. It may not be unworthy the Reader's Notice, to obferve fomething briefly concerning the Skilful, Cowardly, and Ignorant Swordfmen. Firft, as I before obferv'd, the Artift, with Courage, has undeniably the Advantage, becaufe he has Two to One; but Skill, without Courage, lofes its greateft Benefit: However, an Artift, if reputed fo, tho' a Coward, has the Advantage, (provided his Cowardice be undifcovered,) of living peaceably and undifturb'd; for I experimentally know, that the better a Man is acquainted with this Art, the lefs Occafion he will have to ufe his Sword. Befides, there is fomething fhocking in the Character of a good Swordfman, efpecially to the Ignorant, allowing even his Cowardice to be expos'd: For, as it is not impoffible to provoke a reputed Cowardly Artift to draw his Sword, fo is it very poffible for him to get the better, as many Inftances have fhewn us, at the Expence of his Adverfary's Life; therefore it is not fafe to infult fuch a Man's Cowardice.

"BUT *was a Man never to fight with his Sword, no Exercife is more wholfome, and delightful to the learner, than this of* Fencing: *For, by working all the Parts of the Body, it ftrengthens the Limbs, opens the Cheft, gives gives a good Air, and handfome Deportment to the Body, a majeftick Tread; and makes him active, vigorous, and lively; and alfo enables him to ferve his Friend, and Country: In fine,* Air *in* Wearing, *and* Skill *in* Ufing *a* SWORD, *are fuch additional Accomplifhments to a Gentleman, that he is never efteem'd polite and well bred without them. I might fay a great deal more in Recommendation and Praife of this Noble Art; and fhew particularly, how* Great-Britain, *of late Years, has exceeded all other Countries in the Improvements thaye have made therein; but that would tire the Reader's Patience, and is a little out of my prefent Purpofe; therefore I will wave it, and conclude with this Intimation: That I herein lay down fuch Rules, as will be conducive to the Advantage of any Gentlemen, Learners, and Lovers of this Art; who with fome fmall Inftructions therein at firft, may afterwards improve it by this Book: But more efpecially have I compofed and publifhed thefe Inftructions for the Benefit of my Scholars, that they may the fooner and better be perfect in their Leffons; and afterwards find herein whatever they have learn'd of me, if thro' Want of Practice, or Length of Time, any Particulars fhould flip out of the Memory of any Gentleman, that has been, or may be, taught by*

Their Obliged,

Humble Servant,

E. B.

"*Advertifement.*

"THIS Treatife was intended to be publifh'd by Mr. *Blackwell*, in his Life Time, as he himfelf fays, *For the Benefit of his Scholars, That they might be the better and fooner perfect in their Leffons; and to remind them of what might flip out of their Memory, by Want of Practice, or Length of Time:* But his Death put a Stop to fo candid an Undertaking.

"It is now Printed for the Benefit of his Widow and Children: And it is hop'd, all Gentlemen who are Lovers of this Art, efpecially thofe who have reap'd the Benfit of his Inftructions, will, out of Gratitude to the Memory of fo eminent a Profeffor, give Encouragement to his unfortunate Family, by taking fuch of thefe Books as in their Generofity they fhall think fit.

"The Compleat *Swordfman:*
OR,
Tutor of the Small-Sword.
"*Scholar. SIR, The Character you have, in the Mafterfhip of FENCING, induces me to wait upon you, for fome Inftructions in that Noble Science.*
"*Mafter. Sir, No Pains fhall be wanting in me, to accomplifh therein, to your Satisfaction.*

"LESSON I.

"*Giving Directions for keeping a good* Pofture, *and* Guard; *and to* Advance *and* Retire.
"THE Firft thing I am to fhew you, is, to keep a GOOD POSTURE: And to do this, You muft keep your Body upright, your Left Heel right under your Left Groin, and Toe on a Direct Line with your Heel; then fink on your Left Knee, perpendicularly over your Left Toe, your Right Knee level with the Infide of your Left Heel, and at Two Feet Diftance; and your right Knee bent directly over your Right Heel, which being bent but a little, leaves the moft Weight of your Body upon your Left: Then you muft raife your Left Hand, with the Palm out, as high as the Left Ear, and about Six Inches before it, and your Left Elbow on a Line with the Shoulder; and, to keep a thin Body, prefent only your Right Side to your Adverfary.
"*Secondly.* To keep a GOOD GUARD, to defend your Body, your Right Hand muft be extended level with your Breaft, your Arm loofe and eafy, and not ftretch'd out to its Extent, that you may have the greater Command of it; yet it muft be but a little curv'd, that your Adverfary may not have too much Light given him, *viz.* too large Openings, to fend his Thrufts upon you; which a Guard with a very crooked Arm always leaves: Your Fingers muft be grafped round the Gripe, commonly called the Handle; bearing the Weight of your Foil chiefly on your Fore Finger, between the firft and fecond Joint of it, and near the Bar of your Shell; but neither clofe to it, nor beyond it, as is very often practced; your Thumb on the upper Part of the Gripe; the Pummel clofe to your Wrift, with the Infide of your Wrift half turn'd up, which alfo turns up your Infide Edge a little; and this is done to ftrengthen your Guard, and prevent the Foil's being beat out of your Hand; and you muft level your Point with your Wrift, and direct it at your Adverfary's Breaft. There are feveral other Guards and different Poftures taught in the Small-Sword, but I recommend none other to you than this.
"*Thirdly,* TO ADVANCE, and RETIRE, in the fame Guard and Pofture, is what you are next to learn.
"*Scholar.* What is to ADVANCE and RETIRE?
"*Mafter.* To ADVANCE is to take Ground of or march towards your Adverfary, when you are out of Diftance or Reach of him with your Sword: And to do this, lift up your Right Foot, keeping your Knee ftill in the fame Pofition, and ftep ftrong and fwift down, about 7 or 8 Inches forward, bringing up your Left Foot at the fame Time the fame Space of Ground as you carry forward your Right; and in doing of this you muft be ftill in your Guard and Pofture.
"*Scholar.* Muft I lift up my Left Foot as I advance?
"*Mafter.* No, not in this LESSON, becaufe it is eafier to bring up your Left Foot, with a Sweep clofe to the Floor as you advance, than to lay it down in its proper Pofture and Diftance when you lift it up; but hereafter you muft learn to do fo, left you fhould Fence on uneven Ground.
"*Scholar.* Now Sir, I hope you will teach me to RETIRE?

"*Mafter*. Yes Sir, and that is what I am now to fhew you: TO RETIRE is to give Ground, retreat, or go back from your Adverfary, as he advances on you; and muft be thus performed: Lift your Left Foot about feven or eight Inches back, but not clofe to the Floor, as when you advance, but as near it as you can without touching it, and draw your Right Foot after it, keeping ftill in your proper Diftance and Pofture.

"*Scholar*. What Occafion fhall I have at Time to retire?

"*Mafter*. There will, or may be, a Neceffity for you to retire, to prevent your Adverfary's reaching you by his *Longe*, &c. And to retire as he advances, you will hereafter find in many Cafes very requifite.

"LESSON II.
"How to make a true Longe.

"MY SECOND LESSON is to make a true LONGE.

"*Scholar*. Pray what is a LONGE? And how muft it be made?

"*Mafter*. To make a LONGE, you muft firft fling your felf with a lively and graceful Air into your Guard and Pofture; and then lift your Right Foot up about Half a Foot high from the Floor, and fpring to a ftiff Left Knee, keeping clofe your Left Foot, and lighting firm and ftrong on your Right Foot about fifteen or fixteen Inches forward, with your Right Knee over your Inftep; pitching home your Thruft with your Arm at its full Extent, and Shoulder over the Knee, and your Wrift as high as your Face, with your Point flop'd about three Inches lower than your Wrift, throwing back your Left Hand at the fame Time level with your Shoulder; all which done in one Motion will compleat your LONGE: But as you deliver this Thruft, were you to do it with a quick turn'd up Wrift, it would add very much to the Beauty and Swiftnefs of the Thruft.

"*Scholar*. Are all thefe Motions neceffary to make LONGE?

"*Mafter*. Yes, and you can't make a compleat Thruft without them; and I will endeavour to fhew you where their Advantage lies. Firft then, The Reafon of *Longeing* fifteen or fixteen Inches, is, becaufe it is as much Ground as you can take, to compleat a fwift and ftrong Thruft, and recover in Safety; and lefs Ground on your LONGE would leffen the Force of your Thruft; and were you to *Longe* further than about fixteen Inches, or as formerly, and in fome Places yet taught, with your Left Ancle to the Ground, and fometimes your Left Knee, and your Right Foot as far forward as you can ftride, certainly then fuch a LONGE muft be a longer Time in fending home a Thruft, than a LONGE of a fhorter Diftance: Befides, a long LONGE endangers a Man's falling, or ftumbling, which, if he hath the good Fortune to efcape, he can hardly recover in Time to defend himfelf; neither can he, by fuch a tottering LONGE, fupport himfelf ftrong enough, or maintain his Wrift fo ftiff and well mounted as is required in a true LONGE; and alfo finks his Body fo low by over-reaching, that his Thrufts are weak, and generally fall under his Adverfary's Shell; and thofe are eafier Thrufts to be parried than any above the Sword; befides the Rifque the Thrufter runs of rufhing his Face on his Adverfary's Point; which are Motives fufficient, I hope, to diffwade a Gentleman from fuch a ridiculous Piece of Practice; and which Example will give you a more fatisfactory Demonftration of, than I can at prefent.

"*Scholar*. Your Reafon againft a long LONGE feems to be very juft; and I defire you will proceed in your Reafons for the other Performances in this LONGE.

"*Mafter*. The Reafon why the Sole of your Left Foot fhould be clofe to the Ground, is, to prevent your flipping back, or fliding forward, on your LONGE: Your Wrift mounted, and ftiff fupported, as high as your Face, is to keep out any Thruft that can be made above or over the Sword: Your Right Knee bent no further than your Inftep, fupports your Body, and prepares it for a fpeedy Recovery: And fending your Right Shoulder forwad right over your Knee, pitches your Thruft further by abour Half a Foot than were you to keep it ftiff and upright, without bending your Back, which fome Profeffors, in this Art approve of; but I think a Thruft cannot be made fwift or ftrong, without bending the Back a little, which you muft do to fend your Shoulder over your Knee; and that is the Extent of the Pofition your Body ought to be in, on a LONGE: To fling your Left Hand level with your Shoulder, helps alfo to fwiften and ftrengthen your Thruft, and keeps up your Head and Shoulders in an eafy Deportment, and from following your Thruft too far; it alfo gives your Thruft a pretty, genteel Air: And without thefe Helps a Thruft cannot be faid to be compleat.

"*Scholar.* Sir, You have given me a very fatisfactory Explanation herein, which I fhall give my Memory in Charge: But, pray, how fhall I recover from this LONGE?

"*Mafter.* I am very much pleafed that I have reconciled you to my Reafons; and I affure you, Sir, no Pains fhall be wanting in me, to give you as ample Satisfaction in every other Leffon that I fhall have the Honour to teach you. And, to recover from your LONGE, you muft bring up your Body with a Spring, to the fame Pofition your Pofture teaches, dropping your Wrift to it's Guard, and raifing your Left Hand again to it's Place.

"LESSON III.
"To thruft Quarte *and* Tierce.

"QUARTE and TIERCE are the Two chief thrufts on the Sword, and are thus diftinguifh'd. QUARTE is given in on the Infide of the Guard and Arm, at the Adverfary's Breaft; and TIERCE on the Outfide of his Sword, and over his Arm, at his Breaft or Armpit; and are deliver'd thus, *viz.* When You thruft QUARTE, thruft over the Shell of your Adverfary's Foil, and clofe to his Blade; but when you thruft clofe to his Blade, in either QUARTE or TIERCE, it muft be only when he keeps he Guard in the Centre between QUARTE and TIERCE; fo that, by thrufting clofe on his Sword, you open his Guard the more, and the eafier hit him; and as you make your Thruft in QUARTE, turn up your Wrift, with a fudden Twift, as high as your Nofe, and level with it; which guards your Infide, at the fame time you deliver it. And, to thruft TIERCE, you muft alfo make it over the Shell, and clofe to the Blade, (if the Blade fhould be in the Centre, as before obferved) directing your Point then at his Armpit: But in this Truth, your Wrift muft be levelled with your Ear, that your Outfide and over the Sword may then be guarded, as well as your Infide is guarded by levelling your Wrift with your Nofe, in making a QUARTE; and both thefe Thrufts you muft make with a ftiff and well-fupported Wrift, as before fhewn: Tho' feveral Mafters teach TIERCE with a turn'd-down Wrift, by which (they tell you) you may parry and thruft together; which Method of Thrufting I difprove: Firft, becaufe a Round Parade would, as I fhall hereafter fhew you, difarm you, or difable your Wrift, or at leaft bring you to fo great an Open, as would be very difficult for you to parry; befides, you can neither thruft fo ftrong or fwift, with a turn'd down Wrift, without depending on your Adverfary's Sword to fupport your Thruft, which would render you liable to be flipt, whereby your Body would be left too open. And for your further Improvement in thefe Thrufts, I recommend you to QUARTE and TIERCE *againft the Wall*; the Practice of which, will enable you to diftinguifh the Difadvantages that are in Thrufting TIERCE with a turn'd-down Wrift.

"*Scholar*. I will endeavour to make what Difcoveries I fhall be capable of therein; but I obferve, you direct me on my Thruft, whether it be in QUARTE or TIERCE, to turn up my Wrift with a fudden Twift; what Advantage will be of that?

"*Mafter*. That little Flirt or Twift of the Wrift, fends home your Thruft with a hand-fome Spring; and alfo fupports and ftrengthens your Thruft, as before obferv'd, that you fhall hardly be difarm'd by any Parade, or brought to an exceeding great Open.

"*Schol*. I fhall obferve your Directions, Sir; Now, pray what is the Meaning or In-tent of QUARTE and TIERCE *againft the Wall?*

"*Master*. QUARTE and TIERCE *againft the Wall*, are to improve you in the Swiftnefs, Strength, and Truth of your Thrufts, and alfo in the Parades of them; and by repeated Practice herein, you cannot fail to make a handfome Figure in Fencing; but the Neglect of fuch Practice, will caufe you to be defpis'd in a School, and be there efteem'd only a Rambler in Fencing, altho' you may make a tolerable Scuffle in an Af-fault: However, you cannot deliver a Thruft fo ftrong, beautiful, fwift, or eafy, as the frequent Practice of QUARTE *and* TIERCE *againft the Wall*, will teach you.

"*Schol*. What you fay, feems very reafonable; and I intend, if clofe Application to Practice will make me a tolerable Proficient herein, to fpare no Pains.

"*Mafter*. Sir, Your Refolution I very much approve; and doubt not but you'll accomplifh your Defign in a very reafonable Time.

"LESSON IV.

"*To parry* Quarte *and* Tierce.

"TO *parry* QUARTE *and* TIERCE, You muft firft put yourfelf in your Guard, and Pofture; and when you obferve a Thruft coming in QUARTE, catch the weak Part of his Foil, *viz.* any Part between the Point and Middle of it, (which in Fencing is call'd the *Feeble*) and with the *Fort* and Infide Edge of yours, and bear it off towards your Infide, with a ftretch'd out Arm, and Wrift, level with your Stomach. The *Fort* of the Sword, is called, That Part of the Blade between the Middle and Shell: But the Middle of the Blade I think ftrong enough to make any fort of a Parade, or parry any Thruft that can be made; provided you take the Feeble of the Sword Time enough; tho' I think if you were never to take the Feeble in your Parade nearer the Point than within 2 or 3 Inches of the Middle of the Blade, you will be foon enough with your Parade; for, by endeavouring to take the Feeble near the Point, you may happen to make your Parade too foon, and flip over his Point, or entirely mifs it: But when you take his Feeble near the Middle of his Blade, you fecure his Sword, and run no Rifque of miff-ing his Point: And you muft alfo pitch forward your Point with a Spring towards your Adverfary's Right Shoulder, in your *Quarte Parade*, if he fhould be taller than yourfelf, or about your Height; but if lower, level your Point on your Parade with his Right Eye; obferving, as before, that your Wrift at the fame time be raifed no higher than your Stomach: But againft a lower Perfon, there are fafer Parades than the aforemention'd, which you fhall have in due Order. And in thofe Parades which I am now about to fhew you, you muft further obferve on each, that you throw not your Wrift beyond the Limits or Bounds of it, as before fhewn in the Parade for QUARTE: As for Inftance, When you parry QUARTE, you muft throw your Wrift no farther acrofs your Right Breaft than your Stomach: And, to parry TIERCE, you muft do it with your *Fort* and *Quarte-Edge*, as you parry QUARTE; but with the Infide of your Wrift turn'd down, and from you, to your Outfide, about 3 Inches clear of your Shoulder, with your Point levell'd at his Eye, or Shoulder, according to his Stature, as before directed: And thefe are the

Bounds which your Wrift muft be confin'd to, in thofe Parades; obferving, on each Parade, that you ftretch out your Arm to its full extent, tho' you be confin'd to the Limits of each Side, as before exprefs'd.

"*Schol.* I obferve, Sir, according to your Inftruction in the Parades aforemention'd, that my Point muft be mounted higher than my Wrift: Pray, your Reafon why it muft be fo?

"*Mafter.* To make your Parades with your Wrift lower than your Point, is the fafeft Way to fecure your Adverfary's Sword, fo as to prevent it's flipping under the Shell, or Mountain of your Sword; which would very often happen, were your Point and Wrift to be level, on your Parade. But there are alfo other Ways taught, to parry *Quarte* and *Tierce*, which differ but little from the former, *viz.* As the former Parades are made with the Edge of the Foil, both thefe are to be perform'd with the Flat, and without turning the Wrift in *Tierce*, but with the Middle of the Blade, as the other Parade fhewn, and are made with a fwift and ftrong Spring; which I muft own, would bring a man to a very large Open, if the Sword be met with by fuch a Parade. But I think there is great Danger in Parrying fo, left the Parade fhould be flipt, or mifs of it's Stroke at the oppofite Sword, and fhould not recover up Time enough to defend That Open it leaves, by miffing or being flipt, by reafon of the vaft Force that is given to it. Befides, was a man to thruft a *Tierce* clofe and ftrong, along your Foil, the Flat of it would yield and give Way to the Thruft, which the Edge, by a turn'd Wrift, would be ftiff and ftrong to parry off. There are alfo feveral other Parades for *Quarte* and *Tierce*, which differ a great deal from thofe I have fhewn you, but do not yet come under your Obfervation: I therefore advife you to the Practice of thefe two Parades I have fhewn you; for, tho' they are the firft Parades always taught of any on the Sword, yet they are the hardeft to get Mafter of; and to put you in Practice of them, it will be firft neceffary for you to learn to know at Sight when you are within a *Longe*, or *due Diftance* of your Adverfary, and when he is within a reafonable Diftance of you.

"*Scholar.* I am of Opinion that this muft be a very neceffaary Leffon; therefore, pray how is it?

"*Mafter.* By my Computation, Sir, you will find your felf within Diftance when (in your proper Guard and Pofture) your Point feems to be within fifteen Inches of your Adverfary's Breaft.

"*Scholar.* I remember, fifteen Inches is the Ground you advifed me to take on my LONGE: And if there muft be but the fame Diftance between my Point and his Breaft before I *longe*, by that Calculation, if I chance to hit him, I fhall but juft touch him with my Point.

"*Mafter.* I will fatisfy you, Sir, how it is Diftance enough to fend Half a Dozen Inches in him: Be pleafed to obferve, that your Guard requires a curved Arm, which being extended on a Thruft, reaches two Inches further than when it is fo curv'd; and leaning your Shoulder perpendicularly over your Knee on your LONGE, fends your Thruft forward Four Inches more; fo that Six Inches of your *Feeble* is your Adverfary's Lot, which would do his Jobb as well as a Dozen. But to take your Diftance at QUARTE and TIERCE *againft the Wall*, you muft meafure out your Diftance, by making an eafy *Longe*, juft touching your Opponent's Breaft with the Button of your Foil, and recover again to your Guard, and engage him firft in *Quarte*, to difengage quick and clofe under the Fort of your Adverfary's Foil, and thruft *Tierce* with a ftiff and well-mounted Wrift, as before taught; then engage in *Tierce*, and thruft *Quarte*, &c.

"*Schol.* Now Sir, as you have taught me to thruft and parry *Quarte* and *Tierce*, fhew me how to mae the beft Ufe of them.

"*Mafter.* Sir, I will fhew you all the Advantages that you can make, by the few Inftructions you have had as yet, in FENCING, *viz.* If you should be affaulted by any Man, with a Sword, you muft immediately place your felf in your *Guard* and *Pofture*; and if he fhould make a Thruft in *Quarte*, you muft parry him, and thruft *Quarte* again at him, as quick as poffibly you can: for, by Parrying that Thruft he made at you in *Quarte*, you open him in *Quarte:* And if he thrufts *Tierce* at you, you muft parry his Thruft, and make a *Tierce* at him again; for, by your Parade you open him there: And when you intend to make a Thruft at your Adverfary, and fhould not be near enough, or within your *Longe*, advance till you get within due Diftance, elfe your Thruft will be made in vain. Before you can make any other Advantage of thefe Thrufts, and their Parades, it will be neceffary for you to learn more Parades, and other forts of Thrufts.

"*Schol.* How many more Thrufts are there upon the Sword?

"*Mafter.* There are but Two more neceffary now for you to learn, *viz.* SECONDE and FLANCONADE; tho' there are feveral more of Different Names, which have but fmall Difference from thofe abovemention'd.

"*Schol.* How many *Parades* are there, Sir?

"*Mafter.* There are Five other different Parades, and very neceffary ones; tho' but one of them comes under your prefent Obfervation, and this is call'd the *Half-Circle*; by which Parade alone, any Thruft on the Sword may be parried, particularly *Quarte*, when not forc'd upon your Sword, or made higher than your Shell; and when a Thruft is forc'd, or made much higher than your Shell, there are other Means to prevent its getting in, which you are hereafter to learn. But to make your *Half-Circle* Parade, calls next for your Obfervation; and muft be made thus, *viz.* If your Adverfary engages you in *Quarte*, or prefents his Sword at you in *Quarte*, and makes home his Thruft, there drop your *Point* under the *Fort* of his Sword, and with the *Fort* and *Quarte-Edge* of yours, half turn'd up, catch his *Feeble*, and raife your Wrift, with an extended Arm, level with your Nofe, and Point floping towards his Right Thigh; which compleats your Parade: But when he engages you in *Tierce*, and thrufts *Quarte*, you muft follow his Sword clofe, as he difengages to give you his Thruft, and catch his *Feeble*, as before fhewn.

"*Schol.* Why muft my Wrift be raif'd, in this *Parade*, fo high as my Nofe?

"*Mafter.* Becaufe this *Parade* being made under the Sword, wou'd bring the Thruft in your Throat or Face, was your Wrift to be raifed no higher than your Breaft, as in the former *Parades* taught.

"*Schol.* I fhall obferve your Inftructions with all imaginable Caution; and now, Sir, I hope you will fhew how SECONDE and FLANCONADE muft be made.

"LESSON V.

"To thruft Seconde *and* Flanconade.

"SECONDE is a Thruft given in under the Arm, from *Tierce Parade*, *viz.* In Parrying *Tierce*, you open your Adverfary in *Seconde*, efpecially if the Thruft be made with a ftiff and well-mounted Wrift, according to my Inftruction; but when *Tierce* is made with a low Wrift, which happens very often, your Parade then opens him only in *Tierce*; when you have brought him to an Open in *Seconde*, you muft give him the Thruft clofe under his Arm, at his Armpit, with your Body and Wrift in the fame Pofition as you have been taught to thruft *Quarte* and *Tierce*; tho' few Mafters teach this Thruft fo, yet in their Affaults they feldom or never make ufe of that *Scaramouch* Pofture they teach their Scholars to thruft *Seconde* in, *viz.* with Head under the Arm, and turn'd-down Wrift, the Left Hand ftretch'd out under the Right, with the Palm out; which I take to be a weak and awkward Pofture to deliver any Thruft in; befides, the *Half-Circle* Parade would difable or difarm any Thruft made with a turn'd-down Wrift under the Sword.

"*Schol.* Can't I make a Thruft in *Seconde*, 'til my Adverfary firft thrufts *Tierce* at me?

"*Mafter.* Yes, as he prefents his Guard at you, you may put his Sword by to one Side with yours, as you parry *Tierce*; and as that will open his Guard, fo deliver your Thruft; but this being out of our prefent Purpofe, we will leave it, 'til it falls in our way of Courfe: But your only Time to thruft *Seconde*, will be from your *Tierce* Parade, as before directed. Before I teach you FLANCONADE, it wll be neceffary for you to know, that there are Three different *Guards* taught on the *Small-Sword*, and but two of Them generally made ufe of *viz.* the *Strait*, and the *Middle Guard:* The *Strait* is that which I taught you: The *Middle Guard* is with a curv'd Arm and Wrift, Two or Three Inches lower than your Breaft, and Point mounted about Six Inches higher than the Wrift; which is the moft common *Guard* now in Practice, tho' I do not approve it to be fo defenfive a *Guard* as the *Strait*; becaufe the *Middle Guard* is open, both in *Quarte* and *Tierce*, and the *Strait Guard* in *Flanconade* only; which you muft obferve to make thus, *viz.* When the *Strait Guard* is prefented at you, and you intend a *Flanconade* upon it, you muft engage in *Quarte*, and with about the Middle or Eighteen Inches of your Foil, take about Twelve Inches of his *Feeble*, and drop your *Point* of the Outfide of his *Guard*, and clofe under his *Fort*, and force your Thruft home under his Sword and Arm, at his Breaft or Armpit; and as you engage his *Feeble* with your *Fort*, turn it from you a little to your Outfide, that you may fend home your Thruft without Danger of rufhing on his Point: You may alfo make this Thruft with a turn'd-down Wrift, and from the firft Parade in *Quarte*; as for Inftance, When you have made your Parade in *Quarte*, without moving your Foil off his, turn your Sword under his, and bear away his *Feeble*, and home with your Thruft in *Flanconade*, as before fhewn. There is alfo another Way to make *Flanconade*, by the help of the Left Hand; but this can never be done in Safety, but from the firft Parade in *Quarte*: And to do it then, when your Parade is made, turn your *Point* under his Wrift, as before fhewn, and bring up your Left Hand clofe to that Part of your Adverfary's Sword on which your Parade lies, keeping his *Feeble* off with the Palm of it, but with the Back of your Fingers at the fame Time clofe to that Part of your *Fort* which has his Sword fecured; and in this Manner force home your Thruft.

"*Schol.* How are SECONDE and FLANCONADE to be *parried*?

"*Maft.* When he has you open in *Seconde*, your *Point* muft be fuppofed to be a little to the Outfide of his Right Breaft; and as he makes his Thruft, you muft, by a sweep of your Sword clofe over his, fecure his *Feeble* with your *Half-Circle Parade*: And when this Thruft is made at you, in Return of another, you muft recover quick, taking the fame *Circle* with your Arm, and the fame *Parade* as before. There is another fafe and eafy *Parade* for *Seconde*, which is made in this Manner, When you perceive the Thruft coming, drop your *Point* under his *Fort* of his Outfide, and taking his *Feeble* with your *Fort*, bear it off with an extended Arm to your Outfide, giving your Wrift that little Twift up, as in the other Parade taught; but in this, you need not raife it higher than your Shoulder, and about Three Inches to the Outfide of it, with your Point floping towards his Left Thigh: And this Parade being made to the Outfide, much in the fame Manner as t'other is to the Infide, it is called the *Outfide Half-Circle.*

"*Schol.* But why muft not my Wrift be mounted in this Parade as high as in the *Infide Circle?*

"*Mafter.* There is not that Danger of your Face in the *Outfide Half-Circle*, as I obferved to you in the *Infide*; for, the *Outfide Parade* taking no Circle, may be made the quicker; and if you do but clear his Point of your Right Side by it, between your Shoulder and Hip, there will be no Danger of its Hitting any other Part of you; and in this Parade, as well as the *Infide Half-Circle*, you are ftill in a tolerable defenfive *Guard*, which Advantage you have not in any other Parade. There is alfo another *Parade* for *Seconde*, but I do not fo well approve it as the *Half-Circles*; tho' in fome Cafes it is extraordinary ufeful, as fhall be hereafter fhewn you: However, it is a tolerable *Parade* for *Seconde*, and worth your prefent Obfervation, and muft be made as follows: With a turn'd-down Wrift, and Fort of your *Quarte*-Edge, beat his *Feeble* ftrong and from you, throwing your Point with a full ftretch'd-out Arm under his Fort, your Wrift about Three Inches clear of your Shoulder to your Outfide, and about Six Inches lower than your Shoulder, with your Point floping towards your Adverfary's Left Hip: By this you may alfo parry *Quarte* and *Flanconade*; and in Parrying *Quarte* with it, you may probably difarm your Opponent: The Name of this *Parade* is the *Under-Counter.* FLANCONADE may be alfo parried by the *Half-Circles*, by this Obfervation: As you find your *Feeble* prefs'd on, or turn'd afide, by your Opponent's Sword, flip clofe over it, and fecure it of the Infide by your *Half-Circle*; and as he preffes your *Feeble* away, to give you this Thruft, you muft prefs againft him, forcing your Sword clofe under his, raifing his *Feeble* on your Fort to your Outfide, as fhewn in your *Outfide Half-Circle* Parade. And, to parry FLANCONADE with your *Under-Counter*; As you perceive your *Feeble* to be mov'd afide, with a quick turn'd-down Wrift, and with your *Fort* and *Quarte*-Edge and Point under his *Fort*, take the Outfide of his Sword, and turn it off to your Outfide; but if your *Feeble* fhould happen to be fuddenly taken afide, your *Infide Half-Circle* is better, efpecially if you have Room to retire upon it. There is alfo another excellent *Parade* for FLANCONADE, When your *Feeble* is fuddenly put afide, or when you perceive your Adverfary about to clear away your *Feeble*, let it go with him, that he may make home his Thruft, which if made clofe under your Sword, will be fo much the better for your Parade, and keeping your Sword clofe on his, you muft fink your Wrift of the Infide and below his *Feeble*, and fecure it with your *Fort* and *Quarte*-Edge, as you do in the firft Parade in *Quarte*, but with your *Point* no higher mounted than the Breaft; becaufe when you make this Parade, you do it with your Wrift as low as your Belly: This Parade being made in the fame manner as the firft Parade in *Quarte*, tho' with the Guard in a lower Pofition, I know no other Name for it than the *Quarte Parade*; yet no other Thruft than the *Flanconade*, or the *German Thruft*, (which I fhall fhew you in my Sixth Leffon) can be conveniently parried with this Parade, in fo low a Pofition.

"*Schol.* What other *Thrufts* are there, Sir?

"*Mafter.* There are Two more Thrufts, which don't differ much from *Quarte* and *Tierce*, viz. QUARTE *over Arm*, and QUARTE *under Arm*, or *Low* QUARTE: QUARTE *over Arm*, is a *Thruft* given over the Sword or Arm, full at the Breaft, without touching or preffing the Sword; and is feldom made without firft making a Feint in *Quarte*, that the Feint may be anfwer'd by the firft Parade in *Quarte*, which then opens your Adverfary fo much above or over the Sword, that you need not touch his Sword or Arm, in fending home your thruft. LOW QUARTE may be given upon *ftrait Guard*, on your *Half-Circle* Line, thus: In your *Guard* and *Pofture*, engage your Adverfary of the Infide of his *Guard*, with your *Point* a little below his *Fort*, and make home your Thruft clofe to his Sword, and under his Wrift, at his Breaft, bearing his *Feeble* off your Infide with your *Fort*, and mounting your Wrift as high as your Face, as you fend it home; which uyou ought to obferve in every *Thruft*, except the *German Thruft*, which will come by and by under your Obfervation. There is another *Guard*, taught chiefly by the *French*, call'd the *High-Guard*, that is, With your Wrift as high as your Shoulder, and *Point* prefenting at your Adverfary's Face: And LOW QUARTE may be alfo given on this *Guard*, thus, When this *Guard* is prefented at you, You muft take upon you the fame Guard, and prefenting your *Point* at his Face, of his Infide, will probably make him expect your *Thruft* there, which may tempt him to make the firft Parade in *Quarte*; and fuppofing his Parade to be higher than ufual, expecting the *Thruft* in his Face, gives you the opportunity of flipping under his Parade, and making your *Thruft* clofe under his Arm.

"*Schol.* How muft QUARTE *over Arm*, and LOW QUARTE be *parry'd?*

"*Mafter.* QUARTE *Over*, is parry'd by your *Tierce Parade*; and LOW QUARTE by your Half-Circle to the Infide; or, You may parry LOW QUARTE with the *Under-Counter*; but it is not fo fafe a Parade here, as the *Half-Circle*. Having now taught you all the regular *Thrufts*, and ufeful *Parades*, I am next to fhew you their proper Ufe, againft an Occafion calls you to exert your Judgment therein.

"LESSON VI.

"Refpofting, Attacking, and Affaulting.

"RESPOSTING is parrying a *Thruft*, and returning another quick upon that Parade, which fome Mafeters call *Repeating*: But before I proceed in this, I muft fhew you what an *Attack* and an *Affault* are: An *Attack* is, When Two Men prefent their *Guards* at each other, and are out of Diftance, he who marches firft upon his Adverfary, or, if within Diftance, makes the firft Thruft, is faid to take the *Attack*; and if his Opponent parries this *Attack*, and thrufts at him again, this brings it to an *Affault:* And in *Fencing-Schools*, when Gentlemen are afk'd to take an *Affault*, it is, That they may try which is the moft expert Swordfman, and who can give the firft Thruft; and he is faid to make a good *Affault*, who thrufts well on the RESPOST. It will be likewife neceffary before you *affault*, to know how to difpofe your *Looks* in the *Affault*, or upon an *Attack:* When you take the *Attack*, direct your Sight at your Wrift, and over it, at your Adverfary's Face; but oftner obferve the Movement of his Wrift; for, in *Fencing*, that muft be your chief Obfervation; but never let your Eyes be fix'd at any particular Part of him.

"*Schol.* I have heard, that to look a Man in the Face, when I fence with him, is the only Way to difcover where he intends his Thruft?

"*Mafter.* It is a genteel Way, to look the Man in the Face with whom you fence, and may prove very ferviceable to you, if he gives Ground on your *Attack*; for, by Purfuing him with a fierce and angry Countenance, (which you ought to put on, efpecially at fuch a Time) may make him Retreat the fafter; by which Means, you may at laft get in a Thruft, without much Danger.

"*Schol.* But if he fhould Retreat, fafter than I can advance, how fhall I get within Diftance to be in with him?

"*Mafter.* Your Obfervation herein, is good, Sir; for, it is certain, one Man may Retire fafter than another can Advance: And when your Opponent ferves you fo, you muft double your *Attack* upon him, thus: Bring up your Left Foot, and lay it down before your Right, in the fame Pofition and Diftance as when your Right Foot was foremoft, then bring your Right Foot up to it's Pofture, bringing up your Left Foot again before it; and keep Advancing in this Manner, with one Foot before t'other in equal Diftance, and You'll foon get within a *Longe:* But when you deliver home your Thruft, let it be from the Pofition you are in, when your Left Foot is placed before Right, which will fend a Thruft from your Right, which will fend a Thruft from your Pofture; which I think the only Way to come up with a nimble Retreater: Tho' there is another Way more approved of for its Safety, which is this, To bring up your Left Safety, which is this, To bring up your Left Safety, which is this, To bring your Left Inftep clofe or very near to your Right Heel, on your March, keeping ftill your *Guard*; and your *Longe* will be, from that Pofition, about a Yard and Three Inches: But, bring up the Left Foot fo clofe to the Right, makes that a very tottering Pofture; befides, you can't take Ground of your Adverfary, near fo faft by this Method, as by the former; tho' when your Adverfary breaks Meafure, I approve very well of bringing up your Left Inftep clofe to your Right Heel, on your *Longe:* To break Meafure, is, to avoid or fhun a Thruft coming, by fpringing back or to one Side of it; fo that, if your Adverfary ever ferves you fo, as you thruft at him, without Recovering from your *Longe* to your *Guard*, as you do at other Times, bring your Left Inftep quick and clofe up to your Right Heel, then make home your Thruft; and if that does not reach him, bring up your Left Foot in the fame Manner again, and in with him; and by purfuing your active Chap thus, you may at laft chance to nick him.

"*Schol.* Now Sir, that you fhewn me what an *Attack*, and an *Affault* are, and how to double my *Attack*, I hope you will fhew me fomething more concerning RESPOSTING.

"*Mafter.* The Helps I have given you, by this Digreffion, will prepare you the better for the RESPOSTS, which are the moft neceffary Parts of *Fencing:* But there are other Things ftill worthy your Obfervation, before I proceed therein, which are as follow. The firft Thing then that you are to do, when you are about to take an *Affault* with a Gentleman, is, to fling your felf into your Guard and Pofture with as undaunted an Air as poffible, carefully obferving the Pofition of your Adverfary's Guard; for according to that, you muft make your *Attack:* But let the Pofition of his Guard be as it will, if you take the *Attack*, it will be to your Advantage, provided you are ready with a *Parade*, in Cafe your Adverfary fhould fend home a Thruft on your *March:* And if it happens to be the *Middle Guard* you *attack*, march up boldly, and ftamp down your Right Foot ftrong as you march, engaging your Adverfary either in *Quarte* or *Tierce*; for on this Guard, there is Room enough to get in either of thefe Thrufts.

"*Schol.* What Occafion is there for my ftamping fo ftrong on my *March?*

"*Mafter.* It looks bold and daring, and may perhaps ftrike a Terror into your Adverfary: But we may reafonably expect, that it will put him to a *Retreat*, or *Parade* at leaft; and if you bring him to a *Parade*, the Moment you perceive the Manner of it, thruft the contrary; that is, if you march *Quarte* and he goes to his *Firft Parade* there, your Thruft muft be *Quarte over Arm*; but if it be the *Half-Circle* he takes, your Thruft muft be *Seconde*, by changing over the infide of his Wrift, and giving in the Thruft under his Arm of the outfide, as before fhewn: And when you march *Tierce*, and he takes to his *Parade* there, your Thruft muft be given in *Quarte*; but if he retreats as he parrys, and you cannot purfue faft enough to get within Diftance by plain *Advancing*, you muft *double your Attack*, as I firft directed; and if he *breaks Meafure, double* upon him as there fhewn: And I muft further recommend to your Obfervation, that when you engage the *Middle Guard* in *Quarte*, or *Tierce*, and no *Parade* made, if you make home your Thruft clofe to the Sword on the fame Side you engage, it is as effectual a to get in a Thruft as any on the Sword.

"*Schol.* When I give him in a Thruft, am I not in Danger of being hit the fame Time?

"*Mafter.* Yes, he may, upon receiving your Thruft, give another, if you do not fupport your Thruft as before fhewn, and immediately *volt* off as you give it; that is, fpring back with both Feet off the Ground, lighting your Right Foot in the Place where your Left Foot was on your *Longe*, and in your proper *Guard* and *Pofture:* And for your further Security, as you *volt*, beat his Sword off that Side you can get the greateft Purchafe, *viz.* where you can give it the fmarter Blow: And to attack the *Streight Guard*, you may do it thus; as foon as you prefent your Guard, engage in *Quarte* clofe to the Sword, with your Point about Two Inches below the *Fort*; and if no *Parade* be made againft this *Attack*, give him in a *Low Quarte* upon the fame Line, or *Flanconade* with a turn'd-down Wrift; but if he beats you away by the *Half-Circle*, make your Thruft in *Seconde*; or if it be the *Under-Counter* he takes to, give him *Quarte over Arm:* And you may alfo attack the *Streight Guard* of the outfide, and clofe to the Sword, in the fame Manner as you engag'd before of the Infide; and if he takes to no *Parade*, you may get in a *Flanconade* with a turn'd-down Wrift; but if he takes to the outfide *Half-Circle*, you have a full *Quarte* open on him; but I would not advife you to fend home your Thruft there, but rather engage the Sword of the Infide, and try to get in a Thruft there; or, according to the *Parade* made againft you, fend in your Thruft as before directed. There are more Ways to attack the aforefaid Guards, which will come under your Notice in due Order.

"*Schol.* Now Sir, that you have given me thefe Second Helps to enliven and affift me in my *Attacks*, and likewife fhew'd me how to give my Thrufts contrary to the Parade, that may be made ufe of, I hope you have now prepared me for the RES-POSTS.

"*Mafter.* I fhall now, Sir, fhew you your RESPOST Thrufts, according to your *Parades*, *viz.* When you parry *Quarte* by the firft Parade for *Quarte*, your RESPOST Thruft muft be a *Quarte* again, or *Quarte over Arm*, if your Adverfary's Thruft be made with a low Wrift; but if it be made with a well mounted Wrift, you have only a *Flanconade* upon him: And when you parry *Tierce* by the *plain Parade*, *Tierce* again, and *Seconde*, are your RESPOST Thrufts, *viz. Tierce*, when yor Adverfary's Thruft is made with a low Wrift, and Point mounted; and *Seconde*, when the Thruft is made at you with a well mounted Wrift, and floping Point: And when you parry with the Infide and low Parade, *viz* the *Half Circle. Low Quarte* on the Infide Line, or Seconde by chang-ing quick over the Infide of his Wrift, as before fhewn, or *Flanconade* with a turn'd down Wrift, are your RESPOST Thrufts: And when you parry by the *Under-Counter*, your Thrufts on the RESPOST are *Quarte over Arm*, or *Low Quarte* clofe under the Sword between Hilt and Point: And when you parry by the outfide *Low Parade*, *Seconde*, or the *German Thruft*, which comes by and by under your Notice, are your RESPOST thrufts; and always obferve, when you have given a Thruft, to beat your

Adverfary's Sword with a Spring, and *volt* off thus, *viz.* If you hit in *Quarte*, beat on that Side of the Sword which you perceive moft open to your Stroke, *volting* off at the fame Time you give it: And when you have given a Thruft of the Infide of the Sword and under it, beat with your *Under Counter* as you *volt*: And when you have given a Thruft under the Sword of the Outfide, *volt* off with a *Half Circle* Sweep. For your further Affiftance in your RESPOST Thrufts, the following Table will be very convenient, and will inform you of any Part thereof that may at any Time hereafter flip your Memory.

"*The* RESPOST THRUSTS.

"On the Firft Parade in *Quarte*, are Three, *viz. Quarte, Quarte over, Flanconade.*

"On the Infide *Low Parade*, Three, *viz. Low Quarte* on the Infide Line clofe to the Sword, *Seconde, Flanconade* with a turn'd down Wrift.

"On the plain Parade for *Tierce*, Two, *viz. Tierce, Seconde.*

"On the *Under-Counter*, Two, *viz, Quarte over, Low Quarte.*

"On the Outfide *Half-Circle*, Two, *viz. Seconde*, and the *German Thruft.*

"*Schol.* The *German Thruft* you have not yet fhew'd me; What Sort of Thruft is it?

"*Mafter.* This Thruft we borrowed, as it is faid, from the *Germans*, who formerly were accounted famous in the Art of the *Small-Sword*, and from whom this Thruft had its Title; and in my Opinion, is as hitting and fafe a Thruft as is upon the Sword, when made on the *Refpoft*, but dangerous on an *Attack*; nor can you ufe it on the *Refpoft* from any other parade than the Outfide *Half-Circle*; and it muft be made thus, *viz.* As your Sword lies clofe under your Adverfary's in this Parade, bearing his *Feeble* off from you with the *Fort* of yours, and with your Point defcending, and Nails up, as before fhewed in this Parade, keep clofe to his Sword, and turn in your Point at his Arm-Pit with your *Tierce*-Edge up; and as foon as you have given in this Thruft, difengage, and beat his Sword on *Tierce*, and *volt* off; and if you mifs, recover to your Guard, and you may give this Thruft above or under his *Mountain*, according to the Parade he takes to defend it: As for Inftance; if he takes to the *Under-Counter*, which is the moft common Parade for any Thruft made under the Sword, this Thruft muft then be given under the *Mountain*, but with your Point ftill raifed towards the Arm-Pit; and, if he endeavours to parry this *German Thruft* with the *Firft Parade* in *Quarte*, then your Thruft gets in above the *Mountain*, if he happens not to be very familiar with that nice and eafy Turn that belongs to the Parade, when made ufe of againft the *German Thruft*, or *Flanconade.*

"*Schol.* Is there a Manner peculiar in the *Firft Parade* in *Quarte*, when ufed againft thofe Two Thrufts?

"*Mafter.* Yes, and thus it muft be made, *viz.* When the *German Thruft*, or *Flanconade* is made at you, you may remember, that they are both made clofe under the Sword, and as it were bearing it up; which when you find coming under yours, you muft, without quitting his Sword, drop your Wrift quick under his *Feeble*, and bear it off from you with your *Fort*, as in the *Firft Parade* in *Quarte*; and when this Parade is thus perform'd, it is the beft Parade againft thofe Two Thrufts of any upon the Sword.

"*Schol.* In my Opinion, you lie very open in making your *German Thruft*, by Reafon of your Point being raifed higher than your Wrift as you deliver it.

"*Mafter.* We muft be extraordinary fwift in giving this Thruft, elfe we run a Rifque in it; but as you turn your back your Point, as fhewn you in the Pofition of this Thruft, the *Mountain* of your Sword, at the fame Time you raife your Point to give in your

Thruft, preffes his *Feeble* from you, and fecures you from his Point, 'till you can *volt* off to your Guard, by a Beat on his *Tierce*, immediately after you give in your Thruft: But to difcover the Beauties and Dangers that are in every Thruft on the *Small-Sword*, requires a great deal of Experience, as well as good Inftructions; which if you will give me Leave to recommend you to, I hope you will reap an Advantage thereby, as well as enjoy a Pleafure.

"LESSON VII.

"*The* Single *and* Double Feints.

"MY SEVENTH LESSON is, The SINGLE and DOUBLE FEINTS.

"*Schol.* What is the Meaning or Defign of a FEINT, Sir?

"*Mafter.* A FEINT, Sir, is a Term in FENCING, that fignifies an Offer or Motion made with the Point of the Sword at a certain Part of the Body, either above, below, or on one Side of the Sword, without touching it, defigning home a Thruft there; and the Intention of it is, to entice your Adverfary to go to a Parade where you make your FEINT, that you may have the greater Open to make home your Thruft in the contrary, viz. in that Place which he leaves expofed by anfwering your FEINT: As for Inftance, if your FEINT be in *Quarte*, and he takes to his *Firft Parade* in *Quarte*, expecting your Thruft there, the Open which he then leaves you will be in *Tierce*; and when you Feint *Tierce*, and he anfwers it by the *Plain Parade* in Tierce, your Open upon him will be in *Quarte*, which Opens you muft obferve to be very quick in taking, and let nothing move but your Wrift and Point in making a FEINT, that you may fend home your Thruft the quicker; obferving alfo, that you only fhew about Two Inches of your Point in your FEINT, in either *Quarte*, or *Tierce*, and let it be above the Four or Five Inches of the *Mountain* or *Shell* of the Sword, that you may be within true Diftance before you deliver your Thruft; for were you to make your FEINT near the *Feeble*, your Thruft would go fhort of your Mark, without contracting your Arm more than you ought in your FEINT; tho' I will allow that your Arm muft be a little curv'd when you make it, yet no more than as taught in your Guard, that FEINT and Thruft may go together, viz. That you make them in the fame Time of a fingle Thruft; which you cannot compleatly do, without being firft acquainted with your Opponent's general Parades; which you may foon be, if you take this Caution with you, viz. Never to make ufe of a FEINT before you find you can't get in a fingle Thruft; and the making a fingle Thruft will certainly difcover your Opponent's Parade: Though I think it is a danger-ous Practice, ever to make a home Thruft, except on the *Refpoft*, before you make a Trial of your Adverfary's Parade, bya Half Thruft, &c. which you fhall have in your next Leffon. Allowing now, that you have made this Difcovery by your fingle Thrufts, and can't hit him by any one of them, What Advantage then will you make of a FEINT?

"*Schol.* If I make a Thruft in *Quarte*, and my Adverfary parries it by the *Firft Pa-rade* in *Quarte*, I may feint *Quarte*, and thruft *Tierce*; and when I thruft *Tierce*, and he parrys it by the *Plain Parade* in *Tierce*, I muft feint *Tierce*, and thruft *Quarte*, as you have in this Leffon before fhewed me.

"*Mafter.* Sir, your Obfervation is right; and as thofe FEINTS which I have fhew'd you are made above the Sword, they cannot be fo aptly made ufe of againft any other than the *Middle Guard.* You may alfo feint a *Seconde* upon this Guard, but you muft lie in *Tierce* to do it, and pitch down your Point, with a turn'd down Wrift, about a Foot below your adverfe Hilt; which if anfwere'd by the *Under-Counter Parade*, you muft recover up your Point again quick, and give home *Quarte over Arm*; for by baulking his *Under-Counter Parade*, his greateft Open will be there: But before you make your FEINT in *Seconde*, in order to follow it with *Quarte over*, you muft know, that the *Under-Counter* is his general Parade for *Seconde*, that you may feint and thruft as before obferv'd to you: But when you meet with a Chap, that fo, the moft Part ufes the *Half-Circle Parades*, and you feint *Quarte* againft thefe Parades, inftead of making your Thruft in *Tierce*, as when your FEINT in Quarte was anfwer'd by the *Firft Parade* in *Quarte*, your Thruft muft be given in *Seconde*, in the Manner following, *viz.* As you feint *Quarte*, obferve that you always engage your adverfe Sword on the Side oppofite to that where you intend your FEINT, fo that you change under the Sword, from *Tierce*, to feint there, you muft follow your FEINT, and change clofe over the Infide of his Wrift, and under his Arm on the Outfide, give in this Thruft *Seconde*: And when you feint *Tierce*, in Expectation to have your FEINT anfwered by this *Half-Circle Parade*, you muft return back your Point under the Sword, and change quick and clofe over the Infide of his Wrift, and give in *Seconde*, as before fhewed; fo that from your FEINT, in either *Quarte* or *Tierce*, when the *Half-Circle Parade* is againft you, your Thruft muft be *Seconde*; and you muft likewife obferve, that thefe FEINTS, with their refpective Thrufts, can be practiced only againft the *Middle Guard*: FEINTS againft the *Strait Guard* cannot be made with Safety, without firft breaking or difordering the Guard, which you are to be fhewed in your NINTH LESSON; but a FEINT may be play'd on the *Refpoft*, and is a very curious and beautiful Part in FENCING, when nicely perform'd: As for Inftance, When you parry *Quarte* by the *Firft Parade* in *Quarte*, feint *Tierce*, thruft *Quarte*, *viz.* If your FEINT in *Tierce* be anfwer'd by the *Plain Parade* in *Tierce*; and when you parry *Tierce* by the *Plain Parade* in *Tierce*, feint *Seconde*; and if your FEINT be anfwer'd by the *Under-Counter*, thruft *Quarte over Arm:* And when you parry *Quarte* by the *Half-Circle Parade*, you may feint *Quarte*, and thruft *Quarte over*, if your FEINT in *Quarte* be anfwer'd by the *Firft Parade* in *Quarte*; but if your FEINT in *Quarte* be anfwer'd by the *Half-Circle*, *Seconde* muft be your Thruft: And when you make ufe of the *Half-Circle Parade*, which you may do to any Thruft that on the Sword can be made, you may change over the Infide of your adverfe Wrift, and under it on the Outfide feint *Seconde*, and change clofe under and over the Infide of it again, and thruft *Seconde*; but here obferve, that this Sort of a FEINT and Thruft can be only made againft the *Half-Circle Parade*: You may alfo make a FEINT in *Flanconade* from the *Firft Parade* in *Quarte*, thus: When you have made your *Fort* under his *Feeble*, and bearing it off from you, run your Sword clofe under his, as you do when you make this Thruft home, but not above Four or Five Inches forward; which will immediately put him to a Parade, and according to that Parade he takes to, give in your Thruft, *viz.* If it be the *Under-Counter*, *Quarte over Arm*; if the *Half-Circle*, *Seconde* muft be your Thruft; and take this further Obfervation with you, That when you make a FEINT, and intend a Thruft from it, that you make a FEINT, and intend a Thruft from it, that you make your FEINT fo fwift, that no Parade fhould touch your *Feeble* 'til your Thruft be delivered; and when you make your FEINT in *Flanconade*, upon an *Attack* againft the *Strait-Guard*, or the *Refpoft*, mind to do it with all imaginable Swiftnefs, to prevent his flipping his *Feeble* from you as you diforder his Guard by your FEINT, and giving you his Point; which is often done in *Fencing*, by cowardly or unfkilful Swordfmen.

"*Schol.* What is giving a Point?

"*Mafter*. It is extending out a ftreight Arm, with the Point levelled at the Opponent's Body, as this Opponent makes a Thruft at the Giver of the Point; and this is the chief Defence a Man intirely ignorant of the Sword has: And it is often the Practice of many who profefs themfelves Swordfmen, efpecially when they find themfelves a little hard put to it; fo that when one of thefe Gentlemen finds that his Parades begin to fail him, he gives the Point in hopes that his Adverfary will mifs his Thruft at him, and at the fame Time rufh himfelf as he makes it upon his Point; which is all the Chance fuch Sort of Gentlemen have in fuch pinching Circumftances. DOUBLE FEINTS againft the *Middle Guard*, may be ufed upon an Attack, becaufe by the Pofition of the Guard, the Body is expofed on both Sides of the Sword, viz. both *Quarte* and *Tierce*; and when ever you difcover Two Opens in any Guard prefented at you, you may feint both thofe Opens together; but they muft be exceeding fwift, or they are very dangerous, unlefs your Chap retreats much as you attack him: But if he fhould not prove fo cowardly, he may *Time* your DOUBLE FEINT; that is, before you make TWO FEINTS, he may drop a Thruft upon you; and even a SINGLE FEINT may be fo ferved, if not made fwift, and clofe to the Sword.

"*Schol*. Tho'thefe FEINTS may appear very beautiful when in a *Fencing School*, perform'd by a curious Artift, yet it is my Opinion, the beft Artift of them all, was he put to the Sword, would find too little Time upon his Hands from his *Parades* and *Refpofts*, to make a FEINT.

"*Mafter*. Were Two Artifts of equal Skill warmly engaged, I believe they would lay afide their FEINTS: But when a Man finds by exchanging a few Thrufts with his Adverfary, that he either has more Judgment in Fencing, or that his Adverfary's Courage lags, he may then pretty fafely venture a FEINT or Two; otherwife, a neat Thruft on the *Refpoft* is the fafeft Play.

"*Schol*. What Parades, Sir, do you recommend to me againft the SINGLE and DOUBLE FEINTS?

"*Mafter*. Againft the Guard, Sir, which I taught you, being the *Streight-Guard*, no FEINT can be made fufficient to entice you to anfwer it by any other Parades than the *Infide* and *Outfide Half-Circles*, which are fuch clofe Parades, that in making either of them, you hardly difplace the Pofition of your Guard; however, it is fo very little difordered then, that a Thruft can fcarce get in, without bearing upon the Blade of your Sword, which gives you the better Opportunity of ufing thofe Parades; and if your Adverfary fhould happen to diforder your Guard, viz. put it to one Side, or prefs it down, which in *Fencing* is called *breaking the Guard*, and then make his FEINTS, the beft Parades you can ufe to baffle them, and render them ineffectual, are your *Half-Circles*, as before obferved: And you muft always obferve, That if you chance to anfwer a FEINT (which you ought never to do if you can avoid it,) by your Infide *Half-Circle*, and fhould not meet his Sword at the Extent of that Parade, return with a quick Wrift, upon the fame Line, to your Outfide; and you may depend upon it, that One of thofe Two Parades will catch his Thruft, and that his FEINTS will do him no Service.

"LESSON VIII.

"*The* Half-Thrufts.

"THE HALF-THRUFTS are made ufe of as much to difcover Parades, as fending home Thrufts on the Opens which they difcover; and muft be made in this Manner, viz. If you lie in *Quarte*, lift up your foremoft Foot, and ftamp it down ftrong about Two or Three Inches forward, and at the fame Time pitch forth your Arm about Three or

Four Inches with a fudden Spring, and your Wrift a little turn'd up, as you do upon
your Thruft, offering in your Point at your Adverfary's Open, as if you intended home
your Thruft there, to make him the more eagerly go to his Parade, which will give you
an Opportunity of fending in a Thruft on his contrary or oppofite Side: As for Inftance,
If your HALF-THRUST be in *Quarte*, and he fhould anfwer it by the *Firft Parade* in
Quarte, you have your Thruft upon him in *Tierce*, or *Quarte over Arm*; and as he anfwers your HALF-THRUSTS, you may make your Thrufts the fame as have been
fhewn you on the *Feints:* And you muft obferve, that thofe HALF-THRUSTS will
fonner bring a Man to Parades, and with greater Safety, than any other Method on the
Sword; for the Quicknefs of the Motion of your Arm-Wrift, Point, and Foot altogether
compleatly made, appear fo much like a full Thruft, that it makes the HALF-THRUST
fo furprizing, that even an Artift may be deceived by it. You may make your HALF-
THRUST either on the fame Side which you engage your Adverfary, or difengage to
make it, as may feem beft to fuit your Advantage; and when you make it, I advife you
to lie a little while there, to try if your Adverfary will go to a Parade, or thruft upon
your HALF-THRUST: which is very often practiced, through a miftaken Notion of
taking *Time* upon you; for tho' this *Time* upon the Sword is fuch a very curious Piece
of Practice, it is as dangerous as it is nice; and in my Opinion, not fo much as to be
aimed at by any other perfon than one extreamly well vers'd in plain *Fencing, viz.* in
all proper *Parades* amd *Refpoft* Thrufts; but as it is no Part of this LESSON, I will take
no more Time up at prefent about it: However, I muft fhew you how to prevent your
Adverfary of taking Time upon your HALF-THRUST, *To wit,* When you eager to follow it with a full Thruft, left his Thruft and yours fhould hit each of you at the fame
Time; fo that you muft be always prepared upon your HALF-THRUST, remembring,
you cannot make a HALF-THRUST at any Open of your Opponent's, without giving
him an Opportunity to fend in a Thruft upon you at the fame Time; and being thus
prepared upon your HALF-THRUST, to defend his Thruft, you may parry, and thruft
on the *Refpoft*, whichI recommend in chief to your Practice. Before I can proceed to
fhew you the other Advantages that you can make of your HALF-THRUSTS, I muft
teach you to *Bind* the Sword.

"LESSON IX.

"Binding, *or* Preffing *the Sword.*

"BINDING the Sword is, to fecure your Adverfary's Sword, by over-lapping and
preffing down his *Feeble* with about the Middle and *Quarte*-Edge of your Sword, to
bring him to an Open on that Side you *Bind* him: And if you intend to fend home your
Thruft in that Open which you make by BINDING, you muft thruft immediately as you
Bind; for by difordering his Guard, you at the fame Time diforder your own, *viz.* leave
yourfelf open, by bringing him to an Open: As for Inftance, If you *Bind Quarte*, you
are open then in *Tierce*, or *Quarte over Arm*; which Thrufts he has as equal a Chance
to give you, as you have to hit him, in the Open which you make by BINDING; unlefs
when you *Bind*, you do it to tempt him to take the Opportunity of fending in his Thruft
in the Open which you leave by BINDING, that you may parry and *refpoft*; and this
is the Method in this Leffon chiefly practiced, and I think your fafeft Play; fo that if
you *Bind* your adverfe *Quarte*, you muft ftay there a little, to entice him to take your
Open in *Tierce*, which you leave him with that Defign; but you muft take efpecial Care
to be prepared to parry his *Tierce*, which you expect him to thruft, and be very quick
on the *Refpoft*, either in *Tierce* or *Seconde*, which fhall appear moft open upon your

Parade: And when you *Bind Tierce*, you muft be ready to parry *Quarte*; becaufe your greateft Open will then lie there: But here your *Firft Parade* in *Quarte* will not be altogether fo fafe as either your *Under-Counter*, or *Half-Circle Parade*; becaufe if he fhould make a Thruft in *Quarte* at you, which you intend he fhould, his Thruft may be made too low for your *Firft Parade* in *Quarte*; but your *Under-Counter*, or *Half-Circle*, will certainly meet with it, if made at any Part of the Body; and your *Refpoft* Thrufts follow of Courfe, as before taught you.

"*Schol.* When, and againft what Sort of Guard is this Leffon of BINDING the Sword, to be played?

"*Mafter.* Chiefly againft the *Streight Guard*, upon an *Attack*; but you may alfo play this Leffon againft the *Middle Guard*; but obferve when you do, to prefs lightly, and at the fame Time run home your Thruft, fmooth and clofe to your Adverfary's Sword, and on the fame Side you prefs; for by delivering it there, it will be the more furprizing; and I look upon it to be as handfome a Way of Thrufting, on an *Attack*, as any on the Sword: Our School Terms for Thrufts perform'd thus are, GLISCEDES, which you fhall have more of by and by.

"*Schol.* Suppofe, Sir, I fhould *Bind* or *Prefs* the *Middle Guard* in *Quarte*, What are my beft Thrufts to make upon it?

"*Mafter.* As I obferv'd to you before, Sir, there is no other Neceffity to *Bind* the *Middle Guard* than laft mentioned; becaufe it is an open Guard of it felf; and you may make home your Thrufts upon it, without running the Risque of difordering it: But when you *Bind* the *Streight Guard*, (for you will have the greateft Occafion of your BINDINGS there,) your Thrufts muft be the fame then, as your Refpoft Thrufts from your Firft Parade in *Quarte* and *Tierce*; becaufe when you Bind the Sword in *Quarte* and *Tierce*, you do it in the fame Form as when you parry *Quarte* and *Tierce*: But on fome Occafions, you muft *Bind* with a little lower Wrift than when you make your Parade; efpecially when you intend to ftay upon your BINDING, in Order that your Adverfary fhould make a Thruft in the Open which you give him by finking your Wrift when you *Bind*, the greater Open will you leave him in the contrary; which will give him the more Encouragement to make his Thruft there; and fo far he may anfwer your Defign: And particularly obferve, that when you Bind, with an Intent to fend home a Thruft upon it, that you do not prefs down the Sword lower than you generally do in your common Parades for *Quarte* and *Tierce*; and my Reafon for it is is, that if you open his Guard but a Little, the lefs apprehenfive he will be of receiving a Thruft there; but if you open it very wide, he will the readier take to his Parade, in Expectation of a Thruft there, To ufe *Half-Thrufts* on the BINDINGS will be fometimes convenient; efpecially when you can't get in a Thruft by BINDING alone, or invite your Opponent to make a Thruft at you; And to do this, you muft *Bind* as before fhewn; and when you *Bind* in *Quarte*, let it be about Half a Foot lower than the Pofition of his Guard, which we muft fuppofe to be the *Streight Guard*; and having thus confin'd the Guard, make your *Half-Thruft* at the Open which you make by BINDING; which will probably bring him to a Parade there, and give you the greater Open in the contrary. There are alfo other methods to break the *Streight Guard*, *viz.* To open the Guard, that a Thruft may get in; which you may do, by taking your Adverfary's *Feeble* underneath with about the Middle of your Sword, and run it clofe under his, 'til you can get at about Half-Sword, *viz.* when your Point can overlap his Hilt about Fifteen Inches, at the fame Time raifing his *Feeble* as high as your Head, but from you, in the fame manner as you parry

Tierce, which in *Fencing* we call *Roufing Tierce*; and having thus opened the Guard, you may make home your Thruft in *Seconde*; or give him the Opportunity of taking the Open in *Quarte* upon you, which you leave very open as you *Roufe*; and if he fhould make this *Quarte* at you, let your *Under-Counter*, or *Half-Circle*, be the Parades you in fuch Cafes always take to: You may alfo by thefe Parades break or open the *Streight Guard*, and at the fame Time, leave your Adverfary fuch ftrong Invitations to thruft at you, that you can hardly fail of bringing him to *Refpoft Play*: And to perform this, by the *Under-Co unter Parade*, you muft turn down your Point under his *Fort* of the Outfide of his Sword, and bear away his *Feeble* with the *Quarte*-Edge and Middle of your Sword, towards your Outfide, the fame as in your Parade; but not with fo much Strength, or fo great a Spring in your Arm, as when you ufe the Parade on your Defence; and you muft abide there a-while, which leaves you very open in *Quarte*; but that muft be given to invite him to thruft there, that you may have an Opportunity of ufing the fame Parade, and thereby difarm him, or leaft *Refpoft* him, as you have been taught on this Parade; or you may parry that *Quarte*, which the breaking of your adverfe Guard by the *Under-Counter* leaves you open in, by the *Half-Circle* Parade, and *refpoft* accordingly: You may alfo open the *Streight Guard* by the *Half-Circle*, and then the Open you give will be in *Seconde*; which you muft be ready to parry, and *refpoft* according to your Parade.

"*Schol.* But what Parade do you advife me to, if he makes a *Seconde* at me, in the Pofition I fhall be then in, when I open his Guard by the *Half-Circle?*

"*Mafter.* Your infide *Half-Circle*, if you have Room to retire upon it; but if not, your outfide *Half-Circle* is beft; and then you may give him the *German Thruft* on the *Refpoft*: And there are alfo other Methods to break or open a Guard, which in our *Fencing* Terms are called, the BEATS and BATTERS on the Sword.

"*Schol.* Pray how are thofe performed?

"*Mafter.* The *Beats* are performed by a brisk Spring or Flirt of your Arm, with about the Middle or *Quarte*-Edge of your Sword on his *Feeble*; which is a very expeditious Way to open a Guard, provided you hit his Sword in doing it; for as you attempt to break your Adverfary's Guard, by beating or ftriking at his Sword, the Motion of your Arm is fo plain and eafy to be obferved, that before the Stroke be given, he has Time to flip his Sword away from it, and give you a Thruft in the Open which you leave by being fo flip'd; fo that you muft always be prepared, when you intend to play This Leffon on your Opponent, to guard the Open which you leave, in Cafe you fhould be flip'd: And your Defign would be good in this Leffon, were you to give him the Opportunity, as you offer to beat his Sword, to flip you, and make his Thruft at the Open you leave him, that you may parry and *refpoft* as ufual; and this is one of the moft inviting Ways on the Sword to bring a Man to his Play.

"*Schol.* But is it not proper to make a Thruft in the Open which I make by a *Beat?*

"*Mafter.* Yes, you may fend in a Thruft as you beat, when you are not flip'd: As for Inftance, If you beat *Quarte*, thruft the fame immediately upon it; or you may difengage quick, and thruft *Quarte over Arm*: And when you beat *Tierce*, you may thruft *Tierce*, or plain *Quarte*: You may alfo beat up the *Streight Guard* in *Tierce*; but when you do it, let it be rather to induce your Adverfary to flip you, and thruft at your Open which you leave in *Quarte* by being thus flip'd, that you may ufe then the *Under-Counter*, or *Half-Circle Parade*, with the fame Advantages as taught you in *roufing* or *binding Tierce*, and waiting there for your Adverfary's *Quarte* at you; for the Open you leave by beating up *Tierce*, is equal to that you leave by *roufing Tierce*; becaufe *roufing* and beating up *Tierce* bring the Guard to the fame Open; fo that the Parades made ufe of in Defence of the Open that is left by beating up or *roufing* the Guard, ought to be the fame. You may alfo ufe *Feints* with your Beats, thus: Beat *Quarte*, feint *Tierce*, and thruft *Quarte*; beat Tierce, feint *Seconde*, and thruft *Quarte over Arm:* But when we feint thus, we muft fuppofe our Opponent ignorant of any other Parades, than the three common Parades for *Quarte*, *Tierce*, and *Seconde*, viz. the *Firft Parade* in *Quarte*, and *Firft Parade* in *Tierce*, and *Under-Counter*; but if you find him to ufe the *Half-Circle*, or any other Parades, your Thrufts muft be made according to the Parades he anfwers your Feints with, as taught you in my SEVENTH LESSON.

"*Schol.* How fhall I difcover when my Adverfary attempts to *bind* or *beat* my Sword?

"*Mafter.* You may difcover it by the Motion of his Arm, if you have Day-Light when you Fence, efpecially when he is about to beat your Sword; becaufe, as I obferved to you before, the Motion of the Arm in Beating is greater than in *Binding* the Sword, and confequently more eafily difcovered: Or you may find his Defign outby *Preffing* his Sword upon yours; which as foon as you feel, you muft imediately flip away from his to your Guard; and if you difcover him by the Motion of his Arm, you muft flip his Stroke as you perceive it coming, and to your Guard immediately.

"*Schol.* Now Sir, If you will teach me how to flip my Sword away from thofe Dangers, I fhall be tolerably prepared againft this Leffon, unlefs you have more Ways to prevent the Dangers of it than you have fhewed me.

"*Mafter.* The Slips I muft teach you; and likewife all the Defenfives, as well as Offenfives, that I am Mafter of, as they occur to my Memory, in their due Places: But give me leave firft to recommend this general Obfervation to you, viz. That when you *bind* the Sword, in order for your Adverfary to thruft at the Open, you then leave him, and if he fhould be afraid or unwilling to accept the Invitation, make a Half-Thruft at the Open you bring him to by BINDING; and if that fails to bring him to a Parade, try the *Beats* or *Batters* upon him, which you may do againft any Guard that can be prefented at you; and if none of thofe will anfwer your Purpofe, open his Guard, which I fuppofe to be *Streight*, by the *Under-Counter*, or *Half-Circle*, as before fhewn; and if he refufes to take the Open then given, make a Half-Thruft at the Open you bring him to; and if none of thefe Incentives prove fufficient to excite him to accept fuch fair Invitations, they are all loft upon him; and fuch a Man you ought to leave to fight alone, as not being worth your Notice; and indeed I wifh you may never meet with a more dangerous Adverfary. Tho' I have before in this Leffon given you thefe Inftructions, yet in this Laft Paragraph they are more concife and comprehenfive than in the former.

"*Schol.* The *Batters* you have not yet fhewed me the Ufe of, nor how they muft be made.

"*Mafter.* They are proper to find out your Opponent's Play; and that is all the Ufe I ever thought fit to make of them: For when you *batter*, you are not fuppofed to be within a *Longe*, becaufe you only beat your *Feeble* againft his *Feeble*; and this you do to provoke him to attack you.

"*Schol.* There feems to be but very little Difference between the *Beats* and *Batters*.

"*Mafter.* They differ, Sir, in two Points; and one of them is very material, which is this, viz. You are within Diftance when you beat the Sword; tho' it is the *Feeble* you *beat*, yet it is done with the Middle of yours, which brings you within Diftance.

"*Schol.* I now apprehend: When I *beat* the Sword, I muft be within Diftance, and *beat* with the Middle of my Sword; and when I *batter*, I muft do it with *Feeble* againft *Feeble*, which will be out of Diftance of a Thruft; and this Diftinction I hope to retain. Now Sir, if you pleafe to teach me the SLIPS, I think my felf ready for them.

"*Mafter.* My next LESSON fhall inftruct you therein.

"LESSON X.
"*The* Slips.

"THE SLIPS are good againft the *Bindings, Beats,* and *Batters,* as I have given you a fmall Inftance in my laft Leffon; and when you have, by the Rule taught there, dif-cover'd your Adverfary's Play to be depending upon the *Bindings, &c.* as aforemen-tioned, your fafeft Defence will be then to *Slip* him: And to do it, you muft dip down your Point clofe under his Sword as he attempts to touch yours, and raife it on his contrary to your Guard, in readinefs to receive his next Attack, or to attack him, which may feem to fuit with your Conveniency beft: And when you dip down your Point to *Slip,* turn the Infide of your Wrift up a little, with a Spring; but neither raife nor fink it in the Motion from the Pofition of your Guard: And if to bind your Sword be his Project, you may give him leave to prefs a little lightly upon your *Feeble,* to try his Play; and perhaps he may ftay a little while there, to induce you to thruft at his Open, which if you difcover his Defign, you muft half-thruft that Open of his, and give him an Opportunity of feeling your Sword on the Parade he makes, that he may make a Thruft from it at the Open you leave, and you get the Advantage of your *Refpoft* Play: As for Inftance, If he binds you in *Quarte,* in Expectation that you will make home your Thruft in *Tierce,* becaufe there lies your invitation, you muft make your Half-Thruft there, and give him an Open at the fame Time in *Tierce,* or *Seconde*; and ac-cording to the Open you then leave, parry and *refpoft,* as often fhewn you; or when you feel his Sword upon yours, you may difengage, and bind his on the contrary; and that will prevent him of making any Advantage by *Binding,* and be a very ready Way to bring him to Play.

"*Schol.* But fuppofe he makes a Half-Thuft when I fuffer him to *bind* me?

"*Mafter.* To anfwer it is your fafeft Method; tho' by that Means you will leave your felf open in the contrary, which no doubt will be as he would have it; yet you muft be reday to make your Parade in that Open there, and to your *Refpoft,* as ufual: As for the *Beats,* and *Batters,* your only Play is to *Slip* them: But before you venture home a Thruft as you *Slip,* it will be neceffary to make a Half-Thruft at the Open you leave him by *Slipping*; efpecially if your Adverfary be very furious in his *Attacks*; becaufe this half-Thruft will ftop his Purfuit, if it is ever fo eager: Befides the Advantage you make if the Half-Thruft be anfwered, which I have often cited to you, may be confiderable.

"*Schol.* But if I fhould make a Full Thruft at the Open I *Slip* him to, where will be the Danger?

"*Mafter.* There will be no great Danger, if your Thruft be made true, and fwift: But this of making your SLIP and Thruft together, belongs to another LESSON, called *The* TIME, which you fhall have in due Order

"LESSON XI.
"*The* Counter *or* Round Parades

"MY ELEVENTH LESSON is, *The* COUNTER *or* ROUND PARADES.

"*Schol.* What Sort of Parades are they? And when ought they be made ufe of?

"*Mafter.* A COUNTER PARADE is, to go clofe under, and round the Sword, when a Thruft is made at you; and to fecure it on that Side contrary to where the Thruft was made: As for Inftance, When you are engaged in *Tierce*, and a *Quarte* made at you, as he difengages from *Tierce* to give you this *Quarte*, you muft follow his Sword clofe, but under it, 'til raifing it again above his, you fecure his by your *Tierce Parade*; for, altho' the Thruft be made at your Infide, your Parade is made here to your Outfide; And by the fame Rule, if *Tierce* be made at you, go round the Sword clofe, and bring it to a *Quarte Parade*; fo that *Quarte* will be parried by a *Tierce Parade*, and *Tierce* by a *Quarte Parade*. Thefe COUNTER PARADES are very good againft the *Slips*, viz. When your Adverfary *flips* you and you attempt to *bind* him, follow his Sword round, and try to *bind* him there again, which is called *counter-binding*; fo that when he flips your *Binding* in *Quarte*, you muft try to *counter-bind* him in *Quarte* again; and if he flips that, try to bind him in *Tierce*; which if he flips, follow his Sword round as before, and make t'other Trial: But as you endeavour to *counter-bind*, and he continues *flipping* your Attempts, he may, as he *flips*, make home a Thruft at you, which you muft be prepared to parry thus: As you go to *counter-bind* him in *Tierce*, he may *flip*, and thruft *Quarte* over, as you offer to *counter-bind* him in *Quarte*, you muft parry that with your ROUND PARADE for *Tierce*, and *refpoft* accordingly; or when you are at any Time *flip'd* in your *Counter-Bindings*, or in your *Counter-Parades*, your beft Play will be to return quick back to your plain and common Parades for *Quarte* and *Tierce:* As for inftance, When you intend to *counter-bind Quarte*, and he flips you there, and goes home in *Quarte over*, your *Tierce Parade* will be the fafeft; becaufe, were you to parry *Quarte over* by a ROUND PARADE, your Wrift would be fo much tired, that your PARADE would be too flow, by following one COUNTER-PARADE with another; fo that when you offer to *counter-bind*, or counter-parry *Tierce*, and you are *flip'd*, and *Quarte* made at you, your *Half-Circle Parade* will be then your beft; tho' your COUNTER-PARADE for that *Quarte* would do very well, and perhaps difarm him, if you have Room to retire as you make it, but not otherways fafe. But if you fhould fecure his Sword by *Binding*, and give him an Invitation to take your Open in the contrary, and he fhould take it accordingly, your only Parade then will be the ROUND PARADE; efpecially in *binding* his *Quarte*, and leaving him an Open in *Quarte over*; for by this PARADE. you fo fecure his Sword, that he can hardly efcape being hit, if you are any thing quick on the *Refpoft*, either in *Quarte*, *Flanconade*, or *Quarte over Arm*, which are excellent *Refpoft* Thrufts, particularly from this COUNTER PARADE.

"*Schol.* Why are thefe better *Refpoft* Thrufts from this ROUND PARADE, than from the *Firft Parade* in *Quarte?*

"*Mafter.* Becaufe in your ROUND PARADE, you generally parry with a lower Wrift than in plain Parade; which confequently brings your Adverfary to a greater Open, and therefore the eafier he is to be hit; and the lower you bring his Sword by this COUNTER PARADE for *Tierce*, the eafier your *Flanconade* can get in; and the eafier you'll baulk him, by difengaging, and thrufting in *Quarte over:* But when you *bind Tierce*, and he takes the Opportunity of fending you home in *Quarte*, being the Thruft you left him open, I do not fo much recommend the ROUND PARADE here, as your *Half-Circle*; neither will I advife you to ufe it, when you are obliged to Fence in a narrow Room, or Paffage; becaufe this PARADE is made with fuch a Circle, that your Sword may be ftop'd, probably by the Wall, or other Hindrances, and were you not to retire upon it, would be too late to parry a quick Thruft: For its being made Round the Sword muft neceffarily take up a longer time, than a Parade that goes but Half Way, or One Third of the Circle round; which is the Extent that the other parades go. The General Advantage of the COUNTER PARADES is, to baffle and baulk the Defign of all *Half-Thrufts*, and *Single* and *Double Feints*; and are alfo proper PA-RADES, if Occafion calls, for a Defence in the Dark; or at any Time againft a *Scatterer*, viz. in *Fencing* Terms, an irregular *Fencer*. In fine, the *Slips*, and *Counter Parades*, are the beft Defenfives in a Field of any on the Sword: But where you are confin'd, your Under-Counter, and Half-Circles, are the fafeft Parades.

"*Schol.* When the COUNTER PARADES are made ufe of againft me, how muft I manage?

"*Mafter.* You muft go round his Sword thus: As foon as you have difcovered that the ROUND PARADES are thofe which he chiefly makes ufe of, and you intend to give him a *Quarte*, you muft fhew him your Point in *Quarte*, as you do on a *Feint*, and fend it clofe over and round his Sword; and as he endeavours to fecure it by the ROUND PARADE, you may lodge your Thruft in *Quarte*: And to thruft *Tierce* againft his ROUND PARADE, you muft fhew him your Point there, and go quick and clofe round his Sword, and give him in *Quarte over Arm*.

"*Schol.* How fhall I prevent my Adverfary of deceiving me in the like Manner?

"*Mafter.* Your beft Way will be, as in a Part of this Leffon before obferved, *viz.* in the *Slips* upon the *Counter-Bindings*; that is, when you don't meet your Opponent's Sword within the Bounds of your COUNTER PARADE, to return quick back to a plain Parade: As for Inftance, When you counter-parry *Quarte*, and can't touch his Sword within the Circumference of that PARADE, return quick back to your *Firft Parade* for *Quarte*, and there you'll meet it: And likewife in the COUNTER PARADE for *Tierce*, when you don't meet the Sword within the Bounds of its PARADE, return to your *Tierce Parade*, and there you may fecure it. You may alfo *Gather the Sword* by the Help of thefe COUNTER PARADES.

"*Schol.* What is the Meaning of Gathering the Sword?

"*Mafter.* When your Adverfary prefents his Guard in an unufual Pofition, *viz.* with his Point perhaps within a Foot of the Ground, or with a very much curv'd or low Arm, with the Point in conftant Motion, this, tho' a very loofe and open Guard, is the moft dangerous and puzzling to attack of any on the Sword.

"*Schol.* Pray where lies the Danger in attacking this Guard?

"*Mafter.* In thrufting home upon it, you may receive another the fame Time.

"*Schol.* How then muft I manage it?

"*Mafter.* You muft attack it with your COUNTER PARADES, which gives him an Opportunity to fend in a Thruft upon you; and that muft be your Defign; becaufe there is more Safety in Refpofting, than in making the firft Thruft, on any Guard that can be prefented: And this Guard, with a low Point, you muft endeavour to raife to the fame Pofition of your own, by the COUNTER PARADES, *Under-Counter Parades*, or *Half-Circles*, that you may then order it as your LESSON directs: And in *Gathering the Sword*, you muft take Care that your Adverfary does not flip, and get in with you; to prevent which, you muft always be ready to take to a Parade in that Open which you leave by *Gathering*. On this Guard, does it generally with a Defign that a

Thruft fhould be made at him, that he may parry it with his Left Hand, and be in with his Opponent the fame Time: Therefore if you can't *gather* this Guard to fome other Pofition, as before fhewn, a Half-Thruft may make him raife it, or take to a Parade; or a Stroke at his Wrift, with a Flirt of your Point, may probably make him alter his Guard; or if he anfwers your Half-Thruft by his *Left-Hand Parade*, you muft be ready to parry his Thruft, that he fends from that Parade, with your Left Hand, and be in with him if you can.

"LESSON XII.
"*The* Cuts *over the* Point.

"THE CUTS are generally ufed on an *Attack*, againft the *Middle Guard*, thus: When you defign to give in a *Quarte* by *Cutting over*, you muft engage in *Tierce*, and raifing your *Feeble* over your Adverfary's Point, drop in *Quarte*, difengage over his Point, you may go round his Sword, and give him *Quarte over:* And if you engage in Quarte, difengage over his Point, and in with him a Tierce; or go round his Sword, and lodge your Thruft in Quarte. But thefe CUTS, unlefs cautioufly manag'd, are very dangerous; for by drawing in your Arm, and raifing your *Feeble* over his Point, gives him fuch an Open, that he may eafily, as you difengage, get in a Thruft with you; unlefs your Defign is fuch, that he fhould thruft at that Open you leave him as you difengage over his Point, that you may parry, and *refpoft:* If fo, I approve your Intention; for I think it the fafeft Way to play this LESSON; efpecially when you have a brisk Swordfman to encounter: You may alfo *Cut over* your Adverfary's Point, as he binds you in either *Quarte*, or *Tierce*, and make home your Thruft; or make a Half-Thruft as you *Cut over*; and as he anfwers that, give in your Thruft.

"*Schol.* How fhall I parry thefe CUTS OVER THE POINT, when play'd againft me?

"*Mafter.* The *Counter-Parades* are beft when you take upon you the *Middle Guard*; but againft the *Streight Guard*, this LESSON will not much avail, without firft difordering the Guard, which you muft take Care to prevent by the *Slips*.

"LESSON XIII.
"Traverfing.

"THIS LESSON fome Profeffors think not worth their Notice, becaufe it is fo much practiced at *Back-Sword*; but in my Opinion is as neceffary at the *Small*.

"*Schol.* How muft TRAVERSING be perform'd?

"*Mafter.* When your Adverfary waits for your *Attack*, which you may eafily difcover his Defign, if he makes any Delay after prefenting his Guard, by TRAVERSING, you may diforder his Guard, and Pofture, and *Time* him, or tempt him to thruft at you, and then parry, and *refpoft*. To TRAVERSE, you muft ftep with your Right Foot about a Foot towards your Outfide, and about Half a Foot forward, bringing your Left Foot up behind it in your Pofture; and by TRAVERSING thus about to the Right you may obtain your End: And when you TRAVERSE to the Left, ftep with your Right Foot about a Foot beyond, and acrofs your Left, and about Half a foot forward, bringing up your Left quick in its Pofture.

"*Schol.* When a Man TRAVERSES upon me, can I make any Advantage by it?

"*Mafter.* Yes, You may *Time* him on his TRAVERSE, as you fhall by and by fee; or you may ftop his TRAVERSE by a Half-Thruft, and make the beft of that, as you have been often fhewn: And as he TRAVERSES, lift up your Right Foot, turning on the Ball of your Left, and place your Right down in its Pofture, always facing your Adverfary, that you may be ready to receive his *Attack*, and thruft on the *Refpoft*, or Time his TRAVERSE.

"LESSON XIV.
"*The* Gliffades.

"MY FOURTEENTH LESSON is, *The* GLISSADES.

"*Schol*. What is the Meaning of GLISSADE?

"*Mafter*. A GLISSADE is a *French* Word, that fignifies Slipping or Sliding; and in *Fencing*, is a Thruft made clofe to the Sword, which you may give on the *Middle*, or *Streight Guard*, without difengaging: And when fuch a Thruft is parry'd, and a Retreat made on the Parade, by *doubling your Attack*, and thrufting without difengaging, you have a better Chance to get in a Thruft, than you were you to difengage to give it; but as you flip along the Sword, if a Parade be made, your Thruft muft be given in the contrary. You may alfo GLISSADE the *High Guard*, thus: As this Guard is prefented, take upon you the fame as before obferv'd, and advance clofe on the Infide of the Guard, raifing it up a little as you advance, directing your Point at your Adverfary's Face, to make him expect a Thruft there, and take to a Parade, that you may get the Opportunity of Slipping under his Arm towards his Arm-Pit: And if you engage in *Tierce*, and run your Sword clofe along his, raifing it up a little as you march, and pre-fenting your Point at his Face, that he may take to a Parade, you may then flip, and give your Thruft in *Quarte*.

"*Schol*. When the GLISSADES and *Double Attacks* are made againft me, what is my beft Defence?

"*Mafter*. Before I can fully refove you, it will be neceffary for you to learn my Two next LESSONS; however, I will fhew you fome neceffary Rules againft them, which you may learn without their Affiftance: As for Inftance, If your Adverfary engages you in *Quarte*, on your *Streight Guard*, clofe to your Sword, and makes home his Thruft there, as you feel his Sword prefs againft yours, go to your proper Parade for that Thruft, which muft always be according to the Side he makes his Thruft on, *viz*. If he thrufts clofe to your Sword, on the *Streight Guard*, and on the infide Line, your Parade for that muft be your *Half-Circle* to your Infide: And when a Thruft is given of the Outfide on the fame Guard, and clofe to the Sword, your outfide *Half-Circle* is your beft Parade: But if you *break Meafure* as a Thruft your Adverfary makes, that you may difcover the Pofition of his *Longe*, and be the better able to manage him in the *Affault*, he may *double his Attack*, and thruft on the fame Line again; if fo, you muft keep your Ground as he comes up to make the fecond Thruft at you; and as he thrufts on your Infide Line, which on this Guard muft be a *Low Quarte*, you may make the fame Thruft at him as he thrufts; and if your Thruft be ftrong, and clofe to the Sword on that Line, you may clear your felf, and be in with him: And if your Adverfary *doubles his Attack* of the Outfide of your *Streight Guard* you may, as you parry that by the outfide *Half-Circle*, give him the *German Thruft*: You may alfo keep your Ground as he *doubles*, and difarm him, as fhall be in my LAST LESSON fhewn you: And if you keep the *Middle Guard*, and an Attack in Quarte is *doubled* on you, you may Time thus, *viz*. As he makes his Thruft in *Quarte*, if with a low Wrift, you may parry that by the *Firft Parade* in *Quarte*, and make home *Quarte* upon him with Safety the fame Time; but if he makes his *Quarte* with a ftiff and well mounted Wrift, *Flanconade*, by the Help of the Left hand, I take to be the fafeft Thruft you can Time this *Quarte* with; efpecially when you're at Half-Sword, which this *Attack* being *doubled* brings you to:

But when an *Attack* is *doubled* on you in *Tierce*, there is no fafe Way to take *Time* upon it; therefore I muft recommend to you the *Difarms* for that, efpecially if you are con-fin'd; or to your *Left-Handed Parade*, by giving Way with your Sword as he preffes on it to get in his *Tierce*, that you may have the clearer Sweep with your Left Hand, to parry it off, and then be in with him. A *Double Retreat*, where you have Room to make it, is alfo a fafe Defence.

"*Schol.* How muft a *Double Retreat* be made?

"*Mafter.* To *Retreat double*, you muft ftep back with your Right Foot about Twenty Inches behind your Left, then your Left the fame Diftance behind your Right, keep-ing your Feet ftill in the fame Pofition as in your proper Pofture, *viz.* with your Right Toe and Infide of your Left Inftep always facing your Adverfary; and by thus *Retreat-ing*, you have the fame Chance to parry, and *refpoft*, as had your *Retreat* been *fingle*, and the *Attack* not *doubled*.

"LESSON XV.

"*The* Single Time; *and* Counter Time,

or Time againft Time.

"TO TIME, or TAKE TIME, as our *Fencing* Terms run, is to make a full Thruft on your Adverfary on his *March*, or as he attempts to *bind*, *beat*, or diforder your Guard by any Means, to flip his Motion, and make home your Thruft; or as your Adverfary makes a Thruft at you, you may make another at him the fame Time, and be in with him, and fave your felf: And to perform thofe, as aforementioned, you muft manage thus, *viz.* Let your Adverfary take the *Attack*; and if it be the *Middle Guard* he keeps, and marches on you in *Quarte*, keep your Ground, and by a full Thruft in *Quarte*, you may ftop his *March*; or if he engages you in *Tierce* on his *March*, you may run him home *Tierce* clofe to the Sword; for in the *Middle Guard*, you may remember, both *Quarte* and *Tierce* are open; and thofe Thrufts you take the TIME on his *March* with, you fend home without difengaging, which makes them fo fwift, they feldom fail of hitting: But you may take the TIME, by difengaging, thus: On his *March* in *Quarte*, difenage quick and clofe, and you may give *Tierce*; or as he marches in *Tierce*, by the fame Rule, give him *Quarte*: You may TIME the *Streight Guard* on a *March*, by *Low Quarte* on the Infide Line, or *Flanconade*; but this Guard feldom comes within Dif-tance, which makes it difficult to take the TIME upon it. To TIME one Thruft with another, this muft be your Method: When *Quarte* is made at you with a flack and low Wrift, you may make home a Thruft in *Quarte*, you may *Flanconade* him, if his Thruft be made with a ftiff Wrift. You may alfo TIME *Flanconade* with the *German Thruft*, when your Parade is the outfide *Half-Circle*; and when you parry *Flanconade* by the *Quarte Parade* with a low Wrift, you may give him *Flanconade* again, by the Help of your Left Hand. You may take the TIME upon *Quarte* and *Tierce*, without making any Parade with your Sword, thus: When you perceive either of thefe Thrufts coming, turn quick a quarter round on the Ball of your Right Foot to the Left about, ftepping with your Left Foot about Two Feet behind your Right, and fpringing to a ftiff Right Knee, as if you had made your *Longe* backward, bringing the Infide of your Left Toe level with your Right Heel, with your Left Knee bent right over your Toe, leaning your Body a little back to give the Thruft made at you the more Room to pafs by your Body, that you may give your Thuft on the TIME with as little Danger as poffible. The Pofition of this Guard and Pofture cannot be eafily explain'd without the Help of the CUTS, the conveniency of which I have herein laid down, together with the Inftructions you have had of me in the Practical Part of this Art, may make your FENCING appear, to any unprejudic'd and competent Judge, polite and well grounded.

"*Schol.* I have heard it afferted, that a *Feint* may be TIM'D; but I was of a contrary Opinion: Becaufe a *Feint* is, or ought to be made fo fwift, that Thruft never could get in upon it; I therefore appeal to you whether or no I'm right?

"*Mafter.* You may TIME a *Feint* made in *Quarte* with *Quarte*, and a *Feint* in *Tierce* with *Tierce*, and a *Feint under the Arm* with *Quarte over Arm*; and in the like Manner you may TIME a Half-Thruft: But there is great Danger in taking TIME upon either *Feint*, or Half-Thruft, left a Thruft fhould quickly follow the *Feint*, and be in with you the fame Time you hit him; and where Two Perfons engag'd thruft together, they are look'd upon to be rafh and ignorant, befides the unfpeakable bad Confequenes attending it. In *Fencing* Terms, thefe Sort of Thrufts are call'd, *Counter Temps Thrufts*, which look fo ridiculous in a *Fencing School*, that there is a Forfeiture for each Perfon to pay for committing fuch a Blunder; therefore I advife you to be very cautious againft fuch dangerous and hot headed Practice, and mind your *Refpoft* Play, which is your fafeft to prevent *Counter Temps* Thrufts. There are feveral Gentlemen, that efteem it a nice Point in *Fencing*, as his Opponent makes his Thruft at him, to bring up his Right Heel clofe to his Left Inftep, leaning forward with a full ftretch'd Arm, expecting his Adverfary to rufh himfelf on his Point, and reach fhort of him with his Thruft; and this they call TIME *on the Sword*; but in my Opinion, it is properly *Giving a Point*.

"*Schol.* How fhall I prevent my Adverfary of TAKING TIME on me, or *Giving me the Point?*

"*Mafter.* You muft march up to your Adverfary, and give him an Open, as if you did it accidentally; which if he takes, you muft parry, and *refpoft:* Or you may COUNTER-TIME him, *viz.* As he makes a Thruft at you, you may parry and thruft together, thus; When you march in your *Streight Guard*, flope your Point a little, and that gives him an Open in *Low Quarte*, or the Infide Line, or in *Flanconade*; and if he takes *Flanconade*, give the *German Thruft* on your Parade; or if he thrufts on your infide Line, make a full Thruft at him on the fame Line; and thefe Two Thrufts well manag'd are good Parades for *Flanconade*, and *Low Quarte* on the *Half-Circle* Line: So that the COUNTER-TIME is no more than the TIMING one Thruft with another, as before fhewn; and in Effect the fame as quick *Refpofting*. To prevent the *Point being given*, you muft endeavour to entice your Adverfary to make a firft thruft at you, that you may thruft on the *Refpoft*; and if you bring him to that, you put it out of his Power to *Give the Point* as he recovers. But a *Point* may be *given* from the Pofition of any Guard that can be prefented againft you, if you make the firft Thruft upon it, tho' the *Giver of the Point* may receive your Thruft the fame Time; which proves it in fome Refpects like the *Counter Temps* Thrufts, and is full as fcandalous; and feldom practiced, but when Two Perfons are engaged, and One of them finds his Opponent too hard for him, then the One, as his laft Shift, *Gives* his Opponent *the Point*, if he can: And tho' this is practiced very often with *Foils*, yet I dare fay, few or none in his Senfes would fuffer himfelf to be kill'd, for the little Advantage he could propofe by killing another at the fame Time. The farther Affiftance that the Left Hand may be to the Right in the Ufe of the *Small-Sword*, is my next LESSON.

"LESSON XVI.

"*The Advantage that the* Left Hand *may be to the* Right.

"THE PARADES with the Left hand ought not to be aim'd by any but thofe who are well vers'd in plain *Fencing*; for there is more Danger than Safety in them, when ufed by fuch as have not had a great deal of Experience that Way; but to thofe that are capable of making the beft Ufe of them, they are very neceffary, tho' in a *Fencing School* feldom taught or practiced, left it fhould encourage the Leaners to neglect their Parades with the Sword, which are the moft fignificant and chief Defenfives a Man ought to depend upon; and the PARADES wiyth the LEFT HAND only to be ventur'd at on fpecial Occafions; fuch as when your parades with the Sword begin to fail, or more than one Perfon be aginft you in the Engagement: And the fafeft Opportunities to make thefe PARADES are as follow, *viz.* Slide clofe under yur Adverfary's Sword with yours, keeping your Wrift of the Infide of his Guard, and your Point to his Outfide, inviting him to force home a Tierce upon you; which if he takes, you muft let your *Feeble* yield a little to his Prefs, that you may have the clearer Sweep to parry it off with your LEFT HAND, and get in with him in *Quarte:* You may alfo *bind* him in *Quarte*, and by making a fmall Delay there, may probably entice him to fend you *Quarte over Arm*, which you muft parry with your LEFT HAND, and give him a full *Quarte* in Return; and likewife, when you *bind* in *Tierce*, you are open in *Quarte*; and if he thrufts there, go to your LEFT HAND PARADE, and give him in a *Quarte*; aand when he *flips* you, as you endeavour to *bind*, or otherways diforder his Guard, and makes home his Thruft upon it, you may likewife parry that Thruft, whether *Quarte* or *Tierce*, with your LEFT HAND, and fend in a *Quarte*. Obferve, that in parrying with your LEFT HAND, you do it with the Palm and Fingers floping down, and from you to your Outfide; and that your Thruft from that Parade, is plain Quarte only: You may alfo parry fome of his *Refpoft* Thrufts with your LEFT HAND, thus: When you thruft *Tierce*, throw your LEFT HAND with an extended Arm, under your Right Wrift, with the Back of your Hand clofe to it, and fupporting your Thruft there as before taught. give hime only a *Seconde* Open, which your LEFT HAND muft parry, and your Thruft from that Parade as before obferv'd: And when you thruft *Quarte*, you may throw your LEFT HAND in the like Manner, and parry his *Flanconade*, and make your Thruft as before fhewn: But when you parry *Flanconade* with your LEFT HAND, let it be when his Thruft is made at you with a *Foil* rather than a Sword, left the Thruft fhould come in fo clofe under your Arm, as to pin one Arm to the other, or perhaps your Left Arm to your Body. There is yet another Way your LEFT HAND may be ferviceable, *viz.* When your Right Hand is tired in the Engagement, you may flip your Sword into your LEFT HAND; and tho' perhaps you can't handle it there fo dextroufly as with your Right, yet you may make a fhift to defend your felf, 'til your Right Hand recruits a little; but to do this compleatly, might be of vaft Service to you. There ae feveral other Ways the LEFT HAND may be helpful to the Right; but none I think fo fafe as the afore-mentioned, except in the DISARMS, which is my next LESSON.

"*Schol.* But how am I to manage a Man that plays this LESSON againft me?

"*Mafter.* When you fee an Open given you, you may expect it is with a Defign that you fhould thruft there, that he may take an Advantage of it; therefore never thruft home at fuch an Open, but rather, as I obferv'd to you before, make a Half-Thruft there, which will difcover his Defign; and if you find out that his LEFT HAND PARADE is his Play, you muft obferve his Manner of doing it; and the next Open you perceive your Gentleman is fo kind to give you, half-thruft as before; and according to the Manner he andwers that by his LEFT HAND PARADE, give in your Thruft: For perhaps his Method of parrying with his LEFT HAND may be with his Fingers up-right; which, tho' contrary to my Method, is practiced by feveral of my Profeffion, and may anfwer the End as well; and againft that Way of Parrying, you muft difengage, or flip, as you do the *Foil*, and give your Thruft in the contrary: As for Inftance, If you make a Half-Thruft in *Quarte*, and he takes a Sweep with his LEFT HAND below your Sword, in order to parry it to his Outfide, like a *Tierce*, you muft flip his Parade, and thruft *Quarte*: But if he parrys with his Fingers down, and his Elbow a little raif'd, you muft flip over his Wrift to give in your Thruft; and by thrufting clofe to the Sword, will in a great Meafure prevent PARADES with the LEFT HAND.

"LESSON XVII.

"*The* Difarms.

"MY SEVENTEENTH and laft LESSON is, The DISARMS: And tho' there are various Ways of DISARMING, I fhall cite only fuch as are fafeft: As for Inftance, When you parry a Thruft by the *Firft Parade* in *Quarte*, make this Parade with your Wrift about Six Inches lower than your Breaft, and on your Parade make a fhort *Longe*, keeping clofe to your Parade, 'til you bring your Left Hand over and a-crofs it, feizing your Adverfary's *Fort* clofe to the *Shell*, with your Fingers under the *Fort*, and Thumb on the *Shell*; then give a fudden Pull to you with your Left Hand, and at the fame Time, thruft his *Feeble* with the *Fort* of your Sword from you; and that done quick and ftrong, will force him to quit his Gripe. You may DISARM from your *Tierce* and *Under-Counter Parade*, thus: Keep clofe to your Parade, and bring up your Left Foot clofe behind his Right Heel as he is on his *Longe*, and throw your Left Arm over his Sword arm, and with your Left hand feize his Fingers clofe to the *Gripe* of his sword, to prevent his flipping it to his Left Hand; and with a contracted Arm, and Elbow rais'da as high as your Shoulder, prefent your Point at his Breaft, that he may acknowl-edge his Life to be in your Hands, or you will quickly dispatch him. The Reafon your Left Foot ought to be brought up clofe behind his Right on his *Longe*, is, to trip him down, if he refifts after being feiz'd. You may likewife DISARM upon a Thruft in *Quarte* by your *Under-Counter Parade*, without the Help of the Left hand, or any Diforder in your Guard: To perform this, you muft take his Thruft *Quarte* on the *Feeble* with a quick and ftrong *Under-Counter*, and it will feldom fail to drive the sword out of your Adverfary's Hand; and if you fhould fail in it, you are in lefs Danger than when you fail in any other DISARM; for by turning up your Wrift, you are in your Guard again. On your *Half-Circle Parade*, you may DISARM thus: When you make your Parade, keep clofe to it, and direct your Adverfary's Sword, which you have on the *Fort* of yours, under your Left Arm, and ftep up with your Left Foot, turning on the Ball of your Right, and with your Left hand under his Sword Hand, feize his Fingers clofe to his Gripe, or if you feize his *Shell* with your Fingers in the Infide of it, that will do 'til you do his Bufinefs.

"Now, Sir, You have learnt all the LESSONS I think needful in FENCING: Not-withftanding, Sir, I hope you'll keep in Practice what you have learnt, while you have the Opportunity of your prefent Mafter; for when you are depriv'd of him, it is prob-able another Profeffor of this Science may not think thefe Parts of *America* worth his Attendance.

"*Schol.* The Knowledge you have given me in this Art, fufficiently convinces me of the Ufefulnefs of it, and I will take all Opportunities to improve it.

"*Mafter.* There is a great Satisfaction in being prepared for Self-defence, Sir; befides the many other Advantages this Exercife affords, which I hope you'll think fufficient to excite you to the Practice of it.

I am, Sir,

Your very humble Servant,

Edward Blackwell."

* * *

Advertisement for a fencing school, Maryland Gazette, No. 2, 3 May 1745.

"AT *Kent* County School, in *Chefter* Town, *Maryland*, young Gentlemen are boarded, and taught the *Greek* and *Latin* Tongues, Writing, Arithmetic, Merchants Accounts, Surveying, Navigation, the ufe of the Globes, by the largeft and moft accurate Pair in *America*: Alfo any other Parts of the Mathematics, by

CHARLES PEALE.

"*N.B.* Young Gentlemen may be inftructed in Fencing and Dancing by very good Mafters."

* * *

Advertisement for fencing instruction, Virginia Gazette, No. ?, 20 March 1752, supplement.

"The Subfcriber who lodges at Mr. *Finnie*'s, in *Williamsburg*, teaches the Art of Fencing, Dancing, and the *French* Tongue; and is ready to begin as foon as he can get a reafonable Number of Scholars. *Le Chevalier de Peyronny.*"

* * *

John Armstrong, poet, refers to fencing in Armstrong, *The Art of Preserving Health,* 4th ed. (London and Boston: Green & Russell, 1757), 37.

"WHATE'ER you ftudy, in whate'er you fweat,
Indulge your tafte. Some love the manly foils;
The tennis fome; and fome the graceful dance."

* * *

Excerpt from an advertisement for a dancing academy at Upper Marlborough, Maryland, Maryland Gazette, No. 650, 20 October 1757.

"The Subfcriber alfo Teaches the Noble Science of DEFENCE and Purfuit of the SMALL-SWORD, with All the favourite Thrufts, Guards and Parades; the Method of Difarming, and Fencing againft rafh Men (who are not skilful in the Science) with Blunts or Sharps, as now practised in the City of *London*; a Science very neceffary for every Gentleman to know, efpecially in this Time of imminent Danger."

JOHN ORMSBY."

* * *

Charles Carter, Virginia planter, expresses his wish for his grandsons to receive instruction in fencing in his will, 10 September 1762, in "The Will of Charles Carter of Cleve," Virginia Magazine of History and Biography, Vol. 31, No. 1 (January 1923), 62.

"It is my will and meaning that they [his sons John and Landon] shall be continued at school to learn the languages, Mathematicks, Phylosophy, dancing and fencing till they are well accomplished...."

* * *

Advertisement for a fencing academy, Massachusetts Gazette and Boston News-Letter, 13 June 1765, reprinted in Robert Francis Seybolt, *The Private Schools of Colonial Boston* (Cambridge, Mass.: Harvard University Press, 1935), 50-51.

"WILLIAM TURNER

"BEGS LEAVE to acquaint Ladies and Gentlemen of the Town and Country, that he has opened his Dancing and Fencing School, in the Room where his Father formerly taught, —in which he will continue to teach those polite Accomplishments in the Newest Taste, and most approved Method, at the usual Price."

* * *

Advertisement for a fencing school, Boston Gazette and Country Journal, No. 600, 29 September 1766.

"Fencing and Dancing,

"TAught in a genteel, expeditious and reafonable Manner, by WILLIAM POPE, who lately arrived in this City from the *Weft Indies*: Any Gentlemen or Ladies inclinable to employ him, may be waited upon at their Houfes or Lodgings, by fending a Line directed to him at Capt. *Richard Tripe*'s in Ann ftreet, near the Draw Bridge.

"*N.B.* He will attend on a Number of Gentlemen or Ladies, at any Boarding School or Academy within Ten or 15 Miles of the Town, by directing as above."

* * *

Advertisement for fencing instruction, Boston Evening Post, No. 1783, 27 November 1769.

"To lovers of the noble Science of Defence.

"GENTLEMEN who chufe to be inftructed in the Art commonly called the BACK-SWORD, are defired to apply to DONALD McALPINE, formerly Serjeant of the 78th Regiment, who will inftruct them in faid Science to their entire Satisfaction, for *Ten Shillings* Sterling per Month, at his Room in Mr. *Carne*'s House near the Meeting-Houfe, New-Bofton, from Hours of One until Five in the Evening.

"*N.B.* Any Gentlemen who chufe to be inftructed in faid Science privately, may be waited upon by applying to said MacAlpine. —Likewife faid McAlpine will inftruct Gentlemen and Ladies in FRENCH, in a most concife Manner and on reafonable Terms.   DONALD McALPINE."

* * *

Advertisement for a fencing school, Massachusetts Gazette and Boston Weekly News-Letter, 28 June 1770, reprinted in Robert Francis Seybolt, *The Private Schools of Colonial Boston* (Cambridge, Mass.: Harvard University Press, 1935), 61.

"DANCING, Small-sword, Back-sword, and the FRENCH LANGUAGE, taught by WILLIAM POPE, at the the School occupied by Mr. William Turner, opposite to William Vassal, Esq;

"Constant Attendance given at the above School."

"Those who will please to send their Children, to dance may depend that great Care will be taken to Instruct them."

* * *

Advertisement for fencing instruction, Massachusetts Gazette and Boston Weekly News-Letter, No. 3536, 18 July 1771.

"BONTAMPS FARTIER

HEREBY Acquaints the Public, that he keeps his

FENCING SCHOOL

in the Room, formerly Occupied by Mr. William Turner, as a Dancing Room, where he teacheth the SMALL SWORD, on Tuefdays, Wednefdays and Fridays in the Forenoon.

"The faid Fartier lives in the Houfe of Mr. Fofdick, in Milk-Street, oppofite the Door of the Old-South Meeting-Houfe."

* * *

Benjamin Rush, Philadelphia physician, recommends fencing as exercise, circa 1772, in Rush, *Sermons to Gentlemen upon Temperance and Exercise* (Philadelphia: John Dunlap, 1772), 32.

"FENCING calls forth moft of the mufcles into exercife, particularly thofe which move the limbs. The brain is likewife roufed by it, through the avenue of the eyes, and its action, as in the cafe of mufic, is propagated to the whole fyftem. It has long been a fubject of complaint, that the human fpecies has been degenerating for thefe feveral centuries. When we fee the coats of mail of our anceftors, who fought under the Edwards and Henries of former ages, we wonder how they moved, much more how they atchieved fuch great exploits, beneath the weight of fuch maffy coverings. We grant that rum—tobacco-tea—and fome other luxuries of modern invention, have had a large fhare in weakning the ftamina of our conftitutions, and thus producing a more feeble race of men; yet me muft attribute much of our great inferiority in ftrength, fize and agility to our forefathers, to the difufe which the invention of gun-powder and fire arms hath introduced of thofeathletic exercifes, which were fo much practifed in former ages, as a part of military difcipline."

* * *

Advertisement for fencing instruction, Rivington's New-York Gazetteer, No. 61, 16 June 1774.

"A PERSON, well qualified to teach the art of
FENCING,
Would be glad to inftruct fome gentlemen in the fcience; if so will engage, he will undertake it at 20s. per month; and 15s. entrance. For further information enquire of J.L.C. ROOME, Efq."

* * *

Philip Vickers Fithian, tutor at Nomini Hall, Virginia, refers to fencing, August 1774, in Fithian to John Peck, 12 August 1774, in Hunter Dickinson Farish, ed., *Journal and Letters of Philip Vickers Fithian, 1773-1774. A Plantation Tutor of the Old Dominion* (Charlottesville, Va.: University Press of Virginia, 1957 [1943]), 161.

"...because any young gentleman travelling through the Colony, as I said before, is presum'd to be acquainted with Dancing, Boxing, playing the Fiddle, & Small-Sword, & Cards."

* * *

Advertisement for fencing instruction, Rivington's New-York Gazetteer, No. 92, 13 January 1775.

"MUSIC, FENCING and DANCING,
William Charles Hulett,
Very gratefully fenfible of the many Favors he has received from his Friends in the Courfe of a twenty Years Refidence in this City,

Begs Leave to inform them, and the Public in general,
That his School in Broad Street is now re-opened; and that he continues to teach at
Home and Abroad, In MUSIC.] The Violin, Guittar, and German Flute, In DANCING.]
According to the prefent Tafte, both in London and Paris) The Louvre, Minuet,
Minuette Dauphine, Rigadoon, Bretagne, the Allemande, Double Minuet, Minuet by
eight, Hornpipes, the Cotillions, and Englifh Country Dances.

For FENCING.] He has prevailed on a Mafter to attend his School, the Variety and
Fatigues of his other Bufinefs, which he means to go through with Juftice to his Scholars, and permitting him to engage in that Department."

* * *

Advertisement for a fencing academy, Rivington's New-York Gazetteer, No. 103, 6 April
1775, supplement.

"French, Fencing, and Dancing
ACADEMY
They intend to run an Academy for Dancing and Fencing, where Ladies and Gentlemen (each in their department) who have not perfected themfelves in thofe agreeable
accomplifhments, may be taught in fuch a manner, as to add grace and beauty to the
deportment of either fex, in the genteeleft characters in life....

[three-dot triangle upside down] If there is any gentleman in town acquainted with
the art of
fencing, they are defired to call at Mr. Myford's...."

* * *

Jabez Fitch, Connecticut lieutenant, observes fencing on Long Island, 16 June 1777, in
William H. Sabine, ed., *The New-York Diary of Lieutenant Jabez Fitch of the 17th (Connecticut) Regiment, from August 22, 1776 to December 15, 1777* (New York: pvt. ptg.,
1954), 179.

"...then came back to Mrs: Rappellyes Barn, where I see some Sword playing, after
which we came home,...."

* * *

Enos Stevens, Charlestown, New Hampshire loyalist lieutenant, takes fencing instruction,
2 August 1778, in Charles Knowlton Bolton, ed., "A Fragment of the Diary of Lieutenant
Enos Stevens, Tory, 1777-1778," New England Quarterly, Vol. 11, No. 2 (June 1938),
386.

"2^d Lords dy Capt Mcalpian [?] came for to in struct the gentlemen the broad sword
&c. I enterd as one of his [s]collars at the rate of one guinea per month. Now the chief
of our exercise is in the school."

* * *

Alexander Graydon, Philadelphia resident, recalls his fencing, circa 1778, in Graydon,
*Memoirs of His Own Time, With Reminiscences of the Men and Events of the Revolu-
tion,* ed. by John Stockton Littell (Philadelphia: Lindsay & Blakiston, 1846), 111-112.

"The instruction I received from Pike, I considerably improved by practice, and began
to grow vain of my skill, until I met Major Clow (or Clough) of Colonel Baylor's
dragoons, who had been a pupil of Angelo and others of the best masters in Europe.
He soon convinced me that I had still much room for improvement; though he was
pleased to assure me, that I was by far the best fencer he had met with in America, and
much superior to Benson, a fencing master in New York.

"During the time of my being with Pike, Mentges, who was afterwards a Colonel in our service, had opened a fencing school. Among his scholars were Messrs. Robeson and Bradford;.... Coming into the school I was asked to take a foil, and in succession contended with each of these gentlemen; but the result was unlucky for Mentges, as it too plainly evinced his incapacity for the business he had undertaken, and of course, soon deprived him of his pupils."

* * *

Alexander Hewatt, South Carolina historian, refers to fencing in that state, circa 1779, in Hewatt, *An Historical Account of the Rise and Progress of the Colonies of South Carolina and Georgia*, 2 vols., Vol. 2 (London: Alexander Donaldson, 1779), 294.

"They [South Carolinians] difcover no bad tafte for the polite arts, fuch as mufic, drawing, fencing and dancing;...."

* * *

John Brown, student at William and Mary College, Virginia, considers fencing instruction, February 1780, in Brown to his uncle, William Preston, 15 February 1780, in "Glimpses of Old College Life," William and Mary Quarterly, 1st Series, Vol. 9, No. 2 (October 1902), 76.

"I have received yours of the 6th of Jan^r in which you recommended me to spend some time at the Fencing School; this I should chearfully do, as I am very sensible that the knowledge of the sword is a very important accomplishment; but money is so very scarce with me that I doubt it will be out of my my power."

* * *

Advertisement for a fencing manual, [Rivington's] Royal Gazette, No. 581, 24 April 1782.

"Lately arrived from London, the following Book,
    illuminated with very elegant figures and fituations, adapted to the art;
A NEW AND COMPLETE TREATISE
ON THE
Theory and Practice of Fencing,
"Difplaying the intricacies of fmall fword play, and reducing the art to the moft eafy and familiar principles, by regular and progreffive leffons; illuftrated with mathematical figures, reprefenting every material attitude of the art.
By J. M'ARTHUR,
Enquire of the Printer."

* * *

Advertisement for a fencing school, [Rivington's] Royal Gazette, No. 627, 28 September 1782.

"*FENCING*

"A PERSON duly qualified to teach the Science of SMALL SWORD, conformable to the neweft and moft approved manner, practifed in London, Paris, and other European Academies, hereby informs fuch gentlemen as wifh to learn this ufeful and indifpenfible part of a gentleman's education. That after the firft part of October next, the School will be opened as laft winter, enquire at the Printers. Amongft many juft and fenfible remarks of a late very ingenious author on this fubject; the following is quoted, 'The juft application of the theory and practice of this art, can never be viewed in a difadvantageous light by liberal minds; on the contrary, many advantages are derived from the proper cultivation thereof. For it not only infpires the poffeffor with a competent fhare of manly confidence and animation, at the fame time producing and eafy and graceful manner, but confidered as an exercife, it has the peculiar qualities over every other, of being conducive to the moft agile motions, the moft graceful attitudes, a bold and martial air, fufceptibility of feeling, quicknefs of fight, and withall, is particularly conducive to the improvement of health, and mufcularity of body. The ftudy of it in a fcientific manner, tends to conftitute a powerful invention, a quick conception, a penetrating judgment, and lively imagination.'

"The School, for the greater facility of Pupils is provided with elegant Engravings, reprefenting every material attitude of the art. The progrefs of the Gentlemen who attended this School left winter, is a clear demonftration of the truth of the above quotation.

"The Hours of attendance, terms, &c. may be known by applying as above. New-York, Sept. 23, 1782."

* * *

Advertisement for fencing instruction, [Rivington's] Royal Gazette, No. 642, 20 November 1782.

"Such Gentlemen as are defirous of being furnifhed with elegant copies of the fecond edition of the much approved TREATISE on FENCING, by John M'Arthur, of the Royal Navy, now preparing to be publifhed in England, are requefted to fend their names to Mr. Rivington, as foon as poffible.—The work is to be embelliefhed with twenty elegant engravings, painted after drawings from life, (including and emblematical frontifpiece, mathematical figures and attitudes) reprefenting every material attitude of the art.—Fifteen Shillings Sterling to be paid by each fubfcriber, on delivery of the book, to their agent or correfpondent, in any of the principal towns of Great-Britain and Ireland; and *one guinea* to be paid on fubfcribing, by fuch gentlemen as wifh to have the book fent out free of all charges, to any of the colonies in America. —The propofals and conditions to be had at Mr. Rivington's, where a copy of the firft edition of the book is left for public infpection."

* * *

Advertisement for a fencing manual, [Rivington's] Royal Gazette, No. 702, 18 June 1783.

"*On the noble Science of Small Sword.*

"ON the firft of January next, will be PUBLISHED in LONDON, by Subfcription, in One Volume Quarto, on a new Letter, and fine Paper, with a copious Gloffary and Improvements,

[*Price 15s. Sterl. in boards, to be paid on delivery*]
The Second Edition of
The Army and Navy GENTLEMAN'S COMPANION,
Or,
A new and compleat TREATISE on the THEORY
and PRACTICE of FENCING;

Illuftrated by Mathematical Figures, and embellifhed with twenty elegant Engravings, painted from Life, reprefenting every material Attitude of the Art.

By JOHN M'ARTHUR, of the Royal Navy.

A Book is opened at Mr. Rivington's for Subfcriber's Names, where the Propofals and Conditions may be feen.

*** The Critical and Monthly Reviewers for January and February 1780, beftow high Encomiums on the Firft Edition of this Work."

Advertisement for fencing instruction, [Rivington's] Royal Gazette, No. 714, 30 July 1783.

"FENCING,
OR
SMALL SWORD PLAY.

BY particular defire of feveral Gentlemen in this City, Mr. WALL will give LES-SONS at the THEATRE every Day, between the Hours of Eleven and Two, and initiate Gentlemen in thofe much efteemed Principles laid down in Mr. M'ARTHUR's TREATISE on that noble Science.

Mr. Wall's defire being rather to oblige, and affift in rendering this fine accom-plifhment more univerfal, (as well as obtaining in the courfe of conftant practice far-ther improvement to himfelf) than for any *pecuniary* advantage, will take NO Entrance; and his terms for teaching, will be found very reafonable."

Chapter 12

FIELD GAMES

A variety of field games were available to colonial Americans. Versions of golf, field hockey, and soccer existed, as well as hurling and a game called "common." All of these diversions were apparently outdoor sports, played over rugged terrain or on the more level fields of village and city commons, but none of them left much detail in the historical record. As games played with balls, they may have been included in various prohibitions against ball-playing or "play at ball," but the sources are too vague to decide that with any degree of confidence.

Most secondary sources about colonial era sports refer to the game of golf, implying that it was, if not a common game, certainly present in colonies ranging from New Netherland, where it was known as "kolven," to South Carolina, where a formal golf club may have existed in Charleston in 1795. Yet, for golf, there is a surprising scar-city of primary-source records of these colonies. Historians know that golf is an old game, derived from some original game that branched one way toward cricket, the other toward golf. King James I was supposedly a golf enthusiast. By 1754 there were quite formal rules at the famous St. Andrews course in Scotland. There any complete story stops, as it is impossible to discern any straight lineage of early American golf before 1820.

Similarly field hockey, as opposed to that on skates on ice, definitely existed, of-ten under the alternate names of "bandy," "bandy wicket," "shinty," and "shinny." Undoubtedly these were lively contests, perhaps quite injury-filled. The game had its origins in Scots-Irish or Irish locales, but beyond that it is difficult to establish the reach of this diversion. This also applies to hurling, that Irish game that combined rugby, field hockey, and soccer. An advertisement in a New York newspaper implied that there were fairly regular matches in that cities among the Irish immigrants, but corroboration is elusive. Another game, labeled in the same newspaper as "Common," was possibly a variant of hurling or some other field game, as the advertisement was in the exact same format as the one for hurling.

Soccer-like games are quite more documentable. Indigenous peoples apparently were avid "foot-ball" players, and a few early commentators thought it worthy to mention this and praise them for a noncombative style. As for Euroamericans, the game was popular enough to prompt colonial Boston authorities to prohibit the game in the city streets out of concern for the safety of bystanders. It is uncertain whether the "foot-ball" of the time was limited to the feet or was a game that allowed a combination of hand and foot movements. No formal rules appear to have existed or survived. Perhaps like many a folk game, determination of the size and shape of the ball and the field, as well as scoring, penalties, and allowable play techniques, all rested with the assembled participants.

The following documents, albeit a scanty record at best, give some testimony to the existence of those field games enjoyed by colonial Americans.

[Consult the general writings about sports, recreation, and the various colonial, provincial, territorial, and state Sabbath and gaming laws in Chapter One for other sources about the specific sports or games in this chapter.]

GOLF

Ordinance at Fort Orange and Beverwyck, New Netherlands, 6 October 1656, reprinted in A.J.F. van Laer, ed. and trans., *Minutes of the Court of Fort Orange and Beverwyck, 1657-1660* (Albany, N.Y.: University of the State of New York, 1923), 235.

"The honorable commissary and magistrates of Fort Orange and the village of Beverwyck, having heard divers complaints from the burghers of this place against the practice of playing golf along the streets, which causes great damage to the windows of the houses and also exposes people to the danger of being injured and is contrary to the freedom of the public streets; Therefore, their honors, wishing to prevent the same, hereby forbid all persons to play golf in the streets, under penalty of forfeiture of fl.25 for each person who shall be found doing so."

* * *

New York Governor Burnet's inventory, circa 1729, reprinted in Esther Singleton, *Social New York under the Georges* (New York: D. Appleton and Company, 1902), 265.

"Nine gouff clubs, one iron ditto, and seven dozen balls."

* * *

Rules of golf, St. Andrews course, Scotland, 14 May 1754, reprinted in William Perkins Bull, *From Rattlesnake Hunt to Hockey. The History of Sports in Canada and of the Sportsmen of Peel, 1798 to 1934* (Toronto: George J. McLeod, 1943), 175.

"I. You must Tee your Ball within a Club length of the Hole.

"II. Your Tee must be upon the ground.

"III. You are not to change the Ball which you strike off the Tee.

"IV. You are not to remove Stones, Bones, or any Break-club for the sake of playing your Ball, except upon the fair Green, and that only within a Club length of your Ball.

"V. If your Ball come among Water, or any watery filth, you are at liberty to take out your Ball, and throw it behind the hazard, six yards at least; you may play it with any club, and allow your Adversary a stroke for so getting out your Ball.

"VI. If yur Balls be found anywhere touching one another, you are to lift the first Ball till you play the last.

"VII. At holing, you are to play your Ball honestly for the Hole, and not to play upon your Adversary's Ball, not lying in your way.

"VIII. If you should lose your Ball by its being taken up, or in any other way, you are to go back to the spot where you struck last, and drop another Ball, and allow your Adversary a stroke for this misfortune.

"IX. No man, at Holing his Ball, is to be allowed to mark to the Hole with his Club or anything else.

"X. If a Ball be stop'd by any person, Horse, Dog, or anything else, the Ball so stopped must be played where it lies.

"XI. If you draw your Club in order to strike, and proceed so far in the stroke as to be bringing down your Club—if then your Club shall break in any way it is to be accounted a stroke.

"XII. He whose Ball lyes farthest from the Hole is obliged to play first.

"XIII. Neither Trench, Ditch, nor Dyke made for the preservation of the Links, nor the Scholars' holes, nor the Soldiers' lines, shall be accounted a Hazard, but the Ball is to be taken out, Teed, and played with any iron Club."

* * *

Benjamin Rush, Philadelphia physician, recommends golf as a recreation, circa 1772, in Rush, *Sermons to Gentlemen upon Temperance and Exercise* (Philadelphia: John Dunlap, 1772), 33.

"To all thefe fpecies of exercife which we have mentioned, I would add, SKEAT-ING, JUMPING, alfo, the active plays of TENNIS, BOWLES, QUOITS, GOLF*, and the like. The manner in which each of thefe operate, may be underftood from what we faid under the former particulars.

   *Golf is an exercife which is much ufed by the Gentlemen in Scotland. A large common in which there are feveral little holes is chofen for the purpofe. It is played with little leather balls ftuffed with feathers; and fticks made fome-what in the form of a bandy-wicket. He who puts a ball into a given number of holes, with the fewest ftrokes, gets the game. The late Dr. M'KENZIE, Author of the effay on Health and Long Life, ufed to fay, that a man would live ten years the longer for ufing this exercife once or twice a week."

* * *

Advertisement for golf equipment, [Rivington's] Royal Gazette, No. 267, 21 April 1779.

"To the GOLF PLAYERS

"The Seafon for this pleafant and healthy Exercife now advancing, Gentlemen may be furnifhed with excellent CLUBS and the veritable Caledonian BALLS, by enquiring at the Printer's."

George Hanger, Hessian colonel, concerning the Cherokee and Creek indigenous people near Savannah, mentions golf, circa 1780, in Hanger, *The Life, Adventures, and Opinions of Col. George Hanger*, 2 vols., Vol. 1 (New York: Johnson and Stryker, 1801), 175.

"The Indians abstain from women, take physic and prepare their bodies for war, by frequently running and using other manly exercises. In one, not unlike the game we call *goff*, they shew great skill and activity."

SOCCER

Henry Spelman, a Virginian English boy, held captive by the Powhatans, describes soccer playing by the indigenous people, circa 1609, in [Spelman], *Relation of Virginia by Henry Spelman, 1609* (London: James F. Hunnewell, 1872), 57-58.

"They vfe befide football play, wch wemen and young boyes doe much play at. They make ther Gooles as ours only they neuer fight nor pull one another doune"

* * *

William Strachey, British explorer, comments on soccer among the indigenous people in Virginia, circa 1612-14, in Strachey, *The Historie of Travaile into Virginia Britannia; Expressing the Cosmographie and Comodities of the Country, Togither with the Manners and Customes of the People,* ed. by R.H. Major (London: The Hakluyt Society, 1899), 78.

"Likewise they have the exercise of football, in which they only forceably encounter with the foot to carry the ball the one the other, and spurned yt to the goale with a kind of dexterity and swift footmanship, which is the honour of yt; but they never strike up one another's heeles, as we doe, not accompting that praiseworthie to purchase a goale by such an advantage."

* * *

William Wood, English settler, describes soccer concerning indigenous peoples in New England, circa 1634, in Wood, *New Englands Prospect, A True, Lively and Experimentall Defcription of that Part of America, Commonly Called Nevv England. Difcovering the Ftate of that Countrie, Both As It Ftands to Our New-Come* Englifh *Planters; and to the Old Native Inhabitants* (London: Thomas Cotes, 1634), reprinted as *Wood's New-England Prospect, Publications of the Prince Society, Volume 1* (Boston: The Prince Society, 1865), 96-97.

"For their fports of activitie they have commonly but three or foure; as footeball, fhooting, running and fwimming: when they play country againft country, there are rich Goales, all behung with Wampompeage, Mowhackies, Beaver skins, and blacke Otter skinnes. It would exceede the beleefe of many to relate the worth of one Goale, wherefore it fhall be nameleffe. Their Goales be a mile long placed on the fands, which are as even as a board; their ball is no bigger than a hand-ball, which fometimes they mount in the Aire with their naked feete, fometimes it is fwayed by the multitude; fometimes alfo it is two dayes before they get a Goale, then they marke the ground they winne, and beginne there the next day. Before they come to this fport, they paint themfelves, even as when they goe to warre, in pollicie to prevent future mifchiefe, becaufe no man fhould know him that moved his patience or accidentally hurt his perfon, taking away the occafion of ftudying revenge. Before they begin their armes be difordered, and hung upon fome neighbouring tree, after which they make a long fcrowle on the fand, over which the fhake loving hands, and with laughing hearts fcuffle for victorie. While the men play the boyes pipe, and the women dance and fing trophies of their hufbands conquefts; all being done a feaft fummons their departure. It is most delight to fee them play, in fmaller companies, when men may view their fwift footemanfhip, their curious toffings of their Ball, their flouncing into the water, their lubberlike wreftling, having no cunning at all in that kind, one English being able to beate ten *Indians* at footeball."

* * *

Roger Williams, Rhode Island founder, comments on soccer among New England indigenous peoples, circa 1643, in Williams, *A Key into the Language of America, or an Help to the Language of the Natives in That Part of America Called New-England* (London: Gregory Dexter, 1643), 146.

"...: beside, they have great meetings of foot-ball playing, onely in Summer, towne against towne, upon some broad sandy shoare, free from stones, or upon some soft heathie plot because of their naked feet at which they have great stakings, but seldom quarrell."

* * *

Boston selectmen's ordinance, January 1658, in "Second Report of the Boston Records Commissioners," 98, reprinted in Justin Windsor, ed., *The Memorial History of Boston, Including Suffolk County, Massachusetts, 1630-1880,* 4 vols., Vol. 1 (Boston: James R. Osgood and Company, 1880), 229.

"Forasmuch as sundry complaints are made that several persons have received hurt by boys and young men playing at football in the streets, these are therefore to enjoin that none be found at that game in any of the streets, lanes, or enclosures of that town, under penalty of twenty shillings for every such offense."

* * *

John Ogilby, British writer, describes soccer among the indigenous people in the Northeast, circa 1670, in Ogilby, *An Account and Description of America,* 2 vols., Vol. 2 (London, 1670), 156, reprinted in Edward H. Dewey, "Football and the American Indians," New England Quarterly, Vol. 3, No. 4 (October 1930), 739.

"Football is found at the north. Their goals are a mile long placed on the sands, which are as even as a board; their ball is no bigger than a handball, which sometimes they mount in the air with their naked feet, sometimes it is swayed by the multitude, sometimes also it is two days before they get a goal, then they mark the ground they win, and begin there the next day. Before they come to this sport, they paint themselves, even as they go to war."

* * *

John Dunton, London traveler, in Boston, describes soccer among New England indigenous people, circa 1686, in [Dunton], *A Summer's Ramble, Through Ten Kingdomes, Occasionally Written by John Dunton, Citizen of London,* 2 Vols. (London: A. Baldwin, 1686), reprinted as W.H. Whitmore, ed., *Letters Written from New-England, A.D. 1686, by John Dunton* (Boston: The Prince Society, 1867), 285-287.

"But there was that Day a great Game of Foot-Ball to be play'd, which was the occafion of our going thither; There was another Town that play'd againft them, as is fometimes common in England; but they play'd with their bare feet, which I thought was very odd; but it was upon a broad Sandy Shoar, free from Stones, which made it the more eafie. Neither were they fo apt to trip up one anothers heels and quarrel, as I have feen 'em in England....

"Their Play at Foot-Ball, (which you have now feen) is the moft Innocent of all their Sports, but this they only play at in the Summer time; playing generally Town againft Town; and always on fome broad Sandy Shoar, as they now did; or elfe on fome foft healthy Plot, becaufe of their naked feet, (for you fee they play bare-foot) and tho' they lay great Stakes, yet they feldom quarrel about it."

* * *

Juan Mateo Manje, Spanish captain, remarks about soccer among indigeous peoples in southern Arizona, February 1699, in Manje, *Unknown Arizona and Sonora, 1693-1721, From the Francisco Fernandez del Castillo Version of Luz Tierra Incognita by Captain Juan Mateo Manje,* trans. by Harry J. Karns (Tucson, Ariz.: Arizona Silhouettes, 1954), 113.

"They make round balls, the size of a football, out of a black pitch-like substance. These are decorated by sticking several small shells onto them. They play with these balls and make bets. They kick the ball with the tip of the foot, run three or four leagues, and the party that goes around and comes back to the starting point wins."

* * *

Boston Massachusetts town order, circa 1701, in *Several Rules, Orders, and By-Laws Made and Agreed upon by the Free-Holders and Inhabitants of Boston of the Massachu-setts, at their Meeting, May 12 and September 22, 1701* (Boston: Bartolomew Green and John Allen, 1702), 11.

"*For preventing danger by* Foot balls, Squibs *and* Snow-balls.
"*Ordered*
"THat whofoever fhall at any time hereafter ufe the exercife of playing or kicking of Foot ball within any of the Streets or Lanes within the Body of this Town, fhall forfeit and pay the Sum of *One Shilling* for every tranfgreffion of this Order:...."

* * *

Excerpt from a story about a St. Andrew's Day festival in Hanover County mentions soccer playing, Virginia Gazette, No. 68, 11-18 November 1737.

"With divers other confiderable Prizes, for Dancing, Singing, Foot-ball-play, Jumping, Wreftling, &c."

* * *

William Stephens, Georgia Trustee, refers to soccer in that colony, 28 December 1741, in E. Merton Coulter, ed., *The Journal of William Stephens, 1741-1743* (Athens, Ga.: University of Georgia Press, 1958), 24.

"During so great a Pother about Rights and Priviledges, among our wise men of Gotham the Common People (who would be quiet enough, if left to themselves) had no other Contest, but at Foot Ball and Crickett, and resolved to see the utmost extent this day of the Holy days."

* * *

Boston, Massachusetts town by-law, circa 1758, in *The By-Laws and Orders of the Town of Boston; in the Province of Massachusetts-Bay, Now in Force* (Boston: Green and Rusell, 1758), 10.

"8. *And it is further Ordered,* That whoever fhall at any Time hereafter ufe the Exercife of playing or kicking at Foot-Ball, within any of the Streets or Lanes within the Body of this Town, fhall forfeit and pay a Sum of not more than *Four Shillings,* nor lefs than *One Shilling* for every fuch Offence."

* * *

Yale College law, circa 1765, quoted and translated in Clarence Deming, *Yale Yesterdays* (New Haven, Conn.: Yale University Press, 1915), 192.

"Siquis Pila pedali vel palmeria, aut globis, in area academica laserit....multetur non plus sex denariis et damna resarciat." [Playing ball by hand or foot in the college yard was forbidden, under the penalty of making restitution for any damage and a maximum fine of sixpence.]

* * *

Thomas Hutchinson, Massachusetts politician and historian, refers to soccer among New England indigenous peoples, circa 1765, in Hutchinson, *The History of the Province of Massachusetts Bay,* 2nd ed., 2 vols., Vol. 1 (London: M. Richardson, 1765), 470.

"THEY had fome fports and games with which they fometimes diverted themfelves. Football was the chief, and whole cantons would engage one againft another. Their goals were upon the hard fands, as even and firm as a board, and a mile or more in length, their ball not much larger than a hand-ball, which they would mount in the air with their naked feet, and fometimes would be two days together before either fide got a goal."

* * *

Yale College law, circa 1774, in *The Laws of Yale-College, in New-Haven, in Connecticut, Enacted by the President and Fellows* (New Haven, Conn.: Thomas and Samuel Green, 1774), 11.

"9. If any Scholar fhall play at Hand-Ball, or Foot Ball, or Bowls in the College-Yard, or throw any Thing againft College, by which the Glafs may be endangered,... he fhall punifhed fix Pence, and make good the Damages."

* * *

Charleston, South Carolina city ordinance, 22 November 1783, in *Ordinances of the City Council of Charleston in the State of South Carolina, Passed in the First Year of the Incorporation of the City* (Charleston, S.C.: J. Miller, 1784), 19.

"AN ORDINANCE
For the better OBSERVANCE of the LORD'S-DAY, commonly called SUNDAY, and to prevent DISTURB-
ANCES at any Place of PUBLIC WORSHIP
within the City of CHARLESTON.

"And be it further ordained by the authority aforefaid, That no fports or paftimes, as bear-baiting, bull-baiting foot-balls, horfe-racing,... fhall be allowed on the Lord's-Day, and every perfon fo offending fhall forfeit for every fuch offence the fum of Five Pounds."

* * *

OTHER FIELD GAMES

William Strachey, British explorer in Virginia, mentions a game resembling field hockey among the indigenous people, circa 1612-1614, in William Strachey, *The Historie of Travaile into Virginia Britannia; Expressing the Cosmographie and Comodities of the Country Togither with the Manners and Customes of the People,* ed. by R.H. Major (London: The Hakluyt Society, 1899), 77-78.

"A kynd of exercise they have often amongst them much like that which boyes call bandy in English, and may be an auncient game, as yt seemeth in Virgill; for when Æneas came into Italy at his marriage with Lavinia, King Latinus' daughter, yt is said the Troyans taught the Latins scipping and frisking at the ball."

* * *

Simeon Lyman, Sharon, Connecticut soldier, at New London, Connecticut, plays a game of goal, 14 September 1775, in [Lyman], "Journal of Simeon Lyman of Sharon, Aug. 10 to Dec. 28, 1775," in "Orderly Book and Journals Kept by Connecticut Men While Taking Part in the American Revolution, 1775-1778," *Collections of the Connecticut Historical Society,* Vol. 7 (Hartford: Connecticut Historical Society, 1899), 118.

"Thursday, 14th. I wrote letters all the forenoon, and in the afternoon I played goold [goal] and got beat."

* * *

Samuel Shute, New Jersey lieutenant, plays field hockey in central Pennsylvania, 9-22 July 1779, in [Shute], "Journal of Lt. Samuel Shute," in Frederick Cook, ed., *Journals of the Military Expedition of Major General John Sullivan against the Six Nations of Indians in 1779* (Freeport, N.Y.: Books for Libraries Press, reprint of 1885 ed.), 268.

"..., until the 22nd, the time was spent in playing Shinny & Ball."

* * *

Ebenezer Elmer, New Jersey surgeon, plays field hockey in central Pennsylvania, July 1779, in [Elmer], "Journal of Dr. Ebenezer Elmer," in Frederick Cook, ed., *Journals of the Military Expedition of Major General John Sullivan against the Six Nations of Indians in 1779* (Freeport, N.Y.: Books for Libraries Press, reprint of 1885 ed.), 83.

15 July 1779: "Played Shinney with Genl. Maxwell, Colo Dayton & a number of Gentlemen."

16 July 1779: "Played as yesterday. Genl. Sullivan attended & was much pleased with our activity in the performance."

26 July 1779: "Drisly weather in the forenoon, the afternoon of the day more fair — All hands dined at the Colonels to day & after dinner we took a hearty game of Bandy wicket."

* * *

Advertisement for a match at common, [Rivington's] Royal Gazette, No. 570, 16 March 1782.

"COMMON.

"SUCH Sons of ST. PATRICK, as intend to join their Brethren in the diverfion of the ancient and favourite Irifh game of COMMON, on Monday the 18th infant, for a Supper, &c. are defired to leave their names at the Bar of the Royal Punch Houfe, near the Tea-Water Pump, before Monday morning.

"The game to be played at the Jews burying ground, by Sons of St. Patrick only, and will begin at Eleven o'Clock."

* * *

Advertisement for a hurling match, [Rivington's] Royal Gazette, No. 585, 8 May 1782.

"HURLING

"THE Subfcriber at the earneft requeft of a number of Gentlemen has procured a fufficient number of Hurls and Balls for a Match at that ancient and manly Game called HURLING, hereby requefts that faid Gentlemen, and fuch others as chufe to partake of the diverfion will be pleafed to call to-morrow evening at the Royal Punch Houfe, near the Tea Water Pump to appoint a day, and regulate other matters refpecting the Game.   THOMAS M'MULLINS."

Chapter 13

FISHING

From the earliest European travelers' reports onwards, North America appeared to be an angler's paradise. Every account detailed the varieties and abundance of the members of the finny tribe there for the taking. Europeans were fascinated with the indigenous fishing customs and techniques, as they sought their share of the bounty. For Europeans who chronically lacked fish supplies, these descriptions quickened the pulse. Stories, probably apocryphal, of rivers and creeks teeming with so many fish that a person could walk across on their backs without getting wet circulated. Certainly less plentiful, fish abounded enough that some colonies and servant contracts stipulated that masters could not feed fish to servants more than three times a week.

As time passed, fish sources suffered from human need for fish and from deforestation erosion that altered the quality of water. Dams and mills aggravated the fish migration routes and spawning patterns. By the mid-eighteenth century, many colonies restricted fishing by certain means such as by torchlight at night and required dam erectors and millowners to remove their obstructions or provide fish ladders.

Much of the fishing was to provide food, fertilizer, and oil. Some of the fishing was for sustenance, much of the rest for commerce. This might lead some to object, with some justification, that fishing was not sport. The difficulty here is that even the sustenance anglers saw fishing as sport and declared it such. The pleasure doesn't always show through the terse notational prose, but occasionally anglers expressed the joys of angling and hauling the seine. For members of the more affluent classes, fishing was often a pleasant pastime. Even though Izaak Walton and Charles Cotton's seventeenth-century manual, *The Compleat Angler,* was a British book, Americans were familiar with it and devoted followers of the art. Many a local citizen or traveler went fishing, or observed others at angling. Consult, for example, the repeated diary entries of Boston merchant John Rowe, who apparently "lived to fish" in the 1760s. Dry goods stores catered to anglers with stocks of fishing tackle and supplies. Early real estate advertisements emphasized the fishing potential on certain land parcels. Even Benjamin Franklin felt compelled to tell jokes at the expense of the patient worm-drowners. Fishing was clearly a sport, pastime, and diversion for such individuals. The following selections demonstrate the full range of colonial and Revolutionary Americans' attachment to the piscatorial science.

[Consult the general writings about sports, recreation, and the various colonial, provincial, territorial, and state Sabbath and gaming laws in Chapter One for other sources about the specific sports or games in this chapter.]

Izaak Walton, British writer, writes about the joys of fishing, mid-1600s, in Walton, *The Compleat Angler; or, The Contemplative Man's Recreation. Being a Discourse of Fish and Fishing for the Perusal of Anglers* (New York: The Heritage Press, 1948), 15-40.

"THE FIRST DAY.

"*A Conference betwixt an* Angler, *a* Hunter, *and a* Falconer, *each commending his Recreation.*

"*Venator*: I might enlarge myself in the commendation of Hunting, and of the noble Hound especially, as also of the docibleness of dogs in general; and I might make many observations of land-creatures, that for composition, order, figure, and constitution approach nearest to the completeness and understanding of man; especially of those creatures which Moses in the Law permitted to the Jews, Lev. ix. 2-8, which have cloven hoofs and chew the cud, which I shall forbear to name, because I will not be so uncivil to Mr. Piscator as not to allow him a time for the commendation of Angling, which he calls an Art; but doubtless 't is an easy one: and, Mr. Auceps, I doubt we shall hear a watery discourse of it, but I hope 't will not be a long one.

"*Auceps:* And I hope so too, tough I fear it will.

"*Piscator:* Gentlemen, let not prejudice prepossess you. I confess my discourse is like to prove suitable to my recreation, calm and quiet; we seldom take the name of God into our mouths, but it is either to praise him or to pray to him: if others use it vainly in the midst of their recreations, so vainly as if they meant to conjure, I must tell you it is neither our fault nor our custom; we protest against it. But pray remember, I accuse nobody; for as I would not make 'a watery discourse,': so I would not put too much vinegar into it; nor would I raise the reputation of my own art by the diminution or ruin of another's. And so much for the prologue to what I mean to say.

"And now for the Water, the element that I trade in. The Water is the eldest daughter of the creation, the element upon which the Spirit of God did first move, Gen. i. 2, the element which God commanded to bring forth living creatures abundantly; and without which, those that inhabit the land, even all creatures that have breath in their nostrils, must suddenly return to putrefaction. Moses, the great law-giver and chief, skilled in all the learning of the Egyptians, who was called a friend of God, and know the mind of the Almighty, names this element the first in the creation; this is the element upon which the Spirit of God did first move, and is the chief ingredient in the creation: many philosophers have made it to comprehend all the other elements, and most allow it the chiefest in the mixtion of all living creatures.

"There be that profess to believe that all bodies are made of the water, and may be reduced back again to water only; they endeavor to demonstrate it thus:—

"Take willow, or any like speedy-growing plant, newly rooted in a box or barrel full of earth, weigh them all together exactly when all trees begin to grow, and then weigh all together after the tree is increased from its first footing to weigh an hundred pound weight more than when it was first rooted and weighed; and you shall find this augment of the tree to be without the diminution of one drachm weight of the earth. Hence they infer this increase of wood to be from water of rain, or from dew, and not to be from any other element. And they affirm, they can reduce this wood back again to water; and they affirm, also, the same may be done in any animal or vegetable. And this I take to be a fair testimony of the excellency of my element of Water.

"The Water is more productive than the earth. Nay, the earth hath no fruitfulness without showers or dews; for all the herbs and flowers and fruits are produced and thrive by the water; and the very minerals are fed by streams that run underground, whose natural course carries them to the tops of many high mountains, as we see several springs breaking forth on the tops of the highest hills; and this is also witnessed by the daily trial and testimony of several miners.

"Nay, the increase of those creatures that are bred and fed in the water are not only more and more miraculous, but more advantageous to man, not only for the lengthening of his life, but for the preventing of sickness; for 't is observed by the most learned physicians, that the casting off of Lent and other fish days,—which hath not only for the lengthening of his life, but for the preventing of sickness; for 't is observed by the most learned physicians, that the casting off of Lent and other fish days,—which hath not only given the lie to so many learned, pious, wise founders of colleges, for which should be ashamed,—hath doubtless been the chief cause of those many putrid, shaking, intermitting agues, unto which this nation of ours is now more subject than those wiser countries that feed on herbs, salads, and plenty of fish; of which it is observed in story, that the greatest part of the world now do. And it may be fit to remember that Moses, Lev. xi. 9, Deut. xiv. 9, appointed fish to be the chief diet for the best commonwealth that ever yet was.

"And it is observable, not only that there are fish,—as namely, the Whale, three times as big as the mighty Elephant, that is so fierce in battle,—but that the mightiest feasts have been of fish. The Romans in the height of their glory have made fish the mistress of all their entertainments; they have had music to usher in their Sturgeons, Lampreys, and Mullets, which they would purchase at rates rather to be wondered at than believed. He that shall view the writings of Macrobius, or Varro, may be confirmed and informed of this, and of the incredible value of their fish and fish-ponds.

"But, Gentlemen, I have almost lost myself, which I confess I may easily do in this philosophical discourse; I met with most of it very lately, and, I hope, happily, in a conference with a most learned physician, Dr. Wharton, a dear friend, that loves both me and my art Art of Angling. But however, I will wade no deeper in these mysterious arguments, but pass to such observations as I can manage with more pleasure, and less fear of running into error. But I must not yet forsake the waters, by whose help we have so many known advantages.

"And first, to pass by the miraculous cures of our known baths, how advantageous is the sea for our daily traffic, without which we could not now subsist? How does it not only furnish us with food and physic for the bodies, but with such observations for the mind as ingenious persons would not want!

"How ignorant had we been of the beauty of Florence, of the monuments, urns, and rarities that yet remain in and near unto old and new Rome, so many as it is said will take up a year's time to view, and afford to each of them but a convenient consideration; and therefore it is not to be wondered at, that so learned and devout a father as St. Jerome, after his wish to have seen Christ in the flesh, and to have heard St. Paul preach, makes his third wish to have seen Rome in her glory; and that glory is not yet all lost, for what pleasure is it to see the monuments of Livy, the choicest of the historians; of Tully, the best of orators; and to see the bay-trees that now grow out of the very tomb of Virgil! These, to any that love learning, must be pleasing. But what pleasure is it to a devout Christian to see there the humble house in which St. Paul was content to dwell, and to view the many rich statues that are there made in honor of his memory! Nay, to see the very place in which St. Peter and he lie buried together! These are in and near to Rome. And how much more doth it please the pious curiosity of a Christian, to see that place on which the blessed Saviour of the world was pleased to humble himself, ane to take our nature upon him, and to converse with men,—to see Mount Sion, Jerusalem, and the very Sepulchre of our Lord Jesus! How may it beget and heighten the zeal of a Christian, to see the devotions that are daily paid to him at the place! Gentlemen, lest I forget myself I will stop here, and remember you, that, but for my element of Water, the inhabitants of this poor island must remain ignorant that such things ever were, or that any of them have yet a being.

"Gentlemen, I might both enlarge and lose myself in such like arguments; I might tell you that Almighty God is said to have spoken to a fish, but never to a beast; that he hath made a Whale a ship to carry and set his prophet Jonah safe on the appointed shore. Of these I might speak, but I must in manners break off, for I see Theobald's house. I cry you mercy for being so long and thank you for your patience.

"*Auceps:* Sir, my pardon is easily granted you; I except against nothing that you have said; nevertheless, I must part with you at this park-wall, for which I am very sorry; but I assure you, Mr. Piscator, I now part with you full of good thoughts, not only of yourself, but your recreation. And so, Gentlemen, God keep you both!

"*Piscator:* Well, now, Mr. Venator, you shall neither want time nor my attention to hear you enlarge your discourse concerning Hunting.

"*Venator:* Not I, Sir; I remember you said that Angling itself was of great antiquity, and a perfect art, and an art not easily attained to; and you have so won upon me in your former discourse, that I am very desirous to hear what you can say further concerning those particulars.

"*Piscator:* Sir, I did say so, and I doubt not but if you and I did converse together but a few hours, to leave you possessed with the same high and happy thoughts that now possess me of it; not only of the antiquity of Angling, but that it deserves commendations, and that it is an art, and an art worthy the knowledge and practice of a wise man.

"*Venator:* Pray, Sir, speak of them what you think fit, for we have yet five miles to the Thatched House, during which walk I dare promise you my patience and diligent attention shall not be wanting. And if you shall make that to appear which you have undertaken; first, that it is an art, and an art worth the learning, I shall beg that I may attend you a day or two a-fishing, and that I may become your scholar, and be instructed in the art itself which you so much magnify.

"*Piscator:* O Sir, doubt not but that Angling is an art; is it not an art to deceive a Trout with an artificial fly?—a Trout! that is more sharp-sighted than any Hawk you have named, and more watchful and timorous than your high-mettled Merlin is bold? and yet I doubt not to catch a brace or two to-morrow, for a friend's breakfast: doubt not therefore, Sir, but that Angling is an art, and an art worth your learning: the question is rather, whether you be capable of learning it? for Angling is somewhat like Poetry, men are to be born so: I mean with inclinations to it, though both may be heightened by discourse and practice; but he that hopes to be a good Angler must bring a large measure of hope and patience, and a love and propensity to the art itself; but having once got and practised it, then doubt not but Angling will prove to be so pleasant, that it will prove to be like virtue, a reward to itself.

"*Venator:* Sir, I am now become so full of expectation, that I long to have you proceed; and in the order that you propose.

"*Piscator:* Then first, for the antiqity of Angling, of which I shall not say much, but only this: some say it is as ancient as Deucalion's flood; others, that Belus, who was the first inventor of godly and virtuous recreations, was the first inventor of Angling; and some others say, for former times have had their disquisitions about the antiquity of it, that Seth, one of the sons of Adam, taught it to his sons, and that by them it was derived to posterity; others say, that he left it engraven on those pillars which he erected, and trusted to preserve the knowledge of the mathematics, music, and the rest of that precious knowledge, and those useful arts which by God's appointment or allowarnce and his noble industry were thereby preserved from perishing in Noah's flood.

"These, Sir, have been the opinions of several men, that have possibly endeavored to make Angling more ancient than is needful, or may well be warranted; fot for my part, I shall content myself in telling you, that Angling is much more ancient thant the incarnation of our Saviour; for in the Prophet Amos mention is made of fish-hooks; and in the Book of Job, which was long before the days of Amos, for that book is said to be writ by Moses, mention is made also of fish-hooks, which must imply Anglers in those times.

"But, my worthy friend, as I would rather prove myself a gentleman by being learned and humble, valiant and offensive, virtuous and communicable, than by any fond ostentation of riches, or, wanting those virtues myself, boast that these were in my ancestors, —and yet I grant that where a noble and ancient descent and such merits meet in any man, it is a double dignification of that person: —so if this antiquity of Angling, which for my part I have not forced, shall, like an ancient family, be either an honor or an ornament to this virtuous art which I profess to love and practise, I shall be the gladder that I made an accidental mention of the antiquity of it; of which I shall tell you, that in ancient times a debate hath risen, and it remains yet unresolved, whether the happines of man in this world doth consist more in contemplation or action.

"Concerning which, some have endeavored to maintain their opinion of the first, by saying, that the nearer we mortals come to God by way of imitation, the more happy we are. And they say, that God enjoys himself only by a contemplation of his own

Infiniteness, Eternity, Power, and Goodness, and the like. And upon this ground, many cloisteral men of great learning and devotion prefer contemplation before action. And many of the fathers seem to approve this opinion, as may appear in their commentaries upon the words of the Saviour to Martha, Luke x. 41, 42.

"And, on the contrary, there want not men of equal authority and credit, that prefer action to be the more excellent; as namely, experiments in physic, and the application of it, both the ease and prolongation of man's life; by each man is enabled to act and do good to others, either to serve his country, or do good to particular persons: and they may also, that action is doctrinal, and teaches both art and virtue, and is a maintainer of humane society; and for these, and other like reasons, to be preferred before contemplation.

"Concerning which two opinions I shall forbear to add a third by declaring my own, and rest myself contented in telling, my very worthy friend, that both these meet together, and do most properly belong to the most honest, ingenuous, quiet, and harmless art of Angling.

"And first, I shall tell you what some have observed, and I have found it to be a real truth, that the very sitting by the river's side is not only the quietest and fittest place for contemplation, but will invite an Angler to it; and this seems to be maintained by the learned Peter Du Moulin, who, in his discourse of the Fulfilling of Prophecies, observes, that when God intended to reveal any future events or high notions to his prophets, he then carried them either to the deserts of the sea-shore, that having so separated them from amidst the press of people and business, and the cares of the world, he might settle their mind in a quiet repose, and there make them fit for revelation.

"And this seems also to be intimated by the children of Israel, Psal. 137, who, having in a sad condition banished all mirth and music from their pensive hearts, and having hung up their then mute harps upon the willow-trees growing by the rivers of Babylon, sat down upon those banks bemoaning the ruins of Sion, and contemplating their own sad condition.

"And an ingenious Spaniard says, that 'rivers and the inhabitants of the watery element were made for wise men to contemplate, and fools to pass by without consideration.' And though I will not rank myself in the number of the first, yet give me leave to free myself from the last, by offering to you a short contemplation, first of rivers and then of fish; concerning which I doubt not but to give you many observations that will appear very considerable: I am sure they have appeared so to me, and made many an hour pass away more pleasantly, as I have sat quietly on a flowery bank by a calm river, and contemplated what I shall now relate to you.

"And first concerning Rivers; there be so many wonders reported and written of them, and of the several creatures that be bred and live in them, and those by authors of so good credit, that we need not to deny them an historical faith.

"As namely of a river in Epirus, that puts out any lighted torch, and kindles any torch that was not lighted. Some waters being drank cause madness, some drunkenness, and some laughter to death. The river Selarus in a few hours turns a rod or wand to stone; and our Camden mentions the like in England, and the like in Lochmere in Ireland. There is also a river in Arabia, of which all the sheep that drink thereof have their wool turned into a vermilion color. And one of no less credit than Aristotle tells us of a merry river, the river Elusina, that dances at the noise of music, for with music it bubbles, dances, and gows sandy, and so continues till the music ceases, but then it presently returns to its wonted calmness and clearness. And Camden tells us of a well near to Kirby in Westmoreland, that ebbs and flows several times every day; and he tells us of a river in Surrey, it is called Mole, that after it has run several miles, being opposed by hills, finds or makes itself a way under ground, and breaks out again so far off, that the inhabitants thereabouts boast, as the Spaniards do of their river Anus, that they feed divers flocks of sheep upon a bridge. And lastly, for I would not tire your patience, one of no less authority than Josephus, that learned Jew, tells us of river in Judæa that runs swiftly the fix days of the week, and stands still and rests all their Sabbath.

"But I will lay aside my discourse of rivers, and tell you some things of the monsters, or fish, call them what you will, that they breed and feed in them. Pliny the philosopher says, in the third chapter of his ninth book, that in the Indian Sea the fish called the Balæna, or Whirlpool, is so long and broad as to take up more in length and breadth than two acres of ground, and of other fish of two hundred cubits long; and that in the river Ganges, there be Eels of thirty foot long. He says there, that these monsters appear in that sea only when the tempestuous winds oppose the torrents of water falling from the rocks into it, and so turning what lay at the bottom to be seen on the water's top. And he says, that the people of Cadara, an island near this place, make the timbers for their houses of those fish-bones. He there tells us, that there are sometimes a thousand of these great Eels found snapped or interwoven together. He tells us there, that is appears that Dolphins love music, and will come, when called for, by some men or boys, that know and use to feed them, andthat they can swim as swift as an arrow can be shot out of a bow; and much of this is spoken concerning the Dolphin, and other fish, as may be found also in learned Dr. Casaubon's course of 'Of Credulity and Incredulity,' printed by him in about the year 1670.

"I know we islanders are averse to the belief of these wonders; but there be so many strange creatures to be now seen, many collected by John Tradescant, others added by my friend Elias Ashmole, Esq., who now keeps them carefully and methodically at his house near to Lambeth near London, as may get some belief of some of the other wonders I have mentioned.

"I will tell you some of the wonders that you may now see, and not till then believe, unless you think fit.

"You may there see the Hog-fish, the Doliphin, the Coney-fish, and not only other incredible fish, but you may there see the Salamander, several sorts of Barnacles, of Solan geese, the Bird of Paradise, such sorts of Snakes, and such bird's-nests, and of so various forms, and so wonderfully made, as may beget wonder and amusement in any beholder: and so many hundred of other rarities in that collection, as will make the other wonders I spake of the less incredible; for you may note, that the waters are Nature's storehouse, in which she locks up her wonders.

"But, Sir, lest this discourse may seem tedious, I shall give it now a sweet conclusion out of that holy poet, Mr. George Herbert, his divine 'Contemplation on God's Providence.'

> *"Lord! who hath praise enough? Nay, who hath any?*
> *None can express thy works but he that knows them;*
> *And none can know thy works they are so many*
> *And so complete, but only he that owes them!*

"We all acknowledge both thy power and love
To be exact, thanscendent, and divine;
Who dost so strongly and so sweetly move,
Whilst all things have their end, yet none but thine.

> *"Wherefore, most sacred Spirit, I here present*
> *For me, and all my fellows, praise to thee;*
> *And just it is that I should pay the rent,*
> *Because the benefit accrues to me.*

"And as concerning fish in that Psalm, Psal. 104, wherein for height of poetry and wonders the prophet David seems even to exceed himself, how doth he there express himself in choice metaphors, even to the amazement of a contemplative reader, concerning the sea, the rivers, and the fish therein contained!

"And the great naturalist, Pliny, says, 'That Nature's great and wonderful power is more demonstrated in the in the sea than on the land.' And this may appear by the numerous and various creatures inhabiting both in and about that element; as to the readers of Gesner, Rondeletius, Pliny, Ausonius, Aristotle, and others, may be demonstrated. But I will sweeten this discourse also out of a contemplation in divine Du Bartas, who says:

> *"God quickened in the sea ansd in the rivers*
> *So many fishes of so many features,*
> *That in the waters we may see all creatures,*
> *Ev'n all that on the earth are to be found,*
> *As if the world were in deep waters drowned.*
> *For Seas, as well as Skies, have Sun, Moon, Stars;*
> *As well as Air— Swallows, Rooks, and Stares;*
> *As well as Earth —Vines, Roses, Nettles, Melons,*
> *Mushrooms, Pinks, Gilliflowers, and many millions*
> *Of other plants, more rare, more strange than these,*
> *As very fishes living in the seas:*
> *As also Rams, Calves, Horses, Hares, and Hogs,*
> *Wolves, Urchins, Lions, Elephants, and Dogs;*
> *Yea, Men and Maids, and, which I most admire,*
> *The mitred Bishop, and the cowled Friar:*
> *Of which examples but a few years since*
> *Were shown the Norway and Polonian Prince.*

"These seem to be wonders, but have had so many confirmations from men of learning and credit, that you need not doubt them: nor are the number nor the various shapes of fishes more strange or more fit for contemplation, than their different natures, inclinations, and actions; concerning which I shall beg your patient ear a little longer.

"The Cuttle-fish will cast a long gut out of her throat, which, like as an angler doth his line, she sendeth forth and pulleth in again at her pleasure, according as she sees some little fish come near to her; and the Cuttle-fish, being then hid in the gravel, lets the smaller fish nibble and bite the end of it, at which time she by little and little draws the smaller fish so near to her, that she may leap upon her, and then catches and devours her: and for this reason some have called this fish the Sea-Angler.

"And there is a fish called a Hermit, that at a certain age gets into a dead fish's shell, and like a hermit dwells there alone, studying the wind and weather, and so turns her shell that she makes it defend her from the injuries that they would bring upon her.

"There is also a fish called, by Ælian, in his ninth Book of Living Creatures, Ch. 16, the Adonis, or Darling of the Sea; so called because it is a loving and innocent fish, a fish that hurts nothing that hath life, and is at peace with all the numerous inhabitants of that vast watery element: and truly I think most Anglers are so disposed to most of mankind.

"And there are also lustful and chaste fishes, of which I shall give you examples.

"And first, what Du Bartas says of a fish called the Sargus: which because none can express it better than he does, I shall give you in his own words; supposing it shall not have the less credit for being verse, for he hath gathered this and other observations out of authors that have been great and industrious searchers into the secrets of Nature.

> "The adult'rous Sargus doth not only change
> Wives every day in the deep streams, but, strange!
> As if the honey of sea-love delight
> Could not suffice his raging appetite,
> Goes courting she-goats on the grassy shore
> Horning their husbands that had horns before.

"And the same author writes concerning the Cantharus, that which you shall also hear in his own words:—

> "But contrary, the constant Cantharus
> Is ever contant to his faithful spouse;
> In nuptial duties spending his chaste life,
> Never loves any but his own dear wife.

"Sir, but a little longer, and I have done.

"Venator: Sir, take what liberty you think fit, for your discourse seems to be music, and charms me to an attention.

"Piscator: Why then, Sir, I will take a little liberty to tell, or rather to remember you, what is said of Turtle-Doves; first, that they silently plight their troth and marry; and that then the survivor scorns, as the Thracian women are said to do, to outlive his or her mate, and this is taken for a truth, and if the survivor shall ever couple with another, then not only the living but the dead, be it either the he or the she, is denied the name and honor of a true Turtle-Dove.

"And to parallel this land-rarity, and teach mankind moral faithfulness, and to condemn those that talk of religion, and yet come short of the moral faith of fish and fowl; men that violate the law affirmed by St. Paul, Rom ii. 14,15,16 to be writ in their hearts, and which, he says, shall at the last day condemn and leave them without excuse;—I pray hearken to what Du Bartas sings, for the hearing of such conjugal faithfulness will be music to all chaste ears, and therefore I pray hearken to what Du Bartas sings of the Mullet.

> "But for chaste love the Mullet hath no peer;
> For, if the fisher hath surprised her pheer,
> As mad with woe, to shore she followeth,
> Prest to consort him both in life and death.

"On the contrary, what shall I say of the House-Cock, which treads any hen; and then, contrary to the Swan, the Partridge, and Pigeon, takes no care to hatch, to feed, or to cherish his own brood, but is senseless, though they perish.

"And 't is considerable, that the Hen, which, because she also takes any Cock, expects it not, who is sure the chickens be her own, hath by a moral impression her care and affection to her own brood more than doubled, even to such a height, that our

Saviour, in expressing his love to Jeruselem, Matt. xxiii. 37, quotes her for an example of tender affection; as his father had done Job for a pattern of patience.

"And to parallel this Cock, there be divers fishes that cast their spawn on flags or stones, and then leave it uncovered, and exposed to become a prey, and be devoured by vermin, or other fishes; but other fishes, as namely the Barbel, take such care fo the preservation of their seed, that, unlike to the Cock or the Cuckoo, they mutually labor, both the spawner and the melter, to cover their spawn with sand, or watch it, or hide it in some secret place, unfrequented by vermin or by any fish but themselves.

"Sir, these examples may, to you and others, seem strange; but they are testified, some by Aristotle, some by Pliny, some by Gesner, and by many others of credit, and are believed and known by divers, both of wisdom and experience, to be a truth; and indeed are, as I said at the beginning, fit for the contemplation of a most serious and a most pious man. And, doubtless, this made the Prophet David say, Psal, cvii. 23, 24, 'They that occupy themselves in deep waters see the wonderful works of God': indeed, such wonders and pleasures too as the land affords not.

"And that they be fit for the contemplation of the most prudent, and pious, and peaceable men, seems to be testified by the practice of so many devout an contemplative men, as the Patriarchs and Prophets of old, and of the Apostles of our Saviour and our latter times; of which twelve, we are sure he chose four that were simple Fishermen, whom he inspired and sent to publish his blessed will to the Gentiles, and inspired them also with a power to speak all languages, and by their powerful eloquence to beget faith in the unbelieving Jews, and themselves to suffer for that Saviour whom their forefathers and they had crucified; and, in their sufferings, to preach freedom from the incombrances of the law, and a new way to everlasting life. This was the employment of these happy Fishmen, concerning which choice some have made these observations.

"First, that he never reproved these for their employment or calling, as he did scribes and the money-changers. And secondly, he found that the hearts of such men by nature were fitted for contemplation and quietness; men of mild, and sweet, and peaceable spirits, as indeed most Anglers are: these men, our blessed Saviour, who is observed to love to plant grace in good natures, though indeed nothing be too hard for him, yet these men he chose to call from their irreprovable employment of fishing, and gave them grace to be his disciples, and to follow him and do wonders; I say four of twelve. And it is observable, that it was our Saviour's will, that these our four fishermen should have a priority of nomination in the catalogue of his Twelve Apostles, Matt. x, 2-4, Acts i. 13, as namely, first St. Peter, St. Andrew, St. James, and St. John, and then the rest in their order.

"And it is yet more observable, that when our blessed Saviour went up into the mount, when he left the rest of his disciples and chose only three to bear him company at his Transfiguration, that those three were all Fishermen. And it is to be believed, that all the other Apostles, after they betook themselves to follow Christ, betook themselves to be Fisherman too; for it is certain that the greater number of them were found together fishing by Jesus after his Resurrection, as it is recorded inthe twenty-first chapter of St. John's Gospel, v. 3,4.

"And since I have your promise to hear me with patience, I will take a liberty to look back upon an observation that hath been made by an ingenious and learned man; who observes, that God hath been pleased to allow those whom he himself hath appointed to write his holy will in Holy Writ, yet, to express his will in such metaphors as their former affections or practice had inclined them to: and he brings Solomon for an example, who before his conversion was remarkably carnally amorous; and after, by God's appointment, wrote that spiritual dialogue or holy amorous love-song, the Canticles, betwixt God and his church; in which he says his beloved had eyes like the fishpools of Heshbon.

"And if this hold in reason, as I see none to the contrary, then it may be probably concluded, that Moses, who, I told you before, writ the Book of Job, and the Prophet Amos, who was a shepherd, were both Anglers; for you shall in all the Old Testament find fish-hooks, I think, but twice mentioned; namely, by meek Moses, the friend of God, and by the humble Prophet Amos.

"Concerning which last, namely, the Prophet Amos, I shall make but this observation,—that he that shall read the humble, lowly, plain style of the prophet, and compare it with the high, glorious, eloquent style of the Prophet Isaiah, though they be both equally true, may easily believe Amos to be, not only a shepherd, but a good-natured, plain fisherman. Which I do the rather believe by comparing the affectionate, loving, lowly, humble Epistles of St. Peter, St. James, and St. John, whom we know were all Fishers, with the glorious language and high metaphors of St. Paul, who we may believe was not.

"And for the lawfulness of fishing, it may very well be maintained by our Saviour's bidding St. Peter cast his hook into the water and catch a fish, for money to pay tribute to Cæsar. And let me tell you, that Angling is of high esteem, and of much use in other nations. He that reads the Voyages of Ferdinand Mendez Pinto shall find that there he declares to have found a king and several priests a-fishing.

"And he that read Plutarch shall find that Angling was not contemptible in the days of Mark Antony and Cleopatra, and that they in the midst of their wonderful glory used Angling as a principal recreation. And let me tell you, that in the Scripture, Angling is always taken in the best sense; and that, though Hunting may be sometimes so taken, yet it is but seldom to be so understood. And let me add this more,—he that views the ancient Ecclesiastical Canons shall find Hunting to be forbidden to churchmen, as being a turbulent, toilsome, perplexing recreation; and shall find Angling allowed to clergymen, as being a harmless recreation, a recreation that invites them to contemplation and quietness.

"I might here enlarge myself by telling you what commendations our learned Perkins bestows on Angling; and how dear a lover and great a practiser of it our learned Doctor Whitaker was, as indeed many others of great learning have been. But I will content myself with two memorable men, that lived near to our own time.

"The first is Doctor Nowel, sometime Dean of the Cathedral Church of St. Paul in London, where his monument stands yet undefaced: a man that in the Reformation of Queen Elizabeth, not that of Henry VIII., was so noted for his meek spirit, deep learning, prudence, and piety, that the then Parliament and Convocation both chose, enjoined, and trusted him to be the man to make a Catechism for public use, such a one as should stand as a rule for faith and manners to their posterity. And the good old man, though he was very learned, yet knowing that God leads us not to heaven by many nor by hard questions, like an honest Angler, made that good plain, unperplexed Catechism which is printed with our good old Service-Book. I say, this good man was a dear lover and contant practiser of Angling as any age can produce; and his custom was to spend, besides his fixed hours of prayer, those hours which by command of the Church were enjoined the clergy, and voluntarily dedicated to devotion by many primitive Christians,—I say, beside those hours, this good man was observed to spend a tenth part of his time in Angling; and also, for I have conversed with those which have conversed with him, to bestow a tenth part of his revenue, and usually all his fish, amongst the poor that inhabited near to those rivers in which it was caught; saying often, 'that Charity gave life to Religion': and at his return to his house would praise God he had spent that free from worldly trouble both harmlessly, and in a recreation that became a churchman. And this good man was well content, if not desirous, that posterity should know he was an Angler, as may appear by his picture now to be seen, and carefully kept in Brazen-nose College, to which he was a liberal benefactor; in which picture he is drawn leaning on a desk with his Bible before him, and on one hand of him his lines, hooks, and other tackling, lying in a round; and on his other hand are his Angle-rods of several sorts: and by them this is written, 'that he died 13 Feb. 1601, being aged ninety-five years, forty-four of which he had been Dean of St. Paul's Church; and that his age had neither impaired his hearing, nor dimmed his eyes, nor weakened his memory, nor made any of the faculties of his mind weak or useless.' 'T is said that Angling and temperance were great dauses of these blessings, and I wish the like to all that imitate him and love the memory of so good a man.

"My next and last example shall be that undervaluer of money, the late Provost of Eton College, Sir Henry Wotton, a man with whom I have often fished and conversed, a man whose foreign employments int he service of this nation, and whose experience, learning, wit, and cheerfulness made his company to be esteemed one of the delights of mankind. This man, whose very approbation of Angling were sufficient to convince any modest censurer of it, this man was also a most dear lover, and frequent practiser, of the art of Angling; of which he would say, ''T was an employment for his idle time, which was then not idly spent': for Angling was, after tedious study, 'a rest to his mind, a cheerer of his spirits, a diverter of sadness, a calmer of unquiet thoughts, a moderator of passions, a procurer of c'ntentedness'; and 'that it begat habits of peace and patience in those that professed and practised it.' Indeed, my friend, you will find Angling to be the virtue of humility, which has a calmness of spirit, and a world of other blessings attending upon it.

"Sir, this was the saying of that learned man, and I do easily believe that peace, and patience, and a calm content, did cohabit in the cheerful heart of Sir Henry Wotton, because I know that, when he was beyond seventy years of age, he made this description of a part of the present pleasure that possessed him, as he sat quietly in a summer's evening on a bank a fishing. It is a description of the Spring, which because it glided as soft and sweetly from his pen as that river does at this time, by which it was then made, I shall repeat it:—

"This day Dame Nature seemed in love:
The lusty sap began to move;
Fresh juice did stir th' embracing vines,
And birds had drawn their valentines.
The jealous Trout, that low did lie,
Rose at a well-dissembled fly:
There stood my friend, with patient skill,
Attending of his trembling quill.

Already were the eaves possest
With the swift Pilgrim's daubed nest:
The groves already did rejoice
In Philomel's triumphing voice:
The showers were short, the weather mild,
The morning fresh, the evening smiled.
Joan takes her neat rubbed pail, and now
She trips to milk the sand-red cow;

Where, for some sturdy foot-ball swain,
Joan strokes a syllabub or twain.
The fields and gardens were beset
With tulips, crocus, violet:

And now, though late, the modest rose
Did more than half a blush disclose.
Thus all looks gay, and full of cheer,
To welcome the new-liveried year.'

"These were the thoughts that then possessed the undisturbed mind of Sir Henry Wotton. Will you hear the wish of another Angler, and the commendation of his happy life, which he also sings in verse? viz. Jo. Davors, Esq.:

"Let me live harmlessly, and near the brink
Of Trent or Avon have a dwelling-place;
Where I may see my quill or cock down sink
With eager bite of Perch, or Bleak, or Dace;
And on the world and my Creator think:
Whilst some men strive ill-gotten goods t' embrace,
And others spend their time in base excess
Of wine, or worse, in war and wantonness.

> *"Let them that list these pastimes still pursue,*
> *And on such pleasing fancies feed their fill,*
> *So I the fields and meadows green may view,*
> *And daily by fresh rives walk at will,*
> *Among the daisies and the violets blue,*
> *Red hyancinth, and yellow daffodil,*
> *Purple Narcissus like the morning rays,*
> *Pale gander-grass, and azure culver-keys.*

"I count it higher pleasure to behold
The stately compass of the lofty sky,
And in the midst thereof, like burning gold,
The flaming chariot of the world's great eye;
The watery clouds that in the air up-rolled
With sundry kinds of painted colors fly';
And fair Aurora lifting up her head,
Still blushing, rise from old Tithonus' bed;

> *"The hills and mountains raised from the plains,*
> *The plains extended level with the ground,*
> *The grounds divided into sundry veins,*
> *The veins enclosed with rivers running round;*
> *These rivers making way through Nature's chains*
> *With headlong course into the sea profound;*
> *The raging sea, beneath the valleys low,*
> *Where lakes and rills and rivulets do flow;*

"The lofty woods, the forests wide and long,
Adorned with leaves, and branches fresh and green
In whose cool bowers the birds with many a song
So welcome with their quire the Summer's Queen;
The meadows fair where Flora's gift among
Are intermixed, with verdant grass between;
The silver-scaléd fish that softly swim
Within the sweet brook's crystal watery stream.

"All these, and many more of His creation
That made the heavens, the Angler oft doth see;
Taking therein no little delectation,
To think how strange, how wonderful, they be!
Framing thereof an inward contemplation.
To set his heart from other fancies free;
And whilst he looks on these with joyful eye,
His mind is rapt above the starry sky.'

"Sir, I am glad my memory has not lost these last verses, because they are some-what more pleasant and more suitable to May-day than my harsh discourse; and I am glad your patience held out so long as to hear them and me, for both together have brought us within sight of the Thatched House.

"*Venator:* Sir, you have Angled me on with much pleasure to the Thatched House; and now I find your words true, that 'good company makes the way seem short': for trust me, Sir, I thought we had wanted three miles of this house till you showed it to me; but now we are at it, we'll turn into it.

"*Piscator:* Most gladly, Sir, and we'll drink a civil cup to all the Otter-hunters that are to meet you to-morrow.

"*Venator:* That we will, Sir, and to all the lovers of Angling too, of which number I am now willing to be one myself; for, by the help of your good discourse and com-pany, I have put on new thoughts both of the art of Angling, and of all that profess it: and if you will but meet me

to-morrow at the time and place appointed, and bestow one day with me and my friends in hunting the Otter, I will dedicate the next two days to wait upon you, and we two will for that time do nothing but angle, and talk of fish and fishing.

"*Piscator:* 'T is a match, Sir; I'll not fail you, God willing, to be at Amwell Hill to-morrow morning before sun-rising."

* * *

Roger Wolcott, Connecticut lawyer and politician, refers to fishing in a poem, circa 1725, in Wolcott, "Some Improvement of Vacant Hours," in *Poetical Meditations, Being the Improvement of Some Vacant Hours* (New London, Conn.: L. Green, 1725), 32.

"The *Fiſherman* the Fry with Pleaſure gets,
With Seins, Pots, Angles, and his Tramel-pots,
In it Swim *Salmon, Sturgion, Crap* and *Eels*,...."

* * *

Joseph Seccombe, Massachusetts essayist, defends fishing as a spiritual activity, circa 1739, in [Seccombe], *Buſineſs and Diverſion inoffenſive to God and neceſſary for the Comfort and Support of human Society. A Discourse utter'd in Part at Ammauſkeeg-Falls, in the Fiſhing-Seaſon. 1739* (Boston: Kneeland & Green, 1743), 1-7, 16-19, 20-21.

"To the Honourable
Theodore Atkinſon, Eſq;
AND OTHER
The Worthy Patrons of the Fiſhing
AT
AMMUSAUSKEEG.

Gentlemen,

"IT'S not to fignify to others that I pretend to an Intimacy with you, or that I ever had a Share in thofe pleafant Diverfions, which you have innocently indulged your felves in, at the Place where I have taken an annual Tour for fome Years paft. Yet I doubt not but you'l Patronize my Intention, which is to fence againft Bigottry and Superftition. All Excefs I difclaim, but pretend to be a Favourer of Religion, and of Labour as an Ingredient, and of Recreation as a neceffary Attendant.

"I believe the Gentleman who moved me to preach there in fome odd Circum-ftances, and thofe at whofe Defire and Charge this Difcourfe is Printed, (asking their Pardon if my Suggeftion appear to them ungrounded) were moved more from the un-commonnefs in it. I have put off the Importunity for near thefe three Years; but leaft it fhould be, that I fear, it's being feen by the World, I fubmit it to Sight and Cenfure.

"So little as I know you, Gentlemen, I heartily prefent it to you; tho' all the Reafon that I intend to offer is, we have fifhed upon the fame Banks; And tho' I know this will be no Bait, I am fond of being efteemed, in the Affair of Fifhing,

Gentlemen,

your moft Obedient and very humble Servant,

Fluviatulis Pifscator, *alias Joseph Seccomb*

"Bufinefs *and* Diverfion
inoffenfive to GOD.

JOHN XXI. iii.

Simon Peter faith unto them, I go a Fifhing.

"'Tis an odd and vicious Conceit of the Superftitious, who in Popifh Countries are called the Religious; that a folitary Sequeftration from the focial Affairs and Duties of Life, afford a mighty Advantage to Religion: For this is contrary to the Defign of the Creator in the Make and Conftitution of Man; oppofite to the Providence and Precepts of God, and the Examples of holy Men recorded in facred Hiftory. The Inftance in our Text fhows that *Bufinefs,*† or I think Diverfion in proper Portions of Time, and other fuitable Circumsftances, are not hurtful, but very friendly to Religion.

†*For their ftated Bufinefs, was to preach the Gofpel; tho' Fifhing had been their Employment.*

The Apoftles were conftituted Fifhers of Men, to allure and draw Souls to Chrift, from a Pit of Sin and Mifery, to an Ocean of Piety and Pleafure. —An high and really religious Employemnt! And *our Lord* gave them a *Vacancy,* with Reftriction, *but tarry ye at Jerufalem.* They had been commiffioned long before, [Matth. x. 17 and Luke ix.] but before they were to enter upon their Enterprize, in which he fhould be corporally abfent, they muft have a Leifure refrefhing Seafon. To what fhould they in Reafon have devoted this Intermiffon, but Fafting and Mourning, for now the Bridegroom was not always with them? Why, *Obedience is better than Sacrifice, and to hearken, than the Fat of Rams,* I Sam. xv. 22. He who beft knew the Nature of Man, before he was to fend Men upon extraordinary Bufinefs, would give them Leifure; nor was this Space confined wholly to Diverfion. Certainly thefe Saints were as fincerely and pioufly affected to God, as the fuperftitious Biggots to Popery can, with any Shew of Modefty, pretend to be; yet they divert themfelves in fo fuitable a Seafon, and outr Lord not only appoints the Leifure, but fupports them in it; by giving them a lucky Draught of Fifhes. This facred Story leads me to think,

I. In the general, that the common Enterprizes of Life are not inconfiftent with Piety towards God: But that infinite Holinefs may be pleafed with them. And in particular, that

II. Fifhing is innocent as Bufinefs or Diverfion.

"Some may think it ftrange that I give myfelef the Trouble to illuftrate thefe Things, which, to them appear level to the loweft Capacity.

"But all Men are not of the fame Caft or Conftitution. A Propofition which is eafy to one, may be as doubtful and difficult to another; and it is no uncommon Cafe, for Men who have no higher End in their Employments, and have been unfeafonable, unguarded and irregular in their Diverfions, and have no higher End than Self, if they are convinced of their Idolatry and carnality, to exclaim againft the World! Then, when they moft of all need to be diligent in fome good Employment, Diligence is termed Worldly-mindednefs; feafonably and temperately to recreate themfelves, is carnal Pleafure. Thefe Difficulties require no great Depth of Tho't, nor a Multitude of Words for their Solution.

"We may, in an eafy and natural Manner, confider that Religion is all of a Piece, and one Duty does not deftroy another. That Bufinefs and Diverfion, in their proper Place and Time, determined from a good Principle, and performed pioufly and prudently; are fo far from being offenfive, that they are a neceffary Branch of our holy Religion.

"Let us then in the general confider, *Whether the common Enterprizes of human Life, be confiftent with practical Piety.*

"Here we muft tell what we mean, by the common Enterprizes of Life. And we renounce all unjuft and difhonest Methods of obtaining the Riches, Honours, and Pleafures of the World: And all unlawful Games, and thofe which are lawful, when they are unfuitably and irregularly managed.

"We confider Bufinefs or Diverfions, as human Underftandings. By Bufinefs, we mean our ftated Exercifes, r that which we ought to employ moft of our Time in, and moft of our Thoughts about. Diverfion is the turning afide from Bufinefs, in fome proper Period, to refrefh ourfelves, and if it fhould be made evident, that thefe are Parts of our Duty to God, I fuppose they muft be confiftent with real Religion. And this will appear, if we confider, That God is an active Being, and propofes himfelf as our Pattern. It's not only contrary to Scripture, and deep thinking, but common Senfe, to fuppofe the great Creator and Governour of all Worlds, idle and unactive. Every one conceives fomething of his Operation, as the Over-ruler of human Affairs, or Author of all Things. And if God be Agent, he expects thofe to be fuch who are capable of acting: And as he is perfect, and muft act in a moft excellent Manner, according to his own Nature, he muft expect and require his Creatures to act according to the Power with which he has endowed them. And as he has endowed Man with a Capacity of knowing fomething of him, he muft defign his imitating of him in his Meafure and Degree. In this the Image of God in Man confifts. And we are to imitate him in Labour and Reft, as well as in other Refpects. This will be clear to you, if you recollect the Fourth Commandment: *Six Days* fhalt *thou* Labour, for in fix—*the Lord made*—and *refted* on the feventh, &c.

"Indeed, no Man was made for Time, but Time for him: And as God ufes Eternity for his own Glory, according to his infinite Wifdom and Power; fo he expects Man fhould fpend his Time, according to his Capacity—.

"Man's Capacity is the Meafure of his Duty, and the Nature of Man requires Reft and Labour, and a prudent Interchange and Succeffion of each.

"II. *Whether Fifhing is lawful as Bufinefs or Diverfion.*

Not only thofe called Religious, among the *Turks* and *Perfians*, and the *Benjans*, &c. have fcrupled eating of Flefh or Fifh, but fome among ourfelves, fewar whether we ought to take away the Lives of Creatures for our own Support; and are pofitive that we fhould not for Diverfion. Many have a great Averfion to thofe whofe Trade it is to take away the Lives of the lower Species of Creatures. A Butcher is (in their Apprehenfion) a mere Monfter, and a Fifherman, a filthy Wretch.

"It's an ancient Obfervation, that *a merciful Man is merciful to his Beaft. The righteous Man regards the Life of his Beaft*, Prov. xii. 10. Where any have long ufed any Creature, the Tho't of it's Service, and fome fort of Regard contracted to it thereby, is not eafily conquered. But a noble generous Soul hates Barbarity to foreign as well as domeftick Creatures. 'It's not certain [fays my Lord BEACON] that the worthier any Soul is, the larger is it's Compaffion. For contracted degenrate Minds imagine that thofe Things belong not to them: But the Mind that looks upon itfelf as a nobler Portion of the Univerfe, is kindly affected towards inferiour Creatures—'.

"He that takes Pleafure in the Pains and dying Agonies of any lower Species of Creatures, is either a ftupid fordid Soul, or a Murderer in Heart. —He that delighteth to fee a Brute die, would foon take as great Pleafure in the Death of a Man.

"But here, in *Fifhing*, we are fo far from delighting to fee our Fellow-Creature die, that we hardly think whether they live—We have no more of a murderous Tho't in taking them, than in cutting up a Mefs of Herbage. We are taking fomething, which God, the Creator and Proprietor of all, has given us to ufe for Food, as freely as the *green Herb*. Gen. ix. 2, 3.

"He allows the eating them, therefore the mere catching them is no Barbarity. Befides God feems to have carv'd out the Globe on purpofe for a univerfal Supply: In Seas, near Shores, are Banks and Beds made for them;—to furnifh the Lands adjacent—and Lands which lye remote, are more divided into Lakes and Ponds, Brooks and Rivers; and he has implanted in feveral Sorts of Fifh, a ftrong Inftinct [or Inclination] to fwim up thefe Rivers a vaft Diftance from the Sea. And is it not remarkable, that Rivers moft incumbred with Falls, are ever more full of Fifh than others. Why are they directed here? Why retarded by thefe difficult Paffages? But to fupply the Inlands? Does forming and difpofing of thefe Things argue nothing?

"Since the Flood the Earth is more barren, and Vegetables afford not a fufficient Support for Mankind.—So that if the Lives of all thefe are of lefs Confequence, nay, are freely given by him whofe they are, they may be taken and ufed as Food: If they *may* be taken, any may make Bufinefs of taking them fo the Supply of others.

"But if this be innocent as Bufinefs, fome may ftill fcruple it as Diverfion.

"And why not all Diverfion with as good Reafon? The grave and judicious Mr. *Perkins* fays, * 'We are allowed to ufe the Creatures of God, not only for our Neceffity,

See his Works, Vol. 2. p. 140.

but for meet and convenient Delight. This is a confeffed Truth. And therefore to them who fhall condemn fit and convenient Recreation (as fome of the ancient Fathers have done, by Name *Chryfoftom* and *Ambrofe*) it may be faid, be not too righteous, be not too wife, *Eccl.* vii. 16.' But if we confider, that the End of Bufinefs and Diverfion are the fame, we fhall clearly conceive the Truth. The End of both are the Refrefhment and

Support of Man in the Service of God. If I may eat them for Refreſhment, I may as well catch them, if this recreate and refreſh me. It's as lawful to delight the Eye, as the Palate. All Pleaſure ariſes from the Suitableneſs and Agreableneſs between the perceptive Faculties, and the Objects that affect them: And our bountiful Maker, as he has given the animal Life many perceptive Faculties, the Senſes of Seeing, Hearing, Taſting, &c. ſo he has provded ſuitable Objects for all theſe Faculties, and does allow us to gratify ourſelves therewith.

"When the Body has been long wearied with Labour, or the Mind weakened with Devotion, it's requiſite to give them Eaſe; then the uſe of innocent and moderated Pleaſures and Recreations is both uſeful and neceſſary, to Soul and Body; it enlivens Nature, recruits our Spirits, and enders us more able to ſet about ſerious Buſineſs and Employment. For to intermix no Gratifications, nor Diverſions with our more ſerious Affairs, makes the Mind unactive, dull and uſeleſs.≠†

≠ Cito rumpes arcum ſi tenſum habueris.

At ſi laxaris, cum voles, eris utilis,
Sic luſus Animo debet aliquando dari,
Ad cogitandum melior, ut redeat tibi.
————————— Study and eaſe
Together mixt; Sweet Recreation,
And Innocence, which moſt does pleaſe,
                        with Meditation.

† The Phariſees were of this Temper and frequently cenſure and condemn Chriſt for his Recreations, both for the Matter and manner. *The Son of Man came eating and drinking, and they ſay, behold a Man gluttonus and a winebibber, a Friend of Publcans and Sinners.* Math. 11. 19. Luke 7. 34, &c. and Chap. 15. 2. But all Extreams are bad, one leads to another; thoſe who in this Caſe *Strain at a Gnat*, in another will generally *Swallow a Camel.*

"It proceeds either from Pride, ill Nature or Hypocriſy, when People cenſure and are offended at the Liberties which others uſe in thus relaxing their Minds, Sloth and Idleneſs, we have already inveigh'd againſt, and condemn'd; bt thoſe who give feaſonable Hours for their Devotions and know how to diſpatch the proper Buſineſs of Life well and feaſonably enough, and ſtill aim chiefly at the Glory of God, need be under no Apprehenſions of the divine Wrath and Diſpleaſure on the Score of their Diverſions. For this is *good* and *comely*, Eccl. v. 18. And indeed, the Comforts and Enjoyments of this Life, which we receive from the bountiful Hand of God, is a great Subject of our Praiſe and Thankfgiving to God,—*that the Lines are fallen to us in pleaſant Places,—our Heads anointed, our Cup running over.* The Steams [Streams?] lead us up to the Fountain and Spring-Head. Our Diverſion, if rightly uſed, nt only fits us for, but leads us to Devotion; and the Creature brings us to Chriſt. Thus in the Context, the Diſciples go a fiſhing, and Chriſt manifeſts himſelf to them. —Not only countenances them, by fucceeding their Deſign; but excites and draws out their Affections to him, ſo much that *Simon* could not wait 'till the Veſſel came to Shore, but leapt into the Lake, and ſwam ſwift afhore, to greet and converſe with his deareſt Lord.

[Digreſſion on religion and eating and drinking]

"... No Man ſhould make Sports his Buſineſs, nor Paſtimes his Employment, no more than Cordials his Drink, or Sauces his Meat. This deſtroys the very Notion of Diverſion. Says Mr. Lock, 'Some Men may be ſaid never to divert themſelves, they can't *turn afide from Bufinefs*, for they never do any.' *To every Thing there is a Seafon,* Eccl. iii. 1,—4.

"Should we not always in every Enterprize wifh for the Prefence and Bleffing of Chrift? Methinks thofe who love and adore the bleffed Jefus, fhould defire to fee him every where, and in every Thing! who calls for our Devotion and allows our Diverfion! who procured Peace and Pleafure fro wretched finful Men! Don't I owe a *grateful Senfe* of the Grace and Favour of my Benefactor, in the Enjoyment of every Bleffing? This gives a Guft to every Enjoyment, our tafting the Sweetnefs of Chrift in them. — We confider hime as Mediator of the Covenant of Grace, and when we fee every Thing convey'd from God to us by him, then we have a real Relifh for them—. There is no fuitable folid Satisfaction in any temporal Good, but as the Gift of God thro' Chrift. This every good Man, in a good Frame finds and feels—. 'Bufinefs and Diverfions, Cities and Palaces, with their various Ornaments; Fields and Groves; Spring, Summer, and Autumn, with all their flowry Beauties and tafteful Bleffings, are fome of the Delights of the Sons of Men. Books and Learning, and polite Company, and refin'd Science, are the more elegant Joys of ingenious Spirits: Thefe are enticing Gratifications of the Senfes or the Mind of Man; they are all innocent in themfelves, they may be fanctified to divine Purpofes, and afford double Satisfaction if God be among them: But if God be abfent, if he hide his Face or frown upon the Soul, not Palacaes, nor Groves, nor Fields, nor Bufinefs, nor Diverfion, nor all the flowry or tafteful Bleffings of Spring or Summer, nor the more refin'd Joys of Books and Learning, and elegant Company; not all the rich Provifion of Nature and Art, can entertain or refrefh, can fatisfy or please the Soul of a Chriftian—when fmitten with the Love of God.

"To conclude, Let us remember that *we* and *all we have*, is God's, and that we are accountable to him for our Improvement of all, and depend on Chrift for our Acceptance with him in all.   AMEN."

* * *

A children's book draws a moral from fishing, in *A Little Pretty Pocket-Book, Intended for the Instruction and Amusement of Little Master Tommy and Pretty Miss Polly* (London: J. Newbery, 1767), 77.

"FISHING.

THE artful Angler baits his Hook,   RULE *of* LIFE.
and throws it gently in the Brook;   Learn well the Motions of the Mind;
Which the Fifh view with greedy Eyes,   Why you are made, for what defign'd."
And foon are taken by Surprife.

FISHING AMONG INDIGENOUS PEOPLES

Thomas Hariot, British promotional writer, describes fishing customs among Virginia area indigenous peoples, circa 1588, in [Hariot], *A Brief and True Report of the New Found Land of Virginia* (London, 1588), D3 and following unnumbered page.

"The inhabitants vfe to take the[m] two maner of wayes, the one is by a kind of wear made of reedes which in that countrey are very ftrong. The other way which is more ftrange, is with poles made fharpe at one ende, by fhooting them into the fifh after the maner as Irifhmen caft dartes; either as they are rowing in their boates or els as they are wading in the fhallowes for the purpofe."

* * *

Thomas Hariot, British promotional writer, and Theodore DeBry, Dutch illustrator, comment on fishing among Virginia area indigenous peoples, circa 1590, in [Hariot and] DeBry, *A Briefe and True Report of the New Found Land of Virginia* (Frankfurt, 1590), plate 13.

"Their manner of fishynge in Virginia.

"The haue likewife a notable way to catche fishe in their Riuers. for whear as they lacke both yron, and fteele, they fafte vnto their Reedes or longe Rodds, the hollowe tayle of a certaine fishe like to a fea crabb in fteede of a poynte, wehr with by nighte or day they ftricke fishes, and take them opp into their boates. They alfo know how to vfe the prickles, and pricks of other fishes. They alfo make weares, with fettinge opp reedes or twigges in the wter, which they foe plant one within a nother, that they growe ftill narrower, and narrower, as appeareth by this figure. Ther was neuer feene among vs foe cunninge a way to take fish withall, wherof fondrie fortes as they fownde in their Riuers vnlike vnto ours. which are alfo a very good tafte. Dowbtlefs yt is a pleafant fighte to fee the people, fomtymes wadinge, and goinge fomtymes failinge in thofe Riuers, which are shallowe and not deepe, free from all care of heapinge opp Riches for their pofteritie, content with their ftate, and liuinge frendlye together of thofe thinges which god of his bountye hath giuen vnto them, yet without giuinge hym any thankes according to his defarte. So fauage is this people, and depriued of the true knowledge of god. For they haue none other then is mentionned before this worke."

* * *

William Strachey, British explorer, details fishing among the indigenous peoples in Virginia, circa 1610-1612, in Strachey, *The Historie of Travaile into Virginia Britannia; Expressing the Cosmographie and Comodities of the Country Togither with the Manners and Customes of the People,* ed. by R.H. Major (London: The Hakluyt Society, 1899), 75.

"Their fishing is much in boats. These they call quintans, as the West Indians call their canoas. They make them with one tree, by burning and scraping awaye the coales with stones and shells tyll they have made them in forme of a trough. Some of them are an ell deepe, and forty or fifty foote in length, and some will transport forty men; but the most ordinary are smaller, and will ferry ten or twenty, with some luggage, over their broadest rivers. Instead of oares, they use paddles and sticks, which they will rowe faster then we in our barges.

"They have netts for fishing, for the quantity as formerly brayed and mashed as our's, and these are made of barkes of certaine trees, deare synewes, for a kynd of grasse, which they call pemmenaw, of which their women, between their hands and thighes, spin a thredd very even and redily, and this threed serveth for many uses, as about their howsing, their mantells of feathers and their trowses, and they also with yt make lynes for angles.

"Theire angles are long small rodds, at the end whereof they have a clift to the which the lyne is fastened, and at the lyne they hang a hooke, made eyther of a bone grated (as they nock their arrowes) in the forme of a crooked pynne or fishooke, or of the splinter of a bone, and with a threed of the lyne they tye on the bayte. They also use long arrowes tyed in a line, wherewith they shoote at fish in the rivers. Those of Accowmak use staves like unto javelins headed with bone; with these they dart fish, swymming in the water. They have also many arteficyall weeres (before described) in which they take aboundance of fishe."

* * *

Edward Winslow, English settler and chronicler of Plymouth, Massachusetts, mentions the fishing of indigenous peoples, circa 1620s, in [Winslow], "Gov. Bradford's History of Plymouth Colony," in Alexander Young, ed., *Chronicles of the Pilgrim Fathers of the Colony of Plymouth, from 1602 to 1625* (Boston: Charles C. Little and James Brown, 1841), 363.

"The men themselves wholly in hunting, and other exercises of the bow, except at some times they take some pains in fishing."

* * *

William Wood, English settler in New England, discusses fishing by indigenous people, circa 1634, in Wood, *New Englands Prospect, A True, Lively and Experimentall Defcription of that Part of* America, *Commonly Called Nevv England. Difcovering the Ftate of that Countrie, Both As It Ftands to Our New-Come* Englifh *Planters; and to the Old Native Inhabitants* (London: Thomas Cotes, 1634), reprinted as *Wood's New-England Prospect* (Boston: The Prince Society, 1865), 100-101.

"Of their Fifhings.

Of their fifhing, in this trade they may be expert, being experienced in the knowledge of all baites, fitting fundry baites for feverall fifhes, and diverfe feafons; being not ignorant likewife of the removall of fifhes, knowing when to fifh in rivers, and when at rockes, when in Baies, and when at Seas: fince the *Englifh* came they be furnifhed with *Englifh* hookes and lines, before they made them of their owne hempe more curi-oufly wrought, of ftronger materials than ours, hooked with bone hookes: but lazineffe drives them to make of their owne; they make likewife very ftrong Sturgeon nets with which they catch Sturgeons of 12. 14, and 16. fome 18. foote long in the day time, in the night time they betake them to their Burthcen *Cannows*, in which they carry a forty fathome line, with a fharp bearded dart, faftned at the end thereof; then lightning a blazing torch made of Burtchen rindes, they weave it too and againe by their *Cannow* fide, which the Sturgeon much delighted with, comes to them tumbling and playing, turning up his white belly, into which they thruft their launce, his backe being impen-etrable; which done they haile to the fhore their ftrugling prize. They have often re-courfe unto the rockes whereupon the fea beates, in warme weather to looke out for fleepie Seales, whofe oyle they much efteeme, ufing it for for divers things. In fummer they feldome fifh any where but in falt, in winter in the frefh water and ponds; in froftie weater they cut round holes in the yce, about which they wil fit like fo many apes, on their naked breeches upon the congealed yce, catching of Pikes, Pearches, Breames, and other forts of frefh water fifh."

* * *

Peter Lindestrom, Swedish geographer, describes fishing among the Delaware indigenous people, circa 1654-1656, in Lindestrom, *Geographia Americae with An Account of the Delaware Indians Based on Surveys and Notes Made in 1654-1656,* trans. and ed. by Amandus Johnson (Philadelphia: Swedish Colonial Society, 1925), 219-220.

"The savages do not know the use of seines, nets, hooks, trolling rods or trolling-line, but far up in the kills or in the creeks emptying into the river, they arrange their fishing, either where the kills stop [their sources], [up] in the country or at the falls. There they close in the kills right across, leaving only a little opening or entrance for the fish right above like a *kassenoor* [fishtrap]. Now when the river rises and the wa-ter is highest they close up in the opening, but when the water is run out and the ebb is lowest then the fish remains behind in the low water, where they either catch them with their hands or shoot it. Otherwise, they also shoot it in deep water, where they can find it, and thus they obtain fish of all kinds, that are found there in abundance, spend-ing [nothing] on either seines, nets or any fishing implements."

* * *

Samuel Clarke, British writer, concerning fishing among the Virginia and New England area indigenous peoples, circa 1670, in Clarke, *A True and Faithful Account of the Four Chiefest Plantations of the English in America. Of Virginia, New England, Bermudus, Barbados* (London: R. Clavel and T. Passenger, 1670), 9, 49.

"The Women ufe to fpin the Bark of Trees, Deer Sinews, or a kind of Grafs called *Pemmenaud*, of which they make a very good thred, which ferves for many ufes about their houfes, Apparel, Fifhing-nets, Lines for Angles: Their hooks are either a bone grated in the form of a hooked Pin, or of the fplinter of a Bone tied to the cleft of a little ftick, and with the end of the Line they tie on the bait. They alfo ufe long Arrows tied to a Line, with which they fhoot at Fifhes in the River, or Darts which they throw at them.

"They take extream pains in their Huntings and Fifhings, whereunto they are enured from their Child-hood: And by their continual rangings they know all the places and Advantages moft frequented with *Deer, Beafts, Fifhes, Fowls, Rooks, Berries.*"

"They are very expert in fifhing, knowing all kinds of baits fit for each feveral forts of fifh, and for all feafons of the year. They know alfo when to fifh in the Rivers, when at the Rocks, when in the Bayes, and when at the Seas: Before the Englifh furnifhed them with Hooks and Lines, they made Lines of their own Hemp, curiously wrought, ftronger than ours, and ufed bone-hooks; They make alfo ftrong Nets, wherewith they, catch Sturgion; and in the night they go forth in their canooes with a blazing Torch, which they wave up and down, with which the Sturgion being delighted, playes about it, turning up her white belly, into which they thruft a bearded Dart, her back being impenetrable, and fo hale her to the fhoar. They look out alfo for fleeping Seals, whofe Oyl they much efteem, ufing it for divers things."

* * *

John Josselyn, British naturalist, comments on fishing by indigenous peoples in New England, circa 1673, in Josselyn, *An Account of Two Voyages to New-England,* 2nd ed. (London: G. Widdowes, 1675), reprinted in *The Collections of the Massachusetts His-torical Society,* 3rd Series, Vol. 3 (Cambridge, Mass.: E.W. Metcalf and Company, 1833), 306.

"[W]hen they are upon the fishing ground near a Bar of Sand (where the *Sturgeon* feeds upon the small fishes (like *Eals*) that are called Lances sucking them out of the Sands where they lye hid, with their hollow Trunks, for other mouth they have none) the *Indian* lights a piece of dry *Birch-Bark* which breaks out into a flame & holds it over the side of his *Canow*, the *Sturgeon* seeing this glaring light mounts to the

Surface of the water where he is slain and taken with a fisgig. *Salmons* and *lampres* are catch'd at the falls of Rivers."

* * *

Daniel Gookin, Cambridge, Masachusetts missionary, mentions fishing by New England area indigenous peoples, circa 1674, in Gookin, "Historical Collections of the Indians in New England," *Collections of the Massachusetts Historical Society, For the Year 1792. Volume I* (Boston: Munroe & Francis, 1806 [1674]), 149.

"They are much addicted to idleness, especially the men, who are disposed to hunting, fishing, and the war, when there is cause. That little tillage or planting used among them, was principally done by the women. Also in their removals from placeto place, which they are inclined to, for their fishing and hunting at several seasons, the women carry the greatest burthen...."

* * *

Thomas Glover, British surgeon, concerning fishing customs by Virginia indigenous peoples, 20 June 1676, in Glover, *An Account of Virginia, Its Scituation, Temperature, Productions, Inhabitants and Their Manner of Planting and Ordering Tobacco* (London: B.H. Blackwell, 1904 [1676]), 23-24.

"They did formerly catch their fifh after an odd manner before the *Englifh* came amongst them, which was thus: At the head of their *Canoes* they fixed a Hearth, on which in a dark night they would make a blaze of fire put to the fhivers of *Pine tree*; then they would paddle their Canoes along the fhoar in fhoal-water; the fifh feeing the light would come as thick as they could fwim by each other about the head of the *Canoes*; then with fticks that were pointed very fharp at the ends, they would ftrike through them and lift them up into the *Canoe*: But now they have learned of the *Englifh* to catch fifh with a hook and line, and fometimes the *Englifh* do ufe their way in dark nights, only they ftrike with an Inftrument of Iron fomewhat like Mole-tines."

* * *

John Dunton, London traveler, in Boston, discusses fishing by New England indigenous people, circa 1686, in [Dunton], *A Summer's Ramble, Through Ten Kingdomes, Occasionally Written by John Dunton, Citizen of London,* 2 Vols. (London: A. Baldwin, 1686), reprinted as W.H. Whitmore, ed., *Letters Written from New-England, A.D. 1686, by John Dunton* (Boston: The Prince Society, 1867), 186-189.

"As we paff'd along, we had the Sea in View, and faw fome Perfons fifhing thereon, which made me fay to my Companions, 'I have already an Account of the Indians Hunting, and now, to make the way feem lefs tedious, I wou'd defire one of you which beft can, to give me an Account of their way of Fifhing, and what fort of Fifh you have in this Countrey." Then he that was the beft Spokefman, and that gave me an Account of the Weather, &c. when we went to Braintree, thus began.

"'The way of Fifhing which the Indians ufe, has nothing very remarkable to diftinguifh it from that which is uf'd by the Englifh; but the variety of our Fifh may be worth your Knowledge: Which I will therefore give you an account of, as far as my Memory will let me. And becaufe I intend to name 'em all, I fhall name thofe we have in England, as well as thofe that are peculiar to this Countrey.' I bid him proceed without any further preface.

"'The firft,' faid he, 'I fhall name, is the Cod, which is indeed the firft that comes, a little before the Spring; then we have Lampries, which is the firft that comes in the

Spring, into frefh Rivers; we have alfo a Fifh fomewhat like a Herring, but not the same; We have alfo a Fifh call'd a baffe, of the head of which the Indians (and the Englifh too) make a very fine Difh, this Fifh having a great quantity of Brains and Fat, which eats as fweet as marrow: We have likewife great quantities of Sturgeon in this Countrey; which for goodnefs and greatnefs of it, is very much priz'd by the Natives, who upon that fcore refuf'd at firft to furnifh the Englifh either with fo many as they wanted, or fo cheap as they might have been afforded, till the Englifh themfelves got the way of fifhing for them, and now they have [them] cheap enough. The Indians venture one or two in a Canow (which is a Boat made out of the Body of a Tree, of fome fuch-like Inftrument, ftick this Fifh, and fo hale it into their Canow; and fometimes they take them by their Nets, which they make of Hemp, very ftrong. Which Nets they will fet thwart fome little River or Cove wherein they kill Baffe (at the Fall of the Water) with fharp fticks or Arrows, efpecially if headed with Iron gotten from the Eng- lifh, &c."

"'Another Fifh we have is Mackarel; we have alfo Salmon, which the Indians call Redfifh; then we a fat, fweet Fifh fomething like a Hadock: Bream is another of our Fifh, of which there is abundance, which the Indians dry in the Sun and Smoak, and fome of the Englifh begin to falt; both ways they keep all the year; and it is hoped it may be as well accepted as Cod at a Market; and better too, were it once known, it being a better Fifh; we have likewife a Fifh call'd Sheeps-heads, and good ftore of Eels; Porpufes is another of our Fifh, and we have alfo Whales, which in fome places are often caft up: I have feen fome my felf,' faid he, 'but they were not above fixty foot long, which were counted but fmall ones: The Indians cut them out in feveral Parcels, and give and fend it far and near among themfelves, for an acceptable prefent; and as fuch it is taken....."

"'We have alfo here a fort of little Fifh, half as big as fprats, very plentiful in the Winter-Seafon. We have another Fifh, which we call a Winter-Fifh, which comes up in the Brooks and Rivulets, and which fome call Froft Fifh, becaufe they come from the Sea into Frefh Brooks, in times of Froft and Snow: The laft I fhall mention, is what we call a Frefh-Fifh, which when the Indians take, they are forc'd to break the Ice in frefh Ponds, where they alfo take many other forts, for the Countrey yields many other forts of Fifh, befides thofe I have mention'd; but I fear I have tir'd your Patience too much already.'"

* * *

Lamothe de Cadillac, French explorer, comments on fishing by indigenous peoples in the Great Lakes region, circa 1695, in Milo Milton Quaife, ed., "The Memoir of Lamothe Cadillac," in *The Western Country in the Seventeenth Century. The Memoirs of Lamothe Cadillac and Pierre Liette* (Chicago: Lakeside Press, 1947), 12-13.

"I think it would be useless to explain the way in which they fish, since each tribe has its own method. But I think I ought to mention the pleasure of seeing them bring up, in one net, as many as a hundred white fish. This is the most delicate fish in the lake. They are as large as shad in France. They also catch a large number of trout, weighing up to 50 pounds; they are certainly very good eating. Finally, the sturgeon, pike, carp, herring, dory, and a hundred different kinds of fish abound at this part of the lake."

* * *

Juan Mateo Manje, Spanish captain, concerning fishing by indigenous people in southern Arizona, February 1699, in [Manje], *Unknown Arizona and Sonora, 1693-1721, From the Francisco Fernandez del Castillo Version of Luz De Tierra Incognita by Captain Juan Mateo Manje,* ed. by Harry J. Karns (Tucson, Ariz.: Arizona Silhouettes, 1954), 112-113.

"They use fish nets made out of twine like those used in Europe. Out of various fibres they weave mats which they join by the ends, forming a sort of small boat from which they fish for the innumerable fish that abound in the river. There are trout and salmon, which they eat."

* * *

Robert Beverly, Virginia plantation owner and historian, describes fishing customs among the indigenous peoples, circa 1705, in Beverly, *The History and Present State of Virginia,* ed. by Louis B. Wright (Charlottesville, Va.: University Press of Virginia, 1947), 148-149, 310.

"Before the Arrival of the *English* there, the *Indians* had Fish in such vast Plenty, that the Boys and Girls wou'd take a pointed Stick, and strike the lesser sort, as they Swam upon the Flats. The larger Fish, that kept in deeper Water, they were put to a little more Difficulty to take; But for these they made Weyrs; that is, a Hedge of small riv'd Sticks, or Reeds, of the Thickness of a Man's Finger, these they wove together in a Row, with Straps of Green Oak, or other tough Wood, so close that the small Fish cou'd not pass through. Upon High-Water Mark, they pitched one End of the Hedge, and the other they extended into the River, to the Depth of Eight or Ten Foot, fastening it with Stakes, making Cods out from the Hedge on one side, almost at the End, and leaving a Gap for the Fish to go into them, which were contrived so, that the Fish could easily find their Passage into those Cods, when they were at the Gap, but not see their Way out again, when they were in:
Thus if they offered to pass through, they were taken.

"Sometimes they made such a Hedge as this, quite a-cross a Creek at High-Water, and at Low wou'd go into the Run, so contracted into a narrow Compass, and take out what Fish they pleased.

"At the Falls of the Rivers, where the Water is shallow, and the Current strong, the *Indians* use another kind of Weir, thus made: They make a Dam of loose Stone, whereof there is plenty at hand, quite a-cross the River, leaving One, Two, or more Spaces or Trunnels, for the Water to pass thro'; at the Mouth of which they set a Pot of Reeds, wove in Form of a Cone, whose Base is about Three Foot, and perpendicular Ten, into which the Swiftness of the Current carries the Fish, and wedges them so fast, they cannot possibly return.

"The *Indian* Way of Catching Sturgeon, when they came into the narrow part of the Rivers, was by a Man's clapping a Noose over their Tail, and by keeping fast his hold. Thus a Fish finding it self intangled, wou'd flounce, and often pull him under Water, and then that Man was counted a *Cockarouse,* or brave Fellow, that wou'd not let go; till with Swimming, Wading, and Diving he had tired the Sturgeon, and brought it ashore. Thses Sturgeons would also leap into their Canoes, in crossing the River, as many of them do still every Year, into the Boats of the *English.*

"They have also another Way of Fishing like those on the *Euxine* Sea, by the Help of a blazing Fire by Night. They make a Hearth in the Middle of their Canoe, raising it within Two Inches of the Edge; upon this they lay their burning Light-Wood, split into small Shivers, each Splinter whereof will blaze and burn End for End, like a Candle: 'Tis one Man's Work to tend this Fire and keep it flaming. At each End of the Canoe stands an *Indian*, with a Gig, or pointed Spear, setting the Canoe forward with the Butt-end of the Spear, as gently as he can, by that Means stealing upon the Fish, without any Noise, or disturbing of the Water. Then they with great Dexterity, dart these Spears ino the Fish, and so take 'em. Now there is a double Convenience in the Blaze of this Fire; for it not only dazzles the Eyes of the Fish, which will lie still, glaring upon it, but likewise discovers the Bottom of the river clearly to the Fisherman, which the Day-light does not."

"The *Indian* Invention of Weirs in Fishing, is mightily improved by the English besides which, they make use of Seins, Trolls, Casting-Netts, Settings-Netts, Hand-Fishing, and Angling, and in each find abundance of Diversion. I have set in the shade, at the Heads of the Rivers Angling, and spent as much time in taking the Fish off the Hook, as in waiting for their taking it. Like those of the *Euxine* Sea, they also Fish wth Spilyards, which is a long Line staked out in the River, and hung with a great many Hooks on short strings, fasten'd to the main Line, about three or four Foot asunder. The only difference is, our Line is supported by Stakes, and theirs is buoyed up with Gourds."

* * *

Daniel Neal, historian, circa 1720, concerning fishing by New England indigenous peoples, prior to 1700, in Neal, *History of New-England Containing an Impartial Account of the Civil and Ecclesiastical Affairs of the Country to the Year of Our Lord, 1700,* 2 vols., Vol. 1 (London: J. Clark, 1720), 25.

"...; the only Employment of the Men is Hunting and Fifhing; when Provifion is low, they go out into the Wood 50 or 100 in a Company with their Bows and Arrows, and bring in a frefh Supply, or fail down the Rivers in their Canoes to catch Fifh. In the Spring they catch *Lobfters, Clams,* &c. and afterwards *Bafs, Cod, Rock, Blue-Fifh, Salmon,* and *Lampus....* *Bafs, Blue-Fifh,* and *Sturgeon,* they ftrike with a fort of Dart made of Wood, and fharpen'd with a Fifh-Bone, to the End of which they tye a String, with which they drag the Fifh to Shoar."

* * *

Father Joseph François Lafitau, French Jesuit missionary, comments on fishing by American indigenous people, circa 1724, in Lafitau, *Customs of the American Indians Compared with the Customs of Primitive Times,* trans. and ed. by William N. Fenton and Elizabeth L. Moore, 2 vols., Vol. 2 (Toronto: The Champlain Society, 1977), 187.

"HUNTING AND FISHING

"If war is the noblest of all exercises and that on which the Indian prides himself the most, as is usually the case with nations which base their glory on it, hunting and fishing are his most customary exercises, because they are most necessary for for his living and he gets most of what he needs for his maintenance from them; the meats with which he nourishes himself, the clothing with which he covers himself, the oils with which he greases himself and the furs with which he trades. The mobile tribes live almost solely on meat and fish. Part of the year they are fish-eaters, roving ceaselessly on the sea shores, or the lakes and river banks. They spend the rest of the year in the woods, hunting wild beasts.

"I shall not enter here into the details of their different hunting and fishing expeditions, their way of hunting meats, having them dried by fire or the sun or reducing them to powder. These things are too well known and too often repeated to burden this work with them."

* * *

William Byrd, Westover, Virginia planter, describes fishing along the Virginia/North Carolina border, 19 November 1728, in [Byrd], "The History of the Dividing Line," in Louis B. Wright, ed., *The Prose Works of William Byrd of Westover. Narratives of a Colonial Virginian* (Cambridge, Mass.: Harvard University Press, 1966), 316-317.

"About eight miles farther we came to Sturgeon Creek, so called from the dexterity an Occaneechi Indian showed there in catching one of those royal fish, which was performed after the following manner: in the summertime 'tis no unusual thing for sturgeons to sleep on the surface of the water, and one of them, having wandered up into this creek in the spring, was floating in that drowsy condition. The Indian above-mentioned ran up to the neck into the creek a little below the place where he discovered the fish, expecting the stream would soon bring his game down to him. He judged the matter right, and as soon as it came within his reach, he whipped a running noose over his jowl. This waked the sturgeon, which, being strong in its own element, darted immediately under water and dragged the Indian after him. The man made it a point of honor to keep his hold, which he did to the apparent danger of being drowned. Sometimes both the Indian and the fish disappeared for a quarter of a minute and then rose at some distance from where they dived. At this rate they continued flouncing about, sometimes above and sometimes under water, for a considerable time, till at last the hero suffocated his adversary and haled his body ashore in triumph."

* * *

Fray Miguel Venegas, Mexican Jesuit missionary, repeats a decalogue of hunting and fishing commandments and describes fishing customs among indigenous peoples in California, circa 1758, in Venegas, *A Natural and Civil History of California,* 2 vols. (London: James Rivington and James Fletcher, 1759), 1:106-107; 2:275-276.

"His decalogue was as follows, 'That they fhould not eat of their firft hunting or fifhing, under pain of being difqualified from hunting or fifhing hereafter. 2d, That they fhould not eat of fome certain fifh. 3d, That they fhould forbear eating fome particular parts of the game, and thefe were the beft and fatteft, faying, that this fat was that of dead old men; and that by eating it old age would immediately come upon them. Thus the beft pieces fell to the fhare of the old hechiceros [shaman] alledging, that as they were already advanced in years, they had nothing to fear on this head. 4. That they fhould not gather certain fruits, nor take fome fpecies of fifh (and both of thefe were the beft) as they would do them a great deal of hurt; but that nothing injured old people. 5. That if they caught any ftag or fifh of an extraordinary fize, not to offer to eat it, as belonging to the hechiceros.... 9. That in very hot weather, all fhould come out and pay their salutations to the fun, who would not then moleft them in their huntings and fifhings; but on the contrary render every undertaking profperous.'"

"The manner of fifhing among the Indians is very ingenious, eafy, and pleafant. They carry in their boats long and thin poles, and to one of thefe they fix a harpoon a long rope. When they perceive at the bottom near the rocks a fea wolf or any other fifh worth catching, they ftrike it with the harpoon; then vere out the rope, till the fifh being fpent, they draw it afhore if large; and if fmall into the boat. Thus they catch as many fifh as they pleafe."

Jean-Bernard Bossu, French traveler, discusses fishing by the Alabama indigenous people, 2 May 1759, in Seymour Feiler, ed., *Jean-Bernard Bossu's Travels in the Interior of
North America, 1751-1762* (Norman, Okla.: University of Oklahoma Press, 1962), 147.

"The [Alabama] Indians are also skillful fishermen, although they use neither hooks
nor nets. They gather reeds, which are plentiful on the river banks, dry the over a fire
or in the sun, sharpen one end like a dart, and tie to the other end a cord made of bark.
They go out into the lake in their canoes and spear the fish in the water. Others hunt
them with bows and arrows. The wounded fish come to the surface of the water."

* * *

Thomas Hutchinson, Massachusetts politician and historian, describes fishing by New
England indigenous peoples, circa 1765, in Hutchinson, *The History of the Province of
Massachusetts Bay,* 2nd ed., 2 vols., Vol. 1 (London: M. Richardson, 1765), 471.

"Their hunting and fifhing, being all they did, which could becalled labor, for their
maintenance or fupport, ferved alfo as diverfions.... Their ordinary fifhing was with
hooks and lines. They made their hooks of bones, their lines of wild hemp, ftronger and
neater than the Englifh lines*. They had a way of taking Sturgeon by lighting a torch
of birch bark, which waving to and fro by the fide of their canoe, would delight the
Sturgeon, and caufe them to come tumbling and playing, throwing up their white bellies, into which the Indians ftruck their fpears or darts†. The Sturgeons backs were
impenetrable. They had grand fifhings at feveral falls of the rivers, at moft of which
a canton or company of Indians had their chief refidence, and at fixed feafons the
feveral neighbouring cantons met by turns, partly for recreation,...."

*Douglas fays they had no threads of flax, hemp or any other herbs, but the
earlieft accounts of the Maffachufet Indians affert the contrary, and Champlain
fays that it was part of the employment of the Indian women of Canada to twift
the wild hemp and make it into nets for fifhing.

†The natives of the Canary Iflands happened to hit upon the fame way of
taking fifh.

THE CAROLINAS AND GEORGIA

John Norris, South Carolinian, comments on fishing in his province, circa 1712, in
[Norris], *Profitable Advice for Rich and Poor in a Discourse Between* James Freeman,
a Carolina Planter *and* Simon Question, *a* West-Country *Farmer. Containing a Descrip-
tion, or True Relation of South Carolina An* English *Plantation, or Colony, in* America
(London: J. How, 1712), reprinted in Jack P. Greene, ed., *Selling a New World. Two
Colonial South Carolina Promotional Pamphlets* (Columbia: University of South Carolina
Press, 1989), 111.

"I say our Fresh-Water produces *Trouts*, but, Differing from these here; there is Plenty
of *Sturgeon*, which is so valuable here in England amongst Gentry; then we have
Cat-Fish, which is a good Dish, and very plentiful; *Mullet, Mud-Fish, Eels,* and many

more Sorts I cannot now remember. Then, in the Salt-Water Rivers, we have a different Kind of Mullet, and extraordinary plentiful; in Taking of them there is great Pleasure, when in a dark Night we in our Canoes, go a Fishing in the River, and in two or
three hours take great Numbers of them, by Burning Handfulls of the Wood of which
the *Tar* is made, and making a Noise, the Fish are therewithal, and by the Light, so
startled that they leap in great Numbers out of the Water towards the Light, and many
fall into our Canoes[.] I have taken at a time Eight or Ten Dozen, some as big as a
Man's Arm, or Hand-Wrist, others less."

* * *

John Brickell, Irish doctor, refers to fishing in North Carolina, circa 1737, in Brickell, *The
Natural History of North-Carolina* (Dublin: James Carson, 1737), 39.

"The chiefeft Diverfions here are Fifhing, Fowling; and Hunting,...."

* * *

William Stephens, Georgia Trustee, goes fishing, 31 May 1744, in E. Merton Coulter, ed.,
The Journal of William Stephens, 1743-1745, 2 vols., Vol. 2 (Athens, Ga.: University of
Georgia Press, 1958), 108.

"Mr. Summer in Company with 3 or 4 others, having spent a Couple of days at Tybee,
partly to take the Diversion of Fishing,...."

* * *

Warning about fishing on private property, South Carolina Gazette, No. 613, 23 December 1745.

"THIS is to forwarn all Perfons from hunting, Fowling or Fifhing on KIWAH ISLAND
after the Date hereof, if they do they may depend on being profecuted.
December 7th, 1745.   *John Stanyarze*"

* * *

John Marrant, African-American preacher of Nova Scotia, recalls fishing during his young
adulthood near Charleston, South Carolina, circa 1768, in [Marrant], *A Narrative of the
Lord's Wonderful Dealings with John Marrant, A Black, (A Preacher of the Gospel in
Nova Scotia) Born in New-York, in North America,* ed. by Rev. Mr. Aldridge, 3rd ed.
(Yarmouth, Nova Scotia: J. Barnes, 1824), 9.

"....; with her [his mother] I staid two months living without God or hope in the world,
fishing and hunting on the sabbath-day."

* * *

Alexander Hewatt, South Carolina historian, comments on fishing in that province, circa
1779, in Hewatt, *An Historical Account of the Rise and Progress of the Colonies of South
Carolina and Georgia,* 2 vols., Vol. 2 (London: Alexander Donaldson, 1779), 303.

"Thofe planters who had arrived at eafy or affluent circumftances employed overfeers;
and having little to do but to ride round their fields now and then, to fee that their
affairs were not neglected, or their flaves abufed, indulge themfelves in rural
amufements, fuch as racing, muftering, hunting, fifhing, or focial entertainments. "

* * *

Johann David Schoepf, German physician, in North Carolina, December 1783, in
Schoepf, *Travels in the Confederation. Pennsylvania, Maryland, Virginia, the Carolinas,
East Florida, the Bahamas,* trans. and ed. by Alfred J. Morrison, 2 vols., Vol. 2 (Cleve-
land: Arthur H. Clark, 1911), 120.

December, 1783: "However, fish attempt the leap, but if they fall short are flung against the rocks and fall dead below. In the spring towards the end of April or the beginning of May so vast a number of fish crowd together below the falls that in their confusion they do themselves injury and may be killed with sticks. Rock-bass especially come up the river in millions to spawn, and being checked at the falls spring and tumble so that the water foams with them. This commonly lasts for several days and is called the 'Rock-fight.' Fishermen take good advantage of the opportunity."

MARYLAND AND VIRGINIA

John Rolfe, English settler in Virginia, notes the fishing, circa 1616, in [Rolfe], "Virginia in 1616," The Virginia Historical Register, and Literary Advertiser, Vol. 1 (1848), 106.

"About two years since, Sir Thomas Dale...found out two seasons in the year to catch fish, namely, the spring and the fall. He himself tooke no small passes in tryall, and at one hall with a scryne caught five thousand three hundred of them, as big as codd. The least of the residue or kind of salmon trout, two foote long; yet durst he not adventure on the mayne skull for breaking his nett. Likewise, two men with axes and such like weapons, have taken and kild neere the shoare and brought home fortie as great as codd in two or three hours space,...."

* * *

Unknown writer advises prospective Maryland settlers on fishing gear, 8 September 1635, in A Relation of Maryland; Together, With a Map of the Countrey, the Conditions of Plantation, His Majefties Charter to Lord Baltemore, Tranflated into Englifh (London: William Peasley, 1635), 51.

"Provifion for Fifhing and Fowling.

"*Inprimis*, neceffaries for a boate of 3. or 4. Tunne, as Spikes, Nayles, Pitch, Tarte, O-come, Canuis for a fayle, Ropes, Anchor, Iron for the Ruther: Fifhing-lines for Cod and Macrills, &c. Cod-hookes, and Macrill-hookes, a Seane or Baffe-net, Herring-netts, Leade, Fowling-pieces of fixe foote; Powder and Shott, and Flint Stones; a good Water-Spaniell, &c."

* * *

John Hammond, British traveler, comments on fishing in Virginia, circa 1656, in Hammond, Leah and Rachel, or, the Two Fruitful Sisters Virginia, and Mary-land. Their Present Condition, Impartially Stated and Related (London: T. Mabb, 1656), 12-13.

"The Country is fruitfull, apt for all and more then *England* can or does produce, the usual diet is such as in *England*, for the rivers afford innumerable sortes of choyce fish, (if they will take the paines to make wyers or hier the Natives, who for a small matter will undertake it,) winter and summer, and that in many places sufficient to serve the use of man, and to fatten hoggs,...."

* * *

George Alsop, British writer, remarks on fishing in Maryland, circa 1666, in Alsop, *A Character of the Province of Maryland* (Cleveland: The Burrows Brothers Company, 1904 [1666]), 41.

"As for Fish, which dwell in the watry tenements of the deep, and by a providential greatness of power, is kept for the relief of several Countries of the world (which would else sink under the rigid enemy of want), here in *Mary-Land* is a large sufficiency, and plenty of almost all sorts of Fishes, which live and inhabit within her several Rivers and Creeks, far beyond the apprehending or crediting of those that never saw the same, which with very much ease is catched, to the great refreshment of the Inhabitants of the Province."

* * *

John Fontaine, Irish Huguenot immigrant, fishes near Germannatown, Virginia, 12 September 1716, in Edward Porter Alexander, ed., *The Journal of John Fontaine. An Irish Huguenot Son in Spain and Virginia, 1710-1719* (Williamsburg, Va.: Colonial Williamsburg Foundation, 1972), 108.

"Germanna town. After breakfast went a fishing in Rappahannoc and took seven fish which we had for dinner."

* * *

John Clayton, Virginia botanist and Gloucester County, Virginia clerk, mentions fishing, March 1739, in Clayton to Samuel Durrent, 21 March 1739, reprinted in "Virginia Game, and Field Sports," Virginia Magazine of History and Biography, Vol. 7, No. 2 (October 1899), 174.

"We have also great pleanty and variety of fish w'ch we take with nets and by Angling as is practised in England,...."

* * *

Robert Rose, Virginia Anglican minister, goes fishing, March 1747, June 1748, June 1750, and May 1751, in Ralph Emmett Fall, ed., *The Diary of Robert Rose. A View of Virginia by a Scottish Colonial Parson, 1746-1751* (Falls Church, Va.?: McClure Press, 1977), 8, 33, 81, 82, 103.

14 March 1747: "Went a fishing without Success—...."

14 June 1748: "Went a fishing and Catched above 5 Doz. of Carp—...."

4 June 1750: "Our people caught a good many fish—...."

23 June 1750: "..., Catched a good Many fish among our twelve Rocks—...."

15 May 1751: "Moderate Weather, went in the afternoon a fishing, I Caught 14 large Carp besides some other Fish at a Draught,...."

* * *

Thomas Walker, Virginia doctor, mentions fishing in western Virginia, 1 April 1750, in [Walker], "The Journal of Doctor Thomas Walker," in J. Stoddard Johnston, ed., *First Explorations of Kentucky, Filson Club Publications No. 13* (Louisville: John P. Morton and Company, 1898), 44.

"The Sabbath. we saw Perch, Mullets, and Carp in plenty, and caught one of the large Sort of Cat Fish."

* * *

Andrew Burnaby, Anglican minister, describes fishing at Williamsburg, Virginia, July 1759, in Burnaby, *Travels through the Middle Settlements in North America, in the Years 1759 and 1760* (London: T. Payne, 1775), 9.

July, 1759: "Thefe waters are ftored with incredible quantities of fifh, fuch as fheeps-heads, rock-fifh, drums, white pearch, herrings, oyfters, crabs, and feveral other forts. Sturgeon and fhad are in fuch prodigious numbers, that one day, within the fpace of two miles only, fome gentlemen in canoes caught above 600 of the former with hooks, which they let down to the bottom, and drew up at a venture when they perceived them to rub againft a fifh; and of the latter above 5000 have been caught at one fingle haul of the feine."

* * *

George Washington, Virginia planter, Revolutionary War general, and later President, chronicles local fishing, April 1760, May and August 1768, April 1769, September 1770, May 1771, July and August 1772, and July 1773, in Donald Jackson and Dorothy Twohig, eds., *The Diaries of George Washington*, 6 vols. (Charlottesville, Va.: University Press of Virginia, 1976, 1978, and 1979), 1:261, 263, 265-266; 2:60, 61, 64, 87, 88, 146, 269; 3:27, 120, 124, 194.

4 April 1760: "Apprehending the Herrings were come Hauled the Sein but catchd only a few of them tho a good many of other sorts. majr. Stewart and Doctr. Johnson came here in the Afternoon and at Night Mr. Richie attended by Mr. Ross solliciting Freight —promisd none."

5 April 1760: "Hauled the Sein again catchd 2 or 3 White Fish more Herring than Yesterday & a great Number of Cats."

10 April 1760: "This Morning my Plows began to Work in the Clover field, but a hard Shower of Rain from No. Et. (where the Wind hung all day) abt. 11 Oclock, stopd them for the Remainder of the day. I therefore Employd the hands in making two or three hauls of the Sein, & found that the Herrings were come."

11 April 1760: "Abt. 11 Oclock set the People to Hauling the Sein and by Night and in the Night Catchd and dressed [ ] Barrels of Herring and 60 White Fish.

"Observed that the Flood tide was infinitely the best for these Fish."

10 May 1768: "Rid to Brick House & returnd to Dinner —after which went a dragging for Sturgeon."

12 May 1768: "White fish began to Run. Catching 60 or 70 at a Haul with some Her[rin]g."

13 May 1768: "Went after Sturgeon & a Gunning."

16 May 1768: "Fishing for Sturgeon from Breakfast to Dinner but catchd none."

18 May 1768: "Began fishing for Herrings with Carpenter's &ca."

30 May 1768: "Went fishing & dined under Mr. L. Washingtons Shore."

23 August 1768: "Hauling the Sein under Mr. Lawrence Washington's shore."

25 August 1768: "Hauling the Sein upon the Bar of Cedar point for Sheeps heads but catchd none. Run down below the Mouth of Machodack & came to."

27 August 1768: "Hauling the Sein upon Hollis's Marsh Bar & elsewhere for Sheeps heads but catchd none."

30 August 1768: "Hauling the Sein on the Bars near Hollis's Marsh & other places."

11 April 1769: "The white fish ran plentifully at my sein landing having catchd abt. 300 at one Hawl."

22 April 1769: "The herring run in great abundance."

8 September 1770: "A Fishing along towards Sheridine Point. Dined upon the Point."

18 May 1771: "Rid to the Brick House with the Family. Hauld the Sein & returnd to Dinner after which went to Mr. Davis's & Drank Tea."

25 July 1772: "Went a fishing and dined at the Fish House at the Ferry Plantation."

11 August 1772: "Went with those Gentlemn. a Fishing and Dined undr. the Bank at Colo. Fairfax's near his White Ho[use]. Found Mrs. Cox here when we returnd."

17 July 1773: "Went down to Colo. Fairfax's White House to haul the Sein. Returnd to Dinner."

* * *

John Ferdinand Dalziel Smyth, British traveler, comments on fishing with Virginians, November? December? 1772?, January? February? 1773?, in Smyth, *A Tour in the United States of America. Containing an Account of the Present Situation of that Country,* 2 vols., Vol. 1 (London: G. Robinson, 1784), 131-132.

November? December? 1772? January? February? 1773?: "I accuftomed myfelf to go out along with them a hunting, fifhing, fwimming, fowling, &c. for my amufement and diverfion."

* * *

Philip Vickers Fithian, tutor at Nomini Hall, Virginia, chronicles local fishing, March, July, September, and October 1774, and in Augusta County, Virginia, December 1775, in Hunter Dickinson Farish, ed., *Journal and Letters of Philip Vickers Fithian, 1773-1774. A Plantation Tutor of the Old Dominion* (Charlottesville, Va.: University Press of Virginia, 1957 [1943]), 75, 145, 189, 192, 206; and Robert Greenhalgh Albion and Leonidas Dodson, eds, *Philip Vickers Fithian. Journal, 1775-1776, Written on the Virginia-Pennsylvania Frontier and in the Army around New York* (Princeton, N.J.: Princeton University Press, 1934), 151.

10 March 1774: "Breakfasted with us Mr Warden, at twelve, with Mr Randolph, I went a fishing, but we had only the luck to catch one apiece."

16 July 1774: "I have forgot to remark before that from the time of our setting out as we were going down Machodock, & along the Potowmack-Shore, & especially as we were rowing up Nominy we saw Fishermen in great numbers in Canoes, & almost constantly taking in Fish Bass & Perch—This was beautiful!—The entrance of Nomini is very shoal, & stony, the Channel is very narrow, & lies close to the Easternmost Side—On these edges of the shoals, or in Holes between the Rocks is plenty of Fish."

11 September 1774: "Towards evening, I took a book in my hand, & strolled down the Pasture quite to the Bank of the River—Miss *Stanhope, Priss, Nancy, Fanny* & *Betsy Carter* were just passing by—They walked to the *Mill*; there they entered a Boat, & for exercise & amusement were rowed down the River quite to the granary, & then went to angling—I walked to the, & together we all marched Home to *Coffee.*"

18 September 1774: "The Morning was fine, & Nomini-River alive with Boats Canoes &c some going to Church some fishing some Sporting—...."

16 October 1774: "We spent the Day in our chamber til towards evening when with the young Ladies we took a turn down the River Many we saw fishing—...."
25 December 1775: "In Summer they tell me here are Plenty of Fish, & fine Angling."

* * *

John Harrower, an indentured servant, in Virginia, goes fishing, 11 June 1774, in Edward Miles Riley, ed., *The Journal of John Harrower, An Indentured Servant in the Colony of Virginia, 1773-1776* (Williamsburg, Va.: Colonial Williamsburg, 1963), 46.

"At 9 AM left the school and went a fishing on the River with the Colonel his eldest [son] and another Gentleman in two Canoes. Mrs. Dangerfield another lady and the other two Boys mett us at Snow Creek in the Chair at 2 pm when we all dined on fish under a tree."

* * *

Robert Honyman, Scottish doctor resident of Virginia, records fishing in eastern Maryland, 5 March 1775, in Philip Padelford, ed., *Colonial Panorama, 1775. Dr. Robert Honyman's Journal for March and April* (San Marino, Cal.: The Huntington Library, 1939), 9.

"About 8 miles from Rockhall I came to a mill Dam & a small Run from it; in crossing which, I observed the fish to flounce about & Jump among my horses feet & several threw themselves ashore & could scarce get off again: I rid up & down the Run & still found them in the same abundance, though the run was so shallow, they were obliged in many places to swim slanting on their sides, & I might easily with my hands have catched numbers of very fine fish without the water coming over my shoes. They were yellow Perch & very large. I was told they were in equal plenty in many runs & especially in the mill dams, & that the Hogs were the principal devourers of them, & that they fattened them mightily. —I smelt the Fish before I got to the run I have mentioned."

* * *

Marquis de Chastellux, French officer, observes fishing near Westover in Virginia, 29 April 1782, in [de Chastellux], *Travels in North-America, in the Years 1780, 1781, and 1782 by the Marquis de Chastellux*, 2nd ed., 2 vols., Vol. 2 (London: G.G.J. and J. Robinson, 1787), 168-172.

"The 29th, the whole of which day I fpent at Weftover, furnifhes nothing interefting in this journal, except fome information I had the opportunity of acquiring refpecting two forts of animals, of very different fpecies, the *fturgeon* and the *hummingbird*. As I was walking by the river-fide, I faw two negroes carrying an immenfe fturgeon, and on my afking them how they had taken it, they told me that at this feafon, they were fo common as to be taken eafily in a fean (a fort of fifhing-net), and that fifteen or twenty were found fometimes in the net; but that there was a much mre fimple method of taking them, which they had juft been ufing. This fpecies of monsters, which are fo active to a great height above the furface of the water, ufually fleep profoundly at mid-day†. Two or three negroes then proceed in a little boat, furnifhed with a long cord, at the end of which is fharp ironcrook, which they hold fufpended like a log line. As foon as they find this line ftopped by fome obstacle, they draw it forcibly towards them, fo as to ftrike the hook into the fturgeon, which they either drag out of the water, or which, after fome ftruggling, and lofing all its blood, floats at length upon the furface, and is eafily taken.

†From General Washington's houfe, which ftands on the lofty banks of the Potowmack, in a fituation more magnificent than I can paint to an European imagination, I have feen for feveral hours together in a fummer's evening, hundreds, perhaps I might fay thoufands of fturgeon, at a great height from the water at the fame inftant, fo that the quantity in the river muft have been inconceivably great; but notwithftanding the rivers in Virginia sabound with fifh, they are by no means plentiful at table, fuch is the indolence of the inhabitants!"

NEW ENGLAND

James Rosier, British gentleman, notes fishing along with the George Waymouth expedition near the Maine coast, May and June 1605, in Rosier, *A Trve Relation of the Moft Profperous Voyage* Made this Prefent Yeere *1605, by Captain* George Waymouth, *in the Difcouery of the Land of* Virginia (London: George Bishop, 1605), B2, C4.

22 May 1605: "This day our boat went out about a mile from our fhip, and in fmall time with two or three hooks was fifhed fufficiently for our whole Company three bayes, with great Cod, Haddocke, and Thornebacke.

"And towards night we drew with a fmall net of twenty fathoms very nigh the fhore: we got about thirty very good and great Lobfters, many Rockfifh, fome Plaife, and other fmall fifhes, and fifhes called Lumpes, verie pleafant to the tafte: and we generally obferved, that all the fifh, of what kinde foeuer we toke, were well fed, fat, and fweet in tafte."

4 June 1605: "Tuefday, the fourth of June, our men tooke Cod and Hadocke with hooks by our fhip fide, and Lobfters very great: which we had not tried."

* * *

John Smith, English settler and leader in Virginia, describes fishing possibilities, concerning New England, circa 1614-1616, in [Smith], *A Description of New England. Or the Observations, and Difcoueries of Captain* Iohn Smith *(Admirall of that Country) in the North of America, in the Year of Our Lord 1614* (London: Humfrey Lownes and Robert Clerke, 1616), 21-22.

"What pleasure can be more, then...to recreate themfelues before their owne doores, in their owne boates vpon the Sea, where man, woman and childe, with a small hooke and line, by angling, may take diuerfe forts of excellent fish, at their pleasures? And is it not pretty sport, to pull vp two pence, six pence, and twelve pence, as fast as you can hale and veare a line? He is a very bad fisher, cannot kill in one day with his hooke and line, one, two, or three hundred Cods: which dressed and dryed; if they be sould there for ten shillings the hundred, though in *England* they will giue more then twentie; may not both the seruant, the master, and marchant, be well content with this gaine? If a man worke but three dayes in seauen, he may get more then hee can spend, vnlesse he will be excessiue. Now that Carpenter, Mason, Gardiner, Taylor, Smith, Sailer, Forgers, or what other, may not make this a pretty recreation though they fish but an houre in a day, to take more then they eate in a weeke: or? if they will not eate it, because there is so much better choise; yet sell it, or change it, with the fisher men, or marchants, for any thing they want. And what sport doth yeeld a more pleasing content, and lesse hurt or charge then angling with a hooke, and crossing the sweete ayre from Ile to Ile, ouer the silent streames of a calme Sea? wherein the most curious may finde, pleasure, profit, and content. Thus, though all men be not fishers: yet all men, whatsoeuer, may in other matters doe as well....

"For Gentlemen, what exercise should more delight them, then ranging dayly those vknowne parts, vsing fowling and fishing, for hunting and hauking?"

* * *

George Morton?, British settler at Plymouth, Massachusetts, goes fishing, November 1620 and March 1621, [Morton?], *Mourt's Relation or Journal of the Plantation at Plymouth*, ed. by Henry Martyn Dexter (Boston: John Kimball Wiggin, 1865), 4, 97.

11 November 1620: "...; for Cod we affayed, but found none, there is good ftore no doubt in their feafon. Neither got we any fifh all the time we lay there, but fome little ones on the fhore."

24 March 1621: "Fryday was a very faire day, *Samofet* and *Squanto* ftill remained with vs, *Squanto* went at noone to fifh for Eeles, at night he came home with as many as he could well lift in one hand, which our people were glad of, they were fat & sweet, he trod them out with his feet, and fo caught them with his hands without any other Instrument."

* * *

Samuel Sewall, Boston magistrate, goes fishing off Boston, July 1687 and July 1705, in Boston, July 1713, and in Rhode Island, September 1718, in M. Halsey Thomas, ed., *The Diary of Samuel Sewall, 1674-1729, Volume I. 1674-1708* (New York: Farrar, Straus and Giroux, 1973), 143, 525; and M. Halsey Thomas, ed., *The Diary of Samuel Sewall, 1674-1729, Volume II. 1709-1729* (New York: Farrar, Straus and Giroux, 1973), 721, 901.

12 July 1687: "Go with them to Alderton's Point, and with our Boats beyond, quite out of the Massachusetts Bay, and there catch'd fresh Cod."

17 July 1705: "I go a fishing in Capt. Bonners Boat, Joseph, Edw. Oakes and Capt. Hill with us; went out at Pulling Point, between the Graves and Nahant, Catch'd but 3 Cod. I was sick and vomited;...."

28 July 1713: "Govr, Mr. Commissary and others went to Notimmy [Menotomy, now Arlington] this day a-fishing."

8 September 1718: "Govr Shute went to the Horse-Race. Fishing to Canonicut."

* * *

Account of a freakish fishing accident, Boston News-Letter, No. 429, 30 June–7 July 1712.

"*Pifcataqua* July 4. An uncommon accident fell out here, Benjamin Gatchell in a Barque bound a fifhing to Cape Sables, on a fudden fprung a Leake, which oblig'd him to return home, and in fearching the Veffel they found in her bottom part of the fword of a fifh (call'd the Sword Fifh) run through the plank, which was two Inches thick, and glancing by a Timber Shatter'd the plank, which caufed her Leakinefs."

* * *

Joshua Hempstead, New London, Connecticut carpenter, chronicles the local fishing, May and June 1713, September 1714, November 1719, April 1734, July 1735, and April 1747, in [Hempstead], *Diary of Joshua Hempstead of New London, Connecticut Covering a Period of Forty-Seven Years from September, 1711, to November, 1758, Collections of the New London County Historical Society, Volume I* (New London, Conn.: New London County Historical Society, 1910), 23-24, 38, 93, 272, 291, 480.

4 May 1713: "Ebe is gone to to Block Island a fishing."

9 May 1713: "Ebe came. hath got about 50 fish."

18 May 1713: "Ebe a fishing."

22 June 1713: "I was a fishing to Jno Harris's with Griffing Jas. Trumn & Danll Way & our wives...."

6 September 1714: "...Will Pendal Drownded a fishing... fell out of a Small Boat in ye horserace Catching bluefish."

20 November 1719: "I went to fishers Iland with Nathanael & Stephn to catch to catch blue fish but there being none Wee went to Stonington for 3 bbs."

24 April 1734: "Molly fell in ye River at Cunner Island yesterday a fishing."

24 July 1735: "John went to fishers Island with Elijah Hide & others fishing."

27 April 1747: "Josh & adm went Alewife brook to Catch alewives. got abot 4 dozn."

* * *

Advertisement for fishing equipment, Boston News-Letter, No. 521, 5-12 April 1714.

"ALL Sorts of Cordage from Cables of eight Inches and an half, a Spunyarn, Boltrope of all Siezes, Hollands Duck of Sundry Sorts, Canvas of Sundry Sorts for fmall Sails, and mending, Junks of all Siezes, Fifhing Anchors of feveral Siezes, and Fifhing Tackle of all Sorts: To be Sold by Meffieurs *John George* and *Nathan Howe* at their Warehoufe on Bofton Peer, near the South Gapp."

* * *

Cotton Mather, Boston, Massachusetts Congregationalist minister, recounts a fishing mishap, August 1716, in Worthington Chauncey Ford, ed., *Diary of Cotton Mather, 2* vols., Vol. 2 (New York: Frederick Ungar Publishing Company, 1911), 366-367.

"This Day, a singular Thing befel me. My God, Help me to understand the Meaning of it! I was prevailed withal, to do a Thing, which I very rarely do; (not once in Years) I rode abroad with some Gentlemen, and Gentlewomen, to take the country Air, and to divert ourselves, at a famous Fish-pond. In the Canoe, on the Pond, my Foot slipt, and I fell overboard into the Pond. Had the Vessel been a little further from the Shore, I must have been drown'd. But I soon recovered the Shore, and going speedily into a warm Bed, I received no sensible HARM."

* * *

James Jeffry, Salem, Massachusetts resident, goes fishing, 25 July 1724, in [Jeffry], "James Jeffry's Journal for the Year 1724," Essex Institute Historical Collections, Vol. 37 (October 1900), 336.

"Mad^m went ot Stage Point on fryday with Mrs Hufk &c^a to meet Col^o &c^a went a fifhing."

* * *

Accounts of fishing accidents, Boston News-Letter, 1731.

"On Monday Evening laft about 9 a Clock, a young Man of this Town named *Thomas Marfhall* an only Son, a Cooper by Trade, and lately Free, having been out a Fifhing with another, and returning back, the faid *Marfhall* being at the Head of the Boat, fell over and was drowned; the other being at the Stern, did not mifs him, till he had call'd to him twice and having no Anfwer, he ran forward, but faw nothing of him, only his Hat fwiming on the Water. His Body was found Yefterday between the Caftle and Spectacle Ifland, and brought up hither."   (No. 1429, 10-17 June 1731)

"We are informed that on Friday the 11th Inftant, as fome Men were Fifhing in a Pond at Brantree, one of the Men loft his Line, &C. and afterwards mentioning it to feveral Lads at a Houfe in the Town, and offering fomething of a Reward to any one of them that would find the fame, one of the Lads taking more notice than the reft, went immediately alone to the faid Pond, and getting into a Canoe, and fearching for faid Line, tis fuppofs'd he pitch't over into the Water, for he was foon after found Drowned therein."   (No. 1430, 17-24 June 1731)

* * *

Account of a fishing accident, Boston News-Letter, No. 1473, 13-20 April 1732.

"We are inform'd that on Wednefday laft Mr *Bodge* of Charlftown went out in Canoe a Fifhing, and that Night or the next Morning the Canoe was found near Col. *Phipps's* Farm and the Body of the faid *Bodge* dead in the fame; 'tis fuppos'd he was feiz'd with a Fit, part of his Body hanging over the fide of the Canoe."

* * *

Account of a fishing accident, Boston News-Letter, No. 1534, 14–21 June 1733.

"On Thurfday laft *Charles Cutting*, an Apprentice to Mr. *Cord Wing*, of this Town Shipwright, went off in a fmall Boat a fifhing in the Harbour; and upon his Return, his Oar fliping out of the fculling Hole, he fell over into the Water, fank down and never rofe again."

* * *

Account of a fishing accident, Boston News-Letter, No. 1583, 30 May-6 June 1734.

"We hear from *Plympton*, That a forrowful Accident fell out there the beginning of laft Week: Three young Men venturing off in an old broken Canoe to Fifh in a Pond there, the Canoe fill'd with Water and funk down, when they had got but a few Rods from the Shoar, and they were all drowned:....."

* * *

Harvard College law, circa 1734, in "College Laws, 1734, Chapter 8th, Concerning Miscellaneous Matters," in *Harvard College Records, Part I. Corporation Records, 1636-1750, Publications of the Colonial Society of Massachusetts*, Vol. 15 (Boston, 1925), 154.

"15. No Undergraduate shall keep a Gun or pistol in the College, or any where in Cambridge; nor shall he go a guning, fishing, or Scating over deep waters, without leave from the President or one of the Tutors, under the penalty of three Shillings. And if any scholar shall fire a Gun or pistol, within the College walls Yard, or near the College; he shall be fined not exceeding ten Shillings; or be admonishe[d] degraded or expelled, according to the Aggravation of the Offence."

* * *

Ebenezer Parkman, Westborough, Massachusetts minister, chronicles local fishing, May 1745, June 1746, January 1751, January 1753, and August 1754, in Francis G. Walett, ed., *The Diary of Ebenezer Parkman, 1703-1782* (Worcester, Mass.: American Antiquarian Society, 1974), 117, 137, 231, 267, 279.

1 May 1745: "Ebenezer [his son] went afishing at the great Pond this Evening, this being almost the very beginning of their Fishing this Season."

10 June 1746: My Cattle grow very troublesome by breaking in upon my Corn, whilst Ebenezer and Thomme [his sons] were gone a fishing."

17 January 1751: "Mr. [Ebenezer] Rice's Young Man (Dudley) and his wife's brethren, had been at the Great Pond, though foul Weather: and caught a great Number of fine Fish—the Pickrell, Some of them very large. They made me an handsome Present of 3 large ones."

12 January 1753: "William [his son] and many more go afishing at the great Pond—they catch a great Number of Pickerell."

17 August 1754: "Concern'd about Billy [his son] who went from his Brother's to Mr. [Hezekiah] How[e']s—and hence out upon the Great Pond a fishing, and did not return to them till Even[ing], till Dark...."

* * *

Francis Goelet, New York merchant, fishes at Milton, Massachusetts, 13 October 1750, in [Goelet], "Extracts from Capt. Francis Goelet's Journal, Relative to Boston, Salem and Marblehead, &c., 1746-1750," New-England Historical and Genealogical Register, Vol. 24, No. 1 (January 1870), 55.

"..., about Ten Yards from the House is a Beautifull Cannal, which is Supply'd by a Brook, which is well Stockt with Fine Silver Eels, we Caught a fine Parcell and Carried them Home and had them drest for Supper...."

* * *

John Adams, Massachusetts lawyer, politician, and later United States President, near Boston, June 1760, in [Adams], *Diary and Autobiography of John Adams, Vol. 1. Diary, 1755-1770*, ed. by Lyman H. Butterfield (Cambridge, Mass.: Harvard University Press, 1962), 140-141.

25 June 1760: "Went out with the Coll., in his Canoe, after Tom Codd. Rowed down, in a still calm, and smooth Water, to Rainsford Island, round which we fished in several Places, but had no Bites. Then we went up the Island, and round the Hill....

"...and then we dined expecting with much Pleasure an easy sail Home before the Wind, which hen bread fresh at East. After Diner we boarded and hoisted sail, and sailed very pleasantly a Mile, when the Wind died away into a Clock Calm and left us to row against the Tide, and presently against the Wind too for that sprung up at south, right a Head of us, and blew afresh. This was hard work. Doubtful what Course to steer, whether to Nut Island, or to Half Moon, or to Hangmans Island or to Sunken Island, Coll. Q. grew sick which determined us to go to ashore at Hangmans for that was nearest.... When the Coll. awoke and found himself strengthened and inspired, we rowed away, under Half Moon, and then hoisted sail and run home. So much for the Day of Pleasure, The fishing frolick, and the Water frolick. We had none of the Pleasure of Angling, very little of the Pleasure of Sailing. We had much of the fatigue of Rowing, and some of the Vexation of Disappointment. However the Exercise and the Air and smell of salt Water is wholesome."

* * *

John Rowe, Boston merchant, chronicles his fishing, September and October 1764, May, June, and July 1765, May, June, July, August, and September 1766, April, May, June, July, August, and October 1767, April, May, June, July, August, and September 1768, June 1769, May 1770, June 1771, June 1772, and May, June, and July 1773, in Anne Rowe Cunningham, ed., *Letters and Diary of John Rowe, Boston Merchant, 1759-1762, 1764-1779* (Boston: W.B. Clarke Company, 1903), 62, 63, 66, 81, 82, 83, 84, 85, 86, 87, 95, 96, 97, 99, 100, 101, 102, 103, 105, 106, 107, 108, 110, 111-112, 129, 131, 132, 133, 134, 135, 136, 137, 138, 139, 140, 142, 143, 144, 160, 161, 163, 164, 166, 170, 173, 174, 187, 202, 203, 216, 229, 230, 246, 247.

15 September 1764: "Sept. 15. A beautiful morning. went a fishing at Jamaica Pond. had poor luck."

17 September 1764: "Sept. 17. Rose very early before six, went with Mrs Rowe to Flax pond in comp^y with Mr Inman & S. Mr Jon^a Simpson & the Revd Mr Walter. were Joyned by John Lane & Henry Ayres & Capt Tracy of Newberry. had very Good Sport. in the afternoon I lost the Top of my Rod Line & Hooks by a very large Pickerell."

21 September 1764: "Sept. 21. Went to Flax pond at twelve of Clock arr^d there at four in the afternoon. Rained very fast. had tolerable good luck."

22 September 1764: "Sept. 22. Rose early this morning, went to Flax pond, fished with Mr Saml Calef had great sport. caught two Pickerell one was two foot long & weighed three pounds & three quarters & about four dozen large Pond Perch, one measured fourteen inches."

13 October 1764: "Oct. 13. Went with Henry Ayres to Monomy pond, had very bad sport,...."

18 October 1764: "Oct. 18. Went a fishing for Smelts with Mr Fenton but got none."

1 May 1765: "May 1. Set out early this morning, reached Pembroke went fishing had bad luck, began to rain which was much wanted. got to Duxbury Mills, went a fishing, had tolerable luck. dined at Mr Nath. Ray Thomas on a mess of Trout."

3 May 1765: "May 3. Breakfasted at Capt Whites. Went a fishing with Mr Wm Watson, had very good sport. I caught one very large Trout & several other very fine ones."

11 May 1765: "May 11. Went fishing at Manotomy Pond with Saml Calef had very good Sport, dined at Winship's, the tavern there & fished there in the afternoon had also very Good Sport, we caght at least ten doz^n of Pond Perch & several Pickerel,...."

25 May 1765: "May 25. Rose very early, went to Flax Pond & breakfasted there with Miss Becky, went a fishing, had great sport,....."

4 June 1765: "June 4. King's Birthday. Went early in the morning with Wm Sheaff & Saml Calef to Manotomy pond. had very Good Sport fishing —were joyned by Solo. Davis * Geo. Bethune —we all dined together at Wyndships —Mr Sheaff & I went fishing at Fresh Pond in the afternoon."

19 June 1765: "June 19. This morning our Fishermen caught a large fish in the shape of a Shark Twenty foot long. his Teeth were different from a Shark's teeth —Went after dinner to Jamaica pond with Capt Jacobson, had pretty good Sport."

20 June 1765: "June 20. This day they cut up the Fish & filled two large hogshead with his Liver. Went in the afternoon to Fresh Pond with Saml Calef."

25 June 1765: "June 25. Went after dinner to Fresh Pond with Sam. Calef & Geo. Apthorp, found Mr James Perkins & Lady there —had pretty sport. I hooked a Turtle to the best of my Judgement must weigh 30 pounds."

28 June 1765: "June 28.... Paid a visit to several of my Friends & came away about six got to Flax Pond alias Gravesend & there met Mr Saml Calef. wee fished & supped & stayed there all night —very agreeably entertained."

3 July 1765: "July 3. Rose very early this morning & went with Mr Saml Calef to Natick Pond. was obliged to stop three hours at Pratt's at Needham it rained so hard, however wee had very good sport. Dined at Bullard's on Fish which Mrs Bullard dressed very well."

13 July 1765: "July 13. Rose very early this morning, went to Monotomy Pond with the Revd Mr Auchmooty & Mr Sam Calef had great sport, we caught above sixteen doz^n of pond & sea perch—...."

20 July 1765: "July 20. Rose very early this morning. Mr Calef, the Revd Mr Auchmooty & myself went to a pond beyond the Blue Hills & put up at Mr Joseph Gooch—went fishing—had very fine Diversion—the weather very hot—...."

27 July 1765: "July 27. Rose very early this morning. went with M Saml Calef to Capt Kendrick's on Charles River a fishing —had very good sport."

14 May 1766: "May 14. Rose early. I went & tryed to get some trout but could not."

20 May 1766: "May 20... Mr Calef & I went to the Great Worcester pond & caught Two doz^n of fine Perch which wee Brought to Furnefs' & supp^d on."

23 May 1766: "May 23. After doing my Business Major Golthwait Mr Calef & I set out for Rutland from Hardwick We reached Colo. Murray's & dined there... —after dinner we went & caught a mess of Trout."

7 June 1766: "June 7. I went this forenoon to Needham a fishing with Mr Saml Calef, Mr Thos Knights, Mr John Stevenson & Mr Archib^d McNeal—we had middling luck —there is a Trout Brook empties itself into Charles River ab^o a mile & half beyond Dedham Island Crossway—dined under a large apple tree & fished again."

21 June 1766: "21 June. Went with Mr Saml Calef to Monotomy Pond, din'd there & went fishing, had very Good Sport, caught seven doz^n of Perch."

23 June 1766: "23 June.... After dinner I went to Monotomy Pond with Archib'^{d} Mr Neal & Mr Knight had pretty Good Sport."

26 June 1766: "June 26.... We went fishing at Natick Pond & had very good sport. Dined at Bullard's with Capt Jacobson went down to Charles River & fished there. wee had very Good Sport."

28 June 1766: "June 28.... I spent two hours with Capt Jacobson on Jamaica Pond, wee had poor Luck."

5 July 1766: "5 July.... Spent ab^o an hour a fishing with Capt Jacobson, had Little Sport."

8 July 1766: "July 8. Rose very early & went with Mr Armiel to Fresh Pond. had very poor Sport, caught but a dozen of Perch."

29 July 1766: "July 29. Capt Jacobson & I went to Flax Pond, had very Good Sport. Caught twelve dozen Perch in two hours."

2 August 1766: "2 Aug.... Afterwards to a pond ab^o a mile from Colo Dotys with Mr John Lovell jun^r & Saml Calef. wee had Good Sport & caught a great many fish tho they were small."

12 August 1766: "Aug. 12. Went with Cornelius White, Ed^{wd} Winslow, & Young Bradford also Capt Ashburn to South Pond a fishing—had very good sport. I caught a very large Perch—measured 18 inches & weighed three pounds & a half."

18 August 1766: "18 Aug.... We stopt at Colo. Doty's Pond & caught Eight Dozen of Perch."

20 August 1766: "Aug. 20. After I had done my Business Mr Laughton & I set out for to come home. We overtook Mr Calef, Mr Armiel, & Wm Speakman at Winnesconnet Pond—they had caught a great many Fish which wee dined on at Howard's at Easton."

21 August 1766: "21 Aug. Wee Rose early this morning and went a fishing had Good Sport."

23 August 1766: "23 Aug.... went in the afternoon to Jamaica Pond & fished there with Capt Jacobson had pretty Good Sport...."

30 August 1766: "Aug. 30. Mr. Core came early this morning & we went to Capt Kendricks a fishing. wee were joyned by Major Golthwait, Mr Armiel & Mr Calef."

11 September 1766: "Sept. 11.... Mr Quincy & I went a fishing."

30 September 1766: "30 Sept. Rose very early this morning & went a fishing with James Perkins & Saml Calef wee din'd together under a tree on the Causeway beyond Dedham Island. Wee had very great sport."

28 April 1767: "Apr 28. Set out early from Halls & got to Duxbury Mills. Stopt here & fished, had very Good Sport. caught five Dozen Trout."

12 May 1767: "May 12.... Reached Martin's at Northborough, breakfasted there, Reached Furnace's, stopt at the bridge & got half a Doz^n Trout."

13 May 1767: "May 13. Finished what I had to do, set out with Mr John Greene for home. called at Worcester Bridge, caught one Trout & half a Dozen perch. went forward and stopt at a Brook two miles this side of Shrewsbury. caught ten Trout."

23 May 1767: "May 23.... Wee set out after dinner for Spot Pond & fished there. We had but poor Sport. Wee caught ab^o 4 dozen of small perch, a few pickerel & three Eylls."

30 May 1767: "May 30.... Spent an hour fishing with Dr Calef and Mr Brattle on Jamaica Pond."

2 June 1767: "June 2. I rose very early this morning & Routed up my companions & set out for Bullard's pond at Natick, where went a fishing, had extraordinary Sport. We did not weigh the fish, I guess wee caught about Eighty weight. I caught 25 3/4 lbs weighed at Kendrick's."

6 June 1767: "6 June. Still very hot. I went to Monotomy with Saml Calef & din'd at Newalls there, with him, with him & Andrew Hall, after dinner wee went a fishing & Caught ab^o 4 dozen of middling Perch."

8 June 1767: "8 June.... Called on Henry Vafsall & Mr Trollet, went to Freshpond a fishing, had good Sport—...."

16 June 1767: "June 16....—in the afternoon Wm Speakman & I went to Jamaica Pond a fishing, had poor Sport."

6 July 1767: "6 July.... Wee Reached Mr Furnace's at Shrewsbury. Wee caught a Good mefs of Perch supped & slept there."

7 July 1767: "7 July. Caught another mefs of Fish,...."

8 July 1767: "8 July. Set out for home with Major Goldthwait. Wee stopt at Shrewsbury Pond, caught a Mefs of Perch & din'd at Mr Barnes at Marlborough. Set out for Sudbury fish'd there, had good sport,...."

24 July 1767: "24 July. Went with Mr Tim^o Fitch to Flax pond, had very Great Sport, caught upwards of Twenty doz^n...."

1 August 1767: "Aug. 1. We went to Punkapong Pond & fished there caught 26 Dozen of Pond Perch before ten of Clock. (2 gentlemen, Mr John Boylston & himself) John Boylston is a Good Companion but very Fretful & Uneasy in his make. I should be very Glad to accompany him at any Time on a party of fishing, especially when the fish Bite fast."

29 August 1767: "Aug. 29. I went with Wm Speakman to Kendrick's after dinner wee went fishing."

1 October 1767: "Oct. 1. Set out with Capt Ashborne for Salem. Stopt at Flax Pond. I caught two dozen of fine large Perch & threee Pickerell."

2 October 1767: "Oct. 2. Went to Mr West's Fish Fence. Bought his Fish, did some other Business—in my way home stopt at Flax Pond & fished there. Left my Fishing Rod & Leather Dram Bottle there."

3 October 1767: "3 Oct. Breakfasted with Capt Wood at home. Wee set out for Richards wee fished at Dedham Caufsway had good Sport...."

27 April 1768: "27 April. Reached Dr. Halls Pembrooke, wee Breakfasted there, from thence to Duxbury; fished there & caught upwards five Dozen of fine Trout."

28 April 1768: "28 Aprill.... About three of Clock wee Returned to Duxbury, had good Sport, I caught about a Dozen fine Trout."

29 April 1768: "29 Aprill. Mr Pelham Winslow joynd us wee went a fishing had but poor Luck."

30 April 1768: "30 Aprill. Wee went to Cushings Brook. Mr Knights caught the finest Trout I ever saw."

28 May 1768: "28 May. Went a fishing with Mr Thos Knights & Mr Saml Calef at Mr Days at Strawberry Hill in Springfield had but poor Sport,...."

1 June 1768: "First June. Went to Flax pond with Mr Saml Calef, Capt Handfield Mr Thos Jackson Senr. Wee had good Sport, wee were joynd by M^r McKneal from Surrinam & Archibald McKneal...."

2 June 1768: "2nd June. Wee breakfasted at Colo Higginson's Returnd to Flax Pond. had but Ordinary Sport—...."

18 June 1768: "June 18. Went to Mr Ballard's at Natick Pond, there I met Capt Jacobson & Mr Sam. Calef, wee fished there, had Great Sport —we caught several Perch Fifteen Inches Long & one Sixteen Inches."

15 July 1768: "July 15. Went to Flax Pond. we fished there and had pretty good sport."

16 July 1768: "July 16. Rose early & went fishing."

17 August 1768: "Aug. 17. After Dinner I set out with Capt Jacobson & Saml Calef for Colo. Dotys—wee fished on Punkapaud Pond—...."

18 August 1768: "Aug. 18. Wee went again to fish—had great sport, caught upwards of twenty dozen & some Large Fish—...."

10 September 1768: "10 Sept. I went out to Richards with Saml Calef a fishing on the Cofsway—was very Lucky—caught many Perch & fine ones—Lost severall fine Hooks & Snoods."

3 June 1769: "June 3. Went with Mr James Perkins & Mr Saml Calef to Spot Pond a fishing—we were joyned by Major Vassall & Mr Thompson of Medford—Wee had very great luck—I never saw such large Perch, before Caught there, many of them ab^o 12 inches."

23 May 1770: "May 23. Sandwich—Wee rose early & set out for Mashby an Indian Town—... Wee fished there, found it a wild place—Wee had Good Sport—...."

24 May 1770: "May 24. Wee Rose early & set out for Plymouth—... after dinner I went down to the River & Caught Ten Trout —The Largest I ever saw several of them eighteen Inches in Length."

11 June 1771: "June 11. Wee fishd again no Great Sport—"

5 June 1772: "June 5. I went to Richards with Thos Knight, Jos. Green & J^{no} Williams wee fished wee had but middling Luck. Thos Knight caught Twenty Two Trout. I sent the Admirall a Dozen of Trout & Perch."

19 June 1772: "June 19. Wee went to Flax Pond, wee fished there, wee had the Best Sport I ever was at, wee caught very near a hundred Weight of Fish & the Largest Perch I ever saw there."

29 May 1773: "May 29. I rose very early this morning in order to get Hunter away. afterward I went to Richards a fishing with Tuthill Hubbard, James Perkins, Saml Calef & Wm Davis."

8 June 1773: "June 8.... I stopt at Richards & at Robin's Walpole & at eleven I reached Wrentham. I went a fishing with the Admiral & Capt Jordan. Wee caught a great many but very small."

9 June 1773: "June 9. I rose very early & went afishing with the Admiral. The Admiral caught 173 Perch."

28 June 1773: "July 28. Went with Mrs Rowe to Salem—Wee stopt at Newalls Lynn from thence to Flax Pond—I fished there. I had very good sport."

* * *

Yale College law, circa 1774, in *The Laws of Yale-College, in New-Haven, in Connecticut, Enacted by the President and Fellows* (New Haven, Conn.: Thomas and Samuel Green, 1774), 14.

"19. If any Scholar fhall go a Fifhing or Sailing, or undrefs himfelf for Swimming, in any Place expofed to public View...he may be fined not exceeding two Shillings;...."

* * *

William Coit, Connecticut captain, at Cambridge, Massachusetts, refers to fishing, 3 July 1775, in [Coit], "Orderly Book for Capt William Coits Company Campt at Cambridge, April 23^d AD 1775," in "Orderly Book and Journals Kept by Connecticut Men While Taking Part in the American Revolution, 1775-1778," *Collections of the Connecticut Historical Society*, Vol. 7 (Hartford: Connecticut Historical Society, 1899), 33.

"Article 10th No Parsons Whatever is allowed to go to the Fresh pond a Fishing or on any other [l]ocation as there May be Danger of Introducing the Small Pox into the army"

* * *

John Joseph Henry, Pennnsylvania rifleman, observes fishing in Maine, October 1775, in Henry, "Campaign against Quebec", in Kenneth Roberts, comp., *March to Quebec. Journals of the Members of Arnold's Expedition* (New York: Doubleday, Doran & Company, 1938), 313.

2 October 1775: "*October 2nd....* From cautionary motives our guns, though not uncared for, were considered as useless, in the way of obtaining food. Several of our company angled successfully for trout, and a delicious chub, which we call a fallfish...."

3 October 1775: "*October 3rd.* The evening brought us to our encampment, on the south side of the river. Angling was resorted to for food. Sergeant Boyd observing low ground on the other side of the river, and an uncommon coldness in the water, passed over, and in an hour returned with a dozen trout, of extraordinary appearance, long, broad, and thick. The skin was of a very dark hue, beautifully sprinkled with deep crimson spots. Boyd had caught these in a large and deep spring-head. Contrasting them with those we caught in the river, they were evidently of a different species. The river trout were of a pale ground, with pink spots, and not so flat or broad."

* * *

Abner Stocking, Connecticut soldier, remarks on fishing in Maine, 4 October 1775, in Stocking, "Journal of Abner Stocking As Kept by Himself, During His Long and Tedious March Through the Wilderness to Quebec, Until His Return to His Native Place," in Kenneth Roberts, comp., *March to Quebec. Journals of the Members of Arnold's Expedition* (New York: Doubleday, Doran & Company, 1938), 549.

"*October 4th....* At the foot of the falls we found fine fishing for salmon trout."

* * *

Joseph Joslin, Jr., South Killingly, Connecticut teamster, goes fishing, June 1777, in [Joslin], "Journal of Joseph Joslin Jr. of South Killingly A Teamster in the Continental Service, March 1777–August 1778," in "Orderly Book and Journals Kept by Connecticut Men While Taking part in the American Revolution, 1775-1778," *Collections of the Connecticut Historical Society*, Vol. 7 (Hartford: Connecticut Historical Society, 1899), 315-316.

21 June 1777: "herrick and I helpt hair Some hides and I had my Shoes tapt and in the afternoon we went a fishing and ketcht 5 Roach and we carried them home on a pole between us and So we Did Sir"

23 June 1777: "in the forenoon it Raind and in the afternoon we went a fishing...."

* * *

Thomas Anburey, British officer, recounts fishing near Mystic, Connecticut, May 1778, in [Anburey], *Travels through the Interior Parts of America*, 2 vols., Vol. 2 (London: William Lane, 1791), 198-199.

20 May 1778: "We have of late been greatly amufed in catching of ell-wives, or alewives, a fpecies of fifh, greatly refembling a herring, both as to make and flavor, but fomewhat fmaller; they come up all the creeks and inlets from the fea at this feafon

to fpawn, floating in with the tide in large fhoals, and proceeding as far as they can for frefh water; when the tide is going out they return, at which time they are caught by means of nets faftened round a hoop, and affixedto a long pole; the nets are very deep, and at one haul you may catch two or three dozen."

* * *

Jeremiah Greenman, Rhode Island soldier and later officer, records fishing in Rhode Island, September 1779, in Robert C. Bray and Paul E. Bushnell, eds., *Diary of a Common Soldier in the American Revolution, 1775-1783. An Annotated Edition of the Military Journal of Jeremiah Greenman* (DeKalb, Ill.: Northern Illinois University Press, 1978), 139, 141.

4 September 1779: "this day went to duches Island a fishing...."
29? September 1779: "went a fishing...."

* * *

Benjamin Gilbert, Brookfield, Massachusetts sergeant, fishes in central Massachusetts, May 1780, in Rebecca D. Symmes, ed., *A Citizen-Soldier in the American Revolution. The Diary of Benjamin Gilbert in Massachusetts and New York,* (Cooperstown, N.Y.: New York State Historical Association, 1980), 68-69.

19 May 1780: "In the morning I came to Joseph Deans and took Breckfirst, Then he & I went afishing but it proving the Darkest Day I ever saw the fish would not bite."
23 May 1780: "I went a fishing with Joseph Dane to west pond and [got] Ten pickerall."

NEW JERSEY, NEW YORK, PENNSYLVANIA

David Pietersz de Vries, Dutch ordnance-master, chronicles fishing in New Netherland, February and March 1633, April or May 1639, and 1642, in de Vries, *Short Historical and Journal Notes of Several Voyages Made in the Four Parts of the World, Namely, Europe, Africa, Asia, and America* (Brekegeest?: Symon Cornelisz, 1655), reprinted in Cornell Jaray, ed., *Historic Chronicles of New Amsterdam, Colonial New York and Early Long Island, First Series, Empire State Historical Publications Series No. 35* (Port Washington, N.Y.: Ira J. Friedman, 1968), 30, 38, 92, 110-111.

February, 1633: "The river has a great plenty of fish, the same as those in our fatherland, perch, roach, pike, sturgeon, and similar fish. Along the sea-coast are codfish, the different kinds of fish which are in our fatherland, and others. After we had taken in some ballast, we went further down the river, and came to its mouth. We fished once with our seines, and caught in one draught as many as thirty men could eat of perch, roach, and pike."

29 March 1633: "Found that our people had caught seven whales, but there were only thirty-two cartels of oil obtained, so that the whale-fishery is very expensive, when such meagre fish are caught. We could have done more if we had had good harpooneers, for they had struck seventeen fish, and secured only seven, which was

astonishing. They had always struck the whales in the tail. I afterwards understood from some Basques, who were old whale-fishers, that they always struck the whales in the fore-part of the back."

April or May, 1639: "The river [Hudson] is about six hundred to seven hundred paces wide at this place, and contains large quantities of fine fish, such as pike, perch, eels, suckers, thickheads, sunfish, shad, striped bass, which is a fish which comes from the sea in the spring, and swims up the river into the fresh water as the salmon does. There are sturgeon, but our people will not eat them; also trout, slightly yellow inside, which I myself have caught, and which are considered in France the finest of fish."

Circa 1642: "*Of the kinds of Fish which frequent the Sea and River as far up as the brackish and fresh water.*

There are different kinds of fine fish on the seacoast for the wants of man, similar to those in Holland, as the codfish (in winter), haddock, plaice, flounders, herring, sole, and many more kinds of which I cannot give the names. There is a species of fish which by our people is called the *twelve* [striped bass], and which has scales like a salmon, and one each side six black streaks, which I suppose is the reason they call it twelve. It is the size of a codfish, very delicate, and good-tasted for eating; the head is the best, as it is full of brains like a lamb's head. The fish comes from the sea into the river in the spring, about the last of March and April, and continues until the last of May. It is caught in large quantities and dried by the Indians, —for at this time the squaws are engaged in sowing their maize, and cultivating the land, and the men go-a-fishing in order to assist their wives a little by their draughts of fish. Sometimes they catch them with seines from seventy to eighty fathoms in length, which they braid themselves, and on which, in place of lead, they hang stones, and instead of the corks which we put on them to float them, they fasten small sticks of an ell in length, round and sharp at the end. Over the purse, they have a figure made of wood, resembling the devil, and when the fish swim into the net and come to the purse, so that the figure begins to move, they then begin to cry out and call upon the *mannetoe*, that is, the devil, to give them many fish. They catch great quantities of this fish; which they also catch in little set-nets, six or seven fathoms long, braided like a herring-net. They set them on sticks in the river, one, and one and a half fathoms deep. There is also another kind of fish on the seacoast, which is called *thirteen* [drumfish] by us, because it is larger than the twelve. The scales of the thirteen are yellow like those of the carp, to which it is not unlike in shape. It is the size of a codfish. Herring also come into the river. There is a species of fish caught on the shore, called by us stone-bream, and by the English *schip-heet*, that is to say, *sheep's-head*, for the reason that its mouth is full of teeth, above and below, like a sheep's head. Sturgeon are numerous in the brackish water, and as high up in the fresh water as Fort Orange. There are many kinds of fish which we have not in our fatherland, so that I cannot name them all. In the fresh waters, are pike, perch, roach, and trout."

* * *

Daniel Denton, British traveler, refers to fishing, concerning the New York area, circa 1670, in Denton, *A Brief Defcription of New-York. Formerly Called New-Netherlands* (London: John Hancock, 1670), 19.

"...and wearied with that [hunting], he may go a Fifhing, where the Rivers are fo furnifhed, that he may fupply himfelf with Fifh before he can leave off the Recreation...."

John Sharpe, minister in Pennsylvania, fishes locally, May 1710, in [Sharpe], "Journal of Rev. John Sharpe," The Pennsylvania Magazine of History and Biography, Vol. 40, No. 3 (1916), 290.

17 May 1710: "prayers I went a fishing before 5 in the morning;...."
24 May 1710: "Wind at South, we catcht much fish."

* * *

Andrew Burnaby, Anglican minister, describes fishing near Philadelphia, July 1760, in Burnaby, Travels through the Middle Settlements in North America, in the Years 1759 and 1760 (London: T. Payne, 1775), 50.

July, 1760: "Their amufements are chiefly dancing, in the winter; and, in the fummer, forming parties of pleafure on the Schuilkil, and in the country. There is a fociety of fixteen ladies, and as many gentlemen, called the fifhing company, which meet once a fortnight on the Schuilkil. They have a very pleafant room erected in a romantic fitu-ation upon the banks of that river, where they generally dine and drink tea. There are feveral pretty walks about it, and fome wild and rugged rocks, which, together with the water, and fine groves that adorn the banks, form a moft beautiful and picturefque fcene. There are boats and fifhing tackle of all forts, and the company divert themfelves with walking, fifhing, going upon the water, dancing, finging, converfing, or juft as they pleafe. The ladies wear an uniform, and appear with great eafe and advantage from the neatnefs and simplicity of it. The firft and moft diftinguifhed people of this colony are of this fociety, and it is very advantageous to a ftranger to be introduced to it, as he thereby gets acquainted with the beft and moft refpectable company in Phila-delphia. In the winter, when there is fnow on the ground, it is ufual to make what they call fleighing parties, or to go upon it in fledges; but as this is a practice well known in Europe, it is needlefs to defcribe it."

* * *

James Kenny, Philadelphia Quaker, fishes near Pittsburgh, June 1761 and March and April 1762, in John W. Jordan, ed., "Journal of James Kenny, 1761-1763," Pennsylvania Magazine of History and Biography, Vol. 37, No. 1 (1913), 7, 45, and No. 2 (1913), 153.

June, 1761: "I Caught some fish with a Rod & Line, one Cat fish that Weigh'd Nine Pounds. I have seen One that Weigh'd fourty One Pounds & they tell me for Certain of some being Catched last Year that Weigh'd One Hundred Weight;...."
23 March 1762: "Caught a Cat fish this Evening;...."
16 April, 1762: "Went over ye River to get home some Shingle Boults; Catched 7 fish;...."

* * *

Samuel Smith, New Jersey historian, comments on fishing in New Jersey, circa 1765, in Smith, The History of the Colony of Nova-Cæsaria, or New-Jersey Containing, An Account of Its First Settlement, Progressive Improvements, The Original and Present Constitution, and Other Events, to the Year 1721. With Some Particulars Since; and a Short View of Its Present-State, 2 vols., Vol. 1 (Burlington, N.J.: James Parker, 1765), 112-113.

"[A]nd fifh in their feafon very plenteous: My coufin Revell and I, with fome of my men, went laft third month into the river to catch herrings; for at that time they came in great fhoals into the fhallows; we had neither rod nor net; but after the Indian fafhion made a round pinfold, about two yards over, and a foot high, but left a gap for the fifh to go in at, and made a bufh to lay in the gap to keep the fifh in; and when that was done, we took two long birches and tied their tops together, and we went about a ftone's caft above our faid pinfold; the hawling thefe birche's boughs down the ftream, where we drove thoufands before us, but fo many got into our trap as it would hold, and then we began to hawl them on fhore as faft as three or four of us could, by two or three at a time; and after this manner, in half an hour, we could have filled a three bufhel fack of as good and large herrings as ever I faw;...."

* * *

Ann MacVicar Grant, an American lady, describes fishing near Albany, New York, circa 1769, in [Grant], *Memoirs of an American Lady. With Sketches of Manners and Scenery in America, As They Existed Previous to the Revolution,* 2 vols., Vol. 1 (London: Longman, Hurst, Rees, and Orme, 1808), 70-71.

"About fix weeks after the paffage of thefe birds, fturgeon of a large fize, and in great quantity, made their appearance in the river. Now the fame ardour [as in hunting pigeons and waterfowl] feemed to pervade all ages in purfuit of this new object. Every family had a canoe; and on this occafion all were launched; and thefe perfevering fifhers traced the courfe of the fturgeon up the river; followed them by torch light; and often continued two nights upon the water, never returning till they had loaded their canoes with this valuable fifh, and many other very excellent in other kinds, that come up the river at the fame time. The fturgeon not only furnifhed them with good part of their food in the fummer months, but was pickled or dried for future ufe or exportation."

* * *

Advertisement for fishing equipment, Rivington's New-York Gazetteer, No. 1, 22 April 1773.

"EDWARD POLE
Has for Sale, Wholesale and Retail,

"At his Store in Second-ftreet, the fecond Door above Cheftnut-ftreet, and a little below Captain RANKIN'S, Philadelphia.

"Fifhing Tackle of all forts, for ufe of either Sea or River.

"RED Cedar, Hazle, Dogwood, &c. Fifhing Rods, for Fly, Trolling and Bottom Fifh.

"6, 8, 10, and 12. Stave Pocket Reels, furnifhed with Lines, &c.

"Trolling Wheels, for Rock, Trout, or Perch, with or without multipliers,

"Bottom or Layout, and Sea Lines, cable laid, from large Dolphin down to Whiting, with Hooks fuitable from Bonetta to the fmalleft Size,

"Beft green or white Hair, Silk, Harveft, Hempen, Flaxen and Cotton Lines, for Angling, Trolling, Deepfeas, and other Fifhing.

"Trimmers, and Man of War Trimmers, and Snap Hooks, with or without Springs, for Pike Fifhing.

"A Variety of Cork Floats of all Sizes,

"Artificial Flies, Moths, and Hackles, with bloes fuitable of any Length,

"Silk Worms, Gut, in Knots, and Quarter Knots,

"Beft Indian Grafs,

"Salmon, Rock, Jack, Trout, and Perch, Box and plain Swivels,

"Deepfeas, with or without Swivels for River Fifhing,

"Leads made of various Patterns, for the Ufe of Black Point, and other Fifhing.

"All Sorts and Sizes of Hooks, without Snooding,

"The beft kind of Fifh Hooks, of various Sizes, made at *Philadelphia*,

"Small Portable Boxes, compleatly furnifhed, with a Variety of Fifhing Tackle,

"Cafting, Minnow, Landing and Scoop Nets.

"Any Perfon inclining to make their own Tackle, may be furnifhed with any Kind of Materials.

"All Kind of Tackle mended at a fhort Notice.

"All Orders from Town and Country will be thankfully received, duly attended to, and carefully executed, as though the Perfons were themfelves perfonally prefent."

* * *

Nicholas Cresswell, British loyalist, observes fishing on the Youghiogheny River in western Pennsylvania, May 1775, in [Cresswell], *The Journal of Nicholas Cresswell, 1774-1777* (Port Washington, N.Y.: Kennikat Press, 1968), 69.

1 May 1775: "After breakfast left Saweekly and stood down the River. Crossed several Fish pots. These fish pots are made by throwing up small stones and gravel something like a mill weir, beginning at the side of the River and proceeding in a diagonal line, till they meet in the middle of the stream, where they fix a thing like the body of a cart, contracted where the water flows in just to admit the fish, but so contrived as to prevent their return or escape."

* * *

William Parsons to Thomas Stretch, governor of the Schuylkill Fishing Company, discusses fishing by the club, 7 May 1775, reprinted in *A History of the Schuylkill Fishing Company of the State in Schuylkill, 1732-1888* (Philadelphia: Members of the State in Schuylkill, 1889), unpaginated facsimile following page ?.

"...And as to what relates to the Fishery of the several Waters within the limitts of their Embafsy they have been very afsiduous not only in searching for and catching but in drefsing and eating of Fish...."

* * *

Bayze Wells, Farmington, Connecticut soldier, notes fishing near Fort Ticonderoga in eastern New York, 14 July 1775, in [Wells], "Journal of Bayze Wells of Farmington, May, 1775–February, 1777 At the Northward and in Canada," in "Orderly Book and Journals Kept by Connecticut Men While Taking Part in the American Revolution, 1775-1778," *Collections of the Connecticut Historical Society*, Vol. 7 (Hartford: Connecticut Historical Society, 1899), 255.

"Orders for 14th July.... The Fifhing to Carred on for the futer by A non Commifhn[d] Offiecar with 5 or 6 men who Are to fifh Every morning and the fifh when taken to be Delivered to the Comefary who is to Provide A hurdle to Receve them and Deliver them out to the Companys according to their Number the Sien forthwith to be hanged upon Stakes and Dried then Delivered to the Care of the Comefery in the Store to be ufed no more that Day without Liberty and if Ufed in the afternoon to be hung upon Stakes and if not Dry before to hang all Night but if Dri to be houfed as Above"

* * *

Jonathan Odell, New Jersey loyalist, publishes a song about fishing and politics, circa 1776, Odell, "Song," in Winthrop Sargent, ed., *The Loyal Verses of Joseph Stansbury and Doctor Jonathan Odell; Relating to the American Revolution* (Albany, N.Y.: J. Munsell, 1860), 9-10.

"SONG FOR A FISHING PARTY
NEAR BURLINGTON, ON THE DELAWARE, IN 1776

"HOW fweet is the feafon, the fky how ferene;
On Delaware's banks how delightful the fcene;
The Prince of the Rivers, his waves all afleep,
In filence' majeftic glides on to the Deep.

"Away from the noife of the Fife and the Drum,
And all the rude din of Bellona we come;
And a plentiful ftore of good humor we bring
To feafon our feaft in the fhade of Cold Spring.

"A truce to all whig and tory debate;
True lovers of Freedom, contention we hate:
For the Demon of difcord in vain tries his art
To poffefs or inflame a true *Proteftant* heart.

"True Proteftant friends to fair Liberty's caufe,
To decorum, good order, religion and laws,
From avarice, jealoufy, perfidy, free;
We wifh all the world were as happy as we.

"We have wants, we confefs, but are free from the care
Of thofe that abound, yet have nothing to fpare:
Serene as the fky, as the river ferene,
We are happy to want envy, malice and fpleen.

"While thoufands around us, mifled by a few,
The Phantoms of pride and ambition purfue,
With pity their fatal delufion we fee;
And wifh all the world were as happy as we!"

* * *

Jeduthan Baldwin, Brookfield, Massachusetts officer, fishes in eastern New York near Fort Ticonderoga, 6 May 1776, in Thomas Williams Baldwin, ed., *The Revolutionary Journal of Col. Jeduthan Baldwin, 1775-1778* (Bangor, Me.: The De Burians, 1906), 40.

"at Evning we caught a plenty of Fish."

* * *

Jabez Fitch, Connecticut lieutenant, observes fishing on Long Island, June, July, and August 1777, in W.H. Sabine, ed., *The New-York Diary of Lieutenant Jabez Fitch of the 17th (Connecticut) Regiment from August 22, 1776 to December 15, 1777* (New York: pvt. ptg., 1954), 179-180, 184, 193, 198.

16 June 1777: "...; Our Ld: Ld: proposed to go to the Bay for Fish, & taking us with him, accordingly we made the necessary preparation, & at about 9 oClock we went down to the Water, but finding the Craft which we Expected was gon, we were obleged to Omit our Voige for the present;...."

17 June 1777: "Early in the morning Majr: Hatfield call'd us up with design to go a Fishing again;... At about 7 oClock we went from our Quarters down to the Widdw: Vendeveres Mill, where Lt: Loring & Ensn: Bradford Joind us, & we Embark'd in a large Battoe, in which we went down the Creek, & into the Bay, we then Steered our

course Southward, almost to Rockway Beech, where we made a Tryal to catch some Fish &c.

"After several Unsuccesfull attempts to catch some Fish, we came back to a Bar,...."

29 June 1777: "...; We had a very curious Dinner this Day on fresh Fish, our Ld: Ld: having been in the bey Yesterday a Fishing;...."

26 July 1777: "...; Our Ld: Ld: & his Son went into the Bay afishing, tho' with but poor success."

9 August 1777: "At one, we Dine'd on a Dish of Sheepshead, our Ld: Ld: having yesterday been into the Bey a fishing, & had good success;...."

* * *

Advertisement for fishing equipment, [Rivington's] Royal Gazette, No. 163, 4 April 1778.

"Fifhing Tackle,
SOLD by
JAMES RIVINGTON,
Confifting of the following Articles.

"RODS of three and four joints, fpun lines of fix, eight, ten, twelve, twenty, and thirty yards each, without a fingle knot; knotted by lines, of fix, eight, ten, and twelve yards; ftave reels for fix, eight, and ten filk and hair lines completely fitted for immediate execution; brafs winches, lines with flies, imitated from the reptiles of Long-Ifland; and an ample ftore of the true *Trout taking old Kirby.*"

* * *

Luke Swetland, Pennsylvania captive, fishes among the Seneca in western New York, June 1779, in [Swetland], *A Narrative of the Captivity of Luke Swetland, in 1778 and 1779, among the Seneca Indians* (Waterville, N.Y.: James J. Guernsey, 1875), 22.

"Caught some eels, killed some hawks, some shitepokes and some muskrats, and I thought we lived exceedingly well."

* * *

Henry Dearborn, New Hampshire officer, goes fishing in north central Pennsylvania, July and August 1779, in Lloyd A. Brown and Howard H. Peckham, *Revolutionary War Journals of Henry Dearborn, 1775-1783* (Freeport, N.Y.: Books for Libraries Press, 1969 [1939]), 162, 169.

23 July 1779: "I went with several other Gentlemen 8 miles up the River, to an old settlement call'd Lachawanee. to fish & hunt dear—...."

24 July 1779: "came home with but few fish.—...."

2 August 1779: "we took a number of fine fish with a sean to day —such as bass, pike, chubs, &c &c—...."

* * *

Samuel Shute, New Jersey lieutenant, fishes in central Pennsylvania, 7 July 1779, in [Shute], "Journal of Lt. Samuel Shute," in Frederick Cook, ed., *Journals of the Military Expedition of Major General John Sullivan against the Six Nations of Indians in 1779* (Freeport, N.Y.: Books for Libraries Press, reprint of 1885 ed.), 268.

"was spent in fish and had extraordinary luck."

* * *

Advertisement for fishing equipment, [Rivington's] Royal Gazette, No. 572, 23 March 1782.

"The Seafon being now commenced for
"The PISCATORS DIVERSION,
"FISHING RODS, of all defcriptions, for Adepts, and young Practitioners.
"Likewife Lines, Hooks, Winches, Reels, &c. are to be had of the Printer."

* * *

Philip van Cortlandt, Cortlandt, New York brigadier general, goes fishing at Honeoye Lake, New York, summer, 1779 and in the Hudson River valley, spring, 1783, in [van Cortlandt], "Autobiography of Philip van Cortlandt," Magazine of American History, Vol. 2 (1878), 290, 298.

Summer, 1779: "Here [Honeoye Lake] I took nine catfish, which was a great relief, for our mess had our scanty provision of three days stolen from us two nights before,...."
Spring, 1783: "I set off, and arrived at the farm, at the mouth of Croton River, where I was joined in a short time by Captains Hamtramck and Vanderburgh, and also by Daniel Pryer, whom I had invited to stay with me until we could go into New York, and they were happily employed, sometimes gunning and fishing, &c., &c."

* * *

Johann David Schoepf, German physician, in New Jersey near the Hudson River in July 1783, in Schoepf, Travels in the Confederation. Pennsylvania, Maryland, Virginia, the Carolinas, East Florida, the Bahamas, trans. and ed. by Alfred J. Morrison, 2 vols., Vol. 1 (Cleveland: Arthur H. Clark, 1911), 29.

July 1783: "In the Hudson they [shad] follow the main channel and tributaries for a distance of 150 miles from the coast. They come, if the weather is mild, in early April; cold weather often holds them back until later; but by the end of April or the beginning of May, the mouths of all the rivers are generally full of them. At this season fishermen line the riverbanks, cast their seines with the flush tide, and at times catch during a running several hundred pounds' worth. The many thousands taken (in all rivers, inlets, and creeks) amount to a very small part of the host, which apparently begins to be diminished only when, far inland, the danger from the nets cannot so easily be escaped in the narrower and shallower streams. That they are all caught is not to be believed, although few are seen descending, and those thin and often dead."

* * *

Francesco dal Verme, Italian count, observes fishing near Lake George in eastern New York, July 1783, in Elizabeth Cometti, trans. and ed., Seeing America and Its Great Men. The Journal and Letters of Count Francesco dal Verme, 1783-1784 (Charlottesville, Va.: University Press of Virginia, 1969), 13-14.

22 July 1783: "We counted on our skill as anglers to provide food, and in the course of a fourteen-mile sail we caught enough fish for dinner."
25 July 1783: "Our Catch of fish was so plentiful that we kept only the best of them. The most common fish is a kind of perch, but in running streams there are also pike and some red trout."

* * *

Jeremiah Greenman, Rhode Island soldier and later officer, records fishing in eastern New York, September 1783, in Robert C. Bray and Paul E. Bushnell, eds., Diary of a Common Soldier in the American Revolution, 1775-1783. An Annotated Edition of the Military Journal of Jeremiah Greenman (DeKalb, Ill.: Northern Illinois University Press, 1978), 268.

6 September 1783: "ketched 20 Salmon and piched our tent—...."

OTHER LOCALES

Richard Mather, Puritan minister, tells of fishing on the Atlantic crossing, circa 1635, in [Mather], *Journal of Richard Mather, 1635. His Life and Death, 1670* (Boston, 1670), reprinted as *Collections of the Dorchester Antiquarian and Historical Society,* No. 3 (Boston, 1850), 15.

"This morning about seven of ye clocke or seamen stroke a great porpuyse, and haled it with ropes into ye ship; for bignesse not much lesse than an hogge of 20 or 25 shillings a piece, and not much unlike for shape, with flesh fat and leane, like in color to the fat and leane of an hogge.... The seeing of him haled into ye ship... was wonderful to us all, and marvellous merry sport and delightful to or women and children, so good was or God unto, in affording us the day before spiritual refreshing to our soules, and ys day morning also delightful recreation to or bodyes, at ye taking and opening of ye huge and strange fish."

* * *

Jean Claude Allouez, French Jesuit missionary, chronicles the fishing north of Lake Superior, 20-22 May 1667, in [Allouez], "Father Allouez's Journey to Lake Superior, 1665-1667," in Louise Phelps Kellogg, ed., *Early Narratives of the Northwest, 1634-1699* (New York: Barnes & Noble, 1917), 136.

"On the twentieth, finding nothing in our nets, we continued our journey, munching some grains of dry corn. On the following day, God refreshed us with two small fishes, which gave us new life. Heaven's blessings increased on the next day, our savages catching so many sturgeon that they were obliged to leave part of them at the water's edge."

* * *

Henri Joutel, French explorer, notes fishing with the La Salle expedition, in the lower Mississippi River valley, March 1685, in [Joutel], *Joutel's Journal of La Salle's Last Voyage* (Chicago: The Caxton Club, 1896 [reprint of 1714 edition]), 47-48.

"Having one Day obferv'd, that the Water work'd and bubbled up, and afterwards perceiving it was occafion'd by the Fifh skipping from Place to Place, I caufed a Net to be brought, and we took a prodigious Quantity of Gilt-Heads, Mullets and others about as big as a Herring, which afforded us good Food for feveral Days. This fifhery, which I caufed to be often followed, was a great Help towards our Subfiftance."
"Another more unlucky Accident befell us, one of our Fifhermen fwimming about the Net to gather the Fifh, was carry'd away by the Current, and could not be help'd by us."
"Our Men fometimes went about feveral little Salt Water Lakes, that were near our Fort, and found on the Banks a Sort of flat Fifhes, like Turbots afleep, which they ftruck with fharp pointed Sticks, and they were good Food."

* * *

Samuel Sewall, Boston magistrate, at Gravesend, England, lists an angling rod among his shipboard possessions, August 1689, in M. Halsey Thomas, ed., *The Diary of Samuel Sewall, 1674-1729, Volume I. 1674-1708* (New York: Farrar, Straus and Giroux, 1973), 235.

13 August 1689: [In a list of Sewall's possessions aboard America]: "One Angling Rod:"

Father Paul du Ru, Jesuit missionary, goes fishing among the Natchez on the Mississippi River, 8 March 1700, in Ruth Lapham Butler, trans., *The Journal of Paul du Ru [February 1 to May 8, 1700] Missionary Priest to Louisiana* (Chicago: The Caxton Club, 1934), 30.

"The weather is fine. I am going fishing. My dinner tomorrow depends on it. The brill do not bite because the musket shots have frightened them. Hunters spoil a fisherman's business. I lost more than one fish on that account."

* * *

A geographer of Nova Scotia, describes fishing in that province, circa 1749, in *A Geographical History of Nova Scotia* (London: Paul Vaillant, 1749), 48, 49.

"In *December*, or rather in the two laft Moons of the Year, a Fifh called *Ponamo*. comes to fpawn upon the Ice, and you may catch as many as you pleafe. I take this to be a Species of the *Dog-Fifh*."

"Towards the End of *March*, the Fifh begin to fpawn, and crowd into the Rivers in fuch Shoals, as is incredible to any one that has not feen it. The firft that comes in is the *Smelt*, which is three times as big here as in *Europe*....

"After thefe, the *Sturgeon* and the *Salmon* bring in warm Weather;...."

"...; and if thefe [indigenous] People would till and fow their Land, feed their Cattle, and raife Poultry; Fifhing, Fowling and Hunting might be ufed only for Exercife and Diverfion."

* * *

Robert Rogers, British officer, reports on fishing on the north side of Lake Ontario, September 1760, in [Rogers], *Journals of Major Robert Rogers. Containing An Account of the feveral Excurfions he made under the Generals who commanded upon the Continent of North America, during the late war* (London: J. Millan, 1765), 204-205.

28 September 1760: "Some of us fifhed with them [Mississaugua indigenous people] in the evening, being invited by them, and filled a bark-canoe with falmon in about half an hour. Their method of catching fifh is very extraordinary. One perfon holds a lighted pine-torch, while a fecond ftrikes the fifh with a fpear. This is the feafon in which the falmon fpawn in thefe parts, contrary to what they do in any other place I ever knew them before."

29 September 1760: "Plenty of fifh was catched here alfo."

* * *

Benjamin Mifflin, Philadelphia merchant, fishes near Dover, Delaware, 6 August 1762, in Victor Hugo Paltsits, ed., *Journal of Benjamin Mifflin. The Record of a Tour from Philadelphia to Delaware and Maryland, July 26 to August 14, 1762* (New York: The New York Public Library, 1935), 16.

"...—towards the Middle of the afternoon went back to Dover with V.L. & from thense went a Fishing on Dover river in C^O with Th^O Parke & The^O Maurice. Caught 14 Fine Perch—...."

* * *

William Roberts, British historian, circa 1763, concerning fishing on the Hernando de Soto expedition, in Florida, August? 1541, in Roberts, *An Account of the First Discovery, and Natural History of Florida* (London: T. Jefferys, 1763), 64.

"Thefe marfhes were fo full of fifh, that the foldiers could take as many as they pleafed with their hands."

George Washington, Virginia planter, Revolutionary War general, and later President, chronicles fishing along the Ohio River, October 1770, in Donald Jackson and Dorothy Twohig, eds., *The Diaries of George Washington*, 6 vols., Vol. 2 (Charlottesville, Va.: University Press of Virginia, 1976, 1978, 1979), 299.

25 October 1770: "About half way in the long reach we Incampd, opposite to the beginning of a large bottom on the East side of the River [the Ohio River]. At this place we through out some lines at Night & found a Cat fish of the size of our largest River cats hookd to it in the Morning, tho it was of the smallest kind here."

* * *

John Ferdinand Dalziel Smyth, British traveler, comments on fishing in the Ohio River Valley, 1774?, in Smyth, *A Tour in the United States of America. Containing an Account of the Present Situation of that Country*, 2 vols., Vol. 1 (London: G. Robinson, 1784), 337.

1774?: "Fifh are innumerable in the rivers here, fuch as perch, pike, eels, trout, roch, fhads, old-wives, cat-fifh, &c. &c. very fat, and fo aftonifhingly large, credibility is endangered in relating it, for it is a fact, that of the cat-fifh fome are from twelve to eighteen inches between the eyes, and are eafily caught."

* * *

Nicholas Cresswell, British loyalist, observes fishing while traveling near Barbados, July and August 1774, in [Cresswell], *The Journal of Nicholas Cresswell, 1774-1777* (Port Washington, N.Y.: Kennikat Press, 1968), 31-32.

29 July 1774: "This morning the Captn. killed a Jew Fish with the gig. It weighed 74 lbs and measured 5 feet long. Something like a Cod. Eats very well."

14 August 1774: "Quite calm and smooth water, the people bathed in the Sea. They had not been on board half an hour before a Shark came alongside. We baited a hook, but he would not take it."

* * *

Du Roi the Elder, German lieutenant and adjutant, describes fishing near Newfoundland, May 1776, and at Quebec, January 1777, in Charlotte S.J. Epping, ed., *Journal of Du Roi the Elder Lieutenant and Adjutant, in the Service of the Duke of Brunswick, 1776-1778* (New York: D. Appleton and Company, 1911), 28, 59.

3 May 1776: "We shortened sail, and with great delight we took out our fishing tackle. These are long lines on the end of which hook's are fastened. Small pieces of meat are put on these hooks, and cannon balls attached hold them under water. Every one joined in and was full of expectation, and in about twnty minutes we saw a codfish, weighing a little more than six pounds, brought to the deck."

9 January 1777: "This is the time for hunting and fishing, and I must mention a peculiar way of fishing, customary in this part of the country. Whole caravans start out right after Christmas and up to twelfth day, to go fishing in the streams Trois Rivières, Batiscan and St. Anne. They cut holes in the ice, and their only implements are boxes, with holes in them, tied to strings. These are let down into the water and fish (Morue, Codfish), which at this season of the year go out of the lakes down the streams, are caught in such quantities that not only the people, but also the pigs, and what seems incredible to Europeans, the cows and horses live on this food for considerable time."

* * *

Henry Dearborn, New Hampshire officer, goes fishing in the St. Lawrence River valley, May 1776, in Lloyd A. Brown and Howard H. Peckham, *Revolutionary War Journals of Henry Dearborn, 1775-1783* (Freeport, N.Y.: Books for Libraries Press, 1969 [1939]), 86.

23 May 1776: "Having no wind we Catched plenty of fish—"

* * *

Jeremiah Greenman, Rhode Island soldier and later officer, records fishing as a prisoner in Quebec, June 1776, in Robert C. Bray and Paul E. Bushnell, eds., *Diary of a Common Soldier in the American Soldier, 1775-1783. An Annotated Edition of the Military Journal of Jeremiah Greenman* (DeKalb, Ill.: Northern Illinois University Press, 1978), 28.

12 June 1776: "13 or forteen prisoners ware takin out to go fishing...."

* * *

Thomas Anburey, British officer, recounts fishing near Newfoundland, September 1776, in [Anburey], *Travels through the Interior Parts of America,* 2 vols., Vol. 1 (London: William Lane, 1791), 9-10.

11 September 1776: "When we found we were upon thefe Banks, which is perceptible without founding, as the water changes from an azure blue to a white fandy color, we laid-to in order to fifh for cod, the procefs of which is no lefs entertaining than furprizing to Europeans.

"After baiting the hooks with the entrails of a fowl, in a few minutes we caught a fifh, when the failors made ufe of fome part of the entrails, as being a better bait, and then drew up the cod as faft as you can poffibly imagine; for though we remained there only half an hour, we caught as many as would ferve the fhip's crew the reft of the voyage.

"You may wonder by what means they are certain of having caught a fifh, with fo many fathom of line out. When it has been a little while in the water, they gently pull it with the finger and thumb, and if there is a fifh, the ftruggling of it occafions a vibration of the line, which is very perceptible, though fo many fathoms deep. They then haul it in, and as foon as the fifh comes in view, the water magnifies it to fuch a fize, that it appears almoft impoffible to get it on board; and indeed it requires some dexterity, for on hauling them out of the water they ftruggle with fuch violence, as frequently to work themfelves off the hooks, by entangling the line in the rigging, before they can be got up the fhip's fide."

* * *

Hessian staff officers at Batiscan, and Ste. Anne, Quebec, remark on fishing, November 1776 and March? April? 1777, in Ray W. Pettengill, trans., *Letters from America, 1776-1779. Being Letters of Brunswick, Hessian, and Waldeck Officers with the British Armies during the Revolution* (Port Washington, N.Y.: Kennikat Press, 1964 [1924]), 21, 62-64.

2 November 1776: "Every *habitant* is a huntsman and fisherman. Hunting and fishing are free; there are no fishponds."

March? April? 1777: "About January 6th there begins a special fishing season for four weeks. The little codfish ascend the St. Lawrence at this season in incredible numbers, go up beyond Montreal and enter all the tributaries. Hence people cut holes in the ice, take a stick, tie to it ten or twelve bits of twine, and to each string a piece of raw meat —preferably lung; then they hang these without any hook at all in the water, pull it out after a second, shake off on the ice the fish which have taken the meat, and let them freeze stiff. It is unbelievable what mountains of fish are caught thus and how many thousand bushel are shoveled into sleighs and hauled home....

"When the big river is completely frozen over, they catch sturgeon five and more ells long from under the ice. This year they have been scarce. Eels are also caught in special eel traps at ebb tide in great quantities. They are hung for a day in the smoke, then frozen. The carp are no good; they have a dry, fibrous meat. The bass (or perch) are as good as at home. The river pike are very excellent and very large. Trout and salmon trout are found in the rapids of all the small rivers.... Poissons dorés and masquinonges are a particular kind of six or eight pound fishes which taste very delicate and are caught in great quantities in the parishes St. François and Masquinonge that they are shipped frozen through all Canada. Thus far I have seen no crucian, gudgeon, or loach. Anyway, there are in Canada no fishponds, pounds, or preserves; consequently no fish baskets and fish thieves; whoever knows how to catch fish from the rivers is lord and master of the fish."

* * *

John Ledyard, British corporal with Captain James Cook, fishes in Alaskan waters, 12 May 1778, in James Kenneth Munford, ed., *John Ledyard's Journal of Captain Cook's Last Voyage* (Corvallis, Oregon: Oregon State University Press, 1963), 78-79.

"..., and finding the weather as yet to be tolerable we slung out the boats and sent them on shore to fish with the seine, but caught nothing."

* * *

John Adams, Massachusetts lawyer, politician, and later United States President, near Newfoundland, July 1779, in [Adams], *Diary and Autobiography of John Adams, Vol. 2, Diary, 1771-1781,* ed. by Lyman H. Butterfield (Cambridge, Mass.: Harvard University Press, 1962), 399.

17 July 1779: "It is surprizing to me, that We have not seen more Fish. A few Whales, a few Porpoises and two Sharks are all We have seen. The two Sharks, We caught, with a Shark Hook and a Bit of Pork for a Bait. We cutt up the first, and threw over board his Head and Entrails, all of which the other, which was playing after the Ship, snatched at with infinite Greediness and swallowed down in an instant. After We had taken him, We opened him, and found the Head and Entrails of his Companion in him."

Chapter 14

GYMNASTICS, RUNNING, AND WALKING

Throughout the earlier centuries of American experience, the human penchant for movement, action, speed, and grace was active and exuberant. The Olympic classical tradition of athletics, track and field, and gymnastics all found some expression during the colonial period. Commercialized calisthenics probably existed at some early circuses and animal exhibitions, but only William Byrd's quick notation of tumblers at an afternoon's entertainment give a glimpse of such here.

There was yet another source of athletic activity contributing to American gymnastic skills and physical contests. Indigenous peoples and frontier settlers, mostly unaware of Greek traditions, were avid leapers, jumpers, throwers, runners and all-around ebullient athletes. From Connecticut to California holidays, social gatherings, and other festivities gave excuses to people, already eager, to indulge in these exuberant activities. Whether the games were spontaneous or part of pre-planned gatherings and rituals, the human thirst for activity found ready outlets. Many travelers and commentators depicted indigenous youth and adults, as well as backwoods settlers, as energetic enthusiasts for any wrestle, any jumping match, any foot race.

Running was one quite common outlet for these physical impulses. Colonial and Revolutionary observers reported on foot races, often in conjunction with fairs and horse races, in Virginia, Maryland, South Carolina and New York. Commentators speculated if Europeans could outrace indigenous people in the short run, but most accorded distance superiority to the tribal runners, accustomed to striding as part of war, trade, and hunting. Unfortunately few descriptions of races among slaves or former slaves exist, beyond one intriguing reference to a race for "negro girls." Similarly, the contemporary accounts are frustratingly short on detail about running techniques, race tracks and distances, typical and record times (although horse racing accounts contain such.) Clearly early Americans loved a good run and occasionally celebrated a champion, such as in Alexander Graydon's remembrance of a famous runner at his school.

If the record is correct and complete enough, walking, either for pleasure or race-walking, elicited little enthusiasm from these same Americans. Aside from comments by John Adams and Benjamin Rush recommending walking as healthful recreation, there was little else in the record to predict the later American fascinations with pedestrianism and hiking movements. Apparently it was a trifle early for mountain walking and climbing. Colonial and Revolutionary Americans probably found walking a chore and mountains too forbidding for recreation, hunting excepted. The following sources recount the expression of physical culture, running, and walking of the colonial period. [Consult the general writings about sports, recreation, and the various colonial, provincial, territorial, and state Sabbath and gaming laws in Chapter One for other sources about the specific sports or games in this chapter.]

GYMNASTICS

William Byrd, Westover, Virginia planter, observes gymnastics, 15 August 1712, in Louis B. Wright and Marion Tinling, eds., *The Secret Diary of Westover, 1709-1712* (Richmond, Va.: The Dietz Press, 1941), 570.

"One of Captain M-r-l's seamen showed us some feats of activity in tumbling."

An account of a wedding near Saybrook, Connecticut, circa 1726, mentions leaping as a recreation, reprinted in Helen Evertson Smith, *Colonial Days and Ways as Gathered from Family Papers by Helen Evertson Smith of Sharon, Connecticut* (New York: The Century Company, 1901), 180.

"[The men at wedding participated in] rastling, quoits, running, leaping, archery and firing at a mark, but on the last day no muskets were allowed by reason of the Indians."

* * *

John Brickell, Irish doctor, lists leaping as a recreation in North Carolina, circa 1737, in Brickell, *The Natural History of North-Carolina* (Dublin: James Carson, 1737), 40.

"*Wreftling, Leaping*, and fuch Activities are much ufed by them;...."

* * *

Excerpt from an advertisement for a St. Andrew's Day festival in Hanover County, Virginia mentions a jumping contest, Virginia Gazette, No. 68, 11–18 November 1737.

"With divers other confiderable Prizes, for Dancing, Singing, Foot-ball-play, Jumping, Wreftling, &c."

* * *

Benjamin Franklin, Pennsylvania editor, concerning physical education, recommends leaping as recreation, circa 1749, in [Franklin], *Proposals Relating to the Education of Youth in Pensilvania* (Philadelphia: pvt. ptg?, 1749), 10-11.

"That to keep them [pupils] in Health, and to ftrengthen and render active their Bodies, they be frequently exercis'd in Running, Leaping, Wreftling, and Swimming, &c."

* * *

Fray Miguel Venegas, Mexican Jesuit missionary, mentions leaping among other recreations at California rancherias, circa 1758, in Venegas, *A Natural and Civil History of California*, 2 vols., Vol. 1 (London: James Rivington and James Fletcher, 1759), 84.

"To thefe feftivities the rancherias ufually invite one another; and likewife often fend challenges for wreftling, leaping, running, fhooting with their bow, and trials of ftrength; and in thefe and the like fports, days and nights, weeks and months were often fpent in times of peace."

* * *

A children's book draws a moral from leaping, in *A Little Pretty Pocket-Book, Intended for the Amusement and Instruction of Little Master Tommy and Pretty Miss Polly* (London: J. Newbery, 1767), 83.

"HOP, STEP, *and* JUMP.

HOP fhort, and *Step* fafe,   MORAL. This old Maxim take,
    To make your *Jump* long;   T' embellifh your Book;
This Art oft has beat   Think well are [ere?] you talk,
Th' Efforts of the Strong.   And, ere you leap, look."

* * *

Benjamin Rush, Philadelphia physician, advocates jumping as recreation, circa 1772, in Rush, *Sermons to Gentlemen upon Temperance and Exercise* (Philadelphia: John Dunlap, 1772), 33.

"To all thefe fpecies of exercife which we have mentioned, I would add, SKEAT-
ING, JUMPING, alfo, the active plays of TENNIS, BOWLES, QUOITS, GOLF, and
the like. The manner in which each of thefe operate, may be underftood from what we
faid under the former particulars."

* * *

Levi Beardsley, Otsego County, New York lawyer, lists jumping and hopping among
Cooperstown area amusements, circa the 1780s, in Beardsley, *Reminiscences; Personal
and Other Incidents; Early Settlement of Otsego County; Notices and Anecdotes of
Public Men; Judicial, Legal and Legislative Matters; Field Sports; Dissertations and Discussions* (New York: Charles Vinten, 1852), 34.

"Wrestling, running, jumping, and hopping always constituted part of the amusements."

RUNNING AND WALKING

William Wood, English settler, notes running among New England indigenous people,
circa 1634, in Wood, *New England's Prospect. A True, Lively, and Experimental Defcription of that Part of* America, *Commonly Called Nevv England. Difcovering the Ftage of
the Countrie, Both as it Ftands to our New-Come* Englifh *Planters; and to the Old Native Inhabitants* (London: Thomas Cotes, 1634), reprinted as *Wood's New-England's
Prospect, Publications of the Prince Society, Volume 1* (Boston: The Prince Society,
1865), 96-98.

"For their fports of acttivitie they have commonly but three or foure; as footeball,
fhooting, running and fwimming:...."

"It is moft delight to fee them play, in fmaller companies, when men may view their
fwift footemanfhip, their curious toffings of their Ball, their flouncing into the water,
their lubberlike wreftling, having no cunning at all in that kind, one *Englifh* being able
to beate ten *Indians* at footeball."

"For their running it is with much celeritie and continuance, yet I fuppofe there be
many *Englifh* men who being as lightly clad as they are, would outrun them for a fpurt,
though not able to continue it for a day or dayes, being they very ftrong winded and
rightly clad for a race."

* * *

John Dunton, London traveler, in Boston, comments on running by New England indigenous peoples, circa 1686, in [Dunton], *A Summer's Ramble, Through Ten Kingdomes,
Occasionally Written by John Dunton, Citizen of London,* 2 Vols. (London: A. Baldwin,
1686), reprinted as W.H. Whitmore, ed., *Letters Written from New-England, A.D. 1686,
by John Dunton* (Boston: The Prince Society, 1867), 277.

"They are generally very quick on foot; and brought up even from their Mother's
Brefts to running; their Legs being ftretch'd and bound up in a ftrange way in their
Cradle backward, from their Infancy: Which makes fome of them fo excel in running,

that they will run four-fcore or an hundred miles in a Summers Day: and they very often Practice running of Races."

* * *

Virginia Governor Francis Nicholson proclaims a running match, circa 1691, reprinted in "Nicholson's Proclamation about the College and Orders for Prize Games for Bachelors, etc.," William and Mary Quarterly, 1st Series, Vol. 11, No. 2 (October 1902), 87.

"To the Sheriffe of Surry County

"I desire that you give public notice that I will give first and second prizes to be shott for, wrastled, played at backswords, & Run for by Horse and foott, to begin on the 22^d. day of Aprill next s^{et}. [Saint] Georges day being Satterday all which prizes are to be shott for &c by the better sort of Virginians onely, who are Batchelers."

* * *

William Byrd, Westover, Virginia planter, observes running races, April 1709, September and October 1711, and runs for his health, December 1711 and January 1712, in Louis B. Wright and Marion Tinling, eds., The Secret Diary of William Byrd of Westover, 1709-1712 (Richmond, Va.: The Dietz Press, 1941), 25, 405, 415, 417, 461, 468.

24 April 1709: "Mr. W-l-s ran two races and beat John Custis and Mr. [Hawkins]."

14 September 1711: "When I came to Captain Stith's I found Joe Harwood and his troopers which are in good order. I told them of the prizes and set them immediately to running and wrestling. I stayed to see them about an hour and then returned home,...."

3 October 1711: "About 11 o'clock I ate some mutton for breakfast, and several of my captains came to go over the river with me, where we got about 2 o'clock but in the meantime the Major had exercised his men on the north side. Then I ordered the men to be drawn in single [file] along the path where the men were to run for the prize, and John Hatcher, one of Captain Randolph's men, won the pistol. Then I caused the men to be drawn into a square to see the men play at cudgels and Dick O-l-n won the sword, and of the wrestling Will Kennon won the gun. Just as the sun went down our games ended...."

6 October 1711: "About 2 o'clock our prizes began and Will M-r-l got the prize of running and John S-c-l-s the prize of cudgels and Robin Easely the prize [of] wrestling. All was finished about 4 o'clock...."

29 December 1711: "..., and then went out to shoot with bow and arrow till the evening and then I ran to breathe myself...."

11 January 1712: "Before I came in I took a run for my health."

* * *

Resolution of the Yearly Meeting of the New England Society of Friends warns against foot racing, circa 1719, in Society of Friends, The Book of Discipline Agreed on the Yearly-Meeting of Friends For New-England (Providence: John Carter, 1785), 135.

"SPORTS and GAMING.

"ADVISED that fuch be dealt with as run races, either on horfeback or on foot; or otherwife lay wagers, or ufe any kind of gaming, or needlefs and vain fports or paftime: For our time fwiftly paffeth away; and our pleafure and delight ought to be in the law of the Lord. 1719.

"And friends are advifed againft attending fuch places, on any accounts."

An account of a wedding near Saybrook, Connecticut, circa 1726, mentions running as a recreation, reprinted in Helen Evertson Smith, *Colonial Days and Ways as Gathered from Family Papers by Helen Evertson Smith of Sharon, Connecticut* (New York: The Century Company, 1901), 180.

"[The men at wedding participated in] rastling, quoits, running, leaping, archery and firing at a mark, but on the last day no muskets were allowed by reason of the Indians."

* * *

John Brickell, Irish doctor, remarks on the absence of foot races in North Carolina, circa 1737, in Brickell, *The Natural History of North-Carolina* (Dublin: James Carson, 1737), 40.

"*Wreftling, Leaping*, and fuch Activities are much ufed by them; yet I never obferved any Foot Races."

* * *

Excerpt in horse racing advertisement refers to a foot race, Virginia Gazette, No. 61, 30 September–7 October 1737.

"4. That 12 Boys of 12 Years of Age do run 112 Yards for a hat of the Value of 12 Shillings."

* * *

Excerpt from an account about a St. Andrew's Day festival in Hanover County, Virginia, mentions foot racing, Virginia Gazette, No. 70, 2–9 December 1737.

"The Horfe and Foot Races were run; and all or moft of the Prizes contended for, and won."

* * *

Excerpt from an advertisement about a fair and horse racing at Williamsburg announces a running match, Virginia Gazette, No. 175, 30 November–7 December 1739.

"A Pair of Silver Buckles, Value 20 S. to be run for by Men, from the *College* to the *Capitol*. A Pair of Shoes to be given to him that comes in Second. And a Pair of Gloves to the Third."

* * *

Advertisement for running matches, South Carolina Gazette, No. 498, 10 October 1743.

"TO BE RUN for on *York* Courfe, at the *Old Quarter Houfe*, on Thurfday the 13th of this Inftant, *October*, 1743 A handfome fafhionable filver Punch Bowl, Value 90 l. by any Horfe, Mare, or Gelding, the beft in three Heats.

"On the fame Day, a Foot Race will be run, for a very good handfome *French* embroider'd Waiftcoat, Value 90 l. by fix People, more or lefs, who are to run twice round the half Mile Courfe; the firft that comes in with fair Play (no joftling allow'd) is entitled to the Waiftcoat.

"On Friday the 14th of the fame Inft. to be run for, a handfome filver Pint Mug, Value 40 l. by any Horfe, Mare or Gelding, the beft in three Heats.

"On *Saturday* the 15th of the faid Inft. to be run for, a handfome Saddle, Bridle and Furniture, Value 30 l. by any Horfe, Mare or Gelding, the beft in three Heats.

"On the fame Day will be given gratis, a very good filver lac'd hat, to be run for by four Men or more, and to make the beft Way they can, 200 Yards, each Man to be in a Sack, all but his Head; the Perfon that comes in firft fhall have the Hat.

John Hanbury.

Advertisement for foot races, South Carolina Gazette, No. 504, 21 November 1743.

"TO be Run for on *York Courfe*, at the *Old Quarter Houfe*, on *Monday* the 26*th of December*, 1743

"A very handfome fafhionable Silver Punch Bowl, Value 90 *l.* by any Horfe, Mare or Gelding, the beft in three Heats is intitled to the Bowl. No joftling or foul Play allow'd

"Alfo on the 27*th* Inft. will be Run for, a very handfome embroider'd Jacket, Value 90 *l.* by Foot Men, to run the half Mile Courfe, no foul Play being allow'd The firft Perfon that comes to the ftarting Poft, is intitled to the Jacket.

"The fame Day will be given Gratis, a very good Hat, for four Perfons or more, to eat fix Apples each Perfon, out of a Pail of Water, each Perfon to have his Hands tied behind his Back; the Perfon that eats the fixth Apple firft, fhall have the Hat

John Hanbury"

* * *

Advertisements for foot races, South Carolina Gazette, 1747.

"TO BE RUN FOR in the *Ponds Old-Field* near *Dorchefter*, on the fecond Thurf-day in *March*, a very neat Saddle and Bridle with blue Houfing, Value 30 *l.* a Gold Watch a pair of Silver Spurs, and fundry other Things of Value, by any Horfe, Mare or Gelding to carry fuch Weight as fhall be agreed or in the faid Field. Likewife a Foot Race for *One Hundred Pounds*; the Mile Courfe the beft in three Heats. And on the fec-ond Thurfday in April will be divers Races at the fame Place.—Good ftabling to be had at *John Burford*'s in *Dorchefter*."   (No. 672, 2 March 1747)

"TO BE RUN for, at *Parker's Ferry*, on the 22d of *December* next, a Silver Tankard, Value 100 *l.* one Mile 3 Heats, the loweft Horfe to carry 130 *lb.* and all above Weight for Inches, no Horfes excepted. A pair of Silver Spurs, Value 15 *l.* by two Horfes, the Quarter; alfo a Cafe of fafhionable Piftols, by 2 or 3 Horfes, as they can agree. Every Horfe to be entered 10 Days before the Race, at the faid Ferry, where the Plate may be feen. And, a Foot-Race 100 Yards by any two Gentlemen, for a Silver Ladle, Value 15 *l.*   *Stephen Marrauld.*"

(No. 710, 16-23 November 1747)

* * *

Excerpt from an advertisement for a fair in Baltimore advertises racing for African-American girls, Maryland Gazette, No. 124, 8 September 1747.

"On Saturday the third Day, a Hat and Ribbon will be cudgell'd for; a Pair of Pumps wreftled for; and a white Shift to be run for by Negro Girls."

* * *

Benjamin Franklin, Pennsylvania editor, advocates running as physical education, circa 1749, in [Franklin], *Proposals Relating to the Education of Youth in Pensilvania* (Phila-delphia: pvt. ptg?, 1749), 10-11.

"That to keep them [pupils] in Health, and to ftrengthen and render active their Bod-ies, they be frequently exercis'd in Running, Leaping, Wreftling, and Swimming, &c."

* * *

J.C.B., French traveler, comments on running by Ohio Country indigenous tribal peoples, circa 1751-1761, in Sylvester K. Stevens, Donald H. Kent, and Emma Edith Woods, eds.,

Travels in New France by J.C.B. (Harrisburg, Penn.: The Pennsylvania Historical Commission, 1941), 140.

"They are generally fleet of foot. The Illinois and Missouris are reputed to have the best legs. It is claimed that they can outrun bears, buffaloes, and even deer. I cannot verify this statement; but I have seen a footrace on the Ohio shore near Fort Duquesne, where several runners raced with some Illinois and Missouris, and these latter were easy winners."

* * *

Account of a running match, Maryland Gazette, No. 488, 12 September 1754.

"Yefterday a fine Smock was Run for, by Barbara Trot *and* Jenny Parker, *which was won by Mifs* Parker, *who had a good deal of Money given her befide."*

* * *

Fray Miguel Venegas, Mexican Jesuit missionary, mentions running among other recreations at California rancherias, circa 1758, in Venegas, *A Natural and Civil History of California,* 2 vols., Vol. 1 (London: James Rivington and James Fletcher, 1759), 84.

"To thefe feftivities the rancherias ufually invite one another; and likewife often fend challenges for wreftling, leaping, running, fhooting with their bow, and trials of ftrength; and in thefe and the like fports, days and nights, weeks and months were often fpent in times of peace."

* * *

Henry Timberlake, British lieutenant, discusses running by indigenous peoples in eastern Tennessee, January 1762, in [Timberlake], *Lieut. Henry Timberlake's Memoirs, 1756-1765,* ed. by Samuel Cole Williams (Marietta, Ga.: Continental Book Company, 1948 [1765]), 79.

"They are extremely proud, despising the lower class of Europeans; and in some athletick diversions I was once present at, they refused to match or hold conference with any but officers.

"Here, however, the vulgar notion of the Indians uncommon activity was contradicted by three officers of the Virginia regiment, the slowest of which could outrun the swiftest of about 700 Indians that were in the place: but had the race exceeded two or three hundred yards, the Indians would then have acquired the advantage, by being able to keep the same pace a long time together; and running being likewise more general among them, a body of them would always greatly exceed an equal number of our troops."

* * *

Joseph Doddridge, Pennsylvania Episcopalian minister, mentions running as a recreation in the western settlements in Virginia and Pennsylvania, circa 1763-1783, in Doddridge, *Notes on the Settlement and Indian Wars of the Western Parts of Virginia and Pennsylvania from 1763 to 1783, inclusive, together with a Review of the State of Society and Manners of the First Settlers of the Western Country* (Pittsburgh: John S. Ritenour and William T. Lindsey, 1912), 123.

"The athletic sports of running, jumping and wrestling, were the pastimes of boys, in common with the men."

* * *

Thomas Hutchinson, Massachusetts politician and historian, notes running as a sport among New England indigenous peoples, circa 1765, in Hutchinson, *The History of the Province of Massachusetts Bay*, 2nd ed., 2 vols., Vol. 1 (London: M. Richardson, 1765), 471.

"Swimming, running, and wrestling they were, as early [as childhood], accustomed to."

* * *

Alexander Graydon, Philadelphia resident, recounts running during his school days, circa 1760s–1770s, in Graydon, *Memoirs of His Own Time, With Reminiscences of the Men and Events of the Revolution*, ed. by John Stockton Littell (Philadelphia: Lindsay & Blakiston, 1846), 45-46, 55-56.

"..., and there was not a boy in the school in whose welfare and competitions I took so decided an interest; the ardour of which was in almost perpetual requisition, from the circumstance of his being a champion in the gymnastic exercise of running, which was then the rage. The enthusiasm of the turf had pervaded the academy, and the most extravagant transports of that theatre on the triumph of a favourite horse, were not more zealous and impassioned, than were the acclamations which followed the victor in a foot-race round a square. Stripped to the shirt, and accoutred for the heat by a hand-kerchief bound round the head, another round the middle, with loosened knee-bands, without shoes, or with mocasons instead of them, the racers were started; and turning to the left round the corner of Arch street, they encompassed the square in which the academy stands, while the most eager spectators, in imitation of those who scour across the course at a horse-race, scampered over the church burying ground to Fifth street, in order to see the state of the runners as they passed, and to ascertain which was likely to be foremost, on turning Market street corner. The four sides of this square cannot be much less than three-quarters of a mile [editor says more likely less than half a mile]; whereof, bottom in the coursers, was no less essential than swiftness, and in both Lewis bore away the palm from every one that dared enter againmst him. After having in a great number of matches completely triumphed over the academy, other schools were resorted to for racers; but all in vain: Lewis was the Eclipse that distanced every competitor, the swift-footed Achilles, against the vigorous agility of whose straight and well-proportioned form, the long-legged stride of the overgrown, and the nimble step of the dapper, were equally unavailing. I was scarcely less elated with his triumphs, than if I myself had been the victor.... Since the time of those exploits, in which I was too young to enter the lists, I have valued myself upon my own agility in running and jumping; but I have never had the vanity to suppose, that at my best, I could have contended with any chance of success, in so long a race against Lewis."

"In gymnastic exercises, however, my relish was keen and altogether orthodox. For those of running, leaping, swimming and skating, no one had more appetite; and for the enjoyment of these, fatigue and hunger were disregarded."

* * *

John Adams, Massachusetts politician and later United States president, speaks enthusiastically about walking as recreation, 28 June 1771, in Lyman H. Butterfield, ed., *Diary and Autobiography of John Adams, Volume 2. Diary, 1771-1781* (Cambridge, Mass.: Harvard University Press, 1962), 42.

"At York. Yesterday I spent in Walking, one Way and another, to view the Town. I find that Walking serves me much. It sets my Blood in Motion much more than Riding."

Benjamin Rush, Philadelphia physician, recommends walking as healthful recreation and discusses running, circa 1772, in Rush, *Sermons to Gentlemen upon Temperance and Exercise* (Philadelphia: John Dunlap, 1772), 30, 31.

"OF ACTIVE EXERCISE.

"WALKING is the moft gentle fpecies of it we are acquainted with. It promotes perfpiration, and if not continued too long, invigorates and ftrengthen the fyftem. As the moft fimple and wholefome drink, namely water, is within every body's reach, fo this fpecies of fimple and wholefome exercife is in every body's power, who has ufe of his limbs. It is to be lamented, that cariages are fubftituted too often in the room of it. In Pekin in China, we are told, that none but the Emperor, and a few of firft officers of ftate, are fuffered to ufe chariots. Although the intention of this law was to fupprefs the number of horfes, in order to make room for the increafe and fupport of the human fpecies, in the number of which the riches of all countries confift, yet we find it attended with good effects otherwife; for the rich and the great, by being obliged to walk in common with the poor people, enjoy with them the common bleffing of health, more than people of the fame rank in other countries. To fuch as can bear it, I would recommend walking frequently up a hill. The inhabitants of mountainous countries are generally healthy and long lived. This is commonly attributed to the purity of the air in fuch places. Although this has a chief fhare in it, yet I cannot help thinking, that the frequent and neceffary exercife of climbing mountains, which thefe people are obliged to undergo, adds much to their health and lives. Every body knows how much walking up a hill tends to create an appetite. This depends upon its increafing the infenfible perfpiration—a fecretion with which the appetite, and the ftate of the ftomach in general, are much connected."

"RUNNING is too violent to be ufed often, or continued for any length of time. The running footmen in all countries are fhort-lived—Few of them efcape confumptions before they arrive at their thirty-fifth year.—Sweating and perfpiration, according to Sanctorius, have been found to be incompatible.—The former always fuppreffes the latter. Upon this account, I would recommend it to be ufed as feldom as poffible."

* * *

Philip Vickers Fithian, tutor at Nomini Hall, Virginia, races, 26 January 1774, in Hunter Dickinson Farish, ed., *Journal and Letters of Philip Vickers Fithian, 1773-1774. A Plantation Tutor of the Old Dominion* (Charlottesville, Va.: University Press of Virginia, 1957 [1943]), 59.

"In the Evening I ran a Foot Race with Ben & Harry fo[r] exercise, & a prize of ten Apples to the winner. We ran from the School-House round the stable, & Kitchen & Great-House which Distance is about 70 Rod—I came out first about One Rod; but almost wholly spent; I went to my Chamber and lay down, sick, fainty, & quite distressed. I puked several times; after having rested a while, however, I revived & went well to Supper...."

* * *

Tench Tilghman, Maryland lieutenant-colonel, comments on foot racing among the Onondagas in New York, circa 1775, in [Tilghman], *Memoir of Lieut. Col. Tench Tilghman, Secretary and Aid to Washington* (Albany, N.J.: Joel Munsell, 1876), 94-95.

"We then put up two laced Hats and a silver arm Band to be run for. I think I have seen white men who would have outstripped these Champions, as their mode of running seemed more calculated for a long distance than for swiftness, their strides are long and strong. Their Race I think was about a quarter of a mile."

* * *

John Long, American trader, discusses running by indigenous peoples in the Great Lakes region, circa 1777, in Milo Milton Quaife, ed., *John Long's Voyages and Travels in the Years 1768-1788,* (Chicago: Lakeside Press, 1922), 48.

"The savages are esteemed very active and nimble-footed, but admitting this general opinion to prevail, it is well known the Europeans are more swift in running a small distance. Their chief merit, I am of opinion, consists in their being able to continue a long time in one steady pace, which makes them useful in going express through the woods;...."

* * *

George Hanger, Hessian colonel, mentions running among the Cherokee and Creek indigenous people near Savannah, circa 1780, in Hanger, *The Life, Adventures, and Opinions of Col. George Hanger,* 2 vols., Vol. 1 (New York: Johnson and Stryker, 1801), 175.

"The Indians abstain from women, take physic and prepare their bodies for war, by frequently running and using other manly exercises."

* * *

Advertisement for a foot race by women, [Rivington's] Royal Gazette, No. 430, 11 November 1780.

"Alfo to be run for on Tuefday, the fecond Day of the Races by Women, a Holland Smock and a Chintz Gown, full-trimmed; to run the beft two in three quarter mile heats, the firft to have the Smock and Gown, of Four Guineas value, the fecond beft a Guinea, and the third beft Half a Guinea—To ftart precifely at 1 o'Clock."

* * *

Levi Beardsley, Otsego County, New York lawyer, concerning the Cooperstown area, mentions running as a sport, circa the 1780s, in Beardsley, *Reminiscences; Personal and Other Incidents; Early Settlement of Otsego County; Notices and Anecdotes of Public Men; Judicial, Legal and Legislative Matters; Field Sports; Dissertations and Discussions* (New York: Charles Vinten, 1852), 34.

"Wrestling, running, jumping, and hopping always constituted part of the amusements."

Chapter 15

HORSE RACING

Beginnning with Columbus's second voyage, in 1493, Europeans reintroduced the horse to the American continents. Relatively quickly the horse, in many ways, changed the cultures of many indigenous peoples, allowing them mobility beyond former capabilities and an animal which conferred much wealth and status upon the owner. For the Europeans the horse was also important, for transportation, as a beast of burden, and as a draft animal for farm tasks. And, the horse brought the prospect of entertainment in the form of the horse race.

Euroamericans became inveterate horse racers who loved a good race. Opposition to racing did exist. The Puritans frowned on the pastime and the Quakers similarly warned against consorting with horse racers (to the point that the Quakers secured restrictions on running races too close to Quaker meetinghouses). Ministers chastised the horse fanciers for idleness and submergence in the vices that attached themselves to the races. Several colonies and states outlawed it, especially during the Sabbath. During the Revolutionary War, the Continental Congress tried to prohibit horse racing as disrespectful to the patriotic aims of the conflict. But these controls did little to dampen the longrunning American love affair with horse flesh.

If horse racing was indeed "the Sport of Kings," colonial Americans considered themselves royalty. But only the very affluent owned the superior race horses and won much of the prize money, but any settler with a nag or a mule was likely to challenge somebody else to a race. In the 1670s, Virginia tried to restrict this democratization by taking to court a tailor for indulging in a pleasure above his station. Horse racing still flourished wherever there were horses. As historians T. H. Breen and Rhys Isaac have shown about the Chesapeake region, horses, horse racing, gambling, and an assortment of merriment became embedded in a cultural matrix of major importance to the elite and the common who followed the sport. But what was occurring in Virginia and Maryland was only a magnification of the penchant for horse racing in the other regions. The Carolinas and Georgia soon rivaled the upper South, and despite some blue laws in the North, horse racing made serious inroads into New Jersey, Pennsylvania, and New York, and even into New England.

During the succeeding decades Americans began to formalize the sport. Fairs became more organized and regular. Breeders paid more attention to domestic bloodlines and imported more and faster British horses to develop the sleeker thoroughbreds and saddlebreds. Newspapers carried many advertisements of famous stallions who would cover mares for a handsome fee. Prize money increased steadily, or race organizers divided the purse into several types of races. Race grounds which were mere clearings in the woods gave way to permanent courses, and crowd numbers increased. The following selections illustrate the pervasiveness of horse racing in the Southern colonies by the 1730s and 1740s and the progressive growth of the pastime northward and westward.

[Consult the general writings about sports, recreation, and the various colonial, provincial, territorial, and state Sabbath and gaming laws in Chapter One for other sources about the specific sports or games in this chapter.]

A letter from Wilmington, North Carolina, reports a Continental Congress prohibition on horse racing, 26 November 1774, reprinted in Francis Barnum Culver, *Blooded Horses of Colonial Days. Classic Horse Matches* in *America before the Revolution* (Baltimore: pvt. ptg., 1922), 139.

"The Continental Congress lately held at Philadelphia, representing the several American colonies from Nova Scotia to Georgia, associated and agreed among other things, for themselves and their constituents, to 'discontinue and discourage every species of extravagance and dissipation, especially all horse-racing, and all kinds of gaming, cockfighting, exhibitions of shows and plays and other expensive diversions and entertainments.'"

THE CAROLINAS

Advertisements for horse races, South Carolina Gazette, 1736.

"To be RUN for
ON Monday the 9th of *February* next at the Quarter houfe
A fine large Pacing Horfe with Saddle and Bridle, value l. 100.
BY any Horfes, Mares or Geldings carrying 10 Stones weight one half mile 3 heats.To enter one Week before the Race and to pay at the Entrance to Mrs *Partridge* at the Quarter Houfe 10 l. In cafe there be not 10 Horfes, the faid sum of 100 l to be made up by as many as will enter. The faid Horfe will be at the Quarter-houfe one Week before the Race, to be view'd.
To ftart at 2 o'clock precifely."

(No. 103, 10-17 January 1736)

"To be Run for
On Saturday the 3d of *April* next at the Bowling Green, a large filver hilted fmall Sword, value 30 *l* by any 3 Horfes, Mares or Geldings, one half mile one heat, or the Quarter 3 heats, to ftart precifely at 3 a clock. *NB* The faid Sword to be feen on Thurfday next at the Bowling-Green, and the Money to be paid on the Day of the Race."

(No. 113, 20-27 March 1736)

Advertisement for a horse race, South Carolina Gazette, No. 170, 23–30 April 1737.

"ON the firft Thurfday in *May* next at the Fair which then will be holden at *Afhley-Ferry*, will be a Ball. *Tickets to be had at the Door at* 40 *s. each*
   There will alfo be a Race for a Saddle value 20 l the fame Day.
   The fame Ball & Race will be at *Strawberry* Fair next."

* * *

John Brickell, Irish doctor, comments on horse racing in North Carolina, circa 1737, Brickell, *The Natural History of North-Carolina* (Dublin: James Carson, 1737), 39.

"*Horfe-Racing* they are fond of, for which they have Race-Paths, near each Town, and in many parts of the Country. Thofe Paths, feldom exceed a Quarter of a Mile in length, and only two Horfes ftart at a time, each Horfe has his peculiar Path, which if he quits, and runs into the other, loofes the Race. This is agreed on to avoid Jockying. Thefe Courfes being fo very fhort, they ufe no manner of Art, but pufh on with all the fpeed imaginable; many of thefe Horfes are very fleet.
   "It is common for People to come and go from this Province to *Virginia,* to thefe publick Diverfions."

* * *

Advertisement for a horse race, South Carolina Gazette, No. 268, 24 March 1739.

"On Tuefday the 2d Day of *April* next, will ftart at Mrs. *Sureau's*, two Horfes, viz. *Ja Abercromby* Efq's Horfe *Cherokee*, againft *Wm. Walter* Efq's Colt call'd *Bright*, the firft two Heats in three for 200 l. Currency, to ftart exactly at four o'Clock, and run the Quarter. Any Perfons inclinable to bring their Horfes to proof, may meet with Opportunity for any Sum not exceeding the above Bett."

* * *

Advertisement for a horse race, South Carolina Gazette, No. 445, 27 September–4 October 1742.

"Notice is hereby given, that the *Fair* at *Childsbury*, will be kept as ufual, which is on the *laft Tuefday* in October next, at which Time there will *ran for a* Saddle and Briddle, Whip, Boots, and Jockey Cap, and an Ox given *Gratis*."

* * *

Advertisements for horse races, South Carolina Gazette, 1743.

"To be RUN for,

ON THURSDAY the tenth Day of *March* next, on *York* Courfe, at the old Quarter-Houfe, a handfome and fafhionable filver Punch Bowl, Value *One Hundred Pounds*, by any Horfe, Mare, or Gelding, the Riders to carry 10 Stone, over or under, to allow the Rules of Jockeyfhip, as by the Articles to be produced on the Entry of the faid Horfes,   *John Hanbury.*
"On the 11th of the fame Inftant, a Gold Watch, Value 140 *l.* is to be run for."
(No. 464, 14 February 1743)

"To be *RUN* for,

"ON the fecond Tuefday of *March* next, at *George Town, Winyaw*, a very fafhionable Piece of Silver Plate, Value *One Hundred* and *Fifty Pounds* Currency, by any 20 Horfes.
   "*N.B.* The Rules and Articles of the Race to be feen at *George Town*, where the Horfes muft be entered."   (No. 465, 21 February 1743)

"A MATCH to be run at the *York* Courfe at the old Quarter-Houfe, on Thurfday the 21ft Inftant, between the Hours of Two and Four in the Afternoon. All Difputes or Controverfies that may arife, to be determin'd by the Judges or Tryers appointed for the fame.

"*N.B.* Another Match to be run for on the 30th Inftant."

(No. 473, 18 April 1743)

"To be RUN for,

"ON *York* Courfe, on Monday the 23d Inftant, at *John Hanbury's* Quarter Houfe, a Saddle, Bridle, & Furniture, trimm'd with Gold, Value 80 *l*.

"The next Day will be run for, at the fame Place, a Saddle, Bridle and Furniture, trimm'd with Silver, Value 60 *l*."   (No. 477, 16 May 1743)

"*TO be RUN for, by any Horfe, Mare or Gelding, at New Market Courfe at Goofe Creek, on Wednefday the 3d of Auguft, a Silver Tankard, Value about £. 100. And on Friday the 5th, another of the fame Value. Subfcriptions are taken ar Mr Ric: Price's in Charleftown, or at the faid Plantation, where Gentlemen may be accomodated in the publick Way, by*   Their humble Servant,

Robert Parker."

(No. 486, 18 July 1743)

"ON Thurfday the 4th of *Auguft*, next will be RUN for, on *York Courfe*, at the old Quarter-Houfe, by any Horfe, Mare or Gelding, *FIFTY POUNDS* Currency.

"*N.B.* They are to run three Heats."   (No. 488, 1 August 1743)

"TO BE RUN FOR, by Subfcription, at *New Market Courfe* at *Goofe Creek*, by any Horfe, Mare, or Gelding, on Thurfday the 29th of *September*, a Silver Tankard, Value ONE HUNDRED POUNDS, for the firft Horfe. And a Pint Pot, Value FIFTY POUNDS, for the fecond Horfe. And,

"On Tuefday the 18th of *October*, two Pieces of PLATE of the fame Value, where Gentlemen may be accommodated in the publick Way, by

Their humble Servant,

ROBERT PARKER.

"*N.B.* The Horfes excepted againft are, Mr. *Raper's*, Mr *McKever's*, Mr. *Carter's* Chucklehead, and Mr. *Butler's* Roger."   (No. 490, 15 August 1743)

"TO BE RUN for, on *York-Courfe*, at the old Quarter Houfe, a handfome and fafhionable Silver Punch Bowl, Value *Ninety five* Pounds, by any Horfe, Mare or Gelding.

"On the 26th, a Silver Pint Pot, Value *Forty* Pounds.

"*NB* A Gallery for the Ladies."   (No. 494, 12 September 1743)

"TO BE RUN for on *York* Courfe, at the *Old Quarter Houfe*, on Thurfday the 13th of this Inftant, *October*, 1743 A handfome fafhionable filver Punch Bowl, Value 90 l. by any Horfe, Mare, or Gelding, the beft in three Heats

"On the fame Day, a Foot Race will be run, for a very good handfome *French* embroider'd Waiftcoat, Value 90 l. by fix People, more or lefs, who are to run twice round the half Mile Courfe; the firft that comes in with fair Play (no joftling allow'd) is entitled to the Waiftcoat.

"On Friday the 14th of the fame Inft. to be run for, a handfome filver Pint Mug, Value 40 l. by any Horfe, Mare or Gelding, the beft in three Heats.

"On *Saturday* the 15th of the faid Inft. to be run for, a handfome Saddle, Bridle and Furniture, Value 30 l. by any Horfe, Mare or Gelding, the beft in three Heats.

"On the fame Day will be given gratis, a very good filver lac'd hat, to be run for by four Men or more, and to make the beft Way they can, 200 Yards, each Man to be in a Sack, all but his Head; the Perfon that comes in firft fhall have the Hat.

John Hanbury.

(No. 498, 10 October 1743)

"TO *be Run for, by any Mare, Horfe or Gelding*, at New market Courfe, once a *Fortnight, during the Winter Seafon*, the 2d and 4th Saturdays *in every Month*; a Purfe of 30 l. no Exception being made to any Horfe, by Goofe Creek, Oct. 20, 1743

Robert Parker.

"*NB.* In cafe of Rain, 'twill be the *Mondays* following."

(No. 501, 31 October 1743)

"TO be Run for on *York Courfe*, at the *Old Quarter Houfe*, on *Monday* the 26*th of December*, 1743

"A very handfome fafhionable Silver Punch Bowl, Value 90 *l.* by any Horfe, Mare or Gelding, the beft in three Heats is intitled to the Bowl. No joftling or foul Play allow'd

"Alfo on the 27*th* Inft. will be Run for, a very handfome embroider'd Jacket, Value 90 *l.* by Foot Men, to run the half Mile Courfe, no foul Play being allow'd The firft Perfon that comes to the ftarting Poft, is intitled to the Jacket.

"The fame Day will be given Gratis, a very good Hat, for four Perfons or more, to eat fix Apples each Perfon, out of a Pail of Water, each Perfon to have his Hands tied behind his Back; the Perfon that eats the fixth Apple firft, fhall have the Hat

John Hanbury"

(No. 504, 21 November 1743)

"TO be Run for on *York Courfe*, at the *Old Quarter Houfe*, on *Monday* the 26*th of December*, 1743

"A very handfome fafhionable Silver Punch Bowl, Value 90 *l.* by any Horfe, Mare or Gelding, the beft in three Heats is intitled to the Bowl. No joftling or foul Play allow'd

"Alfo on the 27*th* Inft. will be Run for, a very handfome embroider'd Jacket, Value 90 *l.* by Foot Men, to run the half Mile Courfe, no foul Play being allow'd The firft Perfon that comes to the ftarting Poft, is intitled to the Jacket.

"The fame Day will be given Gratis, a very good Hat, for four Perfons or more, to eat fix Apples each Perfon, out of a Pail of Water, each Perfon to have his Hands tied behind his Back; the Perfon that eats the fixth Apple firft, fhall have the Hat.

"*NB* A Match to run the 30th Inftant, by a Horfe nam'd *Roger* from *Stono*, and a Horfe nam'd *Batchelor* from *Afhley River*; the faid Horfes are to run the half Mile Courfe twice round to a Heat, running three Heats, and to rub half an Hour between each Heat, and to ftart precifely at 12 a 'Clock.

John Hanbury"

(No. 506, 5 December 1743)

Advertisements for horse races, South Carolina Gazette, 1744.

"*TO be run for, on York Courfe at the old Quarter Houfe on Friday the 24th Inftant, a fine embroidered Jacket, valued at 90 l by any Horfe, Mare or Gelding, to run twice round the half Mile Courfe; and the Horfe that comes in laft fhall been intituled to the Jacket. each Man to ride his Adverfary's Horfe, 9 Horfes to ftart, more or lefs, making up the Sum of 90 l.*   John Hanbury."

(No. 515, 6 February 1744)

"*Joseph Butler* of *Charles Town*, will run his Gelding CHESNUT, from the Quarter Houfe to Charles Town, with any Horfe, Mare, or Gelding that can be brought againft him by the firft Day of *December* next, for 500 or 1000 *l.* Inch Weight, the loweft Horfe carrying 13 Stone. Enquire of the Printer, who will inform you of one in Charles Town that will enter into the Articles, upon the above Terms, on the Subscriber's Behalf.   *Joseph Butler*"

(No. 546, 10 September 1744)

Tribute to a famous race horse, South Carolina Gazette, No. 526, 23 April 1744.

"The famous running Horfe of *Stono*, named *ROGER*, (after his many notable Races, in which he has had the Honour always to come off Conqueror, with the beft Horfes in the Country he has run with, for feveral years paft) being now in Age, is to live at Eafe the Remainder of his Days and enjoy the Fruits of his Labours, and therefore muft not be challenged after this date.

> For, fince when young and
> ftout, he out run all, with
> Eafe and Plenty his old
> Days (in the Stall) fhall
> now be crown'd; and fince
> he ever hear,
> *STONO PRAISE HIM FOR EVER.*"

* * *

Advertisements for horse races, South Carolina Gazette, 1745.

"*On Tuefday the 24th Inftant, Afhley Ferry* Fair will be held as ufual, where will be a Shoat to be run for, the Property of the Perfon who catches him, and a Goofe to be rid for under Gallop, the Property of him who pulls off his Head, and a Watch and plate to be raffled for, likewife Horfe racing, at the Houfe of

Thomas Stoakes."

(No. 598, 9 September 1745)

"TO be RUN for, on Friday the 20th of December next, at Mr *Thomas Butler's* Race Ground on Charles Town Neck, a Silver Tankard of 140 *l.* Value. The loweft Horfe to be 13 Hands high and to carry 9 Stone Weight, and all higher Horfes to carry 14 *lb.* for the firft Inch, and 7 *lb.* for every Inch after; to run 1 Mile 3 Heats; beginning at 9 o'Clock in the Morning, the Race Ground in an exact Mile round, twenty Feet wide, without any fhort Turn"   (No. 609, 25 November 1745)

* * *

Advertisements for horse races, South Carolina Gazette, 1747.

"TO BE RUN for, at the *Ponds Old-Field* near *Dorchefter*, on the fecond Thurfday in *February* next, a very neat Saddle and Bridle, with blue Houfing, Value *Thirty Pounds*, a pair of Silver Spurs, with fome other Things, by any Horfe, mare or Gelding, one Mile the beft in three Heats. No Horfe carrying lefs than eight Stone Weight. —Good Stabling at *John Burford's* in *Dorchefter*." (No. 667, 26 January 1747)

"TO BE RUN FOR in the *Ponds Old-Field* near *Dorchefter*, on the fecond Thurfday in *March*, a very neat Saddle and Bridle with blue Houfing, Value 30 *l*. a Gold Watch a pair of Silver Spurs, and fundry other Things of Value, by any Horfe, Mare or Gelding to carry fuch Weight as fhall be agreed or in the faid Field. Likewife a Foot Race for *One Hundred Pounds*; the Mile Courfe the beft in three Heats. And on the fecond Thurfday in April will be divers Races at the fame Place. —Good ftabling to be had at *John Burford's* in *Dorchefter*."

(No. 672, 2 March 1747)

"TO BE RUN for, at the Houfe of *Ifaac Peronneau* (where Mr. *Maurice Keating* lately lived) in *Goofe-Creek*, by any Horfe, Mare or Gelding, on Saturday the 23d of *May*, a handfome quilted Buck-fkin feat faddle, Bridle and Houfing, Value 30 *l*. Alfo a handfome filver Watch and feveral other Things To be raffled for."

(No. 680, 20–27 April 1747)

"To be RUN for, on Wednefday the Third Day of *December* next, at Mr. *Fergufon's* MILE COURSE, A VERY GOOD HORSE, Price £100. Whoever has a mind to run for the faid Horfe, may apply to the faid *Fergufon* up the Path, where the Horfe may be feen, and the Conditions known." (No. 708, 2-9 November 1747)

"TO BE RUN for, at *Parker's Ferry*, on the 22d of *December* next, a Silver Tankard, Value 100 *l*. one Mile 3 Heats, the loweft Horfe to carry 130 *lb*. and all above Weight for Inches, no Horfes excepted. A pair of Silver Spurs, Value 15 *l*. by two Horfes, the Quarter; alfo a Cafe of fafhionable Piftols, by 2 or 3 Horfes, as they can agree. Every Horfe to be entered 10 Days before the Race, at the faid Ferry, where the Plate may be feen. And, a Foot-Race 100 Yards by any two Gentlemen, for a Silver Ladle, Value 15 *l*. *Stephen Marrauld*."

(No. 710, 16-23 November 1747)

"TO BE RUN, RAFFLED, OR SHOT FOR, on Friday the 20th of *January* next, at the Houfe of *Ifaac Peronneau* at *Goofe Creek*, a very handfome Silver-mounted *Gun*, with a water Pan, value 140 *l*. Alfo a neat Silver Watch, value 55 *l*. and a handfome Saddle, Bridle, and Houfings, value 25 *l*. with Silver Spurs, Boots and Sundry other Things."

(No. 714, 14–21 December 1747)

* * *

Advertisement for a horse race, South Carolina Gazette, No.716, 28 December 1747-6 January 1748.

"PUT UP by the Subfcriber, to be Run for, on Friday the 20th Inft. at *Afhley*-Ferry, a filver hilted Sword of 40 *l*. Price, a pair of fcrew Barrel Piftols of 30 *l*. and fundry other things. Whoever has a mind to run for the fame, may fee them and know the Conditions, on Application to me at the faid Ferry.

Charles Lowndes."

Advertisements for horse races, South Carolina Gazette, 1749.

"TO BE RUN for, by fix horfes, mares, or geldings, carrying 144 *lb.* weight, two miles three heats (half an hour to be allowed betwixt each heat to rub) the round courfe at *William Marten's* at *Monck's* corner, a purfe value *fixty pounds* and a neat faddle, piftols and furniture value *fifty pounds.* Every horfe, &c. muft be entered at faid *Marten's* by the 20th of *October,* and the race to be on wednefday the firft of *November* next: The ftart to be given at 12 o'clock, the horfe, mare or gelding that wins the two firft heats to have the purfe, the next beft the faddle, &c. but thofe that don't fave their diftance go on no more. Several things of great value to be run or raffled for, the fame day." (No. 802, 18-25 September 1749)

"The Fair at *Childfberry* will begin on the laft Tuefday in this Month, and continue to the Friday following inclufive, when there will be exhibited fome curious and entirely new Diverfions. There will alfo be Horfe races, &c." (No. 805, 9-16 October 1749)

* * *

Advertisements for horse races, South Carolina Gazette, 1750.

"TO be RUN for, on Thurfday the 8th of *February* at *Afhley*-Ferry, by two horfes, one owned at Stono, the other on *Afhley* River, a filver-mounted gun. The fame day, a neat faddle and furniture, and fome valuable plate, will be put up to be run for.

John Gordon."
(No. 818, 15-22 January 1750)

"TO BE RUN *for*
ON the fecond Monday in *November* next, if a fair day, and if nor the firft fair day after, at the houfe of Mr. *Ifaac Peronneau* in *Goofe-Creek,* a three pint filver TANKARD and a filver PUNCH BOWL, value *Two Hundred* and Fifty Pounds, by any nine mares, horfes, or geldings, to run a quarter of a mile and catch riders. Three horfes to run together, and the foremoft, to be put afide till the others run; and afterwards the three beft to run, and the foremoft horfe to win the prize. All perfons inclinable to run for the fame, are defired to give in their names, withe name and colour of their horfes, by the 20th inftant, as there will be no horfes taken in after that day.

"*N.B.* the fame night will be put up a GUINEA, to be *Whiftled* for, by any five perfons who will undertake to whiftle three tunes that fhall be propofed them, and the perfon that whiftles them the beft, cleareft, and without laughing, wins the money." (No. 855, 24 September-1 October 1750)

* * *

Advertisement for a horse race, South Carolina Gazette, No. 1548, 24 March 1764.

"THE STOP-WATCH lately advertifed, will pofitively be run for on the 10th of APRIL; free for any thing bred in CAROLINA, catch riders, the beft of three *one* or *two-mile* heats, as the majority of the fubfcribers fhall agree."

* * *

Josiah Quincy, Jr., Massachusetts lawyer, describes horse racing in Charleston, South Carolina, 16 March 1773, in [Josiah Quincy, Jr.], "Journal of a Voyage to South Carolina," reprinted in [Josiah Quincy], *Memoir of the Life of Josiah Quincy Jun. of Massachusetts. By His Son, Josiah Quincy* (Boston: Cummings, Hilliard, and Company, 1825), 110-111.

"March 16th. Spent the morning, ever since five o'clock, in perusing public records of the province;...; am now going to the famous races.

"The races were well performed—but Flimnap beat Little David (who had won the sixteen last races) out and out. The last heat the former distanced the latter. The first four-mile heat was performed in eight minutes and seventeen seconds, being four miles. Two thousand pounds sterling were won and lost at this race, and Flimnap sold at public venue the same day for 300£ sterling!....

"At the races I saw a fine collection of excellent, though very high-priced horses, and was let a little into the singular art and mystery of the turf!"

* * *

An English traveler in Charleston, South Carolina, mentions horse racing, circa 1774, in "Charleston, S.C., in 1774 as Described by an English Traveller," *Historical Magazine*, Vol. 9 (November 1865), 341-347, reprinted as "Charleston in 1774," in H. Roy Merrens, ed., *The Colonial South Carolina Scene. Contemporary Views, 1697-1774* (Columbia, S.C.: University of South Carolina Press, 1977), 283.

"It [Charleston] is upon the whole rather a gay place, there being public dancing assemblies and plays acted in it, with horse racing about a mile off."

* * *

Alexander Hewatt, South Carolina historian, remarks on race horses, circa 1779, in Hewatt, *An Historical Account of the Rise and Progress of the Colonies of South Carolina and Georgia*, 2 vols., Vol. 2 (London: Alexander Donaldson, 1779), 303.

"Thofe planters who had arrived at eafy or affluent circumftances employed overfeers; and having little to do but to ride round their fields now and then, to fee that their affairs were not neglected, or their flaves abufed, indulge themfelves in rural amufements, fuch as racing,.... The horfes of the country, though hardy and ferviceable animals, make little figure; and therefore, to improve the breed, many have been of late years imported from England. The planters being fond of fine horses, have been at great pains to raife them, fo that they now have plenty of an excellent kind, both for the carriage and the turf."

* * *

Francesco dal Verme, Italian count, attends horse races at Halifax, North Carolina, November 1783, in Elizabeth Cometti, trans. and ed., *Seeing America and Its Great Men. The Journal and Letters of Count Francesco dal Verme, 1783-1784* (Charlottesville, Va.: University Press of Virginia, 1969), 50.

14 November 1783: "Afterward went to a horse race in which small Negroes weighing around one hundred pounds served as jockeys. The purse was 12 dollars on this fourth day of racing. The two-mile course was run in four minutes three seconds." 15 November 1783 "In the afternoon went to another horse race."

* * *

Charleston, South Carolina city ordinance, 22 November 1783, in *Ordinances of the City Council of Charleston in the State of South Carolina, Passed in the First Year of the Incorporation of the City* (Charleston, S.C.: J. Miller, 1784), 19.

"AN ORDINANCE
For the better OBSERVANCE of the LORD'S-DAY, com-
monly called SUNDAY, and to prevent DISTURB-
ANCES at any Place of PUBLIC WORSHIP

within the City of CHARLESTON.

"And be it further ordained by the authority aforefaid, That no fports or paftimes, as bear-baiting, bull-baiting, foot-balls, horfe-racing,...fhall be allowed on the Lord's-Day, and every perfon fo offending fhall forfeit for every fuch offence the fum of Five Pounds."

MARYLAND AND VIRGINIA

An account of Virginia mentions horse racing, in "A Perfect Description of Virginia" (London 1649), reprinted in W.G.S., "Racing in Colonial Virginia," Virginia Magazine of History and Biography, Vol. 2 (1894-1895), 298.

"That there are [in Virginia] of an excellent raise [race] about two hundred Horses and Mares."

* * *

Court order from York County Court, Virginia, 10 September 1674, reprinted in W.G.S., "Racing in Colonial Virginia," Virginia Magazine of History and Biography, Vol. 2 (1894-1895), 294.

"James Bullocke, a Taylor, haveing made a race for his mare to runn w'th a horse belonging to Mr. Mathew Slader for twoe tbousand pounds of tobacco and caske, it being contrary to Law for a Labourer to make a race, being a sport only for Gentlemen, is fined for the same one hundred pounds of tobacco and caske.

"Whereas Mr. Mathew Slader & James Bullocke, by condition under the hand and seale of the said Slader, that his horse should runn out of the way that Bullock's mare might win, w'ch is an apparent cheate, is ord'ed to be putt in the stocks & there sitt the space of one houre."

* * *

Henrico County, Virginia court records, October 1678, August 1683, April and August 1687, August 1689, and April 1698, reprinted in W.G.S., "Racing in Colonial Virginia," Virginia Magazine of History and Biography, Vol. 2 (1894-1895), 294-298, except the 1683 excerpt, which was reprinted in "The Hancock Family," Virginia Magazine of History and Biography, Vol. 33, No. 1 (January 1925), 110-111.

"Bartholomew Roberts, aged 40 years or thereabouts, Deposeth That July last yo'r Deponent being at Bermuda Hundred, there being a horse race run betweene Mr. Abraham Womock & Mr. Rich'd Ligon. Capt. Tho: Chamberlaine being at ye end of ye race he asked whether both horses were ready to run, young Tho: Cocke saying yes, and that Abraham Childers being ordered to start the horses he bid them goe. Tho: Cocke's horse went about 4 or 5 lengths from ye starting place, run out of ye way, and Tho: Cocke rained him in and cryed it was not a faire start & Capt. Chamberlaine calling ye other young man backe, Joseph Tanner made answer ye start is faire, onely oue horse run out of ye way and further yo'r Deponent saith not.

His marke

Oct., 1678.   BARTHOLOMEW B. R. ROBERTS."

"Philip Jones, aged 17 years or thereabouts, Deposeth: That this summer this deponent was at ye Hundred and saw Abraham Womecke and Rich'd Ligon there, and afterwards saw Mr. Chamberlaine's boy upon Abraham Womeck's horse, and Thos: Cocke upon another horse, and ye s'd Cocke told ye other boy that if he did not come in at a word he would leave him behinde, and ye said boy answered him againe that if he did not at a word he would leave him, they being then at ye starting place, or going to ye starting place (which the deponent cannot certainly tell) to run a race, there being a man ordered to start them, who gave a word, at which Mr. Chamberlayne's went, and Tho: Cocke sayed it was not a faire start.

And further sayth not,

Oct, 1678.   PHILLIP JONES."

8 August 1683:

"Johan Hancocke, aged 30 years or thereabouts, sworn and examined saith: That some time this last summer being at Abraham Womack's house I heard Edward Hatcher, James Baugh, William Puckett and Andrew Martin in discussion concerning a horse race and after some time I heard a challenge made between Ed Hatcher and Andrew Martin and Will Puckett and James Baugh that ye said Edw Hatcher's horse that he then had there was to run against ye said Andrew Martin's horse that he had there, horse for horse, the same race that was run there before to the best of my remembrance, and I heard them all swear, done and done, and presently on ye same they start up to go to run; and Richard Lygon called after Edward Hatcher and said my Edward Hatcher my horse shall not run any more today or night one ye wch Edw Hatcher swore by God that he should for he was his horse and took him and ledd him out into ye pasture, and Andrew Martin in company with his horse and gott upon him and Edw Hatcher was a getting up, and Richd Lygon coming and took hold of the horse, and said Edward Hatcher this is my horse, and he shall not run on ye wch ye said Hatcher said If it is your horse take him I can't help it, on ye wch William Puckett and James Baugh and Andrew Martin by consent resolved that ye said Martin should run over the place appointed as he was on the first agreement chosen to to ride his own horse, and Edw Hatcher to ride his own horse, and Andrew Martin ridd away upon his horse, and after some while came riding back again and said that he had been over the race, and said that he had left his knife there, and bid them go and see if they would, and at his return the sd Andrew Martin took Edward Hatcher's Horse, and say'd that he had won him and fasten'd them both together, and then Richd Lygon went and took hold of ye horse and fore-warned him for medding with him for it was not his horse to ye best of my remembrance and further saith not

Johan Hancocke

Jurat in Cur Com Hon p: die A.o 1683 Teste   Henry Randolph
I, the subscriber, do declare the very same onely done, and done, Exeundet and Edward Hatcher's by God   Richard Lygon."

April, 1687: "Richard Blande, aged about 21 years, Deposeth That in the race run between Mr. John Brodnax and Capt. William Soane, now in tryall, the horse belonging to Henry Randolph, on w'ch Capt Soane layed came, after the Start first between the Poles agreed on for their comeing in."

August, 1687: "Chrisopher Branch, aged about 29 years, Deposeth: That being at a Race at Varina [the County C.H.] was present at ye making of another Race between

Hugh Liggon & Stephen Cocke, and did hear say they would run fair horseman's play, w'th severall other words confirming tbe same.   CHRISTOP'R BRANCH. Aug 1st, 1687."

August, 1689: "William Randolph, aged about 38 years, Deposeth That about Saturday last was a fortnight this depon't was at a race at Mawvern hills [Malvern Hill] at w'ch time Mr. Wm. Epes and Mr. Stephen Cocke came to this depon't and desired him to take notice of ye agreem't: w'ch was That ye horse of ye s'd Epes and the horse of Mr. Wm. Sutton was to run that Race for ten Shillings on each side, and each horse was to keep his path, they not being to crosse unlesse Stephen Cocke could gett the other Riders Path at ye start at two or three Jumps (to ye best of this dep'ts knowledge) and also that they were not to touch neither man nor horse, and they further desired his dep't to start the Horses, w'ch this dep't did and to ye best of this dep'ts Judgm't they had a fair start, & Mr Cocke endeavored to gett the other rider's path as afores'd accordh-, to ye agreem't, but to ye best of this dept's Judgm't he did not gett it at two or three Jumps nor many more, upon w'ch they Josselled upon Mr. Epes horse's path all most part of the race.And further saith not,   WM. RANDOLPH August 1st, 1689."

April, 1698: "At a Court held at Varina, Ap'l 1st, 1698, Richard Ward complains against John Stewart, Jun'r, in a plea of debt for that, that is to say the s'd plahltiff & defendant did on the 12th day of June Last, covenant and agree in the following words:

"It is Covenanted and agreed this 12th day of June, 1697, Between Mr. Richard Ward of the one part, in Hen'co Co'ty, & John Steward, Jun'r, of ye other part in ye same Co'ty Witnesseth, that the aforesaid Mr. Richard Ward doth hereby covenant, promise & agree to run mare named Bony, belonging to Thomas Jefferson, Jun'r [Grandfather of the President], ag'st a horse now belonging to Mr. John Hardiman, named Watt, the said horse & mare to Run at the race-place commonly called ye Ware, to run one quarter of a mile. And ye said John Steward, Jun'r, doth hereby Coven't & agree to Run a horse now belonging to Mr. Jno. Hardiman, of Cha: City Co'ty, the said horse named Watt to Run ag'st a mare belonging to Thomas Jefferson, Jun'r, named Bony. The s'd horse to give the s'd mare five horse Lengths, Vizt: that is to say ten yards. And it is further agreed upon by the parties above s'd, that the s'd horse & mare are to Run on the first day of July next Ensuing the date hereof. And it is further agreed upon by the parties above s'd that if the s'd mare doth come within five Lengths of the fores'd Horse, the fores'd John Steward to pay unto Mr. Rich'd Ward tbe sum of five pounds Sterling on Demand, & the s'd Richard Ward doth oblige himself that if the afores'd horse doth come before s'd mare five Lengths, then to pay unto the afores'd John Steward, Jun'r, the sum of six pounds Sterling on Demand. It is further agreed by the p'ties aforesaid, that there be fair Rideing & the Riders to weigh about one hundred & thirty Weight, to the true p'formance of all & singular the p'misses, the p'ties above s'd have hereunto set their hands the day and year above written.

"And the plaintiff in fact saith, That pursuant to tlle afores'd agreement, The s'd horse & mare, to-wit: The horse named Watt, belonging to Mr. John Hardiman, & the mare named Bonny, belonging to Mr. Tho. Jefferson, Jun'r, were by the s'd pl't'f & Def'd't brought upon the afores'd Ground to Run upon the first day of July, and the word being given by the person who was appointed to start the s'd horse & mare, The afores'd mare, with her Rider who weighed about onehundred & thirty weight, Did

Leap off, and out running the afores'd horse came in first between the poles which were placed at the comeing in of the s'd Race, commonly called the Ware, one quarter of a mile distance from the starting place appointed; and was by the s'd mare, with her Rider of about one hund'd & thirty weight as afores'd, fairly Run.

"Wherefore the afores'd pl't'f saith that the afores'd Mare, Bony, with fair Running & Rideing, according to agreement, Did beat the s'd horse Watt, and that according to the true meaning of the s'd agreem't he, the s'd plaintifif, hath Woon the wager, to-witt: the sum of five pounds sterling of the afores'd John Steward And thereupon he brings suit ag'st the afores'd John Steward, Jun'r, & demands Judgem't for the afores'd sum of five p'ds Sterl., witb Co'ts, &c. To which the Defend't, by Mr. Bartholomew Fowler, his attorney, appears and upon oyer of the plaintiff declaracon pleads that he oweth nothing by the covenants, &c., and thereof puts himself upon ye country & ye pl't'f likewise.

"Whereupon, it is ordered that a Jury be impanelled & sworn to try the issue, To-witt Thomas Edwards, Wm. Ballard, Phill Childers, John Watson, Edward Bowman, Will Hatcher, Amos Ladd, John Wilson, Phill. Jones, Edw'd Good, John Bowman.

"Who Returned this Verdict: We find for the plaintiff. Upon the motion of the plaintiffs' attomey the s'd Verdict is Recorded, & Judgement is awarded the s'd pl't'f against the Def'd't for tbe sum of five pounds Sterling, to be p'd with Costs, als Ex'o."

* * *

Virginia Governor Francis Nicholson proclaims a horse race, circa 1691, reprinted in "Nicholson's Proclamation about the College and Orders for Prize Games for Bachelors, etc.," William and Mary Quarterly, 1st Series, Vol. 11, No. 2 (October 1902), 87.

"To the Sheriffe of Surry County

I desire that you give public notice that I will give first and second prizes to be shott for, wrastled, played at backswords, & Run for by Horse and foott, to begin on the 22^d. day of Aprill next s^{et}. [Saint]. Georges day, being Satterday all which prizes are to be shott for &c by the better sort of Virginians onely, who are Batchelers."

* * *

Court case records in Northumberland County, Virginia, 18 May 1705, in "Some Extracts from Northumberland County Records," William and Mary Quarterly, 1st Series, Vol. 21, No. 2 (October 1912), 102-103.

"At a Court held for North^d County; the 18th day of May An^o 1705 p^{r}sent Coll Geo. Cooper, Coll. Rodhm Kenner, Coll. Peter Hack, Capt. Chr: Neale, Mr Peter Coutanceau, Capt. Maurice Jones Justices.

"Thomas Pinkard was attached to answer Joseph Humphreys in a plea of the case and whereupon the plaintiff sheweth that on or about the sixteenth day of October An^o 1703 on the race grounds called ffaire ffeils Race in St Stephens Parish in this County the said Pinkard challenged to run a horse in & belonging to the lower part in Lancaster County with any horse in this County except Maj^r Kenner's horse and thereupon the pl^t accepted the said challenge and the said Pinkard & the plt mutually consented that some horse of Lancaster County, & some horse of this County to be procured by the plt should Run at Scotland Race ground in this County the last Thursday in the month of October for Ten pounds & the said Pinkard to allow twenty shillings to the plt for coming to the said Scotland race ground & it was agreed and consented to by both parties that the horse intended to run should be upon the ground aforesaid (whether faire or fowle weather) by twelve of the clock on the said last Thursday in October and if either pty should ffail to meet with the horse intended to Run on the Said Day perfixed by twelve of the clock as aforesaid the party ffailing should Loose the Wager and the said plt further sheweth that according to his agreement he came to the said Race ground called Scotland with the horse intended to Run agst the Lancaster horse and was there with the sd Horse p^rcisely at twelve of the clock on the said fixed day and then stayed some hours, but the sd Thomas Pinkard did not meet the Plt nor bring nor send the horse intended to Run with this County horse to the said Race place & whereupon the plt caused the horse (intended as aforesaid to Run with the Lancaster horse) to be Rid over the Race ground and departed home whereupon the plt further sheweth that the said Thomas Pinkard by his said failure hath fforfeited to the plt the sum of ten pounds & twenty shillings in all eleven pounds &c. the plaintiff prays judgment (Judgment granted and an appeal allowed before his Excellency the Govr and Hono^ble the Counsell on the 6th day of the next General Court.)"

* * *

William Byrd, Westover, Virginia planter, 27 August 1709, in Louis B. Wright and Marion Tinling, eds., *The Secret Diary of William Byrd of Westover, 1709-1712* (Richmond, Va.: The Dietz Press, 1941), 75.

"I denied my man G-r-l to go to a horse race because there was nothing but swearing and drinking there."

* * *

Hugh Jones, Virginia Anglican minister, comments on horse racing, circa 1724, in Jones, *The Present State of Virginia* (New York: Joseph Sabin, reprint of 1724 ed.), 48-49.

"The common Planters leading eafy Lives don't much admire Labour, or any manly Exercife, except Horfe-racing., nor Diverfion, except Cock-Fighting, in which fome greatly delight. This eafy Way of Living, and the Heat of the Summer makes fome very lazy, who are then faid to be Climate-ftruck."

"The Saddle-Horfes, though not very large, are hardy, ftrong, and fleet; and will pace naturally and pleafantly at a prodigious Rate.

"They are fuch Lovers of Riding, that almost every ordinary Perfon keeps a Horfe; and I have known some spend the morning in ranging feveral miles in the Woods to find and catch their Horfes only to ride two or three miles to Church, to the Court-Houfe, or to a Horfe-Race, where they generally appoint to meet upon Bufinefs; and are more certain of finding thofe that they want to fpeak or deal with, than at their Home."

* * *

Advertisement for a horse race, Virginia Gazette, No. 16, 19-26 November 1736.

"We hear, from *Hanover* County, that on Tuefday next, (being St. *Andrew*'s Day) fome merry-difpos'd Gentlemen of the faid County, defign to celebrate that Feftival, by fetting up divers Prizes to be contended for in the following Manner, (*to wit*,) A neat Hunting Saddle, with a Fine Broad-cloth Houfing, fring'd and flower'd, &c. to be run for (the Quarter,) by any Number of Horfes and Mares: A fine *Cremona* Fiddle to be plaid for, by any Number of Country Fiddlers, (Mr. *Langford*'s Scholars excepted:) With divers other confiderable Prizes, for Dancing, Singing, Foot-ball-play, Jumping, Wreftling, &c. particularly a fine Pair of Silk Stockings to be given to the *handfomeft Maid* upon the Green, to be judg'd of by the Company."

Advertisement for horse racing, Virginia Gazette, No. 47, 24 June-1 July 1737.

"We hear, there is to be Horfe Racing every Saturday till October, at the Race Ground near this City."

* * *

Advertisements for a horse race and subsequent account, Virginia Gazette, 1737.

"Williamsfburg, October 7 We have Advice from *Hanover* County, That on *St. Andrew*'s Day, being the 30th of *November* next, there are to be Horfe Races and feveral other Diverfions, for the Entertainment of the Gentlemen and Ladies, at the *Old Field* near Capt. *John Bickerton*'s in that County, (if permitted by the Hon. *William Byrd,* Esq; Proprietor of the faid Land,) The Subftance of which are as follows, *viz.*

"1. It is propos'd, That 20 Horfes or Mares do run round a Three Miles Courfe, for a Prize of the Value of Five Pounds, according to the ufual Rules of Racing; That every Horfe that runs fhall be firft enter'd with Mr. *Joseph Fox*; and that no Perfon have the Liberty of putting in a Horfe, unless he is a Subfcriber towards defraying the Expence of this Entertainment, and pay to Mr. *Fox* Half a Piftole of it at entring his Horfe.

"2. That a Hat of the Value of 20 s. be cudgell'd for; and that after the firft Challenge made, the Drums are to beat, once every Quarter of an Hour, for Three Challenges, round the Ring; on no Anfwer made, the Perfon challenging to be entitled to the Prize; and none to Play with their Left Hand.

"3. That a Violin be played for by 20 Fiddlers, and to be given to him that fhall be adjudged to play the beft: No Perfon to have the Liberty of playing, unlefs he brings a Fiddle with him. After the Prize is won, they are all to play together, and each a different Tune; and to be treated by the Company.

"4. That 12 Boys of 12 Years of Age do run 112 Yards, for a Hat of the Value of 12 Shillings.

"5. That a Flag be flying on the faid Day, 30 Feet high.

"6. That a handfome Entertainment be provided for the Subfcribers, and their Wives; and fuch of them who are not fo happy as to have Wives, may treat any other Lady. And that convenient Booths be erected for that Purpofe.

"7. That Drums, Trumpets, Hautboys, &c. will be provided, to play at the faid Entertainment.

"8. That after Dinner, the Royal Healths, his Honour the Governor's, &e. are to be drank.

"9. That a Quire of Ballads be fung for, by a Number of Songfters, the beft Songfter to have the Prize, and all of them to have Liquor fufficient to clear their Wind-Pipes.

"10. That a Pair of Silver Buckles be Wrestled for, by a certain Number of brisk young Men.

"11. That a Pair of handfome Shoes be danced for.

"12. That a Pair of handfome Silk Stockings of One Piftole Value, be given to the handfomeft young Country Maid that appears in the Field: With many other Whimfical and Comical Diverfions, too tedious to mention here.

"The Horfe Race is to be run that Day, fair or foul; but if foul, the other Diverfions are to be continued the next Day.

"The Subfcription Money to be paid on the faid Day in the Field; and Notice will be given, who is to receive it.

"And as this Mirth is defign'd to be purely innocent, and void of Offence, all Perfons reforting there are defir'd to behave themfelves with Decency and Sobriety; the Subfcribers being refolv'd to difcountenance all Immorality with the utmoft Rigour.

"As fuch Meetings and Entertainments are fomewhat New, in thefe Parts, it may not be improper to acquaint my Readers with the Occafion of this. *Hanover* County is large, well feated, inhabited by confiderable Number of Gentlemen, Merchants, and creditable Planters, who, being defirous of cultivating Friendfhip, and innocent Mirth, propos'd an annual Meeting of the beft Sort, of both Sexes. Mr. *Auguftine Graham*, Clerk of the County, a generous Batchelor, defirous of effecting fo fociable a Defign, provided a handfome Entertainment for the Gentlemen and Ladies, on the 30th of *November* laft, and for their Diverfion, gave feveral Prizes to be contended for, by feveral Sorts of Exercife and Agility, all at his own Expence; and was honour'd with a great deal of Company; who were fo well pleas'd with the fame, that it was then refolved and concluded on, for keeping up the fame Spirit of Friendfhip, and good Society, to have an annual Meeting at the Expence of the Gentlemen, by Subfcription; accordingly a Subfcription was fet on Foot, and many of the Gentlemen have generoufly contributed towards defraying the Expence of the Entertainment and Diverfions, this Year; and propofe the fame annually."   (No. 61, 30 September-7 October 1737)

"We hear from *Hanover* County, That the Prize to be run for there, on St. *Andrew*'s Day, by 20 Horfes, &c. is a neat Saddle, with a handfome Silver-lac'd and fring'd Houfing: That feveral Gentlemen have already enter'd their Horfes; and 'tis believ'd the whole Number will be made up. The Pofts are already fet up at the Place mention'd in the former Papers; and 'tis exp[ected there will be a great deal of Company."
(No. 67, 11-18 November 1737)

"In fome of our former *Gazettes* we gave an Account that there was to be a Meeting of the Gentlemen and Ladies, in that County [Hanover], on St. *Andrew*'s Day, as well to propagate good Society, as to commemorate that Patron, &c. We can now inform our Readers, that there was accordingly a Meeting at the Time and Place appointed, of a great Number of Gentlemen, Ladies, and others; Booths were fet up, and an extraordinary good Dinner provided for them, with Variety and Plenty of Liquors. The Horfe and Foot Races were ran; and all or moft of the Prizes contended for, and won. The fine Saddle and Houfing were won by a Bay Horfe belonging to one *Tynes*, of *Caroline* County; but 'tis faid Mr. *James Littlepage* is to have it. During the Time a Flag was difplay'd, Drums were beating, Trumpets founding, and other Mufick playing, for the Entertainment of the Company, and the whole was manag'd with as good Order, and gave as great Satisfaction, in general, as cou'd poffibly be expected."
(No. 70, 2-9 December 1737)

* * *

Advertisement for a horse race and subsequent account, Virginia Gazette, 1739.

"AND for the *Entertainment* and *Diverfion* of all Gentlemen and others, that fhall refort thereto, the following PRIZES are given to be contended for, at the [Williamsburg] Fair, *viz.*

"A good Hat to be Cudgell'd for; and to be given to the Perfon that fairly wins it, by the common Rules of Play.

"A Saddle of 40 *S.* Value, to be run for, once round the Mile Courfe, adjacent to this City, by any Horfe, Mare or Gelding, carrying Horfeman's Weight, and allowing

Weight for Inches. A handfome Bridle to be given to the Horfe that comes in Second. And a good Whip to the Horfe that comes in Third.

"A Pair of Silver Buckles, Value 20 *S*. to be run for by Men, from the *College* to the *Capitol*. A Pair of Shoes to be given him that comes in Second. And a Pair of Gloves to the Third.

"A Pair of Pumps to be danc'd for by Men.

"A handfome Firelock to be exercis'd for; and given to the Perfom that performs the Manual Exercife beft.

"A Pig, with his Tail foap'd, to be run after; and to be given to the Perfon that catches him, and lifts him off the Ground fairly by the Tail.

"There will be feveral other Prizes given: And as the Fair is to hold Three Days, there will be Horfe-racing, and a Variety of Diverfions every Day; and the Prizes not here particularly mentioned, (for want of Room) will be then publickly declared, and appropriated in the best Manner.

"The Horfes that run for the Saddle, are to be Enter'd before Ten o'Clock on *Wednefday* Morning next, with Mr. *Henry Bowcock* in *Williamfburg*, thofe that are not Contributors, to pay 2 *S*. 6 *d*. at Entrance. The Horfe that wins the Saddle, not to run for any other Prize this Fair.

"Proper Perfons will be appointed to have the Direction and Management of the Fair, and to decide any Controverfies that may happen, in relation to the Bounties and Prizes to be beftowed." (No. 175, 30 November-7 December 1739)

"The Prizes were all contended for. There was a Horfe Race round the Mile Courfe [at Williamsburg] the Firft Day [of the Fair], for a Saddle of Forty Shillings Value. Eight Horfes ftarted, by Sound of Trumpet; and Colonel *Chifwell*'s Horfe, *Edgecomb*, came in Firft, and won the Saddle: Mr. *Coke*'s Horfe *Sing'd Cat* came in Second, and won the Bridle, of 12 Shillings Value; and Mr. *Drummond*'s Horfe _____ came in Third, and won the Whip.

"The Second Day, a Silver Soop Ladle, of 45 Shillings Value, was run for, the fame Ground; and was won by Mr. *Coke*'s Horfe. Mr. *Gooch*'s Horfe *Fop*, came in Second, and won the Bridle of 12 Shillings Value; and Mr. *Stanhope*'s Horfe won the Whip.

"The Third Day, a Saddle and Bridle, of about 40 Shillings Value, were run for, the fame Ground; Mr. *Gooch*'s Horfe *Fop*, came in Firft, and won the Saddle and Bridle: Mr. *Drummond*'s Horfe came in Second, and won the Bridle, of 12 Shillings Value; and Mr. *Booker*'s Horfe *Tail*, won the Whip." (No. 176, 7-14 December 1739)

* * *

William Byrd, Westover, Virginia planter, chronicles local horse racing, May, August, and October 1740, in Maude H. Woodfin, ed., *Another Secret Diary of William Byrd of Westover, 1739-1741* (Richmond, Va.: The Dietz Press, 1942), 63-64, 93, 107.

1 May 1740: "After dinner we walked to the race but were soon forced to retire for the rain."

8 May 1740: "About 12 the company went to the race and so did my family and I gave them all money and sent a pistole myself by Mr. Hall who brought back two about 4 o'clock."

7 August 1740: "My son was gone to the race...."

30 October 1740: "After dinner we had a race which I went not to but won 20 shillings."

Advertisements for a horse races, Maryland Gazette, 1745.

"NOTICE *is hereby given*,
THAT on Thurfday and Friday, the 30th and 31ft Days of this Inftant *May*, will be Run for at *John Conner's* in *Anne Arundel* County, the Sum of Ten Pounds Currency, the Firft Day; and on the following Day, will be Run for at the fame Place, the Sum of Five Pounds Currency: By any Horse, Mare or Gelding (*Old Ranter* and *Limber-Sides* excepted); to carry 115 Pounds, three Heats, the Courfe two Miles.

The Horses &c., to be Entered with *John Conner*, before 10 o'Clock in the Forenoon of each Day of Running: paying Entrance-Money 15 *s*. the firft Day, and 10 *s*. the Day following." (No. 4, 17 May 1745)

"ON Tuefday the 17th Day of this Inftant *September*, and Wednefday the 18th of the fame Month, a Fair will be kept at Mr. *Murdock's* Old Fields, near *Queen Anne* Town, *Prince George's* County;

"On the firft day of the faid Fair will be run for by any Horfe, Mare, or Gelding, Thirty Pounds Current Money; to run three Heats, two Miles each Heat, and to carry one Hundred and ten Pounds Weight.

"On the Day following will be run for on the fame Courfe, Twenty Pounds Current Money, to run three Heats, and carry the fame Weight; the winning Horfe on the firft Day, to be excepted on the fecond.

"The horses, &c. to be entered with Mr. *William Beall*, at *Queen Anne*, on each Day of Racing; paying Thirty Shillings Entrance each Horfe, &c. for the firft Prize; and Twenty Shillings for the fecond.

"All Differences and Difputes to be determined by *Thomas Harwood*, and *Thomas Brooke, junior*." (No. 20, 6 September 1745)

"ON Thurfday the 10th of *October*, 1745, Friday the 11th, and Saturday the 12th of the fame Month, a Fair will be kept at *Baltimore* Town, in *Baltimore* County.

"On the firft Day of the faid Fair will be run for, by any Horfe, Mare, or Gelding, Ten Pounds Current money; to run three Heats, half a Mile each Heat, and to carry Hundrfed Twenty-five Pounds Weight.

"On the fecond Day will be run for Five Pounds Current Money, to run three Heats the fame Diftance, and to carry the fame Weight; the winning Horfe the firft Day to be excepted on the fecond.

"On the third Day will be run for Three Pounds Current Money, the fame Courfe, three Heats; the winning Horfes on the firft and fecond Days to be excepted.

"The Horfes, &c. to be entered either with *William Hammond*, or *Darby Lux*, at any Time before the Day of Racing; paying Ten Shillings for each Horfe of the firft day, Seven Shillings for each Horfe of the fecond day, and Half a Crown for each Horfe of the third day.

"A Hat and Ribbon of Twenty-five Shillings Value to be cudgelled for on the fecond Day, and a Pair of *London* Pumps to be wreftled for on the third Day.

"All Difputes that may arife, to be determined by *William Hammond, Charles Ridgley*, and *Darby Lux*." (No. 24, 20 September 1745)

"ON Wednefday the 30th of this Inftant *October*, and Thurfday the 31ft of the fame Month, a Fair will be kept in the old Fields near *John Conner*'s in *Anne-Arundel* County.

"On the Firft day of the Fair will be Run for by any Horfe, Mare, or Gelding, Twelve Pounds Current-Money, to run three Heats two Miles each Heat, and to carry one hundred and twelve Pounds.

"On the day following will be run for on the fame Courfe Eight Pounds Current-Money, to run three Heats, and to carry the fame Weight; the winning Horfe, &c. on the firft day, to be excepted on the fecond.

"The Horfes, &c. are to be entered with *John Conner* on each Day of Racing; paying Twenty Shillings Entrance each Horfe, &c. for the firft Prize, and Fifteen for the fecond.

"All Differences and Difputes are to be determined by Mr. *David Weems* and Mr. *Richard Harwood.*

"*N.B.* Thofe Gentlemen that fubfcribe for the Benefit of the Fair, to pay but Half Price for Entrance."   (No. 26, 18 October 1745)

* * *

Advertisement for a horse race, Virginia Gazette, No. 476, 5-12 September 1745.

"A PURSE of Nineteen Piftoles, will be run for, the 3d Thurfday in this prefent Month September, at the Race-Ground near *York* Town, by any Horfe, Mare or Gelding, (that not won a Purfe at the faid Ground before) carrying 130 Pounds, the beft of three Heats, two Miles to a Heat. Whoever hath a Mind to put in a Horfe, *&c.* for the faid Purfe, is defired to enter him or her with *Ifhmael Moody*, in *York* Town, the *Monday* before the ftarting, or muft pay double Entrance. The Subfcribers pay One Piftole Entrance, and the Non-fubfcribers Four."

* * *

Advertisements for horse races, Virginia Gazette, 1746.

"TO be Run for, at *King-William* Court Houfe, on the firft *Wednefday* in *September* next, by any Horfe, Mare, or Gelding, carrying 130 lbs. each, a Purfe of Thirty Piftoles; the Subfcribers to pay one Piftole Entrance, and a Non-fubfcriber four. The Entrance Money to be given to the fecond beft Horfe: The Horfes to be entered with Mr. *John Doncaftle*, three Days before the Race."   (No. 518, 26 June-3 July 1746)

"To be Run for at *Leeds-Town*, on Third *Wednefday* in *September* next,

"A Valuable Purfe, on the following Terms, *viz.* Free to any Horfe, Mare or Gelding, carrying 130 *lbs*. Poneys carrying Weight for Inches under that Weight, at the ufual Allowance of fourteen Pounds for the firft Inch, and feven after. The beft of the Heats (two Miles each) to win and receive 30 Piftoles. The fecond Horfe to have the Remainder of the Subfcription or Entrance Money at Choice: and the third Horfe to have whichever the fecond refufes. All Horfes to entered and meafured in the faid Town by One o'Clock on the *Monday* before the Race, and a Piftole Entrance Money paid down. The Horfes to be at the Starting Pole, by One o'Clock, and to obferve the Rules of fair Racing: No Horfe to win more than one Purfe.

"All Gentlemen Subfcribers who will not be at the Race, are defired to fend their Money for the Advantage of the Town, and Encouragement of Sporting. Due Attendance will be given by

Jofeph Morton.

"*N.B.* The Subfcription is about 40 Piftoles, and is made up by Gentlemen of Honour."   (No. 524, 7-14 August 1746)

Advertisements for horse races, Maryland Gazette, 1747.

"ON the 30th of *April*, a FAIR will begin at *Queen's-Town* in *Queen-Anne*'s County; where will be given, to be run for, by any Horfe, Mare, or Gelding; *viz.*

"On the firft Day of the Fair, Seven Pounds Current Money, the mile, three Heats.

"On the fecond Day, Four Pounds like Money, the Quarter, three Heats.

"Each Horfe to carry 140 Pounds weight. Any Horfe to run the fecond Day, except the winning Horfe of the firft.

"The Horfes muft be Entered with *Benjamin Sutton* in *Queen's Town*, by 10 of the Clock the firft Day of the Fair, paying Seven Shillings for the firft Prize, and four Shillings for the fecond; which Money arifing on the faid Entries, to go to the fecond beft Horfe each Day."   (No. 100, 24 March 1747)

"*May* 6, 1747

"ON the 21ft Inftant, a Fair will be held in *Prince-George*'s County, near Mr. *Kennedy Farrell*'s at *Rock Creek*, in Mr. *Henry Wright Crabb*'s old Field.

"On the firft Day, will be run for, by any Horfe, Mare or Gelding, a Prize of Ten Pounds Currency.

"On the Second Day, a Prize of Six Pounds, like Money; and none to be excepted but the winning Horfe of the firft Day.

"And on the third Day, a Prize of Four Pounds like Money; the two winning Horfes only excepted.

"The Horfes are to run three Heats, two Miles each Heat, and to carry 120 Weight. The Horfes to be entered with Mr. *Farrell*, the Morning of the Race, Paying as many Shillings as Pounds are Run for, each Day. The Diftance 100 Yards.

"All Differences and Difputes, if any arife, to be determined by THOMAS OWING,

H. W. CRABB."

(No. 107, 12 May 1747)

"ON the 29th of *September*, will be Run, on the Race-Ground near *Annapolis*, a Match for Fifty Guineas.

"And the Day following, a Subfcription Race for Twenty Pounds Current Money, by any Horfe, Mare, or Gelding, carrying Nine Stone, the beft of Three Heats. A Non-fubfcriber to pay Twenty Shillings Entrance."   (No. 122, 18 August 1747)

"WHereas there is a Fair appointed by Act of Affembly to be held in *Baltimore-Town*, on the firft Thurfday, Friday, and Saturday, in *October* yearly; the Commiffioners of the faid Town hereby give Notice, that whoever brings to the faid Fair, on the firft Day thereof, the beft Steer, fhall receive Eight Pounds current Money for the fame; alfo a Bounty of Forty Shillings, over and above the faid Eight Pounds. The faid Steer afterwards, on the fame Day, to be run for, by any Horfe, Mare, or Gelding, not exceeding 5 Years old, three Heats, a Quarter of a Mile each Heat, not confined to carry any certain Weight: The winning Horfe to be intitled to the faid Steer, or to Eight Pounds in Money, at the Option of the Owner.

"On Friday the fecond Day of faid Fair, will be run for the Sum of Five Pounds current Money, by any Horfe, Mare, or Gelding, the fame Diftance, not confin'd to carry any certain Weight. Alfo a Bounty of Forty Shillings will be given to any Perfon that produces the beft Piece of Yard wide Country-made white Linnen, the Piece to contain 20 Yards.

"On Saturday the third Day, a Hat and Ribbon will be cudgell'd for; a Pair of Pumps wrestled for; and a white Shift to be run for by Negro Girls.

"The Horfes to be entered with *William Lux*, Clerk of faid Town, any Time before the Day of Running; paying for the firft Day Five Shillings, for the fecond Day Half a Crown. All Difputes that may arife, are to be determined by the Commiffioners of the faid Town: And all Perfons are exempted from any Arrefts, during the faid Fair, and the Day before, and day after; except in Cafes of Felony, and Breaches of the Peace, according to the Tenure of the above-mentioned Act." (No. 124, 8 September 1747)

"ON the 29th of *September*, will be Run, on the Race-Ground near *Annapolis*, a Match for Fifty Guineas.

"And the Day following, a Subfcription Race for Twenty Pounds Current Money, by any Horfe, Mare, or Gelding, carrying Nine Stone, the beft of Three Heats. A Non-fubfcriber to pay Twenty Shillings Entrance." (No. 125, 15 September 1747)

* * *

Robert Rose, Virginia Anglican minister, goes to the horse races, October 1748 and October 1749, in Ralph Emmett Fall, ed., *The Diary of Robert Rose. A View of Virginia by a Scottish Colonial Parson, 1746-1751* (Falls Church, Va.: McClure Press, 1977), 43, 66.

27 October 1748: "Went to Leeds, saw a Race run for 50 pistoles, dined at Joseph Morton's being an Ordinary, returnd at Night—...."

7 October 1749: "Cloudy—Went with Messrs Lomax & Jordan to a race, near Piney River—...."

* * *

Advertisements for horse races, Maryland Gazette, 1749.

"*To be RUN for, at* Frederick-Town, *in* Frederick *County*,

"A Subfcription of Twenty-Eight Pounds Two Shillings and Six Pence, Current Money, on the following Days, *viz.* On Tuefday the 9th Day of *May*, Fifteen Pounds, by any Horfe, Mare, or Gelding, carrying Weight for Inches; each Horfe, &c. being 14 Hands high, to carry 9 Stone, and fo in proportion, allowing *7 lb.* for an Inch; and to pay 15*s.* Entrance.

"On Wednefday the 10th, will be run for the Sum of Ten Pounds; the Horfes, &c. to carry Weight for Inches, and to pay 10*s.* Entrance. And,

"On Thurfday the 11th of the fame Month, will be run for Three Pounds Two Shillings and Six Pence, and the Entrance Money of each Day; the Horfes, &c. to carry Weight for Inches, as on the two preceding Days, and to pay after the Rate of 1*s.* in the Pound Entrance. The winning Horfes to be excepted each Day.

"The Horfes, &c. are to be Entered with *Kennedy Farrell*, by 12 o'Clock the Day before they run. And if any Differences arife, they are to be decided by *John Durnall*, Efq. and Capt. *Nathanael Wickburn*." (No. 208,19 April 1749)

"*TO BE RUN FOR, on the Race Ground near the City of* Annapolis, *on Friday the 29th Day of* September *next,*

"A PURSE of the value of TWENTY POUNDS Currency, Three Heats, by any Horfe, Mare or Gelding, bred in this Province, to carry Seven Stone.

"The faid Horfes, Mares, or Geldings, to be entered the preceding Day, by XII of the Clock, with *Jonas Green* at *Annapolis*, and to pay each Twenty Shillings Entrance, for the Benefit of the Second Beft.

"All Difputes to be determined by the Mayor and Aldermen prefent."

(No. 219, 5 July 1749)

"TO BE RUN FOR,

At LEEDS-TOWN, *in* Virginia, *on Wednefday the 17th of* September *next*,

A Purfe of about Thirty five Pounds Value, by any Horfe, Mare, or Gelding, carrying Weight for Inches; the Heats three Miles. And,

"On Thurfday the 18th of the fame Month, will be Run for at the fame Place, a Plate of about One hundred Pounds Value by any Horfe, & c. to carry 10 Stone, the Heats 4 Miles.

"That Gentlemen may be more particularly informed of the Terms of Running, Copies of each Subfcription will be lodged at the Printing Office in *Annapolis*."

(No. 221, 19 July 1749)

"*TO BE RUN FOR, on the Race-Ground near the City of* Annapolis, *on Friday the 29th Day of* September *next*,

"A PURSE of the value of TWENTY POUNDS Currency, Three Heats, by any Horfe, Mare or Gelding, bred in this Province, to carry Seven Stone.

"The faid Horfes, Mares, or Geldings, to be entered the preceding Day, by XII of the Clock, with *Jonas Green* at *Annapolis*, and to pay each Twenty Shillings Entrance, for the Benefit of the Second Beft.

"All Difputes to be determined by the Mayor and Aldermen prefent."

(No. 223, 2 August 1749)

* * *

Advertisements for horse races, Maryland Gazette, 1750.

"ON Tuefday, the 1ft Day of *May* next, will be Run for at *Upper Marlborough*, in *Prince George's* County, a Prize of THIRTY POUNDS, *Maryland* Currency. And

"On Wednefday, the Day following, will be Run for, at the fame Place, a Prize of, FIFTEEN POUNDS; by any Horfe, Mare, or Gelding; each Horfe, &c. to carry 126 *lb*. Weight; and to run three Heats, two Miles each Heat; the winning Horfe on the firft Day, to be excepted on the fecond.

"The Horfes, &c. to be Enter'd with *Benjamin Barry* and *Benjamin Brookes*, on each Day of Racing, by Ten o'Clock in the Morning; and to pay Thirty Shillings on the firft Day, and Fifteen Shillings on the fecond.

"All Differences and Difputes, if any arife, to be determined by Meff. *Clement Hill* and *Bafil Waring*." (No. 258, 4 April 1750)

"TO BE RUN FOR,

AT *Port-Tobacco*, on Tuefday the 30th Day of this Inftant *October*, THIRTY POUNDS Current Money of *Maryland*, by any Horfe, Mare, or Gelding, belonging to the faid Province; to carry 126 Pounds Weight, and to run three Heats, two Miles each Heat.

"And on Wednesday the 31ft of *October*, will be Run for at the fame Place, TEN POUNDS Current Money, the winning Horfe the Day before to be excepted; and to catch Riders.

"The Horfes, &c. to be Entered the Day before each Race, with Mr. *Hugh Mitchel* at *Port-Tobacco*; paying Twenty Shillings Entrance for the firft Day, and Ten Shillings for the fecond." (No. 285, 10 October 1750)

Advertisements for horse races, Virginia Gazette, 1751.

"A PURSE of Fifty Piftoles will be run for at *Frederickfburg*, the fecond Day of *June* Fair. Each Horfe carrying 140 *lb*. Weight, 4 Miles at a Heat. Thofe who are inclinable to bring their Horfes, muft enter them with the Subfcriber, Six Days before hand."   (No. 15, 11 April 1751)

"To be RUN for, at LEEDS *Town,*

"ON the third *Wednefday* in September, the beft of three, three Mile Heats, a Purfe of about Thirty Seven Piftoles Values, by Subfcribers only.

"The next Day a Purfe of about Ninety Pounds Value, by any Horfe, Mare, &c. that has not already won one of them, the beft of Three four Mile Heats, each Horfe carryingten Stone, a Non-Subfcriber to pay Ten Piftoles Entrance-Money, or by no Means to be entitled to any Part of the Purfe or Stakes, which Entrance-Money is to be for the fecond beft Horfe. Every Horfe that runs muft be fhown at *Leeds* Town, and entered the *Wednefday* Sev'nnight before the Race Day, and the Entrance-Money paid, &c. &c.

"*N.B.* There is alfo a Ferry kept at the faid Town, where all Gentlemen may depend on meeting with quick Difpatch, being provided with good Boats for Horfe and Foot
Mark Talbott."
(No. 32, 8 August 1751)

"To be RUN for, at Dudley's *Ferry, in* King *and* Queen,

ON the firft *Wednefday* of *October* next, the beft Two Mile Heats, a Purfe of about Thirty-two Piftoles Value, all Horfes to carry One Hundred and Thirty Pounds.
Robert Dudley."
(No. 37, 12 September 1751)

* * *

Advertisements for horse races, Maryland Gazette, 1751.

"TO BE RUN FOR,

"*At Mrs.* Crawford's *Old Fields, near* Upper-Marlborough, *in* Prince George's *County,*

"ON the fourteenth Day of *May* next , by any Horfe, Mare or Gelding, A Prize of THIRTY POUNDS, and the Day following, A Prize of FIFTEEN POUNDS, to carry One Hundred and Twenty Six Pounds Weight; each Horfe on the firft Day to pay Thirty Shillings Entrance; and Fifteen Shillings on the fecond Day. The Horfes to be entered with *Benjamin Berry*, junior, and *Benjamin Brooke*, by ten o'Clock each day. To run three Heats, two Miles each Heat. All Difputes and Differences to be determined by Meff. *Clement Hill* and *Basil Waring*.

"The winning Horfe the firft Day to be excepted on the fecond."
(No. 312, 17 April 1751)

"TO BE RUN FOR,

On the RACE-GROUND near ANNAPOLIS,

"ON Tuefday the 22d Day of *October* next, the Sum of TWENTY-FIVE Pounds Currency, by any Horfe, Mare, or Gelding, to carry nine Stone, three Heats. And

"On Wednefday the 23d of the fame Month, will be run for on the faid Courfe, the Sum of FIFTEEN Pounds Currency, by any Horfe, Mare, or Gelding (the winning Horfe the Day before to be excepted); to carry the fame Weight, and to run three Heats.

"The Horses, &c. to be Entered on each Day of Running, by 10 o'Clock in the Forenoon, with *Jonas Green* in *Annapolis*; and to pay Twenty-five Shillings Entrance on the firft Day, Fifteen Shillings on the fecond.

"All Difputes, if any arife, to be decided by *John Gaffaway* and *Daniel Dulany, junior*, Efquires."   (No. 332, 4 September 1751)

* * *

Account of a horse race, Maryland Gazette, No. 315, 8 May 1751.

"ANNAPOLIS.

"Laft Wednefday, being the firft Day of our Fair, a Match was Run on the Race Ground near this City, the beft of three Heats, each Heat being two Miles and a half, between Mr. IGNATIUS DIGGES's Bay Horfe *Vendome*, and Mr. HARRISON's Grey Horfe *Beau*, for Sixty Guineas, which was won by the former, who got the two firft Heats."

* * *

Devereux Jarratt, Anglican rector, Bath Parish, Dinwiddie County, Virginia, writes of his own indulgence in horse racing and subsequent rejection of it, circa 1751, in [Jarratt], *The Life of the Reverend Devereux Jarratt, Rector of Bath Parish, Dinwiddie County, Virginia* (Baltimore: Warner & Hanna, 1806 [1969 reprint]), 23, 41.

"*Cards, racing, dancing*, &c. which are still the favourite sport of the wicked and un-godly, were then much in vogue. In these I partook, as far as my time and circumstances would permit, as well as on Sundays as any other day. In these I vainly sought my felicity, but never found."

"For some time, I had withdrawn myself from the company of the wicked; had quitted dancing, racing, cards, &c...."

* * *

Advertisements for horse races, Maryland Gazette, 1752.

"ON the firft Day of *May* next, a Purfe of FORTY POUNDS Currency, to be run for, by any Horfe, Mare, or Gelding, carrying nine Stone Weight, three Heats, each Heat to be once round the Poles on the Race Ground, near the City of *Annapolis*, and to be won by fuch Horfes, &c. having the beft of the faid Heats: Such Horfes, &c. are to be entered with Jonas Green two Days before the Race Day, and forty Shillings Currency to be paid at the Entrance, which with what further Addition can be made, is defigned for a Race on the fecond Day of *May*."   (No. 356, 20 February 1752)

"ON the 13th Day of *May* next, a Purfe of FORTY POUNDS Currency, to be run for, by any Horfe, Mare, or Gelding, carrying nine Stone Weight, three Heats, each Heat to be once round the Poles on the Race Ground, near the City of *Annapolis*, and to be won by fuch Horfe, &c. having the beft of the faid Heats: Such Horfes, &c. are to be entered with *Jonas Green* two Days before the Race Day, and forty Shillings Currency to be paid at the Entrance, which with what further Addition can be made, is defigned for a Race on the fecond Day of *May*."   (No. 360, 19 March 1752)

"THE Sum to be Run for on the fecond Day of the Fair, near *Annapolis* (the 14th Inftant) will be about Fifteen Pounds. Thofe Horfes, Mares, &c. which are to run for it, muft be entered that Morning by 10 of the Clock, with *Jonas Green*, paying Fifteen Shillings Entrance. The winning Horfe on the preceding Day to be excepted; and to carry the fame Weight."   (No. 367, 7 May 1752)

"To be RUN for,

At UPPER-MARLBOROUGH, *in* Prince George's *County,*

"ON Tuefday the 17th of *October* next, the Sum of THIRTY POUNDS Currency, by any Horfe, Mare, or Gelding, carrying 126 *lb.* Weight; and to pay Thirty Shillings Entrance Money. And,

"On Wednefday the 18th of *October,* will be Run for, at the fame Place, Twenty Pounds Currency, to carry 126 *lb.* Weight, and to pay Twenty Shillings Entrance: The winning Horfe the Day before to be excepted.

"The Horfes, *&c.* to be Entered each Day of Running, by 10 o'Clock in the Forenoon, either with *Benjamin Brooks* or *Benjamin Barry.*

"All Difputes, if any fhould arife, to be determined by Meffieurs *Clement Hill* and *Bafil Waring.*" (No. 382, 20 August 1752)

"ON Monday the 16th of *October* next, will be Run for, at the House of *John Hammond,* on *Elk Ridge,* the Sum of Eight Pounds, by any Horfe, Mare, or Gelding, (the *Englifh* Horfe, Mare, or their Breed, excepted;) to carry 110 Pounds Weight, and to run three Heats, two Miles each Heat: To pay Fifteen Shillings each Horfe, *&c.* Entrance Money.

"On Tuefday the 17th will be Run for, at the fame Place, a Saddle; three Heats, two Miles each Heat, to carry the fame Weight, and to pay Ten Shillings Entrance Money. And,

"On Wednefday the 18th, will likewife be Run for a Saddle; to run three Heats, twice round the Poles to a Heat; Weight and Entrance Money the fame as on the Day before.

"The Horses, *&c.* which are to run the firft Day, to be Entered with the faid *Hammond,* two Days before they run; and thofe which are to run the fecond and third Days, to be entered the Day before they run.

"If any Difputes fhould arife, the fame are to be determined by Capt. *Nicholas Gaffaway* and Mr. *Jofeph Hall.*

"The Horfes, *&c.* to have 15 Minutes allowed, between every two Heats, for Rubbing." (No. 384, 14 September 1752)

* * *

Accounts of horse races, Maryland Gazette, 1752.

"ANNAPOLIS

"Yefterday the Prize of Forty Pounds, was run for on our Race Ground, by Col. *Tafker*'s Mare *Selyma,* and Capt. *Butler*'s Mare *Creeping Kate*; and won by the former.

"This Day the Prize of Twenty Pounds was run for, when feven Horfes ftarted; but Mr. *Hungerford*'s Horfe *Hector* won the Prize." (No. 368, 14 May 1752)

"ANNAPOLIS.

"The two Prizes at *Upper-Marlborough,* in *Prince George*'s County, on Tuefday, and Yefterday, were both won by two Mares belonging to Capt. *Butler.*"

(No. 389, 19 October 1752)

"ANNAPOLIS.

"On the 5th Inftant a great Match was Run at *Gloucefter* Race Ground in *Virginia,* a Four Mile Heat, Col *Byrd*'s Cheftnut Horfe *Trial,* againft any that could be brought for 500 Piftoles. One Horfe and three Mares ftarted againft him, and they came in thus.

Col. *Tafker*'s Bay Mare *Selima*,	1ft
Col. *Byrd*'s Cheftnut Horfe *Trial*,	2d
Col. *Thornton*'s Grey Mare ————— ,	3d
Col. *Tayloe*'s Bay Mare, *Jenny Cameron*,	4th
His Bay Horfe *Childers*,	diftanced"

(No. 398, 21 December 1752)

* * *

Advertisements for horse races, Virginia Gazette, 1752.

"*To be RUN for*, at Dudley's *Ferry*, *in* King *and* Queen *County*,

A PURSE of the Value of 82 Piftoles, by any Horfe, Mare, or Gelding, each carrying 130 Pounds, on the firft *Monday* in *April* next.

Robert Dudley."

(No. 64, 20 March 1752)

"*March* 26, 1752

"*To be RUN for*, *at* York, *on* Thurfday *next*,

"A PURSE of Sixty Three Piftoles, four Mile Heats, the beft two in three, the Rider to weigh 135 *lbs*. to ftart at One o'Clock, to reft half an Hour between each Heat:

"He who fubfcribes Four Piftoles to pay One

"He who fubfcribes Three Piftoles to pay Two

"He who fubfcribes Two Piftoles to pay Three Piftoles at Entrance

"He who fubfcribes One Piftole to Pay Four

"And a Non-fubfcriber to pay Ten

"The Horfes to be enter'd with *John Gibbons*, or *James Mitchell*, five Days before the Race."   (No. 65, 27 March 1752)

"*To be RUN for*, *at* Leeds *Town*,

ON *Tuefday* the 19th of *September* next, a Purfe of about Forty Pounds Value, by any Horfe, Mare, &c. (that has not already won one of them) the beft of three Four Mile Heats, each Horfe carrying ten Stone; a Non-Subfcriber to pay Ten Piftoles Entrance Money, or by no Means to be entitled to any Part of the purfe, or Stakes, which Entrance Money is to be for the fecond beft Horfe: And, on *Thurfday* following a Purfe of about Ninety Pounds Value to be run for, on the Terms aforefaid. Every Horfe that runs muft be fhewn at *Leeds* Town, and enter'd the *Tuefday* Se'nnight before the Race-Day, and the Entrance Money paid, &c.

Mark Talbott.

"*N.B.* As I advanced my own Money laft Year, for Good of Sport, for one of the Purfes, I now lie out of Fifteen Piftoles of my Money: It's to be hoped, that Gentlemen who are Subfcribers to that Purfe will contrive it to

Their humble Servant, *Mark Talbott*"

(No. 84, 7 August 1752)

* * *

Landon Carter, Virginia plantation owner, comments on local horse racing, April 1752 and April 1770, in Jack P. Greene, ed., *The Diary of Colonel Landon Carter of Sabine Hall, 1752-1778*, 2 vols., Vol. 1 (Charlottesville, Va.: University Press of Virginia, 1965), 91, 379.

2 April 1752: "After reading a few bills [in the legislature], adjourned and Went to a Race in York Town Where Colo. Tayloe's Mare, Jenny Cameron, won the Purse."

2 April 1770: "Mr. Carter went up to a sweep stake race that was to be this day at Boyd's hole. Curious weather indeed for a planter lavish of his own health and regardless of his Cropping to be traveling about."

* * *

Advertisements for horse races, Maryland Gazette, 1753.

"To be RUN for,

In Mrs. Crawford's *old Fields, near* UPPER-MARLBOROUGH.

"ON Tuefday the 16th of *October* next, the Sum of TWENTY POUNDS Currency, by any Horfe, Mare, or Gelding, that have belonged to Perfons in this Province 12 Months, carrying 126 *lb*. Weight; and to pay twenty Shillings Entrance Money. And,

"On Wednesfday the 17th of *October*, will be Run for, at the fame Place, TEN POUNDS Currency, to carry 126 *lb*. Weight, and to pay Ten Shillings Entrance: The winning Horfe the Day before to be excepted.

"The Horfes, &c. to be Entered each Day of Running, by 10 o'Clock in the Forenoon, either with *Benjamin Barry*, or *Benjamin Brookes*.

"All Difputes, if any fhould arife, to be determined by Meffieurs *Clement Hill* and *Bafil Waring*."   (No. 434, 30 August 1753)

"ON Thurfday the 18th Day of *October* next, will be Run for, on the Race Ground, near *Bladenfburg*, about two Miles each Heat, a Prize of FIFTEEN POUNDS Currency. And,

"On the Day following, a Prize of FIVE POUNDS Currency, by any Horfe, &c. that never won a Prize of Five Pounds Currency.

"The Horfes, &c. to be enter'd with Mr. *William Beall*, and the Subfcriber, in *Bladenfburg*, on the faid days, by 10 of the Clock in the Forenoon; each Horfe, &c. to carry 126 *lb*. Weight for the firft Day's Prize; and on the fecond Day, what Weight the Owners of the faid Horses, &c. choofe to put on them; the Horfes, &c. to ftart precifely at two o'Clock, P. M. Fifteen Shillings Currency to be paid on Entrance the firft Day, and Five Shillings on the fecond.

"All Differences and Difputes that may arife, to be decided by *John Cooke*, Efq; and Mr. *Bafil Waring*, who are appointed Judges of the faid Race. *Thomas Chittam*."

(No. 437, 20 September 1753)

* * *

Advertisements for horse races, Maryland Gazette, 1754.

"To be RUN for,

On Monday the 15th of *April*,

(Being the Gift of his Excellency,)

"AT *Talbot* County Court-Houfe, a Purfe of TWENTY POUNDS, by any Horfe, Mare or Gelding, (who never then fhall have won a Prize ofabove Seven Pounds,) carrying Nine Stone Weight, the beft of Three Heats, each Heat to be Twice round the Poles on the Race Ground; to rub Half an Hour between each Heat. The Horfes, &c. to be entered with Mr. *Josiah Coleman*, living at *Talbot* Court Houfe, on Saturday the 13th, each paying Twenty Shillings Entrance.

"Such Rules and Orders are to be obferved as are ufual on thefe Occafions; and if an Difputes fhould arife, they are to be determined by Gentle men appointed for that Purpofe, before ftarting; and if the 15th fhould be a rainy Day, the Prize to be run for on the firft fair Day after."   (No. 462, 14 March 1754)

"To be RUN for,

At ANNAPOLIS, *on Tuefday the* 10th *of* September,

(Being the Gift of his Excellency),

"A PURSE of TWENTY POUNDS, by any Horfe, Mare, or Gelding, carrying Nine Stone Weight, the beft of Three Heats, each Heat to be once round the Poles on the Race Ground; to rub Half an Hour between each Heat. The Horfes, &c. to be entered with *Jonas Green* on Monday the 9th, paying Twenty Shillings Entrance; at the Poft Forty Shillings.

"Such Rules and Orders are to be obferved, as are ufual on thofe Occafions; and if any Difputes fhould arife, they are to be determined by Gentlemen appointed for that Purpofe, before ftarting; and if the 10th fhould be a rainy Day, the Prize to be run for on the firft fair Day after."   (No. 488, 15 August 1754)

"To be RUN for,

At Upper-Marlborough, *on Tuefday the* 8th *of* October *next,*

"A PRIZE of Twenty Pounds, by any Horfe, Mare, or Gelding, carrying Nine Stone Weight, the beft of Three Heats, each Heat to be once round the Poles on the Race Ground; and to pay Twenty Shillings Entrance Money. And,

"On Wednesday the 9th, will be run for, the Entrance Money, and what more fhall be fubfcribed; to pay Five Shillings Entrance. The winning Horfe the Day before to be excepted.

"The Horfes, &c. to be entered with *Benjamin Berry* and *Benjamin Brookes,* the Day before each Day of Running.

"All Difputes, if any fhould arife, to be determined by Gentlemen appointed for that Purpofe."   (No. 489, 19 September 1754)

"To be RUN for,

In the Old Fields near Bladenfburg, *on Tuefday the* 22d *of this Inftant,*

"A PRIZE of Ten Pounds Current Money, by any Horfe, Mare, or Gelding, bred in this Province, that never gain'd a Prize exceeding that Sum; each Horfe to carry Nine Stone, Horfe Man's Weight; to run three Heats, three Times round the Poles to each Heat (which is about two Mil"es); and to rub fifteen Minutes between the Heats.

The next Day, a Prize of Five Pounds Current Money, only the winning Horfe the firft Day excepted. The Horfes, &c. to be entered for the firft Day with *Thomas Chittam* the Day before Running, and to pay Ten Shillings Currency Entrance; and Five Shillings the next day, at Starting. All Difputes to be determined by Meffieurs *John Cooke* and *Bafil Waring,* who are to apply the Entrance Money as they think proper."

(No. 492, 10 October 1754)

* * *

George Hume, Virginia surveyor, refers to local horse racing in Culpepper County, Virginia, August 1754, in Hume to his brother, John Hume, 22 August 1754, in "Letters of Hume Family," William and Mary College Quarterly, 1st Series, Vol. 8, No. 1 (July 1899), 89.

"I have no oy^r news to tell you —money is so scarce it is a rare thing to see a dollar, and at publick places where great monied men will bet on cock fights, horse races, etc., ye noise is not now as it used to be—...."

* * *

The officers of William and Mary College, Virginia express their disapproval of horse racing among the students, 29 August 1754, and pass an ordinance against such, 14 September 1754, in "Journal of the Meetings of the President and Masters of William and Mary College," William and Mary Quarterly, 1st Series, Vol. 2, No. 1 (July 1893), 54-55; and Vol. 2, No. 2 (October 1893), 123.

"Aug, 29, 1754.
At a Meeting of the President and Masters of William and Mary College:
Present,
The Rev. W. Stith, President,
Mr Dawson, Mr Robinson, Mr Preston, Mr Graham and Mr Camm.

Mr Dawson is desired to acquaint Mr Kemp y^t ye President and Masters are very uneasy at his encourageing the boys to Engage in Racing, and other Diversions contrary to the Rules of the College, and that if he do not desist for ye future they are determined to make a proper Representation thereof to the Court."

"At a meeting of ye President & Masters of William & Mary College, Sepr ye 14th, 1754, present,

Y^e Revd Mr Stith, President, Mr Dawson, Mr Robinson, Mr Preston & Mr Graham, ye following Orders were unanimously agreed to.

1. Ordered y^t no scholar belonging to any school in the College, of w^t Age, Rank, or Quality, soever, do keep any race Horse, at ye College, in ye Town —or any where in the neighborhood— y^t they not be any way concerned in making races, or in backing, or abetting, those made by others, and y^t all Race Horses, kept in ye neighborhood of ye College & belonging to any of ye scholars be immediately dispatched & sent off, & never again brought back, and all this under Pain of ye severest Animadversion and Punishment."

* * *

Account of a horse race, Maryland Gazette, No. 488, 12 September 1754.

"Tuefday laft his Excellency's Gift of Twenty Pounds was Run for on our Race Ground. There were only Capt Hopper's *Horfe* Pleafure, *and Capt.*Gantt's *Horfe* Buffaloe, *who ftarted for the Prize, and it was won by the latter. And in the Evening there was a public Ball, where there was a fine Appearance of Ladies, and a great number of Gentlemen."*

* * *

Advertisement for a horse race, Virginia Gazette, No. 219, 21 March 1755.

"TO be RUN for, at *York*, on the firft *Thurfday* in *April*, Four Mile Heats, the beft Two in Three, carrying One Hundred and Thirty-five Pounds, a Purfe of Sixty-feven Piftoles.

"He who fubfcribes Four Piftoles, to pay One Piftole at Entrance.

"He who fubfcribes Three Piftoles, to pay Two

"He who fubfcribes Two Piftoles, to pay Three Piftoles at Entrance.

"He who fubfcribes One Piftole, to pay Four

"And a Non-Subfcriber to pay Ten

"The Horfes to be Enter'd, five Days before the Race, with *James Mitchel*, in *York*."

* * *

Advertisements for horse races, Maryland Gazette, 1755.

"To be RUN for,

ON Thurfday the 29th of this Inftant *May*, on the Race-Ground, at *Pig-Point*, the Sum of FIFTEEN POUNDS Current Money, by any Horfe, Mare, or Gelding, that never won a Prize of Ten Pounds Currency (or the Value thereof at any one Time before); each Horfe, &c. to be enter'd with *John Zachariah Allein* the Day before the Race, and to pay Fifteen Shillings Entrance Money, and to carry One Hundred and Twelve Pounds Weight, and to Run Three Heats, and each Heat Three Times round the Poles.

"And alfo to be Run for on Friday the 30th Inftant, the Sum of TEN POUNDS Currency; each Horfe, &c. to pay Ten Shillings Entrance Money. The winning Horfe, &c. the Day before to be excepted; and to Run on the fame Terms as above.

"Any Difputes arifing, to be determined by Gentlemen appointed for that Purpofe."
(No. 523, 15 May 1755)

"To be RUN for,

"ON Thurfday the 6th Day of *November* next enfuing, by any Horfe, Mare, or Gelding, that never won the Sum of Ten Shillings at any one Time, to run from Capt. *Thomas Harwood*'s near Gate on the Road leading to *Jonathan Rawling*'s, by a Stake fix'd for that Purpofe, the Sum of EIGHT POUNDS Current Money; each Horfe, &c.to carry One Hundred and Twenty-fix Pounds, to run Three Heats, the laft Two in Three, faving his Diftance, which is Twenty Yards.

"The fecond Day, the Entrance Money and what can be raifed between this and then, to be Run for, carrying Weight and Diftance as above, &c. &c. All Difputes to be determined by Meffieurs *Ifaac James* and *John Conner*. The Horfes to be entered with *Jonathan Rawlings* the day before the Race, paying Eight Shillings Entrance Money."
(No. 546, 23 October 1755)

* * *

Advertisement for a horse race, Virginia Gazette, No. 294, 27 August 1756.

"TO be run at *Leeds* Town, the third *Thurfday* in *September* next, a Sweep-ftakes Match, for 200 Piftoles, by *America* bred Horfes, five Years old, a four Mile Heat, carrying 10 Stone; and the next Day a Match for 50 Piftoles by *Virginia* bred Horfes.

Mark Talbot."

* * *

Elizabeth Hill Carter Byrd, Virginia planter's wife, informs her husband, stationed in Fort Pitt, of local horse race results, May 1757, in Byrd to William Byrd III, 13 May 1757, reprinted in "Letters of the Byrd Family," Virginia Magazine of History and Biography, Vol. 37, No. 3 (July 1929), 242.

"Your horse Valient has lost the Race, that Mr. Page & Mr. Lewis made with Mr Boothe. My Calista has a very handsome filly."

* * *

Advertisement for a horse race, Maryland Gazette, No. 641, 18 August 1757.

"TOP BE RUN FOR,
On the Second *TUESDAY* of OCTOBER,
at UPPER MARLBOROUGH,

"A PRIZE of THIRTY POUNDS, by any Horfe, Mare, or Gelding, (that never won a Prize of Ten Pounds Value) the beft of Three Heats, Two Miles each Heat, to carry One Hundred and Twenty-fix Pounds.

"And on the Wednefday following, a PRIZE of FIFTEEN POUNDS on the fame Terms as the firft Day; the winning Horfe only to be excepted.

"Any Perfon, not a Subfcriber, to pay Thirty Shillings Entrance the Firft Day, ad Fifteen Shillings the next Day. If a Subfcriber, to pay only Fifteen Shillings the Firft Day, and Seven Shillings and Six Pence the next.

"The Horfes, &c.to be Entered the Day before Running with *Benjamin Berry* or *Benjamin Brooker*, and the Riders to be weighed on the Day of Entrance by the Judges.

"All Difputes to be determined by Meffieurs *John Cooke* and *Jofeph Sim.*"

* * *

Advertisement for a horse race, Virginia Gazette, No. 347, 2 September 1757.

"ON the Third *Thurfday* in September next, the Sweepstakes Race for 100 Piftoles will be run for (as ufual) at *Leeds* Town; and the Day following a Gold Watch of 20 Pounds Value will be fet up by   *Mark Talbot.*"

* * *

Advertisement for a horse race, Maryland Gazette, No. 689, 20 July 1758.

"TO BE RUN FOR,
On the Seventeenth Day of OCTOBER *next*,

"A PURSE of THIRTY PISTOLES, on the Race-Ground near the City of *Annapolis*, by any Horfe, Mare, or Gelding, that never won at one Time, any Purfe or Match above One Hundred Piftoles. The Weight to be 120 *lbs*. The Winner to have the beft of Three Heats. One Piftole and a Half to be paid at Entrance with Jonas Green Four Days before the Race, or Two Piftoles at the Poft. If Three reputed Running Horfes fhould not Enter, to be no Race: If only One or Two Enter, each of them to receive Five Piftoles. All Difputes to be determined by proper Judges, to be appointed.

"*N.B.* 'Tis expected that on the next Day, there will be a Purfe of TWENTY PISTOLES; the winning Horfe on the firft Day to be excluded."

* * *

Advertisement for a horse race, Maryland Gazette, No. 724, 22 March 1759.

"To be RUN for,
On Tuefday the 17th of April *next*,

"AT *Walter Maddox*'s Old-Fields in *Charles* County, by any Horfe, Mare, or Gelding, that never won the Value of Fifty Piftoles (true Bred Horfes only excepted) Five Piftoles to the Purfe, and one Guinea Entrance.   FRANCIS TRIPLETT."

* * *

Andrew Burnaby, Anglican minister, remarks about the horses and horse racing in Virginia, July 1759, in Burnaby, *Travels through the Middle Settlements of North America in the Years 1759 and 1760* (London: T. Payne, 1775), 11.

"The horfes are fleet and beautiful; and the gentlemen of Virginia, who are exceedingly fond of horfe-racing, have fpared no expence or trouble to improve the breed of them by importing great numbers from England."

* * *

Advertisements for a horse race, Maryland Gazette, No. 751, 27 September 1759.

"ON the Twenty-third Day of *October* next, will be Run for, at *Frederick-Town* in *Frederick* County, a Purfe of THIRTY POUNDS, by any Horfe, Mare, or Gelding.

"On the Twenty-fourth, all the Entrance and what other Money may be made up; the winning Horfe the firft Day excepted.

"Each Horfe to carry Nine Stone Weight, to Run Three Heats, Two Miles each Heat.

"If any Difputes fhall arife, the fame to be determined by Meffieurs *James Dixon* and *Chriftopher Edelin.*

"Every Horfe, &c. to be Entered with Mr. *Arthur Charlton* in the Town aforefaid, the Day before the Race, and the Owners to pay Thirty Shillings Entrance Money."

"TO BE RUN FOR,
On the ufual Race-Ground at Upper-Marlborough,

"ON the Firft Tuefday of *November* next, by any Horfe, Mare or Gelding, carrying Nine Stone, a Purfe of THIRTY POUNDS, the beft in Three Heats, about Two Miles each Heat.

"Meffieurs *John Cooke* and *Bafil Warring* are to be Judges of the faid Race, and to determine all Difputes which may arife thereon.

"Each Running Horfe to pay Thirty Shillings Entrance Money, and be Entered with Mr. *Benjamin Berry* or Mr. *Benjamin Brooke*, the Day before the Race.

"And alfo to be Run for the Day following, by any Horfe, Mare or Gelding (the winning Horfe of the Firft Day Excepted) all the Entrance and what other Money may be made up by Subcfription, which, at this Time, is not compleated, carrying the fame Weight, and on the fame Terms, with the Horfes of the Firft Day."

* * *

Advertisements for horse races, Maryland Gazette, 1760.

"TO BE RUN FOR,
At the ufual Race Ground, near Alexandria, *on*
Thurfday, the 29th Day of May *next,*

"A PURSE of THIRTY POUNDS, the beft in three Heats, (three Times round the Ground, which is about two Miles and a Half each Heat), by any Horfe, Mare, or Gelding, 14 Hands to carry ten Stone, or below that Meafure, Weight for Inches.

"And on Friday the 30th will be run for, a Purfe of Fifteen Pounds, by any Horfe, &c. 14 Hands carrying nine Stone, or below that Meafure, Weight for Inches.

"The Horfes to be entered on the Monday before at the Court-Houfe, with Meffrs. *Carlyle, Adams,* and *Hunter,*between the Hours of Two and Six o'Clock in the Afternoon. The Entrance Money to be paid for the firft Race, Thirty Shillings for each Horfe, &c. And for the fecond, Fifteen Shillings each.

"Proper Judges will be appointed to determine any Difputes which may arife.

"Three Horfes to Enter and Start or no Race.   (No. 779, 10 April 1760)

"Queen's-Town, July 12, 1760.

"WHEREAS a RACE for ONE HUNDRED POUNDS, is to be Run for at *Queen's-Town*, on Thurfday the 31ft Inftant, between Mr. *Edward Neale's* Black Horfe, and Mr. *Thomas Hamar's Lively Grey:* The Subfcriber thinks it a Duty incumbent on him to inform his Friends and Cuftomers, That they are to Run the Heats (Half Mile each Heat): The coming in Place is at the Subfcriber's; where all Gentlemen, who are fo kind as to Honour him with the Favour of their Cuftom, may depend on having the beft in Quantity and Quality, from

Their moft humble Servant,
MICHAEL FLOWER."

(No. 793, 17 July 1760)

"TO BE RUN FOR,

On Thurfday the Fourth Day of September, *at the Plantation of Mr.* George Frafer, *about a Mile below* Pifcattaway, *by any Horfe, Mare or Gelding, that never run round the Poles for any Purfe or other Wager,*

"A PURSE of FIFTEEN POUNDS, the Beft in Three Heats, Three Times round the Poles, which is about Two Miles each Heat. A Horfe of Fourteen Hands high to carry Nine Stone Weight, and to rife and fall according to Size.

"The Second Day, a Purfe of Five Pounds, and the Entrance-Money of both Days, to be Run for, by any Horfe the firft Day excepted.

"The Horfes to be Entered the Monday before the Race with Meffieurs *Baynes* and *Bowden.*

"The Entrance Money to be paid for the firft Race, Fifteen Shillings each Horfe, &c. and for the fecond Day Seven Shillings and Six Pence each.

"Proper Judges will be appointed to determine any Difputes which may arife."

(No. 795, 31 July 1760)

"TO BE RUN FOR,

On Thurfday the 30th Day of October, *at the Plantation of Mr.* Thomas Johns, *about three Miles above* George-Town *in* Frederick County, *by any Horfe, Mare, or Gelding, that never ftarted round the Poles for any Purfe or other Wager,*

"A PURSE of TWENTY POUNDS, the beft in Three Heats, Three Times round the Poles, which is about two Miles each Heat. A Horfe of Fourteen Hands to carry Nine Stone Weight, and to rife and fall according to Size.

"The fecond Day the Entrance Money to be Run for, on the fame Terms as the firft Day; the winning Horfe only excepted

"The Horfes, &c. to be Entered the Day before running, with Meffr's *Jofeph Belt* and *John Orme* in *George-Town.* The Entrance Money the firft Day Fifteen Shillings, and Seven Shillings and Six Pence the fecond Day.

"Any Difputes which may arife, are to be determined by Meffrs. *Thomas Johns* and *Walter Evans.*" (No. 803, 25 September 1760)

"TO BE RUN FOR,

At the Race-Ground in Frederick-Town, *on Monday the Twentieth Day of* October, *by any Horfe, Mare, or Gelding,*

"A PURSE of FIFTEEN POUNDS, the beft in Three Heats, which is about Two Miles each Heat, and each Horfe, &c. to carry One Hundred and Forty Pounds.

"On the fecond Day, a Purfe of Ten Pounds to be Run for, on the fame Terms as the firft Day; the winning Horfe only excepted. And,

"On the the Third Day, the Entrance Money of the firft and fecond Days to be Run for on the fame Terms; the winning Horfes only excepted.

"The Horfes, &c. to be Entered the Day before Running with Mr. *Arthur Charlton.*

"The Entrance Money the firft Day Fifteen Shillings, the fecond Day Ten Shillings, and in proportion for the third.

"Any Difputes which may arife, are to be determined by Meffrs. *Chriftopher Edelin* and *John Cary.*" (No. 805, 9 October 1760)

* * *

Account of a horse race, Virginia Gazette?, 11 April 1760, reprinted in "Notes From Colonial Newspapers," Virginia Magazine of History and Biography, Vol. 16, No. 2 (October 1908), 207.

"On the the 3rd Inst. [the] 50£ subscription [race was run] at Warwick.

	Heats
Mr. Hardiman's sorrel h. Pilot	5. 5. I. 0. I
Col. Randolph's Fortunatus	6. I. 2. 0. 2
Mr. Braxton's b. h. Tryall	3. 2. 2.
Mr. Edloe's Silvertail	I. 3. dr.
Mr. Jones's b. h. Page	2. 4. 4. dr.
Mr. Turnbull's bl. h. Othello	4. dist.

First heat was easy. 2nd warmly disputed. 4th couldn't be decided. 5th won by five feet.

Never was finer sport shown."

* * *

Advertisements for horse races, Maryland Gazette, 1761.

"ANNAPOLIS RACES.
ONE HUNDRED & TWENTY DOLLARS.

"TO be Run for, on the OLD RACE-GROUND IN THE CITY OF *ANNAPOLIS*, on Thurfday the Seventh Day of May next, by any Horfe, Mare or Gelding, not extending Four Years old, carrying Eight Stone each, Three Times round the Poles (being about Two Miles) the beft in Three Heats, A PURSE of EIGHTY DOLLARS. Twenty Shillings Entrance to be paid for each Horfe, &c. unlefs belonging to a Perfon who has Subfcribed that Sum at leaft; and to be Entered the Day before the Race, otherwife to pay double Entrance.

"And on the next Day, will be Run for, on the fame Ground, the fame Diftance, and with the fame Weight, by any Horfe, &c. of the above Age (the winning Horfe on the preceding Day only excepted) a PURSE of FORTY DOLLARS. Each paying one Dollar Entrance.

"The Horfes, &c. to be Entered with JONAS GREEN, who is appointed Judge, to determine all Differences that may arife."   (No. 826, 5 March 1761)

"TO BE RUN FOR,
On Thurfday the 28th Day of May, on the ufual
Race Ground at ALEXANDRIA.

"A PURSE of FIFTY POUNDS, Three Times round the Ground (being near three Miles) the beft in Three heats, by any Horfe, Mare, or Gelding, 14 Hands to carry 10 Stone, below that Meafure, Weight for Inches.

"And, on the Day following, will be Run for, on the fame Ground and Diftance, A PURSE of TWENTY-FIVE POUNDS, by Four Year old Colts, 14 Hands to carry Stone, below that Meafure, Weight for Inches

"The Horfes to be Entered on the Monday before the Race with the Managers, Mr. *George Wafhington*, Mr. *John Carlyle*, and Mr. *Charles Digges:* Each Horfe to pay Fifty Shillings Entrance on the Firft Day, and Twenty-five Shillings the Second Day; and thofe who do not enter their Horfes on the Monday aforefaid, to pay double Entrance.

"Three Horfes to Start or no Race.

"All Differences that may arife, will be decided by the Managers."

(No. 833, 23 April 1761)

"TO BE RUN FOR,

On Thurfday the Tenth of September, *at* PIG POINT,

"A PURSE of TEN POUNDS, by any Horfe, Mare, or Gelding, that never Run for 4 *l.* or the Value of 4 *l.* at any one Time, the *Englifh* Blood, and a Sorrel Stallion belonging to John Elliott, excepted, to carry 100 *lb.* Weight, the Beft Two in Three Heats round the Poles. The Horfes, *&c.* to be entered the Day before the Race with

RICHARD WELLS.

"*N.B.* The Entrance Money to be Run for the Second Day, on the fame Terms as above."   (No. 849, 13 August 1761)

"*Leonard-Town, Auguft* 17, 1761.

"TO be Run for, on Tuefday the 29th Day of September, on the ufual Race-Ground at *LEONARD-TOWN*, the beft of Three Heats, twice round the Ground for each Heat, being about Two Miles, A Purfe of FORTY POUNDS, by any Horfe, Mare or Gelding, that never before won a Purfe of Twenty Pounds, or the Value thereof. Horfes of 14 Hands to carry 10 Stone, and below that Meafure, Weight for Inches, feven Pounds to be allowed for each Inch.

"On the Day following will be Run for, on the fame Ground and Diftance, A Purfe of about FIFTEEN POUNDS, by any Colts, not exceeding Four Years old, the winning Horfe the preceding Day only excepted, each Colt to carry eight Stone.

"The Horfes to be Entered on the Day before the Race with *Timothy Bowes*; each Horfe, for the firft Day, to pay Forty Shillings Entrance, (which Entrance Money will be applied towards making up the Purfe for the fecond Day). Ten Shillings to be paid for each Horfe Entered for the fecond Day, which Entrance Money will be given to the Second Beft Horfe. Thofe who do not Enter their Horfes on the Day appointed, to pay double Entrance.

"No Race unlefs Three Horfes Start.

"All Differences that may arife will be determined by Meffieurs *George Plater*, *Normand Bruce*, and *Thompfon Mafon*, Managers."   (No. 850, 20 August 1761)

"TO BE RUN FOR,

On the Third Thurfday in October *next, on the ufual Race-Ground near* GEORGE-TOWN, in *Frederick* County,

"A PURSE of TWENTY-FIVE POUNDS, by any Horfe, Mare, or Gelding, that never ftarted further than a Quarter of a Mile for any Sum.

"And, on the Day following, the Entrance Money of both Days, and what other Money may be made up, on the fame Terms as the firft Day (the winning Horfse the preceding Day only excepted). Horfes 14 Hands high to carry Nine Stone, and to raife or fall according to the common Rules of Racing.

"The Diftance to be Run about Two Miles to a Heat, Three Times round the Poles, the two beft Heats in three to win the Race.

"Three Horfes to Start or no Race.

"The Entrance Money the firft Day Twenty Shillings, and Ten Shillings the fecond Day.

"The Horfes to be Entered the Day before Running, with Meffieurs *Jofeph Belt* and *John Orme,* or pay double Entrance if entered the Day of Running.

"All Differences that may arife will be determined by Meffieurs *Thomas Johns* and *Walter Evans,* who are appointed Managers.

"The Horfes to Start precifely by II o'Clock."   (No. 852, 3 September 1761)

"TO BE RUN FOR,
On the ufual Race-Ground at Upper-Marlborough,

"ON Tuefday the Twentieth of October next, the beft in Three Heats, each Heat three Rounds, by any Horfe, Mare, or Gelding, the Sum of THIRTY POUNDS: Each Horfe, &c. to carry 126 *lbs.* and to pay Forty Shillings Entrance Money, or Twenty Shillings to Subfcribers, and to be Entered the Day before Running, with Mr. *Brookes,* or Mr. *Scott.*

"And on the Day following will be Run for, on the fame Race-Ground, by any Horfe, &c. (the winning Horfe the firft Day excepted) the Entrance Money, and what elfe fhall be made up by Subfcription, to carry 126 *lbs.*

"Entrance the fecond Day Twenty Shillings, or Ten Shillings to Subfcribers.

"Piftoles, Dollars, or Pennfylvania Money to be received and paid.

"All Difputes arifing to be fettled by Judges to be appointed before the Day of Running."   (No. 853, 10 September 1761)

"TO BE RUN FOR,
On Thurfday the Fifteenth of October, *at* JOPPA
in BALTIMORE County,

"A PRIZE of THIRTY POUNDS, by any Horfe, Mare, or Gelding, the Beft of Three Heats, Two Rounds to each Heat, to carry 126 *lbs.* The Horfes, &c. to be Entered with Mr. *Henry James* Three Days before the Race, or to pay double Entrance.

"On Friday the 16th, a PRIZE of FIFTEEN POUNDS, by any Horfe, Mare, or Gelding. (the winning Horfe the preceding Day excepted) to carry the fame Weight. Each Horfe, &c. to pay Fifteen Shillings Entrance, and to be Entered the day before the firft Race, or not allowed to Enter.

"And on Saturday will be Run for, on the fame Ground and Diftance, by any Colts not exceeding four Years old Leaft Spring, all the Entrance Money of the two preceding Days, and to catch Riders."   (No. 853, 10 September 1761)

"Baltimore-Town, Sept. 1, 1761.

TO BE RUN FOR,
On the Second Thurfday, Friday, and Saturday, *in* October *next, on the ufual Race-Ground at* BALTIMORE-TOWN,

"THE PURSES as follows:

"The firft day, the beft in Three Heats, Three Times round the Ground for each Heat, being about Two Miles, a Purfe of TWENTY-FIVE POUNDS, by any Horfe, Mare, or Gelding, to carry Nine Stone.

"The Second Day, to be Run for, on the fame Ground and Diftance, a Purfe of EIGHTEEN POUNDS, by any Horfe, Mare, or Gelding, the winning Horfe the preceding Day only excepted, to carry Weight for Inches, the Standard to be the fame Weight as aforefaid, to carry Fourteen Pounds for the firft Inch, and Seven Pounds for every Inch afterwards.

"The Third Day, on the aforefaid Ground, Twice round for a Heat, to be Run for by any Horfe, Mare, or Gelding, under Four Years old, a Purfe of TWELVE POUNDS, to carry the fame Weight mentioned as above.

"The Horfes, &c. to be Entered the Day before the Race with *William Lux*. Each Horfe, &c. for the firft Day to pay Twenty-five Shillings; for the second day Twenty Shillings; and for the Third Day Twelve Shillings, Entrance Money; which Entrance Money will be applied towards making up higher Purfes for the Second and Third Days.

"Thofe who do not Enter their Horfes on the Day appointed, to pay double Entrance."   WILLIAM LUX, Manager."

(No. 854, 17 September 1761)

"TO BE RUN FOR,

On Thurfday the 29th of October *Inftant, at Mr.* Thomas Chittam'*s Pafture, near* Bladenfburg *in* Prince George's *County,*

"A PURSE of TWENTY POUNDS, by any Horfe, Mare, or Gelding, that never won a Prize of Five Pounds Value by running the Heats (full bred Horfes exepted).

"And the Day following, the Sum of TEN POUNDS, on the fame Terms as the firft Day, (the winning Horfe the preceding Day only excepted).

"Horfes Fourteen Hands to carry Nine Stone, and to raife or fall according to the common Rules of Racing. The Diftance to be Run about Two Miles to a Heat, Three Times round the Poles, the Two Beft Heats in Three to win the Race. The Entrance-Money the firft Day Twenty Shillings, and Ten Shillings the fecond Day. The Horfes to be Entered the Day before Running with Mr. *Thomas Chittam*, or to pay Double Entrance if Entered on the Day of Running.

"All Differences that may arife, will be determined by Meffieurs *Bafil Waring* and *John Hill*, who are appointed Judges.

"The Horfes to ftart precifely by Two o'Clock each Day."

(No. 857, 8 October 1761)

* * *

Joseph Doddridge, Pennsylvania Episcopalian minister, comments on horse racing concerning the western settlements of Virginia, circa 1763-1783, in Doddridge, *Notes on the Settlement and Indian Wars of the Western Parts of Virginia and Pennsylvania from 1763 and 1783, inclusive, together with a Review of the State of Society and Manners of the First Settlers of the Western Country* (Pittsburgh: John S. Ritenour and William T. Lindsey, 1912), 121-122.

"Horse racing is regarded by the statesman as a preparation, in various ways, for the equestrian department of warfare; it is said that the English government never possessed a good cavalry until by the encouragement given to public races, their breed of horses was improved."

* * *

Advertisement for a horse race, Maryland Gazette, No. 1057, 8 August 1765.

"*OXFORD* RACES.

"TO be Run for, over the Courfe of this Town, on Thurfday the Third of *October* next, by any Horfe, Mare, or Gelding, not being more than half bred, A Purfe of EIGHTY DOLLARS, on the following Terms, *viz.* Four Years old to carry 8 Stone 8 Pounds; Five years old, 9 Stone, 4 Pounds; Six Years old and upwards, 10 Stone,

Saddle and Bridle included; to Run Two Mile Heats, the Horfe, &c. winning two Heats, to be intitled to the Purfe. And,

"On the Day following will be Run for, the fame Diftance, and on the fame Terms, A Purfe of THIRTY DOLLARS, by Country Horfes only.

"The Whole to be conducted agreeable to his Majesty's Articles.

"The Horfes to be Entered two Days before the Race, with Mr. *Jacob Bromwell*, and to Pay (if a Subfcriber of Twenty Shillings) Two Dollars, if a Non-Subfcriber, Fur Dollars, or Eight Dollars Entrance at the Poft.

"Proper Certificates of the Age and Pedigree of the Horfes, muft be produced to Qualify them to Start."

* * *

Robert Page, Hanover County, Virginia planters expresses in his will his wishes to keep his sons from horse races, 15 August 1765, reprinted in "Wills of Robert and John Page," Virginia Magazine of History and Biography, Vol. 34, No. 3 (July 1926), 276.

"I desire my brother Mann and John Page with my dearest wife may be my Executors and I desire neither of my sons may ever be allowed to go to Horse Races or Cock Fights, or to any other public diversion as they are only consuming of time & that all my children may be piously brought up to that one and only thing necessary religion. Robert Page, Thursday, Augt. 15, 1765."

* * *

Accounts of horse races, Virginia Gazette, 1766.

"WILLIAMSBURG, April 25.

"Yefterday the Williamfburg purfe of 100l. was run for, and won with eafe by Traveller, the property of the Hon. John Tayloe, Efq; the horfes that ftarted Againft him were John Difmal and Janus, the former belonging to Lewis Burwell, Efq; the latter to Francis Whiting, Efq.; who was withdrawn after the firft heat."

(No. 779, 25 April 1766)

"On Thurfday fe'nnight was run for, at Pride's race ground near Peterfburg, a purfe of 100 l. by Lewis Burwell, Efq. of Glo'fter's bay horfe Janus, who won the firft heat, a bay horfe belonging to Thomas Randolph, Efq. who came in fecond, Col. William Byrd's bay horfe, who was next, and a bay mare the property of Mr George Nicholas; fhe was diftanced the firft heat. Mr. Randolph's horfe won the fecond and third heats; and it was judged the courfe was run fwifter than ever it had been before.

"Merry Tom was fhown on the turf that day, as a covering horfe, with great applaufe."   (No. 782, 16 May 1766)

"WILLIAMSBURG, October 24.

"Yefterday the purfe of 100 l. was run for, at the race ground near this city, by Col. Tayloe's horfe Hero, Col. Byrd's horfe Valiant Tryall, and Mark Anthony, a horfe belonging to Richard Lee, Efquire. There were only two heats, in the firft of which Mark Anthony was diftanced, and the purfe won by Hero."   (No. 805, 24 October 1766)

* * *

Advertisement for a horse race, Virginia Gazette, No. 799, 12 September 1766.

"Frederickfburg Races.

"ON Thurfday the 9th day of *October* a purfe of twenty pounds, ready money, to be run for by any horfe, mare, or gelding, not more than quarter blooded, the beft of three four mile heats, or as near that diftance as the ground will admit of, carrying nine ftone for 14 hands, give and take feven pounds for each inch above or below that fize.

"And on *Friday* the 10th day of *October* a purfe of ten pounds, ready money, to be run for by any horfe, mare, or gelding, that has not any mixture of the *Englifh* or foreign breed, the beft of three two mile heats, or as near that diftance as the ground will admit of, carrying the fame weight, give and take, as for the above purfe.

"The horfes that are to ftart for either of the above purfes are to be entered, fhown, and meafured, at Capt. *George Weedon*'s, on the *Monday* preceding the races, paying for the firft purfe 20 s. and for the fecond 10 s. which entrance money is to be given to the fecond beft horfe, &c. running for each purfe, according to the rules of racing, to be adjudged by Gentlemen appointed by the fubfcribers, who are alfo to regulate every matter on the field, and determine any difputes that may arife.

"Three horfes are to enter and ftart, or no race, and no entrance will be allowed at the pole, or any time after the day fixed for that purpofe. There will alfo be fundry other diverfions; and it is propofed, on the firft race day, to hand about a fubfcription for future races at *Frederickfburg*, on fuch terms as may be moft agreeable to the Gentlemen prefent, who are encouragers of the turf."

* * *

Accounts of a horse race, Rind's Virginia Gazette, 1766.

"The PURSE which was mentioned in this Paper to be run at *Chefter* in *Maryland* by SELIM and YORICK, was won by the former." (No. 30, 4 December 1766)

"Williamsburg, *December* 11.

"We hear from *Cheftertown* in *Maryland*, that the Race there which engaged the fporting Community fo deeply, was won by SELIM, perhaps more by Contrivance than Superiority of Goodnefs; for tho' it was calculated to bring him and YORICK together, it was not made upon equal Terms, he being Seven, and *Yorick* Six Years old, yet both carried equal Weight; wheras, by *Newmarket* Rules, 10 ft fhould have been allowed. This Confideration would have prevented his going over, had not his Owner received a Letter, acquainting him of a Bett of Five Hundred Pounds being made, and that an honeft Groom of Jugment was fent on Purpofe to take Care of the Horfe, knowing the Gentleman's own Groom was then engaged, who, when he got to his Horfe a few Days before running, found he had been abufed by a Fall, and that in Fact no fuch Bett was made, fo that *Yorick* can have loft nothing of his Reputation in the Opinion of good Judges, as he came very near his Antagonift (who ran for a Diftance at the End, under all thofe Difadvantages but admitting him to have been fairly beaten, it can be no Difgrace, when the Pedigree and Performances of the Victor (with all other Circumftances) are duly confidered." (No. 31, 11 December 1766)

* * *

Advertisement for a horse race, Rind's Virginia Gazette, No. 41, 19 February 1767.

"A SWEEPSTAKE RACE
to be run for annually,

"ON the day before the 4th *Thurfday* in *October*, at the Seat of Government in *Virginia*, for the Term of Seven Years, to commence in *October*, 1768, one 4 Mile Heat. Four Years old, carrying Nine Stone, Five Years old Ten Stone, and all above that Age Ten Stone Ten Pounds. Fillies to be allowed Four Pounds in Weight. Any Perfon may enter for any particular Year, paying double Stakes for that Year, and ftanding afterwards as Subfcribers. Free only for Subfcribers to ftart for or receive any Benefit from. The Horfes fhown with proper Certificates on the Monday before running, and the Money then to be depofited with Mr. *Anthony Hay*, and the Owners neglecting to be excluded from any Right to ftart for that or any other Race, but neverthelefs to pay their Subfcriptions yearly. To run fair, agreeable to the King's Plate Rules of Racing at Newmarket, and all Difputes to be decided by the other diftinguifhed Subfcribers.

"Those Gentlemen who have an inclination to become Subfcribers for the above mentioned Race, on the Plan propofed, are defired to fend their Names to Mr. AN-THONY HAY, in *Williamsburg*."

* * *

Accounts of horse races, Virginia Gazette, 1767.

"WILLIAMSBURG, *May* 28.

On Thurfday fe'nnight a purfe of 100l. was run for, at the race ground near Peterfburg, by Col.Baylor's brown colt got by Sober John, 4 years old, Col. John Cocke's bay filly got by Janus, 3 years old, and Col. Alexander Bollings' bay colt of 4 years old, who, being lame, was diftanced the firft heat. It was a fmart race between the other two, but Col. Baylor's colt won both heats." (No. 836, 28 May 1767)

"On Thurfday laft Valiant Tryall, the property of the Hon. William Byrd, Efq. won the 100l. purfe at the race ground near this city, with great eafe, againft Col. Baylor's horfe Britannicus, and Young Briton, belonging to the eftate of the Hon. Philip Ludwell, deceafed." (No. 858, 29 October 1767)

"On Tuefday laft, about one o'clock in the afternoon, ftarted for the Gentlemen's fubfcription purfe of one hundred guineas, carrying nine ftone, the following horfes, viz. Selim, Colt Granby, Old England, and Northumberland. Granby led two miles and a half, then Selim and Old England paffed him; Selim won the heat by a little, and ran in eight minutes. Northumberland was diftanced. The fecond heat Granby did not ftart, and Old England ran Selim fmartly for near three miles, when, being hard pufhed, he flew the courfe, and Selim won the heat eafy.

"Odds at ftarting, three to two Selim againft the field, and two to one Selim beat the Colt Granby the firft heat.

"On Friday laft the Ladies purfe, of fifty pounds, free for three year olds only, to carry eight ftone, was run for by the following horfes, viz. Chatham, by Selim; Nonpareil, by Dove; Lady Legs, by Briton; which was won hollow by the latter.

"Odds at ftarting, five to three Chatham againft the field.

"On Saturday laft the city purfe, of fifty pounds, was run for, weight for age, by the following horfes, viz. Marquis, by Ariel; Tryall, by Othello; Hector, by Ariel; Carelefs, by Bully Rock; Strumpet, by Briton; Fearnought, by Ariel. Strumpet won both heats hollow.

"At ftarting, Strumpet taken againft the field for the firft heat; and fecond, odss three to two fhe won." (No. 859, 5 November 1767)

* * *

Advertisement for a horse race, Virginia Gazette, No. 873, 11 February 1768.

"*Maryland, Jan.* 22, 1768.
"PRINCE-GEORGE's county RACES.

"ON *Wednefday* the 4th of *May* next, will be run for, over the courfe near *Upper Marlborough*, a fubfcription purfe of ONE HUNDRED POUNDS currency, free for any horfe, mare or gelding, rifing 4 years old to carry 8 ftone (bridle and faddle included) if five years old, 8 ftone 10 pounds, if fix, 9 ftone 6 pounds, and if aged, 10 ftone.

"On the day following, will be run for, on the fame terms, a purfe of twenty five pounds currency, the winning horfe, the preceding day, excepted:—To run for the purfes agreeable to the King's plate articles.—Start precifely at 2 o'clock each day, and enter with Mr. *Benjamin Brookes* on *Monday* the fecond, when each party muft name and produce a certificate of the age of what he propofes to ftart.—Each jockey to appear with a neat waiftcoat, cap and half boots. A horfe winning two clear heats, fhall not be obliged to ftart a third. Any jockey detected in unfair behaviour, fhall be deemed diftanced—Non fubfcribers to pay five pounds entrance for the firft day, and twenty five fhillings for the fecond—Subfcribers three pounds for the firft day, and fifteen fhillings for the fecond. Judges will be appointed, to determine all difputes, and the money to be paid as foon as they fhall pronounce their decifion.

"*N.B.* On Tuefday the third, a match will be run over the courfe, for 50 guineas."

* * *

Advertisements for horse races, Maryland Gazette, 1768.

"*January* 22, 1768.
"PRINCE-GEORGE's COUNTY RACES.

"ON Wednefday the 4th Day of *May* next, will be run for, over the Courfe, near *Upper Marlborough*, a SUBSCRIPTION PURSE of ONE HUNDRED POUNDS Currency, free for any Horfe, Mare, or Gelding. If rifing Four Years old, to carry Eight Stone, (Bridle and Saddle included) if Five Years old, Eight Stone Ten Pounds; if Six, Nine Stone Six Pounds; and, if aged, Ten Stone.

"On the Day following will be run for, on the fame Terms, a Purfe of TWENTY-FIVE POUNDS Currency, the winning Horfe the preceding Day excepted.

"To run for the Purfes agreeable to the King's Plate Articles. Start precifely at Two o'Clock each Day, and enter with Mr. BENJAMIN BROOKS, on Monday the Second; when each Party muft name and produce a Certificate of the Age of what he propofes to ftart. Each Jockey to appear with a neat Wiaftcoat, and Half-Boots. A Horfe winning Two clear Heats, fhall not be obliged to ftart a Third. Any Jockey detected in unfair Behaviour, fhall be deemed diftanced. Non-Subfcribers to pay Five Pounds Entrance, for the Firft Day, and Twenty-five Shillings for the Second. Subfcribers, Three Pounds, for the Firft Day, and Fifteen Shillings for the Second, or double at the Poft. Judges will be appointed to determine all Difputes; and the Money to be paid as foon as they fhall pronounce their Decifion.

"N.B. On Tuefday the Third of *May*, a Match will be run over the fame Courfe, for FIFTY GUINEAS. (No. 1181, 28 April 1768)

"ON the 30th Inftant, will be run for, at *Pig-Point*, a SUBSCRIPTION PURSE of TWENTY POUNS Currency, the beft of Three Heats, Three Times round the Ground to each Heat; Four Years old, to carry Eight Stone; Five Years old, Nine Stone; Six Years old, and upwards, Ten Stone, Saddle and Bridle included; the Horfe winning Two Heats, and faving his Diftance the Third, to be entitled to the Purfe.

"On the Day following, will be run for, over the fame Courfe, the Entrance Money of both Days, with what other Money may be made up; on the fame Conditions as the firft Day's Race; the winning Horfe the firft Day only excepted. Twenty Minutes will be allowed for Rubbing, between each Heat. The Horfes to be entered the Saturday before the Race, with Mr. *Richard Wells*, and to pay Twenty Shillings for the Firſt Day, and Fifteen Shillings for the Second Day; or, if entered at the Pole, to pay double Entrance. All Diſputes that may ariſe, to be determined by Judges appointed for that Purpoſe. —The Horſes to ſtart between the Hours of One and Two o'Clock.

"Three reputed Horſes to ſtart, or no Race."　　　　　　(No. 1183, 12 May 1768)

"*April* 18, 1768.

"FREDERICK COUNTY RACES.

"ON Tueſday the 24th of *May* next, will be run for, near *George-Town*, a SUB-SCRIPTION PURSE of TWENTY-FIVE POUNDS, free for any Horſe, mare, or Geld-ing: A Horſe of 14 Hands, to carry One Hundred and Twenty-ſix Pounds, Saddle and Bridle included, and to riſe and fall according to the Rules of Racing. —On the Day following, will be run for, on the ſame Terms, a PURSE of TWELVE POUNDS TEN SHILLINGS, the winning Horſe the preceeding Day excepted: To ſtart between Two and Three o'Clock each Day, and entered with Meſſieurs *Joſeph Belt*, or *John Orme*, the preceding Day of each Race. A Horſe winning Two clear Heats, and ſaving his Diſ-tance the Third, ſhall be entitled to the Money. Any Jockey detected in unfair Behaviour, ſhall be deemed diſtanced. —To pay One Pound Five Shillings for the firſt day's Entrance, and Twelve Shillings and Six-pence for the Second; or double at the Poſt. Judges will be appointed to determine all Diſputes, and the Money to be paid as ſoon as they ſhall pronounce their Deciſion. Three reputed running Horſes to ſtart, or no Race. To run the Two Mile Heats."　　　　　　(No. 1183, 12 May 1768)

* * *

Accounts of horse races, Maryland Gazette, 1768.

"Yeſterday a Subſcription Purſe of ONE HUNDRED POUNDS Currency, was run over the Courſe near *Upper-Marlborough*, by Four Horſes, who came in as follows:

		1ſt H.	2d H.
FIGURE,	(Dr. *Hamilton*'s)	1	1
————————,	(Col. *Thornton*'s)	3	2
SELIM,	(Mr. *Galloway*'s)	2	3
BUCKSKIN,	(Mr. *Thomas*'s)	4	di."

(No. 1182, 5 May 1768)

"TO THE PRINTERS.

As a Miſtake appears in your laſt Gazette, in publiſhing our Races, we deſire you will publiſh them from the Account herewith ſent. We are

　　　　　　　　　　　　　　　　Your humble Servants
May 7, 1768.　　　　　　　　　　The MANAGERS of the
　　　　　　　　　　　　　　　　Upper-Marlborough RACES.

"On Tueſday, the 3d Inſt., a Match for 50 Guineas was run for, over the *Upper-Marlborough* Course, One four-mile heat, carrying 9 Stone, by a grey Filly, called *Britannia*, got by *Briton*, belonging to his Excellency the Governor, and a black Colt, call'd *Gimcrack*, got by *Ariel*, belonging to *Notley Young*, Esq., and won by the latter. —Odds Two to One on *Gimcrack*, the Filly being lame.

"Wedneſday 4. The following Horſes ſtarted for the Subſcription Purſe of 100 Pounds, *viz.*

			1st H.	2^d H.
Dr. *Hamilton*'s Horfe,	*Figure,*	Wt. 10 St.	1 :	1
Francis Thornton's ^{do}.,	*Merryman,*	do. do.	2 :	2
Sam Galloway's ^{do}.	*Selim,*	do. do.	3 :	3
Mr. *Thomas*'s *Buckfkin,*	5 Y^{rs}. old	8 ft. 10 lb.	4 :	dif.

Odds at Starting, Three to One *Selim* againft the Field; Five to One the Field againft *Figure*; Five to Four *Merryman* would be diftanced in the Heats; and even Bets *Buckfkin* would be diftanced in the firsf Heat. —*Figure* took the Lead from the Poft, and won the Heats with great Eafe. —'Tis remarkable that the laft Heat was run in 8 Minutes and 52 Seconds. The Ground, by a fair Meafurement, is full Four Miles.

"*Thurfday*, 5. A purse of 25 Pounds was run for, by

Mr. *McGill*'s bay Colt *Nonpareil,*	Wt. 8 ftone.	1
Mr. *Bullen*'s brown Horfe, *Liberty**, aged,	10 ft.	2
Dr. *Hamilton*'s bay Filly, *Primrofe,*	8 ftone	dif.
Mr. *Digges*'s mare *Moll Row*, 6 Y^{rs}. old,	9 ft. 6 lb.	dif.

Bets in Favour of *Nonpareil,* who won the Heat with Eafe, and received the Money— *Liberty* not ftarting the Second Heat.

*Formerly TRYALL." (No. 1183, 12 May 1768)

* * *

New York newspaper account of a horse race at Upper Marlborough, Maryland, 16 May 1768, in reprinted in Esther Singleton, *Social New York under the Georges* (New York: D. Appleton and Company, 1902), 268.

"The Hundred Pounds purse at Upper Marlborough, has been won by Dr. Hamilton's English horse Figure, beating the, hitherto, terrific Salem. As many incidents occur in a four mile heat, and we have no particulars of the sport, it is but justice to the gallant American that the public should suspend its decisive opinion until the champions have met at Philadelphia, next October; when the vanquished may recover, or the victor be confirmed in the triumphant past which, to the astonishment of thousands, he has so successfully contended for. Figure was got by a beautiful horse of that name, the property of the Duke of Hamilton; ran five times in England and won one plate; he has also started two years ago against five horses at Annapolis and beat them in four fine heats. Salem, a grandson of Godolphin Arabian, and got by Governor Sharp's valiant Othello, has run about nine times, and till this event proved in every dispute unconquerable. The gentlemen of Philadelphia have raised a purse of £100 and two of £50 each, to be run for over their course in the Fall. The particulars adapted to the late increase of fine horses in the Northern Colonies will be advertised very soon."

* * *

Accounts of horse races, Rind's Virginia Gazette, 1768.

"*Maryland*, May 7, 1768.

"ON Tuefday the 3d inftant, was run over the courfe at Upper Marlborough a match —*Notley Young*, Efqr's, black colt *Gimcrack*, got by *Ariel*, beat the Excellency the Governor's grey filly *Britannia*, got by *Briton*, one four mile heat, carrying 9 ftone for fifty guineas.

"Odds at ftarting two to one on the winner, the filly being lame.

"Wednefday, 4th. The following horfes ftarted for the fubfcription purfe of one hundred pounds.

	1ft H.	2d. H
Dr. *Hamilton*'s bay horfe *Figure*, aged, wt. 10 ft.	1	1
Francis Thornton, Efqr's bay horfe *Merryman*, d°. d°.	2	2
Sam. *Galloway*, Efqr's brown horfe *Selim*, d°. d°.	3	3
Mr. *Thomas*'s brown horfe *Buckfkin*, 9 years old, 8 ft. 10 lb.	4	dif.

"Odds at ftarting, three to one *Selim* againft the field, five to one the field againft *Figure*, five to four *Merryman* would be diftanced in the heats, and even bets *Buckfkin* would be diftanced the firft heat. —*Figure* took the lead from the poft, and won the purfe with great eafe. —It is remarked, that the laft heat as run in 8 min. 52 fec. The ground, by a fair meafurement, is full four miles.

"Thurfday, 5th for the 25 l. purfe,

Mr. *McGill*'s bay colt *Nonpareil*, 8 ftone	1
Mr. *Bullen*'s brown horfe *Liberty*,* aged, wt. 10 ftone	2
Dr. *Hamilton*'s bay filly *Primrofe*, 8 ftone	dif.
Mr. *Digges*'s grey mare, *Moll Row*, 6 years old, wt. 9 ft. 6 lb.	dif.

"Bets in favour of *Nonpareil*, who won the heat with eafe, and received the money, *Liberty* not ftarting the fecond heat.

*Formerly called *Tryall*.   (No. 107, 26 May 1768)

"RICHMOND County, July 28.

"The fweepftake race of eleven fubfcribers, of ten pounds each, was won by Dr. William Flood's cheftnut colt, got by Nonpareil. Only four ftarted. Col. Tayloe's filly, Small Hopes, got a kick from Mr. Parker's horfe, in paffing by, foon after ftarting, whereby fhe was fo lame as to be diftanced. Mr. Carter's bridle rein broke at ftarting, and his colt, after running one mile, took out of the courfe, and threw his rider, which left the conteft to Mr. Parker's horfe, who was backed by the knowing ones, and the victor.

"The next day the purfe was run for, and won by Col. Tayloe's cheftnut colt, Nonpareil, five years old, diftancing Mr. Parker's and Mr. Carter's colts, four years old each. The firft heat afforded fport, though Nonpareil was tender footed before ftarting, but took the lead, and kept it hard in hand, having fuperiority in every requifite, befides the advantage of the other two having ftarted the day before. The fecond heat, in the firft mile, Mr. Carter's horfe took the reft, and Mr. Parker's run within a poft in the fecond, juft after turning the winning poft. There was a very genteel and numerous company, and a good ordinary at Garland's. The goodnefs of the ground, with other conveniencies, makes this fpot as proper a place for fport as any in the colony. Therefore, as the fubfcription is now out, the brothers of the bridle, and lovers of the turf, are invited to encourage it by a new fubfcription, which will alfo be doing a favour to a young houfekeeper, whofe diligent ftudy will be to pleafe and oblige. The firft heat was run in four minutes and nine feconds, and the the firft mile of the fecond heat in one minute and fifty-eight feconds."   (No. 117, 4 August 1768)

"Yesterday the Williamfburg purfe of 100l. was run for, by Col. Lewis Burwell of Glo'ter's horfe Remus, and Mr. Roger Gregory's horfe Dimple. Remus won the firft heat with eafe, and diftanced his antagonift the fecond."

(No. 129, 27 October 1768)

* * *

Advertisements for horse races, Rind's Virginia Gazette, 1768.

"We are defired to acquaint the publick that there will be three purfes to be run for over the Center courfe of Philadelphia, in October next, one of 100l. and two of 50l. each." (No. 109, 9 June 1768)

"To be run over Newmarket *ground, at* Richmond *court-houfe, on* Wednefday *the* 20th *inftant,*

A SWEEP-STAKES for £. 110, one four mile heat. And the next day a purfe of forty odd pounds, two mile heats; free for any horfe, mare or gelding foaled in *Virginia,* from a *Virginia* bred mare, carrying weight for age, four years old, eight ftone; five years old, nine ftone; fix years old, ten ftone; and aged horfes, eleven ftone four pounds. Subfcribers paying twenty fhillings, non-fubfcribers ten pounds entrance money. The Horfes to be entered at *Richmond* court-houfe, with *Vincent Garland,* on the *Monday* before the races, with proper certificates of the age and neceffary requifite of each horfe." (No. 114, 14 July 1768)

"To be RUN *for,*
At Aquia, in Stafford *county,* Virginia, *on the*
1ft Thurfday *in September next,*
"A PURSE of TWENTY-FIVE POUNDS, current money, by any horfe, mare or gelding, two mile heats carrying weight for fize, *viz.*horfes of 14 hands high, to carry 126 lbs. and to fize above and below, 7 lbs. for evry inch. The horfes defigned to run muft be entered the day before at *Yelverton Peyton*'s, and meafured by a Gentleman chofen for that purpofe. A fubfcriber pays 20*f.* entrance, a non-fubfcriber pays 40*f.* Any horfe winning two clear heats, and faving the third, fhall be entitled to the purfe. There are Gentlemen appointed truftees, that will chufe judges to decide difputes, in cafe any arife, and will pay the money at the ftake to the Gentleman who wins it." (No. 116, 28 July 1768)

* * *

George Washington, Virginia planter, Revolutionary War general, and later President, attends the horse races locally and in Annapolis, September and November 1768, May 1769, September 1771, October 1772, September 1773, in Donald Jackson and Dorothy Twohig, eds., *The Diaries of George Washington,* 6 vols. (Charlottesville, Va.: University Press of Virginia, 1976, 1978, and 1979), 2:96, 109, 154; 3:54, 136, 205.

29 September 1768: "Went to a Purse Race at Accatinck & returnd with Messrs. Robt. and George Alexander."

17 November 1768: "Went up to a Race by Mr. Beckwiths & lodgd at Mr. Edwd. Paynes."

26 May 1769: "Rid into the Neck and from there went up to a Race at Cameron."

21 September 1771: "Set out with Mr. Wormeley for the Annapolis Races. Dind at Mr. Willm.Digges's & lodgd at Mr. Ignatius Digges's."

4 October 1772: "Set out for the Annapolis Races. Dined and lodged at Mr. Boucher's."

26 September 1773: "I set of for Annapolis Races. Dined at Rollins's & got into Annapolis between five & Six Oclock. Spent the Evening & lodged at the Governors."

* * *

Account of a horse race, Virginia Gazette, No. 936, 27 April 1769.

"This day the Williamsburg purfe of 100l. was run for, at our raceground, by Nonpareil, the property of the Hon. John Tayloe, Efq; Mark Anthony, belonging to Capt. Littlebury Hardyman, and Fanny Murray, the property of Nathaniel Walthoe, Efq. Mark Anthony won the firft heat with eafe (in which Fanny Murray was withdrawn the fecond mile going round) the other heat Nonpareil more warmly contefted, but Mark Anthony came off victor."

* * *

Advertisement for a horse race, Virginia Gazette, No. 949, 27 July 1769.

"*To be* RUN *for*,
At Aquia, Stafford *county*, Virginia,
on the *fecond* Thurfday in September *next*,

"A SUBSCRIPTION PURSE of FORTY THREE POUNDS, by any horfe, mare, or gelding; the two mile heats carrying weight for age, according to the *Englifh* rules of racing. A fubfcriber to pay thirty fhillings entrance, a non-fubfcriber to pay ten pounds; any horfe winning two clear heats to be entitled to the purfe; the fecond beft horfe to have the entrance money. Horfes defigned to run muft be entered at *Yelverton Peyton*'s, the day before the race, with proper certificates of the names and age of the horfes. The purfe is to continue for feven years. Any perfon that inclines to be a fubfcriber, may by a line; or otherwife, at any time before the day of the race. The Gentlemen already fubcribed, moft of them defign to run horfes; and have fubfcribed five pounds each, fo that there is no doubt but that the whole money will be collected on the fpot. In cafe any difpute arifes, it will be decided by a majority of the fubfcribers then prefent."

* * *

Charles Jeffery Smith, Virginia educator, on plans to forbid horse racing at a new academy at New Kent, Virginia, 1 March 1770, in Smith, "Plans for an Academy at Providence, in New Kent," *William and Mary Quarterly*, 2nd Series, Vol. 3, No. 1 (January 1923), 54.

"The *morals* of the pupils, that capital part of *education*, will be watched with pious vigilance, and formed with unremitting assiduity: But no licentious amusements, which are real vices, however polite and fashionable they may appear to some, will be tolerated or connived at, such as *card-playing, horse-racing, cock-fighting, wrestling, &c.*"

* * *

Advertisements for horse races, Rind's Virginia Gazette, 1770.

"THE FIFTY POUND purfe, at *Aquia*, is to be run for, on the fecond *Thurfday* in *September* next, on the fame terms as the laft *November* purfe, was run for. The fubfcriber is a fubfcriber to the purfe, but has no horfe to run. Any Gentleman that is not a fubfcriber, and has a good horfe may run him on eafy terms, by applying to
YELVERTON PEYTON."
(No. 224, 23 August 1770)

"Frederickburg FAIRS
are altered, by a late act of Affembly, from *June* and *October* to *May* and *November*. The enfuing FAIR will be on the 24th of the month; and on that or the following day, the inhabitants and neighbouring Gentlemen propofe giving a genteel PURSE for a horse race. Particulars will be advertifed in this paper." (No. 224, 23 August 1770)

"THIS is to inform the public, that the new fubfcription purfe is to be run for at *Leeds* town, on the fecond *Monday* in *November* yearly for feven, is now worth eighty pounds, and expected to be more foon. The money is to be paid at the winning poft."

(No. 235, 8 November 1770)

* * *

Account of a horse race, Maryland Gazette, No. 1331, 9 May 1771.

"ANNAPOLIS, May 9.

"On the Firft Inftant was run for over the Courfe near Upper-Marlborough, a Purfe of FIFTY POUNDS, which was won with Eafe by *William Fitzhugh*, Efquire's bay Horfe *Regulus*. —And the Day following was run for over the fame Courfe, a Purfe of THIRTY POUNDS, which was won by *Daniel MCarty*'s bay Horfe *Silverlegs*."

* * *

William Eddis, Maryland resident, comments on the local horse racing, November 1771, in Eddis, *Letters from America* (London, 1792), 106.

"Our races, which are concluded continued four days and afforded excellent amusement to those who are attached to the pleasures of the turf; and, surprizing as it may appear, I assure you there are few meetings in England better attended, or where more capital horses are exhibited."

* * *

Advertisements for horse races, Maryland Gazette, 1772.

"ANNAPOLIS RACES
Will begin on Tuefday the 6th *of* October *next.*

"THERE will be Four Days Sport, a particular Account of which will be fpeedily inferted in this Gazette." (No. 1399, 2 July 1772)

"*Charles* County, *Maryland, Oct.* 6, 1772.
"POMONKEY RACES.

To be run for, at Pomonkey, *on Thurfday the Third Day of* November,

"A PURSE of Twenty Pounds, free for any Horfe, Mare, or Gelding; Heats Three Miles Each.Four Years old to carry Seven Stone, Five Years old to Seven Stone Ten Pounds, Six Years old Eight Stone Seven Pounds, and aged Nine Stone. —On the Day following will be run for at the fame Place, a Purfe of Ten Pounds, with the Entrance Money of both Days free for any Horfe, Mare, or Gelding; the winning Horfe the firft Day only excepted; Heats Two Miles each, carrying Weight for Size. A Horfe Fourteen Hands high to carry 126 lb. Saddle and Bridle included, to rife and fall 14 Pounds the Firft Inch, and 7 Pounds for every Inch they may be higher or lower.

"The Horfes for each Days Purfe, are to be entered on Monday the 2d of *November*, with Mr *Benjamin Douglass*, with proper Certificates of their Ages. Entrance 20 Shillings if a Subfcriber, if a Non-Subfcriber 30 Shillings, and if at the Poft 40 Shillings; and for the 2d Day Subfcribers to pay 15 Shillings, Non-Subfcribers 20 Shillings, and if at the Poft 30 Shillings. The Horfes to be ftarted each Day precifely at One o'Clock. Proper Judges will be appointed to fettle any Difputes that may arife."

(No. 1413, 8 October 1772)

"*Prince-George*'s County, *Maryland, Octob.* 12, 1772.
QUEEN-ANNE RACES.
To be run for, on Tuefday the 27th *Inftant,*

"A PURSE of Twenty Pounds, free for any Horfe, Mare or Gelding; Heats 3 Miles each. Four Years old to carry 7 Stone, 5 Years old 7 Stone 10 lb. 6 Years old * Stone 7 lb. and aged 9 Stone.

—On the Day following, a Purfe of Ten Pounds, free for any Horfe, Mare or Gelding, to run the fame Diftance, and to carry Weight for Size, the winning Horfe the preceding Day excepted; a Horfe of 14 Hands high to carry 126 lb. and to rife or fall 7 lb. for each Inch higher or lower.

"The Horfes to ftart each Day's Purfe to be entered the Day before the Race, with Meff. *Burrell* and *Rofe* in *Queen-Anne*, and to pay 20 Shillings for the firft Day's Entrance if a Subfcriber, in a Non-fubfcriber 30, and if at the Poft 40; and for the fecond Day, Subfcribers to pay 10 Shillings Entrance, Non-fubfcribers 15, and if entered at the Poft to pay 20 Shillings.

"Proper Certificates for the Horfes Ages that ftart the firft Day muft be produced before entered, and proper Judges will be appointed to determine any Difputes that may arife.

"*N.B.* The Horfes to ftart precifely at One o'Clock for each Day's Race, and any Jockey detected in joftling or unfair riding fhall be deemed diftanced."

(No. 1414, 15 October 1772)

* * *

John Ferdinand Dalziel Smyth, British traveler, describes horse racing in Virginia, August 1772?, in Smyth , *A Tour in the United States of America. Containing an Account of the Present Situation of that Country,* 2 vols., Vol. 1 (London: G. Robinson, 1784), 20-23, 67.

"There are races at Williamfburg twice a year; that is, every fpring and fall, or autumn. Adjoining to the town is a very excellent courfe, for either two, three or four mile heats. Their purfes are generally raifed by fubfcription, and are gained by the horfe that wins two four-mile heats out of three; they amount to an hundred pounds each for the firft day's running, and fifty pounds each every day after; the races commonly continuing for a week. There are alfo matches and fweepftakes very often, for confiderable fums. Befides these at Williamfburg there are races eftablished annually, almoft at every town and confiderable place in Virginia; and frequent matches, on which large fums of money depend; the inhabitants, almoft to a man, being quite devoted to the diverfion of horfe-racing.

"Very capital horfes are ftarted here, fuch as would make no defpicable figure at Newmarket; nor is their fpeed, bottom, or blood inferior to their appearance; the gentlemen of Virginia fparing no pains, trouble or expence in importing the beft ftock, and improving the excellence of the breed by proper and judicious croffing.

"Indeed, nothing can be more elegant and beautiful than the horfes bred here, either for the turf, the field, the road, or the coach; and they have always fine, long, full, flowing tails; but their carriage horfes feldom are poffeffed of that weight and power, which diftinguifh thofe of the fame kind in England.

"Their ftock is from old Cade, old Crab, old Partner, Regulus, Babraham, Bofphorus, Devonfhire Childers, the Cullen Arabian, &c. in England; and a horfe from Arabia, named the Bellfize, which was imported into America, and is now in exiftence.

"In the fouthern part of the colony, and in North Carolina, they are much attached to *quarter-racing*, which is always a match between two horfes, to run one quarter of a mile ftreight out, being merely an excurfion of fpeed; and they have a breed that perform it with aftonifhing velocity, beating every other, for that diftance, with great eafe; but they have no bottom. However, I am confident that there is not a horfe in England, nor perhaps the whole world, that can excel them in rapid fpeed: and thefe likewife make excellent faddle horfes for the road.

"The Virginians, of all ranks and denominations, are exceffively fond of horfes, and efpecially thofe of the race breed. The gentlemen of fortune expend great fums on their ftuds, generally keeping handfome carriages, and feveral elegant fets of horfes, as well as others for the race and road; even the most indigent person has his faddle-horse which he rides to every place, and on every occafion; for in this country nobody walks on foot the fmalleft diftance, except when hunting: indeed a man will frequently go five miles to catch a horfe, to ride only one mile upon afterwards. In fhort, their horfes are their pleafure, and their pride."

"They [the Virginians] are all exceffively attached to every fpecies of fport, gaming, and diffipation, particularly horfe-racing, and that moft barbarous of all diverfions, that peculiar fpecies of cruelty, cock-fighting."

* * *

Joseph Pilmore, Methodist itinerant preacher, moralizes about horse racing in Virginia, October 1772, in Frederick E. Maser and Howard T. Maag, eds., *The Journal of Joseph Pilmore Methodist Itinerant For The Years August 1, 1769 to January 2, 1774* (Philadelphia: Message Publishing Company, 1969), 158.

"After dinner, a gentleman came in who looked like a Minister, and, as there was to be an horse-race that afternoon, I began to speak freely of the absurdity of it, and shewed how rediculus it is for gentlemen of sense to ride many miles to see two or three horses run about a field with Negroes on their backs!"

* * *

Accounts of horse races, Maryland Gazette, 1772.

"ANNAPOLIS, October 8.

"On Tuefday laft the *Jockey Club* Purfe of One Hundred Guineas was run for over the Courfe near this City, and won by Col. *Lloyd's* bay Mare *Nancy Bywell:* And, on Wednefday, the *Give and take* Purfe of Fifty Pounds, which was won by Mr. *Mafter's* bay Mare *Black Legs*. The Remainder of the Races with the Particulars, will be in our next." (No. 1413, 8 October 1772)

"ANNAPOLIS, OCTOBER 15.

"On Tuefday the 6th Inftant the Jockey Club Purfe of One Hundred Guineas, and on the Three following Days Purfes of Fifty Pounds each, were run for over the Courfe near this City, the Particulars of which are as follow:

Benjamin Ogle, Efqr's, gray Mare Britannia	4	3	2
Col. Lloyd's bay Mare Nancy Bywell	1	4	1
Maj. Sims's bay Horfe Wildaire	2	di.	
Mr. Mafter's bay Filly Kitty	dift		
W. Fitzhugh, Efqr's bay Horfe Regulus	5	1	dift
Mr. Spotfwood's bay Horfe Apollo	3	2	dift
Dr. Hamilton's bay Mare Harmony	dift		
Wednefday, October 7.			
Dr. Hamilton's bay Mare Primrofe	dift		
Mr. Delancy's bay Horfe Bafhaw	3	dift	
Mr. Mafter's bay Mare Black Legs	1	2	1

Mr. M'Carty's bay Colt Achilles   4   1   2
Mr. Nevin's brown Filly I will if I can   2   dift
                    Thurfday, October 8.
James Delancy, Efqr's bay Mare Sultana   3   1   2
Mr. Water's bay Mare Quaker Lafs   2   dift
W. Fitzhugh, Efq'rs bay Horfe Brilliant   1   3   1
Mr. Ham's bay Colt Garrat   4   2   3
                    Friday, October 9.
W. Fitzhugh, Efqr's bay Horfe Silver Legs   4   3
Sam Galloway, Efqr's brown Horfe Selim   3   2
Mr. Mafter's bay Gelding Sportfman   dift
Mr. Water's bay Mare Nettle   1   1
Maj. Sims's bay Horfe Wildaire   2   4"

                                            (No. 1414, 15 October 1772)

                              * * *

Philip Vickers Fithian, tutor at Nomini Hall, Virginia, chronicles local horse racing, November 1773 and January, April, May, June, August, September, and October 1774, and in Augusta County, Virginia, January 1776, in Hunter Dickinson Farish, ed., *Journal and Letters of Philip Vickers Fithian, 1773-1774. A Plantation Tutor of the Old Dominion* (Charlottesville, Va.: University Press of Virginia, 1957 [1943]), 24-25, 53, 94-95, 108, 121, 161-162, 186-187, 190, 201, 201-202; and Robert Greenhalgh Albion and Leonidas Dodson, eds., *Philip Vickers Fithian. Journal, 1775-1776, Written on the Virginia-Pennsylvania Frontier and in the Army around New York* (Princeton, N.J.: Princeton University Press, 1934), 158.

25 November 1773: "Rode this morning to Richmond Court-house, where two Horses run for a purse of 500 pounds; besides small Betts almost enumerable.

"One of the Horses belonged to Colonel John Taylor, and is called *Yorick*—The other to Dr. Flood, and is called *Gift*—The Assembly was remarkably numerous; beyond my expectation and exceedingly polite in general.

"The Horses started precisely at five minutes past three; the Course was one Mile in Circumference, they performed the first Round in two minutes, third in two minutes & a-half, *Yorick* came out the fifth time round about 40 Rod before *Gift* they were both, when the Riders dismounted very lame; they run five Miles, and Carried 180 lb—...."

8 January 1774: "*Bob* [Robert Carter, Jr.] told us that there was a Race between Mr —— and Colonels Horses—that they run a Mile, & that *Dottrell* belonging to Mr —— won the Race;...."

7 April 1774: "This Gentleman [Colonel Tayloe] owns *Yorick*, who won the prize of 500£ last November from Dr Floods Horse *Gift* —In the Dining-Room, besides many other fine Pieces, are twenty-four of the most celebrated among the English Race-Horses, Drawn masterly, & set in elegant gilt Frames—...."

25 May 1774: "My Land-Lord invited me to a race about four miles off, & as the day grew better I went; the Purse was fifty Dollars."

18 June 1774: "At twelve Bob teaz'd me for leave to go to a Cock-Fight & Horse-Race about two Miles off, I gave him Leave with his promising to be home by Sun Set."

12 August 1774: [Fithian to John Peck] "But whenever you go from Home, whereyou are to act on your own footing, either to a Ball; or to a *Horse-Race*, or to a *Cock-Fight*, or to a *Fish-Feast,* I advise you that you rate yourself very low,...."

8 September 1774: "I informed him [Harry] that he had at once dismiss'd himself from my authority... And therefore that he had general & unbounded Liberty to go not only to the Horse-Race, but *where* & *when* he chose—.... Harry grew sick and refused to go to the Race.... The Colonel on his return, in the evening informed us that the Race was curious, & that the Horses were almost an even match—That the Betts were Drawn & no Money paid—That the Rider of one of the Horses weighed only forty Seven pound—Strange that so little substance in a human Creature can have the strength & skill sufficient to manage a Horse in a Match of Importance—...."

15 September 1774: "He [Ben] has an unconquerable Love for Horses; he often tells me that he should have been a skillful, & useful Groom; that he should be more fond & careful of his favourite Horse than of a *Wife*, or than his *victuals*, or than anything whatever! I never saw a Person, in any Diversion, Recreation or amusement, who seemed so full of Pleasure & enjoyment as he is when on Horse back, or even in the company of a Horse! He seems to possess as warm a regard for them as Dr *Swift* had for the Houyhnnms—But I cannot discover that Ben has so cordial an enmity to Mankind as *Swift* had for the Yahoos.—*Bobs* passion for the same animal is no less strong, but it is furious, & cruel, he rides excessive hard, & would ride always—...."

6 October 1774: "The School presented me with a petition formally drawn up for a holiday to day on account of the race at Mr Turberville's, which I granted—*Priscilla, Nancy, Ben,* & *Bob* go Harry & I , making in my opinion the wisest choice both stay."

6 October 1774: [Fithian to Harry Willis and Robert Bladen Carter]

"I approve highly of the method you have taken in asking for liberty to attend the race this afternoon, and think myself bound to give you an answer in the same manner.

"This Race happening so soon after the other, which was at the same place, and so much like it seems to promise nothing that can require your attendance, it is therefore my desire and advice that you stay contented at home. But if your inclination be stronger than either of these, and you still choose to go, you have my consent provided you return by Sun set in the Evening."

1 January 1776: "At the Col:s Invitation I rode with him to a Muster. Strange how fantastic. Instead of military Exercises, Drinking, Horse-Racing—Hollowing, carousing —but most thirsty for News. O have you heard from poor Boston? Afflicted Sons of Freedom there, in what Manner shall we best contribute to their Relief?"

* * *

Advertisement for a horse race, Maryland Gazette, No. 1516, 29 September 1774.

"ANNAPOLIS RACES.

"ON Tuefday the 15th of November will be run for, the Jockey club purfe of ONE HUNDRED GUINEAS, free only for horfes, &c. belonging to the members of the club.

"On Wednefday and Thurfady following will be two town purfes of FIFTY POUNDS each, one to four years old, the other give and take. And,

"On Friday will be run for, a PURSE, being the furplus money remaining over the five years fubfcription of the Jockey club. Further particulars in the next gazette.

WILLIAM EDDIS, fecretary."

* * *

John Harrower, an indentured servant, observes horse racing in Virginia, October 1774, in Edward Miles Riley, ed., *The Journal of John Harrower, An Indentured Servant in The Colony of Virginia, 1773-1776* (Williamsburg, Va.: Colonial Williamsburg, 1963), 65.

4 October 1774: "I Went to Fredericksbg. & seed a Horse Race for a Hundred Guineas, Gained by Mr. Fitchews [Fitzhugh's] Horse."

5 October 1774: "This day a Horse race at Fredericksburg for Fifty pound, & it was gained by a Horse belonging to Coll. Tailo [Tayloe? Taylor?]."

6 October 1774: "This day a Horse race at Fredericksburg for Fifty pound, & it was gained by a Horse belonging to Mr. Fitchew [Fitzhugh]."

7 October 1774: "The race this day at Fredericksburg for Fifty pound was gained again by another Horse belonging to Mr. Fitchew [Fitzhugh]."

8 October 1774: "This day the races at Fredericksburg was finished and this night finishes the Puppet shows, roape dancings &ca. which has continowed evry night this week in town. I only seed the purse of a Hundred Guineas run for, and that day I hade the Misfortune to have my Horse, saddle and bridle stole from me, while I was doing some bussiness in town. And I never could hear, nor get any intelligence of either of them again."

* * *

Ebenezer Hazard, Postal Inspector for the Continental Congress, comments on the horse racing near Jamestown, Virginia, June 1777, in Fred Shelley, ed., "The Journal of Ebenezer Hazard in Virginia, 1777," Virginia Magazine of History and Biography, Vol. 62 (1954), 411, 414.

10 June 1777: "At Nelson's (where I dined) a Cock Match is to be fought next Thursday: great Betts are depending. Met some Men who were going to race their Horses. Horse-Racing & Cock-fighting seem to be the principal Objects of Attention between Williamsburgh & Smithfield at present.... I find that the Cock Match is between the Counties of Isle of Wight & Surry."

13 June 1777: "The Virginians ...[are] much addicted to Gaming, drinking, swearing, horse-racing, Cock-fighting, & most Kinds of Dissipation."

* * *

Thomas Anburey, British officer, describes horse racing near Charlottesville, Virginia, 12 May 1779, in [Anburey], Travels through the Interior Parts of America, 2 vols., Vol. 2 (London: William Lane, 1791), 349-351.

"A few days ago I went with feveral officers to fee a diverfion peculiar to this country, termed quarter-racing, which is a match between two horfes, to run a quarter of a mile in a ftraight direction; and near moft of the ordinaries there is a piece of ground cleared in the woods for that purpose, where there are two paths about fix or eight yards afunder, which the horfes run in: this diverfion is a great favorite wof the middling and lower claffes; and they have a breed of horfes to perform it with afton-ifhing velocity, beating every other for that diftance with the greateft eafe. I think I can, without the leaft exaggeration, affert that even the famous Eclipse could not excel them in fpeed, for our horfes are fome time before they are able to get into full fpeed, and thefe are trained to fet out in that manner the moment of ftarting. It is the most ridiculous amufement imaginable, for if you happen to be looking another way, the race is terminated before you can turn your head; nothwithftanding which, very confiderable fums are betted at thefe races....

"Thefe races are only among fettlers in the interior parts of this Province, for they are much laughed at and ridiculed by the people in the lower parts, about Richmond and other great towns; at Williamfburg, is a very excellent courfe for two, three, and four mile heats, where there are races every Spring and Fall; they run for purfes are generally raifed by fubfcription, and the horfe that wins two four-mile heats, out of three, is entitled to the prize, which is one hundred pounds the firft day's running, and fifty pounds every other day, and thefe races commonly laft a week; at which very capital horfes are ftarted, that would make no contemptible figure at Newmarket."

* * *

Advertisement for a horse race, Virginia Gazette, No. 29, 28 August 1779.

"AUGUST 16, 1779.

"A PURSE RACE at *Manchefter*, on the laft *Thurfday* of *September* next, free for any horfe, mare, or gelding, running 2 mile heats, agreeable to the rules of racing."

* * *

Jean-Baptiste-Antoine de Verger, French officer, comments on horses and horse racing near Williamsburg, Virginia, 18 January 1782, in [Verger], "Journal of Jean-Baptiste-Antoine de Verger," in Howard C. Rice, Jr. and Anne S. K. Brown, trans. and eds., *The American Campaigns of Rochambeau's Army 1780, 1781, 1782, 1783*, 2 vols., Vol. 1 (Princeton, N.J.: Princeton University Press, 1972), 157.

"There are thoroughbred horses in this country, comparable to the finest in England, which are generally esteemed. They fetch high prices in the French colonies, thus providing still another branch of commerce that is very lucrative.

"The people here are very fond of horse races, on which they bet considerable sums."

* * *

Ludwig von Closen, French baron and captain, discusses horse racing in Virginia, 16 February 1782, in Evelyn M. Acomb, trans. and ed., *The Revolutionary Journal of Baron Ludwig von Closen, 1780-1783* (Chapel Hill, N.C.: University of North Carolina Press, 1958), 176-177.

"There are endless balls; the women love dancing with as much passion as the men hunting and horse-racing,....

"I have gone to several horse-races, which I found entertaining. One of the great sciences and occupations of Virginians is the preparation of horses for racing; they take the greatest care of them and understand them completely. The French have been amused more than once by these races."

* * *

Lucinda Lee Orr, Virginian young woman, remarks on horse racing in Virginia, September and October 1782, in [Orr], *Journal of a Young Lady of Virginia, 1782* (Baltimore: John Murphy and Company, 1871), 11, 24.

19 September 1782: "I have almost determined not to go to the races this Fall: every one appears to be astonished at [me,] but I am sure there is no sollid happiness to be found in such amusements. I don't think I could answer for myself if you were to go; and then I should only go to be with you. I have no notion of sacrificing my own ease and happiness to the Opinion of the world in these matters. They laugh, and tell me, while I am mopeing at home, other girls will be enjoying themselves at races and balls; but I never will, I am determined, go to one, unless I have an inclination."

5 October 1782: "Mr. Pinkard and a Mr. Lee came home to-day from the Fredericksburg Races. How sorry I was to hear 'Republican' was beaten. I was really interested in that race."

An unidentified English gentleman, concerning Virginia, moralizes about horse racing, circa 1782-1787, quoted in Marquis de Chastellux, *Travels in North-America, in the Years 1780, 1781, and 1782,* 2nd ed., 2 vols., Vol. 2 (London: G.G.J. and J. Robinson, 1787), 192.

"The indolence and diffipation of the middling and lower claffes of white inhabitants of Virginia, are fuch as to give pain to every reflecting mind. Horfe-racing, cock-fighting, and boxing-matches, are ftanding amufements, for which they neglect all bufinefs;...."

* * *

Johann David Schoepf, German physician, discusses horse racing in Virginia, September and December 1783, in Schoepf, *Travels in the Confederation. Pennsylvania, Maryland, Virginia, the Carolinas, East Florida, the Bahamas,* trans. and ed. by Alfred J. Morrison, 2 vols. (Cleveland: Arthur H. Clark, 1911), 1:311; 2:65-66, 95.

September, 1783: "The public amusements are horse-racing, play, and dancing;...."
"Horses are a prime object with the Virginians; but they give their attention chiefly to racers and hunters, of which indubitably they have the finest in America, their custom formerly being to keep up and improve the strain by imported English stallions and mares. The pedigree of their horses is carried out with great exactitude.... With the exception of those horses upon which as racers a high value is placed, all others are let run about in the fields for pasture, without giving them in the hardest winter any protection against the inclemencies of the weather...."
December, 1783: "A Virginia youth of 15 years is already such a man as he will be at twice that age. At 15, his father gives him a horse and a negro, with which he riots about the country, attends every fox-hunt, horse-race, and cock-fight, and does nothing else whatever;...."

NEW ENGLAND

Advertisement for a horse race, Boston News-Letter, No. 593, 22-29 August 1715.

"THis is to give Notice that at Cambridge on Wednefday the 21ft day of September next, will be Run for, a Twenty Pound Plate, by any Horfe, Mare or Gelding not exceeding Fourteen and a half hands high, carrying 11 Stone Weight, and any Perfon or Perfons fhall be welcome to Run his Horfe &c. entering the fame with Mr. *Pattoun* at the Green Dragon in Bofton, any of the fix Days preceding the Day of Running, & paying Twenty Shillings Entrance."

* * *

Advertisement for a horse race, Boston News-Letter, No. 709, 11-18 November 1717.

"THefe are to give Notice that there is a Horfe Race Intended to be Run, on Wednefday next the 20th day of this Inftant November, on Rumly-Mafh Beach, for 10 Pounds between Mr. *Thomas Nowell* of Maldon and Mr. *John Lamfon* of Rumly-Mafh, provided it be fair Weather, and not rainy, if fo, then to be Run the next Fair Day."

Samuel Sewall, Boston magistrate in Connecticut, mentions a horse race, 8 September 1718, in M. Halsey Thomas, ed., *The Diary of Samuel Sewall, 1674-1729, Volume II. 1709-1729* (New York: Farrar, Straus and Giroux, 1973) 901.

"Govr Shute went to the Horse-Race."

* * *

Advertisement for a horse race, Boston News-Letter, No. 898, 15-22 May 1721.

"ON the 2d of June next at 4 in the afternoon, A Silver Punch Bowl Value Ten Pounds will be run for on Cambridge Heath, Three Miles, by any Horfe, Mare or Gelding 13 hands 3 inches High, none to exceed 14, carrying Nine Stone Weight: The Horfes that put in for the Plate are to Enter at the Poft-Office in Bofton on the 1ft of June between the Hours of 8 & 12 in the Morning, and pay down Twenty Shillings. The winning Horfe to pay the charge of this Advertifement."

* * *

Joshua Hempstead, New London, Connecticut carpenter, notes some local horse racing, October 1724 and March 1725, in [Hempstead], *Diary of Joshua Hempstead of New London, Connecticut Covering a Period of Forty-Seven Years from September, 1711, to November, 1758, Collections of the New London County Historical Society, Volume I* (New London, Conn.: New London County Historical Society, 1901), 148, 156.

October 19, 1724: "I went to Groton to See ye Horse Pacing between ye Horses of Wm Wheeler & James Harris 100 Rod for £5. Harris gained about 3 foot but they Caveled & then yeilded ye Wage but drew Stakes & afterwards went twice for Nothing. Harris gained."

March 29, 1725: "a Horse Racing today at Champlins. 5 Horses Ran all at once. Each pd down 40s & he that out Run Recd £20 of Majr Bewer, one Bly of Boston Carryed of the mony."

* * *

Advertisement for a horse race, Boston Gazette, No. 283, 19–26 April 1725.

"This is to give Notice to all Gentlemen and others, that there is to be Thirty Pounds in Money Run for on Thurfday the 13th of May next at 9 a clock, by Six Horfes, Mares, or Geldings, Two Miles between Menotomy & Cambridge, to carry 9 Stone weight, the Standard to be 14 hands high, all exceeding to carry weight for Inches. Each one that Runs to have their Number from 1 to 6, to be drawn, and to run by 2 together only as the Lots are drawn, the 3 firft Horfes to run a fecond heat, and the firft of them to have the Money, allowing the 2d, 5l. if he faves his Diftance, which fhall be 100 yards from coming in.

Each Perfon to enter & pay 5l. to Mr. Philip Mufgrave, Poftmafter of Bofton, 15 Days before they Run."

* * *

Advertisement for a horse and pig race and subsequent account, Boston Gazette, 1725

"ON Monday the 27th Inftant between 2 & 3 a Clock in the Afternoon, a Race will be run (for a confiderable Wager) on the Plains at Portfmouth, New Hampfhire, between a Hog and a Horfe."   (No. 301, 30 August-6 September 1725)

"We hear from New-Hampfhire, that on Monday the 27th of Sept. laft, there was a Race Run, for a confiderable Sum of Money, between a Hog and a Horfe, the former of which had the Advantage moft part of the way, which [the party that were] for the

Horfe obferving, it is thought, caufed the hog to be frighten'd, so that with much ado the Horfe got the Advantage."   (No. 305, 27 September-4 October 1725)

* * *

Account of a horse racing accident, Boston News-Letter, No. 1441, 2–9 September 1731.

"We hear from *Windham* in Connecticut Colony, That a few Days fince, One *Jonathan Palmer* of that Place, as he was running a Race with a young Horfe, the Horfe turned out of the Way and threw him down with the back part of his Head againft a Stone, and beat a hole into his Brains, fo that he dy'd immediately upon the Spot."

* * *

Resolution by the Yearly Meeting of the Society of Friends in New England advises Quakers and others to avoid horse races, circa 1739, in Society of Friends, *The Book of Discipline, Agreed on by the Yearly-Meeting of Friends for New England* (Providence, R.I.: John Carter, 1785), 135.

"WE earneftly befeech our friends, and efpecially the youth among us, to avoid all fuch converfation as may tend to draw out their minds into the foolifh and wicked paftimes with which this age aboundeth (particularly balls, gaming-places, horfe-races, and play-houfes) thofe nurferies of debauchery and wickednefs, the burthen and grief of the fober part of other focieties, as well as of our own; practices wholly unbecoming a people under the Chriftian profeffion, contrary to the tenor of the doctrine of the gofpel, and the examples of the beft men in the earlieft ages of the church."

* * *

John Adams, Massachusetts lawyer, politician, and later United States President, refers to horse racing in his argument in Lovell *v.* Ward, October 1760, in [Adams], *Diary and Autobiography of John Adams, Volume I.* Diary, *1755-1770,* ed. by Lyman H. Butterfield (Cambridge, Mass.: Harvard University Press, 1962), 157.

"Suppose I should Agree with a Man, to let him have my Horse to Rhode Island to purchase a Quantity of Goods, and he engages that I shall have one fifth or one Qr. of the Profits of his Journey. Well when he gets upon Seachonk Plain, He finds a Number of People there a horse racing. He challenges every Horse upon the Plain to run. At last they run for 100 Guineas which my Horse wins. Would it not be reasonable that I should have a Proportion of that Prize? Shall the Man that I let him to, run the Hazard of breaking the Neck, or Limbs or Wind of my Horse. Shall he strain, and violently drive him so as uterly to mar him very much; and I have no Recompence at all?"

* * *

Advertisement for a horse race, Boston Gazette and Country Journal, No. 290, 20 October 1760.

"THESE are to notify all Gentlemen that there is a Horfe-Race to be run the 23d Inftant, at a Place called Lynn-Beach for *Fifty Pounds* Sterling, three Heats, a Mile each, the beft two in three to have faid *Fifty Pounds* Sterling. This money is given by private Gentlemen as an Encouragement, in order to procure a good Breed of Horfes. Any Gentleman that pleafes to put in a Horfe, muft depofit *Three Pounds* Sterling as a Referve for Stakes to be run for the next Day. Any Horfe that does not come within the the Diftance by 30 Rod, is not to run again.

[pointing hand] Each Heat ftop half an Hour and rub."

* * *

Jabez Fitch, Connecticut lieutenant, chronicles the horse racing on Long Island, March, October, and November 1777, in William H. Sabine, ed., *The New-York Diary of Lieutenant Jabez Fitch of the 17th (Connecticut) Regiment from August 22, 1776 to December 15, 1777* (New York: pvt. ptg., 1954), 131, 234-235.

31 March 1777: "...; there was also some Running of Horses with the Inhabitants this Day, it being call'd an Holliday with them."

20 October 1777: "In the afternoon I was up at Capt: Elderds, to see a horse race, where I found a considerable collection of men & horses for that purpose, & after several trifling races being Ran, I went with a number of our Offrs:...."

6 November 1777: "At about 1 oClock Mestrs: Brewster & Kalender came to my Quarters, & the Storm being considerably abated, I went with them to Isaac Elderds, with an Intention to see a famous Horserace, that that was agreed to be ran on this day; but being arriv'd at Mr: Eldards, we were Inform'd that the Race was pospon'd while tomorow on act: of the badness of the weather,... [watches a boxing match]; after which I observ'd several trifling horseraces,...."

7 November 1777: "Soon after dinner I went up on to the Plain by Capt: Eldards again to see the horseraces, where I found a very large collection of People, & many small Races were ran soon after I came onto the ground; At about 3 oClock the first Heat of the grand Race was ran by five threeyear old horses, which appear'd very gay, & were bro't onto the ground by the Jockeys with great Ceremony, each cloth'd in a large Cirplis, & demanded equal Respect & attention from this country people to so many Church Priests; They ran round a number of stakes plac'd in a circular manner for that purpose, so as to contain one mile in length; & at the 3rd: Heat an horse belonging to one Thorn belonging some where up the Iseland, won the Purse which contain'd about 100 dollars: After this there was several smaller Races ran, & at a little after sunset the people Retired, without much fighting this day;...."

8 November 1777: "...; soon after which I took a walk up to Capt. Eldards, in Expectation of seeing some more Racing, but finding no compy:...."

* * *

Rhode Island law, September 1777, in Rhode Island General Assembly, *Session Laws, September 1777* (Providence: Attleborough, [1777]), 6.

"AN ACT to prevent *Horfe-racing.*

"WHEREAS the fuffering of Horfes to be run for Bets or Wagers is contrary to a Refolve of the Honorable Continental Congrefs, and is of pernicious Confequences, as it affembles together a great Number of idle Perfons, and is a wafte of Time and Money, to many who are very unable to bear it; and likewife tends greatly to introduce among the People a fet of Sharpers, and other diffolute Perfons;

"WHEREFORE, *Be it Enacted by this General Affembly and by the Authority thereof, it is Enacted,* That, for the future, not any Perfon or Perfons fhall make any Bet, or lay any Wager of any Kind, upon any Horfe, Mare, or Gelding, to ftart or run therefor, under the Penalty of paying, as a Fine, the Sum of One Hundred Pounds, lawful Money: One Half to the Informer, and the other Half to and for the Ufe of the Town where the Offence is committed; to be recovered by Bill, Plaint or Information, in any Court proper to try the fame.

"*AND be it further Enacted, by the Authority aforefaid,* That if any Perfon or Perfons fhall knowingly fuffer or permit any Horfe, Mare, or Gelding, belonging to him or them, to ftart or run for any Bet or Wager; he, fhe, or they, fo offending, fhall forfeit his, her, or their Horfe, Mare, or Gelding, ftarting or running as aforefaid, to and for the Ufe of the Town where fuch Offence is committed, to be recovered in Manner as aforefaid; and that this Act be publifhed in the next *Providence* Gazette."

* * *

Connecticut law, October 1778, in State of Connecticut, *Acts and Laws,* 21 October 1778 (Hartford?, 1778?), 505.

"An Act for the preventing of Horfe-Racing.

"*WHEREAS Horfe-Racing is a growing Evil, productive of Diffipation, Idlenefs, and many other Vices ruinous to Individuals and detrimental to the public Weal.*

Which to prevent:

"*BE it enacted by the Governor, Council, and Representatives, in General Court affembled, and by the Authority of the fame,* That the Owner or Owners of every Horfe or Horfe-Kind, that fhall be ufed, employed, or improved in Horfe-Racing in this State, by his or their Privity or Permiffion, whereon any Stakes are held, or any Bets or Wagers laid or dependant, either directly or indirectly, fhall forfeit every fuch Horfe or Horfe-Kind employed as aforefaid, or the Value thereof. And every Perfon or Perfons concerned in laying any Bet or Bets or Wagers on fuch Race or Races fhall forfeit the Sum of *Forty Shillings* Lawful Money, in all Cafes where the Bet or Wager laid fhall be *Forty Shillings* or under; in all other Cafes the Value of the Bet or Wager laid as aforefaid."

* * *

William Pynchon, Salem, Massachusetts resident, mentions a horse race at Lynn, 24 June 1782, in Fitch Edward Oliver, ed., *The Diary of William Pynchon of Salem* (Boston: Houghton, Mifflin and Company, 1890), 126.

"A clear day and moderate. Grand horse-race to be at Lynn beach. The race was run, but the stakes withdrawn: one of the riders and his horse fell down in the water."

* * *

Francesco dal Verme, Italian count, attends horse races near Portsmouth, New Hampshire, August 1783, in Elizabeth Cometti, trans. and ed., *Seeing America and Its Great Men. The Journal and Letters of Count Francesco dal Verme, 1783-1784* (Charlottesville, Va.: University Press of Virginia, 1969), 22.

19 August 1783: "Dinner with Mr. Sheafe, then went on an excursion by carriage with Mr. Langdon (10 miles) and saw race of their horses."

NEW JERSEY, NEW YORK, PENNSYLVANIA

Advertisement for a horse race, New York Gazette, No. 419, 29 October-5 November 1733.

"To be Run for, on the Courfe at *New-York*, the 8th of this Month, a Purfe upwards of 4 *l.* value, by any Horfe, Mare or Gelding carrying 12 Stone, and paying 5 S.

entrance, which entrance Money is to be given to the fecond Horfe, unlefs diftanced.
[*Note*, All Horfes that have won Plates here, are excepted.]

* * *

Advertisement for a horse race, New York Gazette, No. 569, 20-27 September 1736.

"*A Subfcription Plate.*

On *Wednefday* the 13*th* of *October* next, will be Run for on the Courfe at *New-York*, a Plate of *Twenty Pounds* Value, by any Horfe, Mare or Gelding, carrying ten Stone (Saddle and Bridle included) the beft of three Heats, two Miles each Heat.

Horses intended to Run for this Plate, are to be entr'd the Day before the Race with *Francis Child*, on *Frefh-Water Hill*, paying a half Piftole each, or at the Poft on the Day of Running, paying a Piftole.

And the next day (being the 14*th*) will be Run for, on the fame Courfe, by all or any the Horfes that ftarted for the *Twenty Pound Plate* (the Winning Horfe excepted) The Entrance Money on the Condition above. Proper judges will be named to deter- mine any Difputes that may arife.

All Perfons on Horfe-back or in Chaifes, coming into the Field (the Subfcribers and Winning Horfes only excepted) are to pay *Six Pence* each to the Owner of the Ground."

* * *

New York Postboy account of a horse race on Long Island, 4 June 1750, reprinted in Francis Barnum Culver, *Blooded Horses* of *Colonial Days. Classic Horse Matches* in *America before the Revolution* (Baltimore: pvt. ptg., 1922), 148-149.

"On Friday last there was a great horse-race on Hempstead Plains which engaged the attention of so many of the city of New York that upwards of 70 chairs and chaises were carried over Brooklyn Ferry the day before, besides a far greater number of horses. The number of horses exceeded, it is thought, one thousand."

* * *

Advertisement for a horse race in New Jersey, Pennsylvania Journal, No. 406, 30 Au- gust 1750.

"NOTICE is hereby given: That there is to be given Gratis, at *Mount-Holly* in the County of *Burlington*, on Wednefday the 19th Day of *September* TWENTY Piftoles, to be run for by as many Horfes, Mares, or Geldings as any Perfon or Perfons fhall think fit to put in. They are to put in *Twenty Shillings* for every Horfe, Mare, or Geld- ing, and enter them four Days before the Day of Running. They are to run three Heats, one Mile at a Heat, on a ftraight Courfe, and to carry weight for Inches. A Horfe, Mare, or Gelding to carry fourteen Pound, and for every Inch above that feven Pound; and all Horfes that are under fize to be equivelent to the fame. Any one Horfe, Mare or gelding that fhall win two Heats and fave the Diftance the third, fhall win the Prize. And the next Day the Betts to be run for; every one that faves his Diftance the firft Day, is entitled to Run, the Horfe that wins the Prize excepted. The Horfes to be en- tered at *John Budd*'s or *Caleb Shinn*'s."

* * *

Account of a horse race, New York Gazette, No. 587, 29 April 1754.

"*Tuefday morning laft a confiderable Sum was depending between a Number of Gentlemen in this City, on a Horfe ftarting from one of the Gates of the City to go to Kingsbridge and back again, being fourteen meafured Miles, in Two Hours Time; which he perform'd with one Rider in One Hour and Forty Six Minutes.*"

Account of a race near Jamaica, Long Island, 3 June 1755, reprinted in Esther Singleton, *Social New York under the Georges* (New York: D. Appleton and Company, 1902), 267.

"On Monday last ended the races round Beaver Pond near Jamaica, L. I., for a purse of £12, which was won by a gelding from Maryland belonging to Mr. John Combes of Jamaica."

* * *

Advertisement for a horse race, New York Mercury, No. 314, 21 August 1758.

"TO BE RUN FOR,

At *Elizabeth-Town*, in *Eaft-New-Jerfey*, on

Tuefday the 30th of *October* next,

"BY any Horfe, Mare or Gelding, (excepting thofe bred in Virginia or Maryland) carrying eight Stone, or 112 lb. weight; to run threee Heats, two Miles each, unlefs the fame Horfe gains the two firft Heats; in that Cafe he wins the Prize, if he faves the Diftance the third Heat; and if three different Horfes gain each a Heat, the whole who have faved their Diftance; to run 'till fome one gains two Heats. The Purfe or Plate Value Twenty Pounds.

"Each Horfe, &c. intending to Run, to enter before Noon on Monday (the Day preceding the Race) paying Twenty Shillings Entrance, which Entrance Money to be run for on Thurfday following, by the loofing Horfes, &c. who faved their Diftance. Not lefs than three Horfes to run. N.B. Horses are entered by William Euen."

* * *

Advertisement for a horse race, Maryland Gazette, No. 849, 13 August 1761.

"*Philadelphia, Auguft* 6, 1761.

"For the Encouragement of the BREED of

FINE HORSES:

"On the 14th Day of *October* will be Run for, on the Race Ground called the Center of this City,

"A Purfe of FIFTY PISTOLES, Free for any Horfe, Mare, or Gelding, carrying 10 Stone, Saddle and Bridle included, the beft of Three Heats, Three Times round the Courfe each Heat.

"The Horfe, Mare, or Gelding, that winneth any Two Heats, fhall be intitled to the Purfe.

"Any Rider that is detected in joftling, croffing, or ufing any foul Play, fhall be deemed Diftanced, and have no Title to the Purfe, even tho' he wins the beft of Three Heats.

"All Horfes, Mares, or Geldings, that run for this Purfe, are to be fhewn and entered at the Houfe of Mr. *Peter Robefon*, at the Sign of the *White Horfe* in this City, Four Days before the Race, and to pay Six Dollars Entrance, or Twelve Dollars if entered at the Poft.

"The Entrance Money will be Run for on the 15th by all the Horfes, except the one that wins the Purfe, and thofe that may be Diftanced."

* * *

Joseph Doddridge, Pennsylvania Episcopalian minister, comments on horse racing concerning the western settlements of Pennsylvania, circa 1763-1783, in Doddridge, *Notes on the Settlement and Indian Wars of the Western Parts of Virginia and Pennsylvania from 1763 and 1783, inclusive, together with a Review of the State of Society and Manners of the First Settlers of the Western Country* (Pittsburgh: John S. Ritenour and William T. Lindsey, 1912), 121-122.

"Horse racing is regarded by the statesman as a preparation, in various ways, for the equestrian department of warfare; it is said that the English government never possessed a good cavalry until by the encouragement given to public races, their breed of horses was improved."

* * *

Advertisement for a horse race near Jamaica, Long Island, 23 April 1763, reprinted in Esther Singleton, *Social New York under the Georges* (New York: D. Appleton and Company, 1902), 268.

"N. Y. Freemason Purse of £100 to be run for around the Beaver Pond at Jamaica, L. I., best 2 of 3 heats, each heat 3 times round the pond—whole bred English only excepted."

* * *

Jacob Hiltzheimer, Philadelphia area farmer and politician, chronicles horse racing locally and on Long Island, November 1766, September and October 1767, October 1768, May, September, and November 1769, May, August, and October 1770, September 1772, and April 1783, in Jacob Cox Parsons, ed., *Extracts from the Diary of Jacob Hiltzheimer* (Philadelphia: William Fell Company, 1893), 12, 13, 16 17, 18, 20-21, 22, 23, 24, 56.

12 November 1766: "Five horses started for the £60 purse. Trial, Merry Andrew, Sterling, Valiant, and a mare belonging to Colonel Armstrong. Trial won the purse."

13 November 1766: "Four horses started in the race to-day —Smoker, Merry Andrew, Sampson, and a little roan, belonging to Joseph Richardson. Smoker won."

4 September 1767: "Timothy Matlack, J. Lukens, Palmer, and myself measured the new race track very exact, and find it lacks 144 yards of being two miles."

13 October 1767: Four horses started in the 100 guinea race: Selim, Granby, Old England, and Northumberland. Selim won."

4 October 1768: "This afternoon started for the £100 purse, the gray horse Northumberland, bay horse Granby, and bay mare Strumpet; the gray won two heats."

6 October 1768: "Started for the Ladies' purse, Mr. Morris's colt Luggs; Mr. Coryell's bay mare Bungtown Maid; Mr. Peterson's horse Brinton; my mare Pallas; all three years old. Luggs won; made the first heat in 4 m. 17 s.; second heat, 4 m. 23 s."

8 October 1768: "The City Plate of £50 was run for by Strumpet, Ladylegs, Nancy Dawson, and Granby; Strumpet won."

12 May 1769: "In the morning took a ride with Joseph Redman in my chair. Drank punch with Henry Keppele, Jr., and wished him joy on birth of a son. Afterwards went to see the race between Mr. J——'s horse Sportsman and Dr. Kearsley's black colt, 3 years old, for a quarter cask of wine. Sportsman won."

28 September 1769: "At noon started for the £100 purse the following horses: James DeLancey's bay horse, Lath; Mr. McGill's bay horse, Nonpareil; Governor Sharp's gray mare, Britannia; Richard Tidmarsh's gray mare, Northumberland. Lath won."

29 September 1769: "Started for the £50 plate, Archibald Dick's gray colt, William Baxter's filly, James DeLancey's brown filly, Dr. Kearsley's black colt, and Mr. Leary's Old England. Three heats were run and the gray won."

8 November 1769: "Went with Mr. Vorhees and John Hunt to the race ground, and had a race."

2 May 1770: "A race for £20 was run between Dr. Kearsley's gray mare and Alvaro Diornella's brown mare bred by myself, a single two miles; the brown beat with ease."

31 August 1770: "Early this morning Timothy Matlack and myself went to the race track to see the brown colt Regulus run the two miles, which he did in four minutes and a quarter."

12 October 1770: "At noon started for the £50 purse the following horses:

James DeLancey's b. f. Angelica	1	4	1
Captain McDaniel's bl. f. Blackbird	1	dist.	
Dr. Kearsley's bl. colt Steady	3	2	3
Governor Sharp's c. f. Creeping Kate	4	3	4
J. Hiltzheimer's b. colt Regulus	5	1	2
James Boyd's g. colt Belt	dist."		

29 October 1770: "Went to the race ground, Hempstead Plains [Long Island], where started for the £50 purse the following horses:—

Dr. Kearsley's b. c. Steady, 4 years	1	2
Mr. Hart's b. f. Blackbird, 3 years	2	3
Walters & Hiltzheimer's b. c. Regulus, 4 years	3	1

The rider of Regulus losing his cap his second heat was given to Steady. Lodged at Valentines."

30 October 1770: "At noon five horses ran for another purse of £50. Lodged at William Furman's for the night."

4 September 1772: "Early this morning James Buchanan, with his bay mare, Nancy Dawson, rode a match against time for 20 guineas. He was to ride fifteen miles around our track in one hour, and he performed it in fifty-six minutes."

29 April 1783: "Took a walk with Captain Webster and Captain Joy to look at the former's garden. In the afternoon went to Jacob Meyer's and then to Adam Weber's to see two horses belonging to British officers run a two-mile heat."

* * *

Advertisements for horse races, New York Gazette and Weekly Mercury, 1769.

"Powles-Hook RACES.

"ON Monday the 9th Day of October next, will be run for over the New Courfe at Powles-Hook, by any Horfe, Mare, or Gelding, not more than three Quarters Blood; and thofe lefs than three Quarters Blood, to be allowed 5 lb. The beft of three Heats round faid Courfe, three Times round reckoned for one Heat; three Years old carrying feven Stone; four Years old feven Stone eight Pounds; five Years old eight Stone two Pounds; fix Years old eight Stone eleven Pounds; ad aged Horfes 9 Stone feven Pounds, Saddle and Bridle included; Fillies to be allowed three Pounds. Any Horfe, &c. winning two Heats fhall not be obliged to ftart a third to fave his Diftance. To run according to the King's Plate Articles.

"Tuefday the 10th, the beaten Horfes to run the beft of three Heats for the Stakes.

"Wednefday the 11th, there will be a Fox Hunt in Bergen Woods, and on

"Thurfday the 12th, there will be a Purfe of Twenty Pounds, free for any Horfe, mare, or Gelding, not more than Quarter Blood, Weight for Age as above. The Horfes, &c. to be fhewn and entered at the Starting Poft, the Saturday before running, between the Hours of 3 and 5 in the Afternoon, in Prefence of the Judges, who will be prefent, paying 50s, Entrance for each Horfe, &c. that ftarts for the Plate of 50l. and 20s, for every Horfe, &c. that ftarts for the 20l. Plate. Any Difpute that may arife, to be determined by the Judges to be appointed.

"Good Crafts will be ready at each ferry to convey over all Perfons who incline to fee the Races; good Stables, with excellent hay and Oats, will be provided for the Horfes, and good Accommodations for the Grooms. To ftart at 2 o'Clock precifely, each Day; Certificates of the Ages of the Horfes, &c. to be produced at Entrance, from under the hands of the Breeders.

"It is hoped no Perfons from New-York will, to evade the Ferry, make ufe of their own Boats, (which is not juftifiable by Law) as the greateft Care will be taken by the Ferrymen during the races, to carry ver Gentlemen in the moft expeditious Manner."

(No. 936, 2 October 1769)

"ON Monday next, the 27th Inft., at the FAIR, at RICHMOND TOWN, on Staten-Ifland, will be run for by common Horfes, or thofe 8th Part blooded, that never ftarted for any Purfe before, a PURSE OF TEN POUNDS. —The Horfes to be entered two Days before the Day of Running, with Mr. Simon Swain, of Richmond, paying 10s. Entrance, or double at the Poft. The Entrance Money to be run for the next day by any common Horfes of the Ifland. The fair to be held three Days."

(No. 943, 20 November 1769)

* * *

David McClure, Congregationalist missionary, comments on horse racing habits among Virginian emigrants in western Pennsylvania, 17 December 1772, in McClure, *Diary of David McClure, Doctor of Divinity* (New York: Knickerbocker Press, 1899), 106.

"The manners of the people of Virginia, who have removed to these parts, are different from those of the Presbyterians and the Germans. They are much addicted to drinking parties, gambling, horse races & fighting."

* * *

Advertisements for horse races, Rivington's New-York Gazetteer, 1773.

"NEWMARKET RACES.
On Tuefday May the 4th, will be run for
A PURSE of FIFTY POUNDS

"FREE for any Horfe, Mare, or Gelding, carrying Weight for Age. Four Years old feven Stone. Fives feven Stone twelve Pounds. Sixes eight Stone feven Pounds, and &c. that never won Match or Plate to be allowed four Pounds, according to their Ages. The beft of three four Mile Heats

"ON WEDNESDAY.
A PURSE of THIRTY POUNDS,
And upwards.

"Free for four Years old only. Colts carrying eight Stone, Fillies feven Stone, ten Pounds. Thofe not of full Blood to be allowed five Pounds. The beft of three two Mile Heats. Not lefs than three reputed Running Horfes to ftart, unlefs allowed by the Judges.

"To enter at the Starting Poft on Saturday before running, paying fifty Shillings for the firft, and thirty Shillings Entrance for the fecond Purfe. No Croffing, Joftling, or other foul Play.

"Proper Certificates, under the Hands of the Breeders, of the Age and Blood, to be produced at the Time of Entrance.

"To ftart exactly at twelve o'clock."   (No. 2, 29 April 1773)

"Powles Hook Races

"TO be run for at Powles Hook fometime in September next: a Whim Purfe of One Hundred Dollars, free for any Horfe, Mare, or Gelding, full Bloods excepted carrying Weight for Age, Blood and Inches."   (No. 10, 1 July 1773)

* * *

Account of a horse race, Rivington's New-York Gazetteer, No. 7, 3 June 1773.

"POWLES-HOOK RACES, May 31ft, 1773.

The following horfes ftarted for the weight for age plate.

			Heats.	
Mr. Elfworth's bay Horfe,	Cyrus	5	1	1
Mr. Jackfon's Horfe,	Quickfilver,	1	3	3
Mr. Tallman's grey Mare,	Dove,	4	4	2
Mr. Wicknefs's black Horfe,	Richmond,	3	2	0
Mr. Patterfon's black Horfe,	Gimcrack,	2	dr	0
Mr. Ifrael Water's Horfe,	Valiant, 5 years old	6	dr	0

"And on Tuefday the undermentioned 4 years old, for another 50l. bay Mare, Capt. Ant. Rutgers' bay Colt, Macaroni, a beautiful fon of Wildale out of a daughter of Ariel and old Spark.

		Heats.		
		1	1	0
Mr. Patterfon's bay Mare,	Virgin,	3	2	0
Mr. Ifrael Waters's bay Horfe,	Xanthae,	2	3	0
Mr. Cornell's bay Horfe,	Bafhaw,	4	4	0"

* * *

Advertisements for horse races, Rivington's New-York Gazetteer, 1774.

"POWLES-HOOK RACES.

"TO be run for at Powles-Hook, on Monday the 23d day of May next, a purfe of FIFTY POUNDS, free for any horfe, mare or gelding (full blood excepted) carrying weight for age and blood, as follows, viz. Four years old, half blood, 7 ftone 5 lb. three quarters, 7 ftone 11lb. Five years, half blood, 8 ftone 3 pounds; three quarters, 8 ftone 9pounds. Six years, half blood, 8 ftone 12 pounds; three quarters, 9 ftone 4 pounds. Aged, half blood, 9 ftone, 5 pounds; three quarters, 9 ftone 12 pounds. Every particle of blood between each quarter, in the above race, to carry 6 pounds extraordinary; and AUCTIONEER, the late property of Mr. Waters, and STEADY, the late property of Mr. Cornell, to carry 10 ftone 4 pounds.

"On Tuefday the 24th, a purfe of FIFTY POUNDS, free for any horfe, mare or gelding, carrying weight for age and blood as follows, viz. Four years old, half blood, 7 ftone 4 pounds; three quarters, 7 ftone 10 pounds; full blood, 8 ftone 2 pounds. Five years, half blood, 8 ftone 2 pounds; three quarters, 8 ftone 8 pounds; full blood, 9 ftone. Six years, half blood, 8 ftone 12 pounds; three quarters, 9 ftone 4 pounds; full blood, 9 ftone 10 pounds. Aged, half blood, 9 ftone 7 pounds; three quarters, 9 ftone 13 pounds; full blood, 10 ftone, 5 pounds.

"N.B. AUCTIONEER, the late property of Mr.Waters, to run for the above purfe as a three quarter blood, and no particle of blood in each quarter to be taken notice of, Not lefs than three reputed running horfes to run for the above purfes, and certificates to be produced from the breeders, or fuch as the judges will approve of.

"The firft days purfe to run the beft of three 3 miles heats; and the fecond day to run the beft of three 4 mile heats. All horfes, &c. to be shewn and entered the Saturday before running, at the ftand, paying entrance 3l. 10s. or double at the poft. No owners of horfes to ftart more than one horfe, or to be concerned in any confederacy. If bad weather the race will be poftponed till good."   (No. 48, 17 March 1774)

"Elizabeth-Town Races,
To be Run for on Tuefday next at Elizabeth Town,
A Purfe of twenty-five Pounds, (New-York, currency)
"FREE for any Horfe, Mare, or Gelding, (full Bloods excepted) carrying Weight for Age and Blood, as follows, viz. four Years old, half Blood, 7ft. 5lb. 3 quarters ditto, 7ft. 11lb. five Years old, half blood, 8ft. 3lb. 3 quarters ditto, 8ft. 9lb. fix years old, half Blood, 8ft. 12lb. 3 quarters ditto, 9st. 4 lb. aged, half Blood, 9ft. 6lb. 3 quarters ditto, 9 ft. 12lb. Every Particle of Blood between each quarter, to carry 6lb. extraordinary; the beft of three Two-mile Heats. All Horfes, &c. to be shown and entered at the Stand, the Day before Running, paying twenty-four Shillings Entrance, or double at the Poft. No Owners of Horfes to ftart more than one Horfe, or to be concerned in any Confederacy. Not lefs than three reputed Running Horfes to ftart for the above Purfe, and Certicates to be produced from the Breeders, or fuch as the Judges shall approve of.

"The entrance Money to be run for the following day at the above Race, by all except winning and diftanced Horfes.

"The Horfes to be entered by Jonathan J. Dayton, Broughton Reynolds, and Noah Marfh."   (No. 76, 29 September 1774)

* * *

Robert Proud, historian of Pennsylvania, circa 1776-1780, concerning the Pennsylvania Quakers' antipathy toward horse racing, in Proud, *The Hiftory of Pennfylvania, in North America, from the Original Inftitution and Settlement of that Province, under the firft* Proprietor *and Governor William Penn, in 1681, till after the Year 1742*, 2 vols., Vol. 1 (Philadelphia: Zachariah Poulson, Junior, 1797), 55.

"*First*, Their *difufe of all gaming*, and *vain fports*; as the frequenting of *plays*, *horfe-races*, &c. was a cuftom ftrictly and conftantly adhered to by them; as being moft confiftent with a truly chriftian life; the ufe of thefe, and fimilar things, having, in their eftimation, a manifeft and infallible tendency to draw away, and alienate the human mind from the moft important object of true happinefs,...."

* * *

Advertisement for a horse race, [Rivington's] New-York Royal Gazette, No. 138, 11 October 1777.

"*LONG-ISLAND*
HORSE RACE.
"TO be run for, on Thurfday the 6th of November next, at the New Lots, on Long-Ifland, about feven miles from Brooklyn ferry, a PURSE, value ONE HUNDRED DOLLARS, or upwards, by three years old colts or fillies, the beft of three heats, one

mile to each heat; three quarter blood carrying eight ftone, half blood feven ftone nine pounds, &c. &c. ...All horfes running for the above purfe to pay one guinea entrance; which money will be run for the next day by all except the winning horfe the firft day."

* * *

Advertisement for a horse race, [Rivington's] Royal Gazette, No. 213, 14 October 1778.

"LONG-ISLAND RACES.

"TO be run for, at Polhemus's New Lotts, five miles from Jamaica, a PURSE of TWENTY GUINEAS, free for any Horfe, Mare or Gelding, carrying weight for age and blood, the beft of three heats, twice round the courfe each heat.

"The horfes, &c. to be fhewn and entered on Tuefday the 27th of October, at Polhemus's, and to run the next day at Eleven o'clock.

[hand pointing] Entrance ONE GUINEA, or double at the Poft.

"Four years old, quarter blood, 6 ftone 10 pounds; four years old, half blood, 7 ftone 1 pound; four years old, full blood, 7 ftone 11 pounds. —Five years old, quarter blood, 7 ftone 6 pounds; five years old, half blood, 7 ftone 11 pounds; five years old, one-third blood, 8 ftone 2 pounds; five yeras old, full blood, 8 ftone 7 pounds. —Six years old, quarter blood, 8 ftone 1 pound; fix years old, half blood, 8 ftone 6 pounds; fix years old, three quarter blood, 8 ftone 11 pounds; fix years old, full blood, 9 ftone 2 pounds. —Seven years old, quarter blood, 8 ftone 8 pounds; feven years old, half blood, 8 ftone 13 pounds; feven years old, three quarter blood, 9 ftone, 4 pounds; feven years old, full blood, 9 ftone 9 pounds."

* * *

Race horse breeding notice, [Rivington's] Royal Gazette, No. 254, 6 March 1779.

"TO COVER,

At Mr. John Thorne's at Great-Neck, at Four Pounds the Seafon,

BASHAW,

"The beft blooded and moft fuccefsful covering Horfe in the government, he was got by Wildair, his dam by Cub; grandam by Second, fhe was the dam of Amaranthus, a very excellent racer, great grandam by Starling, fhe was the dam of Leeds, Fop and Flafh, and feveral other good racers, his great grandam by Old Partner, and full fifter to Bandy's dam. He is remarkably ftrong, boney and handfome. Pafturing and great care taken of Mares at Three Shillings per week. He was efteemed the beft Horfe ever got by WILDAIR.

"Wildair at this time covers in England at Thirty Guineas a Mare."

* * *

Advertisements for horse races, [Rivington's] Royal Gazette, 1779.

"NEW-MARKET RACES.

"ON the 4th day of June will be run for over Hampftead courfe,

"The Hunter's SUBSCRIPTION PURSE and SWEEPSTAKES of TEN GUINEAS each, by any Horfe, Mare or Gelding 15 hands, carrying 10 ftone, higher and lower weights in proportion, the beft of three two mile heats.

"On the 5th day of June the Ladies and Gentleman's SUBSCRIPTION PURSE and SWEEPSTAKES of TEN GUINEAS each, by any Horfe, Mare or Gelding 15 hands, carrying 10 ftone, weight for age, and inches in proportion, the beft of three two mile heats.

"On the 6th day of June, the WHIP will be run for, free for any Horfe, Mare or Gelding 15 hands, carrying 10 ftone, higher or lower weight for age and inches in proportion, the beft of one four mile heat.

"No horfe, &c. to be permitted to run that has not been a fortnight in training upon Hampftead courfe before the 4th of June, or entered for what race he runs for at Mr. Rivington's a week before ftarting.

"Subfcriptions to be taken in at Mr. Rivington's, and a judge of the courfe to be chofen by the owners of the horfes.

"The Whip to be purchafed by the fportfmen of the Navy and Army, and the name of the winning horfe engraved upon it." (No. 271, 5 May 1779)

"Jamaica Races.
To be run for on Tuefday the 26th inftant.
A Subfcription Purfe of Twenty Guineas,
"Free for any Horfe, Mare or Gelding, carrying weight for inches, 14 hands, 8 ftone, higher or lower in proportion; feven pounds allowed for every inch, to run the beft of three heats, twice round the Beaver Pond to each heat.

"The Horfes, &c. to be be fhewn and entered on Monday the 25th inft. at Mr. W. Betts's in Jamaica." (No. 319, 20 October 1779)

"New Market Races,
Hampfted Plains.
"ON Monday next, the Firft of November, will be run for a Subcription Purfe of Ten Guineas, free for any horfe, mare, or gelding (the horfe Dulcimore excepted), to carry weight for inches, 14 hands to carry 8 ftone, and 7 lb. for every inch over or under to be allowed, the beft in three one mile heats; each horfe to pay Half a Guinea entrance; the fecond beft horfe to have the ftakes by winning a clear heat.

"N.B. Two very famous horfes will ftart for Four Hundred Guineas precifely at Twelve o'Clock, and the Subfcription Purfe to be run for exactly at One." (No. 322, 30 October 1779)

"New-Market Races,
Hampftead Plains,
"ON Wednefday the 10th inftant, will be run for a Subfcription Purfe of Twenty-Five Guineas, the beft of three two mile circular heats, free for any horfe, mare or gelding, (the horfe Dulcimore excepted) carrying weight for inches, 14 hands to carry eight ftone, and 7lb. to be allowed for every inch over or under, the firft horfe to have 17 Guineas, the fecond 5 Guineas, and the third beft 3 Guineas, with winning each a clear heat, each to pay One Guinea entrance, no lefs than five horfes to ftart, and to ftart precifely at XII o'Clock.

"Alfo to be run for by two noted horfes, a bett of One Hundred Guineas, one two mile heat, to ftart at XI o'clock, likewife a bet of 50 Guineas, to ftart half after XII o'Clock, to run one two mile heat, and a bet for 40 Guineas, one two mile heat.

"N.B. Each horfe to be entered between the hours of IX and XI o'clock at Loofley and Elms's Tent near the Starting Poft, or to pay Two Guineas Entrance, if admitted after the faid time. If any difputes fhould arife, they are to be decided by the majority of the fubfcribers prefent.

"Every perfon who fhall erect a Booth or Tent or retail provifions or liquors on the Plains, will be expected to fubfcribe One Guinea to the Subfcription Purfe. God Save the King." (No. 324, 6 November 1779)

* * *

Race horse breeding notice, [Rivington's] Royal Gazette, No. 371, 19 April 1780.

"TO COVER

"At Philip Platt's, in Flufhing, Long Ifland, at Four Pounds Currency a Mare, Eight Pounds to infure a Colt, or One Guinea a fingle Leap, Mr. Oliver Water's handfome, tall and powerfull, dark

Chefnut HORSE
SPECULATOR,

"He was got by old Col. Baylor's Fearnought, a fon of Regulus, out of which Mr. Warren's famous Roan Mare, which was Dam of Carelefs and Camillus, two of the moft famous Racers fince Childers's time.

"Fearnought's Dam was got by Mr. Greville's celebrated Bajazet, a famed fon of Lord Godolphin's Arabian. Speculator has more of that valuable Stallion's blood n his veins than any Horfe hitherto known upon the American Turf, and, whether for Racing, Fox-Hunting, the Road or Carriage, the likelieft of all Horfes to get excellent ftock out of tolerable Mares.

"Good Grafs for Mares at Six Shillings a Week."

* * *

Christopher Marshall, Lancaster, Pennsylvania soldier, discusses the local horse racing, 25 July 1780, in William Duane, ed., *Extracts from the Diary of Christopher Marshall, Kept by Philadelphia and Lancaster, During the American Revolution, 1774-1781* (Albany, N.Y.: Joel Munsell, 1877), 256.

"The horse race that was begun yesterday, but not ended, was completed this morning. The wager, it's said, was Twenty-five hundred Pounds, won by Gasper Dull's black horse.... More horse racing this afternoon.... Had our government by their officers exerted the authority that they have used with some degree of cruelty on the poor farmers by taking their horses out of their ploughs, &c., they might have collected a great number of useless yet valuable ones to-day and yesterday on the race ground. This would have been praiseworthy by showing they were true friends to government, by *first*, suppressing the breakers of the law of the state,...."

* * *

Advertisement for a horse race, [Rivington's] Royal Gazette, No. 430, 11 November 1780.

"By PERMISSION.
THREE DAYS SPORT,

"On Monday the 13th of November, will be
    Run for on Afket Heath, formerly called
    Flat Land Plains, five mile, from Brooklyn
    Ferry, the Noblemen and Gentlemens

PURSE of SIXTY POUNDS,

"FREE for any Horfe, Mare or Gelding, except the Bay Mare that won the purfe laft feafon at Hampftead Plains, which at that time belonged to Mr. Wortman, and fince that purchafed by Mr. Allen, and alfos the Bay Horfe which won the plate at Beaver Pond laft feafon, carrying weight for age and inches, to run the beft of three two mile heats, the winner to have Fifty Pounds, and the fecond beft Ten Pounds, upon winning a clear Heat.

"Each Horfe &c. to pay *Two Guineas* Entrance and not lefs than FOUR to ftart.

"To ftart precifely at Eleven o'Clock.

"Alfo the fame day will be run for, a Saddle, Bridle, and Whip, of Fifteen Pounds value, by PONIES not exceeding 13 and 1-2 hands high, all under 13 hands to catch weight, 13 hands and an inch to carry feven pounds more than the heavieft catch, and thirteen hands and an half, to carry fourteen pounds more than the heavieft catch, to run the beft of three one mile heats, the firft to have the Saddle and Bridle, the fecond the Whip.

"To pay the TWO DOLLARS Entrance; no lefs than Four to ftart, and to ftart at One o'Clock.

"—On Tuefday the 14th, The LADIES PURSE of FIFTY POUNDS will be run for, on the fame conditions as the firft day's Purfe, the Horfes excepted in the firft day, and the winner of the firft day's Purfe not to ftart, the firft to have FORTY POUNDS, & the fecond beft TEN POUNDS.

"On Wednefday the 15th will be run for, the country fubfcription Purfe of FIFTY POUNDS free for any Horfe, mare or Gelding, carrying weight for blood and age, to run the beft in three two miles heats, to pay two guineas entrance, and no lefs than four to fatrt: The firft horfe to have thirty pounds, the fecond beft fifteen pounds, and the third beft five pounds. To ftart at Eleven o'clock.

"All Horfes to be entered and meafured at Mr. Loofley's Booth, on the Raceground, between Ten and Eleven o'clock in the morning and Four in the afternoon, on Saturday the 11th inftant, or to pay double entrance at the poft.

"If any difpute fhall arife, to be decided by the Judge of the courfe, or the majority of the Subfcribers prefent.

"It is expected that no perfon will attempt to erect a booth, or fell wine, liquors, &c. unlefs firft fubfcribing, at leaft, two guineas towards the Saddle, Bridle and Whip, and other expences attending the races.

"[pointing hand] Gentlemen fond of FOX HUNTING, are requefted to meet at LOOSELY's King's Head Tavern, at Day-break, during the Races.

"Alfo to be run for on Tuefday, the fecond Day of the Races by Women, a Holland Smock and a Chintz Gown, full trimmed, to run the beft two in three, quarter mile heats, the firft to have the Smock and Gown, of Four Guineas value, the fecond beft a Guinea, and the third beft Half a Guinea —To ftart precifely at 1 o'Clock.

"GIVE and TAKE PLATE.

"Seven years old, three quarter blood, to carry 10 ftone, 7 pounds for quarter blood over or under, fix years old 9 ftone 7 pounds, five years old 8 ftone 12 pounds four years old 8 ftone.

"On WEDNESDAY,

A GOLD LACED HAT of five guineas value to be run for by MEN, the beft two in three quarter mile heats, to ftart at 1 o'clock.

"N.B. If foul weather, the races, &c. to be poftponed till the next fair day, when notice will be given by Mr. Loofley's Union Flag being hoifted, by 7 o'Clock in the morning.

"A KENNEL is provided on the race ground for the reception of fuch dogs as may be brought, Gentlemn who will favour the fportfmen with their dogs fhall have them well taken care of.

"N.B. A Band of Musick will attend, and
GOD SAVE THE KING
will be played every Hour during the Races."
* * *
Jeremiah Greenman, Rhode Island officer, as a prisoner on Long Island, goes to a horse race, 7 June 1781, in Robert C. Bray and Paul E. Bushnell, eds., *Diary of a Common Soldier in the American Revolution, 1775-1783. An Annotated Edition of the Military Journal of Jeremiah Greenman* (DeKalb, Ill.: Northern Illinois University Press, 1978), 210.

"...the after noon of the 7th when went to Flat lands [to] a hors race—...."
* * *
Advertisement for a horse race, [Rivington's] Royal Gazette, No. 507, 8 August 1781.

"PRO BONO PUBLICO.

"GENTLEMEN that are fond of Fox Hunting, are requefted to meet at Loofley's Tavern, on Afcot Heath, on Friday morning next between the hours of five and fix, as a pack of Hounds will be there purpofely for a trial of their abilities: Breakfafting and Relifhes until the Races commence. —At Eleven o'clock will be run for an elegant Saddle, &c. value at leaft Twenty Pounds, for which upwards of twelve Gentlemen will ride their own Horfes. —At Twelve, a match will be rode by two Gentlemen, who will alfo ride their own Horfes. —Dinner will be ready at Two o'clock, after which, and fuitable regalements, Racing and other diverfions, will be calculated to conclude the day with pleafure and harmony.   *Brooklyn-Hall, 6th Auguft*, 1781."
* * *
Samuel Dewees, Pennsylvania soldier, describes horse racing at Lancaster, Pennsylvania, circa 1781-1782, in John Smith Hanna, ed., *A History of the Life and Services of Captain Samuel Dewees, A Native of Pennsylvania, and Soldier of the Revolutionary and Last Wars* (Baltimore: Robert Neilson, 1844), 265-266.

Circa 1781-1782: "Some of these officers (the British field-officers) had several very fine English horses, and that were good runners too. Our officers used to run American horses against theirs upon small bets, and would so manage it as that the English horses won the stakes. The American officers by a little management in this way, soon found out the bottom of their own horses, as well as that of the English ones. The American officers would get the English officers to run their horses against time on small bets, and when they found out the greatest speed of the English horses, they then went off some little distance where they would be out of view of the English officers, and ran their (American) horses like distance, and aginst the same time. After they had done this, they would know what the English horses could do, and what their own could do also. The American officers would then take on heavy bets and win them. At last they made up large purses to be run for. The British officers depending upon the bottom of their horses, which they still thought could not be beaten, 'forked over' their yellow-boys (gold) largely into purses. I recollect that our officers, by their Yankee Jonathan management, were always able to best John Bull with their American chargers. Major Varnum's (American) horse came out first, and won the first purse, and Major Green's (American) horse came out second and won the second purse, whilst John Bull came out last and among the missing, or at least his shiners (guineas) were missed, and a good many of them too, they having *absquatulated*, and sought refuge in the pockets of the American officers (as the transferred captives of the captured,) to whom they were of signal service. This was fine fun for the American soldiers and the citizens of Lancaster, for they (the soldiers) laid claim to the merit of their horses in mettle and speed, as they were able to do to the merit of their own bravery upon the battle-fields of their country."

* * *

Advertisements for horse races, [Rivington's] Royal Gazette, No. 1782.

"*PRO BONO PUBLICO.*
Afcot Heath Races.

"TO BE RUN for, on the 24th of April next, a *SWEEP STAKES* of one hundred guineas, each fubfcriber, play or pay, a fingle four mile heat: each horfe to carry ten ftone.

"Any horfe, mare, or gelding, within the lines, will be allowed to run, on the owners depofiting the above fum, on or before the 10th day of April next, at Brooklyn Hall, where the articles of agreement are to be feen. —The horfes to ftart precifely at twelve o'clock.

"The noted horfes Mercury and Gold Finder, are already entered.
NEXT DAY.

"A match of an HUNDRED GUINEAS will be run for betwixt the grey horfe Jupiter, of Brooklyn, and the well known horfe Barney, of Staten-Ifland.

"N.B The grand races for the Hundred Pound purfes, will be run for early in May, of which particulars will be publifhed in future papers." (No. 572, 23 March 1782)

"Horfe Races.

"ON Wednefday next the firft of May will be run on Afscot Heath, between the Horfes
"MERCURY and GOLDFINDER,

The beft of three two mile heats, to carry nine ftone and an half each, for One Hundred Guineas, to ftart precifely at I o'Clock.

"At III o'Clock the fame Day,

Will be run the mile heats, between the two Mares,

"Pink and Petticoats-loofe,

for Fifty Guineas. Befides feveral other fmaller Races." (No. 582, 27 April 1782)

* * *

Advertisements for horse races, [Rivington's] Royal Gazette, 1783.

"*ASCOT RACE.*

"ON Tuefday the 1ft day of April next, a PURSE of ONE HUNDRED GUINEAS, will be run for, on Afcot Heath, between the CALFSKIN Mare, and the Gelding FEARNOUGHT. —The Mare to carry ten ftone, and the Horfe to carry nine ftone. The beft two in three one mile heats. The Horfes to ftart precifely at Twelve o'Clock."

(No. 678, 26 March 1783)

"A RACE.

TO be run for on Wednefday next, round the Beaver Pond, at Jamaica, a purfe of One Hundred Guineas, by the noted Mare Calf Skin, and the noted Black Horfe Loofley, from Bofton.

New-York, June 28, 1783." (No. 705, 28 June 1783)

* * *

Race horse breeding notice, [Rivington's] Royal Gazette, No. 682, 12 April 1783.

"THE FAMOUS HORSE
YOUNG BRUTUS,

YOUNG BRUTUS was got by Mr. Martindale's famous Old Brutus, and out of a Mare called Silver Heels; which was got by the Duke of Devonfhire's Traveller; Traveller's Dam was a Cade Mare, her Grandam by Carelefs; her great Grandam was got by the Godolphin Arabian: Old Brutus was got by Mafh, belonging to the Duke of Cumberland, out of a Mare called Matchlefs. the Pedigree of thefe capital Horfes is fo well known both in England and America, by moft Gentlemen Sportfmen, there is no occafion to fay any thing more Young Brutus, at Five Years old, was matched to Run, at Charleftown, for Five Hundred Guineas, Two Mile Heats, which he won with eafe; and at Six Years old won an Hundred Guineas at Sillcops, Four Mile Heats, beating very capital Horfes, proving himfelf, on thefe occafions, a good Racer, and is very likely to get good Colts.

"This Horfe is a Strawberry Roan, Fifteen Hands and a Half High; Covers at Little-Neck, on Long-Ifland, at Mr. Stephen Hicks's, at Half a Joe the Seafon, Six Pounds a Colt, or One Guinea a fingle Leap. Good Pafturing for Mares (on the faid Neck, which is very well known) at Three Shillings per Week, with proper Care and Attendance."

* * *

Prohibition against horse racing, [Rivington's] Royal Gazette, No. 726, 10 September 1783.

"WHEREAS Complaint has been made, that of late frequent HORSE-RACING, has been on the High Roads near this City, endangering the Lives of Paffengers: This is to forbid all Perfons in future from fuch Practices, under pain of the fevereft Punifhment....

By Order of the Commandant,
JOHN BLUCKE, *Secretary.*

New-York, Auguft 30, 1783."

Chapter 16

HUNTING

Far and away the sport that occurs most frequently in colonial and Revolutionary historical records, often with great detail, is hunting. No other sport can match the number of diary entries, journal accounts, memoir passages, and travel narratives that described the writer's own experiences afield or observed those of others. Objections may arise about calling hunting a sport, but it is a fact that Americans of this period labeled it such, adding other similar words such as pastime, diversion, and amusement. Even when the writer or teller seems to have been recording subsistence or market hunting, most of the hunters spoke about what enjoyment or diversion they were having. Their own words explain why so many men, and fewer women, slogged off into wet forests, soggy swamps, scorching or freezing plains, and dry deserts in search of one particular species or anything available.

Americans hunted then enthusiastically, and by many accounts, with abandon. Nearly every promotional description of the colonies and travel narrative gushed about the prodigious amount of wildlife available. They also discussed the hunting by indigenous peoples, missing the obvious fact about the horticultural nature of most tribes south of the subarctic region. To Europeans who were not aristocrats and thus had little chance to hunt, the colonization of the Americas opened, to their way of thinking, a new form of recreation. For the aristocrats the Americas were yet another playground for hounds and horn. As environmental historians have noted, the impact on American wildlife in these centuries was mostly disastrous. Under the principle of "free taking" guaranteed in many colonial laws or charters, colonists could not restrain themselves. Some of the Puritans, such as John Winthrop, worried about the state of their salvation, if they hunted too often or took too much pleasure in it, but even in New England hunting became lawful recreation every day but the Sabbath. Otherwise Americans shot, as anti-hunters phrase it, at anything that moved. Much of what they killed the hunters ate or stripped of its fur or hides, but clearly some of the shooting was to kill for the sake of killing. Expanding markets for some animal-derived commodities propelled hunters, indigenous and Euroamerican —and even a few African-Americans with the right to have a firearm to hunt— to harvest animals as if they were so many crops in the field. Bounties on predators and vermin added more incentive to kill. Many times whole communities would turn out to chase down solitary predators or stage sweeps through the woods. Newspapers sometimes published "body count" type stories of the astoundingly successful ones.

Yet early in the colonial period, some colonists developed a sense of waste and conservation. Although an outright anti-hunter movement did not exist save a few poets who wrote sympathetic odes to the quarries, most every colony passed legislation stipulating hunting seasons and rudimentary notions of bag limits. Some laws prohibited hunting specific species altogether at certain locales to let populations rebound. Additionally nearly every colony outlawed unsportsmanslike methods of hunting such as firehunting, in which the hunter or his servants carried torches or pans of coals to fan into flames to immobilize the curious or stunned prey at night. Fear of fires in the woods likely was a major thought behind these laws, but the net effect on the wildlife was the same. But clearly there was class conflict afoot as well, as patrician hunters sought to impose control on the unruly lower classes. By the 1780s these ideas were crystallizing into a sportsmanship code, best expressed in *The Sportsman's Companion; or, An Essay on Shooting,* by an unidentified sportsman. Few examples of these laws appear below because of their sheer number and complexity, and space constraints. The following documents, numerous and some lengthy, speak of the longstanding passion for hunting by early Americans.

[Consult the general writings about sports, recreation, and the various colonial, provincial, territorial, and state Sabbath and gaming laws in Chapter One for other sources about the specific sports or games in this chapter.]

John Armstrong, poet, refers to hunting in *The Art of Preserving Health,* 4th ed. (London and Boston: Green & Russell, 1757), 37.

> "WHATE'ER you ftudy, in whate'er you fweat,
> Indulge your tafte. Some love the manly foils;
> The tennis fome; and fome the graceful dance.
> Others, more hardy, range the purple heath,
> Or naked ftubble; where from field to field
> The founding coveys urge their labouring flight;
> Eager amid the rifing cloud to pour
> The gun's unerring thunder: and there are,
> Whom ftill the meed of the green archer charms.
> He chuses beft, whofe labour entertains
> His vacany fancy moft: the toil, you hate,
> Fatigues you foon, and fcarce improves your limbs."

* * *

A children's book moralizes about hunting, in *A Little Pretty Pocket-Book, Intended for the Amusement and Instruction of Little Master Tommy and Pretty Miss Polly* (London: J. Newbery, 1767), 99.

"SHOOTING.

THO' fome *Birds*, too heedlefs,	MORAL. From hence we may learn
Dread no Danger nigh;	That, by one thoughtlefs Trip,
Yet ftill by the *Fowlers*	Strange Accidents happen
They inftantly die.	'Twixt the Cup and the Lip."

* * *

An unidentified gentleman publishes the first systematic statement of the hunter's sportsmanship code, *The Sportsman's Companion; or, An Essay on Shooting* (New York: Robertsons, Mills and Hicks, 1783).

"To the PUBLIC.

"To my brother Sportfmen in particular, to the Public in general, and to fuch young Gentlemen as are defirous of becoming Adepts in the Diverfion of the Field, I beg leave to Addrefs myfelf here.

"GENTLEMEN,

"WHEN I undertook to attempt this fmall ESSAY, at the requeft of fome of my Friends, I muft own that I was difcouraged by the Diffidence of my own Abilities as a Writer upon any Subject;

but, emboldened by the utmoft Confidence and hopes in my Readers Lenity and Indulgence on this Score, I am, on thefe Confiderations, come to the Refolution to prefent it to the World, fuch as it is, with all its Incorrrections and Imperfections.

"As nothing worth the reading on this Subject has appeared in Public, to my Knowledge, and, if any Thing new and ufeful fhould offer itfelf in this Work, it will give the utmoft Pleafure, moft heartfelt Satisfaction, and moft amply Reward,

Gentlemen,

Your moft Obedient and

Moft devoted humble Servant,

The AUTHOR.

"PREFACE.

"THE Author of thefe Sheets much regrets that his Situation, at the Time of writing them, did not admit of his procuring Engravings and Plates, that would be ufeful and ornamental, make the Work complete, and render fome Paffages clear and demonftrative, as well to illuftrate the Dimentions, Length, and Size of the Fuzee, Shot-Bag, Powder-Horn, &c. as to fully comprehend the Nature and different Attitudes of the Sportfman firing at Birds, in different Flights and Directions, as of the various Pofitions of the Pointer, the Shape and Form of the Collar, Chain, Couples,Spring Collar and Cord, Puzzle, Dog Call, Portable Pocket Whip, Pocket Bottle and Bird Net, &c. &c. &c.

"The greateft Pains, however, have been taken to explain the moft minute Circumftances of Materiality, as well to improve, as to guard againft Accidents attending this Amufement..

"The few Incidents and Digreffions quoted here, are not mentioned for their Novelty, or from any Vanity or Fondnefs in the Author, to relate them, but are ftated as abfolute Facts, to fupport the Ideas that ftruck the Writer, as well as to guard againft the like happening to others.

"The Part which relates to the Choice and Treatment of Dogs, may appear trifling and frivoulous to fome; but the Author begs leave to inform his Readers, that that Subject is not handled with half the minutenefs that was originally intended, and it fwelling the Book much above the Size propofed, is the reafon for not entering more particularly on that Head. It is, notwithftanding, humbly prefumed, that the few Hints given, with my Reader's own Pains and Reflection, will be deemed fufficient.

"The Author has prepared his Mind on the Score of the Cenfure and Ridicule thefe Sheets may meet with, as fuch Gentlemen as are already better informed, will be too generous to publicly difapprove of what is here offered; the lefs informed, I hope, will meet with many Things worth their Attention.

"As to the Diction and grammatical Part of the Book, it's hoped, that, to be clearly underftood, is fufficient without the Advantage of the exact Rules of Grammer; that it is to the generous and noble minded Sportfman, that this is dedicated, and not to the Ungenerous.

"If my Readers will think it any degree of Merit that I have invariably adhered to the Principles that my own Obfervations, long Experience, and the Approbation of moft excellent Sportfmen, have affifted me with in the following Effay: I claim it wholly as my own Productions, entirely new, and totally independent of any borrowed Opinion, or Maxims of any other Writer; never having feen or read a Book upon the Subject.

"THE
Sportfman's Companion;
OR, AN
Effay on Shooting
"CHAP. I

"Of the Choice of Pointer Pups, training and keeping them in good Health.

"IN befpeaking a Pup you fhould calculate his age, fo as to have him from *nine* to *twelve* months old, —againft the feafon for poults or young game, as, at that age, birds lie clofe, and the weather is fine and fitter to exercife your Dog.

"IN the choice of this kind of Pups, the greateft care is neceffary in a thorough knowledge of their pedigree and fpecies. Spurious Pups feldom turn out to any advantage.—There are many kind of Pointers, fuch as the heavy Spanifh Dog, the Ruffian rough Dog, the German, the genuine Englifh Pointer, and the fleet Dogs of that country, with the fmall delicate kind, and many others. I would choofe the fleet fpecie, with a dafh of the Ruffian, on account of its furr, rather large and powerful, and from a young Dam and Sire. Some attention is neceffary in the colour; the white, ground and liver colour, and white and red, or yellow, are generally the beft; though I have feen them good of various colours, and I am credibly informed, that there is an excellent breed of black ones in England. I would prefer white, with liver coloured ears, and flea-bitten spots; or white and red, with fpots of the fame; fome are entirely white, whatever the fpots are, white fhould prevail moft, being eafier feen, and lefs fatiguing to the fight, as one is obliged to have a conftant eye to them in ranging. Bitches are commonly the beft and fleeteft; but they are inconvenient and very troublefome, and often rendered ufelefs, and difappoint you, by either being in heat, or with pup, &c.

"SOME difapprove of the firft litter of the Pups, this I leave to the Phyficians.

"ADMITTING you have got a Pup to your liking, and that you have him under your care, his tail fhould be cut when very young, rather long; nothing disfigures a Dog more than a fhort ftumpy tail, efpecially if he is large.—And I muft here, with the utmoft reluctance, enter upon a fubject that I deteft, although its utility obliges me to mention it, viz. cropping or cutting the ears pretty fhort. I have, by long experience, obferved, that the generality of Pointers, in North-America in particular, have their ears tore with briars and other prickly fhrubs; this keeps them in continual torment, and by a perpetual fhaking of the ears, caufe bleeding and dirtying every body about them. I have known them puffed up and bleed fo much as to prevent their hunting for fome time. I own, that the only remedy for this, which is cropping them when very young, is attended with a degree of barbarity, and disfigures the animals very much; but the neceffity of it, where Pointers are ufed in bad cover, leaves no alternative. I have feen one who had the ears cut; he looked very odd, indeed, and ugly, but never was troubled with fore ears.—I had a Dog that was fo much troubled with this complaint, that I was obliged to cut them about the middle; I firft tried feveral things to cure them, but they always bled, and were cankerous.

"YOU fhould choofe fome fhort ftrong word to name your Dog, as it will be eafier pronounced and better heard in calling him to you in the field; fuch as Don, Dafh, Flufh, Fido, Ponto, Sancho, &c. You fhould prevent his going in the ftreet (if living in town) as they are perfect loobies and fubject to many accidents; nor fhould they be permitted to lie clofe to the fire; this chills them: Their food fhould be wholefome, and, in the fhooting feafon, ought to be chiefly meal of fome fort. They are fubject to what is called the diftemper in Dogs (not madnefs); it's either caufed by worms or colds; they run, at the nofe and eyes, with a coughing and choaking, and refufe their food, and fometimes linger out in this manner, daily wafting in flefh, about fix months, though they moft frequently die, if not relieved by medicine, in a few days. Many remedies are ufed for this ficknefs in Dogs, and, as I am no Phyfician, I fhall only mention one, which I have applied often with fuccefs: On the firft appearance of this diftemper, give your Dog, in proportion to his age and ftrength, Crocufmetolorum: This will, perhaps, make him perfpire, emit, and purge; keep him warm for a few days, and repeat the medicine if neceffary. I have loft, in five years time, fix young Dogs, before I made ufe of the Crocus, from the age of two months to eleven, notwithftanding the applications of many remedies; but I have cured feveral with this medicine, effectually fince. After they are done growing they are feldom feized with the diftemper.— Let their bed be clean ftraw or fomething warm.

"ABOUT the age of fix or feven months, you may take out your Pup, fome times to air him, but by no means fatigue him—taking care not to permit him to run after fowls, fheep, cows, horfes, &c.—The firft thing to be taught him, is obedience, by making him come to you, and follow you whenever you pleafe, to make him follow well is a great point gained, as they are very giddy at firft; next make him clofe *down,* and let him remain fo as long as you pleafe—this you may do in the houfe, by laying a piece of meat down before him, and not allow him to touch it until you think proper, then hide the meat and make him hunt for it.—If you have a mind he fhould fetch and carry, never fuffer him to touch a ftone, large bones, or a ftick; or any other hard fub-ftance, this will make him hard mouthed—make a ball of fome fpungy fubtance, and if he is hard in the mouth, fill it with pins, with their points prickling outward, in imi-tation of a hedge-hog's briftles, this will foften his mouth.

"IN Great-Britain and Ireland it is not common for Pointers to fetch your dead or wounded game, but in America or in other woody countries, this is an indifpenfible qualification in them, on account of the immenfe cover and brufh, which caufes the lofs of many birds that are even fhot dead, particularly Quail, when the Dogs have not been taught to fetch and carry.

"WHEN your Dog follows well, is obedient, and fetches his ball well, at the proper feafon for poults, (but never before he is *nine* months or a year old, for fome Dogs are much forwarder than others) take him out alone, or with a very ftaunch Dog, to fome ground where you expect to meet with game, and if he is of a good tractable kind, he will not fail to fcent and hunt them; don't check his beating fleet, and going far out from you at firft, but chaftife him gently for purfuing and chacing the game; don't be in a hurry to make him *point,* he will very likely do that of his own accord, or back the old Dog when you call out, clofe—or down, Sir—you fhould have a fmall ivory dog or cat-call to bring in your Dog, which is much eafier than calling him in the voice.

"I HAVE made a Dog perfectly ftaunch in one day, in this manner; in all this do not take your gun out, nothing but a fmall whip is neceffary, until you have made him quite ftaunch—you fhould then make him quarter and beat the ground to your mind, by figns from your hand. If your Dog is hard to ftop, fiery, and fprings his game, you muft provide a broad leather collar with fmall nails drove through it, pointing inwards to his neck; the collar muft be pretty wide, and fixed fo as to prick him a little on your pulling a long cord faftened to it, for the purpofe of checking him when he offers to run in, which muft trail after him as he beats the ground; if this does not do with a few trials, have patience, and time with the affiftance of this machine, which is very fimple, will make him *point.*—Some very good Dogs are long ere they ftaunch, if they are croffed in the breed by vigorous and high-bred ones.

"WHEN your Dog *ftands* well, take out your gun, and it will be a great ftep towards making him, to fhoot a bird to him the firft time you fire; what is to be done then will be mentioned hereafter.

"IN Scotland, where game-keepers and fowlers find out the Moor-fowl and Par-tridge fitting on the ground when the Dog *points,* and fhoots them for the fake of kill-ing plenty of game,—they teach their Dogs to ftand ftill on their point or fett, on their miffing fire or burning priming—this is absolutely neceffary in the above practice, for if the Dog was permitted to move forward at either of the aforefaid accidents, his very action would fpring game—you may therefore teach him this with a piftol and a little powder, before you begin to take out your gun; you may alfo fire your piftol at game on their rifing, to habituate your Dog not to *chace* when you fire.

"I am fo very averfe to netting birds with fetters, that I fhall avoid faying any thing here about it, it is rather too much known and practifed—' though when done with difcretion in proper places, it is entertaining, and requires excellent Dogs.

"TO prevent your young Dog's acquiring bad tricks, you fhould never lend him until he is thoroughly broke, or let another perfon hunt him, or go out fhooting with bad Pointers, and never with Spaniels.—Some Pointers that do very well alone, have an anxiety and eagernefs from being jealous and wanting the lead of other Dogs, make them fpring your game; it is therefore neceffary to accuftom them to hunt in company with others of equal ftaunchnefs, back and point together: When Dogs know their game, they don't always range in the fame direction, and it often happens that one is ftanding to a point when the other know nothing about the matter; you fhould therefore, adopt fome *word* by which all the Dogs may know that one is fixed at his point; I have made ufe of calling to him that ftands, pretty *loud* by name, fuch as *clofe—* Ponto; the others will immediately hearken, repair to the *point*, and back if ufed to this. If after your Dog is pretty well made, that you obferve him to fnub and ftop at fmall birds and other vermin, and carry his head low in the manner of Spaniels; if he will bear it, ufe the puzzle until he is perfectly cured of this fault.

"YOUR Dog fhould not be fed on the morning you hunt him, unlefs it be a little bread or fomething light; but he ought to have a plentiful fupper and nothing falt; refrefh him about mid-day, when you reft, with bread and milk, or meal and milk.

"CHAP. II.
"Choice of your Gun, Powder, and Shot.

"HERE it may be expected I fhould enlarge upon the different kinds and quality of fowling pieces, in general; but I beg leave to avoid that fubject, and proceed to give my opinion of its fize only: Your gun then fhould never be too light; gentlemen in general choofe light pieces, for the convenience of carrying them, but they ought to be rather heavy and not too fhort, with a ftrong wide barrel and large deep groove at the breech; this facilitates the quicknefs of your aim. I would prefer two guns of equal fize and caliber to the double barrel, the one carried by a fervant accuftomed to this kind of exerfice, who could be entrufted to load it, and who ought therefore to carry powder and fhot.

"YOUR powder fhould be of the beft and drieft kind: For Groufe and Partridge, take fhot, No. 3, 4 and 5; for Quail, Woodchuck and Snipe, ufe No. 7 and 8; and the fhot ought to be varied according to the feafon; when the birds are young, the fmaller your fhot the better; but in the months of November and December, a large kind is neceffary, the game being then in full plumage, are become ftronger, and as the cold increafes, you feldom get fo nigh as you do in fine weather, fome warm fun-fhine days excepted.

"CHAP. III.
"Taking Aim in various Directions, and firft of the Groufe.

"IF you have a *Point* to a pack of Groufe (which you may generally diftinguifh from a fingle bird by the action of your Pointer, if an experienced one, he will fhew greater caution and point fquatter to a pack; covey, or bevy, than to a fingle bird) and that a bird or two rifes too far off, and not to your liking, don't fire; others will, moft likely, follow.—If the bird you fingle out fhould fly ftraight from you, horizontally, if he is too nigh, be fure not to hurry, give him time to gain a proper diftance, that your fhot may fpread and have its proper effect; cover your bird, and, keeping the piece firm againft your fhoulder, pull the trigger the firft glance you have of him—from 35 to 50 paces, which habit will pretty nigh afcertain, is a good diftance, 'though you may kill at fixty paces diftance and more.

"IF your bird flies to your right, aim a little before his head, always taking your time with the utmoft deliberation and compofure, should he be too nigh in this direction, wait until his flight and the trace of your fhot, will bring him to the point of a faliant angle.

"IF he goes to your left, fhoot alfo before him a little, and obferve the fame direction, this is called crofs fhooting, and requires the fteadieft aim. Arched fhots (i.e. when the bird rifes high before he recovers his full flight) are deemed the eafieft and the fureft, therefore if a bird rifes or towers, you may take your own time; always obferving to cock your piece after the bird rifes; many act contrarily, but befides the danger of this, you will always, when you have habituated yourfelf to it, have fufficient time,— therefore never walk with your piece cocked, or with your muzzle carried low, or in a carelefs pofition, or pointing to any perfon in company; after you do cock, keep your thumb upon it till you take aim.

"GROUSE, or Heath-cock, may be juftly deemed the fublimity of fhooting, and it is much to be regretted that any fhould have accefs to this diverfion, but fuch as are at leaft competent judges of fo very Majeftical an amufement.—You should therefore be provided with a brace of the beft Pointers, of the fleet fpecies, large and vigorous.

"IN Scotland and England for the moors, this kind of fhooting is not fo laborious for Dogs as it is in North-America; the brufhy plains on Long-Ifland, is the only place I have feen in that country abounding with Groufe, and it is pretty well known to many good fportfmen refiding in New-York and Long-Ifland. As the cover on faid plains is an under oak-wood, of a ftrong and thick brufhy nature, it certainly requires the very beft of Dogs, and it should be fo contrived in your parties, to have always a frefh brace to hunt, for as your Dogs on that ground are obliged to gallop at a very high rate, and rife powerfully to the cover, they are foon fatigued; they ought to have a very large range, the cover being even and the ground extenfive to a long view, admits of their going well out, and as they are fuppofed to be perfectly ftaunch, you run no rifk of fpringing. Of many Pointers, that I have feen carried to this ground, who were deemed good ones in fmall fhooting, few were, at leaft for the firft two or three days, good for much. You fhould then, previous to the feafon for this game, keep your Dogs in good wind, by frequent exercife, and reducing their fat, by feeding them on meal and light diet; by this attention they will be rendered, in fome meafure, prepared for the great exercife that muft enfue, and for which they would be very ill calculated, were they taken immediately from feeding on the run of the kitchen and ftreet carrion.—I have feen tolerable good Dogs brought there, that never made out a bird in three or four days labour.

"AS for directions for finding this game, the plains are fo very large and extenfive that nothing but patience, perfeverance, and labour, with the addition of guides that know their haunts, can enfure fuccefs.—I fhould here avoid attempting to defcribe the feveral articles of conveniency, fuch as horfes, chairs, provifions, liquors, &c. neceffary for this diverfion; it will be prefumptive in me (who am but a ftranger) to delineate them, they being much better known than I can explain them; yet if I was permitted to choofe, I would make the following arrangement:—Suppofe my party to confift of two Gentlemen, I would provide a fingle horfe-chair (the horfe fhould be accuftomed to the firing of arms,) a Servant in a fecond chair, to carry the Dogs, (of which there fhould be two brace at the leaft) provifions, liquors, tea, fugar, &c. and fpare powder and fhot, &c. &c. &c. fo that between the expences of the Gentlemen, Servant, Horfes, Dogs, &c. I may, within moderate bounds, allow three guineas per diem for the whole, to be a very moderate calculation for the expences of this kind of amufement, exclufive of powder and fhot.

"INDIAN-MEAL, porridge and milk is the common food you can get for the Dogs in that part of the country; it is light and wholefome: This and the exercife, foon reduces them to a proper condition for action—Several Gentlemen in and nigh New-York have excellent Dogs, but I cannot avoid giving the preference, to any that I ever faw, to one which, I believe, was General Birch's; he had been fome years in the poffeffion of a man on the Plains who ferved as a Guide to Gentlemen when Groufeing—he had reduced the Dog fo low, that when I faw him firft, he was a mere fkeleton, I thought he could not ftand upon his legs, but he foon convinced me to the contrary by ranging with admirable agility, and perfect ftaunchnefs; this I entirely imputed to his uncommon practice:—The dog was fo habituated to game (or rather over hunted) and kept fo low, that he fcarcely made any fhow when he came upon birds, and drew with feeming indifference; and if he happened far out from you at a point, he fat upon his backfide until you came up to him —being as I thought too weak to ftand in the attitude of pointing for any confiderable time: He was red and white, and of a middling fize. I think of the fleet fpecies, though he was fo low in flefh that I could form no juft idea of his fhape and make.

"A pack of thefe birds will cover will cover a confiderable extent of ground in evenings and mornings, when difperfed and fcattered about after food, that it very often happens after you have had feveral fhots, may be from more than one point to the fame pack, that fome birds ftill remain on the ground, efpecially if they have not been much difturbed;—you fhould therefore allow your Dogs to make full ranges all round and back-hunt, what you take to be the utmoft limits of the ground the pack occupied;— here the excellency of your Dogs are abfolutely neceffary, not only in picking up the remaining game, but alfo in being perfectly obedient and ftill after you fire, and not moving an inch whilft you are loading; they ought indeed to be very cool in general, particularly upon fuch occafions as the above; without this qualification in your Pointers, you will have the mortification of feeing the Groufe rife and fly in fair fhots all round, when perhaps you have not a gun ready to fire, which will not in general be the cafe if the Dogs lay ftill, for in fine weather, the birds will not fometimes be eafily got up.—I muft here beg leave to quote an inftance in fupport of the preceeding ideas., viz.

"I was the firft that took Mr. L——'s Bull-head (fo called, having a fhort head like one of thofe animals, being of the Spanifh kind) to the Plains, I think in the year 1778: He was made in England, was ftaunch, and of the beft breed, was under good command, and feemed rather timid; it was in the latter end of September: the Dog ftood, but when I fired, Bull-head ran out and gave tongue at a great rate; I imputed this to the long fea-paffage and want of practice; called him in, and only fpoke harfh to him. —The fecond fhot, he however behaved much worfe than the firft, and would not come in, but run after a whole pack of Groufe in fingle birds; yelped and barked without intermiffion. He continued this career for a whole day, and all my addrefs could not bring him in, and confequently fpoilt the day's converfation.

"THE fecond day I gave him to our guide, with a rope faftened from his collar to a bell tied about the man's waift. Upon my firing (being very ftrong) he brought the

fellow down upon his face, and trailed him through the brufh a great way, which exafperated our Guide fo much, as to cut the rope and let him go. I faw no more of
Sancho, only at a diftance, for the reft of the day, and though we had another Dog, now
loft the fecond day's fport, not being able to catch him.

"HAD he been my own I certainly would have fhot him. Notwithftanding, Bull-
head next feafon became one of the beft Dogs I ever faw: He was by no means fleet,
but held out well, and, I believe, all art would not induce him to move an inch from
his point. It will feem (to thofe acquainted with this work) incredible to declare that,
in 1781, I hunted him five days fucceffively on the Plains, and on the fifth day, he
travelled to Brooklyne-Ferry, abov forty miles. On this occafion he found more birds
than General Birch's Dog, owing to his fuperior ftrength. L—— and myfelf loft him
once in a brufhy cover, Quail fhooting, at Bufhwick: We called, fhouted, and whiftled
for him very nigh half an hour, and had no appearance of Sancho; at laft I heard a faint
howl, and, turning about, within three yards of my heels, there was poor Bull-head
fixed at a dead point to a bevy.—He became mine afterwards, but falling down from
a garrat, three ftories high, he died of a bruife in a few days. To a Sportfman of fortune, he was worth forty pounds fterling.

"CHAP. IV.
"Of Partridge, Quail, marking in your Game,
with fome interefting Digreffions, and other Matters.

"THESE birds are apt to rife in a flock, though fometimes one part of them takes
wing confiderably before the others; of this you muft judge from your knowledge of
the ground, and, perhaps, of the covey. Suppofe them to get up pretty numerous, and
that you want to kill many birds, as is the general wifh; in that cafe you fhould, previous to their rifing, poft yourfelf at a proper diftance from where you fuppofe them
to lie, by the Dog's attitude; allowing your Servant or one of the company to fpring
them, and fire among them (always taking aim at a particular bird) juft as they clear
the cover or ground, for they immediately difperfe after rifing. If you choofe a fingle
bird, obferve the former directions refpecting the Groufe; though the Partridge being
a leffer object, and of quicker flight, require a quicker and furer fight; this refers to
Partridges in Europe, particulalrly in Great-Britain and Ireland.

"TO afcertain the diftance of the birds from your Dog, a Pointer, at a moderate diftance, will draw and ftretch himfelf out to a beautiful attitude; but if he is taken fhort,
and comes nearer than he would, before he catches the fcent, he droops and hunches
his back almoft double, or, perhaps, *point*, looking over his fhoulder fide-ways (I have
known cautious Dogs ftand with the bird behind, being fo clofe as for fear of fpringing,
to prevent his turning about); this, you'll fay, may be at a detached bird of the covey;
I grant it may; but when the others take wing, you'll be nigh enough, in the common
occurrences, in fuch a cafe, as the body of the covey is feldom at any confiderable diftance from the ftraggling birds.—I have often feen good chances loft by firing at the
firft birds that got up, efpecially where there was no fecond gun ready loaded.

"WE will now fuppofe you have done execution, and killed your game, don't ftir
an inch from where your fired, until you are loaded, nor fhall your Dog be fuffered to
move forward, until you order him, making him come and lay down clofe to your heels
till you have loaded. My reafon for this precaution will appear obvious to every
Sportfman; but I fhall lay it down here for the information of the lefs experienced.

"I HAVE once myfelf met with the following difappointment, and feen the like
happen to others frequently:—My Dog *Cæfar*, made a ftaunch point at Quails, at a

pretty moderate diftance, in an open field, without any other cover than a little thin grafs: Five birds got up and flew in different directions; I fingled out one, fired, and down he fell, to all appearance dead, upon the ground, at about the diftance of 50 yards; contrary to my ufual manner, not thinking he could by any means get off, I encouraged *Cæfar* to quit his ftation, and go fetch him, and moved forward myfelf without loading; juft as the Dog was going to mouth him, up fprings the Quail from between his feet, and towering to a considerable heighth in the air, fell at a great diftance ftone dead, as I judged, in a very thick cover, with the utmoft affiduity, loft him: Had I been loaded I could have eafily fired at him a fecond time, and could not well mifs him.—Another reafon why you fhould load before you go to pick up your bird, is, that there may be more game ftill nigh you, that may rife upon your moving forward, and give you another chance.

"I HOPE the above example, of which there are many inftances, and the reafon affigned, will be fufficient to reconcile Gentlemen to the utility of loading ere they move from whence they fired; and though this may, in fome inftances, be attended with the lofs of a few birds, that are winged and run away into fome hole or bad cover, yet this method will be, in general, as nineteen to one in your favour; befides it ftaunches your Pointer, gives him breath, and effectually prevents his chacing.

"IT frequently happens that you mortally wound your bird, though he flies and apparently does not feem to be in the leaft hurt, any farther than his giving a fudden bounce, and it is often not without caufe.

"I WAS once on the Brufhy-Plains, in company with two Gentlemen, we fell in with a pack of Groufe or Heath-hens, and had fome fhots; as we turned our backs, and were quitting the ground, I heard a bird rifing behind me; I turned quickly about, and, notwithftanding it flew at a great diftance, I covered him and fired; he immediately towered high in the air, and, after croffing a large wood at a confiderable diftance, difappeared. I infifted upon my hitting him, from his towering fo very high: The other Gentlemen laughed, and faid it was impoffible from the diftance I was at when I fired, that the bird was only frightened. I begged, however, that they would ftay for me, and that I would go back after him, and convince myfelf, if poffible.—I took a boy that faw the bird's flight, and one of the Dogs, and after going nigh half a mile, and through a large piece of wood, the Dog found my bird under our feet, lying ftone dead upon his back. I came back with him in great triumph, fhewing him to the company, but on examining could not find any marks of fhot; this renewed the laugh againft me; but the bird being quite warm, I ws fully convinced it was the fame I fired at:—We brought it to our rendezvous, and plucked him with the utmoft care, but could find no impreffion of fhot; at laft, after many fearches, I difcovered that a fingle grain of fhot had carried the end of a pen-feather through the fpine, and the other end in the mouth of the wound, which prevented our feeing it before.—There muft, undoubtedly, be many efcapes of this nature, in the cafe of body wounds: For Groufe, Partridge and Quail, will carry a great quantity of fhot, and fly ftrong and far, when you don't touch their wings, even if you break their legs.

"I, AT another time, in company with Mr. M——, of the 69th Regiment, fired at a fingle cock Quail in a grafs meadow, at a moderate diftance, and a very deliberate fhot; the bird bounded ftrong and ftruck againft the ground, but, without any delay, rebounded and towered to a great heighth, and flew ftrong and fwift over a very broad and thick cover: I gave him up, but faw he was hit. About an hour afterwards, as the

Dogs were ranging on the other fide the thicket, Ponto made a fudden *point,* very clofe and fquat; I called Mr. M——, and faid I would lay any bett that was the bird I had fired at: We endeavoured to rife our game, but nothing ftirred. All the Dogs by this time backed and confirmed the point. We then went up, and there the poor Quail fat within two feet of the Dog's nofe, alive, but could not rife or move; I took it up, and, upon examining him, one of his thighs was broke, and his guts hanging out, his belly being tore in a very large gafh.—I mention thefe circumftances not as uncommon, and in the marvelous; many others of the fame kind might be quoted: But to caution the young Sportfman to attend particularly to the flight of his bird, after firing and apparently miffing, efpecially if they are feen to tower, bound, or give a fudden ftart or fhake; thefe are fure figns of being hit.

"SHOULD you fire and not kill, or in a Sportfman's term mifs your fhot, have an eye to the flight of the game and mark them in as clofe as poffible, but do not run immediately to find them, ftill having attention to where they alighted by taking fome mark; fuch as a tree, bufh, fhrub, or rock:—There may be more birds between you and them, you fhould therefore with coolnefs beat the intermediate ground towards them; this will give your game time to fettle, befides it may caufe them to take foot to fome other place, which will facilitate your Dog's roading and drawing up to them with greater certainty. Marked birds is hard for a Dog to make out, as he will have no other fcent than fuddenly winding them in beating his ground, and as their time on their new ground has been but fhort, and perhaps did not move an inch from where they firft alighted—confequently their fcent will be weaker than where they perhaps bafked, and roaded, and ftrayed about for a confiderable time; you fhould therefore in general beat againft the wind, particularly in going towards marked game. If your pack, covey, or bevy is fpread on the marked ground they will fquat and lye clofe, this is the effence of fhooting, you fhould therefore beat and re-beat the ground and make the Dog beat alfo very clofe;—fome old Dogs are excellent at picking up birds in fuch a fituation. I have feen from twelve to fourteen different *points* to one bevy of Quails on New-York Ifland after marking them; and I have on the fame ground in the year 1778 feen ten fhots fired from one point, i.e. the Dog ftood at his point in a brufhy cover, and it being a fine calm day in Autumn, all the birds rofe almoft fingly;—two of the Gentlemen that were of the party are Captains in the Navy;—the Dog was Mr. Templeton's Nero: You fhould, therefore, when you perceive Quails to rife fingly, or in two's and three's, beat your ground very clofe.—In all the foregoing cafes, I muft infift upon your keeping your Dog in whilft you are loading, admitting him ever fo ftaunch, his very action in beating about, will rife the game.

"EXCEPTING where the abundance of birds renders Dogs ufelefs, all depends upon the goodnefs of your Pointer.

"I HAVE known the beft fhots, fire a whole day with indifferent Dogs to little pur-pofe, and I have known the fame Gentlemen, out at other times with good Dogs where the birds were not fo plenty, kill every fhot, and bring home feveral brace. This may be eafily accounted for: Calm weather is beft for this diverfion, birds fly unpleafant on windy days.

"CHAP. V.
"Of fhooting Parties and other Matters relative thereto.

"I WOULD recommend the avoiding a large company on fhooting parties; two Gentlemen is fufficient to beat the ground together, there may be more of the fame party at a diftance, and meet occafionally.—Three is commonly attended with fome degree of hurry and heat, and above that number, with guns, is very unfociable, and nothing but confufion can enfue; befides, as every Gentleman is not accuftomed to this amufement, large companies may be attended with many inconveniencies and accidents.

"SUPPOSE our fhooting party to confift of two Gentlemen, their Servants and Dogs, &c. I would recommend the following manner of fhooting to them, viz. That they do not fire together, except when agreed at a covey or bevy, but that, from all *points* of the Dog, they fhoot in turn; that fuppofing the two Gentlemen walking abreaft and the Dogs ftanding of courfe, if the birds take fhort to the right hand, or, in other language, turn upon him, he on that fide, has a right to the fhot, for if the Gentleman on the left was to fire, it would be, perhaps, acrofs his companion. The fame to be inviolably obferved fhould the birds take the left, or turn in upon the Gentleman on that fide. If the Gentleman whofe turn it is to fhoot firft, miffes his bird, it is reafonable the other fhould endeavour to remedy this, by trying his fhot, particularly in ftraight directions, giving fufficient time to diftinguifh the effects of the two difcharges.—Shooting both together at the fame moment at a bird, is little diverfion; it leaves a doubt whofe fhot did execution, fpoil the game if too nigh, and is generally with the cooleft attended with fome emotion; it is much better to give the bird fair play, as Gentlemen, and have ocular demonftration who is the beft fhot. Yet all accidental chances fhould be embraced inftantly, without ceremony, fuch as birds fpringing unexpectedly before you, rifing fide ways, or, as it often happens, behind, for there is fuch a thing as leaving birds behind, though you and the Dogs have almoft trodden upon them; I think this is called overfhooting the game. Woodcocks frequently come ftrait towards you, I would recommend your letting them pafs, and take them at a proper diftance after you turn about on your heel; this is commonly an arched fhot, the bird being high. Other game turn fhort upon you fometimes, efpecially if you hunt with Spaniels, but I have obferved it more peculiar in Woodcocks.

"WHEN you fee your Dog ftand fixed upon his *Point*, don't call out loud and elated to your company to obferve him, *nor fhould you run up to him,* this befides *heating you* and *affecting your nerves,* is apt to caufe an anxiety in your Dog and if not old and ftaunch, may make him move on and fpring your game. Never in any fituation make your Pointer fpring your birds for you, on the contrary, go round him, and if the fun fhines, endeavour to have it to your back, this, when the fun is low, in mornings or evenings, prevents its rays from obftructing your fight along the barrel, which fhould never be bright, but ought to be darkened with fome kind of ftain.

"CHAP. VI.

"Of Improfperous Days for Shooting, with Inftances quoted from undoubted Veracity; the Caufes explained, and Remedy propofed.

"I HAVE frequently remarked that fome days are improfperous to the Sportfman, although he fees many birds, and fires feveral fhot, and fair ones too: I have known a dark horizon, high wind, and other caufes blamed for this, but I have frequenty known the fame to happen in very clear, calm, ferene days; I will not here enter into the feveral caufes, but beg leave to mention what I think fhould be done: When you are unlucky and don't fhoot well, I would reft and refrefh myfelf and Dogs, and repeat this pretty often, until I was quite compofed, for nothing caufes a greater anxiety than difappointments of this kind, when you are confident in your own adroitnefs, the goodnefs of your gun, powder and fhot, &c. It is probably owing to this heat and anxioufnefs that you fire fo badly. I hope my generous reader will pardon me in mentioning a cir-cumftance of this kind, when I declare it to be a fact, upon the ftricteft honour and veracity. My Father was one of the beft fhots that I ever faw, with ball or fmall fhot, and no man would contend the point with him in the part of the world he lived in; he was a very even tempered man, indefatigable and patient; I followed him one day, as I often did when a boy, to a moor that abounded with Moor-fowl or Groufe; it was in September, the day was clear, but rather windy; we had a ftaunch old Dog and a young one, who was rather rude at the firft birds we met, and did not pleafe my Father, he accordingly corrected him, as I imagined, with the utmoft compofure and judgement, (though upon the fequel I believe that he heated himfelf with the Dog) this had a very good effect upon *Pedro*, he backed the old Dog the whole day afterwards. But to our fubject, he fired many fhots, perhaps from fix to ten, very fair ones, and miffed them every one; he expreffed fome wonder and changed his powder and fhot, yet he miffed four or five fhots more; in all this he did not, to our knowledge, touch a feather; we at laft about twelve o'clock, fat down and refrefhed ourfelves, about an hour we be-gan again, and the firft point, he fhot his bird; I faw plainly, young as I was, that the *charm* was expelled, for I never faw him mifs fix times in all his fhooting before that day;—to end my digreffion, I was loaded with twelve brace of Groufe by fun-fet, and in all the afternoon's fhooting, he did not mifs once in firing twenty-four times.

"ANOTHER fhort ftory and then I will end this part:—Bingham, an Irifsman, for-merly a Soldier in the 16th, and lately in the 52d Regiment, and was killed a Serjeant at Bunker's Hill, was the moft indefatigable Sportfman and one of the beft fhots in the world. I have often been out with him at Chatteau-Richie, and the Ifland of Orleans, nigh Quebec. I have frequently feen him fhoot twelve brace of Snipe (before a fiery Spaniel) without miffing once: I faw him one day kill eighteen brace, miffing but twice out of thirty-eight fhots. He would hit the Target, when firing at a mark, with any in-different piece belonging to the Company. His diet when out fhooting, was bread and milk; and he would tire an Indian to follow him, though I have known him at other times guilty of intemperance in drinking.

"I was prefent with faid Bingham one day and faw him fire thirty fhots at Snipe, and fhot but two brace; he owned that he was never in better order, as to his habit of body; the birds flew fair, and we had a calm ferene day. He often threw his piece down, and fwore he would break it: It was a good one, though a very long French barrel; and what added to his choler, was my killing almoft every fhot.—As there muft be fome-thing more than mifchance, or bad-luck in difappointments of this nature, I hope the above inftances, with many more of a fimilar kind that almoft daily occur, are pretty evident demonftrations, that fome heat or too much anxiety, in endeavouring to rem-edy our fhooting fo bad, is moft commonly the caufe of (good fhots) want of fuccefs. —Therefore, as I have already obferved, the beft remedy is to reft a little take breath; talk over the matter, and recollect ourfelves.

"CHAP. VII.
"*Of Woodcocks.*

"AS thefe birds moft commonly keep in ftrong cover, fuch as fwamps, brufhy and clofe fcrubby woods (excepting where they are to be found in wet meadows fprings and open ground) I would recommend the Cocking Spaniel; indeed I have known good Pointers, I fuppofe by reafon of not being ufed to them, that would not take much notice, or *point* to them: As they don't travel much on foot, they are hopping puzzling game for Pointers. Good Spaniels and boys to beat the cover with fticks, are the beft to fpring them: They are an eafy fhot, and generally arched, if you give them time to difentangle and clear themfelves from the cover, and fuffer them to take fair flight; this, however, much depends upon your own fituation.

"IN this kind of fhooting you fhould be very careful how you fire, (I have fhot and was fhot myfelf at this work,) by keeping a conftant talking to your companion, in the wood and cover to prevent accidents happening, not only to yourfelf and party, but to perfons paffing in the line of your fhot, or to Cows, Horfes, &c. Many difagreeable accidents of this kind frequently occur by inattention.—The Woodcock is eafily marked, as he will take but fhort flights, if he has not been often fired at or much dif- turbed; in this cafe I have known them to fly a confiderable way, fometimes half a mile, for though they are loath to quit their haunts, they are a bird of great flight, inftance their long paffages from one climate to another, when they are obliged to fly many leagues without having an opportunity to reft. They have been known to pitch themfelves on the rigging of fhips to take breath and reft.

"CHAP. VIII.
"Of Snipe.

"THESE birds are commonly (being birds of fuction as well as the Woodcock) found in frefh water fprings, wet meadows and deep grafs: They are an eafy fhot, if you give them time to quit their ferpentine windings, which their long bill obliges them to take ere they recover themfelves fufficiently to fly ftreight, you fhould allow them to fly full out, if diftance permits, ere you fire, and then you may eafily kill them.

"SNIPES in proper ground, if not much frightened, will, after taking many turns, pretty high and far diftant, moft commonly, return and alight in fome part of the ground they fprung from: As they are generally in open ground, they are eafily marked.— Whenever you fee a bird rife, efpecially in any kind of wood or cover, you fhould call out *Mark*; this advertifes your companions that game is fprung, and may give fome one of the company a chance: This refers more particularly to Woodcock fhooting.—Span- iels, under good command, will do for Snipe, but Pointers ufed to them are better, un- lefs they are of the delicate kind, in that cafe they are foon knocked with the wet and cold. Large fetters, I prefume, as you can always keep fight of them, are good for this kind of fhooting: There are Pointers, however, that are from habit, good for the feveral kinds of game.

"CHAP. IX.
"Of Intimidating or Cowing Dogs, with a glaring Inftance—
better Treatment recommended.

"ONE thing I beg leave to lay down as a general maxim here, is a careful attention to the natural temper and difpofition of your Dogs. There are fome of thefe animals of fo high bred a kind that they will bear frequent beating and abufe, and will hunt with greater vigour immediately after a chaftifement; others, of a fofter kind, are fo eafily intimidated, and become fo very fulky, that they are rendered ufelefs for ever.

"I HAVE a glaring inftance of this kind now in my poffeffion, and the manner in which I ruined him (for want of knowing his temper) was as follows: —Ponto was imported from Great-Britain to America by a friend of mine, who made me a prefent of him: He is a beautiful animal, of the fleet fpecies of Pointers, of uncommon fagacity, and amazing travel; hunts high, is very ftaunch and obedient. I had him but a few months, when I coupled him one day to a young Dog, to avoid being troublefome in the ftreets, as well as to civilize the young one. Ponto being very eager, made feveral fprings to difentangle himfelf from his companion, as well as to gain the liberty of ranging about. I turned fuddenly about in fome heat, and gave him an unlucky blow on the back with the *but* of my fuzee; obferved he was much hurt, but thought no more about the matter, until I untied him on the field; he immediately hung down his tail, and (inftead of beating about, of which he was very fond) made the beft of his way home.—Upon my returning in the evening, I took no notice of his behaviour, but, by coaxing and making much of him, and forefeeing there was a rifk of his being cowed, I did not take him out for a month afterwards, in order to give him time to forget it; the Dog followed me then, and went on as ufual with the utmoft chearfulnefs, and feemed to me to behave better than formerly;—but the firft time I fpoke rough to the young Dog, *Ponto* fet off home as faft as he could run, and would not come in. He ferved me the fame trick repeatedly afterwards, without any other provocation but my fpeaking harfh to the other Dog, and I could not contrive any thing to break him of it. At laft he once difappointed me in the fame manner, when engaged on a very particular party; I own I was angry; and contrived to get home before him, where I gave him a very fevere flogging; but, inftead of mending the matter, he will not come near me, nor will he even vouchfafe to eat from my hand, let him be ever fo hungry; by which means he is now, though the beft of Dogs, with another perfon, rendered entirely ufe-lefs to me, to my no fmall mortification as you may well fuppofe.

"THIS inftance, with many others that I could afcertain, will, I hope, be a fufficient warning to Gentlemen how to treat their Dogs. I believe if I had ftruck mine with a whip, rod, or pulled his ears, it would have no bad effect upon him. You fhould, there-fore, never kick your Dog, or ufe any heavy hard fubtance to correct him; a gentle pulling of the ears (if not cut) or, which is ftill better, a fmall whip carried for that purpofe, is much better.—Had I bred Ponto, I might have known him better perhaps. Great caution is neceffary in this article. I have known the ftrongeft and moft vigor-ous forward Dogs, fpoiled for a whole day by a violent kick, which, I fuppofe, have hurt them fo much that they could not recover themfelves.—Biting your Dog's ears with your teeth is a barbarous method of correcting, and is generally attended with a corruption and corroding of blood. I have known Dogs to die of an inflammation caufed by violent beatings, efpecially when inflicted on the fmall of the back. I muft, neverthelefs, own, that, on many occafions, their mifdemeanor puts one's humour to the trial, and that a great deal of beating is abfolutely neceffary and indifpenfible to reprove them, but we ought to know them well, and treat them accordingly, and that with fomething fharp and pliable.

"WHENEVER your Dog behaves well, you ought conftantly to praife and clap him, and, by making ufe of certain kind expreffions, encourage him as much as poffible; he will be fond of this, and have a good effect upon him, and, as they are generally very fagacious, this will animate and encourage one of a good difpofition, to behave bet-ter and with greater chearfulnefs and caution.—Some very good Dogs are fond of choofing their own ground, and are very apt to give you the flip, and come to a fly point; in this cafe, don't call or whiftle for them (but endeavour to find them out) unlefs you are obliged to it.

"CHAP. X.

"Shooting Apparatus recommended, method of Loading,
and Precautions to be ufed in returning Home.

"OF thefe, there are great variety, and moft commonly are chofen more from fancy than for utility; fome ufe the fteel fpring chargers for their fhot, I own they are handy and convenient, but, as they weigh almoft as much as the fhot they contain, I would recommend and prefer the pudding fhot bag, with a brafs head, and a horn or leather powder horn, with a fpring top; fuch as have the fpring ftopper infide, wafte and fpill the powder.—I difapprove of loading out of the top of the horn, it is both uncertain and dangerous, by the powder's clogging between the ftopper and head of the horn, and thereby often admits a greater quantity of powder than you intend.—I will here endeavour to explain my method of loading, and hope that habit will make it both expeditious and fafe to fuch as chufe to practife it:—Being provided then with a powder horn and pudding fhot bag, as above defcribed, the former in a pocket on my right fide, with the cord belonging to it on the left fhoulder; my fhot bag on the left fide, flung with its ftrap on the right fhoulder; my bird net fixed pretty high, to avoid catching in the brufh and cover, with a certain number of fquare bits of foft gray paper run through the middle with a thread, and fewed to a convenient part on the right breaft of my coat; a turnkey and couple of fpare flints in my pocket.—I, firft of all, prime. *2dly*, fill the head of my horn with powder, and empty it in the top of my fhot bag, (which fhould contain the exact charge I intend, and ferve as a meafure for powder and fhot, and be equal to the full of my powder horn top) put up my horn, empty the powder in my gun, take one of my fquare papers for wadding, and, ramming it down, I *3dly*, fill my meafure with fhot, put it in the barrel, take another bit of paper, ram it down, and, returning my meafure and rammer, I am ready. All this may, at firft, appear complex and tedious, but, by a little practice, will become eafy, expeditious and fafe: I have invariably loaded in this manner; I found that I was in general, as quick as others.—Many of the beft and moft experienced *fhots*, object to priming firft; I cannot fee wherein the danger confifts, unlefs it may be fuppofed to proceed from the heat of the barrel, or fomething touching the trigger whilft you are loading. How muft it be with the Army, who always prime firft, and fire very often fo quick, that they can fcarcely hold their pieces in their hands, with the heat, yet it's extraordinary to fee one of them go off whilft loading, without fome other caufe than the heat of the piece.—Bad powder leaving a fulphurous fediment in the breech of the barrel, is a more frequent caufe of fuch accidents. I have often feen a Battalion from five to feven hundred men, fire fixty rounds on a field day, without one accident of this nature; though I once faw a whole Grenadier Company's pouches on fire, by a fpark communicating to a broken cartridge in one of the men's pouches; it was in the inftant of firing, and the pouch was open. However, I fhan't infift upon the propriety or impropriety of priming firft or laft, only infift that priming firft is the moft expeditious; and Gentlemen feldom fire fo quick, when fowling, as to endanger any accident of this kind;—it never happened to myfelf;—every one's own difcretion may guide them in this particular as they pleafe.

"IF you have a Servant, when out fhooting, let him carry your fhot bag, (thofe that I have defcribed contain *4lb.* fome more, fome lefs) and you may carry half a dozen fteel fpring chargers in your waiftcoat or jacket pockets, which, being double, will contain twelve charges. Many ufe cartridges contain twelve charges. Many ufe cartridges containing both powder and fhot. I would recommend your carrying a few charges of large fhot, No. 3 and 4, as many opportunities frequently offer of making ufe of them. I fhall conclude this Chapter, by hinting, that the portable pocket bottle, covered with twigs, and the collation of cold meat and bread, or bifcuit, are always fafe and ufeful companions, even for their fhort excurfions, as well as the Sportfman's knife and fork.

"I WILL fuppofe you returning home, loaded with game, be not, however entirely inattentive to your Dogs, for in the evening, birds will run far to feed, and, perhaps, give you chances when you leaft expect them. If you hunt with a brace of Dogs, the *couple* is very ufeful in preventing their ftraggling and lofing them in going through the ftreets, &c. befides, being hungry, they will ftray away after carrion and other ftuff, which coupling effectually prevents, and faves you much trouble.—It is needlefs to caution you againft carrying your piece home loaded; it is dangerous, and fhould be always guarded againft, by either drawing the charge or firing it off.

"CHAP. XI.

"Of Spaniels in General.

"OF thefe there are many kinds; I have heard a Gentleman once defcribe thirteen different fpecies of them; from the Setter, the large *Englifh* Spaniel, and Water Spaniels, down to the little Turnfpit Legged one. The brown coloured Cocking Spaniel, with curly ears, are very good; but, I believe, the fmall Short Legged ones, with a fharp nofe, and pretty fmall ears, that give tongue when they come nigh their game or upon a hot fcent, are the beft: I have known many of thefe, well broke, that exceed any kind of Dogs for fhooting: They are commonly red and white; I have fen fome yellow of the fame kind, and various other colours.

"A GOOD Spaniel, very obedient, that will hunt clofe, is very indefatigable, and certainly better than Pointers in woods and thick cover, becaufe they have the advantage of being able to creep under the bufhes, and hunting chiefly upon the track or roading of the bird: My greateft objection to them is (unlefs they are very well broke indeed) their being very troublefome; you are always obliged to *hey* them, and keep conftantly calling, hollowing, or whiftling to them, and the more you beat fome of them, the more eager they are; yet, for a young man able to follow them, they are by far the beft for fmall fhooting. It is hard to prevent their fpoiling your birds, being in general hard mouthed.

"THERE is another kind that I have known to be very excellent, and not fo fiery as the former, which has a refemblance to *Setters*, but not fo large, though much larger than the little Spaniels, with a fan-tail and pretty large ears: This kind of Dogs ranges well, and will make a fudden ftand, or fhort paufe or point, and, as you come up, bounce in upon, and fpring the game.

"I HAVE alfo obferved, that birds rife more puzzled and confufed before Spaniels, than from a *point*, owing, I fuppofe, to their not having time to take proper flight, by the fudden and furious approach of the Spaniel. You fhould ufe a brace of thefe Dogs.

"CHAP. XII.

"Of ftealing Game Dogs.

"WITH A

"DIALOGUE.

"FORMER Acts of Parliament, and, in particular, a late Act, is very rigorous againft perfons found guilty of this crime: It is generally committed by *Poachers* and the loweft clafs of ruffians, and it is great pity but the Law had made it more heinous:— If a man fteals my Horfe, which may not be worth five Pounds, the Law condemns him to the Gallows. A good Pointer is feldom valued at lefs than ten Guineas, very often twice that fum, and yet the punifment for ftealing one, does not extend to life or limb.

To a perfon fond of thefe animals, it is a great grief and difappointment to lofe one of them; and it is not the value of him alone, but the difficulty of replacing fuch a one as he has loft to his liking: Befides, if the Dog ftolen has been brought up in his family from a Pup, the feeding, training, and breaking him, is an expenfive and troublefome procefs, and no bounds can be fet to his value, and the fatisfaction he yields to his owner. Not only his Mafter, but, perhaps, his whole family, is become exceeding fond of poor *Sancho*, and much attached to the animal, for his great fagacity and affection to them. I have known many inftances of this kind (where the parties concerned had no ridiculous fondnefs for animals) to have caufed great uneafinefs to a whole family. That Gentlemen could be guilty of fo mean and ungenerous an action, would feem incredible, yet, I am forry to fay, that many affuming the appellation, have, to their very great shame, been detected of this crime.

"In Order to enforce my Ideas in the foregoing ESSAY, *I will fuppofe the following* DIALOGUE, *between* Squire JOLLYMAN, Mr. AIMWELL, *and their* SERVANTS.

"Squire JOLLYMAN'S Houfe.

"*Aimwell.* Good morning, Sir; I hope that I am punctual, and did not keep you waiting.

"*Jollyman.* On the contrary, Sir, I have but this moment put on my cloaths —'tis but five o'clock, though let us lofe no time;—come, Sir,—breakfaft is ready—do you drink coffee, chocolate, or tea?

"*Aim.* Neither Sir;—I'll have bread and milk—which way do we travel to-day?

"*Jol.* I will be entirely guided by you, Sir—tho' fuppofe we fpend the morning on the Moor, for Groufe, and the afternoon, in our return, on the Stubble, for Partridge.

"*Aim.* An excellent plan, Sir:—We fhall have a charming day;—what Dogs do you take out?

"*Jol.* There is old *Lafher*, and his grandfon *Primo*, —you know the old *Gentleman*; —but, pray Sir, what Curs are that you have coupled?

"*Aim.* Pardon me, Sir,—they are an excellent brace of ftaunch Pointers, of wonderful travel, *Ponto* and *Dafh*; the latter I had a prefent from his Grace the D—— of B——, and, I am informed, that he has a dafh of the Fox-hound.

"*Jol.* I was only in jeft, Sir;—the Dogs look very beautiful.

"*Aim.* And you will find them, Sir; as good as they look.

"*Jol.* Do we ride or walk to the Moor?

"*Aim.* Juft as you pleafe, Sir,—for my own part, I would prefer walking.

"*Jol.* You are much lighter and a better walker than I am, Sir;—the Moor is fix full miles off, and by riding there we will be frefh to beat the ground.

"*Aim.* Very juftly obferved;—we will ride then.

"*Jol.* Here, boys, take our Horfes—we are now in the very heart of the ground.

"*Aim.* How shall we hunt the Dogs, Sir?

"*Jol.* A brace at once is enough—we will begin with mine if you pleafe.

"*Aim.* Done, Sir—Tom, couple up mine;—your Dogs beat very high, Sir.

"*Jol.* I think that's an advantage, Sir;—I can't bear your fnubbing Dogs.

"*Aim.* I join with you in that, as well as in moft other things.

"*Jol.* Lafher *ftands*, and *Primo* backs him; the old Dog pins them.

"*Aim.* A bird a-piece—I like this—'tis a bad omen to mifs the firft fhot;—they are fine birds—how very plump?

"*Jol.* What think you of my Dogs?

"*Aim.* Charming indeed—elegant—I wifh mine may pleafe you as well, though I have no doubt of it.

"*Jol.* We muft beat the ground clofer—there are more birds here;—how many got up, Billy?

"*William.* Five brace, Sir, with thofe you fhot.

"*Jol.* That's but ten birds, and, as it's a frefh *pack*, they are not all up.

"*Wil.* The young Dog Primo, draws Sir,—there he ftops—and old Lafher is coming to back him.

"*Jol.* Down, *Lafher*;—take heed *there*, Primo.

"*Aim.* I have killed my bird;—did you, mifs, Sir?

"*Jol.* 'Egad, I have fo, though, I believe, he has carried away fome fhot—I faw him ftagger—I gave him too much time, and my fhot fcattered.

"*Aim.* We can't always hit,—if we did, God help the poor Groufe!

"*Jol.* If we all fired like you, Sir, there would be none left to breed: I am rather grown too fat, and fometimes I get pretty warm in coming up to my fhot. The young Dog has led well, I think.

"*Aim.* Admirable!—and he made no offer to chace when they rofe.

"*Wil.* He knows a trick worth two of that, Sir;—he knows what I carry in my pocket.

"*Jol.* Yes,—he has tafted it pretty often;—he was hard to break—being crofs-bred,—but he promifes fair now to make amends.

"*Aim.* Lafher is upon game, sir.

"*Jol.* Hold up, my Dogs; Lafher, get on; *down, Primo*;—there they are, Sir,—a frefh *pack*;—twig, Lafher;—he wants to make a fet of it;—fee how he fquats and looks round him;—he has them on all fides—come Sir, the firft chance is yours;—boys ftand clofe with the guns.

"*Aim.* I have fhot two; what a pity!

"*Jol.* And I my bird—that's a Leafh.

"*Aim.* I never fhot *two* Groufe at a fhot before, or did I fee another do it;—the fecond bird croffed juft as I pulled my trigger.

"*Jol.* 'Tis very uncommon, and fo much the better;—it's murder.

"*Wil.* I have marked a fingle bird, Gentlemen.

"*Aim.* Squire Jollyman, up to him.

"*Wil.* Primo fprung him, Sir.

"*Jol.* Sirrah, 'tis falfe—it can't be—there, firrah, he ftands to him:—*Down, Primo.*

"*Wil.* I might have been miftaken, Sir;—I thought I faw him run in upon him.

"*Jol.* There he lays; go and pick him up;—a plaguy long fhot indeed!

"*Aim.* Wonderfully fo!—I think it's above eighty yards—come let us meafure—exactly feventy-five paces—a decent diftance and the bird *ftone* dead.

"*Jol.* Did you mark the pack?

"*Tom.* Yes Sir,—I have feen them alight, but a great way off—'tis almoft half a mile.

"*Aim.* They have taken a long flight; —they are a little frightened.

"*Jol.* I am a little warm, Sir,—and, as it's juft twelve, fuppofe we reft a while here, and refrefh.

"*Aim.* With all my heart, Sir,—I am both dry and have a keen appetite, though not in the leaft fatigued.

"*Jol.* Come boys, get the cold meat, brandy and water, and give the Dogs fome water.

"*Aim.* 'Tis now clofe upon *one*—I'll let loofe my Dogs and tye up your's, if you pleafe.

"Jol. Do fo;—the pack will be pretty well fettled by this time.

"Aim. Both the Dogs ftand, Sir, in different directions, fo that we are fure of a fhot a-piece.

"Jol. We have both done execution;—I like your Dogs much—Dafh is a great beauty, I muft have a Pup from him and my Clara.

"Aim. You do me honour, Sir;—by all means, and I befpeak a Bitch Pup.

"Jol. It is time to quit this ground, and take Horfes to the Stubble.

"Tom. I rejoice to hear it, for between thefe plaguy Dogs pulling, and the weight of the Groufe, I am in a fine lather.—Back, Lafher—he pulls like a Horfe.

"Aim. Let the poor things loofe, and let them have a run—we may have a *royal point* from all the Dogs.

"Wil. Ponto leads roading——he is very cautious;—the birds are on foot.

"Jol. You judge well—for now they all four ftand;—old Lafher muft lead;—Ponto is very cautious;—fee Primo's beautiful attitude, and Dafh's is admirable!

"Aim. They are Partridge to be fure—I fee them gather, Sir;—we may kill many;—what, the deuce, four brace? that's too many;—I think it's time to return home, and be time enough for tea.

"Jol. Agreed; but none of your tea for me—after my fatigue I chufe a cup of good beer:—Let us fee Tom, how we ftand—fix brace of Groufe and four of Partridge,—pretty well for the fhort time we have hunted; and, I believe, neither we or the Dogs are in the leaft fatigued.

"Tom. I can't join with you there, Sir,— I am very much tired.

"Aim. Come, Sir, we have had a pleafant day's diverfion,—excellent Dogs—plenty of game—and fine weather.

"P.S. Pleafe to take notice, That the Quails in North-America are much larger than thofe in England and that fhooting them, in moft cafes, is Partridge fhooting in min-iature, (which is the reafon they are mentioned in the fame Chapter) with this differ-ence; that, as the under cover is, in general, very bad and almoft inacceffible, the very beft of Dogs fhould be had: A rough, hardy, vigorous Ruffian Dog, I think, would be the beft, though I have feen many fmooth Dogs excellent for them, by being ufed to the cover.

FINIS."

HUNTING AMONG INDIGENOUS PEOPLES

Francisco Gomarra, Spanish historian, concerning Mexico, describes royal hunting, circa 1519-1522, in [Gomarra], *Pleafant Hiftorie of the Conqueft of the VVeaft India, now called new Spayne* (London: Henry Bynneman, 1578), 212-214.

"The recreation of Hunting, vvhiche *Mutezuma* vfed.

"*Mutezuma* had not only al the libertie that he defored in the Title, beeyng prifoner among the *Spanyardes,* but alfo *Cortes* permitted him to hunt and hauke, or to go to the temple, for he was very devoute, and a great hunter.

"When he went a hunting, he was carried vpon mens fhoulders with eyght or ten *Spanyards* in his guard, and three thoufande *Mexicans*, who were Gentlemen, his fervants, and hunters, of whome he hadde a great number, fome to feeke the game, others to beate the covertes, and others to marke. Some of thofe hunters were only for hares and conneys, others for all forts of Deere, Wolves, foxes, and fuch like. They were very precife with theyr bowes, and good markeme', for he that miffed his marke at fourefcore pafes diftanc' was punifhed. It was ftrange to fee the number of people that wente with him on hunting, and to fee the flaughter of beafts killed, with hande, ftaues, nettes, and bowes, fome of thofe beaftes were tame, and other braue and fearefull, as Lyons, Tigers, and Ounces. It is a harde thing to take a fierce Lion in hunting as they do, being in manner a naked people, and the beaft, couragious and ftrong, but yet the Proverbe faith, flight and cunning is better than ftrength.

"It is a more straunge thyng to take any foule that flieth in the ayre as their Fauconers doe, for after they haue once marked and fet eye vpon any foule, the Fauconers of *Mutezuma* will vnder take to catch him, although the foule be neuer fo fwifte of wing, beyng at the leaft fo commaunded by the King. It happened one day that *Mutezuma* ftoode in his gallerie with his Guarde of Spanyards, who had efpied a fayre Hauke foryng in the ayre, oh quoth they what a fayre Hauke flieth yonder, *Mutezuma* hearyng their talke, called unto him certayne of his Faulconers, commaundyng them to followe that Hauke & fo bring him vnto him. The Faulconers wente to fulfill his requeft, and followed that foule with fuch diligence, that in fhorte fpace they brought the Hauke vnto him, who prefented the fame to the Spanyards, a thing truely almoft incredible, but yet certified by worde and wrytings of the prefent witneffes. Their cheifeft and moft pleafant paftime of Hauking was, of Kightes, Ravens, Crowes, Pies, and other birdes of hardie ftomake and flowe in fight, greate and fmall of all fortes, for the which he had Egles, Buyters, and other foule of rapyne marveylous fwifte of wing, and fuche as woulde mounte very high in the ayre, withe whiche they murdered Hares, Wolves, and (as fome fay) Hartes.

"He had other foulers, that vfed Nettes, Snares, and fundry engins. *Mutezuma* vfed much to fhoote in a tronke, and with his bow killed many wilde beaftes. His houfes of pleafure as I haue before declared, ftoode fixe myles from the Citie in pleafant woodes: and always when he went a huntyng after the tyme that he was pryfoner, the fame day he would returne agayne to *Cortes* his lodgyng, although he banketed & feafted with the Spaniardes at his places of fporting and paftime, and would alwayes at his returne to his lodgyng giue fome prefent vnto the', that had accompanied him that day."

* * *

Cabeza de Vaca, Spanish explorer, describes hunting in the Gulf Coast region, circa 1530, and west Texas, circa 1535, in Cyclone Covey, trans., *Cabeza de Vaca's Adventures in the Unknown Interior of America* (Albuquerque, N.M.: University of New Mexico Press, 1983 [1961]), 79, 80, 81, 107.

"Occasionally, these Indians [Yguaces] kill deer [antelope] and take fish;...."

"These Indians [Yguaces] are so used to running that, without rest, they follow a deer from morning to night. In this way they kill many. They wear the deer down and then sometimes overtake them in a race."

"They [Yguaces] also kill deer [antelope] by encircling fires; deprived of pasturage, the animals are forced to seek it where the Indians may trap them.... The Indians kill all the deer and other animals they can the day of their arrival, then consume the whole of their water and wood in cooking and smudge fires."

"As we went through these valleys [in west Texas], every Indian carried a club three palms long and kept alert. When a rabbit jumped (the country teems with these animals), they quickly surrounded him and threw their clubs with amazing accuracy, driving him from one man to another. I cannot imagine a sport that is more fun, as often the rabbit runs right into your hand. By the time we stopped for the night, the Indians had provided us with eight or ten backloads of rabbits apiece.

"The archers, instead of staying with us, deployed in the mountains after deer and came back at dark with five or six for each of us, besides quail and other game. Whatever the Indians killed or found, they brought before us, not daring to eat anything until we had blessed it, even if they were desperately hungry."

* * *

John Smith, British explorer, describes hunting by indigenous peoples in Virginia, circa 1612, in Smith, *A Map of Virginia* (London? 1612), 24-25.

"In their hunting and fifhing they take extreame paines; yet it being their ordinary exercife from their infancy, they efteeme ita pleafure and are very proud to be expert therein. And by their continuall ranging, and travel, they know all the advantages and places moft frequented with Deare, Beafts, Fifh, Foule, Rootes, and Berries. At their huntings they leaue their habitations, andreduce themfelevs into companies, as the *Tartars* doe, and goe to the moft defert places with their families, where they fpend their time in hunting and fowling vp towards the mountaines, by the heads of their riuers, where there is plentie of game. For betwixt the rivers the grounds are fo narrowe, that little commeth there which they devoure not. It is a marvel they can fo directly paffe thefe deferts, fome 3 or 4 daies iourney without habitation. Their huntng houfes are like vnto Arbours couered with mats. Thefe their women beare after them, with Corne, Acornes, Morters, and all bag and baggage they vfe. Whe[n] they come to the place of exercife, euery man doth his beft to fhew his dexteritie, for by their excelling in thofe quallities, they get their wiues. Forty yards will they fhoot leuell, or very neare the mark, and 120 is their beft at Random. At their huntings in the deferts they are commonly 2 or 300 together. Hauing found the Deare, they environ them with many fires, and betwixt the fires they place themfelves. And fome take their ftands in the midft. The Deare being thus feared by the fires and their voices, they chace them fo long within that circle that many times they kill 6, 8, 10, or 15 at a hunting. They vfe alfo to driue them into fome narrowe point of land; when they find that aduantage and fo force them into the riuer, where with their boats they haue *Ambufcadoes* to kill them. When they haue fhot a Deare byland, they follow him like blood hounds by the blood and ftraine and oftentimes fo take them.Hares, Pattridges, Turkies, or Egges, fat or leane, young or old, they devoure all they ca[n]catch in their power. In one of thefe huntings they found Captaine *Smith* in the difcoverie of the head of the river of Chickahamania, where they flew his men, and tooke him prifoner in a Bogmire, where he faw thofe exercifes, & gathered thefe obfervations.

"One Savage hunting alone, vfeth the skinne of a Deare flit on the one fide, and fo put on his arme, through the neck, fo that his hand comes to the head which is ftuffed, and the hornes, head, eies, eares, and every part as arteficially counterfeited as they can devife. Thus fhrowding his body in the skinne by ftalking he approacheth the Deare, creeping on the ground from one tree to another. If the Deare chance to find fault, or ftand at gaze, hee turneth the head with his hand to his beft advantage to feeme like a Deare, alfo grazing and licking himfelfe. So watching his beft aduantage to approach, hauing fhot him, hee chafeth him by his blood and ftraine till he get him."

* * *

William Strachey, British explorer, describes hunting by indigenous peoples in Virginia, circa 1612-1614, in Strachey, *The Historie of Travaile into Virginia Britannia; Expressing the Cosmographie and Comodities of the Country, Togither with the Manners and Customes of the People,* ed. by R.H. Major (London: The Hakluyt Society, 1899), 75-77.

"In the tyme of their huntings, they leave their habitations and gather themselves into companyes, as doe the Tartars, and goe to the most desart places with with their families, where they passe the tyme with hunting and fowling up towards the mountaines, by the heads of their rivers, wher in deed there is plentye of game, for betwixt the rivers the land is not so large belowe that therein breed sufficyent to give them all content. Considering, especyally, how at all tymes and seasons they destroy them, yt maye seeme a marveyle how they can so directly passe and wander in these desarts, sometymes three or fower dayes' journyes, meeting with no habitacions, and, by reason of the woods, not having sight of the sun, wherby to direct them how to coast yt.

"Theire huntinge howses are not soe laboured, substancyall, nor artyficyall as their as their other, but are like soldiers' cabins, the frame sett up in too or three howers, cast over the head, with matts, which the women beare after them as they carry likewise corne, acornes, morters, and all bag and baggage to use, when they come to the place where they purpose for the tyme to hunt.

"In the tyme of hunting every man will strive to doe his best to shew his fortune and dexterity, for by their excelling therin they obteyne the favour of the women.

"At their hunting in the desarts they are comonly two or three hundred togither. With the sun rising they call up on[e] another, and goe forth searching after the heard, which when they have found, they environ and circle with many fiers, and betwixt they place themselves, and there take up their stands, making the most terrible noise thet they can. The deare being thus feared by the fires and their voices, betake them to their heeles, whome they chase so long within that circle, that many tymes they kill six, eight, ten, or fifteen in a morning. They use also to drive them into some narrow point of land, when they find that advantage, and so force them into the river, where with their boats they have ambuscades to kill them. When they shott a deare by land, they followe him (like bloodhounds) like the blood and straine [view or track of a deer], and often tymes so take him. Hares, partriges, turkeys, fatt or leane, young or old, in eggs, in breeding time, or however they devour, at no time sparing any that they can catch in their power.

"On[e] savadge hunting alone useth the skyne of a deare slitt in the one side, and so put upon his arme through the neck, in that sort that the hand comes to the head, which is stuffed, and the hornes, head, eyes, eares, and every part as artaficyall counterfeited as they can devise, thus shrowding his body in the skynne, by stalking he approacheth the deere creeping on the ground from one tree to another; yf the deare chaunce to find fault, or stand at gaze, he turneth the head with the hand to the best advantage to win his shoot; having shott him, he chaseth him by his blood and straine till he gett him.

"In these hunting and fishing exercises they take extreame paines, and they being their ordinary labours from their infancy, they place them amongst their sports and pleasures, and are very prowd to be expert therein, for thereby (as before remembered) they wyn the loves of their women, who wilbe the sooner contented to live with such a man, by the readyness and fortune of whose bow and diligence such provision they perceave they are likely to be fedd with well, especially of fish and flesh,....'

* * *

Edward Winslow, English settler and chronicler of Plymouth, Massachusetts, comments on hunting by New England indigenous peoples, circa 1620s, in [Winslow], "Gov. Bradford's History of Plymouth Colony," in Alexander Young, ed., *Chronicles of the Pilgrim Fathers of the Colony of Plymouth, from 1602 to 1625* (Boston: Charles C. Little and James Brown, 1841), 363.

Circa 1620s: "The [indigenous] men themselves wholly in hunting, and other exercises of the bow, except at some times they take some pains in fishing."

* * *

Thomas Morton, English settler, reports on hunting by indigenous peoples in eastern Massachusetts, circa 1632 (1620s?), in Morton, *New English Canaan, or, New Canaan, Containing An Abstract of New England* (London?: Charles Green, 1632), 48, 51-52.

"I had a Salvage who hath taken out his boy in a morning, and they have brought home their loades about noone.

"I have asked them what number [turkeys] they found in the woods, who have answered Neent Metawna, which is a thousand that day; the plenty of them is such in those parts. They are easily killed at rooste, because the one being killed, the other sit fast nevethelesse, and this is no bad commodity."

"...there is such abundance of them [deer] that the Salvages, at hunting time, have killed of them so many, that they have bestowed six or seaven at a time, upon one English man whome they have borne affection to."

"These [fallow deer] bringe 3. fawnes at a time, spotted like our fallow Deares fawnes; the Salvages say, foure, I speake of what I know to be true; for I have killed, in February, a doe with three fawnes in her belly, all heared, and ready to fall;...."

"The Salvages take these [deer] in trappes made, of their naturall Hempe, which they place in the earth; where they fell a tree for browse, if hee tread on the trapp, he is horsed up by the legg, by meanes of a pole that starts up and catcheth him."

* * *

William Wood, English settler, in New England, comments on hunting by New England indigenous peoples, circa 1634, in Wood, *New Englands Prospect, A True, Lively and Experimentall Defcription of that Part of* America, *Commonly Called Nevv England. Difcovering the Ftate of that Countrie, Both As It Ftands to Our New-Come Englifh Planters; and to the Old Native Inhabitants* (London: Thomas Cotes, 1634), reprinted as *Wood's New-England Prospect, Publications of the Prince Society, Volume 1* (Boston: The Prince Society, 1865), 98-100.

"Of their huntings:

For their hunting, it is to be noted that they have no fwift foote Grayhounds, to let flippe at the fight of the Deere, no deepe mouthed hounds, or fenting beagles, to finde out their defired prey; thenfelves are all this, who in that time of the yeere, when the Deere comes downe, having certaine hunting houfes, in fuch places where they know the Deere ufually doth frequent, in which they keep their randevowes, their fnares and all their accoutraments for that imployment: when they get fight of a Deere, Moofe or Beare, they ftudie how to get the wind of him, and approaching within fhot, ftab their marke quite through, if the bones hinder not. The chiefe thing they hunt after is Deere, Moofes, and Beares, it greeves them more to fee an *Englifh* man take one Deere, than a thoufand Acres of land; they hunt likewife after Wolves, and wild Catts, Rackoones, Otters, Beavers, Mufquafhes, trading both their skinnes and flefh to the *Englifh*. Befides their artillery, they have other devices to kill their game, as fometimes hedges a mile or two miles long, being a mile wide at one end, and made narrower and narrower by degrees, leaving onely a gap of fixe foote long, over againft which, in the day time they lye lurking to fhoot the Deere which come through that narrow gut; fo many as come within the circumference of that hedge, feldome return backee to leape over, unleffe they be forced by the chafing of fome ravenous Wolfe, or fight of fome accidentatall paffinger; in the night at the gut of this hedge, they fet Deere traps, which are fpringes made of young trees, and fmooth wrought coards; fo ftrong as it will toffe a horfe if hee be caught in it. An *Englifh* Mare being ftrayed from her owner, and growne wild by her long fojourning in the Woods ranging up and downe with the wilde crew, ftumbled into one of thefe traps which ftopt her fpeed, hanging her like *Mahomets* tombe, betwixt earth and heaven; the morning being come, the Indians went to look what good fucceffe their Venifon trappes had brought them, but feeing fuch a long fcutted Deere, praunce in their Merritotter, they bade her good morrow, crying out, what cheere what cheere *Englifhmans fquaw* horfe; having no better epithite than to call her a woman horfe, but being loath to kill her, and as fearefull to approach neere the frifcadoes of her Iron heeles, they pofted to the *Englifh* to tell them how the cafe ftood or hung with their *fquaw* horfe, who unhorfes their Mare, and brought her to her former tameneffe, which fince hath brought many a good foale, and performed much good fervice. In these traps Deeres, Moofes, Beares, Wolves, Catts, and Foxes, are often caught. For their Beavers and Otters, they have other kinds of trappes, fo ponderous as is unfupportable for fuch creatures, the maffie burthen whereof either takes them prifoners, or expells their breath from their fquifed bodyes. Thefe kinde of creatures would gnaw the other kind of trappes afunder, with their fharpe teeth: thefe beafts are too cunning for the *Englifh*, who feldome or never catch any of them, therefore we leave them to thofe skilfull hunters whofe time is not fo precious, whofe experience bought-skill hath made them practicall and ufefull in that particuler."

* * *

Father Andrew White, British Jesuit missionary, comments on the hunting skills of indigenous peoples in Maryland, circa 1634, in White, "A Briefe Relation of the Voyage unto Maryland, by Father Andrew White, 1634," in Clayton Colman Hall, ed. *Narratives of Early Maryland, 1633-1684* (New York: Barnes & Noble, Inc., 1918), 43.

"Their weapons are a bow and a bundle of arrowes, an ell long, feathered with turkies feathers, and headed with points of deered hornes, peeces of glasse, or flints, which they make fast with an excellent glew which they have for that purpose. The shaft is a small cane or sticke, wherewith I have seene them kill at 20 yards distance, little birds of the bignesse of sparrows, and they use to practise themselves by casting up small stickes in the aire, and meeting it with an arrow before it come to ground. Their bow is but weake and shoots level but a little way. They daily catch partridge, deere, turkies, squirrels and the like of which there is wonderfull [plenty?],...."

David Pietersz de Vries, Dutch ordnance-master, describes deer hunting by indigenous peoples in New Netherland, circa 1642, in [de Vries], *Short Historical and Journal notes of Several Voyages Made in the four parts of the World, namely, Europe, Africa, Asia, and America* (Alckmaer? Brekegeest?: Symon Cornelisz, 1655), reprinted in Cornell Jaray, ed., *Historic Chronicles of New Amsterdam, Colonial New York and Early Long Island, First Series,* Empire State Historical Publications Series No. 35 (Port Washington, N.Y.: Ira J. Friedman, 1968), 108-110.

Circa 1642: "There are great quantities of deer, which the Indians shoot with their bows and arrows, or make a general hunt of, a hundred more or less joining in the hunt. They stand a hundred paces more or less from each other, and holding flat thigh-bones in the hand, beat them with a stick, and so drive the creatures before them to the river. As they approach the river, they close nearer to each other, and whatever is between any two of them, is at the mercy of their bows and arrows, or must take to the river. When the animals swim into the river, the Indians lie in their canoes with snares, which they throw around their necks, and drag them to them, and force the deer down with the rump upwards, by which they cannot draw breath. At the north, they drive them into a *fuyk* [a type of net leading to a snare], which they make of palisades split out of trees, and eight or nine feet high, and set close to each other, for a distance of fourteen or fifteen hundred paces on both sides, coming together like a fuyk, as is shown in the plates; the opening is one or two thousand paces wide. When the animal is within the palisades, the Indians begin to come nearer to each other, and pursue it with great ardour, as they regard deer-hunting the noblest hunting. At the end of the fuyk it is so narrow that it is only five feet wide, like a large door, and it is there covered with the boughs of trees, into which the deer or animal runs, closely pursued by the Indians, who make a noise as if they were wolves, by which many deer are devoured, and of which they are in great fear. This causes them to run into the mouth of the fuyk with great force, whither the Indians pursue them furiously with bows and arrows, and from whence they cannot escape; they are then easily caught with snares as may be seen in the plate."

* * *

Peter Lindestrom, Swedish geographer, concerning hunting by the Delaware indigenous people, circa 1654-1656, in Lindestrom, *Geographia Americae with An Account of the Delaware Indians Based on Surveys and Notes Made in 1654-1656,* trans. and ed. by Amandus Johnson (Philadelphia: The Swedish Colonial Society, 1925), 213-217.

"Now as soon as the winter bids good night, they begin with their hunts, which is done with a fine innovation. Now at that time of the year the grass which grows there, as has been said, is as dry as hay. When now the sachem wants to arrange his hunt, then he commands his people [to take a position] close together in a circle of 1/2, 1 or 2 miles, according to the number of people at his command. In the first place each one roots up the grass in the position, [assigned to him] in the circumference, to the width of about 3 or 4 ells, so that the fire will not be able to run back, each one then beginning to set fire to the grass, which is mightily ignited, so that the fire travels away, in towards the center of the circle, which the Indians follow with great noise, and all the animals which are found within the circle, flee from the fire and the cries of the Indians, traveling away, whereby the circle through its decreasing is more and more contracted towards the center. When now the Indians have surrounded the center with a small circle, so that they mutually cannot do each other any harm, then they break loose with guns and bows on the animals which they have been blessed with, that not one can escape and thus they get a great multitude of all kinds of animals which are found there....

"In the meantime later in the year, when the grass has thus been burnt off the land, they do not care to arrange any more such hunts, but shoot the animals wherever they find them in the woods, which they have no difficulty in doing, because they have scent of the animals like the dogs; for often the savages say to the Christians, when they follow them in the woods: "Indeed I now feel the scent of deer, if I wanted to bother to go after them." This the Christians did not believe in the beginning, before they followed them, and got to see that they were right. Otherwise they are so perfect in shooting that they do not miss.

"And the savage is so armstrong that he is able to shoot with a bow so far, that no gun can carry that far, when he extends his limbs so that daylight shines through his elbow joints. When a Christian wrestles with a savage if he [the Christian] does not get at his back [he cannot prevail against him], he can do nothing against his arms.

"The savages also use a splendid system for killing pigeons in quantities with great ease. When the pigeons come flying, which [at times] may be a few hundred pairs in a flock, or following, then they usually settle down to rest in the largest and highest tree, which they find. Then they also have the custom that in the tree in which they once used to rest, they will, with preference go there again. When now the savage observes where they have been accustomed to rest, the savage goes and cuts around the tree, so that it stands only on the center. When now the pigeons come there again to sit down, they cannot possibly set themselves so evenly on the tree that they weigh alike on either side, whereby the tree falls over and kills a large number of them, for many cannot save themselves in such a fury of branches and leaves, nor fly away. There is also an abundance of swans and wild geese to shoot."

* * *

Samuel Clarke, British writer, remarks on hunting by indigenous peoples in Virginia and the New England area, circa 1670, in Clarke, *A True and Faithful Account of the Four Chiefest Plantations of the English in America. Of Virginia, New England, Bermudus, Barbados* (London: R. Clavel and T. Passenger, 1670), 9, 36, 48-49.

[In this first segment Clarke apparently plagiarizes John Smith's writings]: "They take extream pains in their Huntings and Fifhings, whereunto they are enured from their Child-hood: and by their continual rangings about, they know all the places and Advantages moft frequented with *Deer, Beafts, Fifhes, Fowls, Rooks, Berries*. At their Huntings they leave their Habitations, and in feveral companies go to the moft Defert places with their Families towards the Mountains, or heads of Rivers where there is plenty of Game. It's a marvel how they can pafs thefe Deferts of three or four dayes journey over, without miffing their way. The Women bear their Hunting Houfes after them with *Corn, Acorns, Mortars*, and *Bagg and Baggage which they ufe*. When they come to the place of Exercife, every man endeavours to fhew his beft Dexterity; for hereby they get their Wives. They will fhoot level about fourty yards, near the Mark, and one hundred and twenty is their beft at Random. When they have found the Deer, they environ them with Fires, and betwixt the Fires they place themfelves; and fome take their ftand in the mid'ft. The Deer being frighted with the Fires, and their voices they chafe them fo long within that Circle, that oftimes they kill fix, eight, ten, or fif-teen at a hunting. Sometimes alfo when they find them in a point of Land, they force them into a River, where with their Boats they kill them. When they have fhot a Dear by Land, they follow him like Blood-hounds, by the blood and ftain, and oftimes fo take him. *Hares, Partridges, Turkies, or Eggs, fat or lean, young or old, they devour all they can come by.*"

"Cormorants are as common as other Fowles, they devour much Fifh. A tame Cormorant, and two or three good Dogs in the water make excellent fport:...."

"The third [type of goose] is a grey Goofe with a black neck, and a black and white head much bigger than our *Englifh*: They are killed both flying and fitting.... The Humilites, or Simplicites rather, be of two forts; The one as big as green Plover, the other is lefs; they are fo fimple that one may drive them on heaps, and then fhoot at them, and the living will fettle themfelves on the fame place again where the dead are, while you fhoot again, fo that fometimes above twelve fcore have been killed at two fhoots."

"They have neither Beagles, Hounds, nor Grayhounds, but fupply all themfelves: In the feafon of the year they have Hunting Houfes in the places to which the Deer refort, in which they keep their *Rendesvouze*, with their Snares, and all the Accoutrements for that imployment. When they fee a Deer Moofe, or bear, they labour to get the wind of him, and coming neer they fhoot him quite through, if the bones hinder not. They hunt alfo Wolves, wild Cats, Rackoones, Otters, Beavers, and Mufquafhes, trading both their Skins and flefh to the *Englifh*. They have alfo other devifes wherewith to kill their game."

* * *

John Josselyn, British naturalist, discusses hunting by indigenous tribal peoples in New England, circa 1673, in Josselyn, *An Account of Two Voyages to New-England,* 2nd ed. (London: G. Widdowes, 1675), reprinted in *The Collections of the Massachusetts Historical Society,* Vol. 3, 3rd Series (Cambridge, Mass.: E.W. Metcalf and Company, 1833), 302-303.

"Their exercises are hunting and fishing, in both they will take abundance of pains. When the snoe will bear them, the young and lustie *Indians*, (leaving their papouses and old people at home) go forth to hunt *Moose, Deer, Bear,* and *Beaver,* Thirty ofr forty miles up into the Countrey; when they light upon a *Moose* they run him down, which is sometimes in a half a day, sometimes a whole day, but never give him over till they have tyred him, the snow being usually four feet deep, and the Beast very heavie he sinks every step, and as he runs sometimes bears down Arms of Trees that hang in his way, with his horns, as big as a mans thigh; other whiles, if any of their dogs (which are but small) come near, jerking out his heels (for he strikes like a horse) if a small Tree be in the way he breaks it quite asunder with one stroak, at last they get up to him on each side and transpierce him with their Lances, which formerly were no other but a staff of a yard and half pointed with a Fishes bone made sharp at the end, but since they put one pieces of sword-blades which they purchase of the *French*, and having a strap of leather fastened to the but end of the staff which they bring down to the midst of it, they dart it into his sides, *hæret latere lethalis arundo,* the poor Creature groans, and walks on heavily for a space, then sinks and falls down like a ruined building, making the Earth to quake; ...."

* * *

Daniel Gookin, Cambridge, Massachusetts Congregationalist missionary, moralizes about the hunting by New England indigenous people, circa 1674, in Gookin, "Historical

Collections of the Indians in New England," *Collections of the Massachusetts Historical Society, For the Year 1792. Volume 1* (Boston: Munroe & Francis, 1806 [1674]), 149.

"They are much addicted to idleness, especially the men, who are disposed to hunting, fishing, and the war, when there is cause. That little tillage or planting used among them, was principally done by the women. Also in their removals from place to place,which they are inclined to, for their fishing and hunting at the several seasons, the women carry the greatest burthen...."

* * *

Charles Wooley, British clergyman, comments on hunting by indigenous people in the New York City area, circa 1678, in W[ooley], *A Two Years Journal in New-York. And Part of its Territories in America* (London: John Wyat and Eben Tracy, 1701), reprinted in Cornell Jaray, ed., *Historic Chronicles of New Amsterdam, Colonial New York and Early Long Island, First Series,* Empire State Historical Publications Series No. 35 (Port Washington, N.Y.: Ira J. Friedman, 1968), 40-41.

"[W]hen they hunt them [bears], they commonly go two or three in company with Guns: for in case one shoot and miss the Bear will make towards them, so they shoot one after another to escape the danger and make the Game sure: But without Guns or any Weapon except a good Cudgel or Stick. I was one with others that have had a very good diversion and sport with them, in an Orchard of Mr. John Robinson's of New-York; where we follow'd a Bear from Tree to Tree, upon which he could swarm like a Cat; and when he got to his resting place, perch'd upon a high branch, we dispatc'd a youth after him with a Club to an opposite bough, who knocking his Paws, he comes grumbling down backwards with a thump upon the ground, so we after him again...."

* * *

An account of New Jersey mentions the hunting by indigenous peoples, circa 1683, in *Brief Account of the Province of East:New:Jarsey in America. Published by the Scots Proprietors Having Interest There* (Edinburgh: John Reid, 1683), 12.

"The *Indian* Natives in this Countrey are but few, Comparative to the Neighbouring Collony, And thefe that are there, are fo far from being formidable, and injurious to the Planters, and Inhabitants, that they are really ferviceable, and advantagious to them, not only in hunting, and taking the Deer, and all other wild Creatures, and catching of Fifh, and Fowl fit for food, in their feafons; but in the killing and deftroying of Bears, Wolves, Foxes, and other Vermine; whofe skins and furrs they bring the *Englifh,* and fell at lefs pryce, then the value of time that people muft fpend to take them."

* * *

John Dunton, London traveler, in Boston, concerning hunting by indigenous people, circa 1686, in [Dunton], *A Summer's Ramble, Through Ten Kingdomes, Occasionally Written by John Dunton, Citizen of London,* 2 vols. (London: A. Baldwin, 1686), reprinted as W.H. Whitmore, ed., *Letters Written from New-England, A.D. 1686, by John Dunton* (Boston: The Prince Society, 1867), 180-183.

"My Seventh Ramble was to *Wiffagufet,* the next Town to Nantafcot, on the South-fide of the Bay: I had but one Friend that accompanied me in this Ramble; and yet I did not want for Company; for his Converfation was fo agreeable that I was very well pleaf'd with it. As we went along we fell into a Difcourfe of the Deers, (which are very numerous in this Countrey,) and of their fwimming over to Deer Ifland; and my Friend told me that they were not fo fubject to be hunted there, as on the main Land; I afk'd

him who it was that ufually hunted them, and he told me it was the Indians: I told him
I had indeed heard that the Indians were great hunters, but had never heard what fort
of Hunting they uf'd; He told me, If I pleaf'd, he wou'd give me an account of it;
having feen 'em hunt himfelf feveral times: I thank'd him, and told him he wou'd
oblige me much with the Relation. He then thus began:

"'The Indians have two feveral Ways of Hunting: Firft, When they purfue their
Game, efpecially Deer, fo which there are abundance: thefe they purfue in twenty, forty,
fifty, yea fometimes in two and three hundred in a Company, as I have feen; when they
drive the Woods before them. A fecond way of Hunting they have is, by Traps of feveral forts: To which purpofe, after they have obferved in fpring time and Summer the
haunt of the Deer, then about Haveft they go ten or twenty together, and many times
more: and withal, unlefs it be too far off, their Wives and Children alfo, where they
build up littel Hunting-Houfes of Barks and Bufhes, not comparable to their dwelling-
Houfes, and fo each Man takes his Bounds of two, three, or four miles, where he fets
thirty, forty, ot fifty Traps, and baits his Traps with that Food the Deer loves; and once
in two Days he walks round to view his Traps, of which they are very tender, where
they lie, and what comes at them: For they fay the Deer, whom the Indians believe to
have a Divine Power in them, will foon fmell, and be gone: And therefore, *Npnow-
waumen*, (which is, I muft go to my Traps) is a ufual Phrafe with them.

"'Nor is it without reafon, that they are fo careful; for fometimes when a Deer has
been taken in their Traps, they have found a Woolf there devouring him; and the Wolf
being greedy of his Prey, they have killed the Wolf: Sometimes the Wolf having glut-
ted himfelf with Eating one half, he leaves the other for his next bait; but the glad
Indian coming in the mean time, prevents him. But it is not the Wolf alone, that will
devour the Deer, but other ravenous Beafts alfo: I remember how a poor Deer, after
having been long chafed by a Stout Wolf, was at laft tired, and the Wolf feized upon
it, and kill'd it; but in the Act of devouring his Prey, two Englifh Sows, big with Pig,
Paft by, and affaulting the Wolf, drove him from his Prey, and devoured fo much of
that poor Deer, that the Swine both furfeited, and died that Night.

"'When a Deer is caught by the Leg in a Trap, fometimes there it lies a whole day
before the Indian comes; and fo the Deer lies a prey to the ranging and ravening Wolf,
and other Wild Beafts, but moft commonly to the Wolf, who fiezeth upon the Deer, and
robbs the Indian (at his firft devouring) of near half his Prey; and if the Indian comes
not the fooner, the Wolf will make a Second Meal, and leave the poor Indian nothing
but the Bones, and the torn Deers Skin; Efpecially if the Wolf brings fome of his
greedy Companions to his bloody Banquet. But the Indian being thus difappointed,
makes a falling Trap with a great Weight of Stones; and fo fometimes knocks the Wolf
on the Head with a gainful Revenge; Efpecially if it be a black Wolf, whofe Skins they
greatly prize. When any Controverfie happens between two Indians, or more, whofe
a Deer fhall be, they commonly divide it, to prevent quarrelling. And when a Deer,
Wolf, or any other Beaft, happens in hunting to run into the Water, and is kill'd there,
the fkin is carried to the Sachim or Prince within whofe Territory it was flain: This they
call *Pumpom*, that is, a Tribute Skin.'

"I gave my Friend many Thanks, for his Relation, but told him they did not hunt
for Pleafure, as we did in England, and indeed throughout Europe, where Hunting is
counted one of the Nobleft Recreations: He told me 'twas true, they did not hunt with
fo much Gallantry, but then it was with lefs hazard and more Profit; and as for Pleafure,

they took as much to find a Deer in a Trap, as the Europeans did to hunt him down, and then their Profit,' faid he, 'which is the Chief thing they aim at, is confiderable. For they don't only get Winter Provifion for their Families, (they hunting for the fkins moft part after Harveft,) but make a great advantage of the Skins, which they fell both to the Englifh and Dutch, for ready money; and is one of the Chief Commodities which the Merchants Export hence.'"

* * *

Baron de Lahontan, French explorer, concerning hunting by indigenous people in Quebec, 8 July 1686, in de Lahontan, *New Voyages to North-America,* ed. by Reuben Gold Thwaites, 2 vols., Vol. 1 (Chicago: A.C. McClurg and Company, 1905) 103-116.

"Laft Winter we had no new Occurrences in the Colony. I fpent the whole Winter at the hunting of Orignals or Elks along with the Savages,....

"The hunting of Elks is perform'd upon the Snow, with fuch *Rackets* as you fee defign'd in the annex'd Cutt. Thefe *Rackets* are two Foot and a half long, and fourteen Inches broad; their ledges are made of a very hard Wood, about an Inch thick, that faftens the Net juft like a Tennis Racket, from which they differ only in this: that thofe for the Tennis are made of Gut-ftrings, whereas the others are made of little thongs of the skins of Harts or Elks. In the Cut, you may perceive two little fpars of Wood, which run a-crofs to render the Net firmer and ftiffer. The hole that appears by the two Latchets, is the place in which they put the Toes and fore-part of the Foot; fo that 'tis tied faft by the two Latchets, which run twice round about the Heel, and every ftep they make upon the Snow, the fore-part of the Foot finks into that hole, as often as they raife their Heel. By the help of this Contrivance they walk fafter upon the Snow, than one can do with Shoes upon a beaten path: And indeed 'tis fo neceffary for them, that 'twould be otherwife impoffible not only to hunt and range the Woods, but even to go to Church, notwithftanding they are fo near; for commonly the Snow is three or four Foot deep in that Country during the Winter. Being oblig'd to march thirty or forty Leagues in the Woods in purfuit of the above-mentioned Animals, I found that the fatigue of the Journey equal'd the pleafure of it.

"The *Orignal* is a fort of Elk, not much different from that we find in *Mufcovy.* 'Tis as big as an *Auvergne* Moyle, and much of the fame fhape, abating for its Muzzle, its Tail, and its great flat Horns, which weigh fometimes 300 and fometimes 400 weight, if we may credit thofe who pretend to have weigh'd them. This Animal ufually reforts to planted Countries. Its Hair is long and brown; and the Skin is ftrong and hard, but not thick. The Flefh of the *Orignal,* efpecially that of the Female fort, eats delicioufly; and 'tis faid, that the far hind Foot of the Female kind, is a Cure for the Falling-Sicknefs; it neither runs nor skips, but its trot will almoft keep up with the running of a Hart. The Savages affure us, that in Summer 'twill trot three Days and three Nights without intermiffion. This fort of Animals commonly gather into a body towards the latter end of Autumn; and the Herds are largeft in the beginning of the Spring, at which time the fhe ones are rutting; but after their heat is over, they all difperfe themfelves. We hunted 'em in the following manner: Firft of all, we went 40 Leagues to the Northward of the River of St. *Laurence,* where we found a little Lake of three or four Leagues in Circumference, and upon the banks of that Lake, we made Hutts for our felves of the barks of Trees, having firft clear'd the Ground of the Snow that cover'd it. In our Journey thither, we kill'd as many Hares and Woodhens, as we could eat. When we had fitted up our Hutts, the Savages went out upon the difcovery of the Elks, fome to the Northward, and fome to the South, to the diftance of two or three Leagues from the Hutts. As foon as they difcover'd any frefh foot-fteps, they detach'd one of their number to give us notice, to the end, that the whole Company might have the pleafure of feeing the chace. We trac'd thefe foot-fteps fometimes for one, and fometimes for two Leagues, and then fell in with five, ten, fifteen or twenty Elks in a body; which prefently betook themfelves to flight, whether a part or in a Body, and funk into the Snow up to their Breaft. Where the Snow was hard and condenfated, or where the froft following wet Weather had glaz'd it above, we came up with 'em after the chace of a quarter of a League: But when the Snow was foft or juft fallen, we were forc'd to purfue 'em three or four Leagues before we could catch 'em, unlefs the Dogs happen'd to ftop 'em where the Snow was very deep. When we came up with them, the Savages fired upon 'em with Fufees. If the Elks be much inrag'd they'll fometimes turn upon the Savages, who covewr themfelves with Boughs in order to keep off their Feet, with which they would crufh 'em to pieces. As foon as they are kill'd, the Savages make new Hutts upon the fpot, with great Fires in the middle; while the Slaves are imploy'd in fleaing 'em, and ftretching out the Skins in the open Air. One of the Soldiers that accompany'd me, told me one Day, that to withftand the violence of the Cold, one ought to have his Blood compof'd of Brandy, his Body of Brafs, and his Eyes of Glafs. And I muft fay, he had fome ground for what he fpoke, for we were forc'd to keep a Fire all round us, all the Night long. As long as the Flefh of thefe Animals lafts, the Savages feldom think of ftirring; but when 'tis all confum'd, they then look out for a new Difcovery. Thus they continue to hunt, till the Snow and Ice are melted. As foon as the great thaw commences, 'tis impoffible for 'em to travel far; fo that they content themfelves with the killing of Hares and Partridges, which are very numerous in the Woods. When the Rivers are clear of the Ice, they make Canows of the Elk-skins, which they fow together very eafily, covering the Seams with a fat fort of Earth inftead of pitch. This work is over in four or five days time, after which they return home in the Canows with all their Baggage.

"This, Sir, was our Diverfion for three Months in the Woods. We took fifty fix Elks, and might have kill'd twice as many, if we had hunted for the benefit of the Skins. In the Summer feafon, the Savages have two ways of killing 'em, both of which are equally troublefom. One confifts in hanging a Rope-gin between two Trees, upon a Pafs furrounded with Thorns; the other is compafs'd by crauling like Snakes among the Trees and Thickets, and approaching to 'em upon the Leeward fide, fo that they may be fhot with a Fufee. Harts and Caribous are kill'd both in Summer and Winter, after the fame manner with the Elks; excepting that the Caribou's, which are a kind of wild Affes, make an eafie efcape when the Snow is hard, by vertue of their broad Feet; whereas the Elk finks as faft he rifes. In fine, I am fo well pleas'd with the hunting of this Country, that I have resolv'd to imploy all my leifure time upon the Exercife. The Savages have promifed, that in three Months time I fhall fee other forts of chafes, which will prove lefs fatiguing, and more agreeable."

"*Being a curious Defcription of the Hunting of divers Animals.*

"I find by your Letter, that you have an agreeable relifh for the curious Elk-Hunting in this Country, and that a further account of our other hunting Adventures, would meet with a welcome Reception. This Curiofity, indeed, is worthy of fo great a Hunts-Man as your felf; but at prefent I muft beg your excufe as to the Beaver-hunting, for I know nothing of it yet but by hear-fay.

"In the beginning of *September*, I fet out in a Canow upon feveral Rivers, Marfhes, and Pools, that difembogue in the Champlain Lake, being accompany'd with thirty or forty of the Savages that are very expert in Shooting and Hunting, and perfectly well acquainted with the proper places for finding Water-foul, Deer, and other fallow Beafts. The firft Poft we took up was upon the fide of a Marfh or Fen of four or five Leagues in Circumference; and after we had fitted up our Hutts, the Savages made Hutts upon the Water in feveral places. Thefe Water-Hutts are made out of the branches and leaves of Trees, and contain three or four Men: For a Decoy they have the skins of Geefe, Buftards, and Ducks, dry'd and ftuff'd with Hay, the two feet being made faft with two Nails to a fmall piece of a light plank, which floats round the Hutt. This place being frequented by wonderful numbers of Geefe, Ducks, Buftards, Teals, and an infinity of other Fowl unknown to the *Europeans*; when thefe Fowls fee the ftuff'd Skins fwim-ming with the heads erected, as if they were alive, they repair to the fame place, and fo give the Savages an opportunity of fhooting 'em, either flying, or upon the Water; after which the Savages get into their Canows and gather 'em up. They have likewife a way of catching 'em with Nets, ftretch'd upon the furface of the Water at the Entries of the Rivers. In a word, we eat nothing but Water-fowl for fifteen Days; after which we refolv'd to declare War againft the Turtle-Doves, which are fo numerous in *Canada*, that the Bifhop has been forc'd to excommunicate 'em oftner than once, upon the ac-count of the Damage they do to the Product of the Earth. With that view, we imbarqued and made towards a Meadow, in the Neighbourhood of which, the Trees were cover'd with that fort of Fowl, more than with Leaves: For juft then 'twas the feafon in which they retire from the North Countries, and repair oto the Southern Climates; and one would have thought, that all the Turtle-Doves upon Earth had chofe to pafs thro' this place. For the eighteen or twenty days that we ftay'd there, I firmly believe that a thoufand Men might have fed upon 'em heartily, without putting thefelves to any trouble. You muft know, that through the middle of this Meadow there runs a Brook, upon which I and two young Savages fhot feveral Snipes, Rayles, and a certain fort of Fowl call'd *Bateurs de faux*, which is as big as a Quail, and eats very delicioufly.

"In the fame place we kill'd fome *Musk-Rats*, or a fort of Animals which refemble a Rat in their fhape, and are as big as a Rabbet. The Skins of thefe Rats are very much valued, as differing but little from thofe of beavers. Their Tefticles fmell fo ftrong of Musk, that no Civet or Antilope that *Afia* affords, can boaft of fuch a ftrong and fweet fmell. We spy'd 'em in the Mornings and Evenings, at which time they ufually appear upon the Water with their Nofe to the Windward, and betray themfelves to the Huntfmen, by the curling of the Water. The *Fouteraux*, which are an amphibious fort of little Pole-Cats, are catch'd after the fame manner. I was likewife entertain'd upon this occafion, with the killing of certain little Beafts, call'd *Siffleurs*, or Whiftlers, with allufion to their wonted way of whiftling or whizzing at the Mouth of their Holes in fair Weather. They are as big as Hares, but fomewhat fhorter, their Flefh is good for nothing, but their Skins are recommended by their coats. The Savages gave me an opportunity of hearing one of thefe Creatures whiftle for an hour together, after which they fhot it. To gratifie the curiofity I had to fee fuch diverfity of Animals, they made a diligent fearch for the Holes or Dens of the *Carcaioux*, and having found fome at the diftance of two or three Leagues from the Fen upon which we were pofted, they con-ducted me to the place. At the break of day we planted our felves round the Holes, with our Bellies upon the Ground; and left fome Slaves to hold the Dogs a Mufket-fhot

behind us. As foon as thefe Animals perceiv'd Day-light, they came out of their Holes,
which were immediately ftop'd up by the Savages, and upon that the Dogs fetch'd 'em
up with eafe. We faw but two of 'em, which made a vigorous defence againft the Dogs,
but were ftrangled after a difpute of half an hour. Thefe Animals are not unlike a Badger, only they are bigger, and more mifchievous. Tho' our Dogs shew'd a great deal
of Courage in attacking the *Carcaioux*, they betray'd their Cowardice the next day in
a rencounter with a Porcupine, which we fpy'd upon a little Tree. To obtain the pleafure
of feeing the Porcupine fall we cut down the Tree: but neither the Dogs nor we durft
go near it: The Dogs only bark'd and jump'd round it; for it darted its long and hard
hair like fo many Bodkins, three or four paces off. At laft we pelted it to death, and
put it upon the fire to burn off its darts; after which we fcalded it like a Pig, took out
the Intrails, and roafted it: But tho' 'twas very fat, I could not relifh it fo well as to
comply with the affertion of the Natives, who alledge, that it eats as well as a Capon
or a Partridge.

"After the Turtle-Doves had all pafs'd over the place, in queft of fome Southern
retreats, the Savages offer'd to fend fome of their number with Canows to conduct me
home, before the Rivers and Lakes were frozen over; for themfelves were to tarry out
for the Elk-hunting; and they imagin'd that the Cold and Hardfhip attending theat Exercife, had made me fick of it the year before. However, we had then a Month good
before the commencement of the Froft, and in that interval of time, they proffer'd to
entertain me with more diverting Game than any I had feen before. They propos'd to
go fifteen or fixteen Leagues further up the Country, affuring me, that they knew of
a certain place that had the moft advantageous fituation in the World, both for Pleafure
and and profit, and that afforded great plenty of Otters, of the Skins of which they
mean'd to make a great Cargoe. Accordingly we pull'd down our Hutts, and having im-
barqu'd in our Canows, fail'd up the River, till we came to a little Lake of two Leagues
in Circumference, at the end of which we faw another greater Lake, divided from this
by an Ifthmus of 150 Paces in length. We pitch'd our Hutts at the diftance of a League
from that Ifthmus; and fome of the Savages fifh'd for Trouts, while the reft were imploy'd in laying Traps for the Otters upon the brinks of the Lake. Thefe Traps are made
of five Stakes plac'd in the form of an oblong Quadrangle, fo as to make a little Chamber, the Door of which is kept up, and fupported by a Stake. To the middle of this Stake
they tye a ftring which paffes thro' a little fork, and has a Trout well faften'd to the
3end of it. Now, when the Otter comes on fhoar, and fees this bait, he puts above half
his Body into that fatal Cage, in order to fwallow the Fifh; but he no fooner touches
the Stake that fupports the Door, upon which an heavy and loaded Door falls upon his
Reins and quafhes him. During our Pilgrimage in that part of the Country, the Savages
took above two hundred and fifty *Canada* Otters; the Skins of which are infinitely
prittier than thofe of *Mufcovy* or *Sweden*. The beft of 'em which are not worth two
Crowns in this place, are fold in *France* for four or five, and fometimes for ten, if they
are black and very rough. As foon as the Savages had fet their Traps, they gave orders
to their Slaves to go round the Lake every Morning, in order to take out the amphibious Animals. After that they conducted me to the above-mentioned Ifthmus, where I
was furpriz'd to fee a fort of a Park or Fence made of Trees, fell'd one upon another,
and interlac'd with Thorns and Branches; with a quadrangular inclofure of Stakes at
the end of it, the entry of which was very narrow. They gave me to know, that they ufed
to hunt Harts in that place, and proms'd to divert me with the fhew, as foon as the

Inclofures were a little mended. In effect, they carry'd me two or three Leagues off, upon fuch Roads as had nothing on either fide but Fens and Marfhes; and after they had difperf'd themfelves, fome on one hand and fome on the other, with a Dog for every Man; I faw a great many Harts running to and again, in queft of places of Safety. The Savage that I kept company with, affur'd me, that he and I had no occafion to walk very faft, becaufe he had took the ftraighteft and the neareft Road. Before us we faw above ten Harts, which were forc'd to turn back, rather than throw themfelves into the Marfh, of which they could never get clear. At laft, after walking a great pace, and running now and then, we arriv'd at the Park, and found the Savages lying flat upon the Ground all round it, in order to fhut up the entry of the ftake Inclofure as foon as the Harts enter'd. We found thirty five Harts in the place, and, if the Park had been better fenc'd, we might have had above fixty; for the nimbleft and lighteft of 'em, skip'd over before they came to enter the Inclofure. We kill'd a great many of 'em, but fpar'd the Dams, becaufe they were great with young. I afk'd of the Savages the Tongues and the Marrow of the Harts, which they gave me very readily. The Flefh was very fat, but not delicious, excepting fome few bits about the Ribs. But after all, this was not our only Game; for two days after we went a Bear-hunting, and the Savages who fpend three parts of four of their life in Hunting in the Woods, are very dexterous at that Exercife, efpecially in fingling out the Trunks of the Trees upon which the Bears Neftle. I could not but admire their knowledge in that Point, when, as we were walking up and down in a Foreft, at the diftance of an hundred Paces one from another, I heard one Savage call to another, *Here's a Bear*. I askt 'em how he knew that there was a Bear upon the Tree which he knock'd with his Axe; and they all reply'd, that 'twas as eafily diftinguifh'd as the print of an Elks foot in the Snow. For five or fix times they never mifs'd; for after they had knock'd two or three times upon the Trunk of the Tree, the Bear came out of its hole, and was prefently fhot. The *Canada* Bears are extream black, but not mifchievous, for they never attack efpecially in the Autumn, that they can fcarce walk: Thofe which we kill'd were extream fat, but their fat is good for nothing but to be burnt, whereas their Flefh, and, above all their Feet are very nice Victuals. The Savages affirm, that no Flefh is fo dleicious as that of Bears; and indeed, I think they rae in the right of it. While we rang'd up and down in queft of Bears, we had the pleafure of fpying fome Martins and wild Cats upon the branches of the Trees, which the Savages fhot in the Head to preferve their Skin. But the moft Comical thing I faw, was the Stupidity of the Wood-hens, which fit upon the Trees in whole Flocks, and are kill'd one after another, without ever offering to ftir. Commonly the Savages fhoot at 'em with Arrows, for they are not worth a fhoot of Powder, which is able to kill an Elk or an Hart. I have ply'd this fort of Fowling in the Neighbourhood of our cantons or Habitations in the Winter time, wth the help of a Dog who found out the Trees by fcent, and then bark'd; upon which I approach'd to the Tree, and found the Fowls upon the Branches."

* * *

Henri Joutel, French explorer, comments on hunting by indigenous peoples while on the La Salle expedition in the lower Mississippi River valley, June 1687, and in the Illinois country, August 1687, in [Joutel], *Joutel's Journal of La Salle's Last Voyage* (Chicago: The Caxton Club, 1896, reprint of 1714 ed.), 136, 162.

21 June 1687: "The other *Indian* feeing his Comrade fick, went a Hunting, and brought a wild Goat; for there are many in that Country. The *Indians* have the Art of dreffing

the Heads of thofe Creatures, which they put upon their own, and imitate them fo exactly, that they can come very near to them, and feldom fail of killing. The fame Method they ufe for Turkeys and other wild Fowl, and fo draw them clofe to them-felves."

7 August 1687: "We proceeded on, continually undergoing the fame Toil, till the Sev-enth, when, we faw the firft Bullock, we had met on our Way, fince our coming among the *Accancea's*. The *Indians*, who had a great Mind to eat Flefh, made a Sign to me, to go kill it. I purfu'd and Shot, but it did not fall, the *Indians* ran after, kill'd, and came to tell us it muft be parch'd, or dry'd, which was accordingly done."

* * *

Lamothe de Cadillac, French explorer, comments on hunting by indigenous peoples in the Great Lakes region, circa 1695, in [de Cadillac], "The Memoir of Lamothe Cadillac," in Milo Milton Quaife, ed., *The Western Country in the Seventeenth Century. The Mem-oirs of Lamothe Cadillac and Pierre Liette* (Chicago: Lakeside Press, 1947), 20-21.

"They have two tests of true men; the first is war and the second hunting. The best warriors and the best hunters are the men most valued, most important, and most praiseworthy among them; so that he who possesses these two qualities seems to be proclaimed as a chief among his tribe.

"The fact that the hunter is accounted the equal of the warrior need cause no sur-prise; for it should be remembered that all the Indians live and maintain their families by their guns or, more properly speaking, by their cleverness, cunning, and skill in catching animals in the snares they lay for them. To succeed in this they must be fa-miliar with the hunting grounds and know the trails, the haunts, and the instinct of wild animals; they must be able to bear fatigue and to be patient, lucky, eager, energetic, bold, and good runners; they must have a keen eye and sound wind. They hunt the elk, moose, hind, bear, roebuck, caribou, beaver, and buffalo. They have to kill these ani-mals in the woods or on the prairies, by surprise or by swiftness of foot.

"Whatever anyone may think, I know that you must have a good pair of legs to play this game. Yet a good hunter sometimes kills a dozen animals in a day, and it is a plea-sure to see the Miami, from time to time, bringing into their village huge bears which they have captured and tamed, driving them before them with switches, like sheep driven to the shambles. It is on such occasions that good hunters show their prowess; and as it is true in every country that those who are fond of hunting pursue it for their own pleasure and satisfaction rather than for profit, money, or gluttony, so, among the Indians, the good hunters profit the least from their hunting."

* * *

Daniel Neal, historian, circa 1720, concerning hunting by New England indigenous peoples prior to 1700, in Neal, *History of New-England Containing an Impartial Account of the Civil and Ecclesiastical Affairs of the Country to the Year of Our Lord, 1700*, 2 vols., Vol. 1 (London: J. Clark, 1720), 25.

"....; the only Employment of the Men is Hunting and Fifhing; when Provifion is low, they go out into the Wood 50 or 100 in a Company with their Bows and Arrows, and bring in a frefh Supply, or fail down the Rivers in their Canoes to catch Fifh."

* * *

John Lawson, Carolina Surveyor-General, chronicles hunting in South Carolina, circa 1700, January and February 1701, and circa 1709, in Lawson, *A New Yoyage to Carolina;*

Containing the Exact Description and Natural History of That Country. Together with the Present State Thereof, and A Journal of a Thousand Miles, Travel'd thro' Several Nations of Indians (London: pvt. ptg., 1709), 10, 12-13, 22-23, 25-27, 44-45, 48, 52, 86, 117, 206-207, 210.

Circa 1700: "As we went up the River, we heard a great Noife, as if two Parties were engag'd againft each other, feeming exactly like fmall Shot. When we approach'd nearer the Place, we found it to be fome *Sewee Indians* firing the Canes swamps, which drives out the Game, then taking their particular Stands, kill great Quantities of both Bear, Deer, Turkies, and what wild Creatures the Parts afford."

January 7, 1701: "We had a very large Swamp to pafs over near the Houfe, and would have hir'd our Landlord to have been our Guide, but he feem'd unwilling; fo we prefs'd him no farther about it. He was the talleft *Indian* I ever faw, being feven Foot high, and a very ftrait compleat Perfon, efteem'd on by the King for his great Art in Hunting, always carrying with him an artificial Head to hunt withal: They are made of the Head of a Buck, the back Part of the Horns being fcrapt and hollow, for Lightnefs of Carriage. The Skin is left to the fetting on of the Shoulders, which is lin'd all around with fmall Hoops, and flat Sort of Laths, to hold it open for the Arm to go in. They have a Way to preferve the Eyes, as if living. The Hunter puts on a Match-coat made of Deer's Skin, with the Hair on, and a Piece of the white Part of a Deer's Skin, that grows on the Breaft, which is faften'd to the Neck-End of this ftalking Head, fo hangs down. In thefe Habiliments an *Indian* will go as near a Deer as he pleafes, the exact Motions and Behaviour of a Deer being fo well counterfeited by 'em, that feveral Times it hath been known for two Hunters to come up with a ftalking Head together, and unknown to each other fo that they have kill'd an *Indian* inftead of a Deer, which hath happen'd fometimes to be a Brother, or fome dear Friend, for which Reafon they allow not that Sort of Practice, where the Nation is populous."

25 January 1701: "This day, one of our Company, with a *Sapona Indian*, who attended *Stewart*, went back for the Horfes. In the meantime, we went to fhoot Pigeons, which are so numerous in thefe Parts, that you might fee many Millions in a Flock; they fometimes fplit off the Limbs of ftout Oaks, and other Trees, upon which they rooft o' Nights. You may find feveral *Indian* Towns, of not above 17 Houfes, that have more than 100 Gallons of Pigeon Oil, or Fat;.... The *Indians* take a Light, and go among them in the Night, and bring away fome houfands, killing them with long Poles, as they rooft in the Trees."

31 January 1701: "..., their *Indian* Guide (who was a Youth of this Nation) having kill'd, in their Way, a very fat Doe, Part of which they brought to us."

1 February 1701: "This day, the King fent out all his able Hunters, to kill Game for a great Feaft,...."

4 February 1701: "All the Indians hereabouts carefully preferve the Bones of the Flefh they eat, and burn them, as being of Opinion, that if they omitted that Cuftom, the Game would leave their Country, and they fhould not be able to maintain themfelves by their Hunting."

Circa 1709: "Some of them hunt and fowl for us at reafonable Rates, the Country being as plentifully provided with all Sorts of Game, as any Part of *America;*...."

Circa 1709: "When thefe Savages go a hunting, they commonly go out in great Numbers, and oftentimes a great many Days Journey from home, beginning at the coming in of the Winter; that is, when the Leaves are fallen from the Trees, and are become dry. 'Tis then they burn the Woods, by fetting Fire to the Leaves, and wither'd Bent and Grafs, which they do with a Match made of the black Mofs that hangs on the Trees in *Carolina*,.... Thus they go and fire the Woods for many Miles, and drive the Deer and other Game into fmall Necks of Land and Ifthmus's, where they kill and deftroy what they pleafe. In thefe Hunting-Quarters, they have their Wives and Ladies of the Camp, where they aet all the Fruits and Dainties of that Country, and live in all the Mirth and Jollity, which it is poffible for fuch People to entertain themfelves withal. Here it is, that they get their Complement of Deer-Skins and Furs to trade with the *Englifh*, (the Deer-Skins being in Seafon in Winter, which is contrary to England.) All fmall Game, as Turkeys, Ducks, and fmall Vermine, they commonly kill with Bow and Arrow, thinking it not worth throwing Powder and Shot after them."

"It is an establifh'd Cuftom amongft all thefe Natives, that the young Hunter never eats of that Buck, Bear, Fifh, or any other Game, which happens to be the firft they kill of that fort; becaufe they believe, if he fhould eat thereof, he would never after be fortunate in Hunting."

* * *

Robert Beverly, Virginia plantation owner and historian, describes the hunting by Virginia indigenous peoples, circa 1705, in Beverly, *The History and Present State of Virginia,* ed. by Louis B. Wright (Charlottesville, Va.: University Press of Virginia, 1947), 153-156, 308-312.

"CHAP. VI
"Of Wild Fowl, and Hunted Game.

"AS in Summer, the Rivers and Creeks are fill'd with Fish, so in Winter they are in many Places cover'd with Fowl. There are such a Multitude of Swans, Geese, Brants, Sheldrakes, Ducks of several Sorts, Mallard, Teal, Blewings, and many other Kinds of Water-Fowl, that the Plenty of them is incredible. I am but a small Sportsman, yet with a Fowling-Peice, have kill'd above Twenty of them at a Shot. In like manner are the Mill-Ponds, and the great Runs in the Woods stor'd with these Wild-Fowl, at certain Seasons of the Year.

"The Shores, Marshy Grounds, Swamps, and Savanna's, are also stor'd with the like Plenty of other Game, of all sorts, as Cranes, Curlews, Herons, Snipes, Wood-cocks, Saurers [Sora?] Ox-eyes, Plovers, Larks, and many other good Birds for the Table that they have not yet found a Name for. Not to mention Beavers, Otters, Musk-Rats, Minxes, and an infinite Number of other wild Creatures.

"Altho' the Inner Lands want these Benefits, (which, however, no Pond or Slash is without,)yet even they, have the advantage of Wild Turkeys, of an incridible Bigness, Pheasants, Partridges, Pigeons, and an Infinity of small Birds, as well as Deer, Hairs, Foxes, Raccoons, Squirrels, Possums. And upon the Frontier Plantations, they meet with Bears, Panthers, Wild-Cats, Elks, Buffaloes, and Wild Hogs, which yield Pleasure, as well as Profit to the Sports-man. And tho' some of these Names may seem fright-ful to the *English*, who hear not of them in their own Country; yet they are not so there; for all these Creatures ever fly from the Face of Man, doing no Damage but to the Cattle and Hogs, which the *Indians*, never troubled themselves about....

"The *Indians* had no other Way of taking their Water or Land-Fowl, but with the Help of Bows,and Arrows: Yet, so great was their Plenty that with this Weapon only, they kill'd what Numbers they pleased. And when the Water-Fowl kept far from Shore, (as in warmer Weather they sometimes did,) they took their Canoes, and paddl'd after them.

"But they had a better Way of killing the Elks, Buffaloes, Deer, and greater Game, by a Method which we call Fire-Hunting: That is, a Company of them wou'd go together back into the Woods, any time in the Winter, when the Leaves were fallen, and so dry, that they wou'd burn; and being come to the Place design'd, they wou'd Fire the Woods, in a Circle of Five or Six Miles Compass; and when they had compleated the first Round, they retreated inward, each at his due Distance, andput Fire to the Leaves and Grass afresh, to accelerate the Work, which ought to be finished with the Day. This they repeat, till the Circle be so contracted, that they can see their Game herded all together in the Middle, panting and almost stifled with Heat and Smoak; for the poor Creatures being frighten'd at the Flame, keep running continually round, thinking to run from it, and dare notpass through the Fire; by which Means they are brought at last into a very narrow Compass. Then the *Indians* let flie their Arrows at them, and (which is very strange) tho' they stand all round quite clouded in Smoak, yet rarely shoot each other. By this means they destroy all the Beasts, collected within that Circle. They make all this Slaughter only for the sake of the Skins, leaving the Carcases to perish in the Woods.

"Father *Verbiast* [Ferdinand Verbiest], in his Description of the Emperor of *China's* Voyage into the Eastern *Tartary*, Anno 1682, gives an Account of a Way of Hunting the *Tartars* have, not much unlike this, only whereas the Indians surround their Game with Fire, the *Tartars* do it with a great Body of armed Men, who having environ'd the Ground they deign to drive, march equally inwards, which, still as the Ring lessens, brings the Men nearer each other, till at length the wild Beasts are incompassed with a living Wall.

"The *Indians* have many pretty Inventions, to discover and come up to the Deer, Turkeys and other Game undiscern'd; but that being an Art, known to very few *English* there, I will not be so accessary to the Destruction of their Game, as to make it publick. I shall therefore only tell you, that when they go a Hunting into the Out-lands, they commonly go out for the whole Season, with their Wives and Family. At the Place where they find the most Game, they build up a convenient Number of small Cabbins, wherein they live during that Season. These Cabbins are both begun, and finished in Two or Three Days, and after the Season is over, they make no further Account of them."

"CHAP. XXI.
"Of the Recreations, and Pastimes used in Virginia.

"FOR their Recreation, the Plantations, Orchards, and Gardens constantly afford 'em fragrant and delightful Walks. In their Woods and Fields, they have an unknown variety of Vegetables, andother rarities of Nature to discover and observe. They have Hunting, Fishing, and Fowling, with which they entertain themselves an hundred ways. Here is the most Good-nature, and Hospitality practis'd in the World, both towards Friends and Strangers: but the worst of it is, this Generosity is attended now and then, with a little too much Intemperance. The Neighbourhood is at much the same distance, as in the Country in *England*: but with this Advantage, that all the better sort of People have been abroad, and seen the World, by which means they are free from that stiffness and formality, which discover more Civility, than Kindness: And besides, the goodness of the Roads, and the fairness of the Weather, bring People oftener together.

"The *Indians*, as I have already observ'd, had in their Hunting, a way of conceal-
ing themselves, and coming up to the Deer, under the blind of a Stalking-Head, in
imitation of which, many People have taught their Horses to stalk it, that is, to walk
gently by the Huntsman's side, to cover him from the sight of the Deer. Others cut
down Trees for the Deer to browze upon, and lie in wait behind them. Others again set
Stakes, at a certain distance within their Fences, where the Deer have been used to leap
over into a Field of Peas, which they love extreamly; these Stakes they so place, as to
run into the Body of the Deer when he Pitches, by which means they Impale him.

"They Hunt their Hares, (which are very numerous) a Foot, with Mungrils or swift
Dogs, which either catch them quickly, or force them to hole in a hollow Tree, whither
all their Hares generally tend when they are closely pursued. As soon as they are thus
holed, and have crawl'd up into the Body of the Tree, the business is to kindle a Fire,
and smother them with Smoak, till they let go their hold, and fall to the bottom stifled;
from whence they take them. If they have a mind to spare their Lives, upon turning
them loose, they will be as fit as ever to hunt at another time; for the mischief done
them by the Smoak, immediately wears off again.

"They have another sort of Hunting, which is very diverting, and that they call
Vermine Hunting; it is perform'd a Foot, with small Dogs in the Night, by the Light
of the Moon or Stars. Thus in Summer-time they find an abundance of Raccoons,
Opossums, and Foxes in the Corn-Fields, and about their Plantations: but at other
times, they must go into the Woods for them. The Method is to go out with three or
four Dogs, and as soon as they come to the place, they bid the Dogs seek out, and all
the Company follow immediately. Where-ever a Dog barks, you may depend upon
finding the Game; and this Alarm, draws both Men and Dogs that way. If this Sport
be in the Woods, the Game by that time you come near it, is perhaps mounted to the
top of an high Tree, and then they detach a nimble Fellow up after it, who must have
a scuffle with with the Beast, before he can throw it down to the Dogs; and then the
Sport increases, to see the Vermine encounter those little Currs. In this sort of Hunting, they also carry their great Dogs out with them, because Wolves, Bears, Panthers,
Wild-Cats, and all other Beasts of Prey, are abroad in the Night.

"For Wolves they make Traps, and set Guns bated in the Woods, so that when he
offers to seize the Bate, he pulls the Trigger, and the Gun discharges upon him. What
Elian and *Pliny* [Roman natural historians Claudius Aelianus and Caius Plinius Secun-
dus] write, of the Horses being benummed in their Legs, if they tread in the Track of
a Wolf, does not hold good here; for I my self, and many others, have rid full Speed
after Wolves in Woods, and have seen live ones taken out of a Trap, and drag'd at a
Horse's Tail; and yet those that follow'd on Horseback, have not perceived any of their
Horses to falter in their pace.

"They have many pretty devices besides the Gun, to take wild Turkeys; And among
others, a Friend of mine invented a great Trap, wherein he at times caught many Turkeys, and particularly seventeen at one time, but he could not contrive it so, as to let
others in after he had entrapped the first flock, until they were taken out....

"Their Fowling is answerable to their Fishing for plenty of Game, in its proper
Season, no Plantation being so ill stored, as to be without a great deal. They have a vast
variety of it, several sorts of which, I have not yet mention'd, as Beaver, Otter, Squirrels, Partridges, Pigeons, and an infinite number of small Birds, &c....

"These Creatures [beavers] have a great deal of Policy, and know how to defeat all the Subtilty and Stratagems of the Hunter, who seldom can meet with them, tho' they are in great numbers all over the Country.

"There is yet another kind of Sport, which the young People take great Delight in, that is, the Hunting of wild Horses; which they pursue sometimes with Dogs, and sometimes without. You must know they have many Horses foaled in the Woods of the Uplands, that never were in hand, and are as shy as any Savage Creature. These having no mark upon them, belong to him, that first takes them. However, the Captor commonly purchases these Horses very dear, by spoiling better in the pursuit; in which case, he has little to make himself amends, besides the pleasure of the Chace. And very often this is all he has for it, for the wild Horses are so swift, that 'tis difficult to catch them; and when they are taken, tis odds but their Grease is melted, or being old, they are so sullen, that they can't be tam'd."

* * *

John Archdale, Carolina proprietor, comments on hunting by Carolina indigenous peoples, circa 1707, in Archdale, "A New Description of That Fertile and Pleasant Province of Carolina, by John Archdale, 1707," in Alexander S. Salley, ed., *Narratives of Early Carolina, 1650-1708* (New York: Barnes & Noble, 1967 [1911]), 289.

"The Indians are great Hunters, and thereby not only serviceable to kill Dear, etc., for to procure Skins for Trade with us, but those that live in Country Plantations procure of them the whole Dear's Flesh, and will bring it many Miles for the Value of about six Pence, and a wild Turky of 40 Pound, for the Value of two Pence Engl. Value. There is also vast Quantities or Numbers of wild Ducks, Geese, Teal, and exceeding Plenty of Fish, etc.,...."

* * *

Thomas Nairne, South Carolina Indian agent, hunts among the Chickasaw near the Mississippi River, 13 April 1708, in [Thomas Nairne], *Nairne's Muskhogean Journals. The 1708 Expedition to the Mississippi River,* ed. by Alexander Moore (Jackson, Miss.: University Press of Mississippi, 1988), 51-55.

"Nothing more contrary to my inclination, than being obliged to travell so slowly, and wait the pace of the Carriors. To make the time slide on as imperceivable as possible I diverted my selfe, by accompanying the hunters at their sports, for the Chicasaws are such excellent forresters, they never mist supplying the Camp with meat enough, and so civill with all, that what ever was killed they threw down to us, that we might order the devission as we pleased....

"When the camp was placed the usuall divertion of the hunters was either to look for Bare, fire a ring for Dear or go to the Clay pitts and shoot Buffeloes, for you must observe that in the spring and all sumer, these cattle eat abundance of Clay.... Though [now] Buffeloe Bulls are not fitt for men to eat, yet in May, June and Jully the Buffeloe Bulls are very fatt and good, the Cows and heifers in the fall and winter. The tongues of these Creatures are extraordinary fine atasting like marrow, and that causes the death of many hundreds of them. Of all hunting deversions, I took most pleasure in fireing rings for in that we never missed 7 or 10 Dear. Three or 4 hours after the ring is fired, of 4 or 5 miles circumferance, the hunters post themselves within as nigh the flame and smoak as they can endure. The fire on each side burns in toward the center and thither the Dear gather from all parts to avoid it, but striving to shun a Death which they might often Escape, by a violent spring, they fall into a Certain one from the Bullets of the hunters who drawing nigher together, as the circle grows less, find an easy pray of the impounded dear, tho seldom kill all for some who find a place wher the Flame is less Violent, Jump out. This sport is the more certain the longer the grownd has been un-burned. If it has not been for 2 or 3 years there are so many dry leaves grass and Trash, that few Creatures within escape, and the men are forced to go out betimes at some slack pace to the leeward. In killing Buffeloes they Aim at the yearlings and heifers, being the tenderest and indeed no Beef exceeds them. After shooting 3 or 4 of these, no remonstrances can prevail with the savages to march farther that day, but the Ketles and spits to work. Sir, A hasty man can worst of any Travell in Company with them, their whole discourse is, here's excellent grownd for bears or Turkeys, in this canepeice we shall surely meet with Buffaloes, and 'twold in their oppinion be perfect folly to pass by without hunting them....

"If then the savages of our Company were cloy'd with dear and Buffeloe, then they went a Bare hunting. This was the time of year in which these Creatures lye in their holes, for from the first of January to the middle of March they sleep and neither eat or Drink. The Indian way of hunting them dureing that time, is only looking in holes under the roots of fallen trees, or up such trees in the swamps, which have a hollow rotten place nigh the Top. In these Large holes the Bears make their nest and repose themselves dureing their sleeping season. The savages when they spy such a hole in a tree presently view it all round and see for the marks of the Bears Claws in going up, thereby looking narrowly are easily seen. They either climb up some small tree that stands by together and prick him out with canes, or else fire the nest, as they come out of the hole, stand ready to shoot him. Thus I saw them take severall.... The hunting law of the Chicasaws is, hat who ever first finds the Bear, has the skin and Belley peice of fatt, and when driving a swamp he who first wounds him, has the same advantage. The rest of the fatt and meat are equally devided among the fires. Of no other meat they make devission as not worth it, each takes what he will."

* * *

Antoine Le Page du Pratz, French traveler, describes hunting by indigenous peoples in Louisiana, circa 1720-1728, in Le Page du Pratz, *The History of Louisiana, or of the Western Parts of Virginia and Carolina. Containing a Description of the Countries that lie on both Sides of the River Mississippi. With an Account of the Settlements, Inhabit-ants, Soil, Climate, and Products* (London: T. Becket, 1774), 254-257, 260-262.

"This buffalo is the chief food of the natives, and of the French alfo for a long time paft; the beft piece is the bunch on the fhoulders, the tafte of which is extremely deli-cate. They hunt this animal in the winter; for which purpofe they leave Lower Loui-fiana, and the river Miffiffippi, as he cannot penetrate thither on account of the thick-nefs of the woods; and befides loves to feed on long grafs, which is only to be found in the meadows of the high lands. In order to get near enough to fire upon him, they go againft the wind, and they take aim aat the hollow of the fhoulder, that they might bring him to the ground at once, for if he is only flightly wounded, he runs againft his enemy. The natives when hunting feldom choofe to kill any but the cows, having ex-perienced that the flefh of the male fmells rank; but this they might eafily prevent, if they did but cut off the tefticles from the beaft as foon as he is dead, as they do from ftags and wild boars. By killing the males there is lefs hazard of diminifhing the fpecies than by killing the females; and befides, the males have much more tallow, and their fkins are the largeft and beft....

"The natives hunt the deer fometimes in companies, and fometimes alone. The hunter who goes ot alone, furnifhes himfelf with the dried head of a deer, with part of the fkin of the neck faftened to it, and this fkin is ftretched out with feveral hoops made of fplit cane, which are kept in their places by other fplits placed along the infide of the fkin, fo that the hands and arms may be eafily put within the neck. Being thus provided, he goes in queft of the deer, and takes all neceffary precautions not to be dif-covered by that animal: when he fees one, he approaches it as gently as poffible, hid-ing himfelf behind a bufh which he carries in his hand, till he be within fhot of it. But if, before he can come near enough, the buck fhakes its head, which is a fign that he is going to make fome capers and run away, the hunter immediately counterfeits the cries of thofe animals when they call each other, in which cafe the buck frequently comes towards him. He then fhews the head which he holds in his hand, and by low-ering and lifting his arm by turns, it amkes the appearance of a buck feeding, and lifting his head from time to time to graze. The hunter ftill keeps himfelf behind the bufh, till the buck comes near enough to him, and the moment he turns his fide, he fires at the hollow of his fhoulder, and lays him dead.

"When the natives want to make the dance of the deer; or if they want to exercife themfelves merrily; or if it fhould happen that the Great Sun inclines to fuch fport, they go about an hundred of them in a company to the hunting of this animal, which they muft bring home alive. As it is a diverting exercife, many young men are generally of the party, who difperfe themfelves in the meadows among the thickets in order to dif-cover the deer. They no fooner perceive one than they advance towards him in a wide crefcent, one point of which may be about a quarter of a league from the other. Part of the crefcent draws near to him, which frightens him away to another point; that part likewife advancing, he immediately flies back to the other fide. He is kept thus run-ning from one fide to another a confiderable time, on urpofe to exercife the young men, and afford diverfion to the Great Sun, or to another Little Sun, who is nominated to fupply his place. The deer fometimes attempts to get out and efcape by the openings of the crefcent, in which cafe theofe who are at the points run forward obliging him to go back. The crefcent then gradually forms a circle: and when they perceive the deer beginning to be tired, part of them ftoop almoft to the ground, and remain in that pof-ture till he approached them, when they rife and fhout: he inftantly flies off to the other fide, where they do the fame; by which means he is at length fo exhaufted, that he is no longer able to ftand on his legs, and fuffers himfelf to be taken like a lamb. Some-times, however, he defends himfelf on the ground with his antlers and forefeet; they therefore ufe precaution to feize upon him begind, and even in that cafe they are fome-times wounded.

"The hunters having feized the deer prefent it to the Great Sun, or in his abfence, to the perfon whom he fent to reprefent him. If he fays, *well*, the roe-buck is imme-diately opened, and its four quarters carried to the hut of the Great Sun, who gives portions of them to the chief men among the hunters."

"The natives, when they meet with any of thofe trees, which they fufpect contains a bear in it, give two or three ftrong blows againft the trunk, and immediately run be-hind the next tree oppofite to the loweft breach. If there be a bear within, he appears in a few minutes at the breach, to look out and fpy the occafion of the difturbance; but upon obferving nothing likely to annoy him, he goes down again to the bottom of his caftle.

"The natives having once feen their prey, gather a heap of dried canes, which they bruife with their feet, that they burn the eafier, and one of them mounting upon a tree adjoining to that in which the bear is, fets fire to the reeds, and darts them one after another into the breach; the other hunters having planted themfelves in ambufcade upon other trees. The bear is quickly burned out of his habitation, and he no fooner appears on the outfide, than they let fly their arrows at him, and often kill him before he gets to the bottom of the tree."

* * *

Sebastien Rasles, French Jesuit missionary, comments on hunting by Quebec area indigenous peoples, 12 October 1723, in "From Father Sebastien Rasles, Missionary of the Society of Jesus in New France, to Monsieur His Brother," reprinted as "The Wanderings of Father Rasles. 1689-1723," in William Ingraham Kip, ed., *The Early Jesuit Missions in North America* (London: Wiley and Putnam, 1847), Part I, 26.

"No sooner have the children begun to walk, than they exercise them in using the bow, and in this they become so skilful that at ten or twelve years of age they scarcely ever fail to kill the bird at which they aim. I was very much surprised, and should have had difficulty in believing it, if I had not myself been a witness of their skill."

* * *

Father Joseph François Lafitau, French Jesuit missionary, describes hunting by American indigenous people, circa 1724, in Lafitau, *Customs of the American Indians Compared with the Customs of Primitive Times,* ed. and trans. by William N. Fenton and Elizabeth L. Moore, 2 vols., Vol. 2 (Toronto: The Champlain Society, 1977), 187.

"HUNTING AND FISHING

"If war is the noblest of all exercises and that on which the Indian prides himself the most, as is usually the case with nations which base their glory on it, hunting and fishing are his most customary exercises, because they are most necessary for for his living and he gets most of what he needs for his maintenance from them; the meats with which he nourishes himself, the clothing with which he covers himself, the oils with which he greases himself and the furs with which he trades. The mobile tribes live almost solely on meat and fish. Part of the year they are fish-eaters, roving ceaselessly on the sea shores, or the lakes and river banks. They spend the rest of the year in the woods, hunting wild beasts.

"I shall not enter here into the details of their different hunting and fishing expeditions, their way of hunting meats, having them dried by fire or the sun or reducing them to powder. These things are too well known and too often repeated to burden this work with them."

* * *

Etienne de Véniard, Sieur de Bourgmont, French army officer and explorer, describes hunting among the Padoucas in the Missouri country, October 1724, in "Journal of the Voyage of Monsieur de Bourgmont, Knight of the Military Order of Saint Louis, Commandant of the Missouri River [which is above That of the Arkansas, and of the Missouri [Country], to the Padoucas [1724]," in Frank Norall, *Bourgmont, Explorer of the Missouri, 1698-1725* (Lincoln, Neb.: University of Nebraska Press, 1988), 149, 159.

October 14th: "M. de Bourgmont, on horseback, killed a bison today with his pistol."

"Manner of hunting of this tribe. The head chief harangues in his village on the day before he wants to send his warriors off on the hunt, to urge them to be ready. He sends out about 50 or 60 mounted warriors, armed with bows and arrows. They ride about two or three leagues from their camp, where they find herds of bison—usually 300 to 400. They start to torment them and run them hard until their tongues stick out a foot. Then they choose the fattest ones and shoot arrows into them which penetrate a foot into the animals' bellies. Choosing the fattest ones in sight, they kill like that all they want. Many of the horses are killed also. They never have colts, for their mares always abort on the hunt."

* * *

Bampfylde Moore Carew, British traveler, hunts among the indigenous people in eastern Pennsylvania near the Delaware River, circa 1730s, in [Carew], *The Surprising Adventures of Bampfylde Moore Carew, King of the Beggars* (Tiverton, England: W. Salter, 1812), 123-124.

"Hunting being the principal employment and diversion of the Indians, at which they are very expert, Mr. Carew had an opportunity of gratifying to the utmost his taste for this diversion, there scarcely passing a day but he was a party amongst them at some hunting match or other, and most generally with the king [chief] himself...."

"One day, being out hunting, they chanced to fall in with some other Indians, near the river Delaware. When the chase was over, they sat down to be merry together,...."

* * *

John Brickell, Irish doctor, describes hunting among indigenous peoples in North Carolina, circa 1737, in Brickell, *The Natural History of North-Carolina* (Dublin: James Carson, 1737), 361-362, 367.

"[T]his [checking a gun for faults] they [indigenous peoples] do before they go to kill *Deer*, or any other kind of Game that is to be met with as they hunt in Woods. It is remarkable in them that they will feldom ftir or go abroad into the Woods to Hunt before the *Sun* is an Hour or two heigh, and hath exhaled moft part of the Dew from the Earth, then are they indefatigable in walking from Morning till Night in purfuit of their Game."

"When they [indigenous peoples] are difpofed to hunt in the Woods, they generally go out in great Numbers together, and feveral Days Journies from home. They always begin thefe Hunting matches at the approach of *Winter*, when the Leaves are fallen from the Trees, and become dry, or when Skins and Furs are beft in Seafon.

"Thus they frequently leave their Houfes and retire into the Woods for four or five Months together..., at which time the Skins are in Seafon, and fet Fire to the Woods for many Miles together to drive out the Deer and other Game into fmall Necks of Lands, and other places where they fix their Guards, by which means they kill and deftroy what they pleafe, efpecially fuch as ftrive to efcape the Fire and get through the paffes they have made for that purpofe.

"In thefe Hunting matches they bring their Wives and Miftreffes along with them, where they eat feveral kinds of Fruits which that Country produces, and live in all the Mirth and Jolity that it is poffible for fuch People to entertain themfelves with. It is in thefe Hunting matches that they get their complement of *Deer-Skins, Furs*, and many other commodities to trade with the *Chriftians*, the *Deer-Skins* being in Seafon here in

Winter, which is contrary in *England* and *Ireland*; moſt of all their ſmall Game they kill with their Bows and Arrows, fuch as *Geefe*, *Turkeys*, *Ducks*, and various kinds of wild Beaſts, as *Raccoons*, *Possums*, *Squirrels*, and feveral other forts of Vermine, judging it not worth throwing Powder and Shot after them."

"It is an eſtabliſhed Cuſtom amongſt all the Natives in theſe Parts, that the young Hunters never eat of that *Buck*, *Bear*, *Fiſh*, or any other fort of Game which happens to be the firſt they kill, becauſe they believe if they ſhould eat thereof, they never would be afterwards fortunate in Hunting."

* * *

William Douglass, British doctor, moralizes about hunting by Northeastern indigenous peoples, circa 1749, in Douglass, *Summary, Historical and Political, of the First Planting, Progressive Improvements, and Present State of the British Settlements in North-America*, 2 vols., Vol. 1 (Boston: Rogers and Fowle, 1749), 153-154.

"...; they do not provide for To-Morrow, their Hunting is their neceſſary Subſiſtence not Diverſion; when they have good Luck in Hunting, they eat and ſleep until all is confumed and then go a Hunting again."

"Like the *wild Iriſh* they dread Labour more than Poverty, like Dogs they are always either eating or ſleeping, excepting in Travelling, Hunting, and their Dances;...."

"The *Indians* have their Hunting, Fowling and Fiſhing Grounds,...."

* * *

A geographer of Nova Scotia, comments on hunting by indigenous people in that province, circa 1749, in *A Geographical History of Nova Scotia* (London: Paul Vaillant, 1749), 47, 48, 49.

"They think it abundantly ſufficient to ſow as much Land as will ordinarily produce Corn enough to ſerve them till next Seaſon, ſo that in caſe the Crop comes to any Miſchance, they live miferably, and ſuffer great Want, even in the Midſt of Plenty, rather than be at the Pains of hunting and killing ſo much Game as would be a comfortable Support."

"In *October* and *November* begins the Chace for the *Caſtor* [beaver] and the *Elk*, which holds a good Part of the Winter.

"*Bears*, *Otters*, and *Hares* make alſo a Part of the Riches of this Seaſon, which is farther improved by ſeveral Sort of Wild Fowl, as *Partridge*, *Duck*, *Teal*, *Buſtard*, and others; and the Rivers and Lakes are cover'd with *Coots*, *Widgeons*, and other River Fowl in all Parts.

"In *January* the *Sea Wolf* [seal?] comes up the River. The Fleſh of this Creature is good eating, neither ill-taſted nor unwholeſome. From the beginning of *February* to the Middle of *March* is the Height of the Seaſon for hunting the *Caribou*, as alſo the *Red* and *Fallow Deer*."

"...; and if theſe People would till and ſow their Land, feed their Cattle, and raife Poultry; Fiſhing, Fowling and Hunting might be uſed only for Exercife and Diverſion."

* * *

Peter Kalm, Swedish naturalist, describes hunting by indigenous people in Quebec, 12 October 1749, in Adolph B. Benson, trans. and ed., *Peter Kalm's Travels in North America*, 2 vols., Vol. 2 (New York: Dover Publications, 1966), 555.

"In the evening of the fourth I arrived here at St. Jean. Several Indians were here who were out on a hunting expedition. When an Indian goes hunting, he does not go alone but takes his whole family with him, also his belongings; that is, his wife, children and dog. He then travels around in the forests shooting all kinds of animals. He eats the meat and preserves the skins to sell, for which he receives in return his clothes and ornaments, also his gunpowder, shot and other articles purchased from the Europeans."

* * *

Fray Miguel Venegas, Mexican Jesuit missionary, repeats part of a decalogue of hunting and fishing commandments among California indigenous peoples, circa 1758, in Venegas, *A Natural and Civil History of California*, 2 vols., Vol. 1 (London: James Rivington and James Fletcher, 1759), 106-107.

"His decalogue was as follows, 'That they fhould not eat of their firft hunting or fifhing, under pain of being difqualified from hunting or fifhing hereafter. 2d, That they fhould not eat of fome certain fifh. 3d, That they fhould forbear eating fome particular parts of the game, and thefe were the beft and fatteft, faying, that this fat was that of dead old men; and that by eating it old age would immediately come upon them. Thus the beft pieces fell to the fhare of the old hechiceros [shaman] alledging, that as they were already advanced in years, they had nothing to fear on this head. 4. That they fhould not gather certain fruits, nor take fome fpecies of fifh (and both of thefe were the beft) as they would do them a great deal of hurt; but that nothing injured old people. 5. That if they caught any ftag or fifh of an extraordinary fize, not to offer to eat it, as belonging to the hechiceros.... 9. That in very hot weather, all fhould come out and pay their salutations to the fun, who would not then moleft them in their huntings and fifhings; but on the contrary render every undertaking profperous.'"

* * *

J.C.B., French traveler, on moose hunting by indigenous peoples in New France, March? 1759, in [J.C.B.], *Travels in New France by J.C.B.*, ed. by Sylvester K. Stevens, Donald H. Kent, and Emma Edith Woods (Harrisburg, Penn.: The Pennsylvania Historical Commission, 1941), 109.

March?, 1759: "...The northern savages have another way of hunting this animal [moose] without any risk. They divide into two bands. One band gets in canoes and, joining in line, they form a half circle, each end touching the shore. The other band on the shore make another large circle and loose their dogs to start up the moose enclosed in this area. The dogs chase the moose before them and force them to plunge into the water. No sooner are they in the water, than fire is opened upon them from all the canoes. They very rarely escape from such an attack."

* * *

Jean-Bernard Bossu, French traveler, details the hunting customs of indigenous people in the Southeast, 2 May 1759, in Seymour Feiler, ed., *Jean-Bernard Bossu's Travels in the Interior of North America, 1751-1762* (Norman, Okla.: University of Oklahoma Press, 1962), 146-147.

"The Indians usually go hunting at the end of October. The Alabamas travel sixty, eighty, and even one hundred leagues from their village, and they take their families with them in their canoes. They come back during the planting season in March....

"These people use some strange tricks to kill deer. They take with them into the woods a dried head of the male of the species. They cover their backs with a deer skin and put an arm through the neck of the dried head, into which they have put little wooden hoops for their hands to grip. They then get down on their knees, while holding the head in view, and imitate the deer's cry. The animals, fooled by this trick, come quite close to the hunters, who kill them easily.

"There are Indians who have used this ruse to kill up to four hundred deer in a single winter. They use the same technique to catch turkeys in the woods. Several of them put the skins of these birds on their shoulders and place on top of their heads a piece of scarlet cloth which flutters in the wind. The disguised Indians attract the turkeys while others shoot them with their arrows rather than with rifles, which would scare off the birds. As long as there are any perched in the trees, the hunters shoot at them with a great deal of skill. The turkeys stay there waiting for those that have been killed to come back. I have often feasted on turkey among the Indians. This bird is excellent in the autumn."

* * *

James Kenny, Philadelphia Quaker, discusses deer-hunting by indigenous people near Pittsburgh, 16 November 1761, in John W. Jordan, ed., "Journal of James Kenny, 1761-1763," Pennsylvania Magazine of History and Biography, Vol. 37, No. 1 (1913), 26-27.

"I am inform'd by Thos Cape, that when ye Indians Kill a Deer in ye Woods & being in haste to follow ye Game, they leave a Cap or some part of their Clothing on ye killed Game untill they return, which hinders ye Buzzards & Vermin to Eat it, also that if they intend to leave it all night where its kill'd they Bark or Blase 3 or four Trees round it & then wets some Powder in their Hand untill it is dissolved then dips their finger in it & Sprinkles it on ye Blazes, which in ye Night will look like Sparks of fire all around, & no Vermin would touch ye Carcase untill it would rot there."

* * *

Henry Timberlake, British lieutenant, concerning indigenous peoples in Tennessee, January 1762, in Samuel Cole Williams, ed., Lieut. Henry Timberlake's Memoirs, 1756-1765 (Marietta, Ga.: Continental Book Company, 1948 [1765]), 71-72, 102-103.

"There are a vast number of lesser sort of game, such as rabbits, squirrels of several sorts, and many other animals, besides turkeys, geese, ducks of several kinds, partridges, pheasants, and an infinity of other birds, pursued only by the children, who, at eight or ten years old, are very expert at killing with a sarbacan or hollow cane, through which they blow a small dart, whose weakness obliges them to shoot at the eye of the larger sort of prey, which they seldom miss."

"They are likewise very dextrous at pantomime dances; several of which I have seen performed that were very diverting. In one of these, two men, dressed in bearskins, came in, stalking and pawing about with all the motions of real bears: two hunters followed them, who in dumb shew acted in all respects as they would do in the wood: after many attempts to shoot them, the hunters fire; one of the bears is killed, and the other wounded; but, as they attempt to cut his throat, he rises up again, and the scuffle between the huntsmen and the wounded bear generally affords the company a great deal of diversion.

"The taking of pigeons at roost was another that pleased me exceedingly; and these, with my walking and observations, furnished me with amusement for some time."

* * *

Alexander Henry, British soldier, discusses hunting among the Chippewa in the Great Lakes region in Michigan, August and December, circa 1763, in Milo Milton Quaife, ed.,

Alexander Henry's Travels and Adventures in the Years 1760-1776 (Chicago: Lakeside Press, 1921), 128-129, 132, 135-136.

"The raccoon was another object of our chase. It was my practice to go out in the evening with dogs, accompanied by the youngest son of my guardian, to hunt this animal. The raccoon never leaves its hiding place till after sunset.

"As soon as a dog falls on a fresh track of the raccoon he gives notice by a cry, and immediately pursues. His barking enables the hunter to follow. The raccoon, which travels slowly and is soon overtaken, makes for a tree on which he remains till shot.

"After the falling of snow nothing is more necessary for taking the raccoon than to follow the track of his feet. In this season he seldom leaves his habitation; and he never lays up any food. I have found six at a time in the hollow of one tree lying upon each other, and nearly in a torpid state. In more than one instance I have ascertained that they have lived six weeks without food. The mouse is their principal prey.

"Raccoon hunting was my more particular and daily employ. I usually went out at the first dawn of day and seldom returned till sunset, or till I had laden myself with as many animals as I could carry. By degrees I became familiar with this kind of life;...."

"A hunting excursion into the interior of the country was resolved; and early the next morning the bundles were made up by the women for each person to carry....

"On the first day of our march we advanced about twenty miles and then encamped. Being somewhat fatigued, I could not hunt; but Wawatam killed a stag not far from our encampment.... On the third day we removed and marched till two o'clock in the afternoon.

"While the women were busy in erecting and preparing the lodges I took my gun and strolled away, telling Wawatam that I intended to look out for some fresh meat for supper. He answered that he would do the same; and on this we both left the encampment in different directions....

"In going down the side of a lofty hill I saw a herd of red deer approaching. Desirous of killing one of them for food, I hid myself in the bushes, and on a large one coming near, presented my piece, which missed fire on account of the priming having been wetted. The animals walked along without taking the least alarm; and having reloaded my gun, I followed them and presented a second time. But now a disaster of the heaviest kind had befallen me; for on attempting to fire I found that I had lost the cock. I had previously lost the screw by which it was fastened to the lock; and to prevent this from being lost also I had tied it in its place with a leather string; the lock, to prevent its catching in the bows, I had carried under my molton coat.

"Of all the sufferings which I had experienced this seemed to me the most severe. I was in a strange country, and I knew not how far I had to go. I had been three days without food. I was now without the means of procuring myself either food or fire. Despair had almost overpowered me: but I soon resigned myself into the hands of that Providence whose arm had so often saved me, and returned on my track in search of what I had lost. My search was in vain, and I resumed my course, wet, cold and hungry, and almost without clothing."

* * *

Thomas Hutchinson, Massachusetts politician and historian, circa 1765, on New England indigenous peoples' hunting in colonial times, in Hutchinson, *The History of the Province of Massachusetts Bay,* 2nd ed., 2 vols., Vol. 1 (London: M. Richardson, 1765), 471.

"Their hunting and fifhing, being all they did, which could be called labor, for their maintenance of fupport, ferved alfo as diverfions. Deer, Moofe, and Bears were their chief objects; Wolves, Wild Cats, Raccoons, Otters, Musquafhes [muskrats], and even Bevers, were not much regarded, until the Englifh, from the value they fet upon their fkins, encouraged the purfuit of them. Befides their bows, they had other devices to take their game, fometimes by double hedges a mile or two in length, and a mile wide at one end, and made narrow, by degrees, until they came to a gap of about fix feet, againft which they lay hid to fhoot the deer, as they came through in the day-time, and, at night, they fet Deer-traps, being fprings made of young trees. They had their traps alfo for Bevers and Otters."

* * *

Miguel Costanso, engineer and cosmographer on the Don Gaspar de Portola expedition, describes hunting by indigenous people in Alta California, circa 1769, in Ray Brandes, trans., *The Costanso Narrative of the Portola Expedition* (Newhall, Cal.: Hogarth Press, 1970 [1770]), 93.

"They are great hunters. To kill deer and antelope, they possess an admirable skill. They preserve the hide of the head and part of the neck of some of these animals, skinned with care and leaving the horns attached to the same hide, which they stuff with grass or straw to keep its shape. They put this shell like cap upon the head and go forth to the woods with this rare equipment. On sighting the deer and antelope, they drag themselves along the ground little-by-little, with the left hand. In the right they carry the bow and four arrows. They lower and raise the head, moving it to one side and the other, and making other movements so like these animals that they attract them without difficulty to the snare, and drawing them near, they discharge their arrows at them with certainty of hitting."

* * *

Samuel Hearne, British explorer in the Canadian Northwest, on indigenous peoples' hunting, 3 March 1771, in Hearne, *Journey from Fort Prince Wales, in Hudson's Bay to the Northern Ocean, for the Discovery of Copper Mines and a North-West Passage, Performed between the Years 1769 and 1772, by Mr. Samuel Hearne* (Philadelphia: Joseph and James Crukshank, 1802), 12.

"In croffing Pike Lake, on the 3rd of March, they came up to a large tent of northern Indians, who had been living there from the beginning of winter, and had employed that long interval in catching deer in a pound. Indeed fo fuccefsful is this method of fporting, in a country where the game is fo abundant, that many families fubfift by it, without having occafion to move their tents above once or twice in the courfe of a whole winter."

* * *

Henry Tufts, Massachusetts criminal, hunts as a refugee among the Abenaki, in Maine? Quebec?, circa 1772-1773, in Edmund Pearson, ed., *Henry Tufts. The Autobiography of a Criminal* (London: Jarrolds Publishers, 1931), 67, 71-72, 77.

"But I had no way to procure money for the purchase, except by hunting with the Indians or setting traps, wherefore to such expeditions I resolved to have recourse. Already had I received pressing invitations to accompany their hunting parties, so that (though hitherto had I declined such proposals) I anticipated no obstacle to the accomplishment of my design. The rigor of the winter was yet too severe for my feelings, but as I had often found profit from being in a state of readiness, I took care to provide a fusee, with good store of amunition. And no sooner had the inclemency of the atmosphere abated in some degree, than I joined a number of the hunters, who were setting out in quest of moose, deer and such other game, as might come to hand. We stayed out upwards of a week; our custom being to traverse the woods in almost every direction, during the day, and at the approach of night, to strike up a large fire, and lie down upon the hemlock boughs, with each man a blanket, but no other covering, than such as the canopy of heaven afforded. To me these hardships were quite irksome; I wished them at an end, although we had vewry good success in our business, for beside killing several moose and deer, we acquired a variety of fur animals. On return to the camps the booty was equalized, in usual manner, among the hunting adventurers."

"Early in February, which is the commencement of the main hunting season, I was positive several parties would set out in quest of moose and deer, because on the improvement of this season, depends, in good measure, their livelihood for the whole year. With a view of joining some or other of those hunters, I carefully provided myself with whatever necessaries might be had, and when the time for departure arrived, we set out loaded with steel and squat-traps, guns, hatchets, ammunition and snowshoes; those accoutrements making up the bigger part of our luggage; since the itinerary provisions we were very little incommoded, our whole viaticum consisting of only a morsel of salt, and a mere trifle of smoked or frozen venison. But, though our dependence for sustenance was altogether on the fruits of the chase, yet were we in no great jeopardy of famishing, for the sagacity of the hunters in starting game, and their dexterity in running it down with their dogs, far exceeds anything of the kind known among civilized people. Our daily stages were from twelve to twenty miles only, except when the heat of the chase tempted us to exceed those limits, as was sometime the case.

"What I disliked most of all, was our cold, uncomfortable mode of lodging, which absolutely forbade the reception of much repose. Our only accommodation of this sort was a parcel of hemlock or spruce twigs thrown upon the snow, on which we lay down, before a large fire, rolled up in our blankets. In this expedition, however, we met with extraordinary good fortune, killing a variety of moose, deer, bears, saple, minks, raccoons, wolverines, etc.,...."

"This same spring I was out upon a hunting match with another Indian, when, happening to espy a female deer at some small distance, I leveled my piece, and dropped her dead upon the spot. The Indian ran toward the game, but presently called aloud for my approach. Drawing near, I descerned, in the bushes, about a rod from the deer, a large buck lying dead also. On examination it appeared, that I killed both of them at the same shot, though the buck had been invisible at the time of fire."

* * *

John Heckewelder, Moravian missionary, on indigenous peoples' hunting in the Muskingum River valley, circa 1773, in Paul A.W. Wallace, ed., *Thirty Thousand Miles with John Heckewelder* (Pittsburgh: University of Pittsburgh Press, 1958), 116.

Circa 1773: "The hunter prefers going out with his gun on an empty stomach; he says, that hunger stimulates him to exertion by reminding him continually of his wants, whereas a full stomach makes a hunter easy, careless, and lazy, ever thinking of his home and losing his time to no purpose. With all their industry, nevertheless, and notwithstanding this strong stimulant, many a day passes over their heads that they have not met with any kind of game, nor consequently tasted a morsel of victuals; still they go on with their chase, in hopes of being able to carry some provisions home, and do not give up the pursuit until it is so dark that they can see no longer.

"The morning and evening, they say, are the precious hours for the hunter. They lose nothing by sleeping in the middle of the day, that is to say, between ten o'clock in the morning and four in the afternoon, except in dark, cloudy, and rainy weather, when the whole day is nearly equally good for hunting. Therefore the hunter, who happens to have no meat in the house, will be off and in the woods before daylight, and strive to be in again for breakfast with a deer, turkey, goose, bear, or raccoon, or some other game then in season."

* * *

Bernard Romans, French captain, details hunting among the Chickasaw and Choctaw, circa 1775, in Romans, *A Concise Natural History of East and West Florida* (New York: pvt. ptg., 1775), 65-67.

"The Chickasaws are esteemed good hunters, have extenfive hunting grounds, and make excellent ufe of them;.... this laft [the Oke Tibehaw River] they regard as their boundary with the Chactaws, but thefe two nations are by no means jealous of each other in this refpect, and hunt in each others grounds without lett or hindrance from either fide; although their country abounds in beaver, they kill none, leaving that to the white men; they think this kind of hunting beneath them, faying any body can kill beaver, but men only deer; this is exactly the reverfe of a northern Indian; they hunt like all their neighbours with the fkin and frontal bone of a deer's head, dried and ftretched on elaftic chips; the horns they fcoup out very curioufly, employing fo much patience on this, that fuch head a head and antlers often do not exceed ten or twelves ounces; they fix this on the left hand, and imitating the motions of the deer in fight, they decoy them within fure fhot. I cannot forbear to mention a merry accident on this occafion; a Chactaw Indian, who was hunting with one of thefe decoys on his fift, faw a deer, and thinking to bring it to him, imitated the deer's motions of feeding and looking round in a very natural way, another favage within fhot, miftaking the head for a real one, fhot the ball through it, fcarcely miffing the fingers of the first; the affair ended in fifty cuffs, but was no farther resented."

* * *

John Long, American trader, concerning indigenous peoples' hunting in the Great Lakes region, circa 1777, in Milo Milton Quaife, ed., *John Long's Voyages and Travels in the Years 1768-1788* (Chicago: Lakeside Press, 1922), 122-123.

"Before I proceed to relate the particulars of my voyage I shall mention the Indian manner of killing the white bear and the buffalo. The large white bear, commonly called the grizzly bear, is a very dangerous animal. When the Indians hunt it they generally go six or eight in a band. The instant they see one they endeavor to surround it by forming a large circle: if it is on the march they fire at it; but it is most frequently discovered, in the winter season, sucking its paws. In that case they approach nearer and form a double row for the animal to run between. One of the party is then sent out, who fires at the bear and generally wounds it. This rouses it to pursue the Indian, who runs between the ranks, and the rest of the band fire and soon despatch it.

"The buffalo I need not describe; it is well known to be a remarkable strong animal. The Indians say its head is bullet proof, and therefore they always fire at the body, endeavoring to hit the heart. When they are in pursuit of this animal they make up small huts of snow in different places, for near a mile in length on each side of the road. In each of these huts an Indian stands with a bow and arrow, to shoot at it as it passes, preferring the mode to powder and ball as it does not alarm the rest of the herd. The snow prevents the buffalo from smelling the Indians, though their scent is very strong and quick. The instant the animal drops they tomahawk it."

THE CAROLINAS AND GEORGIA

Edward Williams, British traveler, reports on potential hunting in Carolina and Georgia, circa 1650, in W[illiams], *Virginia. More Especially the South Part Thereof, Richly and Truly Valued* (London: John Stephenson, 1650), 12, 48.

"That no part of this happy Country may bee ungratefull to the Industrious, The ayre it selfe is often clouded with flights of Pigeons, Partriges, Blackbirds, Thrushes, Dottrels, Cranes, Hernes, Swans, Geese, Brants, Duckes, Widgeons, Oxeyes, infinites of wilde Turkeyes, which have been knowne to weigh fifty pounds weight, ordinarily forty."

"For Provision of flesh, if he can use his peece he may, even at his labour in the Woods, have opportunity of killing Venison, Hares, Wild-foule (in their season innumerable)...."

* * *

William Hilton, Barbados ship captain, hunts in the Cape Fear region of North Carolina, December 1663, in Hilton, "A Relation of a Discovery, By William Hilton, 1664," in Alexander S. Salley, Jr., ed., *Narratives of Early Carolina, 1650-1708* (New York: Barnes & Noble, 1967 [1911]), 53.

"In that time as our businesse called us up and down the River and Branches, we kill'd of wild-fowl, four Swans, ten Geese, twenty nine Cranes, ten Turkies, forty Duck and mallard, three dozen of Parrakeeto's, and six or seven dozen of other small Fowls, as Curlues and plovers, etc."

* * *

Henry Woodward, South Carolina surgeon, hunts in South Carolina, October–November 1674, in Woodward, "A Faithfull Relation of My Westoe Voiage, by Henry Woodward, 1674," in Alexander S. Salley, Jr., ed., *Narratives of Early Carolina, 1650-1708* (New York: Barnes & Noble, 1967 [1911]), 131, 134.

"Here [on the Edisto River] killing a large buck wee took up our rendeavouze wth two mile of the river, glad of the opportunity of lying in two of their hunting hutts.... Wee supped wth two fatt Turkeys to help out wth our parcht corne flower broth.... In the afternoon wee shott a fatt doe which, proportionably divideing amongst them, was carried along by them for our better comons at night.... Thursday wee tooke our journey dew West, passing many large pastorable Savanas, the other and promising very well. This day wee shott two Bucks. The best of both wth a fatt Turkey wee carried along wth us, for our better accomodation at night.

"Ten of them [Westoe tribal people] prepared to accompany mee in my journey home, returning by the same ways that I came, killing much game wth two large she beares uppon the way through much rain the fresshes being mightily encreased."

* * *

Thomas Ashe, South Carolina proprietor, describes potential hunting in South Carolina, circa 1682, in Ashe, "Carolina, or a Description of the Present State of That Country, by Thomas Ashe, 1682," in Alexander S. Salley, Jr., ed., *Narratives of Early Carolina, 1650-1708* (New York: Barnes & Noble, 1967 [1911]), 150-151.

"Birds for Food, and pleasure of Game, are the Swan, Goose, Duck, Mallard, Wigeon, Teal, Curlew, Plover, Partridge, the Flesh of which is equally as good, tho' smaller than ours in England. Pigeons and Parakeittoes. In Winter huge Flights of wild Turkies, oftentimes weighing from twenty, thirty, to forty pound."

* * *

Samuel Wilson, secretary to the Earl of Craven, discusses hunting in South Carolina, circa 1682, in Wilson, "An Account of the Province of Carolina, by Samuel Wilson, 1682," in Alexander S. Salley, Jr., ed., *Narratives of Early Carolina, 1650-1708* (New York: Barnes & Noble, 1967 [1911]), 170-171.

"Here [in the grassy savannahs] you may hunt the Hare, Fox, and deere all day long in the shade, and freely, spur your horse through the Woods to follow the chase.

"The Woods abound with hares, Squirrels, Racoons, Possums, Conyes and Deere, which last are so plenty that an Indian hunter hath kill'd nine fatt Deere in aday all shott by himself, and all the considerable Planters have an Indian hunter which they hire for less than twenty shillings a year, and one hunter will very well find a Family of thirty people with as much Venison and Foul, as they can well eat. Here are also in the woods great plenty of wilde Turkeys, Partridges, something smaller than those of England, but more de[l]icate, Turtle Doves, Paraquetos, and Pidgeons: On the grassy plaines the whistling Plover and Cranes and divers sorts of Birds unknowne in England.

"On the Rivers and brooks are all the winter moneths vast quantitys of Swan, wild Geese, Duck, Widgeon, Teale, Curlew, Snipe, Shell Drake and a certaine sort of black Duck that is excellent meat, and stayes there all the year."

* * *

John Lawson, Carolina Surveyor-General, chronicles hunting in South Carolina, circa 1700, January 1701, and circa 1709, in Lawson, *A New Yoyage to Carolina; Containing the Exact Description and Natural History of That Country. Together with the Present State Thereof, and A Journal of a Thousand Miles, Travel'd thro' Several Nations of Indians* (London: pvt. ptg., 1709), 10, 12-13, 22-23, 25-27, 44-45, 48, 52, 86, 117, 206-207, 210.

Circa 1700: "Here Propriety hath a large Scope, there being no ſtrict Laws to bind our Privileges. A Queſt after Game, being as freely and peremptorily enjoy'd by the meaneſt Planter, as he that is the higheſt in Dignity or wealthieſt in the Province. Deer, and other Game that are naturally wild, being not immur'd, or preferv'd within Boundaries, to ſatisfy the Appetite of the Rich alone. A poor Labourere, that is Maſter of his Gun, &c. hath as good a Claim to have continu'd Coarſes of Delicacies crouded upon his Table, as he that is Maſter of a greater Purſe."

9 January 1701: "We made our felves as merry as we could, having a good Supper with the Scraps of Venifon we had given us by the *Indians*, having kill'd 3 Teal and a Poffum, which Medly all together made a curious Ragoo."

12 January 1701: "Near the Sea-board, the *Indian* kill'd 15 Turkeys this Day; there coming out of the Swamp, (about Sun-rifing) Flocks of thefe Fowl, containing feveral hundreds in a Gang, who feed upon the Acrons, it being the moft Oak that grow in thefe Woods."

"Early the next Morning, we fet forward for the *Congeree-Indians*, parting with that delicious Profpect. By the Way our Guide kill'd more Turkeys, and two Polcats, which he eat, efteeming them before fat Turkeys. Some of the Turkeys which we eat, whilft we ftay'd there, I believe, weigh'd no lefs than 40 Pounds.

"The Land we pafs'd over this Day, was moft of it good, and the worft paffable. At Night we kill'd a Poffum, being cloy'd with Turkeys, made a Difh of that, which tafted much between young Pork and Veal;...."

24 January 1701: "On *Saturday* Morning, we all fet out for *Sapona*, killing, in thefe Creeks, feveral Ducks of a ftrange Kind, having a red Circle about their Eyes, like fome Pigeons that I have feen, a Top-knot reaching from the Crown of their Heads, almoft to the middle of their Backs, and abundance of Feathers of pretty Shades and Colours. They prov'd excellent Meat."

27 January 1701: "At Night, we lay by a fwift Current, where we faw plenty of Turkies, but perch'd upon fuch lofty Oaks, that our Guns would not kill them, tho' we fhot very often, and our Guns were very good. Some of our Company fhot feveral times, at one Turkey, before he would fly away, the Pieces being loaded with large Goofe-fhot."

Circa 1709: "Bear-Hunting is a great Sport in America, both with the *Englifh* and *Indians*. Some years ago, there were kill'd five hundred Bears, in two Counties of Virginia, in one Winter; and but two She-Bears amongft them all, which were not with Young, as I told you of the reft. The *Englifh* have a breed of Dogs fit for this fport, about the fize of Farmers Curs, and, by Practice, come to know the Scent of a Bear, which foon as they found, they run him, by the Nofe, till they come up with him, and then bark and fnap at him, till he trees, when the Huntfman fhoots him out of the Trees, there being, for the moft part, two or three with Guns, left the firft fhould mifs, or not quite kill him. Though they are not naturally voracious, yet they are very fierce when wounded. The Dogs often bring him to a Bay, when wounded, and then the Huntfmen make other Shots, perhaps with the Piftols that are ftuck in their Girdles."

* * *

John Norris, South Carolina resident, describes hunting in that province, circa 1712, in [Norris], *Profitable Advice for Rich and Poor in a Discourse Between* James Freeman, a Carolina *Planter and* Simon Question, *a* West-Country *Farmer. Containing A Description, or True Relation of South Carolina An* English *Plantation, or Colony, in* America (London: J. How, 1712), reprinted in Jack P. Greene, ed., *Selling a New World. Two Colonial South Carolina Promotional Pamphlets* (Columbia, S.C.: University of South Carolina Press, 1989), 111-112.

"We have Plenty of Wild Turkies in our Woods, and continues all the Year, sometimes 40 or 50 together in a Company, they are great Eaters on Pease in the Fields, but often their bodies pays for the Trespass; some say they have kill'd *Turk[e]y-Cocks*, when fat, in the Fall of the year, that have weighed Thirty Pounds, or more, I have kill'd from a Tree, with a single Bullet, a Turk[e]y (weighing Twenty Pounds) whilst looking down on the Dog that Tre[e]d him, which stood Barking underneath till the Turkey fell. About the Middle or latter End of *November* there comes from the Northern frozen Climate great Numbers of *Brant* and *Grey Wild-Geese*, the latter is the best Sort, but the former the most numerous, some Men have kill'd, in a Winter Season, as many Geess whose Feathers fill'd them a good Bed, or more, those who are diligent, often shoot a Dozen, or more, at a Shot amongst the great Numbers of them when Feeding on these Marshes, which they frequent till *February*, and then return. We have, in the Winter, several Sorts of *Wild-Ducks*, and very plentiful, but the *English* kind is the best, which are usually fat, and they are very common, and not hard to come within Shot of them in Ponds and Creeks where they frequent. We have *Widgeon, Teal, Curlew, Shell-Drakes, Cranes, Pelicans, Gannets, Sea-Larks, Snipes, Wild-Pigeons, Partridges*, and many more Sorts of small Land-Birds, three very Noted for the Cage, the *Mock-Bird, Red-Bird*, and *Blue-Bird*, and several other Sorts not here in *England*. A man that is a good Gunner and Fisher may find himself and Family with sufficient of Flesh, Fish, and Fowl, that he may very plentifully kill, whilst he is Recreating himself therein. Some Men hire a Native *Indian* for some Cloathing of small Value and supply them with Powder, Shot, and Bullets, for which they'll supply the Family with Store of either Flesh, Fish, or Fowl thro' the Year, the *Indian* reserving to himself the Skins of the wild Beasts that he destroys."

* * *

Mr. Purry, visitor, mentions hunting in Charleston, South Carolina, September 1731, in "A Description of the Province of South Carolina, Drawn Up at Charles Town, in September, 1731," in Peter Force, ed., *Tracts and Other Papers, Relating Principally to the Origin, Settlement, and Progress of the Colonies in North America, from the Discovery of the Country to the Year 1776*, 4 vols., Vol. 2 (Washington: Peter Force, 1837), 10.

"There is great plenty of Game of all sorts, but especially wild Turkeys, some of which are 30 pound weight, and those who love Fowling, may easily take them."

* * *

An English traveler describes hunting in South Carolina, February, 1734, in *A New Voyage to Georgia. By A Young Gentleman. Giving an Account of his Travels to South Carolina, and Part of North Carolina. To which is added, A Curious Account of the Indians, by an Honourable Person*. (London, 1737), reprinted as "A Gentleman's Account of His Travels, 1733-34," in H. Roy Merrens, ed., *The Colonial South Carolina Scene. Contemporary Views, 1697-1774* (Columbia, S.C.: University of South Carolina Press, 1977), 115, 116.

"But the next morning, when we were in the midst of our work, our companions came back to us, but without one morsel of provision, the oarsmen having eat it all up, so that we were then almost as bad off as before, save only having our guns again, which we had unluckily left in the boat. We made shift to shoot some crows and woodpeckers, which we lived on that day; but inquiring what might be the occasion of their staying so long, they told us one of the men had straggled out in the wood by himself a shooting, and it was with great difficulty they found him again. The next morning we went out with an intent to shoot some venison, but having hunted a considerable time, and not meeting with any, concluded to return to our camp; but in our return met with a wolf in full chase after a deer, and had the good fortune to kill them both; so that we had then provisions sufficient for two days longer, which time we spent very pleasantly; and finding by our companions that there was still a better land higher up, we concluded to see it, trusting to our guns to supply us with provisions, which they did very plentifully."

"The next night we encamped on Bear Bluff,.... That night we had a very odd affair happened. One of our men had killed a venison in the evening, and about 12 o'clock at night as we were all of us fast asleep, one of my companions was waked by a noise he heard at a small distance from him, and as I lay the next to him, he endeavored to wake me as gently as he could: when I awaked, he bid me present my piece, for he had just seen something not above six yards from him, which he did imagine was a bear; we lay in that posture near half an hour, when we heard him coming again, and soon after saw him, when we both fired and shot him dead on the spot: but instead of a bear, it proved to be a wolf, that had stole one quarter of venison before, and was just then come back for a second; and, indeed, it was very lucky for us that we killed him, or otherwise we must have come uo short allowance. On the 20th of February, we set out on our voyage again, and the first night reached Kingston Bluff, where we had the good fortune to kill one bear, some of which we barbicued for our suppers."

* * *

John Brickell, Irish doctor, describes hunting in North Carolina, circa 1737, in Brickell, *The Natural History of North-Carolina* (Dublin: James Carson, 1737), 39, 42, 113-114, 116, 345.

"The chiefeft Diverfions here are Fifhing, Fowling; and Hunting, Wild Beafts, fuch as Deer, Bears, Racoons, Hares, Wild Turkies, with feveral other forts,...."

"The civilized *Indians* are very ferviceable to the Planters in many Cafes,.... Others Hunt and Fowl for them at very reafonable Rates, this Country being as plentifully provided with all forts of Game as any in *America*;...."

"*Bear-hunting* is a very great Diverfion amongft the *Chriftians* and *Indians*, the former have a Breed of Dogs fit for that kind of Sport, about the fize of Farmers Curs; thefe by practice become acquainted with the Scent of the *Bears*, which as foon as they have found, they run him by the Nofe 'till they come up with him, and then bark and fnap at him 'till he Trees. By the Noife of the Dogs the Huntfmen repair to the place, and find the *Bear* in a large Tree, wher they generally fhoot one after another, 'till they kill him: And though they are not naturally voracious, yet are they very fierce, and will fight moft defperately when wounded, for which reafon there are three or four of thefe Huntfmen together with Guns ready, for fear the firft fhot fhould mifs, or not quite kill him.

"If any of thefe Dogs fhould faften on a *Bear*, the Huntfman looks upon him as not good, for the beft Dog in *Europe* is nothing in their Paws, for when ever they get a Dog in their Clutches they either tear him in pieces, or blow the Skin from the Flefh like a Bladder, and fometime kill him; but if he recovers, he is never good for any thing afterwards. As the Paws are accounted the beft Morfel of this Creature, fo is the Head efteemed the worft, and is therefore caft away, for the Brain is faid to be Poifonous. They are not near fo plenty now as they were fome years ago in this Province, where the Planters have kill'd four or five Hundred in one Seafon; the reafon is becaufe they are fo eafily kill'd, for the leaft Dog will make them Tree, where they moft commonly remain 'till fhot, for the Dog continues barking about the Tree 'till the Planters come to their Affiftance."

"[A]nd the fmalleft Dogs will make them [panthers] take up into a Tree, where they generally remain 'till they are fhot by the Huntfmen, and if it happens that they don't kill them outright, thefe and the *Bears* are a very dangerous Enemy when they are wounded, to the Huntfmen; but more efpecially to the Dogs that approach too near them."

"They [mountain cats] will nimbly climb Trees when purfued by Huntfmen and Dogs, where they remain till they are fhot, but if only flightly wounded, will fight moft defperately, tearing the Dogs in pieces that they chance to meet with, which feldom happens, by reafon fo many hunt in a Body together,...."

* * *

William Stephens, Georgia Trustee, recounts a hunting accident, October 1743, and tells of pigeon hunting, December 1744, in E. Merton Coulter, ed., *The Journal of William Stephens, 1743-1745*, 2 vols., Vol. 2 (Athens, Ga.: University of Georgia Press, 1958), 33, 176.

31 October 1743: "Little passed worth Note, but another unlucky Accident happen'd.... His Master sending him on an Errand this Morning about a mile out of Town, the Lad [an orphan apprentice] took his Gun with him and in his way attempting to shoot a Squirrel; another person ...with his Gun also walking that way took Aim at the same Squirrel, not Seeing the Lad, and unhappily threw a great Number of Shot into his breast, Arms, Face, &c, wherewith he was so wounded, that he lies in danger of his life."

6 December 1744: "After some days conflict in the Elements, the Rain ceased and the Frost prevailing continued very Severe, which brought incredible Numbers of Wild Pidgeons from the Northern Regions, to such degree that the Trees of the Woods were filled with them, which our people of all Ranks fed plentifully upon; every body (man or Boy) that would make use of a Gun, taking as many as they pleased, like Quails to the Israelites in the Wilderness."

* * *

An account of hunting by Moravians in North Carolina, circa 1760, in Adelaide L. Fries, ed., *Records of the Moravians in North Carolina,* Vol. 1, 233, reprinted as "Wild Game in the Moravian Settlements, 1760," in Hugh Talmage Lefler, ed., *North Carolina History Told by Contemporaries* (Chapel Hill: University of North Carolina Press, 1934), 75.

"Nov. 2nd it is recorded that there were many bears and wolves about. The Moravians killed several of the former, one weighing 300 pounds.... Also on the 20th neighbors from the South Fork came for their share of corn they had helped to plant. On their way home they found the roosting place of wild pigeons of which there are remarkably many, and they killed 1200, of which they sent us a number. Next week some of the Brethren went off to the same place and brought in 1800. In the morning the pigeons go off in clouds, at sunset return to their camp, crowding so closely together that branches are broken off, and trees that have withstood many a heavy storm fall to the ground. Every night many pigeons come to the ground with the falling branches and trees. People who have often seen wild pigeons before say they have never seen anything like this."

* * *

George Milligen-Johnston, South Carolina doctor, notes the hunting in South Carolina, circa 1763, in [Milligen-Johnston], *A Short Description of the Province of South-Carolina, with An Account of the Air, Weather, and Diseases, at Charles-Town, Written in the Year 1763* (London: John Hinton, 1770), in Chapman J. Milling, ed., *Colonial South Carolina. Two Contemporary Descriptions* (Columbia, S.C.: University of South Carolina Press, 1951), 135.

"In the Autumn, Winter, and Spring, there is Variety and Plenty of Game for the Gun or Dogs; the Gentlemen are not backward in the Chace."

* * *

John Marrant, African-American preacher of Nova Scotia, concerning hunting during his young adulthood near Charleston, South Carolina, circa 1768, in Rev. Mr. Aldridge, ed., *A Narrative of the Lord's Wonderful Dealings with John Marrant, A Black, (A Preacher in Nova Scotia) Born in New-York, in North America,* 3rd ed. (Yarmouth, Nova Scotia: J. Barnes, 1824), 9.

"…; with her [his mother] I staid two months living without God or hope in the world, fishing and hunting on the sabbath-day."

* * *

An unidentified Scotsman lists the local hunting in North Carolina, circa 1773, in *Informations Concerning the Province of North Carolina, Addressed to Emigrants from the Highlands and Western Isles of Scotland, by an Impartial Hand* (Glasgow: James Knox, 1773), in William K. Boyd, ed., *Some Eighteenth Century Tracts Concerning North Carolina* (Raleigh, N.C.: Edwards & Broughton Company, 1927), 438.

"At this season [winter], the country is very agreeable to sportsmen, having plenty of all sorts of game in the greatest perfection; such as deer, which are as numerous as sheep in Scotland; wild turkeys, in flocks, throng as rooks or crows, and weighing about thirty pounds, which shews they are of a large size; geese and ducks, of which last great quantities are taken; eight or ten, when fitting, is but a middling shot. There are also great quantities of partridges, doves, larks, woodcocks, snipes, plovers, and blackbirds, besides a great number of sea fowl; and in the back woodlands, where the chestnut grows, they have the pheasant and the peacock."

* * *

Janet Schaw, Scottish lady, on hunting in eastern North Carolina, April, 1775, in Evangeline Walker Andrews, ed., *Journal of a Lady of Quality; Being the Narrative of a Journey from Scotland to the West Indies, North Carolina, and Portugal in the Years 1774 to 1776* (New Haven, Conn.: Yale University Press, 1922), 175-176.

"The congress has forbid killing Mutton veal or lamb, so that little variety is to be had from the domestick animals; but indulgent nature makes up for every want, by the vast quantities of wild birds, both of land and water. The wild Turkeys, the wild pigeon, a bird which they call a partridge, but above all the rice-bird, which is the Ortalon in its highest perfection, and from the water the finest ducks that possibly can be met with, and so plenty that when on wing sixteen or eighteen are killed at a shot. The beauty of the Summer-duck makes it death almost a murder. The deer now is large, but not so fat as it will be some time hence; it is however in great plenty, and makes good soup…. The gentlemen indeed out of idleness shoot deer, but nothing under a wild turkey is worth a shot. As they are now on the eve of a War, or something else I dare not name, perhaps they save their powder for good reasons; but at Mr Rutherfurd's there is a huntsman, with as many assistants as he pleases, and every day provisions are brought home of those Articles I have mentioned."

* * *

Alexander Hewatt, South Carolina historian, comments on hunting in that state, circa 1779, in Hewatt, *An Historical Account of the Rise and Progress of the Colonies of South Carolina and Georgia*, 2 vols., Vol 2 (London: Alexander Donaldson, 1779), 303.

"Thofe planters who had arrived at eafy or affluent circumftances employed overfeers; and having little to do but to ride round their fields now and then, to fee that their affairs were not neglected, or their flaves abufed, indulge themfelves in rural amufements, fuch as racing, muftering, hunting, fifhing, or focial entertainments. For the gun and dog the country affords fome game, fuch as fmall partridges, woodcocks, rabbits, &c. but few of the planters are fond of that kind of diverfion. To chace the fox or the deer is their favourite amufement, and they are forward and bold riders, and make their way through the woods and thickets with aftonifhing fpeed."

* * *

Francisco de Miranda, Spanish aristocrat, comments on hunting in eastern North Carolina, 23 July 1783, and in Charleston, South Carolina, 6? August 1783, in Judson P. Wood, trans., and John S. Ezell, ed., *The New Democracy in America. Travels of Francisco de Miranda in the United States, 1783-1784* (Norman, Okla.: University of Oklahoma Press, 1963), 15, 23.

23 July 1783: "Deer are plentiful, and deer hunting is the favorite sport of the gentlemen and country folk. I went on some of these excursions and assure you that at every moment I expected one of the participants to have a leg, arm, or head broken. The fashion is to dash forth on horseback behind the discovered buck through a forest covered with branches, the horse sometimes barely having room. The horse is already accustomed to this and, happen what may, charges after the game and acts as the guide; the riders bends down grasping the neck of the horse. There is no lack of mournful reminders of this sport in the region."

6? August 1783: "Hunting, dancing, and smoking tobacco in pipes are the favorite diversions."

* * *

Francesco dal Verme, Italian count, on hunting in North Carolina, November 1783, and in South Carolina, November and December 1783, in Elizabeth Cometti, trans. and ed., *Seeing America and Its Great Men. The Journal and Letters of Count Francesco dal Verme, 1783-1784* (Charlottesville, Va.: University Press of Virginia, 1969), 51, 53-55.

18 November 1783: "Spent the day here hunting."

20 November 1783: "In the evening after supper went fire-hunting. The hunters carry on their left shoulder a pan containing a lighted combustible for spotting the animals' eyes, which are blinded by the light and thus unable to see the hunter who approaches to within firing range of the beast. We came upon the trail of a panther —a fresh prey covered with leaves which had been discovered after dinner; when the panther returned to this spot, the hunter who shot it failed to kill it but only wounded it as was evident from the blood that was spattered about. One of the two deer spotted was killed. This kind of hunting is prohibited because it often results in the killing of domestic animals grazing in the woods."

26 November 1783: "Went hunting and killed a wolf."

27 November 1783: "Rode off to hunt deer and pursued two of them without success."

5 December 1783: "Dinner; afterwards went hunting...."

6 December 1783: "Accompanied Mr. Farrar (11 miles) for a dinner with the Deer Hunt Club composed of twenty-two members, who may invite friends. The hunt is held once in every fifteen days and the members take turns in defraying the cost of the repast."

7 December 1783: "Went fire-hunting in the evening, but the moon kept us from having any success."

13 December 1783: "Rode to the home of Mr. Farr (12 miles). Using his horses, we went deer hunting with the other members of the club. Saw two deer and took one of them."

14 December 1783: "Went out hunting with a gun and took many pigeons, ducks, and a hawk."

* * *

Johann David Schoepf, German physician, in North Carolina, December 1783, in Schoepf, *Travels in the Confederation. Pennsylvania, Maryland, Virginia, the Carolinas, East Florida, the Bahamas,* trans. and ed. by Alfred J. Morrison, 2 vols., Vol. 2 (Cleveland: Arthur H. Clark, 1911), 108.

December, 1783: "The export of their [deer] skins is a considerable item yearly in this province. A proof of the number of these animals is that one man on the New River has been able to shoot 175 head since spring of this year, and simply for the pelts. If one cannot or will not shoot for himself, the game can be bought commonly for one or at most two Spanish dollars the head, which always gives more than a hundredweight of venison."

MARYLAND AND VIRGINIA

Thomas Hariot, British promotional writer, discusses the potential hunting in the Virginia area, circa 1588, in [Hariot], *A Brief and True Report of the New Found Land of Virginia* (London: 1588), unnumbered page before D3.

"Beares which are all of black colour. The beares of this countrey are good meat; the inhabitants in time of winter do vfe to take & eate manie, fo alfo fomtime did wee. They are taken commonlie in this fort. In fome Ilands or places where they are, being hunted for, as foone as they haue fpiall of a man they prefently run awaie, & then being chafed they clime and get vp the next tree they can, from whence with arrowes they are fhot downe ftarke dead, or with thofe wounds that they may after eafily be killed; we fomtime fhotte them downe with our caleevers."

* * *

Virginia martial law against idle hunting, 22 June 1611, in [William Strachey?],"The Summarie of the Marshall Lawes," in *For the Colony in Virginea Britannia. Lavves Diuine, Morall and Martiall, &c.* (London: Walter Burre, 1612), 26.

"41 No Souldier shall vnprofitably waste his pouder, shot, or match, by shooting it idly away, or at birds, beasts, or fowle, but shall giue an account vnto his Corporall of the same, who shall certifie his Captain vpon the peril for his first fault so comitted, to be comitted to prison, there to lie in Irons head & heeles togither eight & forty hours, for the second to be condemned sixe moneths to the Gallies, and for the third offence to be condemned two yeares to the Gallies."

* * *

John Smith, English explorer and leader, discusses the hunting in Virginia, circa 1614-1616, in [Smith], *A Description of New England. Or The Observations, and Discoueries of Captain Iohn Smith (Admirall of that Country) in the North of* America, *in the Year of Our Lord 1614* (London: Humfrey Lownes and Robert Clerke, 1616), 22.

"For Gentlemen, what exercise should more delight them, then ranging dayly those vnknowne parts, vsing fowling and fishing, for hunting and hauking? and yet you shall see the wilde haukes giue you some pleasure, in seeing them stoope (six or seauuen after one another) an houre or two together, at the skuls of fish in the faire harbours, as those a-shore at a foule; and neuer trouble nor torment your selues, with watching, mewing, feeding, and attending them: nor kill horse and man with running and crying, *See you not a hauk?* For hunting also: the woods, lakes, and riuers, affoord not onely chase sufficient, for any that delights in that kinde of toyle, or pleasure; but such beasts to hunt, that besides the delicacy of their bodies for food, their skins are so rich, as may well recompence thy dayly labour, with a Captains pay."

* * *

An unidentified writer advises prospective settlers in Maryland on hunting gear, 8 September 1635, in *A Relation of* Maryland; *Together, With a Map of the Countrey, the Conditions of Plantation, His Majefties Charter to Lord* Baltemore, *Tranflated into Englifh* (London: William Peasley, 1635), 51.

"Provifion for Fifhing and Fowling.

Inprimis, neceffaries for a boate of 3. or 4. Tunne, as Spikes, Nayles, Pitch, Tarte, O-come, Canuis for a fayle, Ropes, Anchor, Iron for the Ruther: Fifhing-lines for Cod and Macrills, &c. Cod-hookes, and Macrill-hookes, a Seane or Baffe-net, Herring-netts, Leade, Fowling-pieces of fixe foote; Powder and Shott, and Flint Stones; a good Water-Spaniell, &c."

* * *

Colonel Henry? Norwood, British traveler, remarks on hunting in Virginia, January 1650, in "A Voyage to Virginia by Colonel Norwood," in Peter Force, ed. *Tracts and Other Papers, Relating to the Origin, Settlement, and Progress of the Colonies in North America, From the Discovery of the Country to the Year 1776,* Vol. 3 (Gloucester, Mass.: Peter Smith, 1963 [1844]), 20, 22-24, 26, 40-41.

"After this sweet refreshment, the captain, myself, and his kinsman crossed the creek in our wherry, invited thither by the cackling of wild-fowl. The captain had a gun charged, and the moon shining bright in his favour, he killed one duck of the flock that flew over us,...."

"All our woodmen and fowlers had powder and shot given them, and some geese were killed for supper."

"Whilst this very cold season continued, great flights of fowl frequented the island, geese, ducks, curlieus, and some of every sort we killed and roasted on sticks, eating all but the feathers."

"One morning, in walking on the shore by the sea side, with a long gun in my hand loaden with small shot, I fired at a great flight of small birds called Oxeyes, and made great slaughter among them, which gave refreshment to all our company."

"...wherefore, that I might be a little recreated, I took a gun in my hand; and hearing the noise of geese on our shore, I approach'd them privately, and had the good hap to be the death of one."

"The king's [the chief's] eldest son, of about eighteen years of age, was hugely enamour'd with our guns, and look'd so wistfully on me, when he saw what wonders they would do, that I could not forbear presenting him with a birding piece [although it was contrary to Virginia law to give an indigenous person a gun].

"I taught his son to shoot at fowls, to charge his gun and clean it, insomuch that in a few minutes, he went among a flock of geese, and firing at random he did execution on one of them to his great joy, and returned to his father with the game in his hand, with such celerity, as if he had borrowed wings of the wind."

* * *

John Hammond, British traveler, discusses potential hunting in Virginia, circa 1656, in Hammond, *Leah and Rachel, or, the Two Fruitful Sisters Virginia, and Mary-land. Their Present Condition, Impartially Stated and Related* (London: T. Mabb, 1656), 13.

"..., water-fowle of all sortes are (with admiration to be spoken of) plentifull in some places then in othersome, Deare all over the Country, and in many places so many, that venison is accounted a tiresom meat, wilde Turkeys are frequent, and so large that I have seen some weigh neer threescore pounds; other beasts there are whose flesh is wholsom and savourie, such as are unknowne to us; and therefore I will not stuffe my book with superfluous relation of their names;...."

* * *

George Alsop, Maryland settler, comments on hunting in that province, circa 1666, in Alsop, *A Character of the Province of Maryland* (Cleveland: Burrows Brothers Company, 1902 [1666]), 35-36, 59.

"Their [deer's] flesh, which in some places of this Province is the common provision the Inhabitants feed on, and which through the extreme glut and plenty of it, being daily killed by the *Indians*, and brought in to the *English*, as well as that which is killed by the Christian Inhabitant, that doth it more for recreation, than for the benefit they reap by it."

"In the Winter time, which lasteth three months (*viz.*) *December*, *January*, and *February*, they do little or no work or imployment, save cutting of wood to make good fires to sit by, unless their Ingenuity will prompt them to hunt the Deer, or Bear, or recreate themselves in Fowling, to slaughter the Swans, Geese, and Turkeys (which this Country affords in a most plentiful manner:) For every Servant has a Gun, Powder and Shot allowed him, to sport him withall on all Holidayes and leasurable times, if he be capable of using it, or be willing to learn."

* * *

John Clayton, Jamestown, Virginia parson, describes hunting in the province, 12 May 1688, in [Clayton], "A Letter from Mr. John Clayton Rector of Crofton at Wakefield in Yorkshire to the Royal Society, May 12, 1688," reprinted in Peter Force, ed., *Tracts and Other Papers, Relating Principally to the Origin, Settlement, and Progress of the Colonies in North America, From the Discovery of the Country to the Year 1776*, Vol. 3 (Gloucester, Mass.: Peter Smith, 1963 [1844]), 35, 38.

"Deer, there are abundance of brave red Deer, so that a good Woodsman, as they call them, will keep a House with Venison; the *Indians*, they say, make artificial sorts of Heads of Boughs of Trees, which they consecrate to their Gods, and these they put on to deceive the Deer when they go a Shooting, or Hunting, as they call it, and by mimicking the Feeding of the Deer, they by degrees get within Shot.

"Every House keeps three or four mungrel dogs to destroy Vermin, such as Wolves, Foxes, Rackoons, Opossums, &c. But they never Hunt with Hounds, I suppose, because there are so many Branches of Rivers, that they cannot follow them. Neither do they keep Grey-hounds, because, they say, that they are subject to break their Necks by running against Trees, and any Cur will serve to run their Hares into a hollow Tree, where after the aforesaid manner they catch them."

* * *

William Byrd, Westover, Virginia planter, chronicles local hunting, September 1709, January 1710, March, May, and November 1711, and January 1712, in Louis B. Wright and Marion Tinling, eds., *The Secret Diary of William Byrd of Westover, 1709-1712* (Richmond, Va.: The Dietz Press, 1941), 85, 128, 317-318, 348, 437, 463.

20 September 1709: "I agreed with John L—— to let him shoot in the marsh provided he brings me the meat and keeps the feathers for himself."

10 January 1710: "I took a walk and endeavored to kill a partridge for my wife but could not."

22 March 1711: "...and I took my gun and endeavored to shoot some partridges but could not."

23 March 1711: "...and I took a walk with my gun to kill some partridge, but could not."

22 May 1711: "Mr. Mumford cut my young horse and then he and I went and shot wild pigeons with bows and arrows...."

13 November 1711: "Then Mr. Graeme and I went out with bows and arrows and shot at partridge and squirrel which gave us abundance of diversion but we lost some of our arrows."

1 January 1712: "Mr. Mumford and I went to shoot with our bows and arrows but shot nothing,...."

* * *

John Fontaine, Irish Huguenot immigrant, hunts in Virginia, November 1715, and August and September 1716, in Edward Porter Alexander, ed., *The Journal of John Fontaine. An Irish Huguenot Son in Spain and Virginia, 1710-1719* (Williamsburg, Va.: Colonial Williamsburg Foundation, 1972), 87, 88-89, 103-104, 104, 107.

18 November 1715: "Monday. Mr. Beverly's son hindered us from proceeding on our journey this day, by promising to set out with us the next morning. So we took our guns and went a hunting. We killed some squirrels and partridge, but did no hurt to the wild turkies nor deer though we see several."

22 November 1715: "Friday. At seven in the morning we mounted our horses and we met upon the road with two huntsmen. We went with them in the woods and in half an hour they shot a buck and a doe and took them on their horses."

31 August 1716: "One of the gentlemen and I, we kept out on one side of the company about a mile to have the better hunting. I see a deer, and off my horse I shot him, but my horse threw me, a terrible fall, and run away. We run after and with a great deal

of difficulty we got him, but we could not after find the deer we shot and we lost ourselves for about two hours before we could come upon the track of our company. About five miles farther we crossed the same river again, and two miles farther we met with a large bear and one of our company shot him and I got the skin. We killed several deer...."

1 September 1716: "We killed three bears this day, which exercised the the horses as well as the the men. About five of the clock we came to a run of water at the foot of a hill where we pitched our tents. We see two bears, but did not pursue them. We killed some deer."

2 September 1716: "We see a bear running down a tree, but it being Sunday we did not endeavour to to kill any thing."

8 September 1716: "We see several bears and deer, and killed some wild turkies."

9 September 1716: "Set out at nine of the clock and before twelve we see several bears. We killed three, one of which attacked one of our men that was riding after him and narrowly missed him, tore his things that he had behind him off his horse, and would have destroyed him had he not been immediately helped by other men and our dogs. Some of the dogs suffered in this engagement."

* * *

William Byrd, Virginia planter, chronicles hunting along the Virginia/North Carolina border, September, October, and November 1728, and near the Roanaoke River in Virginia, September and October 1733, in [Byrd], "The Secret History of the Line," "The History of the Dividing Line," and "A Journey to the Land of Eden," in Louis B. Wright, ed., *The Prose Works of William Byrd of Westover* (Cambridge, Mass.: Harvard University Press, 1966), 97-98, 100, 102-104, 113, 115-118, 120, 122-123, 125-127, 129, 131-133, 135-142, 144, 224-225, 230, 232-236, 239, 241, 243-244, 246, 248-249, 251-253, 255-257, 262-263, 265, 269, 273, 276-279, 283, 285-286, 289, 291, 295-296, 299-300, 304, 306-307, 318, 389-391, 397, 400-401, 403-404.

23 September 1728: "I sent several of the men out a-hunting, and they brought us four wild turkeys. Old Captain Hix killed two of them, who turned his hand to everything notwithstanding his great age,...." ["Secret History"]

"Our hunters brought us four wild turkeys, which at that season began to be fat and very delicious, especially the hens. These birds seem to be of the bustard kind and fly heavily. Some of them are exceedingly large and weigh upwards of forty pounds.... They roost commonly upon very high trees, standing near some river or creek, and are so stupefied at the sight of fire that, if you make a blaze in the night near the place where they roost, you may fire upon them several times successively before they will dare to fly away." ["History"]

24 September 1728: "Our shooters killed four more wild turkeys. Meanwell and Captain Stith pretended to go a-hunting, but their game was eight fresh-colored wenches, which were not hard to hunt down." ["Secret History"]

"In the meantime, they sent out some of their most expert gunners, who brought in four more wild turkeys." ["History"]

28 September 1728: "He [Epaphroditus Bainton] spends most of his time in hunting and ranging the woods, killing generally more than one hundred deer in a year." ["Secret History"]

"We were conducted a nearer way by a famous woodsman called Epaphroditus Bainton. This forester spends all his time in ranging the woods and is said to make great havoc among the deer and other inhabitants of the forest not much wilder than himself." ["History"]

30 September 1728: "By the way a very lean boar crossed us and several claimed the credit of killing it, but all agreed 'was stone-dead before Firebrand fired, yet he took the glory of this exploit to himself,...." ["Secret History"]

"On our way the men roused a bear, which being the first we had seen since we came out, the porr beast had many pursuers. Several persons contended for the credit of killing him, though he was so poor he was not worth the powder." ["History']

1 October 1728: "One of the Indians killed a fawn,...." ["Secret History"]

"One of our Indians killed a large fawn, which was very welcome, though, like Hudibras' horse, it had hardly flesh enough to cover its bones." ["History"]

2 October 1728: "By the way Firebrand had another occasion to show his prowess in killing a poor little wildcat, which had been crippled by two or three before..... The Indians killed two deer and John Evans a third, which made great plenty...." ["Secret History"]

"Here we encamped, and by the time the horses were hobbled our hunters brought us no less than a brace and an half of deer, which made great plenty and consequently great content in our quarters. Some of our people had shot a great wildcat, which was that fatal moment making a comfortable meal upon a fox squirrel, and an ambitious sportsman of our company claimed the merit of killing this monster after it was dead." ["History"]

3 October 1728: "Our Indian killed one deer and William Pool another,...." ["Secret History"]

"Our people had the fortune to killa brace of does, one of which we presented to the Carolna gentlemen,...." ["History"]

4 October 1728: "Robert Hix saw three buffaloes but, his gun being loaden only with shot, could do no execution. Bootes shot one deer, and the Indians killed three more and one of the Carolina men four wild turkeys." ["Secret History"]

"One of our men spied three buffaloes, but his piece being loaded only with goose shot, he was able to make no effectual impression on their thick hides; however, this disappointment was made up by a brace of bucks and as many wild turkeys killed by the rest of the company." ["History"]

7 October 1728: "Tom Short killed a deer, and several of the company killed turkeys." ["Secret History"]

"Our men killed a very fat buck and several turkeys. These two kinds of meat boiled together, with the addition of a little rice or French barley, made excellent soup,.... Our Indian was very superstitious in this matter and told us, with a face full of concern, that if we continued to boil venison and turkey together we should for the future kill nothing, because the spirit that presided over the woods would drive all the game out of our sight. But we had the happiness to find this an idle superstition, and though his argument could not convince us, yet our repeated experience at last, with much ado, convinced him." ["History"]

9 October 1728: "Our Indian killed a mountain partridge, resembling the smaller partridge in the plumage but as large as a hen." ["Secret History"]

"Our Indian killed nothing all day but a mountain partridge, which a little resembled the common partridge in the plumage but was near as large as a dunghill hen." ["History']

10 October 1728: "We began this day very luckily by killing a brace of turkeys and one deer, so that the plenty of our breakfast made amends for the shortness of our supper last night.... Our Indian killed a deer and other men some turkeys, but the Indian begged very hard that our cook might not boil venison and turkey together because it would certainly spoil his luck hunting...." ["Sectret History"]

"The day began very fortunately by killing a fat doe and two brace of wild turkeys; so the plenty of the morning made amends for the short commons overnight." ["History"]

11 October 1728: "Tom Jones killed a buck and the Indian a turkey, but he would not bring it us for fear we should boil it with our venison against his ridiculous superstition." ["Secret History"]

"We encamped about two miles beyond the river, where we made good cheer upon a very fat buck that luckily fell in our way. The Indian likewise shot a wild turkey but confessed he would not bring it us lest we should continue to provoke the guardian of the frest by cooking the beasts of the field and the birds of the air together in one vessel. This instance of Indian superstition, I confess, is countenanced in some measure by the Levitical law, which forbade the mixing things of a different nature together in the same field or in the same garment, and why not, then, in the same kettle? But, after all, if the jumbling of two sorts of flesh together be a sin, how intolerable an offense it must be to make a Spanish olla, that is, a hotchpotch of every kind of thing athat is eatable? And the good people of England would have a great deal to answer for beating up so many different ingredients into a pudding." ["History"]

12 October 1728: "Our men killed a bear of two years old which was very fat." ["Secret History"]

"Our Indian killed a bear, two years old, that was feasting on these grapes." ["History"]

13 October 1728: "...; however, after dinner several of the men ventured to try their fortune and brought in no less than six wild turkeys." ["Secret History"]

"In the afternoon our hunters went forth and returned triumphantly with three brace of wild turkeys." ["History"]

14 October 1728: "However, several of the men went hunting in the afternoon and killed three deer and four turkeys, so that the frying pan was not cool till next morning." ["Secret History"]

"This gave leisure to the most expert of our gunners to go and try their fortunes, and they succeeded so well that they returned about noon with three fat deer and four wild turkeys." ["History"]

15 October 1728: "The men chased a bear into the river, that got safe over, notwithstanding the continual fire from the shore upon him." ["History"]

16 October 1728: "Our Indian killed a deer, and the men knocked down no less than four bears and two turkeys, so that this was truly a land of plenty both for man and beast." ["Secret History"]

"The Indian killed a fat buck, and the men brought in four bears and a brace of wild turkeys, so that this was truly a land of plenty both for man and beast." ["History"]

17 October 1728: "Our dogs catched a young cub, and the Indian killed a young buck." ["Secret History"]

"We untreed a young cub in our march that made a brave stand against one of the best of our dogs. This and a fawn were all the game that came in our way." ["History"]

18 October 1728: "Bearskin killed a fat doe and came across a bear which had been killed and half devoured by a panther." ["Secret History"]

"The Indian killed a very fat doe and came across a bear, which had been put to death and was half devoured by a panther." ["History"]

19 October 1728: "All that our hunters could kill was only one turkey,...." ["Secret History"]

"Indeed, the woods were too thick to show us any sort of game but one wild turkey, which helped to enric our soup." ["History"]

20 October 1728: "Our Indian had the luck to kill a monstrous fat bear,...." ["Secret History']

"At their return they had the very great comfort to behold a monstrous fat bear, which the Indian had killed very seasonably for their breakfast." ["History"]

21 October 1728: "Our Indian shot a bear so prodigiously fat that there way to kill him but by firing in at his ear." ["History"]

22 October 1728: "On the brow of the hill we spied a young cub on the top of a high tree at supper upon some acorns. We were so indiscreet as to take no gun with us and therefore were obliged to halloo to the men to bring one. When it came, Astrolabe undertook to fetch the bear down but missed him. However, the poor beast, hearing the shot rattle about his ears, came down the tree of his own accord and trusted to his heels. It was a pleasant race between Bruin and our grave surveyor, who, I must confess, runs much better than he shoots; yet the cub outran him, even downhill, where bears are said to sidle lest their guts should come out of their mouths. But our men had better luck and killed no less than six of these unwieldy animals." ["Secret History"]

"Here our hunters had leisure to go out and try their fortunes, and returned loaded with spoil. They brought in no less than six bears, exceedingly fat, so that the frying pan had no rest all night. We had now the opportunity of trying the speed of these lumpish animals by a fair course it had with the nimblest of our surveyors." ["History"]

24 October 1728: "The men came off better, for the Indian killed two bears,...." ["Secret History"]

"The Indian had killed two large bears, the fattest of which he had taken napping. One of the people, too, shot a raccoon,...." ["History"]

26 October 1728: "Our men killed two bears, a buck, and a turkey —a very seasonable supply and made us reflect with gratitude on the goodness of Providence." ["Secret History"]

"Our men had the fortune to kill a brace of bears, a fat buck, and a wild turkey, all which paid them with interest for yesterday's abstinence." ["History"]

29 October 1728: "Our men went out a-driving and had the luck to kill two bears, one of which was found by our Indian asleep and never waked." ["Secret History"]

"Notwithstanding the falling weather, our hunters sallied out in the afternoon and drove the woods in a ring, which was thus performed: from the circumference of a large circle they all marched inward and drove the game toward the center. By this means they shot a brace of fat bears, which came very seasonably,...." ["History"]

30 October 1728: "Our Indian killed a deer that was extremely fat, and we picked his bones as clean as a score of turkey buzzards could have done." ["Secret History"]

"The Indian killed a stately, fat buck, and we picked his bones as clean as a score of turkey buzzards could have done." ["History"]

31 October 1728: "We took up our camp at Miry Creek and regaled ourselves with one buck and two bears, which our men killed in their march." ["Secret History"]

"Our hunters killed a large doe and two bears, which made all other misfortunes easy." ["History"]

1 November 1728: "However, we made a shift to go six miles and by the way had the fortune to kill a brace of does, two bears, and one turkey." ["Secret History"]

"As we marched along, we had the fortune to kill a brace of bucks, as many bears, and one wild turkey. But this was carrying our sport to wantonness, because we butchered more than we were able to transport." ["History"]

3 November 1728: "By the way our Indian killed four deer and a bear." ["Secret History"]

"On our way our unmerciful Indian killed no less than two brace of deer and a large bear. We only primed the deer, being unwilling to be encumbered with their whole carcasses." ["History"]

4 November 1728: "John Ellis, who was one of the men we had sent to bring up the tired horses, told us a romantic adventure which he had with a bear on Saturday last. He had straggled from his company and treed a young cub. While he was new priming his gun to shoot at it, the old gentlewoman appeared, who, seeing her heir apparent in distress, came up to his relief. The bear advanced very near to her enemy, reared up on her posteriors, and put herself in guard. The man presented his piece at her, but, unfortunately, it only snapped, the powder being moist. Missing his fire in this manner, he offered to punch her with the muzzle of his gun, which Mother Bruin, being aware of, seized the weapon with her paws and by main strength wrenched it out of his hand. Being thus fairly disarmed and not knowing in the fright but the bear might turn his own cannon upon him, he thought it prudent to retire as fast as his legs could carry him. The brute, being grown more bold by the flight of her adversary, immediately pursued, and for some time it was doubtful whether fear made one run faster or fury the other. But after a fair course of forty yards, the poor man had the mishap to stumble over a stump and fell down at his full length. He now would have sold his life a pennyworth, but the bear, apprehending there might be some trick in this fall, instantly halted and looked very earnestly to observe what the man could mean. In the meantime, he had with much presence of mind resolved to make the bear believe he was dead by lying breathless on the ground, upon the hopes that the bear would be too generous to kill him over again. He acted a corpse in this manner for some time, till he was raised from the dead by the barking of a dog belonging to one of his companions. Cur came up seasonably to his rescue and drove the bear from her pursuit of the man to go and take care of her innocent cub, which she now apprehended might fall into a second distress." ["Secret History"]

"One of the young fellows we had sent to bring up the tired horses entertained us with a remarkable adventure he had met with that day. He had straggled, it seems, from his company in a mist and made a cub of a year old betake itself to a tree. While he was new-priming his piece with intent to fetch it down, the old gentlewoman appeared and, perceiving her heir apparent in distress, advance open-moutthed to his relief. The man was so intent upon his game that she had approached very near him before he perceived her. But finding his danger, he faced about upon the enemy, which immediately reared upon her posteriors and put herself in battle array. The man, admiring at the bear's assurance, endeavored to fire upon her, but by the dampness of the priming his gun did not go off. He cocked it a second time and had the same misfortune. After missing fire twice, he had the folly to punch the beast with the muzzle of his piece; but Mother Bruin, being upon her guard, seized the weapon with her paws and by main strength wrenched it out of the fellow's hands. The man, being thus fairly disarmed, though himself no longer a match for the enemy and therefore retreated as fast as his legs could carry him. The brute naturally grew bolder upon the flight of her adversary and pursued him with all her heavy speed. For some time it was doubtful whether fear made one run faster or fury the other. But after an even course of about fifty yards, the man had the mishap to stumble over a stump and fell down at his full length. He now would have sold his life a pennyworth; but the bear, apprehending there might be some trick in the fall, instantly halted and looked with much attention on her prostrate foe. In the meanwhile, the man had with great presence of mind resolved to make the bear beieve he was dead by lying breathless on the ground, in hopes that the beast would be too generous to kill him over again. To carry on the farce, he acted the corpse for some time without daring to raise his head to see how near the monster was to him. But in about two minutes, to his unspeakable comfort, he was raised from the dead by the barking of a dog belonging to one of his companions, who came seasonably to his rescue and drove the bear from pursuing the man to take care of her cub, which she feared might now fall into a second distress." ["History"]

5 November 1728: "The Indian killed a young buck, the bones of which we picked very clean,...." ["Secret History"]

6 November 1728: "Hamilton wounded a buck, which made him turn upon the dogs and pursue them forty yards with great fury. But he got away from us, choosing rather to give the wolves a supper than to more cruel man. However, our other gunners had better fortune in killing a doe and a two-year-old cub." ["Secret History"]

"One of the men wounded an old buck that was gray with years and seemed by the reverend marks he bore upon him to confirm the current opinion of the animal's longevity. The smart of his wound made him not only turn upon the dogs but likewise pursue them to some distance with great fury. However he got away at last, though by the blood that issued from his wound he could not run far before he fell and without doubt made a comfortable repast for the wolves. However, the Indian had better fortune and supplied us with a fat doe and a young bear two years old." ["History"]

7 November 1728: "The hunters were more fortunate than ordinary, killing no less than four deer and as many turkeys. This made them impatient to encamp early, that they might enjoy the fruits of their good luck." ["Secret History"]

"Our gunners did great execution as they went along, killing no less than two brace of deer and as many wild turkeys." ["History"]

8 November 1728: "The Indian brought us the primings of a fat doe, which he had killed too far for him to carry the whole. This and two turkeys that our men shot made up our bill of fare this evening." ["Secret History"]

"The Indian had killed a fat doe in the compass he took round the elbow of the river but was contented to prime it [select the best parts] only, by reason it was too far off to lug the whole carcass upon his back. This and a brace of wild turkeys which our men had shot made up all our bill of fare this evening...." ["History"]

9 November 1728: "Here our horses made better cheer than we, for the Indian killed nothing but one turkey." ["Secret History"]

"One brace of turkeys were all the game we could meet with,...." ["History"]

10 November 1728: "This being Sunday, we observed the Fourth Commandment; only our hunters went out to provide a dinner for the rest, which was matter of necessity. They fired the woods in a ring, which burning inwards drove the deer to the center, where they were easily killed. This sport is called fire-hunting and is much practiced by the Indians and some English as barbarous as Indians. Three deer were slaughtered in this manner, of which they brought one to the camp and were content only to prime the other two. Besides these, Thomas Short brought in a doe, which made us live in luxury." ["Secret History"]

"In a dearth of provisions our chaplain pronounced it lawful to make bold with the Sabbath and send a party out a-hunting. They fired the dry leaves in a ring of five miles' circumference, which, burning inwards, drove all the game to the center, where they were easily killed. 'Tis really a pitiful sight to see the extreme distress the poor deer are in when they find themselves surrounded with this circle of fire; they weep and groan like a human creature, yet can't move the compassion of those hardhearted people who are about to murder them. This unmerciful sport is called fire-hunting and is much practiced by the Indians and frontier inhabitants, who sometimes, in the eagerness of their diversion, are punished for their cruelty and are hurt by one another when they shoot across at the deer which are in the middle.

"What the Indians do now by a circle of fire the ancient Persians performed formerly by a circle of men; and the smae is practiced at this day in Germany upon extraordinary occasions when any of the princes of the empire have a mind to make a general hunt, as they call it. At such times they order a vast number of people to surround a whole territory. Then, marching inwards in close order, they at last force all the wild beasts into a narrow compass, that the prince and his company may have the diversion of slaughtering as many as they please with their own hands. Our hunters massacred two brace of deer after this unfair way, of which they brought us one brace whole and only the primings of the rest." ["History"]

11 November 1728: "Near this creek our men killed a young buffalo of two years old that was as big as a large ox." ["Secret History"]

"A little wide of this creek, one of the men had the luck to meet with a young buffalo of two years old." ["History"]

12 November 1728: "John Ellis killed a bear in revenge for the fright one of that species had lately put him into." ["Secret History"]

"Our hunters shot nothing this whole day but a straggling bear, which happened to fall by the hand of the very person who had lately been disarmed and put to flight. for which he declared war against the whole species." ["History"]

13 November 1728: "On our way we had the fortune to kill a deer and a turkey, sufficient for our day's subsistence;...." ["Secret History"]

"By the way we shot a fat doe and a wild turkey, which fed us all plentifully." ["History"]

14 November 1728: "The Indian killed a fawn and one of the other men a raccoon,...."
["Secret History"]

"The Indian killed a fawn which, being upon its growth, was not fat but made some amends by being tender. He also shot an otter, but our people were now better fed than to eat such coarse food....

"One of our people shot a large gray squirrel with a very bushy tail,...." ["History"]

16 November 1728: "I also dismissed our honest Indian Bearskin, after presenting him with a note of £3 on Major Mumford, a pound of powder with shot in proportion. He had, besides, the skins of all the deer he had killed in the whole journey and had them carried for him into the bargain.... He killed a fat buck, great part of which he left us by way of legacy; the rest he cut into pieces, toasted them before the fire, and then strung them upon his girdle to serve him for his provisions on his way to Christanna Fort, where his nation lived." ["Secret History"]

20 November 1728: "...one of those that guarded the baggage killed a polecat, upon which he made a comfortable repast." ["History"]

20 September 1733: "Our Indians killed three deer but were so lazy they brought them not to the camp, pretending for their excuse that they were too lean." ["Journey"]

22 September 1733: "While were stayed for that [drying baggage], our hunters knocked down a brace of bucks, wherewith we made ourselves amonds for our scanty supper the aforegoing night.....
"However it was some comfort in the midst of our abstinence to dream of the delicious breakfast we intended to make the next mroning upon a fat doe and two-year old bear our hunters had killed the evening before." ["Journey"]

23 September 1733: "Our Indians, having no notion of the Sabbath, went out to hunt for something for dinner and brought a young doe back along with them." ["Journey"]

30 September 1733: "One of the Indians shot a bear, which he lugged about half a mile for the good of the company. These gentiles have no distinction of days but make every day a Sabbath, except when they go out to war or a-hunting, and then they will undergo incredible fatigues." ["Journey"]

3 October 1733: "One of the Indians shot a wild goose that was very lousy, which nevertheless was good meat and proved those contemptible tasters to be no bad atasters." ["Journey"]

5 October 1733: "We pursued our journey through uneven and perplexed woods and in the thickest of them had the fortune to knock down a young buffalo of two years old. Providence threw this vast animal our way very seasonably just as our provisions began to fail us." ["Journey"]

7 October 1733: "A she-bear had the ill luck to cross our way, which was large enough to afford us several luxurious meals." ["Journey"]

8 October 1733: "In our way we shot a doe, but, she not falling immediately, we had lost our game had not the ravens by their croaking conducted us to the thicket where she fell. We plunged the carcass of the deer into the water, to secure it from these ominous birds till we returned, but an hour afterwards were surprised with the sight of a wolf which had been fishing for it and devoured one side.

"We knocked down an ancient she-bear that had no flesh upon her bones, so we left it to the freebooters of the forest. In coming back to the camp, we discovered a solitary bull buffalo, which boldly stood his ground, contrary to the custom of that shy animal. We spared his life, from a principle of never slaughtering an innocent creature to no purpose." ["Journey"]

* * *

John Clayton, botanist and Clerk of Gloucester County, Virginia, reports on hunting, 21 March 1739, in Clayton to Samuel Durrent, 21 March 1739, reprinted in "Virginia Game, and Field Sports," Virginia Magazine of History and Biography, Vol. 7, No. 2 (October 1899), 173-174.

"To satisfie the Gentleman you mention who is so desirous of Knowing the diversion of hunting and shooting here and the several sorts of game pray give my service to him and tell him, that we have all the tame domestick beasts and fowls that you do in England, and great variety of wild ones as Deer in great pleanty, Bears, Buffaloes, Wolves, Foxes, Panthers, wild Cats, Elks, Hares (smaller than any of y's which run in holes in the earth and hollow trees when pressed by the dogs, and are much like w't you call in England bush Rabbits), Squirrels 3 or 4 sorts, Raccoons, Oppossums, Beavers, Otters, musk rats, Pole cats, minks and there has been two Porcupines killed here, but they are very scarce. Then for fowls, wild Turkey's very numerous, Partridges (the size and colour like y'r Quails), wild Geese, Swans, Brants, Cormorants, Teal, Duck and Mallard, Black Ducks and another sort we call Summer Ducks, Plover 2 or 3 sorts, Soris (a delicious eating bird in Shape and way of living like y'r Water Rails), Heath Fowls (called here improperly Pheasants) 2 sorts, wild Pidgeons in prodigious great flocks, Fieldfares [??], Woodcocks (but what is very strange they come here only in summer) Snipes, Herons, Bitterns, Eagles, Larks 2 sorts one of w'ch are here all the year round, are as big as Quails, the other are seen only in winter and are much like your lark. Now the Gentlemen here that follow the sport place most of their diversion in Shooting Deer; w'ch they perform in this manner they go out early in the morning and being pritty certain of the places where the Deer frequent they send their servants w'th dogs to drive 'em out and to shoot 'em running, the Deer are very swift of foot, larger and longer legged than the English fallow Deer, and less than the red Deer, the diversion of shooting Turkies is only to be had in the upper parts of the Countrey where the woods are of a very large extent, and but few settlements as yet tho' they increase daily. Some hunt the foxes w'th hounds as you do in England, the shooting of water fowl is performed too in the same manner w'th a Water spaniel, as w'th you, and of Partridges; and also the hunting our hares w'h small dogs, who drive 'em presently into the hollow of a tree, then we either cut 'em out w'th an Ax or fill the hole w'th old dead leaves and set fire to 'em, the smoke of w'ch Suffocates the hare, and she drops down; the bears, Panthers, Buffaloes and Elks and wild cats are only to be found among the mountains and desert parts of the countrey where there areas yet but few inhabitants and the hunting there is very toilsome and laborious and sometimes dangerous. Yet the Common Sort of People who live among the Mountains kill great Quantitys of Bears every year; but the greatest destruction of 'em is made in the beginning of the Winter when the bears lay themselves to sleep in the caves and holes among rocks of the mountains at w'ch time the people go to the mouth of the Cave w'th their guns loaded and shoot 'em as they lye in their dens."

* * *

Thomas Lewis, Virginia surveyor, chronicles hunting in the Blue Ridge mountains, Virginia, October and November 1746, in John W. Wayland, ed., The Fairfax Line. Thomas

Lewis's Journal of 1746 (New Market, Va.: The Henkel Press, 1925), 27-28, 33, 37, 50, 54.

10 October 1746: "one of our men Wounded a bair which made his Escape."

12 October 1746: "Some of our Well Disposed hands went ahunting this Day Killd one old Bair & three Cubs."

16 October 1746: "one of our men Kill'd a Deer."

20 October 1746: "Some others went ahunting & killd Dear & Turkey we proved a very Seasonable Relive to us"

28 October 1746: "amonges the Rocks of whch one of our men Surprized & killd a Statly Buck with an axe"

1 November 1746: "this Evening one of our men Killd a turkey"

* * *

George Washington, Virginia planter, Revolutionary War general, and later President, hunts along the Potomac in western Virginia and Maryland, March and April 1748; hunts foxes and birds in Virginia, January, February, March, April, May, August, September, October, November, and December 1768, January, February, March, April, September, and October 1769, January, February, March, April, August, and December 1770; hunts foxes, deer, and birds in Virginia, January, February, March, May, October, November, and December 1771, January, April, May, August, October, and December 1772, January, February, March, October, November, and December 1773, January, February, and April 1774, and January, February, and March 1775, in Donald Jackson and Dorothy Twohig, eds., *The Diaries of George Washington,* 6 vols. (Charlottesville, Va.: University Press of Virginia, 1976, 1978, and 1979), 1:15, 16, 18, 19; 2:30, 31, 32, 36, 37, 38, 39, 40, 44, 45, 46, 47, 52, 53, 60, 61, 83, 84, 93, 94, 95, 96, 99, 100, 109, 110, 111, 114, 115, 116, 119, 120, 121, 126, 127, 128, 129, 136, 140, 141, 181, 182, 183, 186, 187, 188, 207, 209, 210, 212, 213, 214, 215, 219, 221, 222, 223, 226, 264, 284, 329, 332; 3:1, 2, 3, 7, 8, 9, 16, 26, 61, 70, 71, 74, 76, 77, 78, 81, 82, 83, 103, 106, 125, 138, 147, 148, 149, 150, 154, 155, 156, 157, 159, 160, 161, 162, 167, 208, 215, 220, 221, 222, 225, 226, 227, 233, 234, 245, 303, 304, 307, 308, 312.

29 March 1748: "This Morning went out & Survey'd five Hundred Acres of Land & went down to one Michael Stumps on the So. Fork of the Branch. On our way Shot two Wild Turkies."

1 April 1748: "This Morning Shot twice at Wild Turkies but killd none. Run of three Lots & returnd to Camp."

3 April 1748: "Last Night was a much more blostering night than the former. We had our Tent Carried Quite of with the Wind and was obliged to Lie the Latter part of the Night without covering. There came several Persons to see us this day one our Men Shot a Wild Turkie."

7 April 1748: "Rain'd Successively all Last Night. This Morning one of our men Killed a Wild Turkey that weight 20 Pounds."

1 January 1768: "Fox huntg. in my own Neck with Mr. Robt. Alexander, and Mr. Colvill. Catchd nothing. Captn. Posey with us."

7 January 1768: "Fox hunting with the above two Gentn. [Mr. B. Fairfax and Mr. Robt. Alexander] and Captn. Posey. Started but catchd nothing."

8 January 1768: "Hunting again in the same Comp'y. Started a Fox and run him 4 hours. Took the Hounds off at Night."

22 January 1768: "Fox hunting with Capt. Posey, started but catchd nothing."

23 January 1768: "Rid to Muddy hole, and directed paths to be cut for Fox hunting."

24 January 1768: "Rid up to Toulston in order to Fox hunt it."

26 January 1768: "Went out with the Hounds but started no Fox. Some of the Hounds run of upon a Deer."

27 January 1768: "Went out again. Started a Fox abt. 10. Run him till 3 and lost him."

3 February 1768: "Fox hunting with Captn. Posey and Ld. Washington. Started but catchd nothg."

6 February 1768: "Fox hunting with Mr. Alexander and Captn. Posey. Started but catchd nothing."

8 February 1768: "Rid to Muddy hole, Doeg Run and Mill, and in returng. met Mr. Alexander, Mr. Stoddard and Captn. Posey, who had just catchd 2 foxes. Returnd w. them. to Dinner."

9 February 1768: "Went out Hunting again. Started a fox, run him four hours and then lost him. Mr. Stoddard went home. Alexr. stayd."

12 February 1768: "Fox hunting with Colo. Fairfax, Captn. McCarty, Mr. Chichester, Posey, Ellzey & Manley who dind here, with Mrs. Fairfax & Miss Nicholas.—catchd two foxes."

13 February 1768: "Hunting in the same Company. Catchd 2 more foxes. None dind at Mt. Vernon."

18 February 1768: "Went a ducking between breakfast & dinner. In the afternoon Mr. Thruston Mr. Alexander and Mr. Carter from Gloster came in."

20 February 1768: "Fox hunting with Captn. Posey. Catchd a Fox."

23 February 1768: "Fox hunting with Captn. Posey. Catchd a Fox we suppose, but being dark coud not find it."

24 February 1768: "Went a ducking between breakfast & dinner & killd 2 Mallards and 5 bald faces. Found Doctr. Rumney here at Dinner who staid all Night. Mr. Magowan returnd."

25 February 1768: "Doctr. Rumney went away. I went to the Creek but not cross it. Killd 2 Ducks, viz. a sprig tail and Teal."

28 February 1768: "In the afternoon went up to Mr. Robt. Alexander's in order to meet Mr. B. Fairfax and others a fox Huntg. None came this day but Captn. Posey."

1 March 1768: "Went a fox hunting with the two Alexrs. and Posey. Was during the chase (in which nothing was catchd) joind by Mr. Fairfax, Jno. Alexander & Muir."

16 March 1768: "Hunting with Captn. Posey & L[un]d W[ashington]. Started and catchd a fox in abt. three hours."

26 March 1768: "Went Fox hunting, but started nothing. Mr. Lawe. Washington came here, & Miss Ramsay in the Afternoon."

29 March 1768: "Fox hunting, with Jacky Custis & Ld. Washington. Catchd a fox after a 3 hrs. chase."

4 April 1768: "Fox hunting with Messrs. Chichester, the Triplets, Manley, Posey, Peake & Adams. Never started a Fox —but did a Deer."

9 April 1768: "Fox hunting with the two Triplets, Mr. Peake & Mr. Manley. Started, but catchd nothing."

14 April 1768: "Fox hunting with Mr. Chichester Captn. Posey Messrs. Triplet Peake & Adams. Started but catchd nothing. Posey & Adams dind here as did Mr. Digges."

9 May 1768: "Went a Fox hunting and catched a Fox after 35 Minutes chace; returnd to Dinner and found the Attorney his Lady & daughter there."

13 May 1768: "Went after Sturgeon & a Gunning."

19 May 1768: "Went a shooting, & hair huntg. with the Hounds who started a Fox wch. we catchd."

4 August 1768: "Went a fox hunting in the Neck with Lund Washington & Mr. Thos. Triplet. Started nothing."

8 August 1768: "Went a fox hunting, but Started nothing. Visited Plantations in the Neck & Mill."

13 August 1768: "The hounds havg. started a Fox in self huntg. we followed and run it after sevl. hours chase into a hold when digging it out it escapd. The Doctr. went home."

13 September 1768: "Went a fox huntg. with Lord Fairfax Colo. Fairfax & B. Fairfax. Catchd nothg."

14 September 1768: "Mr. B. Fairfax & myself went a huntg. Started a Fox & run it into a hole but did not catch it."

23 September 1768: "Went a fox hunting & catchd a Bitch Fox after abt. 2 Hours Chase."

26 September 1768: "Went Fox huntg. in the Neck. Started and run a Fox or Foxes 3 Hours & then lost."

1 October 1768: "Fox huntg. back of Mr. Barry's with Mr. Robt. Alexander Mr. Manley & Captn. Posey. Started & catchd a bitch Fox. Mr. Stedlar came here in the Afternoon."

8 October 1768: "Went Fox huntg. (in the Neck) in the forenoon. Started but catchd nothing & in the afternoon went up the Ck. after Blew Wings—Killd 7 or 8."

13 October 1768: "Went a fox hunting and catchd a Bitch Fox after two hours chase."

15 October 1768: "Went a hunting with Captn. Posey & Ld. Washington. Catchd a Bitch Fox after a chace of 1 Hour and 10 Minutes."

12 November 1768: "Went Fox huntg. in the Neck. Started & was run out of hearg. of the Dogs—owing to the Wind. Whether they catchd or not is not known."

15 November 1768: "Went a Fox hunting in the Neck; catchd a bitch fox —after an hour and 40 Minutes Chace."

22 November 1768: "Went a fox huntg. with Lord Fairfax & Colo. Fairfax & my Br. Catchd 2 Foxes."

23 November 1768: "Went a huntg again with Lord Fairfax & his Brother, & Colo. Fairfax. Catchd nothing that we knew of. A fox was started."

25 November 1768: "Mr. Bryan Fairfax, as also Messrs. Grayson & Phil. Alexander came here by Sunrise. Hunted & catchd a fox with these and my Lord, his Br. & Colo. Fairfax, all of whom, with Mrs. Fx.& Mr. Watson of Eng'd dind here."

26 November 1768: "Hunted again in the above Compa. but catchd nothing."

29 November 1768: "Went a Huntg. with Lord Fairfax & catchd a Fox."

3 December 1768: "Went a fox huntg. in Company with Lord & Colo. Fairfax Captn. McCarty & Messrs. Henderson & Ross. Started nothg. My Br. came in the Afternoon."

5 December 1768: "Fox hunting with Lord Fairfax & his Brothr. & Colo. Fairfax. Started a Fox and lost it. Dind at Belvoir and came [home] in the Evg."

8 December 1768: "Fox huntg. with Lord Fairfax & Brothr. & Colo Fairfax all of whom dind here. Started nothing."

10 December 1768: "Went a fox hunting in the Neck & catchd a fox. Afterwards went to the Plantatin. there. Doctr. Rumney came to D[inne]r. & Mr. Alexr. in the E[venin]g."

15 December 1768: "Returnd home; by the way (that is near Muddy hole) started & catchd a Fox."

17 December 1768: "Rid out with my Gun but killd nothing. Mary Wilson came to live here as a Ho. keeper a[t] 15*l*. pr. Month."

23 December 1768: "Went a Pheasant Huntg. Carrd. hounds & they started & followed a Deer."

27 December 1768: "Ditto. Do. except Shooting between breakfast & Dinner."

29 December 1768: "Went a fox hunting. Started one but did not catch it. In the Afternoon Messrs. Dalton, Piper & Riddell came here. Also Mr. Mag[owa]n."

31 December 1768: "Went a hunting & catchd a bitch fox—the above Gentlemn.with me."

4 January 1769: "Went a fox huntg. with the above Gentlemen [Col. Carlyle and Mr. Ramsay], & were met by the two Colo. Fairfax's but found nothing. Messrs. C[arlyle] & R[amsay] went home."

10 January 1769: "Went a Fox huntg. with L[und] W[ashington]—Jackey Custis, & Mr. Manley. Found Nothing."

11 January 1769: "Went a fox hunting in the Neck with Mr. Peake, but found nothing."

12 January 1769: "Went out in the Morng. with the Hounds in order to meet Colo. Fairfax but did not. In Hell hole started a fox and after an hours chase run him into a hole, & left him. In the afternoon went to Alexa. to the Monthly Ball."

16 January 1769: "Went a ducking in the forenoon—otherwise at home all day. In the Afternoon Mr. B. Fairfax came here."

17 January 1769: "Fox huntg. in the Neck with Mr. Fairfax Triplet & Peake—started nothing."

18 January 1769: "Fox huntg again in the above Compa. and Harn. Manley—started a Fox and lost it. The above dind here as Mr. Wagener also did."

19 January 1769: "Fox hunting in the same Company—fd. nothing. Mr. Fairfax and Mr. Wagr. dind here."

20 January 1769: "Fox huntg. again with Mr. Wagener Mr. Fairfax and Mr. Clarke. The two last dind here. Mr. Wagener went home."

21 January 1769: "Fox huntg. again upon long Branch with Mr. Fairfax Mr. Clarke Mr. Mac[ar]ty & Mr. Chichester. All went home from the field. Found Doctr. Rumney here."

25 January 1769: "Hunting below Accatinck with Captn. McCarty Mr. Chichester & Mr. Wagener with their dogs. Found a fox & killd it in abt. an hour and 35 Minutes."

28 January 1769: "Went a Huntg. with Mr. Alexander. Traild a fox for two hours and then lost it. Mr. Alexander went home from the field."

3 February 1769: "Went a Gunning up the Creek—killd 7 Ducks. In the Afternoon Colo. F. Lewis & Son Fieldg. & Mr. Rozer came here."

9 February 1769: "Went a Ducking with Colo. Lewis. His Son & Betcy Dandridge went to the Monthly Ball at Alexandria."

10 February 1769: "Went a shooting again. In the Afternoon fieldg. Lewis returnd from the Ball."

11 February 1769: "Ducking till Dinner. Mr. Piper dind here. Betsy Dandridge came home in the Evening."

14 February 1769: "Went a fox hunting—but started nothing. The two Colo. Fairfax's dind here."

17 February 1769: "Rid out with my hounds. Started a fox and lost it, after an hour s chase. Doctr. Rumney came in the Afternoon."

18 February 1769: "Went a hunting with Doctr. Rumney. Started a fox, or rather 2 or 3, & catchd none. Dogs mostly got after Deer and never joind."

27 February 1769: "Fox hunting with Colo. G. Fairfax & Mr. Warnr. Washington. Started and killed a Dog fox, after havg. him on foot three hours & hard runng. an hour and a Qr. Dined at Colo. Fairfax's."

25 March 1769: "Went a fox hunting with Colo. Bassett & Mr. Bryan Fairfax—who also came here last Night. Started & run a fox into a hole after an hours chase. Mr. Fairfax went home after dinner. Dog fox killd."

27 March 1769: "Went a Fox hunting—found and was run out of hearing by some of the Dogs."

28 March 1769: "Hunting again. Found a fox & killd it in an hour and an half. Mr. Magowan & Vale. Crawford came here today."

31 March 1769: "Hunting—found a fox & killd him in an hour. This & the last were both Dog Foxes. Mr. Magowan went to Alexandria."

7 April 1769: "Went a fox hunting in the Morning & catchd a dog fox after running him an hour and treeing twice. After this went to an intended meeting of the Vestry but there was none. When I came home found Mr. Buchanon & Captn. McGachin here— also Captn. Weeden and my Br. Charles."

11 April 1769: "Went a fox hunting & took a fox alive after running him to a Tree. Brot him home."

12 April 1769: "Chased the above fox for an Hour & 45 Minutes when he treed again after which we lost him. Mr. B. Fairfax came this afternoon."

13 April 1769: "Went a Huntg. with him in the Neck & killd a Dog fox, after treeing him in 35 Min[utes]. Mr. W[arner] Washington Dind here & both of them stayd all Night. My Br. & Captn. Weeden went away this Morning."

16 September 1769: "Mr. Robt. Alexander came before Sun Rise this morning and we all went a fox huntg. Started one & run him into a hollow tree in an hour & 20 minutes. Chase him in the afternn. & killd in an h[our] and 1/2."

22 September 1769: "Went a huntg. & killd a bitch fox in abt an hour. Returnd home with an Ague upon me. Mr. Montgomery came to Dinner."

23 September 1769: "Went a huntg. again with the Compy. aforesaid & suppose we killd a fox but could not find it. Returnd with my Ague again. Mr. Wagener went home."

30 September 1769: "Went a Hunting. Catchd a Rakoon but never found a Fox. One Doctr. Harris of Goochland dined here."

5 October 1769: "Went after Blew Wings with Humphrey Peake. Killd 3 & returnd by Muddy hole."

6 October 1769: "Went a hunting but found nothing after which Rid to Muddy hole, D. Run, & Mill."

9 October 1769: "Went a fox hunting & finding a Deer the Dogs ran it to the Water but we never see it. Mr. Alexr. went home."

14 October 1769: "Went a Fox hunting. Started a Dog Fox by old Palmers & Run it back of Mr. Clifton & there catchd it. Went afterwards into the Neck. Mr. Matthew Campbell dined here."

18 October 1769: "Went a Fox huntg. with Mr. Fairfax & Mr. Magowan. Found and killd a Dog Fox."

4 January 1770: "Went a hunting with Jno. Custis & Lund Washington. Started a Deer & then a Fox but got neither."

5 January 1770: "Rid to Muddy hole & Doeg Run. Carrd. the Dogs with me but found nothing. Mr. Warnr. Washington & Mr. Thruston came in the Evening."

8 January 1770: "Went a huntg. with Mr. Alexander, J. P. Custis & Ld. W[ashingto]n, killd a fox (a dog one) after 3 hours chase. Mr. Alexr. went away and Wn. & Thruston came in the Aftern."

9 January 1770: "Went a ducking but got nothing, the Creeks and Rivers being froze. Mr. Robt. Adam dined here & returnd."

10 January 1770: "Mr. W[ashingto]n. & Mr. Thruston set of home. I went a hunting in the Neck & visited the Plantn. there. Found & Killd a bitch fox after treeing it 3 times and chasg. it abt. 3 Hr."

20 January 1770: "Went a hunting with Jacky Custis & catchd a Bitch Fox after three hours chace. Founded it on the Ck. by J. Soals."

23 January 1770: "Went a hunting after breakfast & found a Fox a Muddy hole & killd her (it being a Bitch), after a chace of better than two hours & after treeing her twice the last of which times she fell dead out of the Tree after being therein sevl. minutes apparently we[ll]. Rid to the Mill afterwards. Mr. Semple & Mr. Robt. Adam dind here."

27 January 1770: "Went a hunting, & after trailing a fox a good while the Dogs Raizd a Deer & run out of the Neck with it & did not (some of them at least) come home till the next day."

30 January 1770: "Went a hunting, & having found a Deer by Piney Cover. It run to the head of Accatinck before we coud stop the Dogs. Mr. Peake dined here."

1 February 1770: "Went a huntg. (being joined by Mr. Peake Wm. Triplet & Harrison Manley) & after a Chace of near five hours we killd a Fox. Mr. Piper & Mr. Adam came here this afternoon."

9 February 1770: "Went a hunting—found a Fox and lost it. Mr. Ballendine & the Doctr. still here. Captn. McCarty went from the field."

14 February 1770: "Went to the Neck with Mr. Fairfax a huntg, but was forcd back by Rain. Doctr. Rumney returnd to Alexandria after breakfast this day."

15 February 1770: "Went a huntg. again with Mr. Fairfax & found a fox at the head of the blind Pocoson which we suppose was killd in an hour but coud not find it. Mr. Peake dind here & Mr. R. Alexander came after."

16 February 1770: "Huntg. again—found a bitch fox at Piney branch & killd it in an hour. Mr. Alexr. went away [after] dinner."

24 February 1770: "Went out with the hounds but found nothing."

28 February 1770: "Went out with Guns Returned about 12 Oclock without killg. of anything. My Brothers and the Company that came with them still here."

6 March 1770: "Went out a hunting with Mr. Alexander [and] his Brothers. Found two or three Foxes but killd neither."

7 March 1770: "Went a hunting again. Found a Fox and run it 6 hours & then lost [it]. I returnd home this Evening."

13 March 1770: "Went a huntg. above Darrels Hills & to G. Alexrs. Pocoson. Found a fox by two Dogs in Cliftons Neck but lost it upon joing. the Pack. Returnd abt. 5 Oclock & found Colo. Mason & Mr. Christian here."

16 March 1770: "Went to doeg run and took the hounds with me —found a fox by the Widow Ashfords & soon lost him. Upon my return home found Colo. Lewis my

Br[other] Ch[arle]s & Mr. Brooke here. In the Evening Mr. Jno. West & Mr. Stedlar came—also Mr. Whiting."

21 March 1770: "Joind some dogs that were self hunting & from thence went to the Mill & was levelling all the remainder of the day with Jno. Ball &ca."

26 March 1770: "Went a hunting with the above Gentln. & killd a fox after two hours chace. The two Mr. Triplets Peake &ca. were with us. T. Triplet & H. Manley dind here."

27 March 1770: "Again went a hunting with the above Compy. but found no Fox. Mr. Geo. Alexander & Mr. Peake dind here with the other Compa.—as Mr. Ramsay did."

28 March 1770: "Went a huntg. again and killd a fox. All the Compy. went home from the field."

6 April 1770: "Went a hunting, but found nothing. Returnd to Dinner."

24 August 1770: "Went out a huntg. with Mr. Fairfax. Killd a young fox without running him and returnd to Dinner. Doctr. Rumney dind here & lodged."

8 December 1770: "Went a hunting but found nothing. From the Woods I went to my Mill & so home to Dinner. Doc[tor] Ross Dind here & went away after."

27 December 1770: "Went a fox Hunting and kill'd a fox in Company with the two Mr. Triplets and Mr. Peake who dined here."

29 December 1770: "Went fox hunting in Company with the two Mr. Triplets & Mr. Peake. Found no Fox. Upon my return home found Mr. & Mrs. Cockburn here."

5 January 1771: "My Brother and Mr. Lawe. Washington set of for Frederick. I went a hunting with the two Mr. Triplet's and Mr. Peake, but killd nothing."

12 January 1771: "Went a huntg. with the two Mr. Triplets Mr. Manley and Mr. Peake. Run a Deer to the Water but killd nothing."

19 January 1771: "Went a hunting in Compa. with the two Mr. Triplets, Mr. Manley & Mr. Peake. Killed a Fox after two hours Chase. In the afternoon rid to where my People were at work on the Mill Race."

9 February 1771: "Attempted to go a hunting, but prevented by Rain. Rid to the Mill in the fore and Afternoon."

18 February 1771: "Those two Gentlemen [Charles Washington and William? Thompson] went a Gunning & I rid to my Mill in the forenoon."

19 February 1771: "They [Charles Washington and Thompson] went a Ducking and I again Rid to my Mill in the forenoon."

20 February 1771: "Rid to my Mill. Colo. Thos. Lee came here to Dinner. My Bro. & Mr. Thompson a Ducking."

21 February 1771: "At home all day. Col. Lee still here. The other Gentn. went a Ducking."

26 March 1771: "Rid to my Mill and Mill dam at the head of the Race in the forenoon (after going a hunting in the Morning). In the Afternoon Rid to Posey's."

14 May 1771: "Went into the Fields with Colo. Bassett a shooting—killd sevl. Hares &ca.

5 October 1771: "Went a hunting with Jacky Custis but found nothing. Came home by the Mill. Mr. Rutherford went away after breakfast & Captn. Oliffe dind here."

8 October 1771: "Went a hunting in the Neck and Catchd a Dog fox. Then went to the Plantn. there & came home to Dinr."

16 November 1771: "Went a hunting but found nothing."

28 November 1771: "Went a driving again with Colo. Mason —killed nothing."

30 November 1771: "Went a hunting in the Neck with Mr. Peake—found & killed a Fox. Mr. Johnson still here."

7 December 1771: "Went a fox hunting with the above two [Philip Pendleton and Valentine Crawford] &ca. Killed a Fox and dined with Doctr. Alexander."

14 December 1771: "Went a fox hunting with John Parke Custis Lund Washington & Mr. Manley—killed a Fox."

18 December 1771: "Went to Doeg Run & carried the Dogs with me who found & Run a Deer to the Water."

21 December 1771: "Went a hunting in the Neck with Mr. Peake & Mr. Wm. & Thos. Triplet the first two of whom dind with me. Found nothing."

26 December 1771: "Went a hunting in the Neck early. Killd a Fox and dined with several others at Mr. Peake's."

27 December 1771: "Went a hunting again in the Neck found a Fox and lost it. Dined with others at Mr. Thos. Triplets."

28 December 1771: "Hunted again in the Neck and killed a Fox. Dined at home with the following Person's—the two Mr. Triplets—Mr. Manley, Mr. Peake, young Frans. Adam's and one Stone Street—also Peakes Daughter & Miss Fanny Eldridge."

30 December 1771: "Went a hunting again with the former Compa. but found nothing. Dined at Mr. Wm. Triplets. Miss Peake &ca. went home."

4 January 1772: "Went a Hunting with the above Gentlemen [Thomas Montgomerie, Harry Piper, Robert Harrison, and Bryan Fairfax]. Found both a Bear & Fox but got neither. Went up to Alexandria with these Gentlemen to finish the business with Montgomerie &ca. which was accordg. done."

6 January 1772: "Went a Hunting in the Neck with Mr. Fairfax. Found a fox & run him into a hole near Night, without Killing him. Found Doctr. Rumney and Mr. Magowan here when we returnd."

11 January 1772: "Went a Hunting in the Neck. Found a fox about One Clock and killed it about 3 Oclock. Mr. Magowan return from Colchester to Dinner."

18 January 1772: "Mr. Hanna went away after Breakfast as Mr. Magowan also did. I went a Hunting & killd a Fox—was joind bv Mr. M. Campbell—Mr. Manley & Mr. Peake who dined here and went away afterwds."

25 April 1772: "Went a hunting with Colo. Bassett. Found nothing."

1 May 1772: "Went a Hunting with Mr. Jno. Custis. Found nothing. Returnd to Dinner."

24 August 1772: "Went a Hunting, and into the Neck, but found nothing; came home by 12 Oclock."

31 October 1772: "Went a foxhunting & killd a Fox in Compa. with sevl. others."

3 December 1772: "Went a Fox hunting, found one in Mr. G. Alexanders Pocoson & killd it after 3 hours chase. In the Afternoon Mr. B. Fairfax and Mr. Wagener came here."

4 December 1772: "Went a hunting again but found nothing. Mr. Wagener & Messrs. Tilghman & Dulany went home in the Afternoon."

5 December 1772: "Went a hunting with Mr. Fairfax. Found a Fox between Edd. Williams's & Johnsons which we lost after a Chase of two hours."

9 December 1772: "Went into the Neck abt. 11 Oclock a fox hunting. Touchd the Drag where we found the last but did not move the Fox."

15 December 1772: "Went a Hunting & found two Foxes both of which were killd, but only one got, the Dogs running out of hearg. with the 2d.; found these Foxes on the Hills by Isaac Gates's."

23 December 1772: "Went a Hunting but found nothing. In the Evening Colo. Fairfax came."

28 December 1772: "Went out a hunting. Found a fox back of Captn. Darrells & killd it. Doctr. Rumney & a Lieutt. Winslow Dind here the former stayd all Night."

30 December 1772: "Went a Hunting but found nothing. Messrs. Addison & Carr dining here—as did Mr. Manley."

5 January 1773: "Mr. Gallaway went away. Mr. Magowan & I went a Hunting. Found a fox on Ackatinck just by Lawson Parkers and lost it. In the Afternoon Mr. Dulany came."

9 January 1773: "Mr. Magowan returnd to Maryland. I went a Hunting. Found a Fox near Timber Landing & lost it near Mrs. French's."

11 January 1773: "Went a Hunting with the above Gentlemen. Found a Fox by Gilbt. Simpsons & killd him by Mrs. Frenchs. Mr. P. Pendleton & Mr. M. Campbell dined and lodgd here the others went away."

25 January 1773: "Went a hunting & found a Fox upon the Hills by Edd. Wathings which Run near 4 hours & was either killd or treed—but the wind blowing fresh we were thrown out & coud only judge from Circumstances. Came home to Dinner and found Doctr. Rumney here who stayd all Night."

30 January 1773: "Went a Fox hunting with Lund Washington. Took the drag of a Fox by Isaac Gates, & carrd. it tolerably well to the old Glebe then touchd now & then upon a Cold Scent till we came into Colo. Fairfax's Neck where we found about half after three upon the Hills just above Accotinck Creek. After Running till quite Dark took of the Dogs and came home."

2 February 1773: "Mr. Fairfax and I went out with the hounds—touchd upon the Drag of the Run[nin]g Fox upon the Hills just above Wathings but it being cold, as the day also was, we took the Dogs of and came home."

3 February 1773: "Went out again and touchd upon a Fox upon the Hills by Gates's & found another in Colo. Fairfax's Neck abt. 2 Oclock which was killd after an hours chace. This Fox was found upon the Hills."

6 February 1773: "Rid into the Neck, and taking the Hounds with me, after being at the Plantns. found a fox between the two which was killd in 3/4 of an hour."

9 February 1773: "Doctr. Rumney continued all day, & Night. After an early Dinner I set of to Mr. Robt. Alexanders upon Fox hunting Party & in the Afternoon, Young Mr. Danl. Dulany Revd. Mr. Montgomerie, Mr. Tilghman & Jno. Custis came here & stayd all [night]."

10 February 1773: "Found a Fox in Mr. Phil Alexanders Island, which was lost after a chase of 7 hour's."

11 February 1773: "Found a fox in the same place again which was killd at the end of 6 hours after wch. I came home & found Mr. Dulany & Mr. Custis here."

25 February 1773: "Went a hunting with those Gentlemen [Bryan Fairfax and Robert Alexander], and being join'd by the two Mr. Triplets, Mr. Manley, & Mr. Peake, all came here to Dinner and Mr. Thos. Triplet stayd all Night. Found a Fox in this Neck but did not kill it."

26 February 1773: "Went a Hunting again with the above Company. Found a Fox in Colo. Fairfax's Neck with part of the Dogs but believe it was not killd. Found Mr. Tilghman here upon our Return at Night."

19 March 1773: "Went a hunting. Found a Fox by Muddy hole Plantation and killd it after a chase of two hours & 3 Quarters."

29 March 1773: "Went a hunting with those Gentlemen [Loyd Dulany and Daniel Digges]. Found a Fox by Thos. Baileys & had it killd by Our Dogs in half an hour. Retd. to Dinner Mr. Manley with us."

30 March 1773: "Went a hunting again. Found Nothing. Colo. Fairfax and Mr. Lan. Lee—also Mr. Herbert & Mr. Miller Dined here, the last two stayd all Night."

5 October 1773: "Went a hunting in the Neck with Mr. Custis & Lund Washington. Found a Fox & after runng. it two hours & half lost it."

15 November 1773: "Went a Fox hunting. Found but did not kill. Returnd to Dinner."

22 December 1773: "Went out after Breakfast with the Dogs. Dragd a fox for an hour or two but never found. Returnd to Dinner & found Mrs. Slaughter here."

27 December 1773: "Went out in the Forenoon with the Dogs. Traild a Fox but did not find. Mr. Cato Moore dined here & in the Afternn. Mr. Geo. Digges & Mr. Custis came."

29 December 1773: "Went out with the Dogs. Found a Fox but did not kill it."

31 December 1773: "Went out with Mr. Digges & Mr. Custis a huntg. Found a Fox but did not kill it."

1 January 1774: "Fox hunting with Mr. George Digges, Mr. Robt. Alexr. & Peake who all dind here, together with Mr. Jas. Cleveland. In the Afternoon all went home but Mr. Alexander."

13 January 1774: "Dind here no body but Captn. Posey. I waiked out with my Gun. In the Afternoon Mr. Geo. Young came here to live."

15 January 1774: "Went out a hunting, & killd a dog fox wch. was found in Hell hole, after a chase of 3 hours. At home afterwards alone."

19 January 1774: "Mr. Custis & I went into the Neck a Hunting. Found two Fox's but killd neither. Doctr. Rumney came to Dinr. & stayd all Nt."

21 January 1774: "Doctr. Rumney went away after Breakfast. Mr. Custis & I went a hunting in the Neck and after run[nin]g a Fox 3 hours lost it."

17 February 1774: "Went a Hunting. Found a dog fox in this Neck and killed him after treeing 3 times and running about 2 hours."

19 February 1774: "Went a Hunting in the Neck see three Foxes but killd none. Mr. Lawson went away after Breakfast."

24 February 1774: "Went a huntg. in the Morning and from thence to the Vestry. Mr. Adam going away. Upon my return found Doctr. Craik, Val. Crawford & Mr. Thos. Gist."

14 April 1774: "Went a hunting. Killd a bitch Fox with three young ones almost hair'd. Doctr. Rumney dind here & stayed all Night."

12 January 1775: "Went a fox hunting—found but did not kill."

21 January 1775: "Went a hunting with Mr. Custis. Killd a Dog Fox & returnd to Dinner."

25 January 1775: "Doctr. Rumney visited the Sick & returnd to Dinner. I went a hunting. Found a fox but did not kill it."

1 February 1775: "Went into the Neck to see the sick. Also went fox huntg. Found nothing."

11 February 1775: "Mr. Milner went away. Mr. Custis & myself went a hunting but killd nothing although we found a Fox. Robt. Ashby & bro. lodgd here."

14 February 1775: "Went a Fox hunting—found & killed a Fox. Robt. Phil., & George Alexander came home with us. Mr. Muir Doctr. Rumney & Cap. Harper lodgd here."

15 February 1775: "Went a Huntg. again—found Nothing. None but Mr. Digges came home with me. Doctr. Rumney contd. here all day."

4 March 1775: "Went a Hunting but found nothing. Colo. Harrison and Captn. Wood came here to Dinner."

* * *

Robert Rose, Virginia Anglican minister, observes hunting, October 1748, December 1749, and October 1750, in Ralph Emmett Fall, ed., *The Diary of Robert Rose. A View of Virginia by a Scottish Colonial Parson, 1746-1751* (Falls Church, Va.: McClure Press, 1977), 42, 70, 90.

11 October 1748: "Rode out Toards the Mill with Jno Blyre who killd a large Buck being the first I ever saw killed,...."

7 December 1749: "..., Jno Blyre killed a bear at Night—...."

2 October 1750: "The same weather, this Night about Nine our people killd a bear—...."

* * *

Thomas Walker, Virginia doctor, hunts in western Virginia, June and July 1750, in "Journal of Doctor Thomas Walker," in J. Stoddard Johnston, ed., *First Explorations of Kentucky, Filson Club Publications No. 13* (Louisville: John P. Morton and Company, 1898), 69, 70, 75.

15 June 1750: "We got on a large Creek where Turkey are plenty and some Elks. we went a hunting & killed 3 Turkeys. Hunted & killed 3 Bears & some Turkeys."

16 June 1750: "The Sabbath. We killed a large Buck Elk."

19 June 1750: "We got to Laurel Creek early this morning, and met so impudent a Bull Buffaloe that we were obliged to shoot him, or he would have been amongst us."

13 July 1750: "We killed in the Journey 13 Buffaloes, 8 Elks, 53 Bears, 20 Deer, 4 Wild Geese, about 150 Turkeys, besides small Game. We might have killed three times as much meat, if we had wanted it."

* * *

Landon Carter, Virginia plantation owner, comments on local hunting, March 1772, December 1774, and February 1777, in Jack P. Greene, ed., *The Diary of Colonel Landon Carter of Sabine Hall, 1752-1778,* 2 vols., Vol 2 (Charlottesville, Va.: University Press of Virginia, 1965), 662, 664, 900, 902, 905, and 1087.

28 March 1772: "Nay, this morning when the moisture is so heavy as to be very foggy and threatening to rain, he [his grandson Landon Carter] was out a hunting almost as soon as light."

30 March 1772: "[F]or in all the moist air of Saturday Landon was out till it rained a fox hunting,...."

21 December 1774: "I find Master Landon is incontrolable; he keeps my horse Nicodemus though he tore the Paper which he wrote himself which was an obligation of restraint upon him if he would get that horse. And he still goes out as he used to do

in the same shame of dissipation. Last night no amorous boy could discover more abandoned folly than he did at a Message sent him last night to come to a fox hunt; and out he takes another horse of mine."

24 December 1774: "Landon Carter, the fox hunter, out again today, and so he has been ever since tuesday...."

27 December 1774: "This as well as yesterday turned out a fine day. It seems yesterday whilst I was at Colo. Tayloe's my low grounds were alive with fox hunters Wm. Ball, Bn. Branham, and G. Garland; my fences all pulled down, Cattle drove out of their wits and the wenches obliged to Climb the trees. I could not help writing to the Gent somewhat sharply on the occasion; ...."

27 February 1777: "Ground still covered with snow yet all foxhunting."

* * *

John Ferdinand Dalziel Smyth, British traveler, concerning hunting among the Virginians, November? December? 1772? or January? February? 1773?, in Smyth, *A Tour in the United States of America. Containing an Account of the Present Situation of that Country*, 2 vols., Vol. 1 (London: G. Robinson, 1784), 131-132.

November? December? 1772? January? February? 1773?: "I accuftomed myfelf to go out along with them a hunting, fifhing, fwimming, fowling, &c. for my amufement and diverfion."

* * *

Philip Vickers Fithian, tutor at Nomini Hall, on hunting in Virginia, December 1773, in Hunter Dickinson Farish, ed., *Journal & Letters of Philip Vickers Fithian, 1773-1774. A Plantation Tutor of the Old Dominion* (Charlottesville, Va.: University Press of Virginia, 1957), 43.

29 December 1773: "This Morning our School begins after the Holidays. Bob [Robert Carter,Jr.] seems sorry that he must forsake the Marsh & River when he is daily fowling, & never kills any Game."

* * *

Nicholas Cresswell, British loyalist, notes his hunting in Virginia, January 1775, in Maryland, February 1775, and in western Virginia, May 1775, in Cresswell, *The Journal of Nicholas Cresswell, 1774-1777* (Port Washington, N.Y.: Kennikat Press, 1968, [1924]), 52, 57, 75.

4 January 1775: "Amused myself with shooting wild Geese and Ducks. Here is incredible numbers in the River likewise Swans. It is said they come from the Lakes."

24 February 1775: "At Mr. Marsden's, shooting wild Geese and Ducks, of which there is incredible numbers. I am told 60 ducks have been killed at one shot."

17 May 1775: "Stopped at Bracken Creek and went a hunting as they call it here. Mr. Rice, Johnston and I went together. In a short time Mr. Rice fired at a Buffalo. Johnston and I went to him and found him standing behind a tree loading his Gun and the beast laid down about 100 yds. from him. As soon as he was ready we fired at him again, upon which he got up and run about a quarter of a mile, where our dogs bayed him till we came up and shot him. It was a large Bull, from his breast to the top of his shoulders long hair, from that to the tail as short as a mouse. I am certain he would have weighed a thousand."

* * *

Marquis de Chastellux, French officer, discusses hunting in Virginia, April 1782, in [de Chastellux], *Travels in North-America, in the Years 1780, 1781, and 1782, by the Marquis de Chastellux,* 2nd ed., 2 vols., Vol. 2 (London: G.G.J. and J. Robinson, 1787), 72-74, 104-105, 108-109.

April, 1782: "My fervant always followed me with a fowling-piece, and as it frequently happened that I was obliged to alight to fire at a partridge, or fome other game, our converfation did not prevent me from being always upon the watch. I perceived a large bird which croffed the road, and by the inftinct of a fportfman, I concluded it to be what the inhabitants of the mountains called a *pheafant,* but which refembles much more of a *woodhen.* To alight, call my dog, and take my gun, was the work of a moment; as I was preparing to follow the *woodhen* among the bufhes, one of my fervants pointed out to me two others, perched upon a tree behind him, and which looked at me with great tranquillity. I fired at the one neareft to me, nor did it require much addrefs to kill it. Except that it was perhaps a little bigger, it refembled the one I had been at Newport, where the Americans carry them fometimes to market, in winter, when they defcend from the mountains, and are more eafily killed.... After ordering the woodhen I had killed, for fupper, I tried to find the firft I had feen run into the underwood. I raifed it once, and although I ran immediately, and had an excellent dog, it was impoffible to find it; thefe birds running very faft, like the pheafant and the rail. The mode which the inhabitants of the mountains make ufe of to kill them, is to walk in the woods at fun-rifing and fun-fetting, to attend to the the noife they make in beating their fides with their wings, which may be heard above a mile; they then approach foftly, and ufually find them fitting upon the trunk of fome old tree. It was perhaps lucky that my fhooting did not continue with more fuccefs;...."

April, 1782: "..., I recollect that we had as yet an hour's day light, and that it was juft the time I had feen the wood-hens, of which, they affured me, there was plenty in the neighbourhood, and that there is a critical moment in hunting as well as love. I took my fowling-piece, therefore, and proceeded to the woods; but inftead of wood-hens, I found only a rabbit, which I wounded; but it rolled down into a bottom, where I loft fight of it, till it was difcovered by Mr. Grifby's dogs, which, accuftomed to the report of a gun, found it in a hollow tree, to the top of which it would have fcrambled had its leg not been broken."

April, 1782: "It was near ten o'clock when we arrived at the ferry, and as we approached, ftill following the courfe of the river, I faw an animal, to which I was a ftranger, returning from the fide of the river, and endeavouring to reach the wood. I pufhed my horfe towards it, hoping to frighten and make it climb a tree, for I took it for a racoon; in fact it mounted the neareft tree, but very flowly and aukwardly. I had not great difficulty in killing it, for it did not even endeavour to hide itfelf, like the fquirrel, behind the large branches. When I had taken it from the dogs, among which it had ftruggled hard, and had bitten them pretty fharply;...."

* * *

Jean-Baptiste-Antoine de Verger, French officer, comments on hunting near Williamsburg, Virginia, in [Verger], "Journal of Jean-Baptiste-Antoine de Verger," in Howard C. Rice, Jr. and Anne S.K. Brown, trans. and eds., *The American Campaigns of Rochambeau's Army, 1780, 1781, 1782, 1783,* 2 vols., Vol. 1 (Princeton, N.J.: Princeton University Press, 1972), 158.

"The stags are very much like the deer in our country. The hares are much smaller than the European variety, and some claim they are rabbits. The foxes are also smaller, and the fox-hunts are quite amusing. Several inhabitants keep excellent packs of hounds and hunt on horseback. We went fox-hunting several times a week with M. de Rochambeau. We rarely failed to run two foxes in a day."

* * *

Baron Ludwig von Closen, French captain, describes hunting in Virginia, 16 February 1782, in Evelyn M. Acomb, trans. and ed., *The Revolutionary Journal of Baron Ludwig von Closen, 1780-1783* (Chapel Hill, N.C.: University of North Carolina Press, 1958), 176-177.

"There are endless balls; the women love dancing with as much passion as the men hunting and horse-racing, and sometimes cock-fights too. M. de Rochambeau, who liked hunting very much, amused himself during the whole winter riding through the woods, followed by twenty or so enthusiasts. We ran down more than 30 foxes. The dog packs belonging to the gentlemen of the neighborhood are wonderful. It is only a pity that the species of foxes is not as strong as that in Europe; ordinarily, after an hour of hunting, they are tracked down, sometimes even in less time, and rarely in more. The country around Williamsburg favors this kind of hunting. There are many clear woods and little thickets, across which one can always follow the hounds, and although thereare several creeks and swamps, the fords are not dangerous and are always marked."

* * *

Johann David Schoepf, German physician, in Virginia, December 1783, in Schoepf, *Travels in the Confederation. Pennsylvania, Maryland, Virginia, the Carolinas, East Florida, the Bahamas,* trans. and ed. by Alfred J. Morrison, 2 vols., Vol. 2 (Cleveland: Arthur H. Clark, 1911), 95.

December, 1783: "A Virginia youth of 15 years is already such a man as he will be at twice that age. At 15, his father gives him a horse and a negro, with which he riots about the country, attends every fox-hunt, horse-race, and cock-fight, and does nothing else whatever;...."

NEW ENGLAND

George Morton?, British settler at Plymouth, Massachusetts, notes hunting, November 1620 and February 1621, in [Morton?], *Mourt's Relation or Journal of the Plantation at Plymouth,* ed. by Henry Martyn Dexter (Boston: John Kimball Wiggin, 1865), 29-30, 79.

28 November 1620: "[A]nd as it fell out, wee got three fat Geefe, and fix Ducks to our Supper, which we eate with Souldiers ftomacks, for we had eaten little all that day;...."
9 February 1621: "That evening the mafter going afhore, killed fiue Geefe, which he friendly diftributed among the ficke people; he found alfo a good Deere killed, the

Savages had cut off the hornes, and a Wolfe was eating of him, how he came there we could not conceiue."

* * *

Edward Winslow, English settler and chronicler of Plymouth, Massachusetts, describes hunting deer for Thanksgiving, December 1621, in [Winslow], "Gov. Bradford's History of Plymouth Colony," in Alexander Young, ed., *Chronicles of the Pilgrim Fathers of the Colony of Plymouth, from 1602 to 1625* (Boston: Charles C. Little and James Brown, 1841), 231.

11 December 1621: "Our harvest being gotten in, our governor sent four men on fowling, that so we might, after a special manner, rejoice together after we had gathered the fruit of our labors. They four in one day killed as much fowl as, with a little help beside, served the company almost a week. At which time, amongst other recreations, we exercised our arms, many of the Indians coming amongst us, and among the rest their greatest king, Massasoyt, with some ninety men, whom for three days we entertained and feasted; and they went out and killed five deer, which they brought to the plantation, and bestowed on our governor,...."

* * *

Thomas Morton, English settler, concerning eastern Massachusetts, reports on hunting, circa 1632 (1620s?), in Morton, *New English Canaan, or, New Canaan, Containing An Abstract of New England* (London?: Charles Green, 1632), 47-48, 52.

"I have had often 1000. [geese] before the mouth of my gunne, I never saw any in England for my part so fatt, as I have killed there in those parts, the fethers of them makes a bedd, softer then any down bed that I have lyen on: and there is a very good commodity, the fethers of the Geese that I have killed in a short time, have paid for all the powther and shott, I have spent in a yeare, and I have fed my doggs with as fatt Geese there, as I have euer fed upon myselfe in England."

"Sanderlings are a dainty bird, more full bodied than a Snipe, and I was much delighted to feede on them, because they were fatt, and easie to come by, because I went but a stepp or to for them: and I have killed bewteene foure and five dozen at a shoot which would loade me home."

"Turkies there are, which divers times in great flocks have sallied by our doores: and then a gunne (being commonly in a redinesse,) salutes them with such a courtesie, as makes them take a turne in the Cooke roome. They daunce by the doore so well.

"Of these there hath been killed, that have weighed forty eight pounds a peece.

"They are by mainy degrees sweeter then the tame Turkies of England, feede them how you can."

"I for my part may be bould to tell you, that my howse, was not without the flesh of this sort of Deare winter nor summer, the humbles of which was ever my dogges fee, which by the wesell, was hanged on the barre in the chimney, for his diet only: for hee has brought to my stand a brace in the morning, one after the other before sunne rising, which I have killed."

* * *

William Wood, English settler, in New England, depicts a bear hunt, circa 1634, in Wood, *New Englands Prospect, A True, Lively and Experimentall Defcription of that Part of America, Commonly Called Nevv England. Difcovering the Ftate of that Countrie, Both As It Ftands to Our New-Come Englifh Planters; and to the Old Native Inhabitants* (London:

Thomas Cotes, 1634), reprinted as *Wood's New-England Prospect, Publications of the Prince Society, Volume 1* (Boston: The Prince Society, 1865), 22-23.

"Two men going a fowling, appointed at evening to meete at a certaine pond fide, to fhare equally, and to returne home; one of thefe Gunners having killed a Seale or Sea calfe, brought it to the fide of the pond where hee was to meete his comrade, afterwards returning to the Sea fide for the gaine; and having loaded himfelfe with more Geefe and Duckes, he repaired to the pond, where hee faw a great Beare feeding on his Seale, which caufed him to throw downe his loade, and give the Beare a falute; which though it was but with Goofe fhot, yet tumbled him over and over, whereupon the man fuppofing him to be in a manner dead, ran and beate him with the hand of his Gunne; The Beare perceiving him to be fuch a coward to ftrike him when he was down, fcrambled up, ftanding at defiance with him, fcratching his legges, tearing his cloathes and face, who ftood it out till his fix foot Gunne was broken in the middle, then being deprived of his weapon, he ran up to the fhoulders into the pond, where hee remained till the Beare was gone, and his mate come in, who accompanied him home."

* * *

Rhode Island and Providence Plantations law, circa 1639, September 1641, August 1644, and February 1646, in *Records of the Colony of Rhode Island and Providence Plantations in New England, Volume I, 1636 to 1663*, ed. by John Russell Bartlett (Providence, R.I.: A. Crawford Greene and Brother, 1856), 81, 84-85, 113, 116.

"6. It is further ordered, that all Men who shall kill any Deare (except it be upon his own proper Land), shall bring and deliver half of said Deare into the Treasurie, or pay Forty shillings; and further it is ordered, that the Governour and Deputy Governour shall have authority to give forth a Warrant to some one deputed of each Towne to kill some against the Court times for the Countries use, who shall by his Warrant have Libertie to kill wherever he find; Provided, it be not within any man's enclosure, and to be paid by the Threasurer; Provided, also, that no Indian shall be suffered to kill or destroy [deer] at any time or any where."

17 September 1641: "22. It is ordered and agreed, that no Englishman or other shall sett any Trapps for deare upon the Island, under paine of forfeiting five pounds, except it be within his own inclosed grounds."

29 August 1644: "It is further ordered, that Ousamequin with ten men shall have leave to kill ten deare uppon this Island within the libertie of Portsmouth; and the forementioned deare they shall bring to the towne to Mr. Brenton and Mr. Baulston, and they to view them; and neither Ousamequin nor any of his men shall carry any deere or skins off from the Island, but at the towne of Portsmouth; and to depart from off the Island within five dayes."

4 February 1646: "It is agreed to concur with Newport in an order that there shall be no shootinge of deere for the space of two months; and if any shall shoot, he shall forfeit five pounds; half to him that sueth, and the other halfe to the Treasurie. The reason of this order is, that the wolves themore readily come to bayte that they may be catched for the general good of the Island.

"It is further ordered, that there shall be noe shootinge of deere from the first of May till the first of November; and if any shall shoot a deere within that time he shall forfeit five pounds; one halfe to him that sueth, and the other to the Treasury."

* * *

Samuel Sewall, Boston magistrate, notes a local hunting accident, 9 September 1696, in M. Halsey Thomas, ed., *The Diary of Samuel Sewall, 1674-1729, Volume I. 1674-1708* (New York: Farrar, Straus and Giroux, 1973), 355.

"Purchase Capen had been gunning, or shot a fowl by the by as was at work: charg'd his Gun which others knew not of, laid it down as was about to go home at night; a Lad took it up in sport and held it out, it went off and killed the Owner."

* * *

Josiah Cotton, Haverhill, Massachusetts resident, notes a local hunting accident in Cotton to Rowland Cotton, 17 October 1702, in Robert E. Moody, ed., *The Saltonstall Papers, 1607-1815, Volume 1. 1607-1789* (Boston: Massachusetts Historical Society, 1972), 271.

"Many sad accidents have lately fallen out.... A young fellow also of this Town [Salem] went agunning. The Gunn broke and has miserably shattered his face and it is thought has crackt his Scull, etc."

* * *

Joshua Hempstead, New London, Connecticut carpenter, chronicles local hunting, December 1711, October and November 1713, August and November 1714, October 1716, March 1720, January 1726, and November 1727, January 1742, March and July 1749, and May 1750, in [Hempstead], *Diary of Joshua Hempstead of New London, Connecticut Covering a Period of Forty-Seven Years from September, 1711, to November, 1758, Collections of the New London County Historical Society, Volume I* (New London, Conn.: New London County Historical Society, 1901), 5, 29, 37, 39, 60, 96, 165, 191, 388, 516, 527, 550.

14 December 1711: "...in ye Latter part wee went to hunt wolves in ye Great Swamp but found none."

29 October 1713: "I was a wolf hunting. wee Killed one wolf in a Swamp above ye Millpond field. their was 14 of us. we wounded 2 more."

2 November 1713: "I was hunting wolves. wee kiled 2 in ye Great Swamp near uncle Douglass's. their was 33 of us boys & all."

11 August 1714: "I paid Richard Rogers five Pound wch was in my hands on acctt of 3 wolves killed Last fall."

15 November 1714: "I was wolf hunting most of ye day at Cedar Swamps. got nothing."

11 October 1716: "aftern. Wolf hunting wee kild none."

16 October 1716: "their hath been a Wolfhunting & they have killed 5 Wolves & Wounded 1 or 2 more."

23 March 1720: "James Smith hath kiled 1 old Bitch fox & .4. young ones."

17 January 1726: "a Deer was killed by the marsh at the going on of Mamacock by Holts, Star, Chapman & others. It was wounded by an Indian near Douglases & he followed it & [ ] with him & had ye Skin."

18 November 1727: "Mr Wanton killed a young Buck in the forenoon which wee brot over."

20 January 1742: "Joshua...brot home 2 Stout Rackoons tht he killed in my Swamp with the help of a Hound yt he pickt up Stray in the Town belonged to Colchester. they weighed 8lb & 8 & 3/4 wn Hdressed. I Sold one Carcass for 5s & baked ye other."

21 January 1742: "Josh & Jno Holt kiled another Coon to Day."

24 March 1749: "I was in Town att mr Winthrops most of the Day writing a Bond from Amos Burrows to Mr Winthrop £65 for killing 2 Dear on fishers Island in Sept last for which I had him arrested & bound over to Court at Southold."

7 July 1749: "they killed a Porpoise in ye River here yesterday with Guns Canoos & boats. 500 Guns they Say fired at him before they killed him. I saw him Stretcht out on ye floor in a warehouse 8 foot & 1/2 long."

29 May 1750: "Josha killd above 20 Pidgeons. they are very plenty in Rogers's orchard Eating the Canker worms who have eat the Trees bare."

* * *

Samuel Dexter, Dedham, Massachusetts minister, goes hunting, 20 December 1722, in [Dexter], "Diary of Rev. Samuel Dexter," New England Historical and Geneaological Register, Vol. 13, No. 4 (October 1859), 308.

"I Diverted my self (I hope) with a Lawfull Recreation in Hunting with Mr Barrett. — A moderate Diversion may brighten and be very advantageous by Refreshing ye mind & so giving it ye greater Life in ye performance of Duty —but God always keep me from wasting my precious Time in too long and Unnecessary Receation."

* * *

Ebenezer Parkman, Westborough, Massachusetts minister, goes hunting, August 1723 and August 1726, in Francis G. Walett, ed., The Diary of Ebenezer Parkman, 1703-1782 (Worcester, Mass.: American Antiquarian Society, 1974), 4, 16.

28 August 1723: "I went out hunting with Mr. [Samuel] Barrett, a Young Faun having been Seen not long since—and Flocks of Turkeys. We Search'd the woods but Saw Nothing but Pigeons. We brought home Seven or Eight of Those."

22 August 1726: "I killed 8 Pidgeons (and how many more I know not) at a shot."

* * *

Harvard College law, circa 1734, in "College Laws, 1734, Chapter 8th, Concerning Miscellaneous Matters," in Harvard College Records, Part I. Corporation Records, 1636-1750, Publications of the Colonial Society of Massachusetts, Vol. 15 (Boston, 1925), 154.

"15. No Undergraduate shall keep a Gun or pistol in the College, or any where in Cambridge; nor shall he go a guning, fishing, or Scating over deep waters, without leave from the President or one of the Tutors, under the penalty of three Shillings. And if any scholar shall fire a Gun or pistol, within the College walls Yard, or near the College; he shall be fined not exceeding ten Shillings; or be admonishe[d] degraded or expelled, according to the Aggravation of the Offence."

* * *

John Adams, Massachusetts lawyer, politician, and later United States President, recalls his hunting during his boyhood, circa 1740s, in [Adams], "The Autobiography of John Adams," in Lyman H. Butterfield, ed., Diary and Autobiography of John Adams, Volume 3. Diary, 1782-1804, Autobiography Part One To October 1776 (Cambridge, Mass.: Harvard University Press, 1962), 257-259; and John Adams to Skelton Jones, 11 March 1809, reprinted in Adrienne Koch and William Peden, eds., The Selected Writings of John and John Quincy Adams (New York: Alfred A. Knopf, 1946), 153.

"And I spent my time as idle Children do in making and sailing boats and Ships upon the Ponds and Brooks, in making and flying Kites, in driving hoops, playing marbles, playing Quoits, Wrestling, Swimming, Skaiting and above all in shootng, to which

Diversion I was addicted to a degree of Ardor which I know not that I ever felt for any other Business, Study or Amusement.

"My Enthusiasm for Sports and Inattention to Books, allarmed my father, and he frequently entered into conversation with me upon the Subject.... To this School I went, where I was kindly treated, and I began to study in Earnest. My father soon observed the relaxation of my Zeal for my Fowling Piece, and my daily encreasing Attention to my Books."

"I was about nine or ten years old at that time and soon learn'd the use of the gun and became strong enough to lift it. I used to take it to school and leave it in the entry and the moment it was over went into the field to kill crows and squirrels and I tried to see how many I could kill: at last Mr. Cleverly found this out and gave me a most dreadful scolding and after that I left the gun at an old woman's in the neighborhood. I soon became large enough to go on the marshes to kill wild fowl and to swim and used to beg so hard of my father and mother to let me go that they at last consented and many a cold boisterous day have I pass'd on the beach without food waiting for wild fowl to go over —often l*ying* in wait for them on the cold ground— to hide myself from them. I cared not what I did if I could but get away from school, and confess to my shame that I sometimes play'd truant."

"17. Under my first Latin master, who was a churl, I spent my time in shooting, skating, swimming, flying kites, and every boyish exercise and diversion I could invent. Never mischievous. Under my second master, who was kind, I began to love my books and neglect my sports."

* * *

James Birket, West Indies merchant and sea captain, goes shooting in Connecticut, 4 October 1750, in [Birket], *Some Cursory Remarks Made by James Birket in His Voyage to North America, 1750-1751* (New Haven: Yale University Press, 1916), 32.

"Meantime my Fellow Traveller & Self, went out a Shooting Kill^d some Squirrels and some very pretty birds called Marsh quails Something bigger then a field fare and fine Eatg...."

* * *

James Parker, Shirley, Massachusetts farmer, hunts the local woods, November 1771, in [Parker], "Extracts from the Diary of James Parker of Shirley, Mass." New England Historical and Genealogical Register, Vol. 69 (January 1915), 15.

18 November 1771: "Capt Ivory & Capt Sawtell & fourteen more of us killed in all about 75 Squarreels & Potteridges then we had a set Down at Mr Ivorys."

* * *

John Boyle, Boston printer and merchant, recounts nearby hunting accidents, January and July 1773, in [Boyle], "Boyle's Journal of Occurrences in Boston, 1759-1778," New England Historical and Genealogical Register, Vol. 84 (October 1930), 362, 364.

20 January 1773: "Daniel Burrell and Marshall Lincoln two young men belonging to Hingham being a gunning in a small Canoe off Cohasset Rocks, the Canoe overset and they were both drowned."

24 July 1773: "Henry Knox, Bookseller, being a Gunning on one of the Islands, in firing his Piece it split, and tore his hand in such a Manner that tis feared he will lose it."

* * *

Bayze Wells, Farmington, Connecticut soldier, notes the hunting on the way to Quebec, early August 1775, in [Wells], "Journal of Bayze Wells of Farmington, May, 1775–February, 1777 At the Northward and in Canada," in "Orderly Book and Journals Kept by Connecticut Men While Taking Part in the American Revolution, 1775–1778," *Collections of the Connecticut Historical Society,* Vol. 7 (Hartford: Connecticut Historical Society, 1899), 247.

Early August, 1775: "major Shot a moos through but Could no Get him...."

* * *

Jeremiah Greenman, Rhode Island soldier, in Maine, 3 October 1775, in [Jeremiah Greenman], *Diary of a Common Soldier in the American Revolution, 1775-1783. An Annotated Edition of the Military Journal of Jeremiah Greenman,* ed. by Robert C. Bray and Paul E. Bushnell (DeKalb, Ill.: Northern Illinois University Press, 1978), 14.

"...one of Capt. hendricks Company killed a yong mo[o]se waing 200 wait."

* * *

John Joseph Henry, Pennsylvania rifleman, on hunting in Maine, October 1775, in Henry, "Campaign against Quebec," in Kenneth Roberts, comp., *March to Quebec. Journals of the Members of Arnold's Expedition* (New York: Doubleday, Doran and Company, 1938), 322-323.

11 October 1775: "Hunger drove us along at a cautious but rapid rate. The sterility of the country above had afforded us no game, neither moose, bear, nor wolf: nothing in short but the diver and a red pine squirrel, which was too small and quick to be killed by a bullet. These squirrels did not much exceed our striped ground squirrel. About dusk the lieutenant's canoe, four hundred yards before us, had within view turned a sharp point of land, when we heard the crack of a rifle, and presently another and a huzza. Apprehending an attack from an enemy, we pulled hard to be enabled to support our friends. In a moment or two, observing them pulling for the north shore, which was steep, we looked up for the enemy. Good Heavens! what a sight! We saw a moose-deer falling on top of the bank. A cry of exultation seemed to burst the narrow valley of the river. Steele had struck the deer in the flank, as it was leaving the water, but it had sprung up the bank with agility. Wheeler, with better fortune for us all, pierced its heart as it arrived at the top. Seeing this, you can scarcely imagine the celerity of our movements. We were ashore in a moment. A fire was kindled —the secondary guide cut off the nose and upper lip of the animal, instantly, and had it on the fire. What a feast! But we were prudent. We sat up all night, selecting the fat and tit-bits—frying, roasting, boiling and broiling. Towards morning we slept a few hours, absolutely careless of the consequences. We knew that we had arrived in a land where game was plentiful, and there were no foes superior to our number, to oppose us."

12 October 1775: " We rose after sunrise, and began, according to practice, to examine and prepare our guns. Prepared, mine was placed against a tree; my duty, in course, was of the culinary kind. George Merchant, my coadjutor, had gone to the river for water. He ran back, seized his own gun, and intimated that a bull moose was swimming across the river towards the camp. We jumped to our arms —it so happened that my station was rearward. The enormous animal was coming towards us, and not more than fifty paces off, his head and horns only above water. The sight was animating. Wheeler and some others fired at his head, but without effect. The extreme desire they had to

possess so noble a prey, probably caused a tremor of the hand, or that part of his body was impenetrable to or small balls, which is most likely. The moose turned and swam to the opposite bank. Having got to the verge of the river, his emerging was awaited. My ball struck precisely where it ought to kill. The huge animal rose the bank by several boggling leaps, but seemed unknowing which way to run. We thought he would fall. Wheeler, and some others, getting into the canoes, pursued him by his blood half a mile. When Wheeler returned he overloaded me with praises for the accuracy of the shot, and was confident that the deer was killed. We had no time to spare. We feasted till noon, and in the intermediate moments culled for entrails for the fat: we even broke the bones and extracted the marrow, under the full persuasion that food of an oily nature is one of the strongest mainstays of human life. Of this principle, if we had a doubt, we were shortly afterwards most irrefragably convinced. We departed from our camp joyously, untortured by the fear of starving; our canoe sunk deep by the weight of our venison. Running some miles and suddenly doubling a point, we saw a large grey wolf sitting on his haunches —he was fired at, but the distance was too great. He escaped. Looking down the river we saw a moose swimming from the main to an island; it was soon brought down. It proved to be young —of about 300 weight. Its ears and flanks were much torn by the wolf. It constituted veal in our larder."

* * *

Abner Stocking, Connecticut soldier, on moose-hunting in Maine, 3 October 1775, in Stocking, "Journal of Abner Stocking As Kept by Himself, During His Long and Tedious March Through the Wilderness to Quebec, Until His Return to His Native Place," in Kenneth Roberts, comp., *March to Quebec. Journals of the Members of Arnold's Expedition* (New York: Doubleday, Doran and Company, 1938), 549.

"One of the riflemen of Captain Hendricks' company this day killed a young Moose, which weighed about 200 lbs."

* * *

Colonel Frye Bayley, Vermont officer, goes moose-hunting near Peacham, Vermont, 2 March 1776, in [Bayley], "Col. Frye Bayley's Reminiscences," in *The Upper Connecticut. Narratives of its Settlement and its Part in the American Revolution,* 2 vols., Vol. 2 (Montpelier, Vt.: Vermont Historical Society, 1943), 31-32.

"In our route we discovered signs of moose. About the 2d of March, Abiel and myself went to Peacham, killed 4 moose & brought the meat to my house in Peacham."

* * *

John Allan, American colonel, on moose-hunting in eastern Maine, July and August 1777, in [Allan], "Allan's Journal" and "Col. Allan's Report on the Indian Tribes, in 1793" in Frederick Kidder, ed., *Military Operations in Eastern Maine and Nova Scotia during the Revolution Chiefly Compiled from the Journals and Letters of Colonel John Allan* (Albany: Joel Munsell, 1867), 119-120, 123, 131.

20 July 1777: "Early this morning a large Moose passed with great speed through our camp, the Indians and dogs in pursuit, but did not come up with him."

21 July 1777: "Provisions very scarce—Lewis killed a Moose this morning, which proved of much service."

23 July 1777: "Canoes when about a third of the lake over, went ashore where we found old Pierre Joe, who had killed two moose and wounded a third,...."

31 July 1777: "When in the great Lake, discovered a large moose which we fired at and wounded, but did not get him—...."

23 August 1777: "They [Maine indigenous people] earnestly desired to repossess the once peaceful abodes,...where their hunt was crowned with success in the spoil of the numerous herds of animals that swarm in their woods."

* * *

Joseph Joslin, Jr., South Killingly, Connecticut teamster, on local hunting, November, 1777, in [Joslin], "Journal of Joseph Joslin Jr. of South Killingly A Teamster in the Continental Service, March 1777–August 1778," in "Orderly Book and Journals Kept by Connecticut Men While Taking Part in the American Revolution, 1775-1778," *Collections of the Connecticut Historical Society,* Vol. 7 (Hartford: Connecticut Historical Society, 1899), 333 and 335.

4 November 1777: "...and now Clemmons and herrick is gone hunting Squrrels...."

28 November 1777: " I Shot at a Partridge...."

* * *

Benjamin Gilbert, Brookfield, Massachusetts sergeant, on hunting in central Massachusetts, February 1778, and in the lower Hudson River valley, September, October, and November 1778, and January 1779, in Rebecca D. Symmes, ed., *A Citizen-Soldier in the American Revolution. The Diary of Benjamin Gilbert in Massachusetts and New York* (Cooperstown, N.Y.: New York State Historical Association, 1980), 24, 25, 37, 38, 40-41, 44.

4 February 1778: "in the fore noon I went a Gunning and Killed nothing."

6 February 1778: "A fair Morning. I went a gunning. Killed one Squariel with Shot and k'd two with a single Ball."

7 February 1778: "At Night I went for Patridges but got none."

25 September, 1778: "Sjt. Wheler, Doty and Wilder went a Hunting and kild a Dozen Pigeons."

26 September 1778: "Cloudy weather. I made shot. We Dined on the Pigeons they Killed Yesterday. In the after noon Serjt. Wheeler & I went a Hunting and got 5 pigeons."

28 September 1778: "I went aguning in the afternoon and Wilder and I got four pigeons."

30 September 1778: "I went aguning and killed a number of Squirells...."

2 October 1778: "Serjt. Wheeler & I went out aguning and Killed seven pigeons. My gun Kicked me and made my lip swell very bad. A coming back I sold my Gun for fourteen Dollers."

3 October 1778: "Serjt. Wheeler went aguning and killed three pigeons."

5 October 1778: "Serjt. Wheeler went a Guning and killed Six Squirls."

28 October 1778: "I was some better. I took Capt Hoyts Gun and went a Gunning but saw no Game."

10 November 1778: "In the after noon I went a Hunting Partriages but Killed none."

12 November 1778: "In the after noon Lt Hooker and I went a Hunting but got nothing."

27 January 1779: "Just at sunsett I went for Partriges, but got none."

* * *

Caleb Bingham, American writer, narrates a moose hunt in Vermont in February 1778, in [Bingham], *The Hunters, or the Sufferings of Hugh and Francis in the Wilderness. A True Story* (Hanover, N.H.: Dartmouth Publications, 1954 [1814]), 17-45.

"ABOUT the year 1776, there lived in the city of Montreal a respectable merchant by the name of Holmes. This gentleman had a favourite son named Hugh; of whose education he was very solicitous, and spared no pains or expense to procure him the best instructors the country afforded. The boy was then about twelve years of age, and very promising as to his appearance and attainments. At this time, one of the tutors of Dartmouth College, in New Hampshire, happended to visit at his father's house; and being struck with the appearance of the lad, invited his father to send him home with him, to pursue his education in that seminary. It being troublesome times, and the schools of Montreal not in a very flourishing state, he readily complied. Hugh was accordingly entered at the grammar school connected with the College, and made rapid progress in his learning; being beloved by his preceptors and all his schoolfellows.

"At this time, there was also at the same school an Indian youth from the tribe of St. François, in Canada, by the name of Francis. These lads, coming from the same province, and from places not far distant, contracted a great attachment for each other. Francis was a descendant from Mrs. Williams, who was captivated in her childhood, at Deerfield, Massachusetts, in 1704; and was married and spent her days among the Indians. He was an amiable youth, and made great proficiency in learning. They were in the same class, and were seldom separate from each other at their pastimes. They were both fond of hunting, and spent many of their leisure hours in the woods together. The Indian was four years the oldest, and of course was always pilot in these excursions.

"On the thirteenth of February, 1778, Hugh and Francis petitioned the President, the venerable Dr. [Eleazar] Wheelock, founder of the institution, for permission to go into the wilderness, for five or six days, to hunt the moose, which were said to be plenty, and easily taken at that season. The guardian of the youths addressed them on the occasion as follows: 'My children, I cannot find it in my heart to refuse your request, though I fear the undertaking is too great fior your years and experience. You are good boys; you have studied faithfully, and have been obedient. You may go, and my blessing attends you. Venture not too far into the desert, and do not outstay your time. Remember your prayers daily; and if you tarry over the sabbath, I charge you not to hunt, or recreate yourselves on that sacred day. The Lord be with you in all your ways, and return you in safety to your friends.'

"The next day, they provided themselves with a blanket each, a gun, a hatchet, snow-shoes, provision, &c. Of the latter they took enough for three days only, because they expected to live chiefly upon the game they should kill. Thus equipped, they set forth on their journey. They crossed the Connecticut river at Hanover, and steered their course northwesterly into the then thick and gloomy forests of Vermont. In this part of the country the trees are large, compact, and of immense height. The lofty pines, hemlocks, spruce, and other evergreens, with their spreading branches, almost hide the sun, even in winter, from the traveller's eye. Our young hunters did not reach, on the first day, beyond the frontier inhabitants; but took up their lodging in the last log hut; where they experienced that hospitality, usually found among the poor, in new-settled countries.

"The next morning, they rigged on their *snow-shoes*, and took leave of their friendly host. If the reader be unacquainted with this sort of shoes, I would inform him, that they are in shape and size similar to a kite: an oval bow of wood, interwoven with leather thongs. They are light, and buoy up the wearer on the surface of the snow, into which he would otherwise sink so deep as to prevent his progress. At this time the snow was five feet deep, and our hunters could not move a step without them. But they knew how to use them, and could pursue their course with ease. As their load was heavy, they grew weary towards the close of the day, and began to prepare for the night, before the darkness commenced.

"Reader, how do you think this was done, in this cold climate, at this season of the year? I will tell you. They first made with their hatchet a kind of shovel, with which they dug away the snow to the ground. Then they cut hemlock or spruce boughs, and stuck them all around the spot, fastening the tops together, and forming a sort of booth, or *wigwam*. They also covered the ground with boughs for a bed; gathered a large quantity of dry wood; kindled a great fire by means of their gun, before the door of their wigwam; then laid themselves down and slept quietly; rising in turns, however, once in an hour, to recruit their fire. In this manner did thesse youthful friends pass the second and third night; regardless of danger, and meeting with no unusual occurrence. The weather was cold, but pleasant; and they had hitherto met with no game.

"The courage and perseverance of these lads is surprizing; and it is almost incredible to find them penetrating further and further into the unknown desert, instead of retracing their steps, and seeking once more their friends fire-sides. The enterprize was bold in the first instance, especially for such children; and it hardly to be supposed, that those who had the care of them ever suspected they would dare to push it to such an extremity. Their friends probably concluded that one night would be a sufficient seasoning for them, and they would willingly return in the course of a day or two. But they were not so easily intimidated. They had an object in view, which they thought laudable; and they were determined to accomplish it.

"They had now arrived on the ground, where they expected to find moose in abundance; but they had as yet seen none, nor any signs of them. And to their unspeakable grief, their provisions were all exhausted, and they began to be pinched with hunger. They wandered nearly all the next day in this forlorn condition, expecting soon to perish with want. Just before midnight, they espied the skeleton of a moose, which some hunter had probably shot; from the bones of which the wild beasts had torn all the flesh. The sagacity of the Indian soon found means to turn this unpromising skeleton to a good account. He broke the dry bones between two stones; and from the marrow contained within them they made a comfortable repast.

"The next day, to their great joy, they discovered a large moose, endeavouring to make his escape from them through the great depth of snow. It was all in vain. He could not run so fast as the Indian on his snow-shoes; who soon overtook him, and despatched him with his hatchet. They skinned him; took as much of his flesh as they could carry, with the skin, and marched forward. On this they feasted, after encamping for the night. They would have been glad indeed of a little salt, and bread; but they were very contented, and thankful to Providence for this rich bounty.

"The next day, about noon, they came to a small river, which they wished to cross. Hugh had all this time carried a long carving knife, without a sheath, hanging to his belt by a string. Francis had remonstrated to him, and warned him of his danger. He was advised to guard the point of the knife with a piece of wood. But he was only a child, and did not take heed. They found the trunk of a tree lying across the stream. They attempted to cross upon it. The log was rotten; it broke, and plunged them both into the river! What was the agony of Hugh, what was the horror of Francis, when in dragging his strangled companion to the shore, he found the naked blade of this knife sticking through the thickest part of his thigh, just below the hip!

"Figure to yourself, reader, the forlorn and hopeless situation of these hapless youths! The weather freezing cold; they drenched in water; the one to all appearances mrotally wounded; he hardly fourteen years of age; the other only eighteen; buried in the depths of a howling wilderness, full thirty miles from their friends, and without the least hope of succour from any mortal hand! In this trying our, nothing short of an overruling Providence could save them. The arm of the Almighty was stretched forth to their relief. Francis had the soul of humanity, and the fortitude of a hero. He loved his companion, as Jonathan loved David. He gently drew the steel from the wound; took the lovely youth in his arms; carried him, all streaming with blood, a few rods from the fatal spot; laid him down on the snow; and with all diligence, set about build- ing a fire, and constructing a booth. As soon as it was finished, he placed his suffer- ing companion within it; tore off a piece of his shirt; sought for some balsam of the fir tree; and bound up the wound in the best possible manner.

"Neither Hugh nor Francis got any sleep that night. The wound grew more and more painful; and to add to their other afflictions, the wolves howled around their camp in the most terrific manner, and threatened every moment to devour them. Francis fired his gun at them several times; and endeavoured to sooth his companion by his un- remitted attentions, and encouraging conversation. In the course of two or three days, the thigh and leg of the patient were swelled to an enormous size; and poor Hugh expected nothing but immediate dissolution. His amiable partner was of the same opin- ion; but in pity he concealed it from his friend. The wolves continued their hideous howlings every night; and Francis was confident that he had frequently heard the tre- mendous yell of a *catamount*. Once, by the light of the fire, he saw his glaring eyeballs, within a few yards of the camp, and expected they should both immediately become his prey. But, firing his piece at him, he severely wounded him; and he ran off, yell- ing, and nevermore returned. Francis concealed from his friend that he had ever seen this frightful beast. The howling of the wolves he was accustomed to hear; and he thought the shot was at them.

"After their stock of moose meat was gone, Francis proposed to Hugh to go in search of more game. But the latter would not consent to be left alone. It was in vain also that he proposed to return to the nearest inhabitants for help. Hugh said he should certainly die if left alone. However, Francis, seeing they should starve, if he did not seek food, stole away early one morning; and after travelling two or three miles from the camp, he fell in with a flock of moose, out of which he soon killed three with his hatchet; the snow being so deep that they could not run from him. It is observable that these animals, during a great depth of snow, herd together in a grove of spruce, which they live upon for the time being, treading the snow hard under their feet, like neat cattle in a farmer's barn yard. I have known thirteen killed in such a situation, within a few rods of each other.

"Francis skinned his game, loaded himself with the meat, and hastened to his friend. It was noon before he arrived. At a great distance, his feelings were touched with the lamentation of the disconsolate Hugh; who, believing himself utterly forsaken, was pouring out his soul in such accents as these, 'Lord have mercy on me, a poor forsaken wretch! Have pity, Lord, when no mortal arm can save!' At this moment, Francis sprang in, and caught him in his arms.

"After a while, the wound suppurated, and the swelling began to subside. Francis returned to his carcasses, several times, as they had occasion for a supply of meat. Till at length, growing weary, he proposed to carry his patient to the game, instead of bringing the game to him. Accordingly he built a new hut near the three carcases, in a superior style to the other; covering it partly with bark; and taking Hugh on his shoulders, in the course of a few hours, he landed him safely in his new habitation. The next trip, he transported all his household furniture. They had now meat enough; some of which was hung up to dry; but no bread, no salt, and no pot or kettle to boil their meat, or make a broth for the sick. Poor Hugh would often exclaim, 'I would give the wealth of the Indies for a kettle to make me some broth.' He was emaciated to a skeleton; his pains continuing to be excruciating. Al the linen they had on their backs they appropriated to dressing the wound; and still it was but very little better when March commenced. At this time, the maple trees began to produce their sap. Francis dug out a woode dish with his hatchet and knife, and tapped one of these trees; the juice of which, caught in the dish, afforded them a delicious beverage. Sometimes Francis would kill a patridge; which, broiled on the coals, was a great luxury. Every Saturday, the wood and provision were conscientiously prepared for the Sabbath; which day it is believed was religiously observed, in compliance with the injunction of the President. Francis was unwearied in his attentions to his friend, by day and by night. His genius contrived to convert the moose-skins into soft and pliable leather. This was done by means of ashes, barks, &c. and by scraping them, with great industry, a considerable time, with the sharp edge of a piece of hard wood. After this, they answered a valuable purpose for a bed and covering.

"Towards the latter part of March, Francis began to grow very uneasy. The meat which he had dried and smoked was nearly expended. The wolves and the weather had destroyed the carcasses of the three moose; and it was seldom he could leave Hugh long enough to hunt with any prospect of success. He ardently urged his friend to permit him to go to the nearest inhabitants in quest of assistance. Hugh, who was utterly unable to stand alone, and whose powers of mind were much weakened by the excessive pains in his body, could not be persuaded to consent. At length, however, about the first of April, the Indian, seeing nothing but destruction before them, if they tarried longer in these dreary wilds, told Hugh he would commence the journey with him on his back. To this the exhausted invalid consented. Accordingly, the next morning, the second day of April, Francis collected the remainder of his provisions, his four moose skins, his gun, two pairs of snow-shoes, two blankets, and his hatchet; and with all these on his back, he commenced his march towards home. After travelling a mile or two, he laid down his load, returned and took Hugh on his shoulders, and carried him to the same place. Thus he continued, taking each load alternately, till towards night, when being completely exhausted, they encamped. This being Saturday, Francis prepared his fuel, as usual, for the Lord's day; believing that it would be a profanation to pursue his journey on the morrow.

"Here my readers may be disposed to smile at the simplicity of these unfortunate youths. But let such remember, that though thier [sic] scruples were groundless in this instance, yet their conduct shows the tenderness of their consciences, and their amiable dispositions. On Monday they continued their journey in the same manner. The snow was now chiefly melted away, appearing only in spots. They had a tedious mountain to climb, which made it excessively fatiguing for the generous hearted Francis. He, however, continued his labours until Wednesday night, encamping each day as usual, before dark; when, coming to the foot of another high mountain, his spirits sunk within him, and he yielded. Their provisions were gone, except a patridge, which they ate for their supper. The next morning, Francis told his friend, it was impossible for him to carry him any further; and proposed again to leave him, and go himself for help. Hugh roared aloud at this; and began to crawl up the mountain upon his hands and knees. This he continued to do, until his hands and knees were all worn to the quick, and his track was marked with gore. However, he reached the top of the mountain, and his courage increased. Here Francis clomb a tree, to see what discoveries he could make. He had no sooner reached the top, than with accents of inexpressable joy, he cried out, '*I espy a smoke!*' He judged there must be a house within three miles. This gave them courage and strength; anfd they descended the mountain with rapidity, Francis again carrying Hugh part of the way on his back. And before sunset, they had the unspeakable happiness to enter a log hut, in the confines of Royalton, fourteen miles from the College. Here they met with a kind reception, and had a comfortable night's rest.

"The next morning, the good man, whose name I have forgotten, offered them the only horse he had; which, indeed, was but a poor one, and without saddle or bridle. The latter they supplied with a strip of their leather; and spreading the moose skins upon his back, they both mounted, and set forward. Towards evening of the same day, they entered the village, whence they had departed nearly two months before. Their singular appearance attracted universal attention, and they were soon surrounded by a crowd. Such was their emaciated state, being nothing but skeletons, and scarcely a rag of clothing remaining on them, that it was sometime before their old acquaintances could be persuaded to own them. The reason they had not been sought for, was, the full persuasion of all, that, not having heard from their friends in Canada for several years, on accunt of the war, and having a strong propensity to visit their homes, they had attempted to cross the wilderness for that purpose, and that all search would be in vain.

"The venerable President wept for joy at the sight of his long lost children; and all welcomed their return. The same year, they both entered the freshman class in the College, and pursued their studies to advantage. The year following, the Indian's propensity to visit his tribe led him to desert his station, to which he never afterwards returned. The British gave him a lieutenant's commission, and he made some depredations upon the frontiers; but he always spared to shed blood, and treated his prisoners with humanity. He is now a popular chief of his tribe, and uses great exertions to have his people instructed in religion and the arts.

"Let those who are accustomed to depreciate the character of Indians, and who are more disposed to extirpate them from the face of the earth, than to civilize and christianize them, view the conduct of this child of the desert. They will be able to produce but few examples, in civilized life, more worthy of imitation, than that of the heroic and benevolent Francis.

"Hugh pursued his studies, and graduated in the year 1782. Soon after which, he returned to Montreal; but, alas! how transitory are all sublunary things! His mother was no more! His father had failed in business; his house was burned; and himself reduced to poverty! Notwithstanding, by his own industry and economy, Hugh acquired a handsome estate; and is now the respectable head of a numerous family, on the river Thames, in Upper Canada, near where Gen. [William Henry] Harrison captured Gen. Proctor's army, in 1813."

* * *

Jean-François Landolphe, a French naval captain, describes hunting near New London, Connecticut in January? February? 1780, in Marvin R. Cox, ed., "A French Sea Captain in Revolutionary Connecticut. Extracts from the Memoirs of J.F. Landolphe," Connecticut Historical Society Bulletin, Vol. 47, No. 2 (April 1982), 46.

"These activities [dances and sleighrides] proved very salutary during the cold weather, and we managed to get some hunting in as well. Since hare and partridge are very common in that locality, we bagged large quantities of these. The partridge in these parts is different from its counterpart in Europe, in that it whistles and perches in trees; aside from that the plumage is the same."

* * *

Marquis de Chastellux, French officer, discusses hunting in Lebanon, Connecticut, January 1782, in [de Chastellux], *Travels in North-America, in the Years 1780, 1781, and 1782, by the Marquis de Chastellux,* 2nd ed., 2 vols., Vol. 1 (London: G.G.J. and J. Robinson, 1787), 456-457.

6 January 1782: "But I am got very far from America, where I muft return however, if it be only to hunt a few fquirrels. The Duke de Lauzun entertained me with this diverfion, which is much in fafhion in this country. Thefe animals are large, and have a more beautiful fur than thofe in Europe; like ours, they are very adroit in flipping from tree to tree, and clinging fo clofely to the branches as to become almoft invifible. You frequently wound them, without their falling; but that is a flight inconvenience, for you have only to call or fend for fomebody, who applies the hatchet to the tree, and prefently knocks it down. As fquirrels are not rare, you will conclude them, and very juftly, that trees are very common. On returning from the chace, I dined at the Duke de Lauzun's,...."

NEW JERSEY, NEW YORK, PENNSYLVANIA

David Pietersz de Vries, Dutch ordnance-master, in New Netherland, December 1632, January 1633, October 1634, and circa 1642, in [de Vries], *Short Historical and Journal notes of Several Voyages Made in the four parts of the World, namely, Europe, Africa, Asia, and America* (Alckmaer? Brekegeest?: Symon Cornelisz, 1655), reprinted in Cornell Jaray, ed., *Historic Chronicles of New Amsterdam, Colonial New York and Early Long Island, First Series,* Empire State Historical Publications Series No. 35 (Port Washington, N.Y.: Ira J. Friedman, 1968), 23, 28, 63, 104, 110.

7 December 1632: "As I had a cousin of mine with me from Rotterdam, named Heyndrick de Liefde, and as a large gull was flying over our heads, I told him to shoot

at it once, as he had a fowling-piece with him, and he being a good shot on the wing, brought it down."

January, 1633: "Went out daily, while here, to shoot. Shot many wild turkeys, weighing from thirty to thirty-six pounds. Their great size and very fine flavour are surprising."

15 October 1634: "We caught a hog which had its navel on the back, and his gunner shot thirty-three teal at one shot, at which I was astonished."

Circa 1642: "I then returned home, and on my way, shot a wild turkey weighing thirty pounds, and brought it along with me."

Circa 1642: [after listing numerous waterfowl and game birds] "Nothing is wanted but good marksmen with powder and shot.... I have seen one of our Netherlanders kill, in the commander's orchard at Fort Amsterdam, eighty-four of these birds [pigeons] at one shot. They are good-tasted, and similar to the thrushes in Fatherland. I have also seen, at different times, thirty to thirty-four pigeons killed at one shot, but they are not larger than turtle-doves,...."

* * *

The Dutch Director and Council, New Amsterdam, prohibit hunting on the Sabbath, 29 April 1648, reprinted in Esther Singleton, *Dutch New York* (New York: Benjamin Blom, 1968), 200.

"On the Lord's day of rest, usually called Sunday, no person shall be allowed to do the ordinary and customary labors of his calling, such as Sowing, Mowing, Building, Sawing Wood, Smithing, Bleeching, Hunting, Fishing, or any works allowable on other days, under the penalty of One Pound Flemish, for each person so offending; much less any idle or unallowed exercises and sports, such as Drinking to excess, frequenting Inns or Taphouses, Dancing, Card-playing, Tick-tacking, Playing at ball, Playing at bowls, Playing at nine-pins, taking jaunts in Boats, Wagons, or Carriages, before, between, or during Divine Service, under the penalty of a double fine (Two Pounds, Flemish); and in order to prevent all such accidents and injuries, there shall be a fine of Twelve Guilders for the first offence; Twenty-four Guilders for the second offence; and arbitrary correction for the third offence; the One-third for the Officers; One-third for the Poor; and the remaining One-third for the Prosecutor."

* * *

Jan Baptist van Rensselaer, New Netherlands, discusses hunting dogs, falconry, and guns in van Rensselaer to Jeremias van Rensselaer, September 1651, in A.J.F. van Laer, trans. and ed., *Correspondence of Jeremias van Rensselaer, 1651-1674* (Albany, N.Y.: University of the State of New York, 1932), 9.

"In reply, write me how everything is at home and how the dogs and the birds are, and take good care that the spotted dog does not get lost. My falcon came over in good shape. He is still keen and alert and is king of all New Netherland. He now dares to take a chance against one twice his size, but he soon gives up. Give my compliments to the *peltier* [furrier] and tell him that I shall expect him here with his king's gun [prize gun won in a contest as king of the marksmen], to shoot some geese, for which I have had a yawl made."

* * *

Peter Stuyvesant, New Amsterdam governor, prohibits hunting on the Sabbath, 27 January 1656, reprinted in Esther Singleton, *Dutch New York* (New York: Benjamin Blom, 1968), 302.

"[Sunday is] a day of fasting and prayer for God's blessing protection and prosperity in trade and agriculture but principally for a righteous and thankful use of his blessings and benefits. The which better to observe and practice with greater unanimity, We interdict and forbid, on the aforesaid day of Fasting and Prayer during Divine Service, all labour, Tennis-playing Ball-playing, Hunting, Fishing, Travelling, Ploughing, Sowing, Mowing and other unlawful games as Gambling and Drunkenness, on pain of arbitrary correction and punishment already enacted against the same."

* * *

Daniel Denton, British traveler, writes with enthusiasm about potential hunting in New York, circa 1670, in Denton, *A Brief Defcription of New-York, Formerly Called New-Netherlands* (London: John Hancock, 1670), 18-19.

"And how prodigal, if I may fo fay, hath Nature been to furnifh the Countrey with all forts of wilde Beafts and Fowle, which every one hath an intereft in, and may hunt at his pleafure; where befides the pleafure in hunting, he may furnifh his houfe with excellent fat Venifon, Turkies, Geefe, Heath-Hens, Cranes, Swans, Ducks, Pidgeons, and the like...."

* * *

John Sharpe, minister, hunts in Pennsylvania, September and October 1710, in [Sharpe], "Journal of Rev. John Sharpe," Pennsylvania Magazine of History and Biography, Vol. 40, No. 3 (1916), 295-296.

27 September 1710: "I went a shooting after dinner at the Mayors."

4 October 1710: "I went out a shooting."

23 October 1710: "Govr dined at the Mayors—I went out a shooting."

* * *

Warrant for hunting game by Thomas Stretch, governor of the Schuylkill Fishing Company, Pennsylvania, 29 September 1744, reprinted in *A History of the Schuylkill Fishing Company of the State in Schuylkill, 1732-1888* (Philadelphia: Members of the State in Schuylkill, 1889), 17-18.

"COLONY OF SCHUYLKILL, SS.

To _____

and all other Schuylkillians whom it may concern.

"WHEREAS great quantities of rabbits, squirrels, pheasants, partridges, and others of the game kind, have presumed to infest the coasts and territories of Schuylkill, in a wild, bold and ungovernable manner; THESE are therefore to authorize and require you, or any of you, to make diligent search for the said rabbits, squirrels, pheasants, partridges and others of the game kind, in all suspected places where they may be found, and bring the respective bodies of so many as you shall find, before the Justices, &c. at a general Court to be held on Thursday, the fourth day of October next, there to be proceeded against, as by the said court shall be adjudged; and for your or any of your so doing, this shall be sufficient *warrant*. Witness, myself, the twenty-ninth day of September, in the twelfth year of my Government, and year of our Lord, one thousand seven hundred and forty-four.

[L. S.]   THOMAS STRETCH."

* * *

John Schuyler, Bergen County, New Jersey landowner warns against hunting on his lands, circa 1749, reprinted in Esther Singleton, *Social New York under the Georges* (New York: D. Appleton and Company, 1902), 264.

"Whereas some persons have of late entered the park of the Subscriber, on New Barbadoes Neck, in the County of Bergen, and have there shot and killed some of my deer in said park. These are therefore to forbid all persons to enter into said park, or to carry a musket or firelock on any of my enclosed lands or meadows without my leave first obtained for so doing under the penalty of being prosecuted with the utmost rigour of the law."

* * *

J.C.B., French traveler, on turkey hunting at Presque Isle, Pennsylvania, April 1753, and deer-hunting near Presque Isle, March 1754, in [J.C.B.], *Travels in New France by J.C.B.,* ed. by Sylvester K. Stevens, Donald H. Kent, and Emma Edith Woods (Harrisburg, Penn.: The Pennsylvania Historical Commission, 1941), 33-34, 55.

24 April 1753: "The surroundings of Presque Isle abound in game of various species, such as elk, white-tail deer, mule deer, bear, swans, bustards, ducks, geese, turkeys, red partridges, and pigeons.

"The most frequent yet unusual hunting that I have seen in this place is for turkeys, which are as amusing as they are plentiful. It is usually done in the moonlight, by at least two or three persons. These birds habitually go in flocks, always on an elevation, so that they can readily take wing with a gradual flight; perhaps in case of a surprise. Usually they descend to the ground to drink only when night comes. They choose the tree tops with the most branches to perch on. There, they congregate beside each other, with as many on each branch as it will hold. Sometimes you will find nearly one hundred and fifty turkeys in the same tree.

"When you have located an area where the turkeys live, you approach silently as near as you can to the tree where they are perched. Without speaking or moving, the hunter then fires his gun, usually bringing down four or five turkeys. Those remaining do not fail to awaken at the sound. They then squawk and, if they hear no noise, go back to sleep. You shoot again, and the same thing happens until all are killed, or you find you have enough. If it happens that some turkeys fall, merely wounded, and run away, the hunters ought to let them escape, because those in the tree may otherwise become alarmed and take flight. Thus the hunters lose more. When you finally think you have enough, those killed are gathered up and carried to the canoe. This was brought as near as possible to the hunting ground. Otherwise it would be impossible to take many, since some of them weigh as much as thirty-five pounds. It is only by surprising them, that these birds are killed in daylight. If they are surprised and pursued on the ground, when they cannot fly because of their weight and lack of sufficient space, they use their feet to climb to an elevation with such speed that a dog can hardly follow them. When they are high enough, they take wing on the side toward an open space and fly far away."

25 March 1754: "As we were making a halt one day on the riverbank, while we were going down, we saw several of the white-tail deer and mule deer which abound in this country. I was one of four who seized a gun, intending to kill at least one. I had with me my dog; a very keen creature, full of vigor. When he found the deer scent, he took up the chase farther than he should have; for when it came time to embark, I called my dog without avail."

Isaac Zane, Pennsylvania missionary, recalls hunters in eastern Pennsylvania, 27 May 1758, in Joseph H. Coates, ed., "Journal of Isaac Zane to Wyoming," *Pennsylvania Magazine of History and Biography*, Vol. 30, No. 4 (1906), 420-421.

"and as it grew Dark there Come home 3 young men who had been a hunting & they brough Each of them a Dear with em & they gave us 2 quarters of venson—...."

* * *

Joseph Doddridge, Pennsylvania Episcopal minister, concerning hunting in western Pennsylvania, circa 1763-1783, in Doddridge, *Notes on the Settlement and Indian Wars of the Western Parts of Virginia and Pennsylvania from 1763 to 1783, inclusive, together with a Review of the State of Society and Manners of the First Settlers of the Western Country* (Pittsburgh: John S. Ritenour and William T. Lindsey, 1912), 123.

"A well grown boy at the age of twelve or thirteen years, was furnished with a small rifle and shot pouch. He then became a fort soldier and had his port hole assigned to him. Hunting squirrels, turkeys and raccoons soon made him expert in the use of his gun."

* * *

Samuel Smith, New Jersey historian, on local hunting, circa 1765, in Smith, *The History of the Colony of Nova-Cæsaria, or New-Jersey Containing An Account of Its First Settlement, Progressive Improvements, the Original and Present Constitution, and Other Events, to the Year 1721. With Some Particulars Since; and A Short View of Its Present-State*, 2 vols., Vol. 1 (Burlington, N.J.: James Parker, 1765), 112.

"As for venifon and fowls, we have great plenty: We have brought home to our houfes by the Indians, feven or eight fat bucks of a day; and fometimes put by as many; having no occafion for them;...."

* * *

Samuel Kirkland, Congregationalist missionary, and his brother go hunting in New York Province, February? early March? 1765, in Walter Pilkington, ed., *The Journals of Samuel Kirkland, Eighteenth-century Missionary to the Iroquois, Government Agent, Father of Hamilton College* (Clinton, N.Y.: Hamilton College, 1980), 12, 13.

"In the afternoon my younger Brother very pleasantly & with apparent affection proposed we should take our guns & go out a mile or two into the woods & kill partridges or squirrels. I readily complied....

"I spent the day in our cabbin, except walking out about an hour with my younger Brother to shoot a Squirrel or two."

* * *

Jacob Hiltzheimer, Philadelphia area farmer and politician, fox-hunts in the Philadelphia area, December 1765, January and December 1767, and on Long Island, October 1770, in Jacob Cox Parsons, ed., *Extracts from the Diary of Jacob Hiltzheimer* (Philadelphia: William Fell Company, 1893), 9, 10, 13, 14, 23-24.

23 December 1765: "Breakfasted at five o'clock at Mrs. Gray's, with Enoch Story, Samuel Morris, Dr. John Cox, Mr. Petit, John Cadwalader, and Levi Hollingsworth; then set out for Darby fox-hunting. The number of hunters was thirty, who by eleven o'clock, killed three foxes. Dined at Joseph Rudolph's, and at evening returned home with Hollingsworth. The other hunters remained over night for another hunt in the morning."

27 December 1765: "Set off this morning at five o'clock with Thomas Mifflin, Sam. Miles, Jacob Hollingsworth, and young Rudolph from my house; proceeded to Darby to meet the other gentlemen hunters; from there to Captain Coultas's house, and to the woods. About thirty-five gentlemen attended with thirty dogs, but no fox was secured."

20 January 1767: "Set off from Jonathan Humphrey's to a fox hunt with the following gentlemen: Zeb. Rudolph, Joseph Jones, Mr. Pallard, Cornelius Francis, Charles Willing, Sam. Morris, Anthony Morris, Richard Bache, and James Massey, huntsman. We afterward dined at Massey's house."

12 December 1767: "The gentlemen hunters let a fox loose at Centre Woods, which afforded an agreeable ride after the hounds till dark. The fox ran up a tree on the Schuykill side, and when Levi Hollingsworth climbed up after him, it jumped down and was killed."

26 December 1767: "From Rudolph's the following gentlemen, Samuel Miles, Levi Hollingsworth, Israel Morris, Joseph Jones, Samuel Nichols, Zebulon Rudolph, and Jeremiah Warder, went to Lower Tinicum fox hunting. There we were met by Charles, Richard, and James Willing and after riding about the woods until two o'clock, without the sign of a fox, we returned to Joseph Rudolph's and dined."

30 October 1770: "This morning a number of gentlemen had a fox hunt [on Long Island where he was visiting].

* * *

G. Taylor, English traveler, tells of hunting in eastern New York, late September?, 1? 2? October 1768, in Taylor, *A Voyage to North America, Perform'd by G. Taylor of Sheffield, Eng. in the Years 1768, and 1769* (Nottingham: S. Creswell, 1771), 86-88.

"The Swifs told us they were often vifited by the bear, efpecially in winter in a great ftorm, or when the *Indians* have purfued them; then they come to the plantations for food. Yet are feldom dangerous, except when very hungry or are wounded. 'We are glad (fays he) to fee them, becaufe they not only afford us diverfion in hunting, but food for our families. When the bear is near our habitation our dogs give us warning by their barking and uneafinefs. We have feveral neighbours within a mile or two; and when the alarm is given, we all go out in purfuit, armed with cutlaffes and fmall hatchets, the dogs leading the way. As foon as the dogs view him he flies; but they quickly come up with him, and a fierce engagement enfues, and continues till we come to their affiftance. We immediately furround him, fome laying heavy ftrokes upon his head with the hatchets, whilft others with cutleffes do much execution; fo that he rarely efcapes us. Whenever we apprehend any danger of his getting better, we take the advantage of climbing fome adjacent tree, and call off the dogs. The bear purfues us to the tree, and fiercely attempts to fcale it; which affords us an opportunity of chopping off his fore paws and knocking him on the head, fo that he drops to the ground and is foon difpatched.'...

"The old Gentleman was concluding his ftory of hunting the bear, when his daughter fteps in and tells her father there was a large flight of pigeons juft alighted below the houfe. Upon this, we all charged our pieces, and coming very near them (no lefs than fifteen or fixteen hudred in the flock) we agreed to fire together, when juft upon the wing. At the firft fire, with five guns, we brought down feventy-two. They alighted again at a fmall diftance, and the fecond time we fhot eighty-five."

* * *

Ann MacVicar Grant, an American lady, on hunting near Albany, New York, circa 1769, in *Memoirs of an American Lady. With Sketches of Manners and Scenery in America, as They Existed Previous to the Revolution,* 2 vols., Vol. 1 (London: Longman, Hurst, Rees, and Orme, 1808), 66-67, 70, 124, 201-203.

"Thefe youths were apt, whenever they could carry a gun, (which they did at a very early period,) to follow fome favourite negroe to the woods, and, while he was employed in felling trees, range the whole day in fearch of game, to the neglect of all intellectual improvement, and contract a love of favage liberty which might, and in fome inftances did, degenerate into licentious and idle habits. Indeed, there were three ftated periods in the year when, for a few days, young and old, mafters and flaves, were abandoned to unruly enjoyment, and neglected every ferious occupation for purfuits of this nature...

"If the morning be dry and windy, all the fowlers (that is every body) are disappointed, for then they [pigeons] fly fo high that no fhot can reach them; but in a cloudy morning the carnage is incredible; and it is fingular that their removal falls out at the times of the year that the weather (even in this ferene climate) is generally cloudy. This migration, as it paffed by, occafioned, as I faid before, a total relaxation from all employments, and a kind of drunken gaiety, though it was rather slaughter than fport; and, for above a fortnight, pigeons in pies and foups, and every way they could be dreffed, were the food of the inhabitants. Thefe were immediately fucceeded by wild geefe and ducks, which concluded the carnival for that feafon, to be renewed in September."

"Boys on the verge of manhood, and ambitious to be admitted into the hunting parties of the enfuing winter, exercifed themfelves in trying to improve their fkill in archery, by fhooting birds, fquirrels, and racoons. Thefe petty huntings helped to fupport the little colony in the neighbourhood, which however derived its principal fubfiftence from an exchange of their manufactures with the neighbouring family for milk, bread, and other articles of food."

"Like them [the indigenous people], they [early Euroamerican settlers] delighted in hunting; that image of war, which fo generally, where it is the prevalent amufement, forms the body to athletic force and patient endurance, and the mind to daring intrepidity. It was not alone the timorous deer or feeble hare that were the objects of their purfuit...." [settlers also had to protect their livestock and watch out for marauding indigenous people] "; and as a boy was not uncommonly trufted at nine or ten years of age with a light fowling-piece, which he soon learned to ufe with great dexterity, few countries could produce fuch dexterous markfmen, or perfons fo well qualified for conquering thofe natural obftacles of thick woods and fwamps, which would at once baffle the moft determined European."

* * *

Philip Vickers Fithian, tutor at Nomini Hall, on hunting near the Juniata River in Pennsylvania, August 1775, in Robert Greenhalgh Albion and Leonidas Dodson, eds., *Philip Vickers Fithian. Journal, 1775-1776, Written on the Virginia-Pennsylvania Frontier and in the Army around New York* (Princeton: Princeton University Press, 1934), 114.

22 August 1775: "The Men, for Exercise, play at Quoits, hunt Deer, Turkeys, Pheasants &c—...."

* * *

Nicholas Cresswell, British loyalist, notes his hunting in western Pennsylvania, July and September 1775, in Cresswell, *The Journal of Nicholas Cresswell, 1774-1777* (Port Washington, N.Y.: Kennikat Press, 1968, [1924]), 98, 113.

27 July 1775: "Went shooting and knocked down a Young Turkey."
11 September 1775: "About sundown Mr. A. called out, 'A Panther.' I looked about and saw it set in a tree about twenty yards from me. Fired at it on horseback and shot it through the neck. It is of a Brown colour and shaped like a cat, but much larger. It measured five foot nine inches from Nose end to Tail end. Camped and skinned the Panther. This exploit has raised me in N.esteem exceedingly, tho' I claim no merit from it, being merely accidental."

* * *

Jahiel Stewart, Massachusetts militiaman, hunting near Valcour Island in Lake Champlain, 1 November 1776, in [Stewart], "A Most Unsettled Time on Lake Champlain. The October 1776 Journal of Jahiel Stewart," ed. by Donald Wickman, Vermont History, Vol. 64, No. 2 (Spring 1996), 97.

"This Day I and whorfield and E Spalmon and Jorge Black Set out to go a hunting and just as we [came] out of the Breast work we met Some men that was out giting wood and Said thay See 3 or 4 fox on about 50 Rods from the Breast work and we hunted till about three a Clock but See no game...."

* * *

Bayze Wells, Farmington, Connecticut soldier, notes the hunting in eastern New York, December 1776, in [Wells], "Journal of Bayze Wells of Farmington, May, 1775–February, 1777 At the Northward and in Canada," in "Orderly Book and Journals Kept by Connecticut Men While Taking Part in the American Revolution, 1775-1778," *Collections of the Connecticut Historical Society*, Vol. 7 (Hartford: Connecticut Historical Society, 1899), 290.

9 December 1776: "I with Several others Went Down the Lake A hunting and had Poor Luck Killed Nothing."
10 December 1776: "...we took A morning hunt and had no Luck...."

* * *

Thomas Anburey, British officer, on pigeon shooting near Lake Champlain, 23 June 1777, in [Anburey], *Travels through the Interior Parts of America*, 2 vols., Vol. 1 (London: William Lane, 1791), 244-245.

"Thefe [pigeons] are moft excellent eating, and that you may form some idea as to their number, at one of our encampments, the men for one day wholly fubfifted on them; fatigued with their flight in croffing the lake, they alight upon the firft branch they can reach to: many are fo weary as to drop in the water, and are eafily caught; thofe that alight upon a bough being unable to fly again, the foldiers knock down with long poles.

"During the flights of thefe pigeons, which crofs this lake into Canada, and are continually flying about in large flocks, the Canadians find great amufement in fhooting them, which they do after a very fingular manner: in the day time they go into the woods, and make ladders by the fide of the tall pines, which the pigeons rooft on, and when it is dark they creep foftly under and fire up this ladder, killing them in great abundance; they then ftrike a light, and firing a knot of pitch pine, pick up thofe they have killed, and the wounded ones that are unable to fly.— During the flights of thefe pigeons, which generally laft three weeks or a month, the lower fort of Canadians moftly fubfift on them."

* * *

Jeduthan Baldwin, Brookfield, Massachusetts officer, squirrel-hunting in eastern New York, 10 November 1777, in Thomas Williams Baldwin, ed., *The Revolutionary Journal of Col. Jeduthan Baldwin, 1775-1778* (Bangor, Me.: The De Burians, 1906), 138.

"Hunting squirrils."

* * *

Samuel Dewees, Pennsylvania soldier, tells of hunting near the Lehigh River in Pennsylvania, circa 1778-1779, in John Smith Hanna, ed., *A History of the Life and Services of Captain Samuel Dewees, A Native of Pennsylvania, and Soldier of the Revolutionary and Last Wars* (Baltimore: Robert Neilson, 1844), 147.

Circa 1778-1779: "The Dutchman was fond of fowling, and often used an English gun belonging to the Colonel, the touch-hole of which was bushed with gold. There was a large pond (or mill-dam) on or near to his farm, and it was much visited by wild ducks. The Dutchman often rose before day and went out and laid an ambuscade and waited their approach. He being a good shot, would often kill numbers of them, and generally divided the spoils with the Colonel."

* * *

Luke Swetland, Pennsylvania captive, hunting among the Seneca in western New York, June 1779, in [Swetland], *A Narrative of the Captivity of Luke Swetland, in 1778 and 1779, among the Seneca Indians* (Waterville, N.Y.: James J. Guernsey, 1875), 22.

"Caught some eels, killed some hawks, some shitepokes and some muskrats, and I thought we lived exceedingly well."

* * *

Henry Dearborn, New Hampshire officer, on hunting in north central Pennsylvania, July 1779, in Lloyd A. Brown and Howard H. Peckham, eds., *Revolutionary War Journals of Henry Dearborn, 1775-1783* (Freeport, N.Y.: Books for Libraries Press, 1969 [1939]), 158-159, 162.

1 July 1779: "a number of us discover'd a fine buck to day on an Island which we surrounded & kill'd.—...."
4 July 1779: "—several dear & wild turkeys have been kill'd within a day or two with which this Country abounds.—...."
23 July 1779: "I went with several other Gentlemen 8 miles up the River, to an old settlement call'd Lachawanee. to fish & hunt dear—...."

* * *

James Norris, New Hampshire major, on deer-hunting near the Susquehanna River, Pennsylvania, 3 August 1779, in [Norris], "Journal of Major James Norris," in Frederick Cook, ed., *Journals of the Millitary Expedition of Major General John Sullivan against the Six Nations of Indians in 1779* (Freeport, N.Y.: Books for Libraries, 1972 [1887]), 228.

"Nothing remarkable happened thro this days march —the Deer seemd to be plenty on this ground—a large Fawn that lay Sulking in the Bushes alarmd with the noise of the Troops attempted to make his escape, but being intirely surrounded was taken without a wound—Affording great amusement to the Soldiers & an agreeable Viand to several of the Officers-"

* * *

William Rogers, Pennsylvania chaplain, notes the hunting near Wyalusing, Pennsylvania, 5 August 1779, in [Rogers], "Journal of Rev. William Rogers," in Frederick Cook, ed., *Journals of the Millitary Expedition of Major General John Sullivan against the Six Nations of Indians in 1779* (Freeport, N.Y.: Books for Libraries, 1972 [1887]), 258.

"The country hereabouts is excellent for hunting."

* * *

Marquis de Chastellux, French officer, discusses hunting near Rhinebeck, New York, December 1781, in [de Chastellux], *Travels in North-America, in the Years 1780, 1781, and 1782, by the Marquis de Chastellux*, 2nd ed., 2 vols., Vol. 1 (London: G.G.J. and J. Robinson, 1787), 364-365.

22 December 1781: "Some dogs of a beautiful kind moving about the houfe awakened my paffion for the chace; on afking Mr. Thomas what ufe he made of them, he told me that they were only for hunting the fox; that deer, ftags, and bears were pretty common in the country, but they feldom killed them in except in winter, either by tracing on the fnow, or by tracking them in the woods."

* * *

Philip van Cortlandt, New York brigadier general, on hunting in the Hudson River valley, spring, 1783, in [van Cortlandt], "Autobiography of Philip van Cortlandt," Magazine of American History, Vol. 2 (1878), 298.

"I set off, and arrived at the farm, at the mouth of Croton River, where I was joined in a short time by Captains Hamtramck and Vanderburgh, and also by Daniel Pryer, whom I had invited to stay with me until we could go into New York, and they were happily employed, sometimes gunning and fishing, &c., &c."

* * *

Johann David Schoepf, German physician, in Pennsylvania, August and November 1783, in Schoepf, *Travels in the Confederation. Pennsylvania, Maryland, Virginia, the Carolinas, East Florida, the Bahamas,* trans. and ed. by Alfred J. Morrison, 2 vols. (Cleveland: Arthur H. Clark, 1911), 1:238-239; 2:5.

August, 1783: "Like most inhabitants of these frontiers, he [a western Pennsylvanian] was one of those whose chief occupation is hunting, who from a preference for doing nothing, and an old indifference to many conveniences, neglect and dread the quieter and more certain pursuits of agriculture. These hunters or 'backwoodsmen' live every like the Indians and acquire similar ways of thinking. They shun everything which appears to demand of them law and order, dread anything which breathes constraint. They hate the name of a Justice, and yet they are not transgressors. Their object is merely wild, altogether natural freedom, and hunting is what pleases them. An insignificant cabin of unhewn logs; corn and a little wheat, a few cows and pigs, this is all their riches but they need no more. They get game from the woods; skins bring them in whiskey and clothes, which they do not care for of a costly sort. Their habitual costume is a 'rifle-shirt,' or shirt of fringed linen; instead of stockings they wear Indian leggings; their shoes they make themselves for the most part. When they go out to hunt they take with them a blanket, some salt, and a few pounds of meal of which they bake rough cakes in the ashes; for the rest they live on the game they kill. Thus they pass 10-20 days in the woods; wander far around; shoot whatever appears; take only the skins, the tongues, and some venison back with them on their horses to their cabins, where the meat is smoked and dried; the rest is left lying in the woods. They look upon the wilderness as their home and the wild as their possession; and so by this wandering, uncertain way of life, of which they are vastly fond, they become indifferent to all social ties, and do not like many neighbors about them, who by scaring off the game are a nuisance besides. They are often lucky on the hunt and bring back great freight of furs, the proceeds of which are handsome. Uncompanionable and truculent as this sort of men appear to be, and however they seem half-savage and, by their manner of life, proof against the finer feelings, one is quite safe among them and well treated; they have their own way of being courteous and agreeable which not everybody would take to be what it is."

November, 1783: "Moreover the game which at one time was very plentiful in this region has in great part been frightened off, and there is little to be seen except a few pheasants (*Tetrao Umbellus & Cupido L.*), partridges (*Tetrao virginianus L.*), squirrels, and hares. Everybody having full liberty to shoot, as much as he can or cares to, the larger game is extirpated in the farmed and settled parts, and has taken a last refuge in the wild mountain country."

* * *

Francesco dal Verme, Italian count, on hunting in New Jersey near the Delaware River, September 1783, in Elizabeth Cometti, trans. and ed., *Seeing America and Its Great Men. The Journal and Letters of Count Francesco dal Verme, 1783-1784* (Charlottesville, Va.: University Press of Virginia, 1969), 30.

28 September 1783: "Went to Belvidere (14 miles), the estate of Mr. Hoops, for dinner, afterwards went squirrel hunting. The dogs treed the animals and we took eight of them with a rifle loaded with ball, since the lofty tree were beyond the reach of shot."

OTHER LOCALES

Hernan Gallegos, Spanish notary, reports on hunting bison on the Rodriguez expedition in the Canadian River valley in New Mexico, October? 1582, in [Gallegos], *The Gallegos Relation of the Rodriguez Expedition to New Mexico,* trans. and ed. by George P. Hammond and Agapito Rey (Santa Fe, N.M.: El Palacios Press, 1927 [1582]), 34.

"We killed forty head for our use by means of the harquebuses. They are easily killed, for no matter where wounded they soon stop, and on stopping they are killed. There is such a large number of cattle that there were days when we saw upward of three thousand bulls."

* * *

Humphrey Gilbert, British explorer, discusses hunting in Newfoundland?, circa 1583, in Gilbert, *A True Reporte of the Late Discoveries and Possession Taken in the Right of the Crowne of Englande, of the Newfound Landes.* By That Valiaunt and Worthye Gentleman, *Sir* Humfrey Gilbert *Knight* (London: Iohn Hinde, 1583), reprinted in The Magazine of History, Extra Number, No. 68 (New York: Tarrytown, 1920), 39.

"...and in great store of Beastes, Byrdes, and Fowls both for pleasure and necessarie use of man is to be found.

"And for such as take delight in hunting, there are Stags, Wild Boars, Foxes, Hares, Coneys, Badgers, Otters, & divers other such like for pleasure. Also for such as have delight in Hawking, there are Hawks of sundry kinds, and great store of game, both for Land and River, as Feazaunts, Partridges, Cranes, Heronshaws, Ducks, Mallards, and such like. There is also a kinde of Beast, much bigger than an Ox, whose hyde is more than 18. foote long, of which sort a Countryman of ours, one *Walker*, a Sea man, who was upon that Coast, did for a truth report, in the presence of divers honourable and worshipful persons, that he and his company did find in one Cottage above 240 Hides which they brought away and sold in *France* for xl. shillinges a hyde, and with this agreeth *David Ingram*, and describeth that beast at large, supposing it to be a certain kinde of Buffe; there are likewise beasts and fowls of divers kinds, which I omit for brevitie's sake,...."

* * *

An English traveler describes hunting bulls on Hispaniola, July 1585, in "Anonymous Journal of the 1585 Virginia Voyage [by Sir Richard Greenvile]," in David B. Quinn and Alison M. Quinn, eds., *The First Colonists. Documents on the Planting of the First English Settlements in North America, 1584-1590* (Raleigh, N.C.: North Carolina Department of Cultural Resources, Division of Archives and History, 1982), 16.

5 July 1585: "Which banquet being ended, the Spanyardes in recompense of our curtesie, caused a great herd of white buls, and kyne, to be brought together from the Mounteines, and appointed for every Gentlemen and Captaine that would ride, a horse ready sadled, and then singled out three of the best of them to be hunted by horsemen after their manner, so that the pastime grew very plesant for the space of three houres, wherein all three of the beasts were killed, whereof one tooke the sea, and there was slaine with a musket. After this sport, many rare presents and gifts were given and bestowed on both partes,...."

* * *

Henri Joutel, French explorer, chronicles the hunting on the La Salle expedition, in the lower Mississippi River valley, January and April 1685, June 1686, and June 1687, and in the Illinois country, August and September 1687, in [Joutel], *Joutel's Journal of La Salle's Last Voyage* (Chicago: The Caxton Club, 1896, reprint of 1714 ed.), 28-29, 47, 72, 135-136, 162-165.

January, 1685: "We lay afhore, and our Hunters having that Day, kill'd good Store of Ducks, Buftards and teal, and the next Day two Goats, Monfieur *de la Sale* fent Monfieur *de Beaujeu* Part. We feafted upon the reft, and the good Sort put feveral Gentlemen that were then aboard Monfieur *de Beaujeu*, among whom were Monfieur *du Hamel*, the Enfign and the King's Clerk, upon coming afhore to partake of the Diverfion; but they took much Pains and were not fuccefsful in their Sport."

April, 1685: "...; which [landing] could not be done for fome Days, becaufe of the foul Weather; but in the mean Time we kill'd much Game."

June, 1686: "About that Time, and on *Eafter-day* that Year, an unfortunate Accident befel Monfieur *le Gros*. After Divine Service he took a Gun to go kill Snipes about the Fort. He fhot one, which fell into a Marfh, he took off his Shoes and Stockings to fetch it out, and returning, through Carelefsnefs trod upon a Rattle Snake,.... The Serpent bit him a little above the Ankle, he was carefully drefs'd and look'd after, yet after having endur'd very much, he dy'd at laft,...."

June, 1687: "...Father *Anaftafius*, being a hunting Bullocks with me, and coming too near one I had fhot, and was fallen, the Beaft, as much hurt as he was, ftarted up, attack'd and threw him down; he had much ado to get off, and I to refcue him; becaufe I durft not fhoot for Fear of killing him. The Bullock being weak, fell again; the Father was deliver'd, but lay ill fome Months."

14 August 1687: "We held on our Way till the 14th, when we met a Herd of Bullocks, whereof we kill'd five, dry'd Part of them,...."

27 August 1687: "The 27th, having difcover'd a Herd of Beeves, we went afhore to kill fome; I fhot a Heifer, which was very good Meat, we put a Board the beft of it,...."

September, 1687: "Thus we went on till the 8th, without ftopping any longer than to kill a Bullock,...."

* * *

Father Paul du Ru, Jesuit missionary, observes deer and bison hunting in the lower Mississippi River valley, 28 April 1700, in Ruth Lapham Butler, trans., *The Journal of Paul du Ru [February 1 to May 8, 1700] Missionary Priest to Louisiana* (Chicago: The Caxton Club, 1934), 64.

"There is a consolation in our misfortunes; one of our men has just killed a deer. Another consolation even more substantial! We have discovered a herd of buffalo and we are practically surrounding them. Good heavens, what shooting! There must be at least six or seven buffalo down. I ran toward the shooting and found two dying buffalo."

* * *

Antoine Le Page du Pratz, French traveler in Louisiana, hunts bison, relates an incident concerning a bear, and discusses wood-pigeons, circa 1720-1728, in Le Page du Pratz, *The History of Louisiana, or of the Western Parts of Virginia and Carolina. Containing a Description of the Countries that lie on both Sides of the River Mississippi. With an Account of the Settlements, Inhabitants, Soil, Climate, and Products* (London: T. Becket, 1774), 133-137, 278-279.

"I therefore pitched upon ten Indians, who were indefatigable, robuft, and tractable, and fufficiently fkilled in hunting, a qualification neceffary on fuch journeys....

"For the firft days of our journey the game was pretty rare, becaufe they fhun the neighbourhood of men; if you except the deer, which are fpread all over the country, their nature being to roam indifferently up and down; fo that at firft we were obliged to put up with this fare. We often met with flights of partridges, which the natives cannot kill, becaufe they cannot fhott flying; I killed fome for a change. The fecond day I had a turkey-hen brought to regale me. The difcoverer, who killed it, told me, there were a great many in the fame place, but that he could do nothing without a dog. I have often heard of a turkey-chace, but never had an opportunity of being at one: I went with him and took my dog along with me. On coming to the fpot, we foon defcried the hens, which ran off with fuch fpeed, that the fwifteft Indian would lofe his labour in attempting to outrun them. My dog foon came up with them, which made them take to their wings, and perch on the next trees; as long as they are not purfued in this manner, they only run, and are foon out of fight. I came near their place of retreat, killed the largeft, a fecond, and my difcoverer a third. We might have killed the whole flock; for, while they fee any men, they never quit the tree they have once perched on. Shooting fcares them not, as they only look at the bird that drops, and fet up a timorous cry, as he falls....."

"I longed much to kill a buffalo with my own hand; I therefore told my people my intention to kill one of the firſt herd we ſhould meet; nor did a day paſs, in which we did not fee feveral herds; the leaſt of which exceeded a hundred and thirty or a hundred and fifty in number.

"Next morning we eſpied a herd of upwards of two hundred. The wind ſtood as I could have wiſhed, being in our faces, and blowing from the herd; which is a great advantage in this chace; becauſe when the wind blows from you towards the buffaloes, they come to ſcent you, and run away, before you can come within gun-ſhot of them; whereas, when the wind blows from them on the hunters, they do not fly till they can diſtinguiſh you by ſight: and then, what greatly favours your coming very near to them is, that the curled hair, which falls down between their horns upon their eyes, is ſo buſhy, as greatly to confuſe their ſight. In this manner I came within full gun-ſhot of them, pitched upon one of the fatteſt, ſhot him in the extremity of the ſhoulder, and brought him down ſtone-dead. The natives, who ſtood looking on, were ready to fire, had I happened to wound him but ſlightly; for in that caſe, theſe animals are apt to turn upon the hunter, who thus wounds them.

"Upon feeing the buffalo drop down dead, and the reſt taking to flight, the natives told me, with a ſmile: 'You kill the males, do you intend to make tallow?' I anfwered, I did it on purpſe, to ſhew them the manner of making him good meat, though a male. I cauſed his belly to be opened quite warm, the entrails to be taken out directly, the bunch, the tongue, and chines to be cut out; one of the chines to be laid on the coals, of which I made them all taſte; and they all agreed the meat was juicy, and of an exquifite flavour.

"I then took occaſion to remonſtrate them, that if, inſtead of killing the cows, the difference in point of profit would be confiderable: as, for inftance, a good commerce with the French in tallow, with which the bulls abound; bull's fleſh is far more delicate and tender than cow's; a third advantage is, the felling of the fkins at a higher rate, as being much better; in fine, this kind of game, ſo advantageous to the country, would thereby efcape being quite deftroyed; whereas, by killing the cows, the breed of theſe animals is greatly impaired."

"Two Canadians, whom were on a journey, landed on a fand-bank, when they perceived a bear croffing the river. As he appeared fat, and confequently would yield a great deal of oil, one of the travellers ran forwards and fired at him. Unhappily however he only flightly wounded him; and as the bears in that cafe always turn upon their enemy, the hunter was immediately feized by the wounded bear, who in a few moments fqueezed him to death, without wounding him in the leaft with his teeth, although his muzzle was againft his face, and he muft certainly have been exafperated. The other Canadian, who was not above three hundred paces diftance, ran to fave his comrade with the utmoft fpeed, but he ws dead before he came up to him; and the bear efcaped into the wood. Upon examining the corpfe he found the place, where the bear had fqueezed it, preffed in two inches more than the reſt of the breaſt....

"Bears are feen very frequently in Louifiana in the winter time, and they are ſo little dreaded, that the people fometime make it a diverfion to hunt them. When they are fat, that is abut the end of December, they cannot run fo faft as a man; therefore the hunters are in no danger fhould they turn upon them...."

"The Wood-Pigeons are feen in fuch prodigious numbers, that I do fear to exaggerate, when I affirm that they fometimes cloud the fun. One day on the banks of the

Miffiffippi I met with a flock of them which was fo large, that before they had all paffed, I had leifure to fire with the fame piece four times at them. But the rapidity of their flight was fo great, that though I do not fire ill, with my four fhots I brought down but two.

"Thefe birds come to Louifiana only in the winter, and remain in Canada during the fummer, where they devour the corn, as they eat the acorns in Louifiana. The Canadians have ufed every art to hinder them from doing fo much mifchief, but without fuccefs. But if the inhabitants of thofe colonies were to go a fowling for thofe birds in the manner that I have done, they would infenfibly deftroy them. When they walk among the high foreft trees, they ought to remark under what trees the largeft quantity of dung is to be feen. Thofe trees being once difcovered, the hunters ought to goout when it begins to grow dark, and carry with them a quantity of brimftone which they muft fet fire to in fo many earthen plates placed at regular distances under the trees. In a very fhort time they will hear a fhower of wood-pigeons falling to the ground, which, by the light of fome dried canes, they may gather into facks, as foon as the brimftone is extinguifhed."

* * *

J.C.B., French traveler, on bear hunting in New France, 1753?, on beaver hunting in New France, September 1753, on buffalo hunting in the Ohio country, circa 1757, and on moose-hunting near Lake Champlain, March? 1759, in [J.C.B.], *Travels in New France by J.C.B.*, ed. by Sylvester K. Stevens, Donald H. Kent, and Emma Edith Woods (Harrisburg, Penn.: The Pennsylvania Historical Commission, 1941), 46, 50, 94-95, 109.

1753?: "Three men ordinarily go to hunt bear in this way. One of them strikes the foot of the tree with an ax. The animal inside always scrambles to the top of the trunk, where he puts out his two paws, pokes out his head, and looks down to see what is happening. If he sees danger he goes back in his hollow, and the tree must be cut down to make him come out. Sometimes, however, repeated blows with an ax force him out to climb down backwards. Only when he starts down will the hunter fire a shot into his head; and if wounded, he hurries his descent and, when halfway down, lets himself drop. At the same instant one or two more shots are fired at him. If by chance he is not killed, and has sufficient strength left, he advances on the hunter in sight, who jumps behind a tree and takes aim. The two others then fire and, when thus attacked, the animal is usually laid low. The hunters run up, cut off his paws with an ax, and cut his throat, after which he is disemboweled."

September, 1753: "They [beaver] are hunted in four ways; by net, by chopping, by traps, and by lying in ambush for them. They seldom use the net or ambush, for the tiny eyes of the creature are so sharp and its ears so keen that it is hard to get near enough to shoot it before it plunges into the water, which is seldom far away. Even if wounded, it is lost to the hunter if it is ready to dive in the water, because it never comes up when it dies of its wounds. "More usually the hunters resort to chopping and trapping, because these animals are partial to a diet of tender wood, and go out in the open to look for it. The savages, being aware of this, arrange traps shaped like a figure four along their tracks, and under these traps place small pieces of fresh-cut green wood. The beaver no sooner touches this bait than a heavy log falls on its head, breaking its back. The hunter, who is in hiding, comes out and dispatches it without difficulty. The chopping method requires more care. This is the way it is done. When the ice is only four or five inches thick, a hole is made in it with an ax, and reed-grass is thrown around the edge. The beavers come up in it to breathe more readily. They can be heard from a distance, because they create a great commotion in the water by their breathing. When the creature has reached the hole in the ice, it puts its two forepaws on the edge, and sticks out its head. Then you knock it on the head, and seize one paw to throw it on the ice, where it is beaten to death before it recovers its senses."

Circa 1757: "I have told about hunting turkeys, bears, beavers, and squirrels, and more will be related about some other game. But I shall now tell about hunting buffalo.

"This sport is very enjoyable. This buffalo ordinarily herd together on the prairies, occasionally as many as two or three hundred. When this hunting is to be engaged in, several hunters join up and stretch nets made of whitewood bark or birch bark. These are fastened to stakes driven in the ground in the form of a barrier. After the nets are stretched, the hunters beat the woods, either on foot or on horseback, over a large area, in order to drive buffalo into the nets. As the animals begin to flee, they are followed, and inevitably stopped in their course and thrown by the nets. Some of the hunters, who have been lying in wait, quickly rush to hamstring them with tomahawk blows, thus mastering them. They bleed them immediately.

"At mating time, the animals attack hunters, who skillfully escape by taking refuge behind trees. The buffalo, with its head lowered, rushes furiously and cracks its horns against the tree it was headed for. The hunter waiting with tomahawk in hand, at once aims several blows at its head between the two horns, in order to fell the animal to the ground. As soon as it is down, the buffalo's throat is cut.

"It must not be thought that great numbers of buffalo are taken in the nets; for the nets are often broken by their strength. When they have made an opening, they dash through it and escape. It is, however, a fact that some are always caught. They are also hunted one at a time, and this individual hunting is more difficult, because the anial has a very keen sense of smell. The hunter must go down wind to get near. It is very timid; though it becomes enraged when it is wounded, or when the cows have new-born calves."

March?, 1759: "Then [winter] it is easy to hunt them [moose], but it is even easier when there is strong sunlight. When there is little snow, it is difficult and dangerous to get near a moose because, when wounded, it will become enraged and turn upon the hunter to trample him under its feet. The hunter can escape its fury by throwing his coat to the animal. The moose vents its rage on the coat, while the hunter, hiding behind a tree, can get ready to dispatch it...."

* * *

Thomas Gist, Pennsylvania officer, describes his hunting as a captive, near Detroit, early 1759, and fugitive in the Great Lakes region, September 1759, in Howard H. Peckham, ed., "Thomas Gist's Indian Captivity, 1758-1759," Pennsylvania Magazine of History and Biography, Vol. 80 (1956), 300, 304-309.

Early 1759: "My wounds was well the last two months, part of which I spent in hunting and other innocent devertions in the woods."

12 September 1759: "In this order we continued for the space of ten or twelve miles, when the foremost man saw a feasant. He knew that we ware without provisions, as well as himself. He therefore halted till I came up. He then asked me if we should kill it. I immediately shot it, and we marched very brisk for five or six miles further when we saw an owl. I then took my bow and arrow from the boy, for he having no gun

carried them for me, and with it kill'd the owl. We was not uneasy about provitions now....

"...Soon after we heard some thing walk in the leaves and soon after discovered a very large racoon coming towards us. We soon kill'd him, then threw away the owl,..."

14 September 1759: "We had not march'd far when we saw a bear, and all being hungry we was determined to kill him if posable. McCrary went after him and got a shot at him. He wounded him badly but he took a different course from that we wanted to go so we lost him."

15 September 1759: "About sunrise we shot a bear twice, but he got into the swamp that we was in yesterday but we rather chose to lose him than follow. Being now tolarable hungry, we march'd as fast as we was able, in hopes of getting something to eat. About 12 oclock we kill'd one raccoon.... In the evening we kill'd another raccon...."

17 September 1759: "[I] was suddenly surprised by an old buck, who had been feeding about ten yards behind me, and I suppose either heard or saw us, gave two or three skips amongst the brush.... we soon discover'd what it was, and shot him through the neck, altho: it was hardly yet light, and for fear he should serve us as the bears had done, we tomahawked him in a moment,...."

19 September 1759: "This day kill'd one raccoon in the evening."

24 September 1759: "This morning came three bears within ten or fifteen yards of our fire. McCrary shot at one of them but his gun being damp by the rain...made long fire and missed them all."

28 September 1759: "I kill'd one young turkey, which was not enough to satisfy us."

* * *

Robert Rogers, British officer, hunts deer on the north side of Lake Ontario, September 1760, and near the Muskingum River in the Ohio country, January 1761, in [Rogers], *Journals of Major Robert Rogers. Containing An Account of the feveral Excurfions he made under the Generals who commanded upon the Continent of NORTH AMERICA, during the late War* (London: J. Millan, 1765), 204, 232-234.

27 September 1760: "The 27th of September, being very windy, we fpent the time in deer-hunting, there being plenty of them there,...."

3 January 1761: "This day we killed plenty of deer and turkies on our march, and encamped."

4 January 1761: "This day killed feveral deer and other game, and encamped."

5 January 1761: "This day killed deer and turkies in our march."

6 January 1761: "...killed plenty of game, and encamped by a very fine fpring."

8 January 1761: "The 8th, halted at this town to mend our mogafons, and kill deer, the provifions I brought from Detroit being entirely expended. I went a-hunting with ten of the Rangers, and by ten o'clock got more venifon than we had occafion for."

10 January 1761: "The 10th, abut the fame courfe, we traveled eleven miles, and encamped, having killed in our march this day three bears and two elks."

12 January 1761: "The 12th, travelled fix miles, bearing rather more to the eaft, and encamped. This evening we killed feveral beaver."

* * *

John Rutherfurd, British soldier, hunts as a captive in Michigan, circa 1763, in Rutherfurd, "John Rutherfurd's Captivity Narrative," in Milo Milton Quaife, ed., *The Siege of*

Detroit in 1763. The Journal of Pontiac's Conspiracy and *John Rutherfurd's Narrative of a Captivity* (Chicago: The Lakeside Press, 1958), 242-244.

"On our return to this village we halted near the burying ground I have mentioned, and while my Mistress and I were erecting our hut my Master went out and killed a bear, which we ate of most heartily....

"My Master, or rather my *Father* now, frequently took me hunting with him, which was an amusement I was very fond of. Although this was not the season for killing deer, he was under the necessity of taking a few to subsist his family upon when at camp with the rest of the warriors."

* * *

John Bartram, Philadelphia botanist, notes hunting in Florida, December 1765 and January 1766, in [Bartram], "A Journal Kept by John Bartram of Philadelphia, Botanist to His Majesty for the Floridas; Upon A Journey from St. Augustine up the River St. John's, as Far as the the Lakes," reprinted in [William Stork], *A Description of East-Florida* (London: W. Nicoll, 1769), 3, 18-19.

December 24, 1765: "...landed, and Mr. Davis fhot a deer, and his Negro a turkey." January 14, 1766: "Our hunter killed a large he-bear fuppofed to weigh 400 pounds, was 7 foot long, cut 4 inches thick of fat on the fide, its fore-paw 5 inches broad, his fkin when ftretched meafured five foot and a half long, and 4 foot 10 inches in breadth, and yielded 15 or 16 gallons of clear oil; two of us had never eat an ounce of bears meat before, but we found it to our furprize to be very mild and fweet, above all four-footed creatures, except venifon; although it was on old he-bear, his fat, though I loathed the fight of it at firft, was incomparably milder than hogs-lard, and near as fweet as oil of olives; it was not hunger that engaged us in its favour; for we had a fat young buck and three turkeys frefh fhot at the fame time, and fome boiled with the bear, but we chofe the laft for its fweetnefs and good relifh."

* * *

Fray Juan Crespi writes about hunting on the Don Gaspar de Portola Expedition in Alta California, 7 September 1769, reprinted in Herbert Eugene Bolton, *Fray Juan Crespi. Missionary Explorer on the Pacific Coast, 1769-1774* (Berkeley, Cal.: University of California Press, 1927), 184-185.

"In this valley we saw troops of bears, which kept the ground plowed up and full of holes which they make searching for roots which constitute their food, and on which the heathen also live, for there are some which have a very good flavor and taste. The soldiers went out to hunt and succeeded in killing one with bullets, in doing which they learned the ferocity of these animals. When they feel themselves wounded they attack the hunter at full speed, and he can only escape by the dexterity of his horse. They do not yield until they get a shot in the head or the heart. This one that they killed received nine balls before he fell, which did not happen until one struck him in the head. Some of the soldiers were fearless enough to chase one of these animals mounted on poor beasts. They fired seven or eight shots, and I have no doubt he would die from the balls; but the bear upset two of the mules, and it was only by good fortune that the two mounted on them escaped with their lives."

* * *

George Washington, Virginia planter, Revolutionary War general, and later President, observes hunting along the Ohio River near Pennsylvania and western Virginia, October and November 1770, in Donald Jackson and Dorothy Twohig, eds., *The Diaries of George Washington*, 6 vols., Vol. 2 (Charlottesville, Va.: University Press of Virginia, 1976, 1978, and 1979), 299, 307-308, 329.

22 October 1770: "The River along down abounds in Wild Geese, and severl. kinds of Ducks but in no great quantity. We killd five wild Turkeys today."

25 October 1770: "About half an hour after 7 we set out from our Incampment around which, and up the Creek is a body of fine Land. In our Passage down to this, we see innumerable quantities of Turkeys, & many Deer watering, & brousing on the Shore side, some of which we killd."

October 31, 1770: "Went out a Hunting & met the Canoe at the Mouth of the Big Kanhawa distant only 5 Miles makg. the whole distance from Fort Pitt accordg. to my Acct. 266 Miles."

2 November 1770: "We proceeded up the River with the Canoe about 4 Miles more, & then incampd & went a Hunting; killd 5 Buffaloes & wounded some others —three deer, &ca. This Country abounds in Buffalo & wild game of all kinds; as also in all kinds of wild fowl, the[re] being in the Bottoms a great many small grassy Ponds or Lakes which are full of Swans, Geese, & Ducks of different kinds."

* * *

John Ferdinand Dalziel Smyth, British traveler, concerning hunting in the Ohio River valley, 1774?, in Smyth, *A Tour in the United States of America. Containing an Account of the Present Situation of that Country,* 2 vols., Vol. 1 (London: G. Robinson, 1784), 142, 309, 311, 337.

Circa 1774?: "All thefe licks are generally frequented by hunters with their rifles, at the dawn of day, or on bright moon-fhine nights, who, by this means, feldom fail of killing fome of the deer, elks, or buffaloes, that refort to them at fuch private times, for the greater fecurity."

Circa 1774?: "I Remained on the fummit of this mountain until two o'clock in the afternoon, but was almoft as much furprifed at the inattention and difregard of the young back-wood's-man to the beauties and grandeur of the perfpective, as I was charmed with the enjoyment of it myfelf; for he went down along one of the fides of the mountain, and was abfent from me above an hour; in that time I heard the report of a gun, and when he returned he brought a fine wild turkey which he had fhot;...."

Circa 1774?: "Here we killed another wild turkey, and dreffed it for fupper as before; indeed they were fo very numerous that we could have eafily fubfifted a company of men upon them, and might kill almoft any number we pleafed."

Circa 1774?: Game of all kinds is alfo exceedingly plenty; a man may kill fix or eight deer every day, which many do merely for their fkins, to the great injury and deftruction of the fpecies, and to the prejudice and public lofs of the community at large."

* * *

Thomas Curtis, British voyager to Prince Edward Island, describes hunting on the island and offshore, circa 1775, in Curtis, "Voyage to the Island of St. John's, 1775," in D.C. Harvey, ed., *Journeys to the Island of St. John or Prince Edward Island, 1775-1832* (Toronto: Macmillan, 1955), 62-63.

"When we had got 2 of our Nets in and getting in the third which was made fast to a tree on the Other side Were was a large Black Bear! Being the first I had ever seen and having no Gun in the Boat was fear full he might attack us. We soon concluded to throw the Nets over board and fetch the Gun. Before we had done this the Bear ran into the Woods and we never saw him after thoughwe staid in this place for about a Week.... "When the Fishing Season was allmost over it was Proposed to me to make one of three to go in the Country Shooting for the Family. According we set Sail well Equipt. The first inlett we put in about 7 miles from home we Saw a great number of Geese but could not get a shott. The next day we went on the hills and with a Spying glass could see two fine Bucks a Doe and fawn. We followed them Miles but could get no Shott. We grew tired of our Chace— the Country being Swampy and very thick moss at the bottom which makes it hard Traveling as if it was half leg deep in Snow. When we got near our Wigwam we let the dog have the liberty to hunt about. He soon drove up a partridge. I shot at it and brake booth its Wings which I thought was very Extraordeny the Gun being loaded with three Balls only for Deer or Bears. When we arived home I was greatly Fateagued but had not lost my Appetite. I roasted my bird. My Companions would not Ate any. I finished it though nearly as big as a Hen Pheasant. The next day my companions would go for the Deers again. I was so tired I could not. In the mean time I got the Ax and Cutt a path inside the Wood to gett at the geese. The next morning we Shot 4 of them and after 14 or 15 Ducks then returnd home."

* * *

Nicholas Cresswell, British loyalist, notes his hunting in the Ohio River valley, May and June 1775, in Cresswell, *The Journal of Nicholas Cresswell, 1774-1777* (Port Washington, N.Y.: Kennikat Press, 1968 [1924]), 76-81, 84-91.

19 May 1775: "Saw an Elk and a Bear cross the River, but could not get a shot at them.... Shot at a Panther this afternoon, but missed him."
22 May 1775: "One of the scouts killed a deer."
23 May 1775: "Saw several of them [buffalo] and killed two Calves and a Bull."
24 May 1775: "Surrounded 30 Buffaloes as they were crossing the River, shot two young Heifers and caught two calves alive whose ears we marked and turned them out again."
25 May 1775: "Some of the company shot a Buffalo Bull,...."
26 May 1775: "Shot an old Buffalo Bull that had its ears marked."
28 May 1775: "Saw a great many Buffaloes cross the River above us, all hands went ashore to surround them. I kept on the outside of them and shot a fine young Heifer, some of the rest shot a Cow and Calf."
1 June 1775: "Saw a Gang of Buffaloes cross the River. Shot a Bull. Saw some Deer but killed none."
2 June 1775: "Went about 9 miles and camped, to hunt, shot at some Buffaloes, but killed none."
11 June 1775: "This morning killed a Buffalo Cow crossing the River.... Their sense of smelling is exquisite. If you get to leeward of them you may go up to them, or at least within shot, but if you are to windward, they run long before they see you."
14 June 1775: "Fell down to Grinin's Lick, shot at some Buffaloes but killed none, tho' I am certain we must have wounded a great number. Five of us fired at a herd of two hundred odd not more than twenty yards."
15 June 1775: "proceeded up the Ohio, where we killed a Buffalo and camped."
16 June 1775: "Killed another Buffalo on the Banks of the River."

17 June 1775: "Saw some Buffaloes but killed none.... One of the company shot a Deer."

19 June 1775: "As we sat at dinner, saw two Buffalo Bulls crossing the River. When they were about half way over four of us got into a Canoe and attacked them in the River, the rest went along shore to shoot them, as soon as they came ashore. The River was wide and we had fine diversion fighting them in the water. The man in the head canoe seized one of them by the tail and he towed us about the River for half an hour. We shot him eight times, let him get ashore and he ran away. Our comrades ashore very angry with us and they have a great right to be so.... Saw a Black Wolf pursuing a Faun into the River, the Faun we caught, but the Wolf got away."

23 June 1775: "Saw a Bear cross the River but did not get a shot at her"

24 June 1775: "Three of us stayed at the Lick till the afternoon waiting for the Buffaloes but saw none. When our out Hunters came loaded with meat and informed us they had killed a Buffalo about five miles off, set out and found it, and loaded ourselves and returned to Camp, but never so much fatigued before. Having already experienced the want of victuals, was willing to gurad against it for the future. I believe I have exerted myself more than I can bear. It is judged by the company that I brought between 70 and 80 pound of meat, exclusive of my Gun and Shot pouch. To add to my distress my shoesoles came off and I was obliged to walk bare foot for six miles. Find myself very unwell. Shot a Pole Cat."

27 June 1775: "Killed a Faun. Saw a Bear cross the River, but could not get a shot at her."

* * *

Du Roi the Elder, German lieutenant and adjutant, on the hunting at Quebec, 9 January 1777, in Charlotte S.J. Epping, ed., *Journal of Du Roi the Elder Lieutenant and Adjutant, in the Service of the Duke of Brunswick, 1776-1778,* (New York: D. Appleton and Company, 1911), 60.

"On account of the war and the soldiers billeted, the settlers were prevented from going hunting, and the fur trade did not amount to much this year. Hunting was left almost entirely to the Indians, who live further inland and in the spring take the skins of the killed animals to the European merchants, particularly to Montreal, where the fur business is mostly transacted."

* * *

Hessian staff officers at Batiscan and Ste. Anne, Quebec, on local hunting, November 1776 and March? April? 1777, in Ray W. Pettengill, trans., *Letters from America, 1776-1779. Being Letters of Brunswick, Hessian, and Waldeck Officers with the British Armies during the Revolution* (Port Washington, N.Y.: Kennikat Press, 1964 [1924]), 21-22, 50-55.

2 November 1776: "Every *habitant* is huntsman and fisherman. Hunting and fishing are free; there are no fishponds. An oxhorn is their powder-horn. Every *habitant* has at least one flintlock in the house. Wild duck, snipe, and wild pigeons are plentiful everywhere; bear, rabbits, muskrats, and beaver are shot in winter, but I am not yet well informed on the subject of hunting and will let it pass."

March? April? 1777: "Now, come, we will go hunting.

"You do shoot anything of consequence near the parishes. The *habitans* have killed off all the wild animals near the settlements. Hence a lover of the hunt finds little pleasure in Canada unless he is willing to hunt after the Indian fashion. What you will find in the neighborhood of the parishes is hare [rabbits]. These are small, miserable, and white-haired. Their ears are smaller than those of our hare and their flesh has not the gamey taste. Their life is sad; they do not run in the fields, but lie under a tree or bush and keep in a very small range of a few hundred paces as if they were enchanted there. No on ever uses a charge of powder on them, but catches tremendous quantities in snares. You pay five or six pence a pair, and in case of need can lay a half-dozen of these poor devils roasted on a dish of sauerkraut.

"The second kind of game you can shoot in the parishes is the so-called *perdrix*. The name is utterly false, for they have little resemblance to our partridge [perdrix cinera]. There are really three kinds, of which the first much resemble our hazel-grouse, the second is quite pheasant-like, and the third does almost resemble our partridge in size, but has a very long neck. Some tweny or thirty sit in a tree, and so still you pass underneath ten times without discovering them. If you have a dog along, he will stand under such a tree. All the *perdrix* stretch their necks and look down at the dog. The hunter shoots down the top bird and all the rest sit quiet, meditating about the dog. Then you again shoot the highest bird, and so all of them in turn. The remaining birds will not be disturbed in their philosophical observations over the stupid dog and so find an unexpected death one after the other. But if you shoot into the bottom of the tree, the rattle of the shot and the powder-smoke disturbs them all, the whole troop flies away and settles in a near-by tree. These birds taste fairly good and have a very white, tender flesh. You pay six pence a pair and can get a superabundance.

"Little red squirrels are abundant in the parishes. Since they are only half as large as at home, one lets the little fools live. White, red, and black foxes are met two or three leagues from the settlements, but they rarely venture out of the woods. They are not so rascally as at home. Land and water beaver—the latter fifty per cent better than the former—are found three or five leagues from the settlements. A real black winter beaverskin is now worth a half guinea at least; not less than twelve of these pelts are needed for a good coat. The flesh is eaten, particularly the tail, but this is unnaturally fat. There are still plenty of otter and people often wear caps of their skins. Marten is found only deep in the wilderness; our European marten are as good, if not better, and also cheaper. Black marten is rare, and a lady's coat, if fine, may easily cost twelve guineas without the cloth cover. Muskrats abound in the rivers and their fur is in good demand. Wolves are found only in the forests toward Nova Scotia; they are not so good as at home, also smaller, and the fur is little regarded. Wildcats are plentiful in the great forests, and the Indians commonly use their skins for sheaths for their knives which they wear hanging over their breasts. Black and white bears are found chiefly on the north side toward the land of the Eskimo. There is not a well-to-do *habitant* who doesn't have a few bearskins to spread as a robe in his carriage or sleigh. The flesh of young bears is eaten at the tables of the wealthy. Polecats and weasels are frequent enough, but not in the settlements. Lots of sea wolves are killed at the mouth of the St. Lawrence, the blubber is tried out, and the hides are used to cover trunks and to make winter shoes.

"Above Montreal and off toward the Five Nations there are lots of Canadian wild oxen or buffaloes with long curly hair and a hump on their back. This is the chief hunt of the Indians. They know how to dress the skins admirably, and you will not find a Canadian without several. They are used as carriage-robes and you can sleep on them or use them as covers. A good skin now costs six or eight piaster or ten reichsthaler sixteen groschen. The second major hunt of the natives is for *orignali*. An *orignal* or *orinal* [Canadian elk] is a creature which is almost as large as a camel, has stag's legs, deer's feet, a camel-like neck and hump, tremendous long ears, antlers like a palm-stag, and a cow's body. If caught young, they can be domesticated. Their flesh is much eaten and the skin makes a fine leather. Caribous are another type of animal which has much of the deer and of the ox in its build. I have seen none as yet. There are said to be many in the vicinity. Deer and chamois are only found toward New York; a deer is a great rarity in Canada. What sort of creature a *sauterol*, *vison*, or *minx* may be, I have not yet discovered. I wear a cap from the skins of these animals which cost me ready-made seven and a half piasters. In natural history the Canadians are regular blockheads; it is a shame that no one brought along a dictionary of natural history, for there is no suggestion of a library in Canada. *Carajous* live only on the north side of the river toward the Eskimos; they are a species of great wildcats with a very long tail with which they hold fast to the limbs of trees. They wait for animals passing below, drop on their necks and bite open the jugular vein. Thus they overcome large animals: stag, wild swine, and rabbits.

"From all this I now draw an important corollary; viz., that he who desires a real hunt must go to one or the other Indian tribe, live with them in their wild fashion, eat, sleep, march, swim, and roam four hundred or five hundred leagues in the wilderness. It is incredible what hunting trips the savages make through woods, over mountains, rivers, lakes and marshes, and what means they know of overcoming all difficulties. They go fifty or sixty German miles into the wilderness, erect huts, leave a few people there, and the rest go by twos and threes in every possible direction, hunt and shoot whatever comes in their way, and after four or five weeks return to the huts just as if regular roads led there. Anyway, the savage can take a straight course for many hundred leagues through wildernesses and all natural obstacles and end up in the place he intended. On the trees, leaves, rivers, and other natural objects they can find indications by which they can guide themselves just as accurately as we do by our compasses. They make natural deductions in places where they have never been and predict two days in advance; 'at such and such a place comes a river from such and such a region, but it must turn so and so'; and their statement proves correct. This is a fine instinct which nature simply gave them and which is based but little on reflection or ripe experience. If they are able—as certainly they are—to tell from a man's footprints by what nation they were made, if they can follow these footprints in the dark and use their nose as their only guide, if they can scent as well as our hunting-dogs and bird-dogs, then the best-trained man's reason fails and cannot comprehend the fine animal senses with which God has endowed people whom we term savages."

* * *

John Ledyard, British corporal, on fowling on the Alaskan coast, 12 May 1778, in James Kenneth Munford, ed., *John Ledyard's Journal of Captain Cook's Last Voyage* (Corvallis, Oregon: Oregon State University Press, 1963), 79.

"The pinnace of the Resolution with the first lieutenant, some other gentlemen and myself went to the opposite shore to shoot some wild fowl. We had some success, and being engaged in our sports, and not suspecting the country from its inhospitable appearance to be inhabited were surprized when we saw several large boats full of Indians already close upon us from behind a small island."

Henry Hamilton, British officer, notes the hunting near the Maumee River in Ohio, October 1778, in John D. Barnhart, ed., "The Unpublished Journal of Lieut. Gov. Henry Hamilton," in *Henry Hamilton and George Rogers Clark in the American Revolution* (Crawfordsville, Ind.: R.E. Banta, 1951), 108-109.

11 October 1778: "6 Hurons killed 50 Turkies in a short time, a good omen of plenty for our march— strict orders against firing out of boats excepting the Indians—...."
14 October 1778: "Savages kill a she bear and cub as they were passing below rapide du loup—...."

* * *

David Zeisberger, Moravian missionary, chronicles local hunting in Ohio, October and December 1781, and at New Gnadenhutten on the Clinton River in Michigan, July, August, September, October, and December 1782, January, February, October, November, and December 1783, in Eugene F. Bliss, trans. and ed., *Diary of David Zeisberger, A Moravian Missionary among the Indians of Ohio*, 2 vols. (Cincinnati: Robert Clarke and Company, 1885), 1:30, 51, 105-107, 113-114, 126, 128, 131, 137, 167, 171, 173, 179-182, 194, 203, 207-208, 249-251, 271, 275-276, 278, 280-281, 285-286, 300, 307, 310-311, 321, 341, 352, 357, 364, 378, 380-381, 389-390, 403-405, 455; 2:25, 51, 65, 99, 102, 107, 216, 232-233, 276-277, 290, 314, 329, 375, 427, 446, 497.

26 and 27 October 1781: "We went through deep swamps and troublesome marshes, in the afternoon came upon Indians out hunting, from whom we got some meat, and with whom we passed the night. On the afternoon of the 27th we came out of the camp and met on a creek Indians again out hunting, and here we stayed. Here our Isaac, who went out hunting, shot a deer."

21 December 1781: "Several brothers came home from hunting."

22 July 1782: "The hunting is good, and our Indians shot their first deer to-day."

27 July 1782: "Indian brethren who went hunting several miles up the creek came upon a cedar-swamp and found many traces of bears in the same neighborhood, but the bush in the summer is so wild, overgrown with weeds and thickets, that it is very hard to get through, and consequently is not then good for hunting, for the game gets off before a man has sight of it,...."

2 August 1782: "When now all our hunters were away, so that we could expect no fresh meat, a deer came by our camp to the creek, which old Br. Abraham shot, but which our heavenly Father sent."

24 September 1782: "Chippewas came in who went through here hunting."

3 October 1782: "To-day Chippewas came again on their way hunting,...."

12 December 1782: "The brethren went hunting in a body together, for they hunt in this way; they form a half moon or circle, and go through a district where the deer come within shot of one or another. Our Indians, however, had to learn here hunting over again, for thus far they have not been very lucky in it."

28 December 1782: "Chippewas came in, who are encamped not far off, hunting.... They...plant very little, but live mostly from the bush, hunting, though they like to eat corn and bread."

3 January 1783: "Most of the brethren went out hunting, for some snow had fallen, of which we have had little indeed thus far this winter. Adam straightaway shot three great bucks, when he had hardly got out of town."

26 February 1783: "All the Indian brethren who went off hunting two days ago, a day's journey from here, came home with nothing, for the snow is gone, and all the land is full of water, so flat and even is it. At times they had to go a long way through water and marsh knee-high, and thus were in no condition to accomplish any thing."

22 October 1783: "Chippewas went through here, up creek, on their way hunting.... Our Indian brethren hunting."

14 November 1783: "Since a fine, fresh snow fell last night and the hunters went out, there was brought to-day a fine number of deer, which are now quite fat. Abraham took a rare animal and quite unknown to our Indians. It was larger and heavier than a raccoon; its head and mouth are just the same, but its feet and legs are short and shaped like those of a mole or a beaver's feet. The Chippewas say they run under ground like moles, although they are so big, and they are very fat. This was the English badger."

3 December 1783: "home, and also many of the Indian brethren from the hunt, but they got little, since many Chippewas are also off hunting in that neighborhood. Thus our Indians earn little hunting, and yet they find it necessary, in order to get corn for their families, and they must try to get something by their labor."

NEWSPAPERS ON HUNTING

Advertisement for hunting guns, Boston News-Letter, No. 851, 27 June–4 July 1720.

"TO be Sold by John Pim of Bofton, Gunfmith, at the Sign of the Crofs Guns, in Anne-Street near the Draw Bridge at very reafonable Rates, fundry forts of choice Arms lately arrived from London, viz Handy Muskets, Buccaneer-Guns, Fowling pieces, Hunting Guns, Carbines; feveral forts of Piftols, Brafs and Iron, fafhionable Sword, &c."

* * *

Account of a hunting accident, Boston News-Letter, No. 1029, 10–18 October 1723.

"They write from New London, That on the 23 of Sept. paft in the Morning, Two Men went a Hunting after Deer, at Eaft Hampton on Long Ifland: After they were parted one from the other a little while, One of them faw the Bufhes ftir (the woods being very thick,) fuppofing there was a Deer, difcharged his Gun at a venture, (which was charged with two Bullets and feveral Swan Shot) the Bullets paft thro' his Body, at which the man fpoke thofe words, Lord! *have Mercy on me, You have kill'd me*: Upon which the Man that fhot, ran and catch'd him before he fell to the ground, but the wounded Man died immediately."

* * *

Account of bear hunting, Boston Gazette, No. 301, 30 August–6 September 1725.

"Thurfday laft 3 Bears, one of them very large, were feen at Marblehead, to the great Surprize of the Inhabitants, who to the Number of 500, affembled together to deftroy them, which they foon effected, and their Skins were brought to Town."

* * *

Account of a hunting accident, Boston News-Letter, No. 1442, 9–16 September 1731.

"By a Letter from Barnftable, dated the 10th Inftant, we have the following awful Occurrence of Divine Providence, viz. That on Monday the 6th feveral went out in a Boat to kill Birds, among whom was Mr. *John Sturges* (who married Mrs. *Suf. Lothrop,*) when their Game was over, they prepared to return home; their Boat being a ground upon the Flats, the Company were obliged to run her into the Water; but before they came to this the Perfon mentioned left his Company, and walked away alone to the edge of the Channel, and venturing in, perhaps for fome Game he efpied, found it deeper than he expected, and was drowned,...."

* * *

Accounts of hunting accidents, Boston News-Letter, 1732.

"Hull, April 25. Yeferday one Nathanael Dill, a young Man, in this Place, difcharging a Fowling-Piece, at a Flock of Brants, near his Father's Door, by the fhore fide; the Breech of the Barrel blew out, and is not to be found, the Lock blew off, and the Stock broke, and fplit into feveral pieces. The young Man's Face is very much burned, his right Eye carried quite away, and the upper Orbit and Jaw Bone very much Fifhur'd; He has his Senfes and 'tis hoped will recover."

(No. 1474, 20–27 April 1732)

"We are informed from Exeter that on Tuefday laft two Lads of about 13 years of Age, went out in order to kill fome Birds, and took their Guns with them one of the Lads name was Samuel S*cribner*, the other *William Levit*; and while purfuing their Game *Scribner's* Flint fell out of his Gun, & in putting of it in again he kill'd his Companion *Levit*; the Shot went in at his left Shoulder and carry'd all the back part of his Head away, and he never fpoke one word after. 'Tis remarkable, that this *Samuel Scribner's* Father was kill'd after the fame manner about a Year ago."

(No. 1482, 15–22 June 1732)

* * *

Account of a deer hunt, Boston News-Letter, No. 1505, 30 November–7 December 1732.

"Newport, Nov- 30. A Buck was lately kill'd in the Narraganfet Country, which weighed 69 Pound a Quarter, and is reckoned the largeft Deer that has been killed in thefe Parts for fome Years paft."

* * *

Account of a deer hunt, Boston News-Letter, No. 1542, 9–16 August 1733.

"We have an Account from *Nottingham*, of an exploit performed there lately by a little Girl about Eleven Years old, as follows: The faid Girl having dreamt that fhe had killed a Deer in the Woods, after fhe awoke & got up fhe fharpned a little Knife, and went out, taking her Dogs with her, and in a fhort Time came upon the Track of a great old Buck, which fhe followed with her Dogs about a Mile, when the Dogs feiz'd him, and the Girl got hold of him by Ear, and would have got upon his Back, but he fhook her off, upon which fhe took her Knife and firft cut his Ham String, and then cut his Throat."

* * *

Accounts of hunting accidents, Boston News-Letter, 1733.

"*Philadelphia*, Octo. 25. We hear from Briftol, that on Monday Morning laft, two young Men went out a Hunting in the Woods near that Place, one of them being a little before the other, faw fomething thro' the Bufhes on the other fide of the Creek; upon which he ftepped back to his Companion and faid, Lend me that Gun, for I fee a fine Deer; accordingly he took Aim, and gave Fire; but when he came to the Place he found a Boy about 9 Years of Age. (who had juft been fent out by his Mother for a Can of Water) ftrugling for Life; the Child never fpoke another Word, being fhot in the Breaft, and died immediately. Scrace a Year paffes without one or more of thefe unhappy Accidents, which ought to make People more careful in their Hunting than they commonly are." (No. 1554, 1–8 November 1733)

"One Night in the beginning of this Month, as two Men at Lebanon (in Connecticut) were on a Wheat Field watching for Deer, they difcover'd a Man walking in the fame, and rofe up in order to difcourfe with him; but he fuppofing them to be a Deer, fir'd at them, and dangeroufly wounded one of them in the Back, the other is wounded in the Leg and Hand." (No. 1560, 13–20 December 1733)

* * *

Account of a goose hunt, Boston News-Letter, No. 1556, 15-23 November 1733.

"We hear from *Newbury*, That on Wednefday the 14th Inftant one *Mofes Bradftreet* went to Plumb Ifland a Gunning; where he found a great number of wild Geefe, which being fo fatigued and tired by a Storm, that they were not able to fly, he with a Club kill'd Sixty of them, befides fome which he fhot. The fame Day a Man at *Salisbury* kill'd Thirty after the fame manner."

* * *

Account of a moose hunt, Boston News-Letter, No. 1558, 30 November–6 December 1733.

"We hear from *Salifbury*, on the North fide of *Merrimack*, that they kill'd a fine large Moofe there the laft Week, faid to be feven Foot high."

* * *

Accounts of hunting accidents, Boston News-Letter, 1734.

"We hear that about a Fortnight ago, a Man at *Norton*, as he was fhooting at a Deer, a piece of his Gun fplit off, and flew into his Right Eye, which wounded him in fuch a manner, that tho' it was taken out again, yet his Life is difpaired of." (No. 1564, 10–17 January 1734)

"Some days ago at South-Hampton on Long-Ifland, Mr. Stephen *Hedges*, a young Man about 19, took his Gun and went out to fhoot at fome Crows near his Father's Houfe, and as he was creeping thro' a pair of Bars, and pulling the Gun after him (as is fuppos'd) it went off and fhot him through the Head: The People heard the gun, and after waiting about two Hours for his Return, went to look for him, and found him lying dead in his own Blood." (No. 1566, 24 January–7 February 1734)

"The Death of the other [youth] we hear was as follows, A Veffel being off of Cape Sable, a Man on the Deck feeing a Wild Fowl, call'd to a Youth named *Clark*, about 16 or 17 Years of Age, to hand him a Gun, that was loaded, out of the Cabin, which being cock'd, as he was reaching it up with the Breech foremoft and the Muzzle pointing towards his Body, the Lock happen'd to touch aginft the Companion Door, whereupon the Gun went off, and fhot him thro' the upper part of his Belly, and he fell down and died on the Spot." (No. 1601, 3–10 October 1734)

Account of a hunting accident, New York Gazette, No. 464, 9-16 September 1734.

"We hear that on Tuefday laft one Reynier Sickelfe, at Gravefend on Long-Ifland, being out a Hunting efpied a Fox, which he purfued, and after fome Time thought he faw behind some Bufhes, and fired at it; but when he came to the Place, he found he had fhot a Woman that was gathering fome Berries: This fatal Miftake was occafioned by her wearing an Orange-brown Waft-Coat. The Man is in a very melancholly Condition."

* * *

Advertisement for hunting guns, Virginia Gazette, No. 49, 1-8 July 1737.

"The faid James Geddy has a great Choice of Guns and Fowling-Pieces, of feveral Sorts and Sizes, true bored, which he will warrant to be good, and will fell them as cheap as they are ufually fold in England."

* * *

Advertisement for hunting guns, Virginia Gazette, No. 114, 29 September–6 October 1738.

"GENTLEMEN and Others, may be Fupply'd by the Subfcriber in Williamfburg, with neat Fowling-Pieces, and large Guns fit for Killing Wild Fowl in Rivers, at a reafonable Rate....

James Geddy."

* * *

Account of a hunting accident, New York Gazette, No. 731, 12–19 November 1739.

"Connecticut Nov. 6.

"Last Wednefday John and Benjamin Hubbard in Connecticut, the only Sons of Mr. John Hubbard being out a Hunting, took the Tracks of two deers in the Snow, and the Deers parting, one Brother took the Track of one Deer, and the other took the Track of the other and they Prefently crofsd each other, and the Eldeft Brother John was Shot by his Younger Brother, (by Miftake) fuppofing it to be one of the Deers who expir'd on the fpot; to the great furprize of the faid Younger Brother, who is now almoft out of his Senfes, for grief of fo great and Sorrowful an Accident, and to the great grief of the whole Family."

* * *

Warning against hunting on private property, South Carolina Gazette, No. 613, 23 December 1745.

"THIS is to forwarn all Perfons from hunting, Fowling or Fifhing on KIWAH ISLAND after the Date hereof, if they do they may depend on being profecuted.

December 7th, 1745.

John Stanyarze"

* * *

Advertisement for a found fowling piece, Maryland Gazette, No. 329, 14 August 1751.

"FOUND, a Fowling Piece, pretty old, has a Trumpet Mouth, the Barrel above four Feet long, has a Brafs Plate round the Stock and Barrel, about mid-way between the Lock and Muzzel, has a large near Sight, and is Branded I G, the Letters about three Quarters of an Inch in length, on the Breech. The Owner may know where to get his Piece, by enquiring of the Printer hereof."

* * *

Letter about hunters burning the woods, Maryland Gazette, No. 354, 6 February 1752.

"Mr. GREEN,

I HAVE heard a Bill was formerly brought into the Affembly, to prevent the Practice of Burning the Woods; but it did not pafs the Lower Houfe; by *what Reafon* I could
not learn: If I may be allow'd to give my Opinion, as one of the Community; in a few
Words, I think it is a vile, pernicious, and deftructive Practice, tending to very little or
no Advantage; but, on the contrary, is frequently of unhappy Confequences.

"...I will, however, juft obferve, that it is moftly ufed by the lower Clafs of Planters, and the Deer Hunters:.... Does not the Fire drive the Deer, and deftroy their hiding Places, whence the Danger of killing or driving them all off? And is it not the Care
of every Country to preferve their Breed, and particularly, Do not our Laws make fome
Provifion for them, tho' it feems, not fufficient?....

I am Yours, &c. Y. Z."

* * *

Notice of a hunting accident, Maryland Gazette, No. 379, 30 July 1752.

"PHILADELPHIA, July 2.
Extract of a Letter from Reading, June 29, 1752.

'...On Wednefday evening laft, one Michael Renner, watching at a Deer Lick, in
Bern Townfhip, abut Twilight, faw fomething approaching the Lick, which he took to
be a Deer; but being in Doubt, made a little Noife, that if he was a humane Creature,
it might anfwer him; but the Noife not being heard, and the Object ftill moving about
the Lick, Renner was fully perfwaded it was a Deer, fo fhot at it, and immediately
heard a Voice cry out, *You have fhot me to Death.* He then went for fome of the
Neighbours, and found that it was one John Schutzman, who was quite dead, having
received five Wounds; upon which he delivered himflef up to a Juftice, who committed him to Lancafter Jail.'"

* * *

Notice of an hunting accident, New York City, 1754, reprinted in Esther Singleton, *Social New York under the Georges* (New York: D. Appleton and Company, 1902), 262.

"A melancholy affair happened near this City. One Jacob Kool, in his round a gunning noticed something moving in a thcket of bushes and not readily distinguishing the
object, imagined it to be a bear; and having no bullets about him, withdrew to a neighbouring house and requested a number, telling the people there was such a beast at a
small distance. Upon this two of the inhabitants, one Johan Baltas Dash, and a negro
man, taking down their pieces, they all three loaded with balls, and coming near the
thicket, Kool discharged his gun into the middle of it, as did likewise the others, when
hearing a groan and seeing the motion of a man's leg, they found their mistake. It afterwards proved to be the body of Mr. Cornelius Vonk of this City, who walking out
to refresh himself, laid down under the thicket to rest, where, it is supposed, he fell
asleep. The Jury brought in their verdict Chance medley. (Short-sighted persons are not
fit to go a gunning; they therefore would do well to go to Ohio, where, as they can't
see distinctly, they may kill as many Frenchmen as they please instead of bears.)"

* * *

Advertisement for missing hunting guns, [Rivington's] New-York Gazetteer, No. 20, 2
September 1773.

"TWO FOWLING PIECES LOST,
MIDSLAID, or STOLEN,

Within three or four months paft.

ONE of them a Spanifh barrel, with the ufual Barcelona marks, the whole piece, ftock and barrel, about five feet ten inches, with a gold touch-hole, and a lock made by Wilfon of London.

The other is a cocking-piece, with a lock made by Perkins of New-York. If with any friends of the owner, they are defired to return them; if otherwife, a reward of EIGHT DOLLARS will be given on delivery of them to the Printer."

* * *

Advertisement for a missing following piece, [Rivington's] Royal Gazette, No. 236, 2 January 1779.

"MISSING
AN OLD STEEL MOUNTED
FOWLING PIECE,

Stock and lock Englifh, the name G. JONES upon the lock, which is falt, the barrel Spanifh, upon an Englifh plan, fhort and wide.

If in the hands of a Friend, it will certainly be returned. If offered for fale, for fear in the hands of a fufpected perfon, the Printer will pay Three Guineas to the difcoverer.

Taken lately from the fame place,

a long Steel mounted

FRENCH FUSIL,

With a fmall oval Silver Thumb Piece. The fame reward is offered to the perfon who difcovers the Thief. Enquire of the Printer's."

* * *

Advertisement for a fox hunt on Long Island, [Rivington's] Royal Gazette, No. 317, 13 October 1779.

"HUNTING.

"A Number of excellent Fox Hounds having with great difficulty been collected, notice is hereby given that there will be hunting every Monday, Wednefday and Friday, upon Hampftead Plains. Such gentlemen who wifh to partake of this amufement are defired immediately to pay the fubfcription of One Guinea into the hands of Capt. Maynard.

"N.B. Half a Guinea will be given for every BAG FOX delivered to Cornet Stapleton, at Hampftead, who will likewife give the higheft price for DEAD HORSES."

* * *

Prohibition on fowling in New York City, [Rivington's] Royal Gazette, No. 421, 11 October 1780.

"WHEREAS due attention has not been paid to the Order of the 27th of October last, forbidding perfons going out with

FOWLING PIECES,

to fhoot near the high roads and other places of public refort; thereby rendering it unfafe for paffengers and others frequenting the faid roads.—The Commandant therefore judges it neceffary, for the public fafety, ftrictly to

PROHIBIT ALL FOWLING,

near the environs of the city, or within half a mile of any high road, or public frequented foot path, as the offenders will be anfwerable for the difobedience of this Order.

By Order of the Commandant.
F. METZNER,
Major of Brigade."

* * *

Advertisement for fox hunts near New York, [Rivington's] Royal Gazette, No. 430, 11 November 1780.

"Gentlemen fond of FOX Hunting, are requefted to meet at LOOSELY's King's Head Tavern, at Day-break, during the Races.

"A KENNEL is provided on the race ground for the reception of fuch dogs as may be brought, Gentlemen who will favour the fportfmen with their dogs fhall have them well taken care of."

* * *

Advertisements for fox hunting near New York, [Rivington's] Royal Gazette, 1781.

"PRO BONO PUBLICO.

"GENTLEMEN that are fond of Fox Hunting, are requefted to meet at Loofley's Tavern, on Afcot Heath, on Friday morning next between the hours of five and fix, as a pack of Hounds will be there purpofely for a trial of their abilities: Breakfafting and Relifhes until the Races commence.— At Eleven o'clock will be run for an elegant Saddle, &c. value at leaft Twenty Pounds, for which upwards of twelve Gentlemen will ride their own Horfes.—At Twelve, a match will be rode by two Gentlemen, who will alfo ride their own Horfes.— Dinner will be ready at Two o'clock, after which, and fuitable regalements, Racing and other diverfions, will be calculated to conclude the day with pleafure and harmony.

Brooklyn-Hall, 6th Auguft, 1781." (No. 507, 8 August 1781)

"BROOKLYN-HUNT,

"ON Wednefday next, and Dinner after, as ufual.—A Guinea and expences will be paid for a ftrong Bag Fox, at Charles Loofley's, Brooklyn-Hall."

(No. 532, 3 November 1781)

"BROOKLYN HUNT.

"THE Hounds will throw off at Denyce's Ferry at Nine o'Clock on Thurfday morning. Dinner on the Table at Three o'Clock at Brooklyn Hall.

"A Guinea or more will be given for a good ftrong Bag Fox, by Charles Loofley."

(No. 535, 14 November 1781)

* * *

Prohibition on fowling near highways in the New York area, [Rivington's] Royal Gazette, No. 726, 10 September 1783.

"WHEREAS Complaint has been made, that of late frequent HORSE-RACING, has been on the High Roads near this City, endangering the Lives of Paffengers: This is to forbid all Perfons in future from fuch Practices, under pain of the fevereft Punifhment.

"And Whereas notwithftanding the repeated Orders that have been iffued, forbidding Perfons going out with FOWLING PIECES, to fhoot near the High Roads, this Irregularity ftill continues: It is therefore again Notified, That any Perfon found difobeying this Order, will be taken into Cuftody.

By *Order of the Commandant,*
JOHN BLUCKE, *Secretary.*
New-York, Auguſt 30, 1783."

Chapter 17

INDIGENOUS SPORTS AND GAMES

Well before any Europeans arrived on the North American continent, indigenous tribal peoples played a variety of energetic sports and games. Europeans were fascinated with these games, which often resembled their own contests yet were exotically different. Although many Europeans considered indigenous people savages and dismissed their culture, including games, as so much superstition and childish rowdiness, more astute travelers and missionaries studied the sports and games to ascertain the tribal cultural sophistication. Never free of European biases, these observers produced mostly ethnocentric descriptions and estimates of the sports. Supplemented with archeological evidence and indigenous oral history these accounts remain the best sources on these games.

Lacrosse was the game drawing the most comment and interest from the Europeans. Indigenous peoples across the continent, north and south, played lacrosse, "the little brother of war." The name "lacrosse" is an European bestowal from the French, who looked at the lacrosse sticks and thought they suggested the cross. "Baggataway," in several spellings, was one of the names the native peoples called it. There were several variations of the game, but they all featured two teams whose players, armed with sticks with racket-like pockets at the end, attempted to manuever a ball through the opposition across an end line or into a goal. Field sizes and team numbers varied, and games lasted many hours, or even several days. Injuries and the occasional death were not uncommon. Men and women played their own versions of the sport, but the women shied from playing before strangers. Gambling accompanied the game. Often the game was part of a larger religious ceremony or healing ritual. In one famous instance at Fort Michilimackinac in June 1763, baggataway was a premeditated distraction to seduce the British soldiers to let down their guard, and the fort's gates opened when a game ball "accidentally" flew into the fort; the resulting massacre left only three British alive. It is unclear if any Euroamericans joined in any of the games; the commentators always seem to stumble upon a game and watch from the sidelines. The modern professional, interscholastic, and intercollegiate game of lacrosse is a direct descendant from the game of colonial times, with some minor modifications such as helmets and more padding for the players.

Indigenous people played active games. In Mexico, the Aztecs played *tlachtli,* a highly developed ball game on elaborate courts, in which teams apparently attempted to keep a ball the size of a small bowling ball aloft without the use of hands, directing it through stone rings on the courtsides to win the game or lavish gifts. Southeast tribal peoples enjoyed a game called *chunké*, which involved rolling or slinging stones and throwing lances at them either to hit the stone or come close. Florida indigenous people had an allegedly violent game called *pelota* that the Spanish missionaries tried to suppress in the 1670s and 1680s. Other games concerned retrieving sticks, trundling hoops, or attempting to throw spears through hoops. As with lacrosse, many of these games were associated with religious ritual, a characteristic that differentiated them from European games which, for the most part, were losing association with their feast day origins in medieval or pagan times. All the games intrigued the Euroamerican observers, although the contests were also the focus of cultural conflict as the missionaries branded them heathenish superstitions. The following sources reflect the continuous Euroamerican interest in lacrosse and other indigenous games.

[For sources on indigenous peoples' skill in aquatics, archery, shooting, wrestling, soccer, fishing, running, and hunting, consult the appropriate chapters.]

LACROSSE

William Wood, English settler, concerning New England indigenous people, probably mentions lacrosse, circa 1634, in Wood, *New England's Prospect. A True, Lively, and Experimental Defcription of that Part of* America, *Commonly Called Nevv England. Difcovering the Ftage of the Countrie, Both as it Ftands to our New-Come* Englifh *Planters; and to the Old Native Inhabitants* (London: Thomas Cotes, 1634), reprinted as *Wood's New-England's Prospect, Publications of the Prince Society, Volume 1* (Boston: The Prince Society, 1865), 97.

"It is moft delight to fee them play, in fmaller companies, when men may view their fwift footemanfhip, their curious toffings of their Ball, their flouncing into the water, their lubberlike wreftling, having no cunning at all in that kind, one *Englifh* being able to beate ten *Indians* at footeball."

* * *

Paul Le Jeune, French Jesuit missionary, in Huronia, refers to lacrosse and its connections to tribal medicine, circa 1636 and 1637, in [Le Jeune], "Le Jeune's Relation, 1636" and "Le Jeune's Relation, 1637," in Reuben Gold Thwaites, ed., *The Jesuit Relations and Allied Documents. Travels and Explorations of the Jesuit Missionaries in New France, 1610-1791* (New York: Pageant Book Company, 1959), 10:185, 187; 14: 47.

Circa 1636: "Of three kinds of games especially in use among these Peoples, namely, the games of crosse, dish, and straw,—the first two are, they say, most healing. Is this not worthy of compassion? There is a poor sick man, fevered of body and almost dying, and a miserable Sorcerer will order for him, as a cooling remedy, a game of crosse. Or the sick man himself, sometimes, will have dreamed that he must die unless the whole country shall play crosse for his health; and, no matter how little may be his credit, you will see then in a beautiful field, Village contending against Village, as to who will play crosse the better, and betting against one another Beaver robes and Porcelain collars, so as to excite greater interest.

"Sometimes, also, one of these Jugglers will say that the whole Country is sick, and he asks a game of crosse to heal it; no more needs to be said, it is published immediately everywhere; and all the Captains of each Village give orders that all the young men do their duty in this respect, otherwise some great misfortune would befall the whole Country."

Circa 1637: "On the 19th, we had a real winter day; nearly half a foot of snow fell and the following night it froze very hard. *Sondacouane* lost a little of his repute on this occasion, Two or 3 days before, they had tired themselves to death playing crosse in all the villages around here, because this sorcerer had affirmed that the weather depended only upon a game of crosse; and now our Savages openly declared that he is only a charlatan and an impostor. It is worthy of note, however, that these experiences render them but little wiser."

* * *

Father Du Peron, French Jesuit, in Huronia, lists lacrosse as a recreation among eastern Canadian indigenous peoples, circa 1638-1639, in "F. Du Peron to Joseph," in Reuben Gold Thwaites, ed., *The Jesuit Relations and Allied Documents. Travels and Explorations of the Jesuit Missionaries in New France, 1610-1791*, Vol. 15 (New York: Pageant Book Company, 1959), 155.

"Their recreations are the games of straw, of dish, and of crosse [lacrosse], in which they will lose to the value of two or three hundred écus."

* * *

Pierre Liette, French explorer, describes lacrosse in the Illinois country, circa 1688, in [Liette], "The Memoir of Pierre Liette," in Milo Milton Quaife, ed., *The Western Country in the Seventeenth Century. The Memoirs of Lamothe Cadillac and Pierre Liette* (Chicago: Lakeside Press, 1947), 123-124.

"I have forgotten to say that before they set out for the chase the men play at lacrosse, a few women mingling with them. They make the racket of a stick of walnut about three feet long, which they bend half way, making the end come within a foot of the other end, which serves them for a handle. To keep this shape they fasten a buffalo sinew to the curved end, which, as I have already said, they fasten about a foot from the end which serves as a handle. They lace the interior with more buffalo sinew so that the ball, which is a knot of wood of the size of a tennis ball, cannot pass through.....

"In the middle of the prairie on whose edge their village stands they place two forks about ten paces apart. An old man who is neutral rises and utters a cry which signifies: It is time. Everybody rises and utters cries similar to those they give when they attack the enemy. The old man throws the ball into the air and pell-mell they all try to catch it. They strike their legs so forcibly that they are sometimes crippled, especially when someone manages to get the ball in hand so as to throw it a long way, so that it has sufficient distance to gain momentum and then strikes a player's legs in front. This makes them fall down in such a manner that you might suppose they would never get up again. I have seen men in this state who were thought to be dead. The players rush over them without paying any heed; only their female relatives come and carry them off in a deerskin. Sometimes as much as two months elapse before they can make use of their legs, and often they break them.

"I have seen a bardash [a cross-dressing, possibly homosexual male] who was standing aside like the women to send back the ball to his party, in case it came this way, who was struck so hard by the ball that his eye was knocked out of his head. It is necessary to go and return to win the game."

* * *

Baron de Lahontan, French traveler, comments on lacrosse among northeastern indigenous people, circa 1703, Baron de Lahontan, *New Voyages to North-America,* ed. by Reuben Gold Thwaites, 2 vols., Vol. 2 (Chicago: A.C. McClurg and Company), 432-433.

"They have a third Play with a Ball not unlike our Tennis, but the Balls are very large, and the Rackets refemble ours, fave that the Handle is at leaft three Foot long. The Savages, who commonly play at it in large Companies of three or four Hundred at a time, fix two Sticks at five or fix Hundreds Paces diftance from each other; They divide into two equal Parties, and tofs up the Ball about half way between the two Sticks. Each Party endeavour to tofs the Ball to their fide; fome run to the Ball, and the reft keep at a little diftance on both fides to affift on all Quarters. In fine this Game is fo violent that they tear their Skins, and break their legs very often in ftriving to raife the Ball. All thefe Games are made only for Feafts or other trifling Entertainments; for 'tis to be obferv'd, that as they hate Money, fo they never put it in the Ballance, and one may fay, *Intereft is never the occafion of Debates among them.*"

* * *

Nicolas Perrot, French commandant in the Upper Mississippi River valley and Great Lakes region, describes lacrosse, circa 1718, in Perrot, *Memoir on the Manners, Customs, and Religion of the Savages of North America* [1864], reprinted in Emma Helen Blair, ed. and trans., *The Indian Tribes of the Upper Mississippi Valley and Region of the Great Lakes,* 2 vols., Vol. 1 (Cleveland: Arthur H. Clark Company, 1911), 93-96.

"X. The games and amusements of the savages
I. *The game of crosse*

"The savages have several kinds of games, in which they take delight. They are naturally so addicted to these that they will give up their food and drink, not only to play but to watch the game. There is among them a certain game, called crosse, which has much likeness to our game of long tennis. Their custom in playing it is to oppose tribe to tribe; and if one of these is more numerous than the other, men are drawn from it to render the other equal to it [in strength]. You will see them all equipped with the crosse—which is a light club, having at one end a broad flat part that is netted like a [tennis] racket; the ball that they use in playing is of wood, and shaped very nearly like a turkey's egg. The goals for the game are marked in an open level space; these goals face east and west, south and north. In order to win the game, one of the two parties must send its ball, by driving it [with the racket], beyond the goals that face east and west; and the other [must send] its ball beyond those to the south and north. If the party which has once won sends the ball again beyond the east and west goals from the side that it had to win, it is obliged to recommence the game, and to accept the goals of the opposing party; but if it should succeed in winning a second time, it would have accomplished nothing—for, as the parties are equal in strength, and are quits, they always begin the game again in order to act the part of conqueror; and that party which wins carries away what has been staked on the game.

"Men, women, boys, and girls are received into the parties which are formed; and they bet against one another for larger or smaller amounts, each according to his means.

"These games usually begin after the melting of the winter's ice, and last until seed-time. In the afternoon all the players may be seen, painted with vermilion and decked with ornaments. Each party has its leader, who makes an address, announcing to his players the hour that has been appointed for beginning the games. All assemble in a body, in the middle of the place [selected], and one of the leaders of the two parties, holding the ball in his hand, tosses it into the air. Each player undertakes to send it in the direction in which he must drive it; if it falls to the ground, he endeavors to draw it toward him with his crosse; and, if it is sent outside the crowd of players, the more alert distinguish themselves from the others by closely following it. You will hear the din that they make by striking one another, while they strive to ward off the blows in order to send the ball in a favorable direction. If one of them keeps it between his feet, without allowing it to escape, it is for him to avoid the blows that his adversaries rain incessantly upon his feet; and, if he happens to be wounded in this encounter, that is his own affair. Some of them are seen who [thus] have had their legs or arms broken, and some even have been killed. It is very common to see among them men crippled for the rest of their lives, and who were hurt in games of this sort only as the result of their own obstinacy. When such accidents occur, the player who is so unfortunate as to be hurt retires quietly from the game, if he is in a condition to walk; but, if his injuries will not permit this, his relatives convey him to the cabin, and the game always goes on as if nothing were the matter, until it is finished.

"As for the runners, when the parties are equally strong they will sometimes spend an afternoon without either side gaining the advantage over the other; but sometimes, too, one of them will bear away the two victories which it must have in order to win the game. In this sport of racing, you would say that they looked like two victories opposing parties who meant to fight together. This exercise has much to do with rendering the savages agile, and ready to ward adroitly any blow from a club in the hands of an enemy, when they find themselves entangled in combat; and if one were not told beforehand that they were playing, one would certainly believe that they were fighting together in the open field. Whatever mishap this sport may occasion, they attribute it to the luck of the game, and they feel no hatred to one another. The trouble falls on the the injured persons, who nevertheless put on as contented an aspect as if nothing had happened to them, thus making it appear that they have great courage, and are men. The party that has won carries away what its members staked, and the profit that it has made, and that without any objection on either side when it is a question of paying [the bets], no matter what kind of game it may be. However, if any person who does not belong to the party, or who has not made any bet, should drive the bal to the advantage of one of the two parties, one of the players whom the blow does not favor would attack this man, demanding of him whether this were any of his business, and why he was meddling in it. They have often come to blows over this point, and and if some chief did not reconcile them there would be bloodshed, and even some one would be killed. The best way to prevent this disorderly conduct is to begin the game over again, with the consent of those who are winning; for if they refuse to do so, the responsibility rests on them. But when some one of the influential men interposes, it is not difficult to adjust their dispute and induce them to conform to his decision."

* * *

Antoine Le Page Du Pratz, French traveler, discusses lacrosse in Louisiana, circa 1720-1728, in Le Page du Pratz, *The History of Louisiana, or of the Western Parts of Virginia and Carolina. Containing a Description of the Countries that lie on both Sides of the River Mississippi. With an Account of the Settlements, Inhabitants, Soil, Climate, and Products* (London: T. Becket, 1774), 341.

"Next morning no perfon is feen abroad before the Great Sun comes out of his hut, which is generally about nine o'clock, and then upon a fignal made by the drum, the warriors make their appearance diftinguifhed into two troops, by the feathers which they wear on their heads. One of thefe troops is headed by the Great Sun, and the other by the chief of war, who begin a new diverfion by toffing a ball of deer-fkin ftuffed with Spanifh beard [moss] from one to the other. The warriors quickly take art in the fport, and a violent conteft enfues which of the two parties fhall drive the ball to the hut of the oppofite chief. The diverfion generally lafts two hours, and the victors are allowed to wear the feathers of fuperiority till the following year, or till the next time they play at the ball. After this the warriors perform the war dance; and laft of all they go and bathe; an exercife which they are very fond of when they are heated or fatigued."

* * *

J.C.B., French traveler, notes lacrosse playing in New France, circa 1751-1761, in Sylvester K. Stevens, Donald H. Kent, and Emma Edith Woods, eds., *Travels in New France by J.C.B.* (Harrisburg, Penn.: The Pennsylvania Historical Commission, 1941), 148.

"The game of lacrosse is played with a bat and a ball. Two posts are set up for the bounds, the distance between them depending on the number of players. For example, if there are sixty or eighty players, they will be nearly half a league apart. The players are divided into two teams, and each has a post. The ball is hit to the opposite side, which bats it back without letting it fall to the ground, or is touched by a hand, that side will lose the game. Savages are so skillful in batting the ball, that games sometimes last several consecutive days."

* * *

James Smith, Pennsylvania captive, describes lacrosse among the Shawanese, circa March? April? May? 1757, in William M. Darlington, ed., *An Account of the Remarkable Occurrences in the Life and Travels of Col. James Smith, During His Captivity with the Indians in the Years 1755, '56, '57, '58 and '59* (Cincinnati: Robert Clarke, 1907), 77-78.

"Many of the young men were now exercifing themfelves with a game game refembling foot ball; though they commonly ftruck the ball with a crooked ftick, made for that purpofe; alfo a game fomething like this, wherein they ufed a wooden ball, about three inches diameter, and the inftrument they moved it with was a ftrong ftaff about five feet long, with a hoop net on the end of it, large enough to contain the ball. Before they begin the play, they lay off about half a mile diftance in a clear plain, and the oppofite parties all attend at the centre, where a difinterefted perfon cafts up the ball then the oppofite parties all contend for it. If any one gets it into his net, he runs with it the way he wifhes it to go, and they all purfue him. If one of the oppofite party overtakes the perfon with the ball, he gives the ftaff a ftroke which caufes the ball to fly out of the net; then they have another debate for it; and if the one that gets it can outrun all the oppofite party, and can carry it quite out, or over the line at the end, the game is won; but this feldom happens. When any one is running away with the ball, and like to be overtaken, he commonly throws it, and with this inftrument can caft it fifty or fixty yards. Sometimes when the ball is almft at the one end, matters will take a fudden turn, and the oppofite party may quickly carry it out at the other end. Oftentimes they will work a long while back and forward before they can get the ball over the line, or win the game."

* * *

Jean-Bernard Bossu, French traveler, details lacrosse play among the Choctaw, 30 September 1759, in Seymour Feiler, ed., *Jean-Bernard Bossu's Travels in the Interior of North America, 1751-1762* (Norman, Okla.: University of Oklahoma Press, 1962), 169-170.

"The Choctaws are very fresh and alert. They play a game similar to our tennis and are very good at it. They invite the men of the neighboring villages to play and tease them by shouting insulting remarks at them. The men and the women gather dressed in their best clothing and spend the day dancing and singing. They even dance all night to the sound of drums and rattles. A game takes place on the day after a village lights its own special fire in the middle of a large field. The players agree upon a goal which is sixty steps away and which is marked by two large posts. The aim is to get the ball between these posts. The game is finished as soon one side has sixteen points. There are forty players on a team, and each one has a racket two and one-half feet long, made of walnut or chestnut wood and covered with deerskin. These rackets are shaped almost like ours.

"An old man, standing in the middle of the field, throws up a deerskin ball. The players then run to try to catch the ball in their rackets. It is fun to watch them play naked, painted with all kinds of colors, and with a wildcat's tail tied behind them. The feathers attached to their arms and heads look odd as they wave back and forth in the wind. The players push and throw each other down. Anyone who is skillful enough to get the ball passes it on to a teammate, and his opponents try to get it away from him. Both teams play with such ardor that shoulders are often dislocated in the fray. The players never become angry, and the old men, who act as referees, remind them that they are playing for sport and not for blood. There is a great deal of gambling; even the women bet among themselves.

"When the men's game is finished, the women get together to play to avenge their husbands' losses. Their rackets are different from those that the men use in that they are bent. The women, who are very good at this game, run swiftly and push each other around just as the men do. They are dressed exactly like the men, but with a little more modesty. They put red paint on their cheeks only and apply vermilion instead of powder to their hair.

"After having played hard all day long, everyone goes home in glory or in shame. There is no bitterness as each one promises to play another day when the best man will win. This is how the Indians practice running. They are so swift that I have seen some of them run as fast as deer."

* * *

Henry Timberlake, British lieutenant, mentions observing lacrosse in Tennessee, late January 1762, in Samuel Cole Williams, ed., *Lieut. Henry Timberlake's Memoirs, 1756-1765* (Marietta, Ga.: Continental Book Company, 1948 [1765]), 102.

"I was not a little pleased likewise with their ball-plays (in which they shew great dexterity) especially when the women played, who pulled one another about, to the no small amusement of an European spectator."

An unidentified British observer, comments on lacrosse in Michigan, ? May 1763, in "The Journal of Pontiac's Conspiracy," in Milo Milton Quaife, ed., *The Siege of Detroit in 1763. The Journal of Pontiac's Conspiracy* and *John Rutherfurd's Narrative of a Captivity* (Chicago: The Lakeside Press, 1958), 34-35.

"In order to play his part better and make it appear that neither he nor his followers cherished evil designs any longer, Pontiac invited for four o'clock in the afternoon the good and bad Huron bands and the Potawatomies to come and play lacrosse with his young men. A good many French from each side of the river came to play also, and were well received by the three nations. The game lasted till about seven o'clock in the evening, and when it was over everybody thought of returning home. The French who lived on the Fort side of the river and had been beaten were obliged to recross the river in order to return home."

* * *

Alexander Henry, British soldier, tells of a lethal lacrosse game at Fort Michilimackinac in Michigan, June 1763, in Milo Milton Quaife, ed., *Alexander Henry's Travels and Adventures in the Years 1760-1776* (Chicago: Lakeside Press, 1921), 78-79, 86-87.

"The morning was sultry. A Chipewa came to tell me that his nation was going to play at baggatiway with the Sacs or Saakies, another Indian nation, for a high wager. He invited me to witness the sport, adding that the commandant was to be there, and would bet on the side of the Chipewa. In consequence of this information I went to the commandant and expostulated with him a little, representing that the Indians might possibly have some sinister end in view; but the commandant only smiled at my suspicions.

"Baggatiway, called by the Canadians *le jeu de la crosse*, is played with a bat and a ball. The bat is about four feet in length, curved, and terminating in a sort of racket. Two posts are planted in the ground at a considerable distance from each other, as a mile or more. Each party has its post, and the game consists in throwing the ball up to the post of the adversary. The ball, at the beginning, is placed in the middle of the course and each party endeavors as well to throw the ball out of the direction of its own post as into that of the adversary's.

"I did not go myself to see the match, which was now to be played without the fort, because there being a canoe prepared to depart on the following day for Montreal I employed myself in writing letters to my friends;.... Mr. Tracy had not gone more than twenty paces from my door when I heard an Indian war cry and a noise of general confusion.

"Going instantly to my window I saw a crowd of Indians furiously cutting down and scalping every Englishman they found."

"The game of baggatiway, as from the description above will have been perceived, is necessarily attended with much violence and noise. In the ardor of the contest the ball, as has been suggested, if it cannot be thrown to the goal desired, is struck in any direction by which it can be diverted from that designed by the adversary. At such a moment, therefore, nothing could be less liable to excite premature alarm than that the ball should be tossed over the pickets of the fort, nor that having fallen there, it should be followed on the instant by all engaged in the game, as well the one party as the other, all eager, all struggling, all shouting, all in the unrestrained pursuit of a rude athletic exercise. Nothing could be less fitted to excite premature alarm—nothing, therefore, could be more happily devised, under the circumstances, than a stratagem like this; and this was in fact the stratagem which the Indians employed, by which they had obtained possession of the fort, and by which they had been enabled to slaughter and subdue its garrison and such of its other inhabitants as they pleased. To be still more certain of success they had prevailed upon as many as they could by a pretext the least liable to suspicion to come voluntarily without the pickets, and particularly the commandant and garrison themselves."

* * *

Chippewa chief Kinonchamek speaks to the Ottawa chief Pontiac, in Michigan, ? June 1763, in quoted in "The Journal of Pontiac's Conspiracy," in Milo Milton Quaife, ed., *The Siege of Detroit in 1763. The Journal of Pontiac's Conspiracy* and *John Rutherfurd's Narrative of a Captivity* (Chicago: The Lakeside Press, 1958), 143.

"Like you, we have undertaken to chase the English out of our territory and we have succeeded. And we did it without glutting ourselves with their blood after we had taken them, as you have done; we surprised them while playing a game of lacrosse, at a time when they were unsuspecting."

* * *

John Rutherfurd, British captive, refers to lacrosse in Michigan, circa 1763, in John Rutherfurd, "John Rutherfurd's Captivity Narrative," in Milo Milton Quaife, ed., *The Siege of Detroit in 1763. The Journal of Pontiac's Conspiracy* and *John Rutherfurd's Narrative of a Conspiracy* (Chicago: The Lakeside Press, 1958), 237.

"When they [the indigenous people who captured him] have victuals of any sort in their huts they do nothing but eat, smoke their pipe, and sleep. Sometimes they amuse themselves with a game something like our children's diversion of shinty, where the females play against the men and often come off victorious. It is on this occasion that the beaux and belles make their conquests and dress in their best attire."

* * *

Jonathan Carver, Massachusetts surveyor and agent for Robert Rogers, comments on lacrosse among indigenous peoples in the Great Lakes region, circa 1766-1768, in Carver, *Jonathan Carver's Travels through the Interior Parts of North America in the Years 1766, 1767, and 1768,* 3rd ed. (London: C. Dilly, 1781), 363-365.

"*Of their* GAMES.

"AS I have before obferved, the Indians are greatly addicted to gaming, and will even ftake, and lofe with compofure, all the valuables they are poffeffed of. They amufe themfelves at feveral forts of games, but the principal and most efteemed among them is that of ball, which is not unlike the European game of tennis.

"The balls they ufe are rather larger than those made ufe of at tennis and are formed of a piece of deer-fkin which, being moiftened to render it fupple, is ftuffed hard with the hair of the fame creature and fewed with its finews. The ball-fticks are about three feet long, at the end of which there is fixed a kind of racket, refembling the palm of the hand and fafhioned of things cut from a deer-fkin. In thefe they catch the ball and throw it to a great diftance, if they are not prevented by some of the oppofite party who fly to intercept it.

"They begin by fixing two poles in the ground at about six hundred yards apart, and one of thefe goals belongs to each party of the combatants. The ball is thrown up high in the centre of the ground and in a direct line between the goals towards which each party endeavours to ftrike it, and which ever side firft caufes it to reach their own goal, reckons towards the game.

"They are so exceeding dextrous in this manly exercife that the ball is ufually kept flying in different directions by the force of the rackets, without touching the ground during the whole contention; for they are not allowed to catch it with their hands. They run with amazing velocity in purfuit of each other and, when one is on the point of hurling it to a great diftance, an antagonift overtakes him, and by a fudden ftroke dafhes down the ball.

"They play with fo much vehemence that they frequently wound each other, and fometimes a bone is broken; but notwithftanding these accidents there never appears to be any fpite or wanton exertions of ftrength to effect them, nor do any difputes happen between the parties."

* * *

John Haywood, Tennessee historian, describes lacrosse among the Cherokee, circa 1768, in Haywood, *The Natural and Aboriginal History of Tennessee Up to the First Settlements therein by White People in the Year 1768,* ed. by Mary U. Rothrock (Jackson, Tenn.: McCowat-Mercer press, 1959 [1823]), 267-268.

"Of their Games.

The Cherokees have many games for their amusement, which are common to other tribes of the south. Amongst them is the game called ball-play. It is generally played at the time of the fall season. The moon presides over it as a tutelary spirit. In the time of Te-shy-ah-Natchee, two chiefs made a ball-play, at which all the red people attended, men, women and children. The contest between the parties was very severe for a long time, when one of them got the advantage by the superior skill of a young man. His adversary on the other side, seeing no chance of success in fair play, attempted to cheat, when in throwing the ball, it stuck in the sky and turned into the appearance which the moon hath, to remind the Indians that cheating and dishonesty are crimes. When the moon becomes small and pale, it is because the ball has been handled by unfair play. They therefore for a long time never played at this game but on the full moon. Many of their customs are now disregarded, and the tradition of them is totally lost. The ball is now played for the most part without any regard to custom.

"The mode of playing it is this: Two chiefs meet, and make up the game, each taking his choice of young men, against the others. An open plain is selected, at which the chiefs meet and lay off the ground, about 400 yards in circumference, through which the ball passes. Equidistant from the extremes of the alley, the grappling sticks to catch the ball are placed. Each chief then retires to his party, consisting of equal numbers, from 11 to 30 on each side, who march up to the centre, whooping and yelling as if going to war. The first thing is to make up all the stakes, which are deposited in one pile. Each chief then addresses his party. He animates them with the glory of beating their adversaries, and the advantage of winning the stakes, which are all to be equally divided amongst the warriors. They are admonished to play fair, that the Great Spirit may not be offended with them. The chiefs then take their station, as judges of the game. The parties arrange themselves in the centre, and the ball is thrown up, each grappling it with his sticks, having a bow at the end to catch the ball. Another seizes it with his grappling stick, and runs away with it, to the post of his party, till at length someone, more active and swift gets the ball too far ahead to be overtaken, till he arrives at the goal, which counts for his party one in the game. Thus the game is continued, sometimes one party carrying out the ball, sometimes the other, till the game is finished, which sometimes takes two or three hours; during which they display as much zeal and animation as if they were contending for prizes of the highest value, yelling, and giving each other the most dreadful falls, in order to stop their progress. The dress worn by the players, is a belt or wampum around the waist, with a flap of blue cloth. When the game is ended, the stakes are equally divided by the chiefs of the winning party. The one who carries out the most balls is dubbed a hero, and is huzzaed as if he had conquered an enemy. For to excel in this game is a great mark of prowess in the chase or field of battle."

* * *

James Adair, Scots-Irish trader, discusses lacrosse among Southeastern indigenous peoples, circa 1775, in [Adair], *Adair's History of the American Indians,* ed. by Samuel Cole Williams (New York: Promontory Press, 1973 [1775]), 428-430.

"The Indians are much addicted to gaming, and will often stake everything they possess. Ball-playing is their chief and most favourite game: and is such severe exercise, as to shew it was originally calculated for a hardy and expert race of people, like themselves, and the ancient Spartans. The ball is made of a piece of scraped deer-skin, moistened, and stuffed hard with deer's hair, and strongly sewed with deer's sinews.— The ball-sticks are about two feet long, the lower end somewhat resembling the palm of a hand, and which are worked with deer-skin thongs. Between these, they catch the ball, and throw it a great distance, when not prevented by some of the opposite party, who fly to intercept them. The goal is about five hundred yards in length: at each end of it, they fix two long bending poles into the ground, three yards apart below, but slanting a considerable ways outwards. The party that happens to throw the ball over these, counts one; but, if it be thrown underneath, it is cast back, and played for as usual. The gamesters are equal in number on each side; and, at the beginning of every course of the ball, they throw it high in the center of the ground, and in a direct line between the two goals. When the crowd of players prevents the one who catched the ball, from throwing it off with a long direction, he commonly sends it the right course, by an artful sharp twirl. They are so exceedingly expert in this manly exercise, that, between the goals, the ball is mostly flying the different ways, by the force of the playing sticks, without falling to the ground, for they are not allowed to catch it with their hands. It is surprising to see how swiftly they fly, when closely chased by a nimble footed pursuer; when they are intercepted by one of the opposite party, his fear of being cut by the ball sticks, commonly gives them an opportunity of throwing it perhaps a hundred yards; but the antagonist sometimes runs up behind, and by a sudden stroke dashes down the ball. It is a very unusual thing to see them act spitefully in any sort of game, not even in this severe and tempting exercise.

"Once, indeed, I saw some break the legs and arms of their opponents, by hurling them down, when on a descent, and running at full speed. But I afterward understood, there was a family dispute of long continuance between them: that might have raised their spleen, as much as the high bets they had then at stake, which was almost all they were worth. The Choktah are exceeding addicted to gaming, and frequently on the slightest and most hazardous occasion, will lay their all, and as much as their credit can procure.

"By education, precept, and custom, as well as strong example, they have learned to shew an external acquiescence in every thing that befalls them, either as to life or death, By this means, they reckon it a scandal to the character of a steady warrior to let his temper be ruffled by any accidents,—their virtue they say, should prevent it.

Their conduct is equal to their belief of the power of those principles: previous to this sharp exercise of ball playing, notwithstanding the irreligion of the Choktah in other respects, they will supplicate *Yo He Wah,* to bless them with success. To move the deity to enable them to conquer the arty they are to play against, they mortify themselves in a surprising manner; and, except a small intermission, their female relations dance out of doors all the preceding night, chanting religious notes by their shrill voices, to move *Yo He Wah* to be favourable to their kindred party on the morrow. The men fast and wake from sunset, till the ball play is over the next day, which is about one or two o'clock in the afternoon. During the whole night, they are to forbear sleeping under the penalty of reproaches and shame; which would sit very sharp upon them, if their party chanced to lose the game, as it would be ascribed to that unmanly and vicious conduct. They turn out to the ball ground, in a long row, painted white, whooping, as if Pluto's prisoners were all broke loose: when that enthusiastic emotion is over, the leader of the company begins a religious invocation, by saying *Yah,* short; then *Yo* long, which the rest of the train repeat with a shortaccent, and on a low key like the leader: and thus they proceed with such acclamations and invocations, as have been already noticed, on other occasions. Each party are desirous to gain the twentieth ball, which they esteem a favourite divine gift. As it is the time of laying by the corn, in the very heat of summer, they use this severe exercise, a stranger would wonder to see them hold it so long at full speed, and under the scorching sun, hungry also, and faint with the excessive use of such physic as the button snake root, the want of natural rest, and of every kind of nourishment. But their constancy, which they gain by custom, and their love of virtue, as the sure means of success, enable them to perform all their exercises, without failing in the least, be they ever so severe in the pursuit."

* * *

Bernard Romans, French captain, comments on lacrosse among the Choctaw and Chickasaw in the Southeast, circa 1775, in Romans, *A Concise Natural History of East and West Florida* (New York: pvt. ptg., 1775), 70, 79.

"They [the Chickasaws] are ftrong, and fwift of foot, and their exercife at home is chiefly their ball play, a very laborious diverfion."

"Their [the Choctaws'] play at ball is either with a fmall ball of deer fkin or a large one with woollen rags; the firft is thrown with battledores, the fecond with the hand only; this is a trial of fkill between village and village; after having appointed the day and field for meeting, they affemble at the time and place, fix two poles acrofs each other at about an hundred and fifty feet apart, they then attempt to throw the ball through the lower part of them, and the oppofite party trying to prevent it, throw it back among themfelves, which the firft again try to prevent; thus they attempt to beat it about from one to the other with amazing violence, and not feldom broken limbs or diflocated joints are the confequence; their being almoft naked, painted and ornamented with feathers, has a good effect on the eye of the byftander during this violent diverfion; a number is agreed on for the fcore, and the party who firft gets this number wins.

"The women play among themfelves (after the men have done) difputing with as much eagernefs as the men; the ftakes or betts are generally high. There is no difference in the other game with the large ball, only the men and women play promifcuously, and they ufe no battledores."

William Bartram, Philadelphia naturalist, comments on lacrosse among Southeastern indigenous people, circa 1776, in William Bartram, *Travels through North and South Carolina, Georgia, East and West Florida*, ed. by Mark Van Doren (New York: Dover Publications, [1791]), 398.

"The ball play is esteemed the most noble and manly exercise. This game is exhibited in an extensive level plain, usually contiguous to the town; the inhabitants of one town play against another, in consequence of a challenge, when the youth of both sexes are often engaged, and sometimes stake their whole substance. Here they perform amazing feats of strength and agility. The game principally consists in taking and carrying off the ball from the opposite party, after being hurled into the air, midway between two high pillars, which are the goals, and the party who bears off the ball to their pillar wins the game; each person has a raquet or hurl, which is an implement of a very curious construction, somewhat resembling a ladle or little hoop net, with a handle near three feet in length, the hoop and handle of wood, and the netting of thongs of raw hide, or tendons of an animal."

* * *

John Long, American trader, notes lacrosse among the eastern Canadian indigenous people, circa 1777, in Milo Milton Quaife, ed., *John Long's Voyages and Travels in the Years 1768-1788* (Chicago: Lakeside Press, 1922), 68-69.

"Playing at ball, which is a favorite game, is very fatiguing. The ball is about the size of a cricket ball, made of deer skin and stuffed with hair; this is driven forwards and backwards with short sticks, about two feet long, and broad at the end like a bat, worked like a racket, but with larger interstices. By this the ball is impelled, and from the elasticity of the racket, which is composed of deer's sinews, is thrown to a great distance. The game is played by two parties, and the contest lies in intercepting each other, and striking the ball into a goal, at the distance of about four hundred yards, at the extremity of which are placed two high poles, about the width of a wicket from each other. The victory consists in driving the ball between the poles. The Indians play with great good humor and even when one of them happens, in the heat of the game, to strike another with his stick, it is not resented. But these accidents are cautiously avoided, as the violence with which they strike has been known to break an arm or a leg."

OTHER SPORTS AND GAMES

Francisco Gomarra, Spanish historian, refers to several games among indigenous peoples in Mexico, circa 1519-1522, in Gomarra, *The Pleasant Hiftorie of the Conqueft of the VVeaft India, now called new Spayne* (London: Henry Bynneman, 1578?), 179-180.

"The Tennis play in Mexico.

"Sometimes *Mutezuma* went to the Tennis Courte. Their ball is called *Villamliztli* and is made of the gumme which commeth from a tree called *vlli*. This tree groweth in a hote Countrey. The gumme being kneded togither, and fo made round, is as blacke as pitch, and fomewhat beadle, and very harde for the hande, but yet good and light to rebound, and better than our windballes. They play not at chafes, but at ???, or at check, that is, if the ball touch the wall it lofeth. They maye ftrike the ball with any part of their body, but tehre is alwayes a penaltie if they only ftrike not with the buttoke by fide, whiche is the fineft play: wherefore they ufe a fkynne upon eache buttocke. They play fo many to fo many for a packe of mantels or according to the abilitie of the players. Alfo they play for golde and feathers, and fometime for their own bodyes, as they ufe at *Patolli*, which is there permitted & lawfull. The Tennis Court is called *Tlachti*, and is a hall long and narrow, but wyder upwards, than downewardes, and higher on the fides than at y' ends, which is an induftrie for their play. The houfe is always white and fmooth in the fide walles: they have certain ftones like unto myl-ftones, w' a little hole in the middeft that paffeth through the ftonr, the hole is fo fmall, that fcarcely the ball maye paffe through, but he that chanceth to ftrike the ball into the hole, whiche feldome happneth, winneth the game, and by an auntients lawe and cuf-tome among Tennis players, he ought to have the clokes of all thofe that ftande and beholde the play, on that fide that the ball went in, and in fome Tennis Courtes, the halfe of the garmentes of them that ftande lookyng on. The winner is then bounde to make certayne facrifice to the God of Tennis play, and to the ftone where the ball entred. The beholders of the play woulde faye, that fuche a wynner fhould be a thiefe and an adulterer, or elfe that he fhoulde dye quickly.

"They vfed in the Temple of the Tennis play two Images of the God of the ball, which ftoode vpon the two lower walles. Their Sacrifce was celebrated at midnighte, with many Ceremonies and Witchcraftes, and fongs for that purpofe. Then came a Priefte from the Cathedrall Churche, wyth other Religious perfons to bleffe the Sac-rifice, fying certayne divelifhe prayers, and throwing the ball four tymes in the Ten-nis Court. In thys order was the Tennis play confecrated, and after thys confecration it was lawfull to play, or elfe not for this diligence was firfte to be done when any Tennis Court or play was newly built.

"The owner of the Tennis Courte alfo woulde never fuffer any to play, untill he had firft ffered fomething to the Divell, theyr fuperftition was fo great.

"*Mutezuma* broughte the *Spanyardes* to behold this paftime and gave the' to vnderftande y' he delyghted much in thys game, and alfo to fee our men play at Cardes and Dyce."

* * *

René Laudonniere, French explorer, concerning the Timucua indigenous people in Florida, notes a ball game, circa 1562, in Laudonniere, *History of the First Attempt of the French to Colonize the Newly Discovered Country of Florida*, trans. by Richard Hakluyt, reprinted in B.F. French, ed., *Historical Collections of Louisiana and Florida* (New York: J. Sabin and Sons, 1869), 171.

"They play at ball in this manner: they set up a tree in the midst of a place, which is eight or nine fathoms high, in the top whereof there is set a square mat, made of reeds or bullrushes, which whosoever hitteth in playing thereat winneth the game."

* * *

Fray Bernardino Sahagun, Spanish missionary, refers to the Aztec game of *tlachtli*, circa 1559-1569, in Sahagun, *The Florentine Codex. General History of the Things of New*

Spain, Book 8—Kings and Lords, Monographs of the School of American Research No.
14, Pt. 9, ed. by Arthur J.O. Anderson and Charles E. Dibble, (Santa Fe, N.M.: School
of American Research, 1979), 29.

"They [the rulers] played ball. There were his ball-catchers and his ball-players. They
wagered [in this game] all [manner of] costly goods—gold, golden necklaces, green
stone, fine turquoise, slaves, precious capes, valuable breech clouts, cultivated fields,
houses, leather leg bands, gold bracelets, arm bands of quetzal feathers, duck feather
capes, bales of cacao—[these] were wagered there in the game called tlachtli.

"On the two sides, on either hand, it was limited by walls, very well made, in that
the walls and floor were smoothed. And there, in the very center of the ball court, was
a line, drawn upon the ground. And on the walls were two stone, ball court rings. He
who played caused [the ball] to enter there; he caused it to go in. Then he won all the
costly goods, and he won everything from all who watched there in the ball court. His
equipment was the rubber ball, the eather gloves, girdles, and leather hip guards."

* * *

Fray Diego Duran, Spanish Dominican missionary, describes the Aztec ball game,
tlachtli, circa 1576-1579, in Duran, *The Book of the Gods and Rites and The Ancient Calendar,* trans. and ed. by Fernando Horcasitas and Doris Heyden (Norman, Okla.: University of Oklahoma Press, 1971), 312-317.

"CHAPTER XXIII

"Which treats of the popular and solemn ball game, much played by the lords,
      in which some, after having lost their wealth, staked their own lives.

"MANY of the Indians' games were extremely subtle, clever, cunning, and highly
refined. [It is a pity] that so much heathenism and idolatry was mixed up with them!

"For who will not grant that it is a subtle and skillful thing for a man [on his back]
to balance a thick log about nine feet long upon his feet as nimbly as another with his
hands, playing so many tricks and turns with it, casting it hither and thither and on
high, catching it with the soles of his feet with admirable deftness?

"Who will not wonder on gazing upon a dance in which forty or fifty men appear
around the drum, on stilts six or twelve feet tall, moving and turning with their bodies as if they were walking with their own feet?

"Who will not consider it a skillful and mihty thing that three men walk about upon
one another's shoulders, the lower one dancing with his arms outstretched and his
hands filled with feathers or with flowers, and the one in the middle doing the same,
and the third one doing the same—each without more support than his feet on the
other's shoulders? It is true that this shows not only skill and dexterity but also an
amazing strength in the feet.

"Nor is it less wondrous to see an Indian standing on the top of the 'flying pole'
(for so they call it) anywhere between one hundred eighty and two hundred feet in
height! He stands there with a trumpet in his hand, and, just watching him, those who
observe become giddy. Yet he is so calm and firm that he seems completely at ease.
He walks around at the summit of the pole—a space a few inches wide which barely
accommodates his feet. And after having performed a thousand turns and tricks, he
descends with an expression as serene as if he had done nothing!

"What could be more entertaining than to see a man lying on the ground on his
back with one foot lifted and other men climbing upon the sole of that foot, doing

twenty turns upon it, then jumping down quickly, one after another, so lightly that I cannot understand how the man can tolerate such punishment to his leg, since [the others] jump and turn upon it, yet do not bend it or move it any more than they would a post.

"I have presented this preamble so that we may describe the ball game, which I am going to deal with, as the chapter indicates and the illustration shows. It was a highly entertaining game and amusement for the people, especially for those who held it to be a pastime or entertainment. Among them there were those who played it with such skill and cunning that in one hour the ball did not stop bouncing from one end to the other, without a miss, [the players] using only their buttocks [and knees], never touching it with the hand, foot, calf, or arm. Both teams were so alert in keeping the ball bouncing that it was amazing. If watching a handball game among Spaniards gives us such pleasure and amazement on seeing the skill and lightness with which some play it, how much more are to be praised those who with such cunning, trickery, and nimbleness play it with their backsides or knees! It was considered a foul to touch [the ball] with the hand or any other part of the body except the parts I have mentioned — buttocks and knees. Through this demanding sport excellent players were formed, and, aside from being esteemed by the sovereigns, they were given notable dignities, were made intimates of the royal house and court, and were honored with special insignia.

"Many a time have I seen this game played, and to find out why the elders still extol it [I asked them] to play it in the ancient way. But the most important [factor] was lacking, namely the enclosure where the contest took place, within which it was played, and the rings through which they cast and passed the ball. And it was a foolish insistence of mine to try to see today something which existed in ancient times, as different as the real thing from a picture. So that we can understand its form and begin to appreciate the skill and dexterity with which this game was played, it must be noted that ball courts existed in all illustrious, civilized, and powerful cities and towns, in those ruled by either the community or the lords, the latter stressing [the game] inordinately. A regular competition existed between the two [types of communities]. [The ball courts] were enclosed with ornate and handsomely carved walls. The interior floor was of stucco, finely polished and decorated with figures of the god and demons to whom the game was dedicated and whom the players held to be their patrons in that sport. These ball courts were larger in some places than in others. They were built in the shape that can be seen in the illustration: narrow in the middle and wide at the ends. The corners were built on purpose so that if the player's ball fell into one it was lost and was considered a foul. The height of the wall was anywhere between eight and eleven feet high, running all around the [court]. Because of the heathen custom, around the [wall] were planted wild palms or trees which give red seeds, whose wood is soft and light. Crucifixes and carved images are made of it today. The surrounding walls were adorned with merlons or stone statues, all spaced out. [These places] became filled to bursting when there was a game of all the lords, when warlike activities ceased, owing to truces or other causes, thus permitting [the games].

"The ball courts were anywhere between one hundred, one hundred fifty, and two hundred feet long. In the square corners (which served as ends or goals) a great number of players stood on guard to see that the ball did not penetrate. The main players stood in the center facing the ball, and so did the opponents, since the game was carried out similarly to the way they fought in battle or in special contests. In the middle of the walls of this enclosure were fixed two stones facing one another, and each had a hole in the center. Each hole was surrounded by a carved image of the deity of the game. Its face was that of a monkey.

"As we shall see under *The Calendar,* this feast was celebrated once a year, and to clarify the use of these stones it should be noted that one team put the ball through the hole of of the stone on one side while the other side was used by the other team. The first to pass its ball through [the hole] won the prize. These stones also served as a division, for between them, on the floor, was a black or green stripe. This was done with a certain herb and no other, which is a sign of pagan belief. The ball always had to be passed across this line to win the game, because if the ball, projected by the back-sides or by the knee, went bouncing along the floor and passed the stripe the width of two fingers, no fault was committed; but if it did not pass, it was considered a foul play. The man who sent the ball through the stone ring was surrounded by all. They honored him, sang songs of praise to him, and joined him in dancing. He was given a very special reward of feathers or mantles and breechcloths, something highly prized. But what he most prized was the honor involved; that was his great wealth. For he was honored as a man who had vanquished many and had won a battle.

"All those who played this game were stripped except for their usual breechcloths, on top of which they wore coverings of deerskin to defend their thighs, which were continually being scratched on the floor. They wore gloves so as not to injure their hands, which they constantly set down firmly, supporting themselves against the floor. They bet jewels, slaves, precious stones, fine mantles, the trappings of war, and women's finery. Others staked their mistresses. It must be understood that this took place, as I have described, among the nobility, the lords, captains, braves, and important men. Countless lords and knights attended this game and played it with such pleasure and enjoyment, changing places with one another occasionally, taking their turns so that everyone could take part in that pleasant sport, to the point that sometimes the sun set upon them while they enjoyed themselves.

"Some of these men were taken out dead from that place for the following reason. Tired and without having rested, [they ran] after the ball from end to end, seeing it descending from above, in haste and hurry to reach it first, but the ball on the rebound hit them in the mouth or the stomach or the intestines, so that they fell to the floor instantly. Some died of that blow on the spot because they had been too eager to touch the ball before anyone else. Some took a special pride in this game and performed so many feats in it that it was truly amazing. There is one trick especially that I wish to describe. I saw it done many times by skillful Indians. They employed a bounce or curious hit. On seeing the ball come at them, at the moment that it was about to touch the floor, they were so quick in turning their knees or buttocks to the ball that they returned it with an extraordinary swiftness. With this bouncing back and forth they suffered terrible injuries on their knees or thighs so that the haunches of those who made use of these tricks were frequently so bruisd that those spots had to be opened with a small blade, whereupon the blood which had clotted there because of the blows of the ball was squeezed out.

"As some may have seen, this ball was as large as a small bowling ball. The material that the ball [was made of] was called *ollin,* which in our own Castilian tongue I have heard translated as *batel,* which is the resin of a certain tree. When cooked it becomes stringy. It is very much esteemed and prized by these people, both as a medicine for the ailing and for religious offerings. Jumping and bouncing are its qualities, upward and downward, to and fro. It can exhaust the pursuer running after it before he can catch up with it.

"Having described the manner in which the nobleman played this ball game for recreation and sport, we shall now deal with those who played it for profit and as a vice, their endeavors and happiness depending upon not losing but winning, like professional gamblers, whose only occupation and job this was, and no other, who depended upon this for their food. Their wives and children...lived constantly on borrowed bread, asking alms of their neighbors, bothering this one and that one, such as some Spaniards do, sending here for bread today, there for vinegar tomorrow, another day for oil, and so on. In this way these men usually went about poor and ill-fortuned, without sowing or reaping. It is rare [even today] to find one of these players prosperous, and they have nothing to show for their efforts. Thus moved and torn by greed and desire of gain, they performed a thousand ceremonies and superstitious acts, invented ways of fortunetelling and idolatrous beliefs which I shall explain here.

"In the first place, it should be known that, when night had fallen, these players took the ball and placed it in a clean bowl, together with the protective leather breechcloth and gloves, and hung it all on a pole. Squatting before these accouterments of the game, they worshiped them and addressed to them certain supersititious words and magic spells; devotedly they besought the ball to be lucky on that day. During the incantation to the ball they invoked the hills, the water, the springs, the cliffs, the trees, the wild animals and snakes; the sun, the moon, and the stars; the clouds, the rainstorms —in sum, all created things, together with the gods which had been invented for each of these.

"When that cursed heathen prayer terminated, [each player] took a handful of incense, cast it into a small incense burner which existed for this purpose, and offered a sacrifice to the ball and to the leather gear. While the copal burned, [the player] went forth to bring food, consisting of bread, a humble stew, and wine, and offered these things in front of the paraphernalia, leaving them there until dawn. When day broke, he ate that simple fare which he had offered and went out to seek someone to play with. They went along, each so sure of winning that if someone suggested to either that he was to lose his faith was such that he would come to mortal blows with [that person] and seven times over defend his heathen belief, something I doubt he would do today in defending our True Faith."

* * *

Robert Sandford, Barbados lieutenant-colonel, describes a type of bowling and running game among the indigenous people in the Cape Fear region of North Carolina, June 1666, in Sandford, "A Relation of a Voyage on the Coast of the Province of Carolina, 1666, by Robert Sandford," in Alexander S. Salley, Jr., ed., *Narratives of Early Carolina, 1650-1708* (New York: Barnes & Noble, 1967 [1911]), 91-92.

"Before the Doore of their Statehouse is a spacious walke rowed with trees on both sides, tall and full branched, not much unlike to Elms, which serves for the Exercise and recreation of the men, who by Couple runn after a marble bowle troled out alternately by themselves, with six foote staves in their hands, which they tosse after the bowle in their race, and according to the laying of their staves wine or loose the beeds they contend for; an excercise approveable enough in the winter, but some what too violent (mee thought) for that season and noontime of the day. From this walke is another lesse aside from the round house for the children to sport in."

* * *

John Lederer, German traveler, notes a game of slinging stones among the Oenock indigenous peoples near the Catawba River, Carolina, 16 June 1669, in [Lederer], *The Discoveries of* John Lederer, *In three feveral Marches from Virginia, to the Weft of Carolina, and other parts of the Continent. Begun in* March 1669, *and ended in* September 1670 (London: Samuel Heyrick, 1672; University Microfilms reprint, 1966), 15.

"Their Town is built round a field, where in their Sports they exercife with fo much labour and violence, and in fo great numbers, that I have feen the ground wet with the fweat that dropped from their bodies: their chief Recreation is Slinging of ftones."

* * *

Fray Juan de Paiva, Spanish Franciscan missionary in Florida, comments on the game of pelota among the Apalachee and Ustaqua indigenous peoples, 23 September 1676, reprinted in Amy Bushnell, "'That Demonic Game.' The Campaign to Stop Indian *Pelota* Playing in Spanish Florida, 1675-1684," The Americas, Vol. 35, No. 1 (July 1978), 7, 15.

"They go after one another with all their might, falling to the ground on top of each other and piling up. Others, to enter in, climb up the bodies as though they were stairs, stepping upon faces, heads and bellies without hesitation: now giving kicks to a face, to a body, to whatever; in other places pulling at arms and legs as though to pull them off. Others are having their mouths filled with dirt. When this heap begins to come untangled, over there are four or five stretched out like tuna fish; there, others with the breath choked out of them, because since they tend to swallow [the ball], the rest make them vomit it up by choking them or kicking their bellies. Over there are others witha broken leg or arm."

"They went about looking for players, entertaining and flattering them, which is like flattering viscious and indolent men, for ordinarily a great pelota player is a great rascal.... They would dig his field, build his house and storehouse. He had license for any kind of misconduct. because the caciques and principales would hide and cover it from the *religioso* and the teniente, without regard to the law of God, fearing that if he were punished he would leave for another place."

"By the love of God, by His Most Holy Mother, by the wounds of our father St. Francis, tell me one single good thing about the game of pelota which they play and for that one I am shown I will be still. (They will not tell me any and so I will not be still....) This game was invented by the devil and by its consequences it can be known.... Behold the abuses, idolatries, discords! It is the center of lasciviousness and the consuming of the substance of these poor creatures,.... [now] so docile and reduced [in number] that my heart weeps to see it."

* * *

Henri Joutel, French explorer with the La Salle expedition, describes a game of stick in the Illinois country, October 1687, in [Joutel], *Joutel's Journal of La Salle's Last Voyage* (Chicago: The Caxton Club, 1896, [rpt. of 1714 edition]), 175.

"A good Number of Prefents ftill remaining, they divide them into feveral Lots, and play at a Game, call'd of the Stick, to give them to the Winner. That Game is play'd, taking a fhort Stick, very fmooth and greas'd, that it may be the Harder to hold it faft.

One of the Elders throws that Stick as far as he can, the young Men run after it, fnatch it from each other, and at laft, he who remains poffefs'd of it, has the firft Lot. The Stick is then thrown again, he who keeps it then has the fecond Lot, and fo on to the End. The Women, whofe Husbands have been flain in War, often perform the fame Ceremony, and treat the Singers and dancers whom they have before invited."

* * *

Father Paul du Ru, Jesuit missionary, observes a type of ball game and comments on betting among the Muskogeans in Mississippi, February and April 1700, in Ruth Lapham Butler, trans., *Journal of Paul du Ru [February 1 to May 8, 1700] Missionary Priest to Louisiana* (Chicago: The Caxton Club, 1934), 21, 52.

27 February 1700: "We walked to the village where there were games and a great dance. The men play in pairs; one of them has a ball in his hand and throws it ahead. Both of them run as fast as they can, throwing a big stick after this ball and, as well as I could make out, the one whose stick is closest to the ball wins the play. Then the one who wins throws the ball the next time. This is a rather strenuous game; neverthe-less, it is played by both old and young. The women have a game also. They separate into two parties between two large posts in the square. Somebody throws a little ball in the center, and the one who seizes it first tries her best to run around the post on her side three times, but she is prevented by the women of the opposite party who seize her if they can. When she can no longer resist them, she throws the ball to her people who make a similar effort to run around their post. Sometimes the ball falls into the hands of the other side which then tries the same manoeuvre. The games are very long and ordinarily when they are over the women plunge into the water to refresh them-selves. Sometimes the men play this game also."

4 April 1700: "I have observed that these people are great gamblers. One has no sooner given a present than he finds it in the middle of the square staked in a game; they will wager everything on the outcome of a ball game. I refer to the game I have already mentioned. It is astonishing how calmly they gamble. Apparently winning or losing is alike to them. I have enjoyed watching them to notice how impossible it would be to judge the course of the play by their expressions, particularly in the games that call for little movement."

* * *

Juan Mateo Manje, Spanish captain, concerning indigenous people in southern Arizona, describes a game called patole, circa 1701, in [Manje], *Unknown Arizona and Sonora, 1693-1721, From the Francisco Fernandez del Castillo Version of Luz De Tierra Incog-nita by Captain Juan Mateo Manje*, ed. by Harry J. Karns (Tucson, Ariz.: Arizona Silhou-ettes, 1954), 242.

"They have another game called *patole*, in which four pieces of cane, cut and stripped to a *jeme* in length, are used. They throw these pieces on top of a stone so that they bounce and fall to the floor which is marked in lines, and the first one who reaches the determined score wins."

* * *

Robert Beverly, Virginia plantation owner and historian, comments on games among Virginia indigenous peoples, circa 1705, in Beverly, *The History and Present State of Virginia*, ed. by Louis B. Wright (Charlottesville, Va.: University Press of Virginia, 1947), 221.

456

"Of the Sports, and Pastimes of the Indians.

"THEIR Sports and Pastimes are Singing, Dancing, Instrumental Musick, and some boisterous Plays, which are perform'd by Running, Catching and Leaping upon one another; they have also one great Diversion, to the practising of which, are requisite whole handfuls of Sticks or hard Straws, which they know how to count as fast, as they can cast their Eyes upon them, and can handle with a surprizing dexterity."

* * *

Antoine Le Page du Pratz, French traveler, discusse a stone and throwing game in Louisiana, circa 1720-1728, in Le Page du Pratz, *The History of Louisiana, or of the Western Parts of Virginia and Carolina. Containing a Description of the Countries that lie on both Sides of the River Mississippi. With an Account of the Settlements, Inhabitants, Soil, Climate, and Products* (London: T. Becket, 1774), 347.

"All nations are not equally ingenious at inventing feafts, fhews, and diverfions, for employing the people agreeably, and filling up the void of their ufual employments. The natives of Louifiana have invented but a very few diverfions, and thefe perhaps ferve their turn as well as a greater variety would do. The warriors practife a diverfion which is called the game of *the pole*, at which only two play together at a time. Each has a pole about eight feet long, refembling a Roman f, and the game confifts in rolling a flat round ftone, about three iches diameter and an inch thick, with the edge fomewhat floping, and throwing the pole at the fame time in fuch a manner, that when the ftone refts, the pole may touch it or be near it. Both antagonifts throw their poles at the fame time, and he whofe pole is neareft the ftone counts one, and has the right of rolling the ftone. The men fatigue themselves much at this game, as they run after their poles at every throw; and fome of them are fo bewitched by it, that they game away one piece of furniture after another. These gamefters however are very rare, and are greatly difcountenanced by the reft of the people."

* * *

Father Joseph François Lafitau, French Jesuit missionary, discusses several ball games other than lacrosse among American indigenous people, circa 1724, in Lafitau, *Customs of the American Indians Compared with the Customs of Primitive Times,* ed. and trans. by William N. Fenton and Elizabeth L. Moore, 2 vols., Vol. 2 (Toronto: The Champlain Society, 1977), 196-200.

"Ball Games

[In the first three paragraphs, Lafitau discussed ball games among the ancient Mediterraneans]

"I shall say nothing here except what has what has some connection with the games of our Indians who have four or five varieties of it.

"The first is played in this way. After marking two goals far enough apart, as much as five hundred paces, the players assemble in the middle between these limits. The player who is to begin the game holds in his hand a ball larger but less compact than those used in our tennis games. He is supposed to throw it in the air as perpendicularly as he can in order to catch it when it falls again. All the others form a circle around him, holding their hands high above their heads to catch it also when it falls. The player who has been able to make himself master of it tries to reach one of the distant goals. The attention of the others is given to blocking him, barring his way, keeping him from their goals, pushing him always back to the centre, finally to seizing him and taking the ball from him. But he, watching all their moves, dodges now to one side, now to the other, holding the ball always firmly grasped, seeking always to evade his pursuers, pushing and jostling all those who are in his way, until he sees himself in danger of being caught without possibility of escape. Then he is supposed to throw it to one of the fastest of the team who is in a position to defend it. But, to lengthen the match, he makes his skill consist in throwing it to those behind him farthest from the goal towards which he was moving, in deceiving them even, pretending to look one way and throwing it another. After this, from being pursued, he becomes in turn the pursuer and loses no hope of again catching the ball which passes in this way from hand to hand. This makes a very quick and agreeable diversion and one requiring skill. It continues until at last some more fortunate player reaches one of the goals. This constitutes the winning of the game which the players then begin over again in the same way.

"The beginning of this game is like the one the ancients called $Ovρανια$ which consisted, according to Pollux description of it, in one of the player's throwing the ball in the air while others tried to catch it, jumping up until it fell to earth again. But either this description is quite imperfect or this game was cooler if that was all there was to it. This writer believed that it was the one which Homer had the Phoaecians play; (but I am inclined to dispute it), as it could only be played by two, as they made Halius and Laodamia play it at the home of Alcinous; that is why I think that it is more nearly the game called *phaininda, phenina,* or *phennida,* that Pollux distinguished from the episcyrus of which I shall speak soon. According to this same author's view, it got its name likewise, either from Phenindus its inventor or from the Greek word, $φευακιξειν,$ because, in this game, they seek to deceive in throwing the ball to one side after pretending to throw it to the other side.

"The poet Antiphanes seems also to describe it in a manner quite close to that cited by Athenaeus. This is the gist: (of his description) 'The one taking the ball, throws it gaily to another, ducking at the same time the latter's throw, pushing him out of his place, and crying with all his strength to his opponent to get up.' In Basse Bretagne [Lower Brittany] they still play today a game much like it which is quite well known in the country under the name of *la soule.*

"The second kind of ball game of the Indians is the lacrosse. Its rules are exactly the same as those of the epicyrus which Pollux describes in this way. 'The players are divided according to their number and distributed into two teams as equal in number as possible. Then a line is drawn in the centre of the field which they call $οκυροσ$ on which they put the ball. In the same way, two other lines are drawn, far apart to serve as limits, behind each of these two teams. Those to whom the lot has fallen, first throw the ball towards the opposing side which makes, on its side, every effort to throw it back to where it comes from. The game goes on in this way, until one or the other has driven his adversary to the limit or the line which he is to defend.'

"The only difference that there can be between the game of lacrosse and the *epicyrus* or *harpastum* is that, in the former, to throw the ball the players use bent sticks at the end of which many Indians have kinds of rackets whereas in the latter type of game they do not seem to have used either one for, except for armlets with which the ancients played ball, we find no trace of any implement which they used in their ball games. It seems, nevertheless, that one can infer not only from the antiquity of the game of lacrosse that it is not possible that the ancients did not know it since it is today as widespread in Europe as far as to the extremties of Lapland as it is in all

America from the North to Chile; but one can also concludethat they knew it from the description which Pollux makes of it, since he states that the ball was brought down on the scyros, or the middle line, and from the epithet of *poudreux* [dusty] which Martial gives to the *harpastum* every time that he speaks of it, as well as that of *arenaria* (sandy) which occurs in St. Isidore of Seville which signifies to us that this ball always rolled in the dust. The Mingrelians play this game on horseback and the description which the author of the *Relation of the Colchidians* makes of it is excellent.

"The third kind of Indian ball is an exercise with a small ball. This game is played very little except by the girls. The rules are no different, I believe, than those of the trigonal of the Romans. It may be played with two, three or four players. The ball has to be always in the air and the player who lets it fall loses the game.

"A fourth kind is found among the Abenaki. Their ball is only a blown up bladder which is also to be kept always in the air. Indeed, it is held up a long time by the numbers of hands which keep on returning it. This game makes an agreeable spectacle.

"The Floridians have a fifth kind. They erect a mast several arms' lengths high above which they put a willow basket which turns on its pivot. The skill consists in touching this cage with the ball and making the ball turn the basket several exchange.

"Their balls have no elasticity and cannot be caught on the bounce. The lacrosse ball is made of leather full of deer or moose hair like that of the ancients, whence has come the word *pila* or *pilis* according to Saint Isidore's definition; it is a little flattened so that it rolls less well. The others may be also of the same material, but usually the Indians make them of corn husk or leaves, without using anything else, so that they are extremely light, with this difference that the trigonal ball is much smaller."

* * *

John Brickell, Irish doctor, notes a ball game in North Carolina, circa 1737, in Brickell, *The Natural History of North-Carolina* (Dublin: James Carson, 1737), 336.

"Their [indigenous peoples'] manner of playing *Ball* is after this manner, *viz.* they place a fquare *Mat* made of *Reeds* or *Bullrufhes* at the top of a Tree eight or nine Fathom from the Ground, and whoever hitteth the *Mat* in playing thereat, winneth the Game."

* * *

Henry Timberlake, British lieutenant, describes chunké among the Cherokee in Tennessee, January 1762, in Samuel Cole Williams, ed., *Lieut. Henry Timberlake's Memoirs, 1756-1765* (Marietta, Ga.: Continental Book Company, 1948 [1765]), 79.

"Some days after my reception at Chilhowey, I had an opportunity of seeing some more of their diversions. Two letters I received from some officers at the Great Island occasioned a great assembly at Chote, where I was conducted to read them; but the Indians finding nothing that regarded them, the greater part resolved to amuse themselves at a game they call nettecawaw [chunkey]; which I can give no other description of, than that each player having a pole about ten feet long, with several marks or divisions, one of them bowls a round stone, with one flat side, and the other convex, on which the players all dart their poles after it, and the nearest counts according to the vicinity of the bowl to the marks on his pole."

* * *

Joseph Doddridge, Pennsylvania Episcopal minister, concerning western Pennsylvania, describes tomahawk-throwing contests by Euroamerican youths imitating indigenous people, circa 1763-1783, in Doddridge, *Notes on the Settlement and Indian Wars of the Western Parts of Virginia and Pennsylvania from 1763 to 1783, Inclusive, Together with a Review of the State of Society and Manners of the First Settlers of the Western Country* (Pittsburgh: John S. Ritenour and William T. Lindsey, 1912), 123.

"Throwing the tomahawk was another boyish sport, in which many acquired considerable skill. The tomahawk with its handle made a certain length will make a given numbers of turns in a given distance. Say in five steps it will srike with the edge, the handle downwards; at the distance of seven and a half, it will strike with the edge, the handle upwards, and so on. A little experience enabled the boy to measure the distance with his eye, when walking through the woods, and strike a tree with his tomahawk in any way he chose."

* * *

Pedro Fages, Spanish soldier, describes a stone and throwing game among indigenous people near San Luis Obispo, California, circa 1772, in Herbert Ingram Priestley, trans. and ed., *A Historical, Political, and Natural Description of California by Pedro Fages, Soldier of Spain* (Berkeley, Cal.: University of California Press, 1939), 76.

"Finally, there are other games that they play which give good exercise, depending not at all upon chance, but contributing entirely to dexterity or industry. [They prepare] a quadrilateral space, very level and smooth, and ten yards long with a width sufficient so that two Indians may run in it side by side, the whole place being enclosed with a hedge of branches and grass a little more than a span in height. Into [this enclosure] two players enter, one on each side, face to face, each of them carrying in his hand a stake four yards long, ending in a good point. One of the Indians throws up a little wheel made of strong straps fastened together so as to leave in the center a hole about the size of a *real* [the size of a dime]; they both instantly hurl their stakes, measuring the shot so as to catch the wheel or thread it upon the stake before it falls to the ground. He who first does this, or who does it oftenest, overcomes his adversary, and wins the game."

* * *

James Adair, Scots-Irish trader, observes chunké among Southeastern indigenous peoples, circa 1775, in [Adair], *Adair's History of the American Indians*, ed. by Samuel Cole Williams (New York: Promontory Press, 1973 [1775]), 430-431.

"The warriors have another favourite game, called *Chungke*; which, with propriety of language, may be called 'Running hard labour.' They have near their state house, a square piece of ground well cleaned, and fine sand is carefully strewed over it, when requisite to promote a swifter motion to what they throw along the surface. Only one, or two on a side, play at this ancient game. They have a stone bout two fingers broad at the edge, and two spans round: each party has a pole of about eight feet long, smooth, and tapering at each end, the points falt. They set off a-breast of each other at six yards from the end of the play ground; then one of them hurls the stone on its edge, in as direct a line as he can, a considerable distance toward the middle of the other end of the square: when they have ran a few yards, each darts his pole anointed with bear's oil, with a proper force, as near as he can guess in proportion to the motion of the stone, that the end may lie close to the stone—when this is the case, the person counts two of the game, and, in proportion to the nearness of the poles to the mark, one is counted, unless by measuring, both are found to be at an equal distance from the stone. In this manner, the players will keep running most part of the day, at half speed, under the violent heat of the sun, staking their silver ornaments, their nose, finger, and ear rings; their breast, arm, and wrist plates, and even all of their wearing apparel, except that which barely covers the middle. All the American Indians are much addicted to this game, which to us appears to be a task of stupid drudgery: it seems however to be of early origin, when their fore-fathers used diversions as simple as their manners. The hurling stones they use at present, were time immemorial rubbed smooth on the rocks, and with prodigious labour; they are kept with the strictest religious care, from one generation to another, and are exempted from being buried with the dead. They belong to the town where they are used, and are carefully preserved."

* * *

Bernard Romans, French captain, comments on chunké among the Chickasaw and Choctaw, circa 1775, in Romans, *A Concise Natural History of East and West Florida* (New York: pvt. ptg., 1775), 70, 79-80.

"Their favourite game of *chunké* is a plain proof of the evil confequences of a violent paffion for gaming upon all kinds, claffes and orders of men; at this they play from morning till night, with an unwearied application, and they bet high; here you may fee a favage come and bring all his fkins, ftake them and lofe them; next his pipe, his beads, trinkets and ornaments; at laft his blanket, and other garment, and even all their arms, and after all it is not uncommon for them to go home, borrow a gun and fhoot themfelves; an inftance of this happened in 1771 at *Eaft Yafoo* a fhort time before my arrival. Suicide has alfo been practifed here on other occafions, and they regard the act as a crime, and bury the body as unworthy of their ordinary funeral rites.

"The manner of playing this game is thus: They make an alley of about two hundred feet in length, where a very fmooth caly [clay] ground is laid, which when dry is very hard; they play two together having each a sftreight pole of about fifteen feet long; one holds a ftone, which is in fhape of a truck, which he throws before him over this alley, and the inftant of its departure, they fet off and run; in running they caft their poles after the ftone, he that did not throw it endeavours to hit it, the other ftrives to ftrike the pole of his antagonift in its flight fo as to prevent its hitting the ftone; if the firft fhould ftrike the ftone he counts one for it, and if the other by the dexterity of his caft fhould prevent the pole of his opponent hitting the ftone, he counts one, but fhould both mifs their aim the throw is renewed; and in the cafe a fcore is won the winner cafts the ftone and eleven is up; they hurl this ftone and pole with wonderful dexterity and violence, and fatigue themfelves much at it."

* * *

John Long, American trader, mentions a type of hoop and archery game among indigenous peoples in the Great Lakes region, circa 1777, in Milo Milton Quaife, ed., *John Long's Voyages and Travels in the Years 1768-1788* (Chicago: Lakeside Press, 1922), 69-70

"The boys are very expert at trundling a hoop, particularly the Cahnuaga Indians, whom I have frequently seen excel at this amusement. The game is played by any number of boys who may accidentally assemble together, some driving the hoop, while others with bows and arrows shoot at it. At this exercise they are surprisingly expert, and will stop the progress of the hoop when going with great velocity, by driving a pointed arrow into its edge; this they will do at a considerable distance, and on horseback as well as on foot."

George Hanger, Hessian colonel, concerning the Cherokee and Creek indigenous people near Savannah, refers to game resembling golf, circa 1780, in Hanger, *The Life, Adventures, and Opinions of Col. George Hanger,* 2 vols., Vol. 1 (New York: Johnson and Stryker, 1801), 175.

"The Indians abstain from women, take physic and prepare their bodies for war, by frequently running and using other manly exercises. In one, not unlike the game we call *goff,* they shew great skill and activity."

Chapter 18

WINTER SPORTS

The long, cold winters that usually cover much of the northern reaches of what were the Dutch, French, and English colonies provided early American settlers with numerous opportunities for wintertime outdoor diversions. Sources record much enjoyment in skating, sliding, sledding (or tobogganing), and sleighing. There is little primary source record of ice hockey, given the stereotype of hockey as the Canadian national game. Secondary sources mention that ice hockey probably appeared in Canada by the early 1800s. It was played much earlier in New Netherland, but the record is mute except for the solitary selection below—an oddity considering the image of Dutch boys born to skate!

Accounts of skating for pleasure are more numerous, although still surprisingly scanty for New Netherland. The British had a fondness for it, on the northern ponds and rivers and even as far south as Virginia, as the skating escapades of William Byrd and Philip Vickers Fithian's charges illustrate. But skating was dangerous. Skaters could fall through the ice and drown all too easily, as an accident near Boston in 1696 demonstrated. Colleges and towns thus passed some restrictions on unsupervised skating. Some colonists were apparently expert skaters. One, Alexander Graydon of Philadelphia, was knowledgeable enough to discuss American versus European skating styles. Occasionally, the recreation on ice did not involve skates but consisted of simply gliding across the surface, something called sliding.

Snow, especially too much of it, discouraged skating, but it brought out the sleds and sleighs. Sledding was a favorite pastime of boys, although the commentators thought it much effort for the little amount of pleasure. Sleighing trips for pleasure were likewise popular. Modern Americans might wonder at classifying this as sport, but the several witnesses to this diversion all referred to it as sport. At a time when people relied on sleighs for human transportation and hauling goods, those with leisure and the wherewithal chartered sleighs to launch expeditions, stopping at taverns and parties on the way, often staying away all the night. Men and women seemed to enjoy this amusement equally. This practice drew both applause and criticism, as recorders either considered it a wonderful way to while away long winter hours or sharply criticized it as idle frivolity, quite possibly unhealthy as well. Whatever the case, colonial Americans loved sleighing.

Overall, winter appears not to have isolated everyone inside by the fire. Although it was too early for skiing, snowboarding, ice sailing, ice snowmobiling, snowshoe racing, and other current American diversions, winter in colonial times was a time for sport as the following selections detail.

[Consult the general writings about sports, recreation, and the various colonial, provincial, territorial, and state Sabbath and gaming laws in Chapter One for other sources about the specific sports or games in this chapter.]

ICE HOCKEY

Court case in Fort Orange, New Netherland, 20 March 1657, in "Ordinary Session held in Fort Orange, March 20 Anno 1657," reprinted in A.J.F. van Laer, ed. and trans., *Minutes of the Court of Fort Orange and Beverwyck, 1657-1660* (Albany: University of the State of New York, 1923), 23.

"The officer, plaintiff, against
  Claes Hendericksen
  Meeuwes Hoogenboom   defendants
  Gusbert van Loenen
"The plaintiff says that Jan Daniel, the under-sheriff, reported to him on the 7th of March, being the day of prayer ordered by the honorable director general of New Netherland and proclaimed here, the defendants played hockey on the ice, demanding therefore that said defendants be condemned to pay the fine indicated in the ordinance.

"The defendants, appearing, maintain that they did not play hockey and promise to prove it.

"The parties having been heard, the court orders the defendants to produce their evidence on the next court day."

SKATING AND SLIDING

Charles Wooley, British clergyman, notes skating in New York City, circa 1678, in W[ooley], *A Two Years Journal in New-York. And Part of its Territories in America* (London: John Wyat and Eben Tracy, 1701), reprinted in Cornell Jaray, ed., *Historic Chronicles of New Amsterdam, Colonial New York and Early Long Island, First Series,*

Empire State Historical Publications Series No. 35 (Port Washington, N.Y.: Ira J. Friedman, 1968), 60.

"And upon the Ice its admirable to see Men and Women as it were flying upon their Skates from place to place, with markets on their Heads and Backs."

* * *

Samuel Sewall, Boston magistrate, discusses a skating accident, 30 November 1696, in M. Halsey Thomas, ed., *The Diary of Samuel Sewall, 1674-1729, Volume I. 1674-1708* (New York: Farrar, Straus and Giroux, 1973), 360.

"Many Scholars [at Harvard College] go in the Afternoon to Scate on Fresh-pond; William Maxwell, and John Eyre fall in and are drown'd. Just about Candle-lighting the news of it is brought to Town, which affects persons exceedingly. Mr. Eyre the father cryes out bitterly."

* * *

Increase Mather, Harvard College president, refers to the skating deaths of two Harvard students, December 1696, in *A Discourse Concerning the Uncertainty of the Times of Men, and the Neceffity of being Prepared for Sudden Changes and Death. Delivered in a Sermon Preached at Cambridge in New England, Decemb. 6, 1696. On Occafion of the Sudden Death of Two Scholars belonging to Harvard College* (Boston: Bartholomew Green and John Allen, 1697), 39-40.

"3*ly*, and Finally, be always able to give a good Anfwer to this Queftion, *What am I doing?* Is the thing that I am about a Lawful thing? Am I ufing Recreations for my Health fake? And is it Lawful Recreation, which no Law neither of God nor man has forbidden? The two young men that were Drowned the other day, Death found them in Recreation: It's well, it was a Lawful one *Skating* on the ice is fo, if ufed feafonably & with due difcretion and moderation. But how difmal is it when Death fhall furprife Perfons when they are diverting themfelves with *Scandalous Paftimes*."

* * *

William Byrd, Westover, Virginia planter, goes skating, December 1709, in Louis B. Wright and Marion Tinling, eds., *The Secret Diary of William Byrd of Westover, 1709-1712* (Richmond, Va.: The Dietz Press, 1941), 123, 124.

28 December 1709: "Then we walked about the plantation and took a slide on the ice." 29 December 1709: "Then we took a walk and I slid on skates, notwithstanding there was a thaw."

* * *

John Adams, Boston Congregationalist minister, writes a poem concerning a skating accident, 8 January 1728, in Adams, *Poems on Several Occasions, Original and Translated* (Boston: D. Gookin, 1745), 79-80.

"XXV. *On the fudden Death of Meffieurs* George *and* Nathan Howell, *the only Children of Madam* SEWALL, *who were loft as they were fkating on the Ice,* January 8*th.* 1727, 8.

"Two charming Youth in all their Bloom, The beauteous Product of one Womb, To try the flattering Ice defign'd, Nor thought their Deftiny to find. Joyful, methinks, I hear them fay,

How fmooth the Waters fhine to Day, O'er the bright Floor we'll rapid glide, Nor dread the under-moving Tide. They went with Expectation flufht, To Fate's refiftlefs Vigour pufht:

Their Eyes with fparkling Spirits fhine,
Their heaving Vitals danc'd within.
Their fhining Irons on they tie,
And o'er the flippery Surface fly:
Nor driving Winds with fwifter Bound,
Brufh o'er the Surface of the Ground.
Too far they run, too quick their Speed,
To the dark Regions of the Dead.
For foon the bending Glafs conteft

Th' unequal Force by which 'twas preft:
The trembling Youth their Danger fee
And ftrive, but ftrivein vain to flee.
To Heav'n they raife their dying Prayers,
To Heav'n they cry with piteous Tears:
Too late they pray, too late they weep,
Hov'ring impendent o'er the Deep,
But quickly reach the Goal of Death,
And dropping thro' refign their Breath."

* * *

Harvard College law, circa 1734, in "College Laws, 1734, Chapter 8th, Concerning Miscellaneous Matters," in *Harvard College Records, Part I. Corporation Records, 1636-1750, Publications of the Colonial Society of Massachusetts*, Vol. 15 (Boston, 1925), 154.

"15. No Undergraduate shall keep a Gun or pistol in the College, or any where in Cambridge; nor shall he go a guning, fishing, or Scating over deep waters, without leave from the President or one of the Tutors, under the penalty of three Shillings. And if any scholar shall fire a Gun or pistol, within the College walls Yard, or near the College; he shall be fined not exceeding ten Shillings; or be admonishe[d] degraded or expelled, according to the Aggravation of the Offence."

* * *

Account of a skating accident, New York Gazette, No. 588, 10-17 February 10-17, 1737.

"*Bofton, Jan.* 31. Laft week a Boy was skeiting very fwiftly upon *Charles-River*, he hapned to fall into an Air Hole, and funk down immediately; but rifing prefently afterward, about five yards off of the Place where he fell in, happen'd to dart his Head exactly against a Place where the Bouy of a Ship had been taken out of the Ice the fame Day, and altho' the Ice was firm, the Force wth which he came up, brake it, and his head appear'd; by which accident, & the fpeedy help of fome People who ran to his affiftance, his Life was wonderfully preferved."

* * *

John Adams, Massachusetts lawyer, politician, and later United States President, refers to skating during his boyhood, circa 1740s, [John Adams], "The Autobiography of John Adams," in Lyman H. Butterfield, ed., *Diary and Autobiography of John Adams, Volume 3. Diary, 1782-1804, Autobiography, Part One To October 1776* (Cambridge, Mass.: Harvard University Press, 1962), 257; and Adams to Skelton Jones, 11 March 1809, reprinted in Adrienne Koch and William Peden, eds., *The Selected Writings of John and John Quincy Adams* (New York: Alfred A. Knopf, 1946), 153.

"[A]nd I spent my time as idle Children do in making and sailing boats and Ships upon the Ponds and Brooks, in making and flying Kites, in driving hoops, playing marbles, playing Quoits, Wrestling, Swimming, Skaiting and above all in shooting, to which Diversion I was addicted to a degree of Ardor which I know not that I ever felt for any other Business, Study or Amusement."

"17. Under my first Latin master, who was a churl, I spent my time in shooting, skating, swimming, flying kites, and every boyish exercise and diversion I could invent. Never mischievous. Under my second master, who was kind, I began to love my books and neglect my sports."

* * *

Peter Kalm, Swedish naturalist, observes skating in Philadelphia, 9 January 1750, in Adolph B. Benson, trans. and ed., *Peter Kalm's Travels in North America,* 2 vols., Vol. 2 (New York: Dover Publications, 1966), 677-678.

"*The Delaware River* was now frozen in most places at Philadelphia. For the last three days there had been a large number of young men and boys on the ice, some walking but most of them skating. There was still an open place here and there in the middle of the River; nevertheless, to-day at eleven I saw a man successfully driving a horse and sleigh on the ice directly in front of the city. The next day was mild and beautiful, when a section of the ice before the town suddenly broke up and began to move downstream. There were a good many people on this piece of ice; booths had been set up to sell brandy and such things to the skaters, and now they all found something else to do besides enjoying themselves. People rushed away precipitously, and fortunately all reached *terra firma* safely. The ice remained, but for a few days no one dared go out on it. There had been some people on the other side of the river starting to cross when the ice began to loosen, but these were obliged to turn back. On the 13th of this month the river was wholly open again so that ships could move in and out. The English youth is very fond of skating, and so are men of thirty years or over. Men of all classes have a passion for this sport. They would sometimes go three or four miles to each a place where the ice was safe. Sheltered spots were flooded with men skaters, but I saw no women on the ice here."

* * *

Alexander Graydon, Philadelphia resident, discusses skating, circa 1760s-1770s, in Graydon, *Memoirs of His Own Time, With Reminiscences of the Men and Events of the Revolution,* ed. by John Stockton Littell (Philadelphia: Lindsay & Blakiston, 1846), 55, 58-61.

"In gymnastic exercises, however, my relish was keen and altogether orthodox. For those of running, leaping, swimming and skating, no one had more appetite; and for the enjoyment of these, fatigue and hunger were disregarded."

"The exercises of swimming and skating were so much within the reach of boys of Philadelphia, that it would have been surprising, had they neglected them, or even had they not excelled in them....

"With respect to skating, though the Philadelphians have never reduced it to rules like the Londoners, nor connected it with their business like Dutchmen, I will yet hazard the opinion, that they were the best and most elegant skaters in the world. I have seen New England skaters, Old England skaters, and Holland skaters, but the best of them could but 'make the judicious grieve.' I was once slightly acquainted with a worthy gentleman, the quondam member of a skating club in London, and it must be admitted that he performed very well for an Englishman. His *High Dutch,* or as he better termed it, his *outer edge* skating, might, for aught I know, have been exactly conformable to the statutes of this institution: To these, he would often appeal; and I recollected the principal one was, that each stroke should describe an exact semicircle. Nevertheless, his style was what we should deem a very bad one. An utter stranger to the beauty of bringing forward the suspended foot towards the middle of the stroke, and boldly advancing it before the other, at the conclusion of it, thus to preserve throughout his course, a continuity of movement, to rise like an ascending wave to its acme, then, gracefully like a descending one, to glide into the succeeding stroke without effort, either real or apparent—every change of foot with this gentleman, seemed a beginning of motion, and required a most unseemly jerk of the body; and unequivocal evidence of the want of that power, which depends upon a just balance, and should never be lost—which carries the skater forward with energy without exertion; and is as essential to his swift and graceful career, as is a good head of water to the velocity of a mill wheel. Those who have seen good skating will comprehend what I mean, still better those who are adepts themselves; but excellence in the art can never be gained by geometrical rules. The two reputed best skaters of my day, were General Cadwallader and Massey the biscuit baker; but I could name many others, both of the academy and Quaker school who were in no degree inferior to them; whose action and attitudes were equally graceful, and like theirs, no less worthy of the chisel than those, which in other exercises, have been selected to display the skill of the eminent sculptors of antiquity. I here speak, be it observed, of what the Philadelphians *were,* not what they *are,* since I am unacquainted with the present state of the art, and as from my lately meeting with young men, who, though bred in the city had not learned to swim, I infer the probability, that skating may be equally on the decline."

* * *

John Barnard, Marblehead, Massachusetts clergyman, circa 1767, concerning a 1696 skating accident, in Barnard, "Autobiography of the Rev. John Barnard [1767]," *Collections of the Massachusetts Historical Society,* Third Series, Vol. 5 (Boston, 1836), reprinted in John Demos, ed., *Remarkable Providences. Readings on Early American History* (Boston: Northeastern University Press, 1991), 75-76.

"There were two accidents which happened while I was an undergraduate, that somewhat startled and awakened me. The one [occurred] in the winter of my freshmanship, when a number of went a skating upon what is called Fresh Pond in Watertown. Two lovely young gentlemen, John Eyre, of our class, son of Justice Eyre of Boston, and Maxwell, [of] the class above me, a West Indian (which two only of all the company had asked leave of the Tutors to go out of town upon the diversion), being both good skaters, joined hand in hand, and flew away to the farther end of the pond, and as they were in like manner returning, they ran upon a small spot in the middle of the pond called the boiling hole (because rarely frozen over), which was open the day before but now had a skim of ice upon it about half an inch thick, and both of them broke the thin ice and plunged into the water. Maxwell rose not again, it being supposed he rose under the ice, Eyre rose in the hole they had broken [and] attempted to get upon the ice, but it gave way under him and plunged him [in] anew. I, who happened to be nearest to them, ran towards the hole, called to Eyre only to keep his head above water by bearing his arms upon the thin ice, and we would help him with boards, which the rest of the company ran to fetch from a new house building by the edge of the pond, not twenty rods off, but he kept on his striving to get up, till it worried him he sunk and rose no more, and thus both were drowned. It threw me into grievous anguish of mind to think I was so near my dear friend, within two rods, and yet it was impossible for me to help him. I went to the utmost edge of the thick ice, and raised my foot to take another step, but saw I must fall in as they had done. The boards arrived to the place within five minutes of Eyre's last sinking."

* * *

Ann MacVicar Grant, an American lady, mentions observing skating in Albany, New York, circa 1769, in [Grant], *Memoirs of An American Lady. With Sketches of Manners and*

Scenery in America, As They Existed Previous to the Revolution, 2 vols., Vol. 1 (London: Longman, Hurst, Rees, and Orme, 1808), 104.

"In winter the river, frozen to a great depth, formed the principal road through the country, and was the fcene of all thofe amufements of fkating and fledge races, common to the north of Europe."

* * *

Benjamin Rush, Philadelphia physician, recommends skating as recreation, circa 1772, in Rush, *Sermons to Gentlemen upon Temperance and Exercise* (Philadelphia: John Dunlap, 1772), 33.

"To all thefe fpecies of exercife which we have mentioned, I would add, SKEATING, JUMPING, alfo, the active plays of TENNIS, BOWLES, QUOITS, GOLF, and the like. The manner in which each of thefe operate, may be underftood from what we faid under the former particulars."

* * *

Philip Vickers Fithian, tutor at Nomini Hall, Virginia, observes skating, January 1774, in Hunter Dickinson Farish, ed., *Journal and Letters of Philip Vickers Fithian, 1773-1774. A Plantation Tutor of the Old Dominion* (Charlottesville, Va.: University Press of Virginia, 1957 [1943]), 54-56.

13 January 1774: "Mr Cunngingham came before Noon to skait—At twelve we all went down to Mr Carters Millpond—none had skaits but Mr Cunningham—we diverted ourselves on the Ice til two, when we went up to dinner—...."

16 January 1774: "Bob [also] informed me that the *Parson*, Mr *Blain*, *Cunningham*, *Balantine*, & others are come to Captain *Turburvilles* Millpond to Skate before they go to the Ball—."

* * *

Jacob Hiltzheimer, Philadelphia politician, watches skaters in that city, January 1774 and January 1782, in [Jacob Hiltzheimer], "Extracts from the Diary of Jacob Hiltzheimer, 1768-1798," Pennsylvania Magazine of History and Biography, Vol. 16, No. 1 (1892), 96, and Jacob Cox Parsons, ed., *Extracts from the Diary of Jacob Hiltzheimer* (Philadelphia: William Fell Company, 1893), 48.

22 January 1774: "Very cold. With my two sons, went with Charles Massey to Schuylkill to see him skate, as it is admitted he is one of the very best at that exercise."

31 January 1782: "While walking along Front Street met George Mifflin, who took me to Joseph Morris's to see his brother the General, who had come in from the Falls, but we learned that he had gone on the river to skate, in which exercise, by all accounts, he is very expert."

* * *

John Adams, Braintree, Massachusetts lawyer, politician, and later United States President, refers to skating in a letter to his wife, Abigail, 26 September 1775, in Lyman H. Butterfield, ed., *Adams Family Correspondence, Volume I. December 1761–May 1776* (New York: Atheneum, 1965), 285-286.

"I have seen the Utility of Geometry, Geography, and the Art of drawing so much of late, that I must intreat you, my dear, to teach the Elements of those Sciences to my little Girl and Boys. It is as pretty an Amusement, as Dancing or Skaiting, or Fencing, after they have once acquired a Taste for them.

James Hadden, British lieutenant, comments on skating in Quebec, winter, 1776-1777, in [Hadden], *A Journal Kept in Canada and Upon Burgoyne's Campaign in 1776 and 1777, by Lieut. James M. Hadden, Roy. Art.* (Albany, N.Y.: Joel Munsell's Sons, 1884), 42.

"*Skating* may sometimes offer but tho' there is plenty of *Ice* you cannot always find a clear spot. To obviate this, the officers at many places hired people to sweep away the S*now* as it fell upon certain situations fixed for that exercise."

* * *

Thomas Anburey, British officer, discusses skating at Montreal, 6 April 1777, in [Anburey], *Travels through the Interior Parts of America,* 2 vols., Vol. 1 (London: William Lane, 1791), 169.

"Among the various amufements we enjoyed while away this long winter, I forgot to mention that fkating is one, which thofe who are fond of that diverfion are amply indulged in, there being fuch a conftancy and large extent of ice. There are feveral officers in the regiment, who being exceeding fond of it, have inftituted a fkating club, to promote diverfion and conviviality.

"The Canadians fkate in the manner of the Dutch, and exceedingly faft, but the Indians dart along like lightning. Some years fince, for a confiderable wager, three Indians fet off from this place at day light, and before dark arrived at Quebec, which is 60 leagues; their fatigue, however, was fo great, that two expired shortly after their arrival, and the third did not furvive above a week."

* * *

Enos Reeves, Pennsylvania lieutenant, writes of sliding near Norfolk, Virginia, in January or February 1782, in "Extracts from the Letter-Books of Lieutenant Enos Reeves, of the Pennsylvania Line," Pennsylvania Magazine of History and Biography, Vol. 21, No. 3 (1897), 382.

"During the night it snow'd, hail'd, rain'd, and froze, all at once. We had the Ladies out on the ice sliding, falling and playing, as it is a thing very unusual in this part of the world, to have such a sleet."

* * *

Francesco dal Verme, Italian count, near New York City, refers to skating, 5 July 1783, in Elizabeth Cometti, trans. and ed., *Seeing America and Its Great Men. The Journal and Letters of Count Francesco dal Verme, 1783-1784* (Charlottesville, Va.: University Press of Virginia, 1969), 8.

"In the morning went to the artillery park near a pond on the north end of the city where everyone goes ice-skating in winter."

* * *

Advertisement for skates, [Rivington's] New-York Gazette, and Universal Advertiser, No. 756, 24 December 1783.

"SKATING.

GENTLEMEN fond of this healthy and delectable amufement, may be provided with
SKATES,
Of excellent conftruction, feven different forts and prices, with ready fixed leather ftraps, for the ufe of fleeting adepts, as well as young practitioners.
Sold by *James Rivington.*"

SLEDDING AND SLEIGHING

Alexander Mackraby, Scottish visitor, comments enthusiastically about sleighing in Philadelphia, 2 January 1769, in "Extracts from Letters of Alexander Mackraby," Pennsylvania Magazine of History and Biography, Vol. 11, No. 3 (1887), 286.

"I had a very clever one [sleighing party] a few days ago. Seven sleighs with two ladies and two men in each, preceded by fiddlers on horseback, set out together upon a snow of about a foot deep on the roads, to a public house a few miles from town, where we danced, sung, and romped and eat and drank, and kicked away care from morning till night, and finished our frolic in two or three side-boxes at the play.

"You can have no idea of the state of the pulse seated with pretty women, mid deep in straw, your body armed with furs and flannell, clear air, bright sunshine, and spotless sky, horses galloping, every feeling turned to joy and jollity!"

* * *

Ann MacVicar Grant, an American lady, on sledding in Albany, New York, circa 1769, in [Grant], Memoirs of An American Lady. With Sketches of Manners and Scenery in America, As They Existed Previous to the Revolution, 2 vols., Vol. 1 (London: Longman, Hurst, Rees, and Orme, 1808), 104, 105-107.

"In winter the river, frozen to a great depth, formed the principal road through the country, and was the fcene of all thofe amufements of fkating, and fledge races, common to the north of Europe....

"In town all the *boys* were extravagantly fond of a diverfion that to us would appear a very odd and childifh one. The great ftreet of the town, in the midft of which, as has been formerly mentioned, ftood all the churches and public buildings, floped down from the hill on which the fort ftood, towards the river; between the buildings was an unpaved carriage road, the foot-path befide the houfes being the only part of the ftreet which was paved. In winter this floping defcent, continued for more than a quarter of a mile, acquired firmnefs from the froft, and became extremely flippery. Then the amufement commenced. Every boy and youth in town, from eight to eighteen, had a little low fledge, made with a rope like a bridle to the front, by which it could be dragged after one by the hand. On this one or two at moft could fit, and this floping defcent being made as fmooth as a looking-glafs, by fliders' fledges, &c. perhaps a hundred at once fet out in fucceffion from the top of this ftreet, each feated in his little fledge with the rope in his hand, which, drawn to the right or the left, ferved to guide him. He pufhed it off with a little ftick, as one would launch a boat; and then, with the moft aftonifhing velocity, precipitated by the weight of the owner, the little machine glided paft, and was at the lower end of the ftreet in an inftant. What could be fo peculiarly delightful in this rapid and fmooth defcent, I could never difcover; thugh in a more retired place, and on a fmaller fcale, I have tried the amufement: but to a young Albanian, flaying, as he called it, was one of the firft joys of life, though attended by the drawback of walking to the top of the declivity dragging his fledge every time he renewed his flight, for fuch it might well be called. In the managing this little machine fome dexterity was neceffary: an unfkilful Phæton was fure to fall. The conveyance was fo low, that a fall was attended with little danger, yet with much difgrace, for an univerfal laugh from all fides affailed the fallen charioteer. This laugh was from a very full chorus, for the conftant and rapid fucceffion of this proceffion, where every one had a brother, lover, or kinfman, brought all the young people in town to the porticos, where they ufed to fit wrapt in furs till ten or eleven at night, engroffed by this delectable fpectacle. What magical attraction it could poffibly have, I never could find out; but I have known an Albanian, after refiding fome years in Britain, and becoming a polifhed refined gentleman, join the fport, and flide down with the reft. Perhaps, after our laborious refinements in amufement, being eafily pleafed is one of the great fecrets of happinefs, as fas as it is attainable in this 'frail and feverifh being.'"

* * *

Patrick M'Robert, Scottish traveler, describes sleighing in Elizabethtown, New Jersey, circa 1775, in M'Robert, *A Tour through Part of the North Provinces of America. Being, A Series of Letters Wrote on the Spot, in the Years 1774, and 1775* (Edinburgh, pvt. ptg., 1776), reprinted as Patrick M'Robert, *A Tour through Part of the North Provinces of America*, ed. by Carl Bridenbaugh (New York: Arno Press, 1968), 34.

"Their manner of travelling here in winter is very pleasant after the snow falls, which being generally so deep that coaches or other wheel-carriages cannot pass, they use sleighs or sledges, made light with a seat on them like an open chair: in these they sit and drive themselves with great rapidity. The young ladies and gentlemen are so fond of this, as a diversion, that whenever the snow gives over falling, tho' it be after sun-set, they will not wait till next day, but have their sleigh yoked directly, and drive about without the least fear of catching cold from the night air. Large parties of pleasure are often formed amongst them,when perhaps ten or twelve sleighs will drive in company (with four in each sleigh) to dine and drink tea, and return in the evening. About New York this sleighing is much used, and large parties of pleasure are often formed to drive to the country.."

* * *

James Hadden, British lieutenant, mentions sleighing in Quebec, winter, 1776-1777, in [Hadden], *A Journal Kept in Canada and Upon Burgoyne's Campaign in 1776 and 1777, by Lieut. James M. Hadden, Roy. Art.* (Albany, N.Y.: Joel Munsell's Sons, 1884), 41-42.

"Upon the whole the Winter in Canada may be passed very pleasantly the weather being in general settled, and the amusement of *Cabrioling* (or driving in a Carriage without Wheels supported by pieces of wood shod with Iron) which is healthy and much followed by all Ranks above the very poor. They can enjoy every fine day, and necessity is the parent of many home Amusements."

* * *

Jean-François Landolphe, a French naval captain, describes sleighing near New London, Connecticut, January? February? 1780, in Marvin R. Cox, ed., "A French Sea Captain in Revolutionary Connecticut. Extract from the Memoirs of J.F. Landolphe," Connecticut Historical Society Bulletin, Vol. 47, No. 2 (April 1982), 46.

"The crew and passengers were visibly satisfied to see the success of my plans. Every evening they treated themselves to dancing and other forms of diversion. The inhabitants of New London took us out on five or six league sleigh rides, often to Norwich. The ladies, wrapped up in fine furs, footwarmers at their feet, ardently partook of this pleasure. Each sleigh held eight people and was drawn by two beautiful, bell-festooned coursers, astride which sat two nimble grooms who drove them at a fast and constant trot. We always set out at six or seven in the evening—under a lovely moon. On arrival at the place in town to which we'd been invited, we would eat and then dance through the night. At five in the morning the host would serve tea and *café au lait* with little cakes. One or two hours later we would set out again, and go to New London to rest after the rigors of the trip. There were eight sleighs at a time for the parties, each of which carried four men and four ladies."

* * *

An unidentified traveler mentions sleighing near Philadelphia, circa 1783, in *The Polite Traveller. Being a Modern View of the Thirteen United States of America* (London: John Fielding, 1783), 74-75.

"In the winter, when there be fnow on the ground, it is ufual to make what they call fleighing parties, or to go upon it in fledges."

SELECTED BIBLIOGRAPHY

PRIMARY SOURCES

Due to the dispersion of information about colonial and early Republic sports in America, it is impossible to suggest easily accessible or compact collections of primary sources. Interested readers should remain alert for other primary sources about sports in manuscript collections, pre-1820 newspapers, travelers accounts, memoirs and autobiographies, state historical society journals, sermons, and other such potential provenances not included in this volume. The individual headnotes above each document provide primary source citations whenever possible.

SECONDARY SOURCES

The following secondary sources contain popular and scholarly interpretations of the development and place of sports in North America during colonial and early Republic times. Because this particular era was neglected by sport historians and historians in general, secondary sources are meager. Several provide more information on the British context of the sport than that of America.

There is a vast literature, mostly anthropological and quite technical, about Mesoamerican ball games. Scarborough and Wilcox's edited anthology listed below contains a substantial bibliography on these games.

GENERAL RECREATION/MULTIPLE SPORTS

Dennis Brailsford, *Sport and Society. Elizabeth to Anne* (London, 1969).

R. Brasch, *How Did Sports Begin? A Look at the Origins of Man at Play* (New York, 1970).

Jane Carson, *Colonial Virginians at Play* (Charlottesville, Va., 1965).

Bruce Daniels, *Puritans at Play. Leisure and Recreation in Colonial New England* (New York, 1995).

Thomas Robert Davis, "Sport and Exercise in the Lives of Selected Colonial Americans. Massachusetts and Virginia, 1700-1775" (Ph.D. diss., University of Maryland, 1970).

Foster Rhea Dulles, *A History of Recreation. America Learns to Play,* 2nd ed. (New York, 1965 [1940]).

John Durant and Otto Bettmann, *Pictorial History of American Sport. Colonial Times to the Present* (Cranbury, N.J., 1965).

William Clinton Ewing, *The Sports of Colonial Williamsburg* (Richmond, Va., 1937).

Marvin H. Eyler, "Origins of Contemporary Sports," *The Research Quarterly of the American Association for Health, Physical Education, and Recreation,* Vol. 32, No. 4 (December 1961), 480-489.

David Hackett Fischer, *Albion's Seed. Four British Folkways in America* (New York, 1989).

Allen Guttmann, *A Whole New Ball Game. An Interpretation of American Sports* (Chapel Hill, N.C., 1988).

Jennie Holliman, *American Sports, 1785-1835* (Durham, N.C., 1931).

J. Thomas Jable, "Pennsylvania's Early Blue Laws. A Quaker Experiment in the Suppression of Sport and Amusements, 1682-1740," *Journal of Sport History*, Vol. 1 (Spring 1974), 107-122.

June A. Kennard, "Maryland Colonials at Play. Their Sports and Games" (MA thesis, University of Maryland, 1969).

John A. Krout, *Annals of American Sport* (New Haven, Conn., 1929).

John A. Lucas and Ronald A. Smith, *The Saga of American Sport* (Philadelphia, 1978).

Robert W. Malcolmson, *Popular Recreations in English Society, 1700-1850* (Cambridge, 1973).

Herbert Manchester, *Four Centuries of American Sport, 1490-1890* (New York, 1968 [1931]).

O. Paul Monckton, *Pastimes in Time Past* (Philadelphia, 1913).

H. Telfer Mook, "Training Day in New England," *New England Quarterly*, Vol. 11 (December 1938), 675-697.

Edmund S. Morgan, *Virginians at Home. Family Life in the Eighteenth Century* (Charlottesville, Va., 1952).

Morris Mott, ed., *Sports in Canada. Historical Readings* (Toronto, 1989).

Roberta J. Park, "'Embodied Selves.' The Rise and Development of Concern for Physical Education, Active Games and Recreation for Women, 1776-1865," *Journal of Sport History*, Vol. 5 (Summer 1978), 5-41.

Charles Peverelly, *Book of American Pastimes* (New York, 1866).

Winton U. Solberg, *Redeem the Time. The Puritan Sabbath in Early America* (Cambridge, Mass., 1977).

Betty Spears and Richard A. Swanson, *History of Sport and Physical Activity in the United States*, 2nd ed. (Dubuque, Iowa, 1983).

Julia Cherry Spruill, *Women's Life and Work in the Southern Colonies* (New York, 1969 [1938]).

Bonnie Sue Stadelman, "Amusements of Revolutionary War Soldiers" (Ph.D. diss., University of Texas, 1969).

Jesse Frederick Steiner, *Americans at Play* (New York, 1970 [1933]).

Nancy Struna, *People of Prowess. Sport, Leisure, and Labor in Early Anglo-America* (Urbana, Ill., 1996).

Joseph Strutt, *The Sports and Pastimes of the People of England* (London, 1867).

Wells Twombly, *Two Hundred Years of Sport in America. A Pageant of a Nation at Play* (New York, 1976).

Hans-Peter Wagner, *Puritan Attitudes toward Recreation in Early Seventeenth-Century New England* (Frankfurt a. M., 1982).

Robert B. Weaver, *Amusements and Sports in American Life* (Chicago, 1939).

Harry B. and Grace M. Weiss, *Early Sports and Pastimes in New Jersey* (Trenton, N.J., 1960).

BASEBALL AND SIMILAR BALL GAMES

Robert W. Henderson, *Ball, Bat, and Bishop. The Origin of Ball Games* (New York, 1947).

BLOOD SPORTS

Richard E. Powell, Jr. "Sport, Social Relations and Animal Husbandry. Early Cockfighting in North America," *International Journal of the History of Sport*, Vol. 10 (December 1993), 295-312.

B.W.C. Roberts, "Cockfighting. An Early Entertainment in North Carolina," *North Carolina Historical Review*, Vol. 42, No. 3 (Summer 1965), 306-314.

BOWLING AND PITCHING SPORTS

Edmund Berkeley, Jr., "Quoits, the Sport of Gentlemen," *Virginia Cavalcade*, Vol. 15, No. 1 (Summer 1965), 11-21.

Soeren Stewart Brynn, "Some Sports in Pittsburgh during the National Period, 1775-1860," *Western Pennsylvania Historical Magazine,* Vol. 51, No. 4 (October 1968), 345-363.

Ulrich Troubetzkoy, "Bowls and Skittles," *Virginia Cavalcade*, Vol. 9, No. 4 (Spring 1960), 11-16.

CONTACT SPORTS

Nat Fleischer, *The Heavyweight Championship. An Informal History of Boxing from 1719 to the Present* (New York, 1961).

Elliott Gorn, "'Gouge and Bite, Pull Hair and Scratch.' The Social Significance of Fighting in the Southern Backcountry," *American Historical Review*, Vol. 90 (February 1985), 18-43

_____, *The Manly Art of Boxing. Bare-Knuckle Prize Fighting in America* (Ithaca, N.Y., 1986).

Alexander Johnston, *Ten—and Out! The Complete Story of the Prize Ring in America,* 3rd ed. (New York, 1947).

Tom Parramore, "Gouging in Early North Carolina," *North Carolina Historical Review*, Vol. 52, No. 2 (May 1974), 55-62.

FIELD GAMES

R. Clark, *Golf. A Royal and Ancient Game* (Edinburgh, 1875).

Edward H. Dewey, "Football and the American Indians," *New England Quarterly*, Vol. 3, No. 4 (October 1930), 736-740.

Harold H. Hilton and Garden G. Smith, eds., *The Royal and Ancient Game of Golf* (London, 1912).

Zander Hollander, ed., *The American Encyclopedia of Soccer* (New York, 1980).

J. Ninian MacDonald, *Shinty. A Short History of the Ancient Highland Game* (Inverness, 1932).

FISHING

Charles Elliott Goodspeed, *Angling in America* (Boston, 1939).

GYMNASTICS

Ludwig H. Joseph, "Gymnastics from the Middle Ages to the Eighteenth Century," *CIBA Symposia*, Vol. 10, No. 5 (March-April, 1949).

HORSE RACING

Allen E. Begnaud, "Hoofbeats in Colonial Maryland," *Maryland Historical Magazine*, Vol. 65, No. 3 (Fall 1970), 207-238.

Timothy H. Breen, "Horses and Gentlemen. The Cultural Significance of Gambling among the Gentry of Virginia," *William and Mary Quarterly*, 3rd Series, Vol. 34 (April 1977), 243-256.

Elbert Chance, "Fast Horses and Sporting Blood," *Delaware History*, Vol. 11 (October 1964), 149-181.

Francis Culver, *Blooded Horses of Colonial Days* (Baltimore, 1922).

Fairfax Harrison, "The Equine FFV's. A Study of the Evidence of the English Horses Imported into Virginia before the Revolution," *Virginia Magazine of History and Biography*, Vol. 35 (October 1927), 329-370.

John Hervey, *Racing in America, 1665-1865*, 2 vols. (New York, 1944).

Roger Longrigg, *The History of Horse Racing* (New York, 1972).

William H. Robertson, *The History of Thoroughbred Racing in America* (Englewood Cliffs, N.J., 1964).

W. G. Stanard, "Racing in Colonial Virginia," *Virginia Magazine of History and Biography*, Vol. 2 (January 1895), 293-305.

John Austin Stevens, "Early New York Racing History," *Wallace's Monthly Magazine*, Vol. 3 (October 1877), 782-788.

HUNTING

Michael Brander, *Hunting and Shooting from Earliest Times to the Present Day* (New York, 1971).

Matt Cartmill, *A View to a Death in the Morning. Hunting and Nature through History* (Cambridge, Mass., 1993).

Fairfax Harrison, "The Genesis of Foxhunting in Virginia," *Virginia Magazine of History and Biography*, Vol. 37 (April 1929), 155-157.

INDIGENOUS SPORTS AND GAMES

Kendall Blanchard, "Stick Ball and the American Southeast," in Edward Norbeck and Claire R. Farrer, eds., *Forms of Play of Native North Americans* (St. Paul, Minn., 1979).

Stewart Culin, *Games of the North American Indians* (New York, 1975 [1907]).

Bil Gilbert, "Sports Were Essential to the Life of the Early North American Indian," *Sports Illustrated*, Vol. 65, No. 24, 1 December 1986, unpaginated.

Vernon L. Scarborough and David R. Wilcox, eds., *The Mesoamerican Ball Game* (Tucson, Ariz., 1991).

Thomas Vennum, *American Indian Lacrosse. Little Brother of War* (Washington, 1994).

Roger L. Wulff, "Lacrosse among the Seneca," *The Indian Historian*, Vol. 10. No. 2 (Spring 1977), 16-22.

INDEXES

INDEX OF NAMES

INDEX OF SUBJECTS

INDEX OF INSTITUTIONS

INDEX OF GEOGRAPHIC AND PLACE NAMES

FROM ACADEMIC INTERNATIONAL PRESS*

THE RUSSIAN SERIES Volumes in Print

2 **The Nicky-Sunny Letters, Correspondence of Nicholas and Alexandra, 1914-1917**

7 Robert J. Kerner **Bohemia in the Eighteenth Century**

14 A. Leroy-Beaulieu **Un Homme d'Etat Russe (Nicholas Miliutine)...**

15 Nicolas Berdyaev **Leontiev** (In English)

17 **Tehran Yalta Potsdam. The Soviet Protocols**

18 **The Chronicle of Novgorod**

19 Paul N. Miliukov **Outlines of Russian Culture Vol. III** Pt. 1. The Origins of Ideology

20 P.A. Zaionchkovskii **The Abolition of Serfdom in Russia**

21 V.V. Vinogradov **Russkii iazyk. Grammaticheskoe uchenie o slove**

22 P.A. Zaionchkovsky **The Russian Autocracy under Alexander III**

23 A.E. Presniakov **Emperor Nicholas I of Russia. The Apogee of Autocracy**

25 S.S. Oldenburg **Last Tsar! Nicholas II, His Reign and His Russia** (OP)

28 S.F. Platonov **Ivan the Terrible** Paper

30 A.E. Presniakov **The Tsardom of Muscovy**

32 R.G. Skrynnikov **Ivan the Terrible**

33 P.A. Zaionchkovsky **The Russian Autocracy in Crisis, 1878-1882**

34 Joseph T. Fuhrmann **Tsar Alexis. His Reign and His Russia**

36 R.G. Skrynnikov **The Time of Troubles. Russia in Crisis, 1604–1618**

38 V.V. Shulgin **Days of the Russian Revolutions. Memoirs From the Right, 1905–1907.** Cloth and Paper

40 J.L. Black **"Into the Dustbin of History"! The USSR From August Coup to Commonwealth, 1991. A Documentary Narrative**

41 E.V. Anisimov **Empress Elizabeth. Her Reign and Her Russia, 1741–1761**

44 Paul N. Miliukov **The Russian Revolution** 3 vols.

THE CENTRAL AND EAST EUROPEAN SERIES

1 Louis Eisenmann **Le Compromis Austro-Hongrois de 1867**

3 Francis Dvornik **The Making of Central and Eastern Europe** 2nd edition

4 Feodor F. Zigel **Lectures on Slavonic Law**

THE ACADEMIC INTERNATIONAL REFERENCE SERIES

The Modern Encyclopedia of Russian and Soviet History 58 vols.

The Modern Encyclopedia of Russian and Soviet Literatures 50 vols.

The Modern Encyclopedia of Religions in Russia and the Soviet Union 30 vols

Soviet Armed Forces Review Annual

Russia & Eurasia Facts & Figures Annual

Russia & Eurasia Documents Annual

USSR Calendar of Events (1987- 1991) 5 vol. set

USSR Congress of Peoples's Deputies 1989. The Stenographic Record

Documents of Soviet History 12 vols.

Documents of Soviet-American Relations

Gorbachev's Reforms. An Annotated Bibliography of Soviet Writings. Part 1 1985–1987

Military Encyclopedia of Russia and Eurasia 50 vols.

China Facts & Figures Annual

China Documents Annual

Sino-Soviet Documents Annual

Encyclopedia USA. The Encyclopedia of the United States of America Past & Present 50 vols.

Sports Encyclopedia North America 50 vols.

Sports in North America. A Documentary History

Religious Documents North America Annual

The International Military Encyclopedia 50 vols.

SPECIAL WORKS
S.M. Soloviev **History of Russia** 50 vols.
SAFRA Papers 1985-

*Request catalogs